GAVILAN COLLEGE LIBRARY

GAVILAN COLLEGE LIBRARY

GAVILAN COLLEGE LIBRARY

CITY CRIME RANKINGS

Crime in Metropolitan America

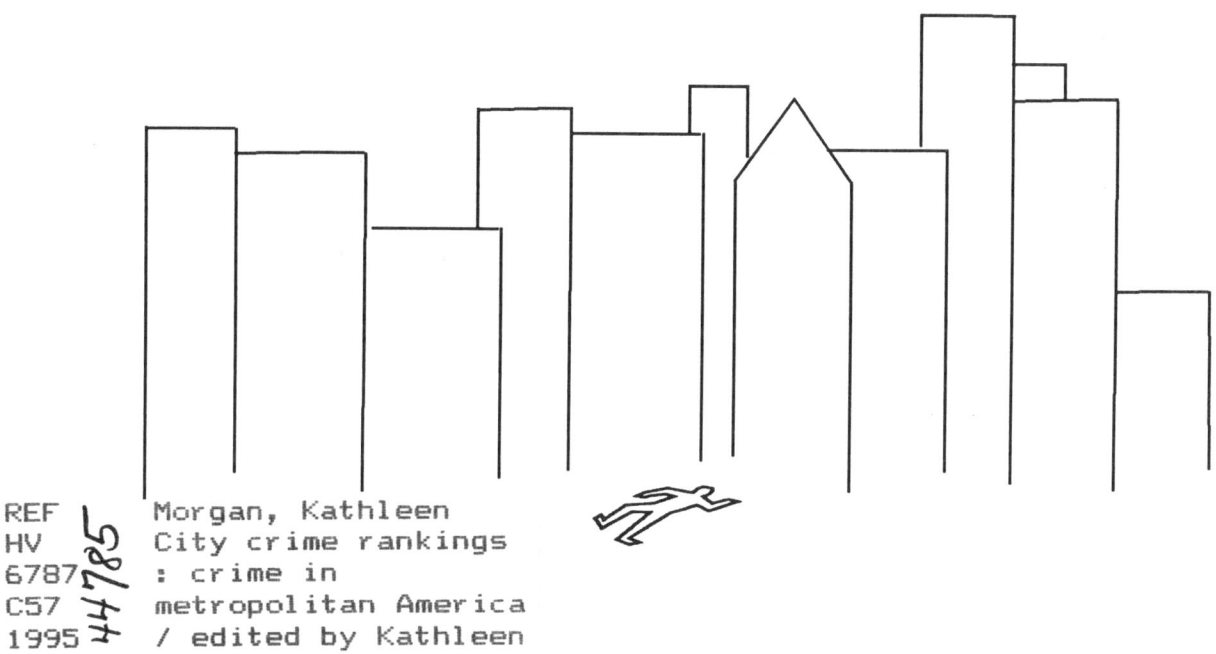

REF
HV
6787
C57
1995

Morgan, Kathleen
City crime rankings
: crime in
metropolitan America
/ edited by Kathleen

Kathleen O'Leary Morgan, Scott Morgan and Neal Quitno, Editors

Morgan Quitno Corporation
© Copyright 1995, All Rights Reserved

WITHDRAWN

512 East 9th Street, P.O. Box 1656
Lawrence, KS 66044
800-457-0742 or 913-841-3534

GAVILAN COLLEGE LIBRARY

© Copyright 1995 by
Morgan Quitno Corporation
512 East 9th Street, P.O. Box 1656
Lawrence, Kansas 66044

800-457-0742 or 913-841-3534

All Rights Reserved

No part of this book may be reproduced in any form, by photostat, microfilm, xerography, or any other means, or incorporated into any information retrieval system, electronic or mechanical, without the express permission of the copyright owner. Copyright is not claimed in any material from U.S. Government sources. However, its arrangement and compilation along with all other material are subject to the copyright. If you are interested in reprinting some of our material, please call or write. We are generally pleased to grant permission.

ISBN: 1-56692-307-7

City Crime Rankings sells for $19.95 (we pay shipping). For those who prefer state ranking information, we also offer Crime State Rankings. This is a much more in depth view of crime from the state level. This 540 page volume sells for $43.95. If you are interested in state health care statistics, please ask about our Health Care State Rankings ($43.95). For a general view of state data, please ask about our annual State Rankings ($43.95). All of our data are also available in machine readable format.

First Edition
Printed in the United States of America
February 1995

PREFACE

One public opinion poll after another shows that crime is the #1 concern in the minds of Americans today. It scares us, angers us, turns us inward and away from our neighbors and saps our communities of their cohesiveness. Yet for all the toll it takes on us as individuals and as a society, few Americans know how bad or not so bad crime is in their hometowns.

City Crime Rankings seeks to fill this void. Using the expertise we have gained in bringing state facts to thousands of readers in our well-reviewed *State Rankings* series, we have put together this easy-to-understand volume laying out crime statistics in a simple, straightforward format. Presented are key crime data as of 1993 for 274 U.S. metropolitan areas and 100 largest cities. In addition, statistics on the number of police patrolling the streets of the 100 largest cities are included.

Our intent in compiling this book is to take the muddle out of searching for crime numbers. We have tracked down answers to questions in which we ourselves have interest: How bad is violent crime in my city? How does that compare with other cities? Has the crime situation improved over the last five years? Since last year? Not only do we provide hard numbers for hard questions, we present all data in alphabetical order and in rank order. You can easily find crime information for your hometown and can just as easily find which cities rank above or below it.

Important Notes About *City Crime Rankings*

City Crime Rankings is organized into three sections: Part I reports crime statistics for metropolitan areas; Part II reports crime statistics and police data for the 100 largest U.S. cities; and Part III consists of appendices that provide population tables for cities and metro areas as well as cross reference tools that describe which cities and counties make up specific metropolitan areas. All statistics in this book are derived from *Crime in the United States 1993,* an annual publication from the FBI that reports crime statistics gathered under the Uniform Crime Reporting (UCR) Program. This program is a nationwide effort under which 16,000 city, county and state law enforcement agencies report data on crimes committed in their jurisdictions. In 1993, approximately 95% of Americans lived in areas participating in the UCR program.

The 1993 statistics presented in *City Crime Rankings* are the most recent non-preliminary, full year numbers available from the FBI. They were released in December 1994. All rankings appearing in this book are reported in order from highest to lowest. Any ties are listed alphabetically by city. Numbers and rates shown in parentheses are negative. Data reported as "NA" were not available or could not be calculated. The national totals and rates appearing at the top of each table are for the entire United States -- both metropolitan and nonmetropolitan areas. Specific totals for metropolitan areas and the 100 largest cities are provided in the appendix, just inside the back cover.

The metropolitan areas for which crime information is reported are those which meet two criteria. First, at least 75% of law enforcement agencies must have reported crime statistics, and second, the central city/cities must have submitted 12 months of data in 1993. There are a few metro areas that did not meet these criteria in 1993 and thus are not included in the 1993 report. In addition, the states of Kansas and Illinois are in the process of converting their crime reporting systems to the FBI's new, expanded National Incident-Based Reporting System. During this transition period, 1993 statistics were not reported for a number of jurisdictions in these two states. Most notable, Chicago metropolitan area data are unavailable as are statistics for the Kansas City, KS-MO and St. Louis MO-IL metropolitan areas. Other large metropolitan areas missing from the 1993 report are Omaha, Nebraska; Cleveland, Ohio and Wichita, Kansas.

PREFACE (continued)

The 100 largest cities for which data are presented in *City Crime Rankings* are those 100 cities with the highest populations *for which statistics were reported in 1993 by the FBI.* From a straight population standpoint, Omaha, Nebraska and Hialeah, Florida are normally included in the list of the 100 largest U.S. cities. However, crime data were not available for these cities for 1993. Consequently, Omaha and Hialeah are not found in the portion of the book reporting crime in the nation's 100 largest cities. Instead, Fort Wayne, Indiana and San Bernardino, California, the next two largest cities for which crime data were available, were added.

Finally, a word of caution. You will not find crime rankings such as those contained in *City Crime Rankings* in any publication of the U.S. Department of Justice or the FBI. Officials of these federal agencies are concerned that rankings may create misleading perceptions. Specifically, the FBI and Justice Department note that the different demographic and geographic make-up of cities and metropolitan areas have much to do with crime and fear that citizens will judge the effectiveness of their community police force solely on the city's crime ranking.

We agree that crime ranking information must be considered carefully and do not want to be irresponsible in our presentation of the rankings. However, we also believe that these crime rankings tell not only an interesting, but also very important story regarding the incidence of crime in this country. The *Safest Metropolitan Area* and *Safest City Awards* that follow are the only subjective rankings in this book. Even in this case, however, we explain how we determined the rankings so that others can decide if they agree or take issue with our findings. We ask our readers to use and enjoy our rankings, but also to keep in mind that the rankings comprise one of many factors used in assessing crime in the United States.

THE EDITORS

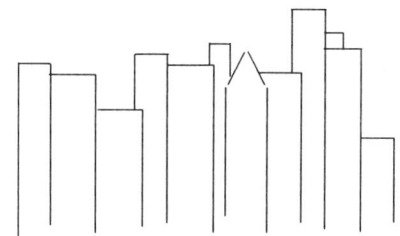

SAFEST METROPOLITAN AREA
and
SAFEST CITY

While we pride ourselves on presenting data in a clear and objective manner, with each of our rankings books we can't the resist the temptation to take the numbers and determine which city or state is the "best" in a subjective set of categories. With this book we make no exception. In the next six pages we present our version of the *Safest Metropolitan Area* and *Safest City Awards*. Congratulations to the citizens of metropolitan Wausau, Wisconsin and those living in the city of Huntington Beach, California, this year's big winners.

First a word on our methodology. Our formula is very simple. We considered six categories: Violent Crime Rate, Property Crime Rate, Murder Rate, Rape Rate, Robbery Rate and Aggravated Assault Rate and averaged the individual rankings for each of the six categories as they are reported in *City Crime Rankings*. It is based on these averages that we determine our award. The averages are ranked from lowest to highest (the opposite of the rankings found in the book, where data in all tables are ranked from highest to lowest.) Thus, the lower the average, the safer the metro area or city. Only those cities or metro areas for which we had complete data for all six categories were considered.

Rounding out the top five for the Safest Metropolitan Area Award are Eau Claire, WI in second place; followed by Altoona, PA; Appleton-Oshkosh-Neenah, WI and Johnstown, PA. Bringing up the rear of those metro areas for which we have complete data are Little Rock-North Little Rock, AR in 256th; Jacksonville, FL in 255th; Miami, FL in 254th; Baton Rouge, LA in 253rd and Tallahassee, FL in 252nd. It is important to remember that there are a number of significant metro areas (such as Chicago and Detroit) for which complete data are not available this year.

In the award among the 100 largest cities, Glendale, CA comes in second; Fremont, CA in third; Honolulu, HI in fourth and Virginia Beach, VA in fifth. At the other end of the scale, Atlanta, GA comes in 93rd; preceded by St. Louis, MO in 92nd; Newark, NJ in 91st, Little Rock, AR in 90th and Kansas City, MO in 89th. Again, please note that a few significant cities (such as Chicago, Detroit and Houston) did not have complete data and were not ranked for purposes of this particular award.

We realize people find awards such as these intriguing, sometimes irritating and perhaps even enlightening. We hope that they help to bring focus to the reality of crime in communities throughout the United States. Others can use the data found in this book and reach a different conclusion. Such is the nature of statistics. They tell part of the story, but not all.

Again, congratulations to Wausau and Huntington Beach!

THE EDITORS

Safest Metropolitan Area Award

RANK	METRO AREA	AVG RANK	RANK	METRO AREA	AVG RANK	RANK	METRO AREA	AVG RANK
139	Abilene, TX	144.83	28	Cheyenne, WY	48.83	214	Fort Worth-Arlington, TX	195.50
92	Akron, OH	98.67	–	Chicago, IL**	NA	243	Fresno, CA	217.33
233	Albany, GA	210.50	84	Chico-Paradise, CA	92.17	217	Gadsden, AL	198.17
–	Albany, NY**	NA	113	Cincinnati, OH-KY-IN	120.83	245	Gainesville, FL	221.00
237	Albuquerque, NM	213.67	133	Clarksville-Hopkinsville, TN-KY	140.83	220	Galveston-Texas City, TX	200.17
203	Alexandria, LA	186.50	–	Cleveland, OH**	NA	201	Gary-Hammond, IN	186.00
3	Altoona, PA	16.50	116	Colorado Springs, CO	122.33	40	Glens Falls, NY	57.50
154	Amarillo, TX	150.67	78	Columbia, MO	85.33	143	Goldsboro, NC	145.83
212	Anchorage, AK	194.50	238	Columbia, SC	214.33	–	Grand Forks, ND-MN**	NA
–	Ann Arbor, MI**	NA	125	Columbus, GA-AL	132.17	–	Grand Rapids-Muskegon-Holland, MI**	NA
196	Anniston, AL	183.00	180	Columbus, OH	166.17	68	Greeley, CO	75.00
4	Appleton-Oshkosh-Neenah, WI	16.67	200	Corpus Christi, TX	185.67	33	Green Bay, WI	51.67
69	Asheville, NC	75.33	23	Cumberland, MD-WV	45.00	164	Greensboro-Winston Salem-High Point, NC	158.33
155	Athens, GA	152.17	230	Dallas, TX	209.00	234	Greenville, NC	210.67
210	Atlanta, GA	194.33	6	Danbury, CT	21.17	193	Greenville-Spartanburg-Anderson, SC	178.83
205	Atlantic City, NJ	189.33	76	Danville, VA	82.67	21	Hagerstown, MD	40.83
135	Augusta-Aiken, GA-SC	141.50	161	Daytona Beach, FL	156.33	71	Harrisburg-Lebanon-Carlisle, PA	75.83
151	Austin-San Marcos, TX	149.83	134	Dayton-Springfield, OH	141.00	87	Hartford, CT	94.67
185	Bakersfield, CA	169.50	52	Decatur, AL	61.67	62	Hickory-Morganton, NC	70.33
242	Baltimore, MD	217.00	157	Denver, CO	154.50	77	Honolulu, HI	85.00
17	Bangor, ME	34.50	60	Des Moines, IA	68.00	80	Houma, LA	88.50
88	Barnstable-Yarmouth, MA	96.83	–	Detroit, MI**	NA	–	Houston, TX**	NA
252	Baton Rouge, LA	232.50	118	Dothan, AL	123.83	37	Huntington-Ashland, WV-KY-OH	55.83
224	Beaumont-Port Arthur, TX	202.00	43	Dubuque, IA	58.33	145	Huntsville, AL	146.67
72	Bellingham, WA	76.33	–	Duluth-Superior, MN-WI**	NA	–	Indianapolis, IN**	NA
–	Benton Harbor, MI**	NA	39	Dutchess County, NY	56.33	–	Jackson, MI**	NA
45	Bergen-Passaic, NJ	59.67	2	Eau Claire, WI	10.33	221	Jackson, MS	200.50
11	Binghamton, NY	28.17	223	El Paso, TX	201.67	250	Jackson, TN	231.50
227	Birmingham, AL	205.83	97	Elkhart-Goshen, IN	105.17	254	Jacksonville, FL	241.00
13	Bismarck, ND	30.83	137	Enid, OK	144.33	53	Jacksonville, NC	61.83
34	Bloomington, IN	52.83	63	Erie, PA	71.83	35	Janesville-Beloit, WI	53.17
58	Boise, ID	65.50	75	Eugene-Springfield, OR	81.83	170	Jersey City, NJ	161.50
120	Boston, MA-NH	124.83	73	Evansville-Henderson, IN-KY	77.17	12	Johnson City-Kingsport-Bristol, TN-VA	28.67
45	Boulder-Longmont, CO	59.67	–	Fargo-Moorhead, ND-MN**	NA	5	Johnstown, PA	19.67
47	Brazoria, TX	60.17	249	Fayetteville, NC	230.50	56	Joplin, MO	63.33
57	Bremerton, WA	63.67	18	Fayetteville-Springdale-Rogers, AR	37.17	–	Kalamazoo-Battle Creek, MI**	NA
129	Bridgeport, CT	137.33	123	Fitchburg-Leominster, MA	131.00	–	Kansas City, MO-KS**	NA
117	Brockton, MA	122.67	–	Flint, MI**	NA	101	Kenosha, WI	111.17
146	Brownsville-Harlingen-San Benito, TX	147.00	27	Florence, AL	48.17	147	Killeen-Temple, TX	148.83
112	Bryan-College Station, TX	120.50	235	Florence, SC	211.67	66	Kokomo, IN	73.83
136	Buffalo-Niagara Falls, NY	142.83	53	Fort Collins-Loveland, CO	61.83	–	La Crosse, WI-MN**	NA
99	Canton-Massillon, OH	108.17	210	Fort Lauderdale, FL	194.33	29	Lafayette, IN	49.83
91	Charleston, WV	98.33	149	Fort Myers-Cape Coral, FL	149.67	103	Lafayette, LA	111.33
204	Charleston-North Charleston, SC	187.50	174	Fort Pierce-Port St. Lucie, FL	162.50	209	Lake Charles, LA	194.17
49	Charlottesville, VA	60.50	85	Fort Smith, AR-OK	92.33	208	Lakeland-Winter Haven, FL	193.17
238	Charlotte-Gastonia-Rock Hill, NC-SC	214.33	47	Fort Walton Beach, FL	60.17	16	Lancaster, PA	33.17
175	Chattanooga, TN-GA	163.17	86	Fort Wayne, IN	93.50	–	Lansing-East Lansing, MI**	NA

Source: Morgan Quitno Corporation
Based on average 1993 rankings of cities in six categories: Violent Crime Rate, Property Crime Rate, Murder Rate, Rape Rate, Aggravated Assault Rate and Robbery Rate. The lower the rate, the closer to a ranking of one (and the safer the metro area.)
***Not available. These cities were missing at least one of the six categories considered.*

Safest Metropolitan Area Award (continued)

RANK	METRO AREA	AVG RANK	RANK	METRO AREA	AVG RANK	RANK	METRO AREA	AVG RANK
144	Laredo, TX	146.50	59	Olympia, WA	67.50	163	Seattle–Bellevue–Everett, WA	157.50
222	Las Vegas, NV–AZ	201.17	–	Omaha, NE**	NA	9	Sheboygan, WI	24.00
100	Lawrence, MA–NH	108.67	109	Orange County, CA	115.00	106	Sherman–Denison, TX	113.50
157	Lawton, OK	154.50	215	Orlando, FL	196.67	231	Shreveport–Bossier City, LA	209.17
10	Lewiston–Auburn, ME	27.00	40	Owensboro, KY	57.50	186	Sioux City, IA–NE	172.50
141	Lexington, KY	145.33	191	Panama City, FL	177.67	73	Sioux Falls, SD	77.17
106	Lincoln, NE	113.50	125	Philadelphia, PA–NJ	132.17	173	South Bend, IN	162.33
255	Little Rock–North Little Rock, AR	241.50	187	Phoenix–Mesa, AZ	173.83	114	Spokane, WA	121.67
183	Longview–Marshall, TX	169.17	244	Pine Bluff, AR	219.33	–	Springfield, MA**	NA
236	Los Angeles–Long Beach, CA	212.33	65	Pittsburgh, PA	73.00	55	Springfield, MO	63.00
105	Louisville, KY–IN	113.33	22	Pittsfield, MA	42.00	50	Stamford–Norwalk, CT	60.83
166	Lubbock, TX	159.33	36	Portland, ME	53.33	30	Steubenville–Weirton, OH–WV	50.17
67	Lynchburg, VA	74.67	162	Portland–Vancouver, OR–WA	156.67	241	Stockton–Lodi, CA	216.83
127	Macon, GA	136.17	70	Providence–Fall River–Warwick, RI–MA	75.50	–	St. Cloud, MN**	NA
38	Madison, WI	56.17	14	Provo–Orem, UT	31.33	83	St. Joseph, MO	92.00
25	Manchester, NH	46.83	202	Pueblo, CO	186.17	–	St. Louis, MO–IL**	NA
111	Mansfield, OH	120.33	32	Punta Gorda, FL	50.83	215	Sumter, SC	196.67
152	McAllen–Edinburg–Mission, TX	150.00	82	Racine, WI	90.83	30	Syracuse, NY	50.17
95	Medford–Ashland, OR	102.50	138	Raleigh–Durham–Chapel Hill, NC	144.50	212	Tacoma, WA	194.50
246	Memphis, TN–AR–MS	222.33	101	Rapid City, SD	111.17	251	Tallahassee, FL	232.00
127	Merced, CA	136.17	50	Reading, PA	60.83	226	Tampa–St. Petersburg–Clearwater, FL	204.33
253	Miami, FL	238.83	119	Redding, CA	124.00	197	Texarkana, TX–AR	183.83
20	Middlesex–Somerset–Hunterdon, NJ	40.50	168	Reno, NV	160.33	169	Toledo, OH	160.83
121	Milwaukee–Waukesha, WI	125.83	93	Richland–Kennewick–Pasco, WA	99.83	124	Trenton, NJ	131.67
–	Minneapolis–St. Paul, MN–WI**	NA	149	Richmond–Petersburg, VA	149.67	199	Tucson, AZ	184.50
189	Mobile, AL	177.17	225	Riverside–San Bernardino, CA	202.50	179	Tulsa, OK	165.17
192	Modesto, CA	178.00	64	Roanoke, VA	72.00	206	Tuscaloosa, AL	191.00
19	Monmouth–Ocean, NJ	38.67	–	Rochester, MN**	NA	206	Tyler, TX	191.00
182	Monroe, LA	168.50	79	Rochester, NY	86.50	26	Utica–Rome, NY	47.50
178	Montgomery, AL	164.83	159	Rocky Mount, NC	155.17	153	Vallejo–Fairfield–Napa, CA	150.33
219	Myrtle Beach, SC	199.83	188	Sacramento, CA	176.00	81	Ventura, CA	89.67
171	Naples, FL	161.67	–	Saginaw–Bay City–Midland. MI**	NA	148	Victoria, TX	149.33
15	Nashua, NH	31.83	90	Salem, OR	97.83	229	Vineland–Millville–Bridgeton, NJ	207.67
240	Nashville, TN	216.67	130	Salinas, CA	138.67	131	Visalia–Tulare–Porterville, CA	139.83
23	Nassau–Suffolk, NY	45.00	96	Salt Lake City–Ogden, UT	104.67	247	Waco, TX	224.33
132	New Bedford, MA	140.50	122	San Angelo, TX	130.17	165	Washington, DC–MD–VA–WV	158.67
110	New Haven–Meriden, CT	119.83	194	San Antonio, TX	179.50	104	Waterbury, CT	112.33
44	New London–Norwich, CT–RI	59.50	177	San Diego, CA	163.83	98	Waterloo–Cedar Falls, IA	105.67
248	New Orleans, LA	229.17	189	San Francisco, CA	177.17	1	Wausau, WI	4.17
232	New York, NY	210.17	94	San Jose, CA	100.33	–	West Palm Beach–Boca Raton, FL**	NA
176	Newark, NJ	163.50	61	San Luis Obispo–Atascadero, CA	69.83	172	Wichita Falls, TX	162.00
42	Newburgh, NY–PA	57.67	89	Santa Barbara–Santa Maria–Lompoc, CA	97.67	7	Williamsport, PA	21.50
167	Norfolk–Va Beach–Newport News, VA–NC	159.83	115	Santa Cruz–Watsonville, CA	122.00	155	Wilmington, NC	152.17
228	Oakland, CA	207.00	108	Santa Rosa, CA	114.50	–	Worcester, MA–CT**	NA
197	Ocala, FL	183.83	181	Sarasota–Bradenton, FL	166.50	184	Yakima, WA	169.33
160	Odessa–Midland, TX	156.00	195	Savannah, GA	182.83	140	Yolo, CA	145.17
218	Oklahoma City, OK	198.67	8	Scranton–Wilkes-Barre–Hazleton, PA	23.17	142	Yuba City, CA	145.50

Source: Morgan Quitno Corporation

Based on average 1993 rankings of cities in six categories: Violent Crime Rate, Property Crime Rate, Murder Rate, Rape Rate, Aggravated Assault Rate and Robbery Rate. The lower the rate, the closer to a ranking of one (and the safer the metro area.)
**Not available. These cities were missing at least one of the six categories considered.

Safest Metropolitan Area Award (continued)

RANK	METRO AREA	AVG RANK	RANK	METRO AREA	AVG RANK	RANK	METRO AREA	AVG RANK
1	Wausau, WI	4.17	47	Fort Walton Beach, FL	60.17	95	Medford–Ashland, OR	102.50
2	Eau Claire, WI	10.33	49	Charlottesville, VA	60.50	96	Salt Lake City–Ogden, UT	104.67
3	Altoona, PA	16.50	50	Reading, PA	60.83	97	Elkhart–Goshen, IN	105.17
4	Appleton-Oshkosh-Neenah, WI	16.67	50	Stamford–Norwalk, CT	60.83	98	Waterloo–Cedar Falls, IA	105.67
5	Johnstown, PA	19.67	52	Decatur, AL	61.67	99	Canton–Massillon, OH	108.17
6	Danbury, CT	21.17	53	Fort Collins–Loveland, CO	61.83	100	Lawrence, MA–NH	108.67
7	Williamsport, PA	21.50	53	Jacksonville, NC	61.83	101	Kenosha, WI	111.17
8	Scranton–Wilkes-Barre–Hazleton, PA	23.17	55	Springfield, MO	63.00	101	Rapid City, SD	111.17
9	Sheboygan, WI	24.00	56	Joplin, MO	63.33	103	Lafayette, LA	111.33
10	Lewiston–Auburn, ME	27.00	57	Bremerton, WA	63.67	104	Waterbury, CT	112.33
11	Binghamton, NY	28.17	58	Boise, ID	65.50	105	Louisville, KY–IN	113.33
12	Johnson City–Kingsport–Bristol, TN–VA	28.67	59	Olympia, WA	67.50	106	Lincoln, NE	113.50
13	Bismarck, ND	30.83	60	Des Moines, IA	68.00	106	Sherman–Denison, TX	113.50
14	Provo–Orem, UT	31.33	61	San Luis Obispo–Atascadero, CA	69.83	108	Santa Rosa, CA	114.50
15	Nashua, NH	31.83	62	Hickory–Morganton, NC	70.33	109	Orange County, CA	115.00
16	Lancaster, PA	33.17	63	Erie, PA	71.83	110	New Haven–Meriden, CT	119.83
17	Bangor, ME	34.50	64	Roanoke, VA	72.00	111	Mansfield, OH	120.33
18	Fayetteville–Springdale–Rogers, AR	37.17	65	Pittsburgh, PA	73.00	112	Bryan–College Station, TX	120.50
19	Monmouth–Ocean, NJ	38.67	66	Kokomo, IN	73.83	113	Cincinnati, OH–KY–IN	120.83
20	Middlesex–Sommerset–Hunterdon, NJ	40.50	67	Lynchburg, VA	74.67	114	Spokane, WA	121.67
21	Hagerstown, MD	40.83	68	Greeley, CO	75.00	115	Santa Cruz–Watsonville, CA	122.00
22	Pittsfield, MA	42.00	69	Asheville, NC	75.33	116	Colorado Springs, CO	122.33
23	Cumberland, MD–WV	45.00	70	Providence–Fall River–Warwick, RI–MA	75.50	117	Brockton, MA	122.67
23	Nassau–Suffolk, NY	45.00	71	Harrisburg–Lebanon–Carlisle, PA	75.83	118	Dothan, AL	123.83
25	Manchester, NH	46.83	72	Bellingham, WA	76.33	119	Redding, CA	124.00
26	Utica–Rome, NY	47.50	73	Evansville–Henderson, IN–KY	77.17	120	Boston, MA–NH	124.83
27	Florence, AL	48.17	73	Sioux Falls, SD	77.17	121	Milwaukee–Waukesha, WI	125.83
28	Cheyenne, WY	48.83	75	Eugene–Springfield, OR	81.83	122	San Angelo, TX	130.17
29	Lafayette, IN	49.83	76	Danville, VA	82.67	123	Fitchburg–Leominster, MA	131.00
30	Steubenville–Weirton, OH–WV	50.17	77	Honolulu, HI	85.00	124	Trenton, NJ	131.67
30	Syracuse, NY	50.17	78	Columbia, MO	85.33	125	Columbus, GA–AL	132.17
32	Punta Gorda, FL	50.83	79	Rochester, NY	86.50	125	Philadelphia, PA–NJ	132.17
33	Green Bay, WI	51.67	80	Houma, LA	88.50	127	Macon, GA	136.17
34	Bloomington, IN	52.83	81	Ventura, CA	89.67	127	Merced, CA	136.17
35	Janesville–Beloit, WI	53.17	82	Racine, WI	90.83	129	Bridgeport, CT	137.33
36	Portland, ME	53.33	83	St. Joseph, MO	92.00	130	Salinas, CA	138.67
37	Huntington–Ashland, WV–KY–OH	55.83	84	Chico–Paradise, CA	92.17	131	Visalia–Tulare–Porterville, CA	139.83
38	Madison, WI	56.17	85	Fort Smith, AR–OK	92.33	132	New Bedford, MA	140.50
39	Dutchess County, NY	56.33	86	Fort Wayne, IN	93.50	133	Clarksville–Hopkinsville, TN–KY	140.83
40	Glens Falls, NY	57.50	87	Hartford, CT	94.67	134	Dayton–Springfield, OH	141.00
40	Owensboro, KY	57.50	88	Barnstable–Yarmouth, MA	96.83	135	Augusta–Aiken, GA–SC	141.50
42	Newburgh, NY–PA	57.67	89	Santa Barbara–Santa Maria–Lompoc, CA	97.67	136	Buffalo–Niagara Falls, NY	142.83
43	Dubuque, IA	58.33	90	Salem, OR	97.83	137	Enid, OK	144.33
44	New London–Norwich, CT–RI	59.50	91	Charleston, WV	98.33	138	Raleigh–Durham–Chapel Hill, NC	144.50
45	Bergen–Passaic, NJ	59.67	92	Akron, OH	98.67	139	Abilene, TX	144.83
45	Boulder–Longmont, CO	59.67	93	Richland–Kennewick–Pasco, WA	99.83	140	Yolo, CA	145.17
47	Brazoria, TX	60.17	94	San Jose, CA	100.33	141	Lexington, KY	145.33

Source: Morgan Quitno Corporation
Based on average 1993 rankings of cities in six categories: Violent Crime Rate, Property Crime Rate, Murder Rate, Rape Rate, Aggravated Assault Rate and Robbery Rate. The lower the rate, the closer to a ranking of one (and the safer the metro area.)
**Not available. These cities were missing at least one of the six categories considered.

Safest Metropolitan Area Award (continued)

RANK	METRO AREA	AVG RANK	RANK	METRO AREA	AVG RANK	RANK	METRO AREA	AVG RANK
142	Yuba City, CA	145.50	189	Mobile, AL	177.17	236	Los Angeles–Long Beach, CA	212.33
143	Goldsboro, NC	145.83	189	San Francisco, CA	177.17	237	Albuquerque, NM	213.67
144	Laredo, TX	146.50	191	Panama City, FL	177.67	238	Charlotte–Gastonia–Rock Hill, NC–SC	214.33
145	Huntsville, AL	146.67	192	Modesto, CA	178.00	238	Columbia, SC	214.33
146	Brownsville–Harlingen–San Benito, TX	147.00	193	Greenville–Spartanburg–Anderson, SC	178.83	240	Nashville, TN	216.67
147	Killeen–Temple, TX	148.83	194	San Antonio, TX	179.50	241	Stockton–Lodi, CA	216.83
148	Victoria, TX	149.33	195	Savannah, GA	182.83	242	Baltimore, MD	217.00
149	Fort Myers–Cape Coral, FL	149.67	196	Anniston, AL	183.00	243	Fresno, CA	217.33
149	Richmond–Petersburg, VA	149.67	197	Ocala, FL	183.83	244	Pine Bluff, AR	219.33
151	Austin–San Marcos, TX	149.83	197	Texarkana, TX–AR	183.83	245	Gainesville, FL	221.00
152	McAllen–Edinburg–Mission, TX	150.00	199	Tucson, AZ	184.50	246	Memphis, TN–AR–MS	222.33
153	Vallejo–Fairfield–Napa, CA	150.33	200	Corpus Christi, TX	185.67	247	Waco, TX	224.33
154	Amarillo, TX	150.67	201	Gary–Hammond, IN	186.00	248	New Orleans, LA	229.17
155	Athens, GA	152.17	202	Pueblo, CO	186.17	249	Fayetteville, NC	230.50
155	Wilmington, NC	152.17	203	Alexandria, LA	186.50	250	Jackson, TN	231.50
157	Denver, CO	154.50	204	Charleston–North Charleston, SC	187.50	251	Tallahassee, FL	232.00
157	Lawton, OK	154.50	205	Atlantic City, NJ	189.33	252	Baton Rouge, LA	232.50
159	Rocky Mount, NC	155.17	206	Tuscaloosa, AL	191.00	253	Miami, FL	238.83
160	Odessa–Midland, TX	156.00	206	Tyler, TX	191.00	254	Jacksonville, FL	241.00
161	Daytona Beach, FL	156.33	208	Lakeland–Winter Haven, FL	193.17	255	Little Rock–North Little Rock, AR	241.50
162	Portland–Vancouver, OR–WA	156.67	209	Lake Charles, LA	194.17	–	Albany, NY**	NA
163	Seattle–Bellevue–Everett, WA	157.50	210	Atlanta, GA	194.33	–	Ann Arbor, MI**	NA
164	Greensboro–Winston Salem–High Point, NC	158.33	210	Fort Lauderdale, FL	194.33	–	Benton Harbor, MI**	NA
165	Washington, DC–MD–VA–WV	158.67	212	Anchorage, AK	194.50	–	Chicago, IL**	NA
166	Lubbock, TX	159.33	212	Tacoma, WA	194.50	–	Cleveland, OH**	NA
167	Norfolk–Va Beach–Newport News, VA–NC	159.83	214	Fort Worth–Arlington, TX	195.50	–	Detroit, MI**	NA
168	Reno, NV	160.33	215	Orlando, FL	196.67	–	Duluth–Superior, MN–WI**	NA
169	Toledo, OH	160.83	215	Sumter, SC	196.67	–	Fargo–Moorhead, ND–MN**	NA
170	Jersey City, NJ	161.50	217	Gadsden, AL	198.17	–	Flint, MI**	NA
171	Naples, FL	161.67	218	Oklahoma City, OK	198.67	–	Grand Forks, ND–MN**	NA
172	Wichita Falls, TX	162.00	219	Myrtle Beach, SC	199.83	–	Grand Rapids–Muskegon–Holland, MI**	NA
173	South Bend, IN	162.33	220	Galveston–Texas City, TX	200.17	–	Houston, TX**	NA
174	Fort Pierce–Port St. Lucie, FL	162.50	221	Jackson, MS	200.50	–	Indianapolis, IN**	NA
175	Chattanooga, TN–GA	163.17	222	Las Vegas, NV–AZ	201.17	–	Jackson, MI**	NA
176	Newark, NJ	163.50	223	El Paso, TX	201.67	–	Kalamazoo–Battle Creek, MI**	NA
177	San Diego, CA	163.83	224	Beaumont–Port Arthur, TX	202.00	–	Kansas City, MO–KS**	NA
178	Montgomery, AL	164.83	225	Riverside–San Bernardino, CA	202.50	–	La Crosse, WI–MN**	NA
179	Tulsa, OK	165.17	226	Tampa–St. Petersburg–Clearwater, FL	204.33	–	Lansing–East Lansing, MI**	NA
180	Columbus, OH	166.17	227	Birmingham, AL	205.83	–	Minneapolis–St. Paul, MN–WI**	NA
181	Sarasota–Bradenton, FL	166.50	228	Oakland, CA	207.00	–	Omaha, NE**	NA
182	Monroe, LA	168.50	229	Vineland–Millville–Bridgeton, NJ	207.67	–	Rochester, MN**	NA
183	Longview–Marshall, TX	169.17	230	Dallas, TX	209.00	–	Saginaw–Bay City–Midland, MI**	NA
184	Yakima, WA	169.33	231	Shreveport–Bossier City, LA	209.17	–	Springfield, MA**	NA
185	Bakersfield, CA	169.50	232	New York, NY	210.17	–	St. Cloud, MN**	NA
186	Sioux City, IA–NE	172.50	233	Albany, GA	210.50	–	St. Louis, MO–IL**	NA
187	Phoenix–Mesa, AZ	173.83	234	Greenville, NC	210.67	–	West Palm Beach–Boca Raton, FL**	NA
188	Sacramento, CA	176.00	235	Florence, SC	211.67	–	Worcester, MA–CT**	NA

Source: Morgan Quitno Corporation
Based on average 1993 rankings of cities in six categories: Violent Crime Rate, Property Crime Rate, Murder Rate, Rape Rate, Aggravated Assault Rate and Robbery Rate. The lower the rate, the closer to a ranking of one (and the safer the metro area.)
**Not available. These cities were missing at least one of the six categories considered.

Safest City Award

RANK	CITY	AVG RANK	RANK	CITY	AVG RANK
–	Akron, OH**	NA	20	Louisville, KY	27.33
50	Albuquerque, NM	48.83	15	Lubbock, TX	22.83
–	Anaheim, CA**	NA	6	Madison, WI	8.17
22	Anchorage, AK	28.67	74	Memphis, TN	66.33
14	Arlington, TX	21.33	11	Mesa, AZ	18.83
93	Atlanta, GA	90.50	87	Miami, FL	79.33
41	Aurora, CO	43.67	38	Milwaukee, WI	40.33
21	Austin, TX	27.83	74	Minneapolis, MN	66.33
23	Bakersfield, CA	30.00	41	Mobile, AL	43.67
88	Baltimore, MD	80.50	18	Montgomery, AL	26.67
84	Baton Rouge, LA	78.50	67	Nashville-Davidson, TN	63.00
83	Birmingham, AL	76.67	79	New Orleans, LA	68.33
69	Boston, MA	63.50	56	New York, NY	53.83
74	Buffalo, NY	66.33	91	Newark, NJ	84.33
80	Charlotte, NC	72.17	30	Newport News, VA	34.67
–	Chicago, IL**	NA	44	Norfolk, VA	45.67
54	Cincinnati, OH	52.50	85	Oakland, CA	78.83
65	Cleveland, OH	61.83	62	Oklahoma City, OK	60.67
13	Colorado Springs, CO	20.17	78	Orlando, FL	67.33
11	Columbus, GA	18.83	37	Philadelphia, PA	39.67
47	Columbus, OH	46.50	35	Phoenix, AZ	39.00
33	Corpus Christi, TX	36.17	41	Pittsburgh, PA	43.67
77	Dallas, TX	67.17	66	Portland, OR	62.83
72	Dayton, OH	65.50	16	Raleigh, NC	24.17
36	Denver, CO	39.17	72	Richmond, VA	65.50
9	Des Moines, IA	14.50	49	Riverside, CA	48.33
–	Detroit, MI**	NA	53	Rochester, NY	52.17
28	El Paso, TX	33.17	46	Sacramento, CA	45.83
27	Fort Wayne, IN	32.00	31	San Antonio, TX	35.17
68	Fort Worth, TX	63.33	85	San Bernardino, CA	78.83
3	Fremont, CA	6.50	24	San Diego, CA	31.00
58	Fresno, CA	55.83	55	San Francisco, CA	52.83
–	Garland, TX**	NA	8	San Jose, CA	13.83
2	Glendale, CA	6.00	29	Santa Ana, CA	33.83
–	Grand Rapids, MI**	NA	52	Seattle, WA	52.00
24	Greensboro, NC	31.00	59	Shreveport, LA	56.33
4	Honolulu, HI	7.67	19	Spokane, WA	27.17
–	Houston, TX**	NA	60	Stockton, CA	59.83
1	Huntington Beach, CA	5.50	92	St. Louis, MO	85.00
61	Indianapolis, IN	60.33	31	St. Paul, MN	35.17
71	Jackson, MS	65.00	57	St. Petersburg, FL	54.83
63	Jacksonville, FL	61.33	70	Tacoma, WA	64.33
47	Jersey City, NJ	46.50	82	Tampa, FL	75.67
89	Kansas City, MO	82.00	39	Toledo, OH	40.83
26	Las Vegas, NV	31.33	40	Tucson, AZ	43.50
17	Lexington-Fayette, KY	25.17	44	Tulsa, OK	45.67
7	Lincoln, NE	13.17	4	Virginia Beach, VA	7.67
90	Little Rock, AR	82.83	81	Washington, DC	73.50
51	Long Beach, CA	49.83	34	Wichita, KS	38.17
64	Los Angeles, CA	61.50	10	Yonkers, NY	15.50

Source: Morgan Quitno Corporation

Based on average 1993 rankings of cities in six categories: Violent Crime Rate, Property Crime Rate, Murder Rate, Rape Rate, Aggravated Assault Rate and Robbery Rate. The lower the rate, the closer to a ranking of one (and the safer the city.)

**Not available. These cities were missing at least one of the six categories considered.

Safest City Award (continued)

RANK	CITY	AVG RANK		RANK	CITY	AVG RANK
1	Huntington Beach, CA	5.50		51	Long Beach, CA	49.83
2	Glendale, CA	6.00		52	Seattle, WA	52.00
3	Fremont, CA	6.50		53	Rochester, NY	52.17
4	Honolulu, HI	7.67		54	Cincinnati, OH	52.50
4	Virginia Beach, VA	7.67		55	San Francisco, CA	52.83
6	Madison, WI	8.17		56	New York, NY	53.83
7	Lincoln, NE	13.17		57	St. Petersburg, FL	54.83
8	San Jose, CA	13.83		58	Fresno, CA	55.83
9	Des Moines, IA	14.50		59	Shreveport, LA	56.33
10	Yonkers, NY	15.50		60	Stockton, CA	59.83
11	Columbus, GA	18.83		61	Indianapolis, IN	60.33
11	Mesa, AZ	18.83		62	Oklahoma City, OK	60.67
13	Colorado Springs, CO	20.17		63	Jacksonville, FL	61.33
14	Arlington, TX	21.33		64	Los Angeles, CA	61.50
15	Lubbock, TX	22.83		65	Cleveland, OH	61.83
16	Raleigh, NC	24.17		66	Portland, OR	62.83
17	Lexington-Fayette, KY	25.17		67	Nashville-Davidson, TN	63.00
18	Montgomery, AL	26.67		68	Fort Worth, TX	63.33
19	Spokane, WA	27.17		69	Boston, MA	63.50
20	Louisville, KY	27.33		70	Tacoma, WA	64.33
21	Austin, TX	27.83		71	Jackson, MS	65.00
22	Anchorage, AK	28.67		72	Dayton, OH	65.50
23	Bakersfield, CA	30.00		72	Richmond, VA	65.50
24	Greensboro, NC	31.00		74	Buffalo, NY	66.33
24	San Diego, CA	31.00		74	Memphis, TN	66.33
26	Las Vegas, NV	31.33		74	Minneapolis, MN	66.33
27	Fort Wayne, IN	32.00		77	Dallas, TX	67.17
28	El Paso, TX	33.17		78	Orlando, FL	67.33
29	Santa Ana, CA	33.83		79	New Orleans, LA	68.33
30	Newport News, VA	34.67		80	Charlotte, NC	72.17
31	San Antonio, TX	35.17		81	Washington, DC	73.50
31	St. Paul, MN	35.17		82	Tampa, FL	75.67
33	Corpus Christi, TX	36.17		83	Birmingham, AL	76.67
34	Wichita, KS	38.17		84	Baton Rouge, LA	78.50
35	Phoenix, AZ	39.00		85	Oakland, CA	78.83
36	Denver, CO	39.17		85	San Bernardino, CA	78.83
37	Philadelphia, PA	39.67		87	Miami, FL	79.33
38	Milwaukee, WI	40.33		88	Baltimore, MD	80.50
39	Toledo, OH	40.83		89	Kansas City, MO	82.00
40	Tucson, AZ	43.50		90	Little Rock, AR	82.83
41	Aurora, CO	43.67		91	Newark, NJ	84.33
41	Mobile, AL	43.67		92	St. Louis, MO	85.00
41	Pittsburgh, PA	43.67		93	Atlanta, GA	90.50
44	Norfolk, VA	45.67		-	Akron, OH**	NA
44	Tulsa, OK	45.67		-	Anaheim, CA**	NA
46	Sacramento, CA	45.83		-	Chicago, IL**	NA
47	Columbus, OH	46.50		-	Detroit, MI**	NA
47	Jersey City, NJ	46.50		-	Garland, TX**	NA
49	Riverside, CA	48.33		-	Grand Rapids, MI**	NA
50	Albuquerque, NM	48.83		-	Houston, TX**	NA

Source: Morgan Quitno Corporation

Based on average 1993 rankings of cities in six categories: Violent Crime Rate, Property Crime Rate, Murder Rate, Rape Rate, Aggravated Assault Rate and Robbery Rate. The lower the rate, the closer to a ranking of one (and the safer the city.)

**Not available. These cities were missing at least one of the six categories considered.

TABLE OF CONTENTS

TABLE OF CONTENTS (continued)

Table: **Page:**

100 LARGEST CITIES CRIME STATISTICS

TABLE OF CONTENTS (continued)

I. METROPOLITAN AREA CRIME STATISTICS

1. Crimes in 1993

National Total = 14,140,952 Crimes*

RANK	METRO AREA	CRIMES	RANK	METRO AREA	CRIMES	RANK	METRO AREA	CRIMES
221	Abilene, TX	5,758	250	Cheyenne, WY	3,199	23	Fort Worth-Arlington, TX	105,885
79	Akron, OH	30,547	–	Chicago, IL**	NA	43	Fresno, CA	65,838
159	Albany, GA	10,242	166	Chico-Paradise, CA	9,549	210	Gadsden, AL	6,519
–	Albany, NY**	NA	36	Cincinnati, OH-KY-IN	75,947	104	Gainesville, FL	19,468
57	Albuquerque, NM	47,537	–	Cleveland, OH**	NA	116	Galveston-Texas City, TX	16,474
172	Alexandria, LA	9,068	92	Colorado Springs, CO	23,593	70	Gary-Hammond, IN	35,182
251	Altoona, PA	3,170	217	Columbia, MO	6,004	235	Glens Falls, NY	4,157
128	Amarillo, TX	14,798	73	Columbia, SC	33,083	216	Goldsboro, NC	6,090
120	Anchorage, AK	16,140	125	Columbus, GA-AL	15,262	–	Grand Forks, ND-MN**	NA
–	Ann Arbor, MI**	NA	30	Columbus, OH	84,262	–	Grand Rapids-Muskegon-Holland, MI**	NA
209	Anniston, AL	6,536	78	Corpus Christi, TX	30,981	199	Greeley, CO	7,384
148	Appleton-Oshkosh-Neenah, WI	11,585	252	Cumberland, MD-WV	2,905	195	Green Bay, WI	7,713
185	Asheville, NC	8,107	8	Dallas, TX	200,577	41	Greensboro-Winston Salem-High Point, NC	66,968
161	Athens, GA	9,754	227	Danbury, CT	5,496	175	Greenville, NC	8,935
4	Atlanta, GA	244,965	247	Danville, VA	3,231	55	Greenville-Spartanburg-Anderson, SC	49,626
82	Atlantic City, NJ	27,936	88	Daytona Beach, FL	25,272	246	Hagerstown, MD	3,249
95	Augusta-Aiken, GA-SC	21,834	53	Dayton-Springfield, OH	50,787	100	Harrisburg-Lebanon-Carlisle, PA	20,232
40	Austin-San Marcos, TX	69,684	231	Decatur, AL	4,975	52	Hartford, CT	51,024
64	Bakersfield, CA	38,805	22	Denver, CO	107,059	138	Hickory-Morganton, NC	12,886
10	Baltimore, MD	178,776	94	Des Moines, IA	22,650	46	Honolulu, HI	56,405
255	Bangor, ME	2,399	–	Detroit, MI**	NA	200	Houma, LA	7,367
218	Barnstable-Yarmouth, MA	5,937	211	Dothan, AL	6,484	–	Houston, TX**	NA
49	Baton Rouge, LA	54,047	248	Dubuque, IA	3,211	168	Huntington-Ashland, WV-KY-OH	9,393
85	Beaumont-Port Arthur, TX	27,048	–	Duluth-Superior, MN-WI**	NA	108	Huntsville, AL	18,698
198	Bellingham, WA	7,428	187	Dutchess County, NY	8,000	–	Indianapolis, IN**	NA
–	Benton Harbor, MI**	NA	230	Eau Claire, WI	5,021	–	Jackson, MI**	NA
56	Bergen-Passaic, NJ	48,913	54	El Paso, TX	50,163	75	Jackson, MS	32,092
177	Binghamton, NY	8,787	193	Elkhart-Goshen, IN	7,806	205	Jackson, TN	6,823
48	Birmingham, AL	54,663	239	Enid, OK	3,928	31	Jacksonville, FL	83,092
249	Bismarck, ND	3,203	162	Erie, PA	9,673	207	Jacksonville, NC	6,736
234	Bloomington, IN	4,204	119	Eugene-Springfield, OR	16,246	197	Janesville-Beloit, WI	7,472
123	Boise, ID	15,403	146	Evansville-Henderson, IN-KY	11,933	68	Jersey City, NJ	36,257
11	Boston, MA-NH	164,388	–	Fargo-Moorhead, ND-MN**	NA	135	Johnson City-Kingsport-Bristol, TN-VA	13,157
143	Boulder-Longmont, CO	12,323	93	Fayetteville, NC	23,321	240	Johnstown, PA	3,793
204	Brazoria, TX	7,013	192	Fayetteville-Springdale-Rogers, AR	7,807	225	Joplin, MO	5,585
181	Bremerton, WA	8,521	213	Fitchburg-Leominster, MA	6,315	–	Kalamazoo-Battle Creek, MI**	NA
89	Bridgeport, CT	25,132	–	Flint, MI**	NA	–	Kansas City, MO-KS**	NA
145	Brockton, MA	12,010	242	Florence, AL	3,723	206	Kenosha, WI	6,769
97	Brownsville-Harlingen-San Benito, TX	21,371	183	Florence, SC	8,355	136	Killeen-Temple, TX	13,093
196	Bryan-College Station, TX	7,697	188	Fort Collins-Loveland, CO	7,985	238	Kokomo, IN	3,929
45	Buffalo-Niagara Falls, NY	63,495	18	Fort Lauderdale, FL	117,550	–	La Crosse, WI-MN**	NA
107	Canton-Massillon, OH	18,911	96	Fort Myers-Cape Coral, FL	21,628	203	Lafayette, IN	7,016
152	Charleston, WV	11,022	121	Fort Pierce-Port St. Lucie, FL	16,135	115	Lafayette, LA	16,735
71	Charleston-North Charleston, SC	34,565	182	Fort Smith, AR-OK	8,397	144	Lake Charles, LA	12,027
219	Charlottesville, VA	5,916	220	Fort Walton Beach, FL	5,829	66	Lakeland-Winter Haven, FL	37,494
27	Charlotte-Gastonia-Rock Hill, NC-SC	89,577	98	Fort Wayne, IN	21,208	141	Lancaster, PA	12,447
90	Chattanooga, TN-GA	23,953				–	Lansing-East Lansing, MI**	NA

Source: U.S. Department of Justice, Federal Bureau of Investigation
  "Crime in the United States 1993" (Uniform Crime Reports, December 4, 1994)
*Includes murder, rape, robbery, aggravated assault, burglary, larceny-theft and motor vehicle theft.
**Not available.

1. Crimes in 1993 (continued)

National Total = 14,140,952 Crimes*

RANK	METRO AREA	CRIMES	RANK	METRO AREA	CRIMES	RANK	METRO AREA	CRIMES
157	Laredo, TX	10,465	180	Olympia, WA	8,607	15	Seattle-Bellevue-Everett, WA	142,982
42	Las Vegas, NV-AZ	66,409	–	Omaha, NE**	NA	236	Sheboygan, WI	4,155
130	Lawrence, MA-NH	14,075	16	Orange County, CA	135,212	228	Sherman-Denison, TX	5,451
212	Lawton, OK	6,384	26	Orlando, FL	99,448	80	Shreveport-Bossier City, LA	30,420
237	Lewiston-Auburn, ME	4,141	245	Owensboro, KY	3,560	184	Sioux City, IA-NE	8,210
99	Lexington, KY	21,179	155	Panama City, FL	10,722	223	Sioux Falls, SD	5,699
126	Lincoln, NE	15,153	6	Philadelphia, PA-NJ	216,429	118	South Bend, IN	16,272
58	Little Rock-North Little Rock, AR	47,281	9	Phoenix-Mesa, AZ	186,384	91	Spokane, WA	23,879
142	Longview-Marshall, TX	12,439	221	Pine Bluff, AR	5,758	–	Springfield, MA**	NA
2	Los Angeles-Long Beach, CA	644,758	37	Pittsburgh, PA	75,414	134	Springfield, MO	13,382
59	Louisville, KY-IN	44,867	253	Pittsfield, MA	2,889	133	Stamford-Norwalk, CT	13,406
129	Lubbock, TX	14,190	158	Portland, ME	10,254	254	Steubenville-Weirton, OH-WV	2,782
214	Lynchburg, VA	6,228	24	Portland-Vancouver, OR-WA	102,464	60	Stockton-Lodi, CA	43,430
106	Macon, GA	18,922	61	Providence-Fall River-Warwick, RI-MA	43,218	–	St. Cloud, MN**	NA
113	Madison, WI	17,095	150	Provo-Orem, UT	11,518	224	St. Joseph, MO	5,698
202	Manchester, NH	7,131	194	Pueblo, CO	7,776	–	St. Louis, MO-IL**	NA
167	Mansfield, OH	9,475	243	Punta Gorda, FL	3,717	208	Sumter, SC	6,680
74	McAllen-Edinburg-Mission, TX	32,663	170	Racine, WI	9,316	83	Syracuse, NY	27,549
173	Medford-Ashland, OR	8,957	47	Raleigh-Durham-Chapel Hill, NC	55,587	62	Tacoma, WA	42,843
33	Memphis, TN-AR-MS	77,667	232	Rapid City, SD	4,521	87	Tallahassee, FL	26,766
153	Merced, CA	10,958	147	Reading, PA	11,782	12	Tampa-St. Petersburg-Clearwater, FL	162,845
3	Miami, FL	275,080	191	Redding, CA	7,893	189	Texarkana, TX-AR	7,940
67	Middlesex-Sommerset-Hunterdon, NJ	36,417	110	Reno, NV	18,079	65	Toledo, OH	38,530
32	Milwaukee-Waukesha, WI	77,854	201	Richland-Kennewick-Pasco, WA	7,290	114	Trenton, NJ	17,015
–	Minneapolis-St. Paul, MN-WI**	NA	51	Richmond-Petersburg, VA	51,242	44	Tucson, AZ	65,363
77	Mobile, AL	31,013	7	Riverside-San Bernardino, CA	204,408	63	Tulsa, OK	40,453
81	Modesto, CA	29,358	164	Roanoke, VA	9,661	140	Tuscaloosa, AL	12,496
69	Monmouth-Ocean, NJ	35,904	–	Rochester, MN**	NA	149	Tyler, TX	11,541
160	Monroe, LA	10,000	50	Rochester, NY	52,756	163	Utica-Rome, NY	9,669
112	Montgomery, AL	17,329	176	Rocky Mount, NC	8,859	84	Vallejo-Fairfield-Napa, CA	27,236
132	Myrtle Beach, SC	13,612	25	Sacramento, CA	100,865	86	Ventura, CA	26,937
169	Naples, FL	9,381	–	Saginaw-Bay City-Midland, MI**	NA	226	Victoria, TX	5,549
233	Nashua, NH	4,269	109	Salem, OR	18,265	174	Vineland-Millville-Bridgeton, NJ	8,949
35	Nashville, TN	76,142	105	Salinas, CA	19,188	103	Visalia-Tulare-Porterville, CA	19,748
29	Nassau-Suffolk, NY	89,155	39	Salt Lake City-Ogden, UT	70,349	127	Waco, TX	14,894
165	New Bedford, MA	9,583	229	San Angelo, TX	5,334	5	Washington, DC-MD-VA-WV	240,295
76	New Haven-Meriden, CT	32,031	17	San Antonio, TX	118,798	154	Waterbury, CT	10,911
171	New London-Norwich, CT-RI	9,222	13	San Diego, CA	161,878	215	Waterloo-Cedar Falls, IA	6,205
21	New Orleans, LA	107,328	20	San Francisco, CA	110,022	244	Wausau, WI	3,680
1	New York, NY	649,309	38	San Jose, CA	71,654	–	West Palm Beach-Boca Raton, FL**	NA
19	Newark, NJ	112,459	178	San Luis Obispo-Atascadero, CA	8,752	179	Wichita Falls, TX	8,751
151	Newburgh, NY-PA	11,395	111	Santa Barbara-Santa Maria-Lompoc, CA	18,044	241	Williamsport, PA	3,780
28	Norfolk-Va Beach-Newport News, VA-NC	89,203	131	Santa Cruz-Watsonville, CA	14,048	139	Wilmington, NC	12,726
14	Oakland, CA	159,061	101	Santa Rosa, CA	20,204	–	Worcester, MA-CT**	NA
137	Ocala, FL	13,057	72	Sarasota-Bradenton, FL	34,230	122	Yakima, WA	16,101
117	Odessa-Midland, TX	16,294	102	Savannah, GA	19,985	156	Yolo, CA	10,658
34	Oklahoma City, OK	76,273	124	Scranton-Wilkes-Barre-Hazleton, PA	15,347	186	Yuba City, CA	8,012

Source: U.S. Department of Justice, Federal Bureau of Investigation
"Crime in the United States 1993" (Uniform Crime Reports, December 4, 1994)
*Includes murder, rape, robbery, aggravated assault, burglary, larceny-theft and motor vehicle theft.
**Not available.

1. Crimes in 1993 (continued)

National Total = 14,140,952 Crimes*

RANK	METRO AREA	CRIMES	RANK	METRO AREA	CRIMES	RANK	METRO AREA	CRIMES
1	New York, NY	649,309	48	Birmingham, AL	54,663	95	Augusta-Aiken, GA-SC	21,834
2	Los Angeles–Long Beach, CA	644,758	49	Baton Rouge, LA	54,047	96	Fort Myers–Cape Coral, FL	21,628
3	Miami, FL	275,080	50	Rochester, NY	52,756	97	Brownsville–Harlingen–San Benito, TX	21,371
4	Atlanta, GA	244,965	51	Richmond-Petersburg, VA	51,242	98	Fort Wayne, IN	21,208
5	Washington, DC-MD-VA-WV	240,295	52	Hartford, CT	51,024	99	Lexington, KY	21,179
6	Philadelphia, PA-NJ	216,429	53	Dayton–Springfield, OH	50,787	100	Harrisburg–Lebanon–Carlisle, PA	20,232
7	Riverside–San Bernardino, CA	204,408	54	El Paso, TX	50,163	101	Santa Rosa, CA	20,204
8	Dallas, TX	200,577	55	Greenville–Spartanburg–Anderson, SC	49,626	102	Savannah, GA	19,985
9	Phoenix-Mesa, AZ	186,384	56	Bergen–Passaic, NJ	48,913	103	Visalia–Tulare–Porterville, CA	19,748
10	Baltimore, MD	178,776	57	Albuquerque, NM	47,537	104	Gainesville, FL	19,468
11	Boston, MA-NH	164,388	58	Little Rock–North Little Rock, AR	47,281	105	Salinas, CA	19,188
12	Tampa–St. Petersburg–Clearwater, FL	162,845	59	Louisville, KY-IN	44,867	106	Macon, GA	18,922
13	San Diego, CA	161,878	60	Stockton-Lodi, CA	43,430	107	Canton-Massillon, OH	18,911
14	Oakland, CA	159,061	61	Providence–Fall River–Warwick, RI-MA	43,218	108	Huntsville, AL	18,698
15	Seattle–Bellevue–Everett, WA	142,982	62	Tacoma, WA	42,843	109	Salem, OR	18,265
16	Orange County, CA	135,212	63	Tulsa, OK	40,453	110	Reno, NV	18,079
17	San Antonio, TX	118,798	64	Bakersfield, CA	38,805	111	Santa Barbara–Santa Maria–Lompoc, CA	18,044
18	Fort Lauderdale, FL	117,550	65	Toledo, OH	38,530	112	Montgomery, AL	17,329
19	Newark, NJ	112,459	66	Lakeland–Winter Haven, FL	37,494	113	Madison, WI	17,095
20	San Francisco, CA	110,022	67	Middlesex–Sommerset–Hunterdon, NJ	36,417	114	Trenton, NJ	17,015
21	New Orleans, LA	107,328	68	Jersey City, NJ	36,257	115	Lafayette, LA	16,735
22	Denver, CO	107,059	69	Monmouth-Ocean, NJ	35,904	116	Galveston–Texas City, TX	16,474
23	Fort Worth-Arlington, TX	105,885	70	Gary-Hammond, IN	35,182	117	Odessa-Midland, TX	16,294
24	Portland-Vancouver, OR-WA	102,464	71	Charleston–North Charleston, SC	34,565	118	South Bend, IN	16,272
25	Sacramento, CA	100,865	72	Sarasota-Bradenton, FL	34,230	119	Eugene-Springfield, OR	16,246
26	Orlando, FL	99,448	73	Columbia, SC	33,083	120	Anchorage, AK	16,140
27	Charlotte–Gastonia–Rock Hill, NC-SC	89,577	74	McAllen–Edinburg–Mission, TX	32,663	121	Fort Pierce–Port St. Lucie, FL	16,135
28	Norfolk–Va Beach–Newport News, VA-NC	89,203	75	Jackson, MS	32,092	122	Yakima, WA	16,101
29	Nassau-Suffolk, NY	89,155	76	New Haven-Meriden, CT	32,031	123	Boise, ID	15,403
30	Columbus, OH	84,262	77	Mobile, AL	31,013	124	Scranton–Wilkes-Barre–Hazleton, PA	15,347
31	Jacksonville, FL	83,092	78	Corpus Christi, TX	30,981	125	Columbus, GA-AL	15,262
32	Milwaukee-Waukesha, WI	77,854	79	Akron, OH	30,547	126	Lincoln, NE	15,153
33	Memphis, TN-AR-MS	77,667	80	Shreveport–Bossier City, LA	30,420	127	Waco, TX	14,894
34	Oklahoma City, OK	76,273	81	Modesto, CA	29,358	128	Amarillo, TX	14,798
35	Nashville, TN	76,142	82	Atlantic City, NJ	27,936	129	Lubbock, TX	14,190
36	Cincinnati, OH-KY-IN	75,947	83	Syracuse, NY	27,549	130	Lawrence, MA-NH	14,075
37	Pittsburgh, PA	75,414	84	Vallejo–Fairfield–Napa, CA	27,236	131	Santa Cruz-Watsonville, CA	14,048
38	San Jose, CA	71,654	85	Beaumont–Port Arthur, TX	27,048	132	Myrtle Beach, SC	13,612
39	Salt Lake City-Ogden, UT	70,349	86	Ventura, CA	26,937	133	Stamford-Norwalk, CT	13,406
40	Austin-San Marcos, TX	69,684	87	Tallahassee, FL	26,766	134	Springfield, MO	13,382
41	Greensboro–Winston Salem–High Point, NC	66,968	88	Daytona Beach, FL	25,272	135	Johnson City–Kingsport–Bristol, TN-VA	13,157
42	Las Vegas, NV-AZ	66,409	89	Bridgeport, CT	25,132	136	Killeen-Temple, TX	13,093
43	Fresno, CA	65,838	90	Chattanooga, TN-GA	23,953	137	Ocala, FL	13,057
44	Tucson, AZ	65,363	91	Spokane, WA	23,879	138	Hickory-Morganton, NC	12,886
45	Buffalo–Niagara Falls, NY	63,495	92	Colorado Springs, CO	23,593	139	Wilmington, NC	12,726
46	Honolulu, HI	56,405	93	Fayetteville, NC	23,321	140	Tuscaloosa, AL	12,496
47	Raleigh–Durham–Chapel Hill, NC	55,587	94	Des Moines, IA	22,650	141	Lancaster, PA	12,447

Source: U.S. Department of Justice, Federal Bureau of Investigation
"Crime in the United States 1993" (Uniform Crime Reports, December 4, 1994)
*Includes murder, rape, robbery, aggravated assault, burglary, larceny-theft and motor vehicle theft.
**Not available.

1. Crimes in 1993 (continued)

National Total = 14,140,952 Crimes*

RANK	METRO AREA	CRIMES	RANK	METRO AREA	CRIMES	RANK	METRO AREA	CRIMES
142	Longview-Marshall, TX	12,439	189	Texarkana, TX-AR	7,940	236	Sheboygan, WI	4,155
143	Boulder-Longmont, CO	12,323	190	Clarksville-Hopkinsville, TN-KY	7,906	237	Lewiston-Auburn, ME	4,141
144	Lake Charles, LA	12,027	191	Redding, CA	7,893	238	Kokomo, IN	3,929
145	Brockton, MA	12,010	192	Fayetteville-Springdale-Rogers, AR	7,807	239	Enid, OK	3,928
146	Evansville-Henderson, IN-KY	11,933	193	Elkhart-Goshen, IN	7,806	240	Johnstown, PA	3,793
147	Reading, PA	11,782	194	Pueblo, CO	7,776	241	Williamsport, PA	3,780
148	Appleton-Oshkosh-Neenah, WI	11,585	195	Green Bay, WI	7,713	242	Florence, AL	3,723
149	Tyler, TX	11,541	196	Bryan-College Station, TX	7,697	243	Punta Gorda, FL	3,717
150	Provo-Orem, UT	11,518	197	Janesville-Beloit, WI	7,472	244	Wausau, WI	3,680
151	Newburgh, NY-PA	11,395	198	Bellingham, WA	7,428	245	Owensboro, KY	3,560
152	Charleston, WV	11,022	199	Greeley, CO	7,384	246	Hagerstown, MD	3,249
153	Merced, CA	10,958	200	Houma, LA	7,367	247	Danville, VA	3,231
154	Waterbury, CT	10,911	201	Richland-Kennewick-Pasco, WA	7,290	248	Dubuque, IA	3,211
155	Panama City, FL	10,722	202	Manchester, NH	7,131	249	Bismarck, ND	3,203
156	Yolo, CA	10,658	203	Lafayette, IN	7,016	250	Cheyenne, WY	3,199
157	Laredo, TX	10,465	204	Brazoria, TX	7,013	251	Altoona, PA	3,170
158	Portland, ME	10,254	205	Jackson, TN	6,823	252	Cumberland, MD-WV	2,905
159	Albany, GA	10,242	206	Kenosha, WI	6,769	253	Pittsfield, MA	2,889
160	Monroe, LA	10,000	207	Jacksonville, NC	6,736	254	Steubenville-Weirton, OH-WV	2,782
161	Athens, GA	9,754	208	Sumter, SC	6,680	255	Bangor, ME	2,399
162	Erie, PA	9,673	209	Anniston, AL	6,536	–	Albany, NY**	NA
163	Utica-Rome, NY	9,669	210	Gadsden, AL	6,519	–	Ann Arbor, MI**	NA
164	Roanoke, VA	9,661	211	Dothan, AL	6,484	–	Benton Harbor, MI**	NA
165	New Bedford, MA	9,583	212	Lawton, OK	6,384	–	Chicago, IL**	NA
166	Chico-Paradise, CA	9,549	213	Fitchburg-Leominster, MA	6,315	–	Cleveland, OH**	NA
167	Mansfield, OH	9,475	214	Lynchburg, VA	6,228	–	Detroit, MI**	NA
168	Huntington-Ashland, WV-KY-OH	9,393	215	Waterloo-Cedar Falls, IA	6,205	–	Duluth-Superior, MN-WI**	NA
169	Naples, FL	9,381	216	Goldsboro, NC	6,090	–	Fargo-Moorhead, ND-MN**	NA
170	Racine, WI	9,316	217	Columbia, MO	6,004	–	Flint, MI**	NA
171	New London-Norwich, CT-RI	9,222	218	Barnstable-Yarmouth, MA	5,937	–	Grand Forks, ND-MN**	NA
172	Alexandria, LA	9,068	219	Charlottesville, VA	5,916	–	Grand Rapids-Muskegon-Holland, MI**	NA
173	Medford-Ashland, OR	8,957	220	Fort Walton Beach, FL	5,829	–	Houston, TX**	NA
174	Vineland-Millville-Bridgeton, NJ	8,949	221	Abilene, TX	5,758	–	Indianapolis, IN**	NA
175	Greenville, NC	8,935	221	Pine Bluff, AR	5,758	–	Jackson, MI**	NA
176	Rocky Mount, NC	8,859	223	Sioux Falls, SD	5,699	–	Kalamazoo-Battle Creek, MI**	NA
177	Binghamton, NY	8,787	224	St. Joseph, MO	5,698	–	Kansas City, MO-KS**	NA
178	San Luis Obispo-Atascadero, CA	8,752	225	Joplin, MO	5,585	–	La Crosse, WI-MN**	NA
179	Wichita Falls, TX	8,751	226	Victoria, TX	5,549	–	Lansing-East Lansing, MI**	NA
180	Olympia, WA	8,607	227	Danbury, CT	5,496	–	Minneapolis-St. Paul, MN-WI**	NA
181	Bremerton, WA	8,521	228	Sherman-Denison, TX	5,451	–	Omaha, NE**	NA
182	Fort Smith, AR-OK	8,397	229	San Angelo, TX	5,334	–	Rochester, MN**	NA
183	Florence, SC	8,355	230	Eau Claire, WI	5,021	–	Saginaw-Bay City-Midland, MI**	NA
184	Sioux City, IA-NE	8,210	231	Decatur, AL	4,975	–	Springfield, MA**	NA
185	Asheville, NC	8,107	232	Rapid City, SD	4,521	–	St. Cloud, MN**	NA
186	Yuba City, CA	8,012	233	Nashua, NH	4,269	–	St. Louis, MO-IL**	NA
187	Dutchess County, NY	8,000	234	Bloomington, IN	4,204	–	West Palm Beach-Boca Raton, FL**	NA
188	Fort Collins-Loveland, CO	7,985	235	Glens Falls, NY	4,157	–	Worcester, MA-CT**	NA

Source: U.S. Department of Justice, Federal Bureau of Investigation
"Crime in the United States 1993" (Uniform Crime Reports, December 4, 1994)
*Includes murder, rape, robbery, aggravated assault, burglary, larceny-theft and motor vehicle theft.
**Not available.

2. Crime Rate in 1993

National Rate = 5,482.9 Crimes per 100,000 Population*

RANK	METRO AREA	RATE	RANK	METRO AREA	RATE	RANK	METRO AREA	RATE
174	Abilene, TX	4,684.1	197	Cheyenne, WY	4,161.0	63	Fort Worth–Arlington, TX	6,880.9
181	Akron, OH	4,573.0	–	Chicago, IL**	NA	19	Fresno, CA	8,099.6
10	Albany, GA	8,703.3	155	Chico–Paradise, CA	5,017.8	76	Gadsden, AL	6,483.0
–	Albany, NY**	NA	166	Cincinnati, OH–KY–IN	4,833.6	3	Gainesville, FL	10,131.2
35	Albuquerque, NM	7,547.8	187	Clarksville–Hopkinsville, TN–KY	4,382.3	51	Galveston–Texas City, TX	7,083.6
59	Alexandria, LA	6,920.0	–	Cleveland, OH**	NA	122	Gary–Hammond, IN	5,649.2
252	Altoona, PA	2,403.4	137	Colorado Springs, CO	5,442.9	3	Gainesville, FL	
34	Amarillo, TX	7,573.0	152	Columbia, MO	5,094.1	226	Glens Falls, NY	3,420.8
81	Anchorage, AK	6,437.5	58	Columbia, SC	6,926.5	127	Goldsboro, NC	5,565.4
–	Ann Arbor, MI**	NA	133	Columbus, GA–AL	5,483.5	–	Grand Forks, ND–MN**	NA
129	Anniston, AL	5,549.3	107	Columbus, OH	6,012.8	–	Grand Rapids–Muskegon–Holland, MI**	NA
223	Appleton–Oshkosh–Neenah, WI	3,510.9	16	Corpus Christi, TX	8,384.9	142	Greeley, CO	5,280.8
200	Asheville, NC	4,041.3	247	Cumberland, MD–WV	2,836.7	212	Green Bay, WI	3,796.3
85	Athens, GA	6,314.7	45	Dallas, TX	7,290.9	97	Greensboro–Winston Salem–High Point, NC	6,109.4
32	Atlanta, GA	7,594.5	230	Danbury, CT	3,380.3	22	Greenville, NC	7,967.1
14	Atlantic City, NJ	8,498.4	245	Danville, VA	2,911.4	117	Greenville–Spartanburg–Anderson, SC	5,746.0
165	Augusta–Aiken, GA–SC	4,835.9	110	Daytona Beach, FL	5,906.4	251	Hagerstown, MD	2,564.3
33	Austin–San Marcos, TX	7,584.5	147	Dayton–Springfield, OH	5,245.4	232	Harrisburg–Lebanon–Carlisle, PA	3,344.6
74	Bakersfield, CA	6,536.3	219	Decatur, AL	3,636.9	164	Hartford, CT	4,841.9
48	Baltimore, MD	7,275.4	100	Denver, CO	6,090.8	193	Hickory–Morganton, NC	4,239.2
222	Bangor, ME	3,547.6	130	Des Moines, IA	5,549.1	80	Honolulu, HI	6,442.9
191	Barnstable–Yarmouth, MA	4,329.8	–	Detroit, MI**	NA	206	Houma, LA	3,935.1
4	Baton Rouge, LA	9,856.1	168	Dothan, AL	4,807.9	–	Houston, TX**	NA
50	Beaumont–Port Arthur, TX	7,172.8	217	Dubuque, IA	3,665.0	242	Huntington–Ashland, WV–KY–OH	2,961.6
144	Bellingham, WA	5,271.3	–	Duluth–Superior, MN–WI**	NA	108	Huntsville, AL	5,998.8
–	Benton Harbor, MI**	NA	241	Dutchess County, NY	3,028.8	–	Indianapolis, IN**	NA
213	Bergen–Passaic, NJ	3,760.1	220	Eau Claire, WI	3,557.3	–	Jackson, MI**	NA
233	Binghamton, NY	3,279.0	26	El Paso, TX	7,827.7	25	Jackson, MS	7,842.2
86	Birmingham, AL	6,288.0	162	Elkhart–Goshen, IN	4,852.6	17	Jackson, TN	8,381.0
216	Bismarck, ND	3,716.5	60	Enid, OK	6,913.3	11	Jacksonville, FL	8,598.0
214	Bloomington, IN	3,747.4	225	Erie, PA	3,444.3	180	Jacksonville, NC	4,587.6
175	Boise, ID	4,672.5	134	Eugene–Springfield, OR	5,473.4	148	Janesville–Beloit, WI	5,187.2
163	Boston, MA–NH	4,844.6	196	Evansville–Henderson, IN–KY	4,178.7	75	Jersey City, NJ	6,484.6
154	Boulder–Longmont, CO	5,027.4	–	Fargo–Moorhead, ND–MN**	NA	244	Johnson City–Kingsport–Bristol, TN–VA	2,917.8
231	Brazoria, TX	3,373.9	18	Fayetteville, NC	8,277.5	255	Johnstown, PA	1,568.4
204	Bremerton, WA	3,956.7	228	Fayetteville–Springdale–Rogers, AR	3,415.8	201	Joplin, MO	4,028.5
128	Bridgeport, CT	5,549.6	177	Fitchburg–Leominster, MA	4,609.8	–	Kalamazoo–Battle Creek, MI**	NA
160	Brockton, MA	4,877.4	–	Flint, MI**	NA	–	Kansas City, MO–KS**	NA
37	Brownsville–Harlingen–San Benito, TX	7,520.6	248	Florence, AL	2,741.3	156	Kenosha, WI	5,007.4
104	Bryan–College Station, TX	6,031.2	57	Florence, SC	6,967.8	153	Killeen–Temple, TX	5,038.3
141	Buffalo–Niagara Falls, NY	5,283.8	209	Fort Collins–Loveland, CO	3,916.2	205	Kokomo, IN	3,947.3
173	Canton–Massillon, OH	4,705.9	6	Fort Lauderdale, FL	8,904.1	–	La Crosse, WI–MN**	NA
190	Charleston, WV	4,334.3	103	Fort Myers–Cape Coral, FL	6,055.4	194	Lafayette, IN	4,215.1
78	Charleston–North Charleston, SC	6,467.5	109	Fort Pierce–Port St. Lucie, FL	5,992.5	172	Lafayette, LA	4,719.3
189	Charlottesville, VA	4,334.6	178	Fort Smith, AR–OK	4,597.3	55	Lake Charles, LA	6,986.5
47	Charlotte–Gastonia–Rock Hill, NC–SC	7,277.0	215	Fort Walton Beach, FL	3,744.8	9	Lakeland–Winter Haven, FL	8,820.9
135	Chattanooga, TN–GA	5,466.5	183	Fort Wayne, IN	4,534.0	246	Lancaster, PA	2,852.7
						–	Lansing–East Lansing, MI**	NA

Source: U.S. Department of Justice, Federal Bureau of Investigation
  "Crime in the United States 1993" (Uniform Crime Reports, December 4, 1994)
*Includes offenses of murder, forcible rape, robbery, aggravated assault, burglary, larceny-theft and motor vehicle theft.
**Not available.

2. Crime Rate in 1993 (continued)

National Rate = 5,482.9 Crimes per 100,000 Population*

RANK	METRO AREA	RATE	RANK	METRO AREA	RATE	RANK	METRO AREA	RATE
61	Laredo, TX	6,912.8	169	Olympia, WA	4,770.8	62	Seattle-Bellevue-Everett, WA	6,887.6
73	Las Vegas, NV–AZ	6,588.6	–	Omaha, NE**	NA	208	Sheboygan, WI	3,920.4
171	Lawrence, MA–NH	4,756.2	138	Orange County, CA	5,386.5	124	Sherman-Denison, TX	5,623.0
146	Lawton, OK	5,256.8	38	Orlando, FL	7,513.2	20	Shreveport-Bossier City, LA	8,098.4
202	Lewiston-Auburn, ME	3,978.2	203	Owensboro, KY	3,971.4	56	Sioux City, IA–NE	6,983.1
114	Lexington, KY	5,814.9	24	Panama City, FL	7,886.5	211	Sioux Falls, SD	3,841.4
65	Lincoln, NE	6,875.1	188	Philadelphia, PA–NJ	4,355.3	82	South Bend, IN	6,432.7
7	Little Rock-North Little Rock, AR	8,884.8	27	Phoenix-Mesa, AZ	7,787.9	96	Spokane, WA	6,130.9
99	Longview-Marshall, TX	6,101.9	72	Pine Bluff, AR	6,670.1	–	Springfield, MA**	NA
53	Los Angeles-Long Beach, CA	7,049.6	236	Pittsburgh, PA	3,111.2	167	Springfield, MO	4,815.4
179	Louisville, KY–IN	4,593.9	243	Pittsfield, MA	2,932.4	199	Stamford-Norwalk, CT	4,066.9
90	Lubbock, TX	6,216.8	186	Portland, ME	4,386.3	254	Steubenville-Weirton, OH–WV	1,953.6
237	Lynchburg, VA	3,092.4	88	Portland-Vancouver, OR–WA	6,244.5	12	Stockton-Lodi, CA	8,528.3
91	Macon, GA	6,204.6	184	Providence-Fall River-Warwick, RI–MA	4,517.0	–	St. Cloud, MN**	NA
182	Madison, WI	4,538.3	198	Provo-Orem, UT	4,077.2	116	St. Joseph, MO	5,767.4
192	Manchester, NH	4,273.2	98	Pueblo, CO	6,105.4	–	St. Louis, MO–IL**	NA
139	Mansfield, OH	5,366.1	238	Punta Gorda, FL	3,072.3	87	Sumter, SC	6,270.9
31	McAllen-Edinburg-Mission, TX	7,609.6	151	Racine, WI	5,143.5	218	Syracuse, NY	3,639.9
119	Medford-Ashland, OR	5,698.0	105	Raleigh-Durham-Chapel Hill, NC	6,021.7	69	Tacoma, WA	6,759.2
39	Memphis, TN–AR–MS	7,408.6	145	Rapid City, SD	5,266.0	2	Tallahassee, FL	10,756.3
118	Merced, CA	5,736.0	227	Reading, PA	3,418.7	30	Tampa-St. Petersburg-Clearwater, FL	7,617.1
1	Miami, FL	13,500.4	158	Redding, CA	4,957.6	79	Texarkana, TX–AR	6,453.9
224	Middlesex-Sommerset-Hunterdon, NJ	3,453.0	77	Reno, NV	6,475.5	89	Toledo, OH	6,222.5
140	Milwaukee-Waukesha, WI	5,355.8	185	Richland-Kennewick-Pasco, WA	4,434.2	150	Trenton, NJ	5,153.6
–	Minneapolis-St. Paul, MN–WI**	NA	123	Richmond-Petersburg, VA	5,633.1	5	Tucson, AZ	9,219.9
93	Mobile, AL	6,184.8	49	Riverside-San Bernardino, CA	7,203.6	132	Tulsa, OK	5,484.1
40	Modesto, CA	7,353.2	195	Roanoke, VA	4,205.7	21	Tuscaloosa, AL	8,038.5
221	Monmouth-Ocean, NJ	3,554.0	–	Rochester, MN**	NA	42	Tyler, TX	7,331.1
64	Monroe, LA	6,875.2	161	Rochester, NY	4,855.7	240	Utica-Rome, NY	3,044.6
126	Montgomery, AL	5,599.9	84	Rocky Mount, NC	6,355.3	121	Vallejo-Fairfield-Napa, CA	5,674.6
8	Myrtle Beach, SC	8,838.6	54	Sacramento, CA	7,038.4	210	Ventura, CA	3,883.8
125	Naples, FL	5,613.2	–	Saginaw-Bay City-Midland, MI**	NA	52	Victoria, TX	7,063.7
249	Nashua, NH	2,661.8	95	Salem, OR	6,146.2	83	Vineland-Millville-Bridgeton, NJ	6,413.4
41	Nashville, TN	7,331.8	149	Salinas, CA	5,157.0	111	Visalia-Tulare-Porterville, CA	5,904.4
229	Nassau-Suffolk, NY	3,392.4	102	Salt Lake City-Ogden, UT	6,072.6	29	Waco, TX	7,625.2
131	New Bedford, MA	5,488.3	143	San Angelo, TX	5,278.1	136	Washington, DC–MD–VA–WV	5,462.4
120	New Haven-Meriden, CT	5,691.1	15	San Antonio, TX	8,450.9	112	Waterbury, CT	5,886.4
239	New London-Norwich, CT–RI	3,060.7	94	San Diego, CA	6,160.5	159	Waterloo-Cedar Falls, IA	4,929.1
13	New Orleans, LA	8,511.7	71	San Francisco, CA	6,697.5	250	Wausau, WI	2,659.6
36	New York, NY	7,532.9	176	San Jose, CA	4,640.3	–	West Palm Beach-Boca Raton, FL**	NA
115	Newark, NJ	5,803.5	207	San Luis Obispo-Atascadero, CA	3,928.0	70	Wichita Falls, TX	6,700.5
234	Newburgh, NY–PA	3,256.0	170	Santa Barbara-Santa Maria-Lompoc, CA	4,756.4	235	Williamsport, PA	3,124.1
113	Norfolk-Va Beach-Newport News, VA–NC	5,871.0	106	Santa Cruz-Watsonville, CA	6,020.1	66	Wilmington, NC	6,873.6
43	Oakland, CA	7,329.6	157	Santa Rosa, CA	4,987.5	–	Worcester, MA–CT**	NA
92	Ocala, FL	6,187.9	68	Sarasota-Bradenton, FL	6,764.5	23	Yakima, WA	7,957.8
67	Odessa-Midland, TX	6,835.4	44	Savannah, GA	7,319.5	46	Yolo, CA	7,285.5
28	Oklahoma City, OK	7,692.7	253	Scranton-Wilkes-Barre-Hazleton, PA	2,392.5	101	Yuba City, CA	6,085.2

Source: U.S. Department of Justice, Federal Bureau of Investigation
   "Crime in the United States 1993" (Uniform Crime Reports, December 4, 1994)
*Includes offenses of murder, forcible rape, robbery, aggravated assault, burglary, larceny-theft and motor vehicle theft.
**Not available.

2. Crime Rate in 1993 (continued)

National Rate = 5,482.9 Crimes per 100,000 Population*

RANK	METRO AREA	RATE	RANK	METRO AREA	RATE	RANK	METRO AREA	RATE
1	Miami, FL	13,500.4	48	Baltimore, MD	7,275.4	95	Salem, OR	6,146.2
2	Tallahassee, FL	10,756.3	49	Riverside–San Bernardino, CA	7,203.6	96	Spokane, WA	6,130.9
3	Gainesville, FL	10,131.2	50	Beaumont–Port Arthur, TX	7,172.8	97	Greensboro–Winston Salem–High Point, NC	6,109.4
4	Baton Rouge, LA	9,856.1	51	Galveston–Texas City, TX	7,083.6	98	Pueblo, CO	6,105.4
5	Tucson, AZ	9,219.9	52	Victoria, TX	7,063.7	99	Longview–Marshall, TX	6,101.9
6	Fort Lauderdale, FL	8,904.1	53	Los Angeles–Long Beach, CA	7,049.6	100	Denver, CO	6,090.8
7	Little Rock–North Little Rock, AR	8,884.8	54	Sacramento, CA	7,038.4	101	Yuba City, CA	6,085.2
8	Myrtle Beach, SC	8,838.6	55	Lake Charles, LA	6,986.5	102	Salt Lake City–Ogden, UT	6,072.6
9	Lakeland–Winter Haven, FL	8,820.9	56	Sioux City, IA–NE	6,983.1	103	Fort Myers–Cape Coral, FL	6,055.4
10	Albany, GA	8,703.3	57	Florence, SC	6,967.8	104	Bryan–College Station, TX	6,031.2
11	Jacksonville, FL	8,598.0	58	Columbia, SC	6,926.5	105	Raleigh–Durham–Chapel Hill, NC	6,021.7
12	Stockton–Lodi, CA	8,528.3	59	Alexandria, LA	6,920.0	106	Santa Cruz–Watsonville, CA	6,020.1
13	New Orleans, LA	8,511.7	60	Enid, OK	6,913.3	107	Columbus, OH	6,012.8
14	Atlantic City, NJ	8,498.4	61	Laredo, TX	6,912.8	108	Huntsville, AL	5,998.8
15	San Antonio, TX	8,450.9	62	Seattle–Bellevue–Everett, WA	6,887.6	109	Fort Pierce–Port St. Lucie, FL	5,992.5
16	Corpus Christi, TX	8,384.9	63	Fort Worth–Arlington, TX	6,880.9	110	Daytona Beach, FL	5,906.4
17	Jackson, TN	8,381.0	64	Monroe, LA	6,875.2	111	Visalia–Tulare–Porterville, CA	5,904.4
18	Fayetteville, NC	8,277.5	65	Lincoln, NE	6,875.1	112	Waterbury, CT	5,886.4
19	Fresno, CA	8,099.6	66	Wilmington, NC	6,873.6	113	Norfolk–Va Beach–Newport News, VA–NC	5,871.0
20	Shreveport–Bossier City, LA	8,098.4	67	Odessa–Midland, TX	6,835.4	114	Lexington, KY	5,814.9
21	Tuscaloosa, AL	8,038.5	68	Sarasota–Bradenton, FL	6,764.5	115	Newark, NJ	5,803.5
22	Greenville, NC	7,967.1	69	Tacoma, WA	6,759.2	116	St. Joseph, MO	5,767.4
23	Yakima, WA	7,957.8	70	Wichita Falls, TX	6,700.5	117	Greenville–Spartanburg–Anderson, SC	5,746.0
24	Panama City, FL	7,886.5	71	San Francisco, CA	6,697.5	118	Merced, CA	5,736.0
25	Jackson, MS	7,842.2	72	Pine Bluff, AR	6,670.1	119	Medford–Ashland, OR	5,698.0
26	El Paso, TX	7,827.7	73	Las Vegas, NV–AZ	6,588.6	120	New Haven–Meriden, CT	5,691.1
27	Phoenix–Mesa, AZ	7,787.9	74	Bakersfield, CA	6,536.3	121	Vallejo–Fairfield–Napa, CA	5,674.6
28	Oklahoma City, OK	7,692.7	75	Jersey City, NJ	6,484.6	122	Gary–Hammond, IN	5,649.2
29	Waco, TX	7,625.2	76	Gadsden, AL	6,483.0	123	Richmond–Petersburg, VA	5,633.1
30	Tampa–St. Petersburg–Clearwater, FL	7,617.1	77	Reno, NV	6,475.5	124	Sherman–Denison, TX	5,623.0
31	McAllen–Edinburg–Mission, TX	7,609.6	78	Charleston–North Charleston, SC	6,467.5	125	Naples, FL	5,613.2
32	Atlanta, GA	7,594.5	79	Texarkana, TX–AR	6,453.9	126	Montgomery, AL	5,599.9
33	Austin–San Marcos, TX	7,584.5	80	Honolulu, HI	6,442.9	127	Goldsboro, NC	5,565.4
34	Amarillo, TX	7,573.0	81	Anchorage, AK	6,437.5	128	Bridgeport, CT	5,549.6
35	Albuquerque, NM	7,547.8	82	South Bend, IN	6,432.7	129	Anniston, AL	5,549.3
36	New York, NY	7,532.9	83	Vineland–Millville–Bridgeton, NJ	6,413.4	130	Des Moines, IA	5,549.1
37	Brownsville–Harlingen–San Benito, TX	7,520.6	84	Rocky Mount, NC	6,355.3	131	New Bedford, MA	5,488.3
38	Orlando, FL	7,513.2	85	Athens, GA	6,314.7	132	Tulsa, OK	5,484.1
39	Memphis, TN–AR–MS	7,408.6	86	Birmingham, AL	6,288.0	133	Columbus, GA–AL	5,483.5
40	Modesto, CA	7,353.2	87	Sumter, SC	6,270.9	134	Eugene–Springfield, OR	5,473.4
41	Nashville, TN	7,331.8	88	Portland–Vancouver, OR–WA	6,244.5	135	Chattanooga, TN–GA	5,466.5
42	Tyler, TX	7,331.1	89	Toledo, OH	6,222.5	136	Washington, DC–MD–VA–WV	5,462.4
43	Oakland, CA	7,329.6	90	Lubbock, TX	6,216.8	137	Colorado Springs, CO	5,442.9
44	Savannah, GA	7,319.5	91	Macon, GA	6,204.6	138	Orange County, CA	5,386.5
45	Dallas, TX	7,290.9	92	Ocala, FL	6,187.9	139	Mansfield, OH	5,366.1
46	Yolo, CA	7,285.5	93	Mobile, AL	6,184.8	140	Milwaukee–Waukesha, WI	5,355.8
47	Charlotte–Gastonia–Rock Hill, NC–SC	7,277.0	94	San Diego, CA	6,160.5	141	Buffalo–Niagara Falls, NY	5,283.8

Source: U.S. Department of Justice, Federal Bureau of Investigation
"Crime in the United States 1993" (Uniform Crime Reports, December 4, 1994)
*Includes offenses of murder, forcible rape, robbery, aggravated assault, burglary, larceny-theft and motor vehicle theft.
**Not available.

2. Crime Rate in 1993 (continued)

National Rate = 5,482.9 Crimes per 100,000 Population*

RANK	METRO AREA	RATE	RANK	METRO AREA	RATE	RANK	METRO AREA	RATE
142	Greeley, CO	5,280.8	189	Charlottesville, VA	4,334.6	236	Pittsburgh, PA	3,111.2
143	San Angelo, TX	5,278.1	190	Charleston, WV	4,334.3	237	Lynchburg, VA	3,092.4
144	Bellingham, WA	5,271.3	191	Barnstable-Yarmouth, MA	4,329.8	238	Punta Gorda, FL	3,072.3
145	Rapid City, SD	5,266.0	192	Manchester, NH	4,273.2	239	New London-Norwich, CT-RI	3,060.7
146	Lawton, OK	5,256.8	193	Hickory-Morganton, NC	4,239.2	240	Utica-Rome, NY	3,044.6
147	Dayton-Springfield, OH	5,245.4	194	Lafayette, IN	4,215.1	241	Dutchess County, NY	3,028.8
148	Janesville-Beloit, WI	5,187.2	195	Roanoke, VA	4,205.7	242	Huntington-Ashland, WV-KY-OH	2,961.6
149	Salinas, CA	5,157.0	196	Evansville-Henderson, IN-KY	4,178.7	243	Pittsfield, MA	2,932.4
150	Trenton, NJ	5,153.6	197	Cheyenne, WY	4,161.0	244	Johnson City-Kingsport-Bristol, TN-VA	2,917.8
151	Racine, WI	5,143.5	198	Provo-Orem, UT	4,077.2	245	Danville, VA	2,911.4
152	Columbia, MO	5,094.1	199	Stamford-Norwalk, CT	4,066.9	246	Lancaster, PA	2,852.7
153	Killeen-Temple, TX	5,038.3	200	Asheville, NC	4,041.3	247	Cumberland, MD-WV	2,836.7
154	Boulder-Longmont, CO	5,027.4	201	Joplin, MO	4,028.5	248	Florence, AL	2,741.3
155	Chico-Paradise, CA	5,017.8	202	Lewiston-Auburn, ME	3,978.2	249	Nashua, NH	2,661.8
156	Kenosha, WI	5,007.4	203	Owensboro, KY	3,971.4	250	Wausau, WI	2,659.6
157	Santa Rosa, CA	4,987.5	204	Bremerton, WA	3,956.7	251	Hagerstown, MD	2,564.3
158	Redding, CA	4,957.6	205	Kokomo, IN	3,947.3	252	Altoona, PA	2,403.4
159	Waterloo-Cedar Falls, IA	4,929.1	206	Houma, LA	3,935.1	253	Scranton-Wilkes-Barre-Hazleton, PA	2,392.5
160	Brockton, MA	4,877.4	207	San Luis Obispo-Atascadero, CA	3,928.0	254	Steubenville-Weirton, OH-WV	1,953.6
161	Rochester, NY	4,855.7	208	Sheboygan, WI	3,920.4	255	Johnstown, PA	1,568.4
162	Elkhart-Goshen, IN	4,852.6	209	Fort Collins-Loveland, CO	3,916.2	–	Albany, NY**	NA
163	Boston, MA-NH	4,844.6	210	Ventura, CA	3,883.8	–	Ann Arbor, MI**	NA
164	Hartford, CT	4,841.9	211	Sioux Falls, SD	3,841.4	–	Benton Harbor, MI**	NA
165	Augusta-Aiken, GA-SC	4,835.9	212	Green Bay, WI	3,796.3	–	Chicago, IL**	NA
166	Cincinnati, OH-KY-IN	4,833.6	213	Bergen-Passaic, NJ	3,760.1	–	Cleveland, OH**	NA
167	Springfield, MO	4,815.4	214	Bloomington, IN	3,747.4	–	Detroit, MI**	NA
168	Dothan, AL	4,807.9	215	Fort Walton Beach, FL	3,744.8	–	Duluth-Superior, MN-WI**	NA
169	Olympia, WA	4,770.8	216	Bismarck, ND	3,716.5	–	Fargo-Moorhead, ND-MN**	NA
170	Santa Barbara-Santa Maria-Lompoc, CA	4,756.4	217	Dubuque, IA	3,665.0	–	Flint, MI**	NA
171	Lawrence, MA-NH	4,756.2	218	Syracuse, NY	3,639.9	–	Grand Forks, ND-MN**	NA
172	Lafayette, LA	4,719.3	219	Decatur, AL	3,636.9	–	Grand Rapids-Muskegon-Holland, MI**	NA
173	Canton-Massillon, OH	4,705.9	220	Eau Claire, WI	3,557.3	–	Houston, TX**	NA
174	Abilene, TX	4,684.1	221	Monmouth-Ocean, NJ	3,554.0	–	Indianapolis, IN**	NA
175	Boise, ID	4,672.5	222	Bangor, ME	3,547.6	–	Jackson, MI**	NA
176	San Jose, CA	4,640.3	223	Appleton-Oshkosh-Neenah, WI	3,510.9	–	Kalamazoo-Battle Creek, MI**	NA
177	Fitchburg-Leominster, MA	4,609.8	224	Middlesex-Somerset-Hunterdon, NJ	3,453.0	–	Kansas City, MO-KS**	NA
178	Fort Smith, AR-OK	4,597.3	225	Erie, PA	3,444.3	–	La Crosse, WI-MN**	NA
179	Louisville, KY-IN	4,593.9	226	Glens Falls, NY	3,420.8	–	Lansing-East Lansing, MI**	NA
180	Jacksonville, NC	4,587.6	227	Reading, PA	3,418.7	–	Minneapolis-St. Paul, MN-WI**	NA
181	Akron, OH	4,573.0	228	Fayetteville-Springdale-Rogers, AR	3,415.8	–	Omaha, NE**	NA
182	Madison, WI	4,538.3	229	Nassau-Suffolk, NY	3,392.4	–	Rochester, MN**	NA
183	Fort Wayne, IN	4,534.0	230	Danbury, CT	3,380.3	–	Saginaw-Bay City-Midland, MI**	NA
184	Providence-Fall River-Warwick, RI-MA	4,517.0	231	Brazoria, TX	3,373.9	–	Springfield, MA**	NA
185	Richland-Kennewick-Pasco, WA	4,434.2	232	Harrisburg-Lebanon-Carlisle, PA	3,344.6	–	St. Cloud, MN**	NA
186	Portland, ME	4,386.3	233	Binghamton, NY	3,279.0	–	St. Louis, MO-IL**	NA
187	Clarksville-Hopkinsville, TN-KY	4,382.3	234	Newburgh, NY-PA	3,256.0	–	West Palm Beach-Boca Raton, FL**	NA
188	Philadelphia, PA-NJ	4,355.3	235	Williamsport, PA	3,124.1	–	Worcester, MA-CT**	NA

Source: U.S. Department of Justice, Federal Bureau of Investigation
   "Crime in the United States 1993" (Uniform Crime Reports, December 4, 1994)
Includes offenses of murder, forcible rape, robbery, aggravated assault, burglary, larceny-theft and motor vehicle theft.
**Not available.*

3. Percent Change in Crime Rate: 1992 to 1993

National Percent Change = 3.1% Decrease*

RANK	METRO AREA	% CHANGE	RANK	METRO AREA	% CHANGE	RANK	METRO AREA	% CHANGE
43	Abilene, TX	2.04	225	Cheyenne, WY	(14.44)	230	Fort Worth–Arlington, TX	(18.97)
181	Akron, OH	(7.15)	–	Chicago, IL**	NA	183	Fresno, CA	(7.29)
147	Albany, GA	(4.98)	149	Chico–Paradise, CA	(5.20)	124	Gadsden, AL	(3.74)
–	Albany, NY**	NA	165	Cincinnati, OH–KY–IN	(6.44)	158	Gainesville, FL	(5.82)
68	Albuquerque, NM	(0.11)	173	Clarksville–Hopkinsville, TN–KY	(6.76)	195	Galveston–Texas City, TX	(8.83)
53	Alexandria, LA	1.09	–	Cleveland, OH**	NA	155	Gary–Hammond, IN	(5.68)
4	Altoona, PA	12.48	117	Colorado Springs, CO	(3.45)	119	Glens Falls, NY	(3.56)
60	Amarillo, TX	0.61	168	Columbia, MO	(6.57)	64	Goldsboro, NC	0.07
194	Anchorage, AK	(8.77)	61	Columbia, SC	0.58	–	Grand Forks, ND–MN**	NA
–	Ann Arbor, MI**	NA	46	Columbus, GA–AL	1.76	–	Grand Rapids–Muskegon–Holland, MI**	NA
114	Anniston, AL	(3.19)	169	Columbus, OH	(6.63)	130	Greeley, CO	(4.07)
175	Appleton–Oshkosh–Neenah, WI	(6.86)	135	Corpus Christi, TX	(4.37)	73	Green Bay, WI	(0.77)
218	Asheville, NC	(12.36)	187	Cumberland, MD–WV	(8.05)	62	Greensboro–Winston Salem–High Point, NC	0.10
223	Athens, GA	(13.33)	224	Dallas, TX	(13.73)	118	Greenville, NC	(3.48)
133	Atlanta, GA	(4.25)	126	Danbury, CT	(3.86)	47	Greenville–Spartanburg–Anderson, SC	1.71
182	Atlantic City, NJ	(7.16)	71	Danville, VA	(0.64)	67	Hagerstown, MD	(0.09)
227	Augusta–Aiken, GA–SC	(17.56)	79	Daytona Beach, FL	(1.22)	190	Harrisburg–Lebanon–Carlisle, PA	(8.35)
171	Austin–San Marcos, TX	(6.72)	137	Dayton–Springfield, OH	(4.50)	202	Hartford, CT	(9.40)
87	Bakersfield, CA	(1.80)	142	Decatur, AL	(4.90)	29	Hickory–Morganton, NC	3.85
83	Baltimore, MD	(1.45)	189	Denver, CO	(8.18)	20	Honolulu, HI	5.30
72	Bangor, ME	(0.66)	213	Des Moines, IA	(10.92)	96	Houma, LA	(2.43)
156	Barnstable–Yarmouth, MA	(5.74)	–	Detroit, MI**	NA	–	Houston, TX**	NA
130	Baton Rouge, LA	(4.07)	176	Dothan, AL	(7.03)	201	Huntington–Ashland, WV–KY–OH	(9.38)
164	Beaumont–Port Arthur, TX	(6.42)	3	Dubuque, IA	16.64	160	Huntsville, AL	(6.14)
166	Bellingham, WA	(6.46)	–	Duluth–Superior, MN–WI**	NA	–	Indianapolis, IN**	NA
–	Benton Harbor, MI**	NA	–	Dutchess County, NY**	NA	–	Jackson, MI**	NA
–	Bergen–Passaic, NJ**	NA	113	Eau Claire, WI	(3.10)	128	Jackson, MS	(4.05)
15	Binghamton, NY	7.36	180	El Paso, TX	(7.14)	107	Jackson, TN	(2.95)
121	Birmingham, AL	(3.60)	8	Elkhart–Goshen, IN	10.72	162	Jacksonville, FL	(6.23)
200	Bismarck, ND	(9.36)	13	Enid, OK	7.86	54	Jacksonville, NC	0.95
38	Bloomington, IN	2.70	34	Erie, PA	3.38	203	Janesville–Beloit, WI	(9.44)
108	Boise, ID	(2.96)	56	Eugene–Springfield, OR	0.81	–	Jersey City, NJ**	NA
–	Boston, MA–NH**	NA	161	Evansville–Henderson, IN–KY	(6.21)	157	Johnson City–Kingsport–Bristol, TN–VA	(5.75)
210	Boulder–Longmont, CO	(10.09)	–	Fargo–Moorhead, ND–MN**	NA	208	Johnstown, PA	(9.89)
217	Brazoria, TX	(12.30)	59	Fayetteville, NC	0.70	–	Joplin, MO**	NA
218	Bremerton, WA	(12.36)	228	Fayetteville–Springdale–Rogers, AR	(17.59)	–	Kalamazoo–Battle Creek, MI**	NA
206	Bridgeport, CT	(9.70)	–	Fitchburg–Leominster, MA**	NA	–	Kansas City, MO–KS**	NA
220	Brockton, MA	(12.40)	–	Flint, MI**	NA	86	Kenosha, WI	(1.58)
30	Brownsville–Harlingen–San Benito, TX	3.79	205	Florence, AL	(9.64)	45	Killeen–Temple, TX	1.78
82	Bryan–College Station, TX	(1.44)	36	Florence, SC	2.92	14	Kokomo, IN	7.45
–	Buffalo–Niagara Falls, NY**	NA	–	Fort Collins–Loveland, CO**	NA	–	La Crosse, WI–MN**	NA
40	Canton–Massillon, OH	2.52	24	Fort Lauderdale, FL	4.43	177	Lafayette, IN	(7.11)
102	Charleston, WV	(2.56)	129	Fort Myers–Cape Coral, FL	(4.06)	100	Lafayette, LA	(2.51)
35	Charleston–North Charleston, SC	3.08	109	Fort Pierce–Port St. Lucie, FL	(2.98)	–	Lake Charles, LA**	NA
7	Charlottesville, VA	10.76	55	Fort Smith, AR–OK	0.90	69	Lakeland–Winter Haven, FL	(0.19)
159	Charlotte–Gastonia–Rock Hill, NC–SC	(5.90)	75	Fort Walton Beach, FL	(0.92)	213	Lancaster, PA	(10.92)
103	Chattanooga, TN–GA	(2.57)	152	Fort Wayne, IN	(5.59)	–	Lansing–East Lansing, MI**	NA

Source: Morgan Quitno Corporation using data from U.S. Department of Justice, Federal Bureau of Investigation
   "Crime in the United States 1993" (Uniform Crime Reports, December 4, 1994)
Includes murder, rape, robbery, aggravated assault, burglary, larceny-theft and motor vehicle theft.
**Not available.*

3. Percent Change in Crime Rate: 1992 to 1993 (continued)

National Percent Change = 3.1% Decrease*

RANK	METRO AREA	% CHANGE	RANK	METRO AREA	% CHANGE	RANK	METRO AREA	CHANGE
184	Laredo, TX	(7.55)	22	Olympia, WA	5.14	51	Seattle–Bellevue–Everett, WA	1.43
95	Las Vegas, NV–AZ	(2.39)	–	Omaha, NE**	NA	119	Sheboygan, WI	(3.56)
–	Lawrence, MA–NH**	NA	134	Orange County, CA	(4.31)	144	Sherman–Denison, TX	(4.92)
63	Lawton, OK	0.09	104	Orlando, FL	(2.67)	21	Shreveport–Bossier City, LA	5.24
18	Lewiston–Auburn, ME	6.51	12	Owensboro, KY	9.13	–	Sioux City, IA–NE**	NA
50	Lexington, KY	1.58	32	Panama City, FL	3.57	23	Sioux Falls, SD	5.01
199	Lincoln, NE	(9.19)	90	Philadelphia, PA–NJ	(1.95)	58	South Bend, IN	0.71
42	Little Rock–North Little Rock, AR	2.35	26	Phoenix–Mesa, AZ	4.33	93	Spokane, WA	(2.22)
78	Longview–Marshall, TX	(1.14)	2	Pine Bluff, AR	16.94	–	Springfield, MA**	NA
140	Los Angeles–Long Beach, CA	(4.83)	149	Pittsburgh, PA	(5.20)	138	Springfield, MO	(4.77)
105	Louisville, KY–IN	(2.77)	112	Pittsfield, MA	(3.05)	122	Stamford–Norwalk, CT	(3.61)
177	Lubbock, TX	(7.11)	231	Portland, ME	(21.33)	74	Steubenville–Weirton, OH–WV	(0.91)
127	Lynchburg, VA	(3.96)	97	Portland–Vancouver, OR–WA	(2.48)	25	Stockton–Lodi, CA	4.36
94	Macon, GA	(2.33)	89	Providence–Fall River–Warwick, RI–MA	(1.85)	–	St. Cloud, MN**	NA
209	Madison, WI	(9.96)	125	Provo–Orem, UT	(3.84)	1	St. Joseph, MO	19.34
–	Manchester, NH**	NA	77	Pueblo, CO	(0.96)	–	St. Louis, MO–IL**	NA
109	Mansfield, OH	(2.98)	–	Punta Gorda, FL**	NA	212	Sumter, SC	(10.51)
97	McAllen–Edinburg–Mission, TX	(2.48)	169	Racine, WI	(6.63)	163	Syracuse, NY	(6.26)
5	Medford–Ashland, OR	11.60	192	Raleigh–Durham–Chapel Hill, NC	(8.47)	65	Tacoma, WA	0.05
31	Memphis, TN–AR–MS	3.68	187	Rapid City, SD	(8.05)	80	Tallahassee, FL	(1.26)
6	Merced, CA	10.91	143	Reading, PA	(4.91)	130	Tampa–St. Petersburg–Clearwater, FL	(4.07)
10	Miami, FL	9.44	37	Redding, CA	2.83	28	Texarkana, TX–AR	3.91
–	Middlesex–Sommerset–Hunterdon, NJ**	NA	44	Reno, NV	1.84	116	Toledo, OH	(3.41)
186	Milwaukee–Waukesha, WI	(7.81)	229	Richland–Kennewick–Pasco, WA	(17.72)	185	Trenton, NJ	(7.66)
–	Minneapolis–St. Paul, MN–WI**	NA	105	Richmond–Petersburg, VA	(2.77)	11	Tucson, AZ	9.36
–	Mobile, AL**	NA	115	Riverside–San Bernardino, CA	(3.38)	167	Tulsa, OK	(6.56)
9	Modesto, CA	9.56	221	Roanoke, VA	(12.60)	48	Tuscaloosa, AL	1.63
–	Monmouth–Ocean, NJ**	NA	–	Rochester, MN**	NA	196	Tyler, TX	(9.00)
193	Monroe, LA	(8.49)	151	Rochester, NY	(5.23)	198	Utica–Rome, NY	(9.10)
85	Montgomery, AL	(1.49)	152	Rocky Mount, NC	(5.59)	139	Vallejo–Fairfield–Napa, CA	(4.79)
19	Myrtle Beach, SC	5.87	52	Sacramento, CA	1.19	206	Ventura, CA	(9.70)
148	Naples, FL	(5.18)	–	Saginaw–Bay City–Midland, MI**	NA	179	Victoria, TX	(7.12)
123	Nashua, NH	(3.62)	84	Salem, OR	(1.46)	81	Vineland–Millville–Bridgeton, NJ	(1.40)
16	Nashville, TN	6.64	90	Salinas, CA	(1.95)	174	Visalia–Tulare–Porterville, CA	(6.79)
–	Nassau–Suffolk, NY**	NA	197	Salt Lake City–Ogden, UT	(9.01)	17	Waco, TX	6.62
–	New Bedford, MA**	NA	226	San Angelo, TX	(15.02)	92	Washington, DC–MD–VA–WV	(1.96)
211	New Haven–Meriden, CT	(10.35)	215	San Antonio, TX	(10.93)	99	Waterbury, CT	(2.49)
76	New London–Norwich, CT–RI	(0.94)	172	San Diego, CA	(6.74)	–	Waterloo–Cedar Falls, IA**	NA
66	New Orleans, LA	(0.01)	145	San Francisco, CA	(4.94)	216	Wausau, WI	(12.00)
–	New York, NY**	NA	101	San Jose, CA	(2.53)	–	Wichita, KS**	NA
–	Newark, NJ**	NA	–	San Luis Obispo–Atascadero, CA**	NA	154	Wichita Falls, TX	(5.60)
–	Newburgh, NY–PA**	NA	111	Santa Barbara–Santa Maria–Lompoc, CA	(3.00)	136	Williamsport, PA	(4.39)
141	Norfolk–Va Beach–Newport News, VA–NC	(4.84)	41	Santa Cruz–Watsonville, CA	2.44	–	Worcester, MA–CT**	NA
70	Oakland, CA	(0.46)	39	Santa Rosa, CA	2.59	232	Wilmington, NC	(22.44)
191	Ocala, FL	(8.45)	204	Sarasota–Bradenton, FL	(9.56)	57	Yakima, WA	0.74
222	Odessa–Midland, TX	(13.31)	49	Savannah, GA	1.59	27	Yolo, CA	4.32
88	Oklahoma City, OK	(1.84)	146	Scranton–Wilkes-Barre–Hazleton, PA	(4.96)	33	Yuba City, CA	3.42

Source: Morgan Quitno Corporation using data from U.S. Department of Justice, Federal Bureau of Investigation
"Crime in the United States 1993" (Uniform Crime Reports, December 4, 1994)
*Includes murder, rape, robbery, aggravated assault, burglary, larceny-theft and motor vehicle theft.
**Not available.

11

3. Percent Change in Crime Rate: 1992 to 1993 (continued)

National Percent Change = 3.1% Decrease*

RANK	METRO AREA	% CHANGE	RANK	METRO AREA	% CHANGE	RANK	METRO AREA	% CHANGE
1	St. Joseph, MO	19.34	48	Tuscaloosa, AL	1.63	95	Las Vegas, NV–AZ	(2.39)
2	Pine Bluff, AR	16.94	49	Savannah, GA	1.59	96	Houma, LA	(2.43)
3	Dubuque, IA	16.64	50	Lexington, KY	1.58	97	McAllen–Edinburg–Mission, TX	(2.48)
4	Altoona, PA	12.48	51	Seattle–Bellevue–Everett, WA	1.43	97	Portland–Vancouver, OR–WA	(2.48)
5	Medford–Ashland, OR	11.60	52	Sacramento, CA	1.19	99	Waterbury, CT	(2.49)
6	Merced, CA	10.91	53	Alexandria, LA	1.09	100	Lafayette, LA	(2.51)
7	Charlottesville, VA	10.76	54	Jacksonville, NC	0.95	101	San Jose, CA	(2.53)
8	Elkhart–Goshen, IN	10.72	55	Fort Smith, AR–OK	0.90	102	Charleston, WV	(2.56)
9	Modesto, CA	9.56	56	Eugene–Springfield, OR	0.81	103	Chattanooga, TN–GA	(2.57)
10	Miami, FL	9.44	57	Yakima, WA	0.74	104	Orlando, FL	(2.67)
11	Tucson, AZ	9.36	58	South Bend, IN	0.71	105	Louisville, KY–IN	(2.77)
12	Owensboro, KY	9.13	59	Fayetteville, NC	0.70	105	Richmond–Petersburg, VA	(2.77)
13	Enid, OK	7.86	60	Amarillo, TX	0.61	107	Jackson, TN	(2.95)
14	Kokomo, IN	7.45	61	Columbia, SC	0.58	108	Boise, ID	(2.96)
15	Binghamton, NY	7.36	62	Greensboro–Winston Salem–High Point, NC	0.10	109	Fort Pierce–Port St. Lucie, FL	(2.98)
16	Nashville, TN	6.64	63	Lawton, OK	0.09	109	Mansfield, OH	(2.98)
17	Waco, TX	6.62	64	Goldsboro, NC	0.07	111	Santa Barbara–Santa Maria–Lompoc, CA	(3.00)
18	Lewiston–Auburn, ME	6.51	65	Tacoma, WA	0.05	112	Pittsfield, MA	(3.05)
19	Myrtle Beach, SC	5.87	66	New Orleans, LA	(0.01)	113	Eau Claire, WI	(3.10)
20	Honolulu, HI	5.30	67	Hagerstown, MD	(0.09)	114	Anniston, AL	(3.19)
21	Shreveport–Bossier City, LA	5.24	68	Albuquerque, NM	(0.11)	115	Riverside–San Bernardino, CA	(3.38)
22	Olympia, WA	5.14	69	Lakeland–Winter Haven, FL	(0.19)	116	Toledo, OH	(3.41)
23	Sioux Falls, SD	5.01	70	Oakland, CA	(0.46)	117	Colorado Springs, CO	(3.45)
24	Fort Lauderdale, FL	4.43	71	Danville, VA	(0.64)	118	Greenville, NC	(3.48)
25	Stockton–Lodi, CA	4.36	72	Bangor, ME	(0.66)	119	Glens Falls, NY	(3.56)
26	Phoenix–Mesa, AZ	4.33	73	Green Bay, WI	(0.77)	119	Sheboygan, WI	(3.56)
27	Yolo, CA	4.32	74	Steubenville–Weirton, OH–WV	(0.91)	121	Birmingham, AL	(3.60)
28	Texarkana, TX–AR	3.91	75	Fort Walton Beach, FL	(0.92)	122	Stamford–Norwalk, CT	(3.61)
29	Hickory–Morganton, NC	3.85	76	New London–Norwich, CT–RI	(0.94)	123	Nashua, NH	(3.62)
30	Brownsville–Harlingen–San Benito, TX	3.79	77	Pueblo, CO	(0.96)	124	Gadsden, AL	(3.74)
31	Memphis, TN–AR–MS	3.68	78	Longview–Marshall, TX	(1.14)	125	Provo–Orem, UT	(3.84)
32	Panama City, FL	3.57	79	Daytona Beach, FL	(1.22)	126	Danbury, CT	(3.86)
33	Yuba City, CA	3.42	80	Tallahassee, FL	(1.26)	127	Lynchburg, VA	(3.96)
34	Erie, PA	3.38	81	Vineland–Millville–Bridgeton, NJ	(1.40)	128	Jackson, MS	(4.05)
35	Charleston–North Charleston, SC	3.08	82	Bryan–College Station, TX	(1.44)	129	Fort Myers–Cape Coral, FL	(4.06)
36	Florence, SC	2.92	83	Baltimore, MD	(1.45)	130	Baton Rouge, LA	(4.07)
37	Redding, CA	2.83	84	Salem, OR	(1.46)	130	Greeley, CO	(4.07)
38	Bloomington, IN	2.70	85	Montgomery, AL	(1.49)	130	Tampa–St. Petersburg–Clearwater, FL	(4.07)
39	Santa Rosa, CA	2.59	86	Kenosha, WI	(1.58)	133	Atlanta, GA	(4.25)
40	Canton–Massillon, OH	2.52	87	Bakersfield, CA	(1.80)	134	Orange County, CA	(4.31)
41	Santa Cruz–Watsonville, CA	2.44	88	Oklahoma City, OK	(1.84)	135	Corpus Christi, TX	(4.37)
42	Little Rock–North Little Rock, AR	2.35	89	Providence–Fall River–Warwick, RI–MA	(1.85)	136	Williamsport, PA	(4.39)
43	Abilene, TX	2.04	90	Philadelphia, PA–NJ	(1.95)	137	Dayton–Springfield, OH	(4.50)
44	Reno, NV	1.84	90	Salinas, CA	(1.95)	138	Springfield, MO	(4.77)
45	Killeen–Temple, TX	1.78	92	Washington, DC–MD–VA–WV	(1.96)	139	Vallejo–Fairfield–Napa, CA	(4.79)
46	Columbus, GA–AL	1.76	93	Spokane, WA	(2.22)	140	Los Angeles–Long Beach, CA	(4.83)
47	Greenville–Spartanburg–Anderson, SC	1.71	94	Macon, GA	(2.33)	141	Norfolk–Va Beach–Newport News, VA–NC	(4.84)

Source: Morgan Quitno Corporation using data from U.S. Department of Justice, Federal Bureau of Investigation "Crime in the United States 1993" (Uniform Crime Reports, December 4, 1994)
Includes murder, rape, robbery, aggravated assault, burglary, larceny-theft and motor vehicle theft.
**Not available.*

3. Percent Change in Crime Rate: 1992 to 1993 (continued)

National Percent Change = 3.1% Decrease*

RANK	METRO AREA	% CHANGE	RANK	METRO AREA	% CHANGE	RANK	METRO AREA	CHANGE
142	Decatur, AL	(4.90)	189	Denver, CO	(8.18)	–	Bergen-Passaic, NJ**	NA
143	Reading, PA	(4.91)	190	Harrisburg-Lebanon-Carlisle, PA	(8.35)	–	Boston, MA-NH**	NA
144	Sherman-Denison, TX	(4.92)	191	Ocala, FL	(8.45)	–	Buffalo-Niagara Falls, NY**	NA
145	San Francisco, CA	(4.94)	192	Raleigh-Durham-Chapel Hill, NC	(8.47)	–	Chicago, IL**	NA
146	Scranton-Wilkes-Barre-Hazleton, PA	(4.96)	193	Monroe, LA	(8.49)	–	Cleveland, OH**	NA
147	Albany, GA	(4.98)	194	Anchorage, AK	(8.77)	–	Detroit, MI**	NA
148	Naples, FL	(5.18)	195	Galveston-Texas City, TX	(8.83)	–	Duluth-Superior, MN-WI**	NA
149	Chico-Paradise, CA	(5.20)	196	Tyler, TX	(9.00)	–	Dutchess County, NY**	NA
149	Pittsburgh, PA	(5.20)	197	Salt Lake City-Ogden, UT	(9.01)	–	Fargo-Moorhead, ND-MN**	NA
151	Rochester, NY	(5.23)	198	Utica-Rome, NY	(9.10)	–	Fitchburg-Leominster, MA**	NA
152	Fort Wayne, IN	(5.59)	199	Lincoln, NE	(9.19)	–	Flint, MI**	NA
152	Rocky Mount, NC	(5.59)	200	Bismarck, ND	(9.36)	–	Fort Collins-Loveland, CO**	NA
154	Wichita Falls, TX	(5.60)	201	Huntington-Ashland, WV-KY-OH	(9.38)	–	Grand Forks, ND-MN**	NA
155	Gary-Hammond, IN	(5.68)	202	Hartford, CT	(9.40)	–	Grand Rapids-Muskegon-Holland, MI**	NA
156	Barnstable-Yarmouth, MA	(5.74)	203	Janesville-Beloit, WI	(9.44)	–	Houston, TX**	NA
157	Johnson City-Kingsport-Bristol, TN-VA	(5.75)	204	Sarasota-Bradenton, FL	(9.56)	–	Indianapolis, IN**	NA
158	Gainesville, FL	(5.82)	205	Florence, AL	(9.64)	–	Jackson, MI**	NA
159	Charlotte-Gastonia-Rock Hill, NC-SC	(5.90)	206	Bridgeport, CT	(9.70)	–	Jersey City, NJ**	NA
160	Huntsville, AL	(6.14)	206	Ventura, CA	(9.70)	–	Joplin, MO**	NA
161	Evansville-Henderson, IN-KY	(6.21)	208	Johnstown, PA	(9.89)	–	Kalamazoo-Battle Creek, MI**	NA
162	Jacksonville, FL	(6.23)	209	Madison, WI	(9.96)	–	Kansas City, MO-KS**	NA
163	Syracuse, NY	(6.26)	210	Boulder-Longmont, CO	(10.09)	–	La Crosse, WI-MN**	NA
164	Beaumont-Port Arthur, TX	(6.42)	211	New Haven-Meriden, CT	(10.35)	–	Lake Charles, LA**	NA
165	Cincinnati, OH-KY-IN	(6.44)	212	Sumter, SC	(10.51)	–	Lansing-East Lansing, MI**	NA
166	Bellingham, WA	(6.46)	213	Des Moines, IA	(10.92)	–	Lawrence, MA-NH**	NA
167	Tulsa, OK	(6.56)	213	Lancaster, PA	(10.92)	–	Manchester, NH**	NA
168	Columbia, MO	(6.57)	215	San Antonio, TX	(10.93)	–	Middlesex-Sommerset-Hunterdon, NJ**	NA
169	Columbus, OH	(6.63)	216	Wausau, WI	(12.00)	–	Minneapolis-St. Paul, MN-WI**	NA
169	Racine, WI	(6.63)	217	Brazoria, TX	(12.30)	–	Mobile, AL**	NA
171	Austin-San Marcos, TX	(6.72)	218	Asheville, NC	(12.36)	–	Monmouth-Ocean, NJ**	NA
172	San Diego, CA	(6.74)	218	Bremerton, WA	(12.36)	–	Nassau-Suffolk, NY**	NA
173	Clarksville-Hopkinsville, TN-KY	(6.76)	220	Brockton, MA	(12.40)	–	New Bedford, MA**	NA
174	Visalia-Tulare-Porterville, CA	(6.79)	221	Roanoke, VA	(12.60)	–	New York, NY**	NA
175	Appleton-Oshkosh-Neenah, WI	(6.86)	222	Odessa-Midland, TX	(13.31)	–	Newark, NJ**	NA
176	Dothan, AL	(7.03)	223	Athens, GA	(13.33)	–	Newburgh, NY-PA**	NA
177	Lafayette, IN	(7.11)	224	Dallas, TX	(13.73)	–	Omaha, NE**	NA
177	Lubbock, TX	(7.11)	225	Cheyenne, WY	(14.44)	–	Punta Gorda, FL**	NA
179	Victoria, TX	(7.12)	226	San Angelo, TX	(15.02)	–	Rochester, MN**	NA
180	El Paso, TX	(7.14)	227	Augusta-Aiken, GA-SC	(17.56)	–	Saginaw-Bay City-Midland, MI**	NA
181	Akron, OH	(7.15)	228	Fayetteville-Springdale-Rogers, AR	(17.59)	–	San Luis Obispo-Atascadero, CA**	NA
182	Atlantic City, NJ	(7.16)	229	Richland-Kennewick-Pasco, WA	(17.72)	–	Sioux City, IA-NE**	NA
183	Fresno, CA	(7.29)	230	Fort Worth-Arlington, TX	(18.97)	–	Springfield, MA**	NA
184	Laredo, TX	(7.55)	231	Portland, ME	(21.33)	–	St. Cloud, MN**	NA
185	Trenton, NJ	(7.66)	232	Wilmington, NC	(22.44)	–	St. Louis, MO-IL**	NA
186	Milwaukee-Waukesha, WI	(7.81)	–	Albany, NY**	NA	–	Waterloo-Cedar Falls, IA**	NA
187	Cumberland, MD-WV	(8.05)	–	Ann Arbor, MI**	NA	–	West Palm Beach-Boca Raton, FL**	NA
187	Rapid City, SD	(8.05)	–	Benton Harbor, MI**	NA	–	Worcester, MA-CT**	NA

Source: Morgan Quitno Corporation using data from U.S. Department of Justice, Federal Bureau of Investigation "Crime in the United States 1993" (Uniform Crime Reports, December 4, 1994)
*Includes murder, rape, robbery, aggravated assault, burglary, larceny-theft and motor vehicle theft.
**Not available.

4. Percent Change in Crime Rate: 1989 to 1993

National Percent Change = 4.5% Decrease*

RANK	METRO AREA	% CHANGE	RANK	METRO AREA	% CHANGE	RANK	METRO AREA	% CHANGE
201	Abilene, TX	(17.96)	125	Cheyenne, WY	(6.46)	222	Fort Worth–Arlington, TX	(28.06)
–	Akron, OH**	NA	–	Chicago, IL**	NA	113	Fresno, CA	(4.75)
75	Albany, GA	0.81	137	Chico–Paradise, CA	(8.06)	2	Gadsden, AL	40.96
–	Albany, NY**	NA	91	Cincinnati, OH–KY–IN	(1.10)	21	Gainesville, FL	14.94
156	Albuquerque, NM	(10.62)	43	Clarksville–Hopkinsville, TN–KY	6.07	128	Galveston–Texas City, TX	(6.66)
18	Alexandria, LA	16.52	–	Cleveland, OH**	NA	41	Gary–Hammond, IN	7.21
98	Altoona, PA	(2.99)	181	Colorado Springs, CO	(14.29)	27	Glens Falls, NY	11.82
66	Amarillo, TX	1.80	146	Columbia, MO	(9.10)	–	Goldsboro, NC**	NA
17	Anchorage, AK	17.71	62	Columbia, SC	2.04	–	Grand Forks, ND–MN**	NA
–	Ann Arbor, MI**	NA	106	Columbus, GA–AL	(3.83)	–	Grand Rapids–Muskegon–Holland, MI**	NA
8	Anniston, AL	23.62	155	Columbus, OH	(10.36)	129	Greeley, CO	(6.67)
73	Appleton–Oshkosh–Neenah, WI	0.89	117	Corpus Christi, TX	(5.24)	99	Green Bay, WI	(3.07)
193	Asheville, NC	(16.16)	34	Cumberland, MD–WV	9.33	35	Greensboro–Winston Salem–High Point, NC	8.75
70	Athens, GA	1.29	227	Dallas, TX	(33.33)	–	Greenville, NC**	NA
208	Atlanta, GA	(19.95)	32	Danbury, CT	9.84	165	Greenville–Spartanburg–Anderson, SC	(12.23)
182	Atlantic City, NJ	(14.33)	10	Danville, VA	22.62	87	Hagerstown, MD	(0.33)
201	Augusta–Aiken, GA–SC	(17.96)	187	Daytona Beach, FL	(15.13)	–	Harrisburg–Lebanon–Carlisle, PA**	NA
169	Austin–San Marcos, TX	(12.53)	147	Dayton–Springfield, OH	(9.13)	176	Hartford, CT	(13.69)
92	Bakersfield, CA	(1.28)	40	Decatur, AL	7.32	–	Hickory–Morganton, NC**	NA
22	Baltimore, MD	14.29	135	Denver, CO	(7.62)	58	Honolulu, HI	3.38
198	Bangor, ME	(16.68)	177	Des Moines, IA	(13.91)	–	Houma, LA**	NA
–	Barnstable–Yarmouth, MA**	NA	–	Detroit, MI**	NA	–	Houston, TX**	NA
11	Baton Rouge, LA	22.13	180	Dothan, AL	(14.18)	119	Huntington–Ashland, WV–KY–OH	(5.33)
79	Beaumont–Port Arthur, TX	0.52	76	Dubuque, IA	0.80	131	Huntsville, AL	(7.04)
121	Bellingham, WA	(5.54)	–	Duluth–Superior, MN–WI**	NA	–	Indianapolis, IN**	NA
–	Benton Harbor, MI**	NA	–	Dutchess County, NY**	NA	–	Jackson, MI**	NA
178	Bergen–Passaic, NJ	(13.93)	140	Eau Claire, WI	(8.71)	4	Jackson, MS	31.53
74	Binghamton, NY	0.86	206	El Paso, TX	(19.18)	23	Jackson, TN	14.15
24	Birmingham, AL	14.14	122	Elkhart–Goshen, IN	(5.95)	97	Jacksonville, FL	(2.89)
48	Bismarck, ND	5.30	20	Enid, OK	15.34	46	Jacksonville, NC	5.69
139	Bloomington, IN	(8.52)	100	Erie, PA	(3.31)	59	Janesville–Beloit, WI	2.47
55	Boise, ID	3.83	154	Eugene–Springfield, OR	(10.30)	188	Jersey City, NJ	(15.16)
–	Boston, MA–NH**	NA	153	Evansville–Henderson, IN–KY	(10.24)	158	Johnson City–Kingsport–Bristol, TN–VA	(10.84)
194	Boulder–Longmont, CO	(16.20)	–	Fargo–Moorhead, ND–MN**	NA	–	Johnstown, PA**	NA
191	Brazoria, TX	(15.48)	136	Fayetteville, NC	(7.79)	167	Joplin, MO	(12.43)
–	Bremerton, WA**	NA	218	Fayetteville–Springdale–Rogers, AR	(23.72)	–	Kalamazoo–Battle Creek, MI**	NA
171	Bridgeport, CT	(12.81)	120	Fitchburg–Leominster, MA	(5.37)	–	Kansas City, MO–KS**	NA
–	Brockton, MA**	NA	–	Flint, MI**	NA	31	Kenosha, WI	10.15
37	Brownsville–Harlingen–San Benito, TX	7.94	151	Florence, AL	(9.41)	53	Killeen–Temple, TX	4.31
221	Bryan–College Station, TX	(26.35)	3	Florence, SC	38.59	26	Kokomo, IN	11.88
42	Buffalo–Niagara Falls, NY	7.05	197	Fort Collins–Loveland, CO	(16.56)	–	La Crosse, WI–MN**	NA
49	Canton–Massillon, OH	5.24	82	Fort Lauderdale, FL	0.38	19	Lafayette, IN	15.80
51	Charleston, WV	4.47	13	Fort Myers–Cape Coral, FL	20.92	126	Lafayette, LA	(6.63)
30	Charleston–North Charleston, SC	10.23	211	Fort Pierce–Port St. Lucie, FL	(21.07)	44	Lake Charles, LA	5.94
89	Charlottesville, VA	(0.80)	50	Fort Smith, AR–OK	5.04	163	Lakeland–Winter Haven, FL	(11.80)
138	Charlotte–Gastonia–Rock Hill, NC–SC	(8.32)	78	Fort Walton Beach, FL	0.58	44	Lancaster, PA	5.94
88	Chattanooga, TN–GA	(0.67)	213	Fort Wayne, IN	(21.88)	–	Lansing–East Lansing, MI**	NA

Source: Morgan Quitno Corporation using data from U.S. Department of Justice, Federal Bureau of Investigation
"Crime in the United States 1993" (Uniform Crime Reports, December 4, 1994)
*Includes offenses of murder, forcible rape, robbery, aggravated assault, burglary, larceny-theft and motor vehicle theft.
**Not available.

4. Percent Change in Crime Rate: 1989 to 1993 (continued)

National Percent Change = 4.5% Decrease*

RANK	METRO AREA	% CHANGE	RANK	METRO AREA	% CHANGE	RANK	METRO AREA	CHANGE
209	Laredo, TX	(19.99)	52	Olympia, WA	4.41	143	Seattle-Bellevue-Everett, WA	(8.76)
95	Las Vegas, NV-AZ	(1.91)	–	Omaha, NE**	NA	28	Sheboygan, WI	10.92
114	Lawrence, MA-NH	(4.80)	148	Orange County, CA	(9.31)	215	Sherman-Denison, TX	(22.20)
7	Lawton, OK	24.21	173	Orlando, FL	(13.10)	162	Shreveport-Bossier City, LA	(11.65)
161	Lewiston-Auburn, ME	(11.20)	84	Owensboro, KY	0.32	110	Sioux City, IA-NE	(4.14)
68	Lexington, KY	1.53	5	Panama City, FL	25.68	77	Sioux Falls, SD	0.77
81	Lincoln, NE	0.39	132	Philadelphia, PA-NJ	(7.08)	–	South Bend, IN**	NA
47	Little Rock-North Little Rock, AR	5.51	150	Phoenix-Mesa, AZ	(9.35)	134	Spokane, WA	(7.56)
86	Longview-Marshall, TX	(0.02)	15	Pine Bluff, AR	20.37	–	Springfield, MA**	NA
116	Los Angeles-Long Beach, CA	(5.05)	118	Pittsburgh, PA	(5.28)	219	Springfield, MO	(24.32)
115	Louisville, KY-IN	(4.87)	–	Pittsfield, MA**	NA	204	Stamford-Norwalk, CT	(18.63)
186	Lubbock, TX	(15.06)	220	Portland, ME	(24.40)	–	Steubenville-Weirton, OH-WV**	NA
217	Lynchburg, VA	(23.40)	192	Portland-Vancouver, OR-WA	(15.64)	71	Stockton-Lodi, CA	1.22
184	Macon, GA	(14.88)	212	Providence-Fall River-Warwick, RI-MA	(21.45)	–	St. Cloud, MN**	NA
183	Madison, WI	(14.57)	–	Provo-Orem, UT**	NA	33	St. Joseph, MO	9.77
226	Manchester, NH	(30.31)	145	Pueblo, CO	(9.05)	–	St. Louis, MO-IL**	NA
108	Mansfield, OH	(4.02)	–	Punta Gorda, FL**	NA	–	Sumter, SC**	NA
16	McAllen-Edinburg-Mission, TX	20.36	175	Racine, WI	(13.21)	164	Syracuse, NY	(12.12)
25	Medford-Ashland, OR	13.88	64	Raleigh-Durham-Chapel Hill, NC	1.91	168	Tacoma, WA	(12.44)
61	Memphis, TN-AR-MS	2.32	67	Rapid City, SD	1.56	14	Tallahassee, FL	20.67
12	Merced, CA	21.31	–	Reading, PA**	NA	160	Tampa-St. Petersburg-Clearwater, FL	(11.06)
102	Miami, FL	(3.65)	149	Redding, CA	(9.33)	157	Texarkana, TX-AR	(10.65)
107	Middlesex-Sommerset-Hunterdon, NJ	(3.95)	144	Reno, NV	(9.02)	174	Toledo, OH	(13.14)
122	Milwaukee-Waukesha, WI	(5.95)	223	Richland-Kennewick-Pasco, WA	(28.84)	196	Trenton, NJ	(16.55)
–	Minneapolis-St. Paul, MN-WI**	NA	79	Richmond-Petersburg, VA	0.52	–	Tucson, AZ**	NA
124	Mobile, AL	(6.32)	–	Riverside-San Bernardino, CA**	NA	172	Tulsa, OK	(13.00)
56	Modesto, CA	3.74	199	Roanoke, VA	(16.91)	9	Tuscaloosa, AL	23.56
101	Monmouth-Ocean, NJ	(3.40)	–	Rochester, MN**	NA	111	Tyler, TX	(4.43)
29	Monroe, LA	10.90	133	Rochester, NY	(7.48)	36	Utica-Rome, NY	8.64
63	Montgomery, AL	1.92	–	Rocky Mount, NC**	NA	112	Vallejo-Fairfield-Napa, CA	(4.56)
–	Myrtle Beach, SC**	NA	83	Sacramento, CA	0.33	65	Ventura, CA	1.83
207	Naples, FL	(19.67)	–	Saginaw-Bay City-Midland, MI**	NA	6	Victoria, TX	24.82
216	Nashua, NH	(23.36)	93	Salem, OR	(1.62)	39	Vineland-Millville-Bridgeton, NJ	7.55
1	Nashville, TN	43.10	60	Salinas, CA	2.42	38	Visalia-Tulare-Porterville, CA	7.56
142	Nassau-Suffolk, NY	(8.75)	159	Salt Lake City-Ogden, UT	(11.02)	189	Waco, TX	(15.24)
169	New Bedford, MA	(12.53)	224	San Angelo, TX	(29.22)	90	Washington, DC-MD-VA-WV	(0.85)
179	New Haven-Meriden, CT	(13.96)	210	San Antonio, TX	(20.26)	127	Waterbury, CT	(6.65)
203	New London-Norwich, CT-RI	(18.47)	195	San Diego, CA	(16.32)	103	Waterloo-Cedar Falls, IA	(3.67)
96	New Orleans, LA	(2.02)	85	San Francisco, CA	0.12	190	Wausau, WI	(15.36)
185	New York, NY	(14.99)	109	San Jose, CA	(4.11)	–	West Palm Beach-Boca Raton, FL**	NA
166	Newark, NJ	(12.37)	–	San Luis Obispo-Atascadero, CA**	NA	225	Wichita Falls, TX	(30.04)
–	Newburgh, NY-PA**	NA	130	Santa Barbara-Santa Maria-Lompoc, CA	(6.71)	–	Williamsport, PA**	NA
105	Norfolk-Va Beach-Newport News, VA-NC	(3.75)	54	Santa Cruz-Watsonville, CA	4.26	205	Wilmington, NC	(18.72)
94	Oakland, CA	(1.74)	57	Santa Rosa, CA	3.50	–	Worcester, MA-CT**	NA
200	Ocala, FL	(17.92)	152	Sarasota-Bradenton, FL	(9.75)	141	Yakima, WA	(8.72)
214	Odessa-Midland, TX	(22.04)	72	Savannah, GA	1.13	–	Yolo, CA**	NA
104	Oklahoma City, OK	(3.74)	–	Scranton-Wilkes-Barre-Hazleton, PA**	NA	69	Yuba City, CA	1.30

Source: Morgan Quitno Corporation using data from U.S. Department of Justice, Federal Bureau of Investigation
   "Crime in the United States 1993" (Uniform Crime Reports, December 4, 1994)
*Includes offenses of murder, forcible rape, robbery, aggravated assault, burglary, larceny-theft and motor vehicle theft.
**Not available.

4. Percent Change in Crime Rate: 1989 to 1993 (continued)

National Percent Change = 4.5% Decrease*

RANK	METRO AREA	% CHANGE	RANK	METRO AREA	% CHANGE	RANK	METRO AREA	% CHANGE
1	Nashville, TN	43.10	48	Bismarck, ND	5.30	95	Las Vegas, NV–AZ	(1.91)
2	Gadsden, AL	40.96	49	Canton-Massillon, OH	5.24	96	New Orleans, LA	(2.02)
3	Florence, SC	38.59	50	Fort Smith, AR–OK	5.04	97	Jacksonville, FL	(2.89)
4	Jackson, MS	31.53	51	Charleston, WV	4.47	98	Altoona, PA	(2.99)
5	Panama City, FL	25.68	52	Olympia, WA	4.41	99	Green Bay, WI	(3.07)
6	Victoria, TX	24.82	53	Killeen-Temple, TX	4.31	100	Erie, PA	(3.31)
7	Lawton, OK	24.21	54	Santa Cruz-Watsonville, CA	4.26	101	Monmouth-Ocean, NJ	(3.40)
8	Anniston, AL	23.62	55	Boise, ID	3.83	102	Miami, FL	(3.65)
9	Tuscaloosa, AL	23.56	56	Modesto, CA	3.74	103	Waterloo-Cedar Falls, IA	(3.67)
10	Danville, VA	22.62	57	Santa Rosa, CA	3.50	104	Oklahoma City, OK	(3.74)
11	Baton Rouge, LA	22.13	58	Honolulu, HI	3.38	105	Norfolk-Va Beach-Newport News, VA–NC	(3.75)
12	Merced, CA	21.31	59	Janesville-Beloit, WI	2.47	106	Columbus, GA–AL	(3.83)
13	Fort Myers-Cape Coral, FL	20.92	60	Salinas, CA	2.42	107	Middlesex-Sommerset-Hunterdon, NJ	(3.95)
14	Tallahassee, FL	20.67	61	Memphis, TN–AR–MS	2.32	108	Mansfield, OH	(4.02)
15	Pine Bluff, AR	20.37	62	Columbia, SC	2.04	109	San Jose, CA	(4.11)
16	McAllen-Edinburg-Mission, TX	20.36	63	Montgomery, AL	1.92	110	Sioux City, IA–NE	(4.14)
17	Anchorage, AK	17.71	64	Raleigh-Durham-Chapel Hill, NC	1.91	111	Tyler, TX	(4.43)
18	Alexandria, LA	16.52	65	Ventura, CA	1.83	112	Vallejo-Fairfield-Napa, CA	(4.56)
19	Lafayette, IN	15.80	66	Amarillo, TX	1.80	113	Fresno, CA	(4.75)
20	Enid, OK	15.34	67	Rapid City, SD	1.56	114	Lawrence, MA–NH	(4.80)
21	Gainesville, FL	14.94	68	Lexington, KY	1.53	115	Louisville, KY–IN	(4.87)
22	Baltimore, MD	14.29	69	Yuba City, CA	1.30	116	Los Angeles-Long Beach, CA	(5.05)
23	Jackson, TN	14.15	70	Athens, GA	1.29	117	Corpus Christi, TX	(5.24)
24	Birmingham, AL	14.14	71	Stockton-Lodi, CA	1.22	118	Pittsburgh, PA	(5.28)
25	Medford-Ashland, OR	13.88	72	Savannah, GA	1.13	119	Huntington-Ashland, WV–KY–OH	(5.33)
26	Kokomo, IN	11.88	73	Appleton-Oshkosh-Neenah, WI	0.89	120	Fitchburg-Leominster, MA	(5.37)
27	Glens Falls, NY	11.82	74	Binghamton, NY	0.86	121	Bellingham, WA	(5.54)
28	Sheboygan, WI	10.92	75	Albany, GA	0.81	122	Elkhart-Goshen, IN	(5.95)
29	Monroe, LA	10.90	76	Dubuque, IA	0.80	122	Milwaukee-Waukesha, WI	(5.95)
30	Charleston-North Charleston, SC	10.23	77	Sioux Falls, SD	0.77	124	Mobile, AL	(6.32)
31	Kenosha, WI	10.15	78	Fort Walton Beach, FL	0.58	125	Cheyenne, WY	(6.46)
32	Danbury, CT	9.84	79	Beaumont-Port Arthur, TX	0.52	126	Lafayette, LA	(6.63)
33	St. Joseph, MO	9.77	79	Richmond-Petersburg, VA	0.52	127	Waterbury, CT	(6.65)
34	Cumberland, MD–WV	9.33	81	Lincoln, NE	0.39	128	Galveston-Texas City, TX	(6.66)
35	Greensboro-Winston Salem-High Point, NC	8.75	82	Fort Lauderdale, FL	0.38	129	Greeley, CO	(6.67)
36	Utica-Rome, NY	8.64	83	Sacramento, CA	0.33	130	Santa Barbara-Santa Maria-Lompoc, CA	(6.71)
37	Brownsville-Harlingen-San Benito, TX	7.94	84	Owensboro, KY	0.32	131	Huntsville, AL	(7.04)
38	Visalia-Tulare-Porterville, CA	7.56	85	San Francisco, CA	0.12	132	Philadelphia, PA–NJ	(7.08)
39	Vineland-Millville-Bridgeton, NJ	7.55	86	Longview-Marshall, TX	(0.02)	133	Rochester, NY	(7.48)
40	Decatur, AL	7.32	87	Hagerstown, MD	(0.33)	134	Spokane, WA	(7.56)
41	Gary-Hammond, IN	7.21	88	Chattanooga, TN–GA	(0.67)	135	Denver, CO	(7.62)
42	Buffalo-Niagara Falls, NY	7.05	89	Charlottesville, VA	(0.80)	136	Fayetteville, NC	(7.79)
43	Clarksville-Hopkinsville, TN–KY	6.07	90	Washington, DC-MD-VA-WV	(0.85)	137	Chico-Paradise, CA	(8.06)
44	Lake Charles, LA	5.94	91	Cincinnati, OH–KY–IN	(1.10)	138	Charlotte-Gastonia-Rock Hill, NC–SC	(8.32)
44	Lancaster, PA	5.94	92	Bakersfield, CA	(1.28)	139	Bloomington, IN	(8.52)
46	Jacksonville, NC	5.69	93	Salem, OR	(1.62)	140	Eau Claire, WI	(8.71)
47	Little Rock-North Little Rock, AR	5.51	94	Oakland, CA	(1.74)	141	Yakima, WA	(8.72)

Source: Morgan Quitno Corporation using data from U.S. Department of Justice, Federal Bureau of Investigation "Crime in the United States 1993" (Uniform Crime Reports, December 4, 1994)
*Includes offenses of murder, forcible rape, robbery, aggravated assault, burglary, larceny-theft and motor vehicle theft.
**Not available.

4. Percent Change in Crime Rate: 1989 to 1993 (continued)

National Percent Change = 4.5% Decrease*

RANK	METRO AREA	% CHANGE	RANK	METRO AREA	% CHANGE	RANK	METRO AREA	CHANGE
142	Nassau–Suffolk, NY	(8.75)	189	Waco, TX	(15.24)	–	Chicago, IL**	NA
143	Seattle–Bellevue–Everett, WA	(8.76)	190	Wausau, WI	(15.36)	–	Cleveland, OH**	NA
144	Reno, NV	(9.02)	191	Brazoria, TX	(15.48)	–	Detroit, MI**	NA
145	Pueblo, CO	(9.05)	192	Portland–Vancouver, OR–WA	(15.64)	–	Duluth–Superior, MN–WI**	NA
146	Columbia, MO	(9.10)	193	Asheville, NC	(16.16)	–	Dutchess County, NY**	NA
147	Dayton–Springfield, OH	(9.13)	194	Boulder–Longmont, CO	(16.20)	–	Fargo–Moorhead, ND–MN**	NA
148	Orange County, CA	(9.31)	195	San Diego, CA	(16.32)	–	Flint, MI**	NA
149	Redding, CA	(9.33)	196	Trenton, NJ	(16.55)	–	Goldsboro, NC**	NA
150	Phoenix–Mesa, AZ	(9.35)	197	Fort Collins–Loveland, CO	(16.56)	–	Grand Forks, ND–MN**	NA
151	Florence, AL	(9.41)	198	Bangor, ME	(16.68)	–	Grand Rapids–Muskegon–Holland, MI**	NA
152	Sarasota–Bradenton, FL	(9.75)	199	Roanoke, VA	(16.91)	–	Greenville, NC**	NA
153	Evansville–Henderson, IN–KY	(10.24)	200	Ocala, FL	(17.92)	–	Harrisburg–Lebanon–Carlisle, PA**	NA
154	Eugene–Springfield, OR	(10.30)	201	Abilene, TX	(17.96)	–	Hickory–Morganton, NC**	NA
155	Columbus, OH	(10.36)	201	Augusta–Aiken, GA–SC	(17.96)	–	Houma, LA**	NA
156	Albuquerque, NM	(10.62)	203	New London–Norwich, CT–RI	(18.47)	–	Houston, TX**	NA
157	Texarkana, TX–AR	(10.65)	204	Stamford–Norwalk, CT	(18.63)	–	Indianapolis, IN**	NA
158	Johnson City–Kingsport–Bristol, TN–VA	(10.84)	205	Wilmington, NC	(18.72)	–	Jackson, MI**	NA
159	Salt Lake City–Ogden, UT	(11.02)	206	El Paso, TX	(19.18)	–	Johnstown, PA**	NA
160	Tampa–St. Petersburg–Clearwater, FL	(11.06)	207	Naples, FL	(19.67)	–	Kalamazoo–Battle Creek, MI**	NA
161	Lewiston–Auburn, ME	(11.20)	208	Atlanta, GA	(19.95)	–	Kansas City, MO–KS**	NA
162	Shreveport–Bossier City, LA	(11.65)	209	Laredo, TX	(19.99)	–	La Crosse, WI–MN**	NA
163	Lakeland–Winter Haven, FL	(11.80)	210	San Antonio, TX	(20.26)	–	Lansing–East Lansing, MI**	NA
164	Syracuse, NY	(12.12)	211	Fort Pierce–Port St. Lucie, FL	(21.07)	–	Minneapolis–St. Paul, MN–WI**	NA
165	Greenville–Spartanburg–Anderson, SC	(12.23)	212	Providence–Fall River–Warwick, RI–MA	(21.45)	–	Myrtle Beach, SC**	NA
166	Newark, NJ	(12.37)	213	Fort Wayne, IN	(21.88)	–	Newburgh, NY–PA**	NA
167	Joplin, MO	(12.43)	214	Odessa–Midland, TX	(22.04)	–	Omaha, NE**	NA
168	Tacoma, WA	(12.44)	215	Sherman–Denison, TX	(22.20)	–	Pittsfield, MA**	NA
169	Austin–San Marcos, TX	(12.53)	216	Nashua, NH	(23.36)	–	Provo–Orem, UT**	NA
169	New Bedford, MA	(12.53)	217	Lynchburg, VA	(23.40)	–	Punta Gorda, FL**	NA
171	Bridgeport, CT	(12.81)	218	Fayetteville–Springdale–Rogers, AR	(23.72)	–	Reading, PA**	NA
172	Tulsa, OK	(13.00)	219	Springfield, MO	(24.32)	–	Riverside–San Bernardino, CA**	NA
173	Orlando, FL	(13.10)	220	Portland, ME	(24.40)	–	Rochester, MN**	NA
174	Toledo, OH	(13.14)	221	Bryan–College Station, TX	(26.35)	–	Rocky Mount, NC**	NA
175	Racine, WI	(13.21)	222	Fort Worth–Arlington, TX	(28.06)	–	Saginaw–Bay City–Midland, MI**	NA
176	Hartford, CT	(13.69)	223	Richland–Kennewick–Pasco, WA	(28.84)	–	San Luis Obispo–Atascadero, CA**	NA
177	Des Moines, IA	(13.91)	224	San Angelo, TX	(29.22)	–	Scranton–Wilkes-Barre–Hazleton, PA**	NA
178	Bergen–Passaic, NJ	(13.93)	225	Wichita Falls, TX	(30.04)	–	South Bend, IN**	NA
179	New Haven–Meriden, CT	(13.96)	226	Manchester, NH	(30.31)	–	Springfield, MA**	NA
180	Dothan, AL	(14.18)	227	Dallas, TX	(33.33)	–	Steubenville–Weirton, OH–WV**	NA
181	Colorado Springs, CO	(14.29)	–	Akron, OH**	NA	–	St. Cloud, MN**	NA
182	Atlantic City, NJ	(14.33)	–	Albany, NY**	NA	–	St. Louis, MO–IL**	NA
183	Madison, WI	(14.57)	–	Ann Arbor, MI**	NA	–	Sumter, SC**	NA
184	Macon, GA	(14.88)	–	Barnstable–Yarmouth, MA**	NA	–	Tucson, AZ**	NA
185	New York, NY	(14.99)	–	Benton Harbor, MI**	NA	–	West Palm Beach–Boca Raton, FL**	NA
186	Lubbock, TX	(15.06)	–	Boston, MA–NH**	NA	–	Williamsport, PA**	NA
187	Daytona Beach, FL	(15.13)	–	Bremerton, WA**	NA	–	Worcester, MA–CT**	NA
188	Jersey City, NJ	(15.16)	–	Brockton, MA**	NA	–	Yolo, CA**	NA

Source: Morgan Quitno Corporation using data from U.S. Department of Justice, Federal Bureau of Investigation "Crime in the United States 1993" (Uniform Crime Reports, December 4, 1994)
*Includes offenses of murder, forcible rape, robbery, aggravated assault, burglary, larceny-theft and motor vehicle theft.
**Not available.

5. Violent Crimes in 1993

National Total = 1,924,188 Violent Crimes*

RANK	METRO AREA	CRIMES	RANK	METRO AREA	CRIMES	RANK	METRO AREA	CRIMES
177	Abilene, TX	915	250	Cheyenne, WY	162	24	Fort Worth–Arlington, TX	12,689
83	Akron, OH	3,116	–	Chicago, IL**	NA	39	Fresno, CA	8,816
153	Albany, GA	1,165	186	Chico–Paradise, CA	836	151	Gadsden, AL	1,184
–	Albany, NY**	NA	37	Cincinnati, OH–KY–IN	9,012	94	Gainesville, FL	2,553
43	Albuquerque, NM	8,021	126	Clarksville–Hopkinsville, TN–KY	1,568	114	Galveston–Texas City, TX	1,914
99	Alexandria, LA	2,402	–	Cleveland, OH**	NA	54	Gary–Hammond, IN	5,568
243	Altoona, PA	263	112	Colorado Springs, CO	1,963	217	Glens Falls, NY	519
150	Amarillo, TX	1,202	214	Columbia, MO	542	184	Goldsboro, NC	861
102	Anchorage, AK	2,213	56	Columbia, SC	5,393	–	Grand Forks, ND–MN**	NA
–	Ann Arbor, MI**	NA	127	Columbus, GA–AL	1,555	–	Grand Rapids–Muskegon–Holland, MI**	NA
134	Anniston, AL	1,394	33	Columbus, OH	9,561	227	Greeley, CO	418
238	Appleton–Oshkosh–Neenah, WI	351	93	Corpus Christi, TX	2,586	206	Green Bay, WI	585
198	Asheville, NC	665	224	Cumberland, MD–WV	426	45	Greensboro–Winston Salem–High Point, NC	7,715
176	Athens, GA	923	11	Dallas, TX	26,035	163	Greenville, NC	1,094
8	Atlanta, GA	29,800	244	Danbury, CT	232	35	Greenville–Spartanburg–Anderson, SC	9,328
90	Atlantic City, NJ	2,750	241	Danville, VA	290	234	Hagerstown, MD	366
87	Augusta–Aiken, GA–SC	2,920	78	Daytona Beach, FL	3,388	100	Harrisburg–Lebanon–Carlisle, PA	2,344
63	Austin–San Marcos, TX	4,853	58	Dayton–Springfield, OH	5,325	61	Hartford, CT	5,209
60	Bakersfield, CA	5,222	239	Decatur, AL	347	161	Hickory–Morganton, NC	1,109
5	Baltimore, MD	33,322	23	Denver, CO	12,862	97	Honolulu, HI	2,501
255	Bangor, ME	85	149	Des Moines, IA	1,214	167	Houma, LA	1,046
154	Barnstable–Yarmouth, MA	1,161	–	Detroit, MI**	NA	–	Houston, TX**	NA
40	Baton Rouge, LA	8,284	165	Dothan, AL	1,061	183	Huntington–Ashland, WV–KY–OH	867
82	Beaumont–Port Arthur, TX	3,189	245	Dubuque, IA	219	92	Huntsville, AL	2,624
240	Bellingham, WA	344	–	Duluth–Superior, MN–WI**	NA	–	Indianapolis, IN**	NA
–	Benton Harbor, MI**	NA	179	Dutchess County, NY	911	–	Jackson, MI**	NA
65	Bergen–Passaic, NJ	4,690	252	Eau Claire, WI	129	80	Jackson, MS	3,308
209	Binghamton, NY	569	48	El Paso, TX	6,607	166	Jackson, TN	1,054
30	Birmingham, AL	9,969	187	Elkhart–Goshen, IN	818	20	Jacksonville, FL	13,722
251	Bismarck, ND	151	226	Enid, OK	420	224	Jacksonville, NC	426
214	Bloomington, IN	542	164	Erie, PA	1,086	233	Janesville–Beloit, WI	378
157	Boise, ID	1,123	175	Eugene–Springfield, OR	945	49	Jersey City, NJ	6,397
9	Boston, MA–NH	26,366	133	Evansville–Henderson, IN–KY	1,400	168	Johnson City–Kingsport–Bristol, TN–VA	1,044
207	Boulder–Longmont, CO	577	–	Fargo–Moorhead, ND–MN**	NA	219	Johnstown, PA	503
202	Brazoria, TX	635	85	Fayetteville, NC	3,033	235	Joplin, MO	363
200	Bremerton, WA	655	222	Fayetteville–Springdale–Rogers, AR	448	–	Kalamazoo–Battle Creek, MI**	NA
86	Bridgeport, CT	3,004	158	Fitchburg–Leominster, MA	1,122	–	Kansas City, MO–KS**	NA
117	Brockton, MA	1,805	–	Flint, MI**	NA	209	Kenosha, WI	569
111	Brownsville–Harlingen–San Benito, TX	1,965	236	Florence, AL	358	119	Killeen–Temple, TX	1,747
199	Bryan–College Station, TX	660	147	Florence, SC	1,254	221	Kokomo, IN	459
36	Buffalo–Niagara Falls, NY	9,070	204	Fort Collins–Loveland, CO	621	–	La Crosse, WI–MN**	NA
115	Canton–Massillon, OH	1,903	22	Fort Lauderdale, FL	13,273	213	Lafayette, IN	543
170	Charleston, WV	1,031	96	Fort Myers–Cape Coral, FL	2,535	108	Lafayette, LA	2,056
62	Charleston–North Charleston, SC	5,044	106	Fort Pierce–Port St. Lucie, FL	2,084	121	Lake Charles, LA	1,683
230	Charlottesville, VA	399	194	Fort Smith, AR–OK	780	68	Lakeland–Winter Haven, FL	4,184
18	Charlotte–Gastonia–Rock Hill, NC–SC	14,826	208	Fort Walton Beach, FL	571	172	Lancaster, PA	981
76	Chattanooga, TN–GA	3,652	124	Fort Wayne, IN	1,596	–	Lansing–East Lansing, MI**	NA

Source: U.S. Department of Justice, Federal Bureau of Investigation
    "Crime in the United States 1993" (Uniform Crime Reports, December 4, 1994)
*Violent crimes are offenses of murder, forcible rape, robbery and aggravated assault.
**Not available.

5. Violent Crimes in 1993 (continued)

National Total = 1,924,188 Violent Crimes*

RANK	METRO AREA	CRIMES	RANK	METRO AREA	CRIMES	RANK	METRO AREA	CRIMES
162	Laredo, TX	1,104	223	Olympia, WA	427	25	Seattle–Bellevue–Everett, WA	12,366
32	Las Vegas, NV–AZ	9,671	–	Omaha, NE**	NA	253	Sheboygan, WI	123
116	Lawrence, MA–NH	1,838	21	Orange County, CA	13,456	220	Sherman–Denison, TX	466
185	Lawton, OK	848	19	Orlando, FL	14,801	74	Shreveport–Bossier City, LA	3,711
248	Lewiston–Auburn, ME	191	247	Owensboro, KY	199	141	Sioux City, IA–NE	1,333
88	Lexington, KY	2,765	169	Panama City, FL	1,040	216	Sioux Falls, SD	532
155	Lincoln, NE	1,158	6	Philadelphia, PA–NJ	32,908	128	South Bend, IN	1,509
44	Little Rock–North Little Rock, AR	7,733	15	Phoenix–Mesa, AZ	19,308	113	Spokane, WA	1,941
135	Longview–Marshall, TX	1,390	178	Pine Bluff, AR	914	–	Springfield, MA**	NA
2	Los Angeles–Long Beach, CA	153,876	34	Pittsburgh, PA	9,535	189	Springfield, MO	800
50	Louisville, KY–IN	6,213	228	Pittsfield, MA	406	174	Stamford–Norwalk, CT	951
131	Lubbock, TX	1,465	211	Portland, ME	563	212	Steubenville–Weirton, OH–WV	549
188	Lynchburg, VA	806	26	Portland–Vancouver, OR–WA	11,679	55	Stockton–Lodi, CA	5,559
130	Macon, GA	1,466	71	Providence–Fall River–Warwick, RI–MA	3,846	–	St. Cloud, MN**	NA
160	Madison, WI	1,112	229	Provo–Orem, UT	401	232	St. Joseph, MO	379
242	Manchester, NH	276	118	Pueblo, CO	1,788	–	St. Louis, MO–IL**	NA
129	Mansfield, OH	1,484	231	Punta Gorda, FL	385	146	Sumter, SC	1,256
81	McAllen–Edinburg–Mission, TX	3,218	191	Racine, WI	796	105	Syracuse, NY	2,090
197	Medford–Ashland, OR	667	52	Raleigh–Durham–Chapel Hill, NC	5,822	53	Tacoma, WA	5,589
27	Memphis, TN–AR–MS	11,629	237	Rapid City, SD	356	70	Tallahassee, FL	3,847
152	Merced, CA	1,183	143	Reading, PA	1,317	10	Tampa–St. Petersburg–Clearwater, FL	26,155
3	Miami, FL	43,526	190	Redding, CA	798	172	Texarkana, TX–AR	981
84	Middlesex–Somerset–Hunterdon, NJ	3,050	123	Reno, NV	1,616	75	Toledo, OH	3,698
47	Milwaukee–Waukesha, WI	7,009	201	Richland–Kennewick–Pasco, WA	638	103	Trenton, NJ	2,133
–	Minneapolis–St. Paul, MN–WI**	NA	59	Richmond–Petersburg, VA	5,262	57	Tucson, AZ	5,347
67	Mobile, AL	4,289	7	Riverside–San Bernardino, CA	30,924	51	Tulsa, OK	5,909
69	Modesto, CA	3,961	195	Roanoke, VA	763	125	Tuscaloosa, AL	1,569
91	Monmouth–Ocean, NJ	2,661	–	Rochester, MN**	NA	148	Tyler, TX	1,234
132	Monroe, LA	1,416	72	Rochester, NY	3,819	192	Utica–Rome, NY	784
95	Montgomery, AL	2,541	171	Rocky Mount, NC	1,003	73	Vallejo–Fairfield–Napa, CA	3,730
137	Myrtle Beach, SC	1,348	28	Sacramento, CA	11,544	77	Ventura, CA	3,471
144	Naples, FL	1,298	–	Saginaw–Bay City–Midland, MI**	NA	205	Victoria, TX	612
249	Nashua, NH	175	181	Salem, OR	883	142	Vineland–Millville–Bridgeton, NJ	1,330
29	Nashville, TN	11,410	89	Salinas, CA	2,759	101	Visalia–Tulare–Porterville, CA	2,224
46	Nassau–Suffolk, NY	7,293	66	Salt Lake City–Ogden, UT	4,379	108	Waco, TX	2,056
122	New Bedford, MA	1,659	203	San Angelo, TX	628	4	Washington, DC–MD–VA–WV	33,935
79	New Haven–Meriden, CT	3,314	38	San Antonio, TX	8,851	196	Waterbury, CT	689
181	New London–Norwich, CT–RI	883	13	San Diego, CA	22,959	218	Waterloo–Cedar Falls, IA	513
17	New Orleans, LA	16,551	16	San Francisco, CA	17,875	254	Wausau, WI	92
1	New York, NY	160,804	42	San Jose, CA	8,102	–	West Palm Beach–Boca Raton, FL**	NA
14	Newark, NJ	19,977	159	San Luis Obispo–Atascadero, CA	1,120	180	Wichita Falls, TX	902
140	Newburgh, NY–PA	1,339	110	Santa Barbara–Santa Maria–Lompoc, CA	1,973	246	Williamsport, PA	214
31	Norfolk–Va Beach–Newport News, VA–NC	9,915	120	Santa Cruz–Watsonville, CA	1,704	138	Wilmington, NC	1,346
12	Oakland, CA	24,685	104	Santa Rosa, CA	2,119	–	Worcester, MA–CT**	NA
98	Ocala, FL	2,409	64	Sarasota–Bradenton, FL	4,726	145	Yakima, WA	1,294
139	Odessa–Midland, TX	1,341	107	Savannah, GA	2,058	193	Yolo, CA	781
41	Oklahoma City, OK	8,212	136	Scranton–Wilkes-Barre–Hazleton, PA	1,378	156	Yuba City, CA	1,131

Source: U.S. Department of Justice, Federal Bureau of Investigation
"Crime in the United States 1993" (Uniform Crime Reports, December 4, 1994)
*Violent crimes are offenses of murder, forcible rape, robbery and aggravated assault.
**Not available.

5. Violent Crimes in 1993 (continued)

National Total = 1,924,188 Violent Crimes*

RANK	METRO AREA	CRIMES	RANK	METRO AREA	CRIMES	RANK	METRO AREA	CRIMES
1	New York, NY	160,804	48	El Paso, TX	6,607	95	Montgomery, AL	2,541
2	Los Angeles–Long Beach, CA	153,876	49	Jersey City, NJ	6,397	96	Fort Myers–Cape Coral, FL	2,535
3	Miami, FL	43,526	50	Louisville, KY–IN	6,213	97	Honolulu, HI	2,501
4	Washington, DC–MD–VA–WV	33,935	51	Tulsa, OK	5,909	98	Ocala, FL	2,409
5	Baltimore, MD	33,322	52	Raleigh–Durham–Chapel Hill, NC	5,822	99	Alexandria, LA	2,402
6	Philadelphia, PA–NJ	32,908	53	Tacoma, WA	5,589	100	Harrisburg–Lebanon–Carlisle, PA	2,344
7	Riverside–San Bernardino, CA	30,924	54	Gary–Hammond, IN	5,568	101	Visalia–Tulare–Porterville, CA	2,224
8	Atlanta, GA	29,800	55	Stockton–Lodi, CA	5,559	102	Anchorage, AK	2,213
9	Boston, MA–NH	26,366	56	Columbia, SC	5,393	103	Trenton, NJ	2,133
10	Tampa–St. Petersburg–Clearwater, FL	26,155	57	Tucson, AZ	5,347	104	Santa Rosa, CA	2,119
11	Dallas, TX	26,035	58	Dayton–Springfield, OH	5,325	105	Syracuse, NY	2,090
12	Oakland, CA	24,685	59	Richmond–Petersburg, VA	5,262	106	Fort Pierce–Port St. Lucie, FL	2,084
13	San Diego, CA	22,959	60	Bakersfield, CA	5,222	107	Savannah, GA	2,058
14	Newark, NJ	19,977	61	Hartford, CT	5,209	108	Lafayette, LA	2,056
15	Phoenix–Mesa, AZ	19,308	62	Charleston–North Charleston, SC	5,044	108	Waco, TX	2,056
16	San Francisco, CA	17,875	63	Austin–San Marcos, TX	4,853	110	Santa Barbara–Santa Maria–Lompoc, CA	1,973
17	New Orleans, LA	16,551	64	Sarasota–Bradenton, FL	4,726	111	Brownsville–Harlingen–San Benito, TX	1,965
18	Charlotte–Gastonia–Rock Hill, NC–SC	14,826	65	Bergen–Passaic, NJ	4,690	112	Colorado Springs, CO	1,963
19	Orlando, FL	14,801	66	Salt Lake City–Ogden, UT	4,379	113	Spokane, WA	1,941
20	Jacksonville, FL	13,722	67	Mobile, AL	4,289	114	Galveston–Texas City, TX	1,914
21	Orange County, CA	13,456	68	Lakeland–Winter Haven, FL	4,184	115	Canton–Massillon, OH	1,903
22	Fort Lauderdale, FL	13,273	69	Modesto, CA	3,961	116	Lawrence, MA–NH	1,838
23	Denver, CO	12,862	70	Tallahassee, FL	3,847	117	Brockton, MA	1,805
24	Fort Worth–Arlington, TX	12,689	71	Providence–Fall River–Warwick, RI–MA	3,846	118	Pueblo, CO	1,788
25	Seattle–Bellevue–Everett, WA	12,366	72	Rochester, NY	3,819	119	Killeen–Temple, TX	1,747
26	Portland–Vancouver, OR–WA	11,679	73	Vallejo–Fairfield–Napa, CA	3,730	120	Santa Cruz–Watsonville, CA	1,704
27	Memphis, TN–AR–MS	11,629	74	Shreveport–Bossier City, LA	3,711	121	Lake Charles, LA	1,683
28	Sacramento, CA	11,544	75	Toledo, OH	3,698	122	New Bedford, MA	1,659
29	Nashville, TN	11,410	76	Chattanooga, TN–GA	3,652	123	Reno, NV	1,616
30	Birmingham, AL	9,969	77	Ventura, CA	3,471	124	Fort Wayne, IN	1,596
31	Norfolk–Va Beach–Newport News, VA–NC	9,915	78	Daytona Beach, FL	3,388	125	Tuscaloosa, AL	1,569
32	Las Vegas, NV–AZ	9,671	79	New Haven–Meriden, CT	3,314	126	Clarksville–Hopkinsville, TN–KY	1,568
33	Columbus, OH	9,561	80	Jackson, MS	3,308	127	Columbus, GA–AL	1,555
34	Pittsburgh, PA	9,535	81	McAllen–Edinburg–Mission, TX	3,218	128	South Bend, IN	1,509
35	Greenville–Spartanburg–Anderson, SC	9,328	82	Beaumont–Port Arthur, TX	3,189	129	Mansfield, OH	1,484
36	Buffalo–Niagara Falls, NY	9,070	83	Akron, OH	3,116	130	Macon, GA	1,466
37	Cincinnati, OH–KY–IN	9,012	84	Middlesex–Sommerset–Hunterdon, NJ	3,050	131	Lubbock, TX	1,465
38	San Antonio, TX	8,851	85	Fayetteville, NC	3,033	132	Monroe, LA	1,416
39	Fresno, CA	8,816	86	Bridgeport, CT	3,004	133	Evansville–Henderson, IN–KY	1,400
40	Baton Rouge, LA	8,284	87	Augusta–Aiken, GA–SC	2,920	134	Anniston, AL	1,394
41	Oklahoma City, OK	8,212	88	Lexington, KY	2,765	135	Longview–Marshall, TX	1,390
42	San Jose, CA	8,102	89	Salinas, CA	2,759	136	Scranton–Wilkes-Barre–Hazleton, PA	1,378
43	Albuquerque, NM	8,021	90	Atlantic City, NJ	2,750	137	Myrtle Beach, SC	1,348
44	Little Rock–North Little Rock, AR	7,733	91	Monmouth–Ocean, NJ	2,661	138	Wilmington, NC	1,346
45	Greensboro–Winston Salem–High Point, NC	7,715	92	Huntsville, AL	2,624	139	Odessa–Midland, TX	1,341
46	Nassau–Suffolk, NY	7,293	93	Corpus Christi, TX	2,586	140	Newburgh, NY–PA	1,339
47	Milwaukee–Waukesha, WI	7,009	94	Gainesville, FL	2,553	141	Sioux City, IA–NE	1,333

Source: U.S. Department of Justice, Federal Bureau of Investigation
  "Crime in the United States 1993" (Uniform Crime Reports, December 4, 1994)
*Violent crimes are offenses of murder, forcible rape, robbery and aggravated assault.
**Not available.

5. Violent Crimes in 1993 (continued)

National Total = 1,924,188 Violent Crimes*

RANK	METRO AREA	CRIMES	RANK	METRO AREA	CRIMES	RANK	METRO AREA	CRIMES
142	Vineland–Millville–Bridgeton, NJ	1,330	189	Springfield, MO	800	236	Florence, AL	358
143	Reading, PA	1,317	190	Redding, CA	798	237	Rapid City, SD	356
144	Naples, FL	1,298	191	Racine, WI	796	238	Appleton–Oshkosh–Neenah, WI	351
145	Yakima, WA	1,294	192	Utica–Rome, NY	784	239	Decatur, AL	347
146	Sumter, SC	1,256	193	Yolo, CA	781	240	Bellingham, WA	344
147	Florence, SC	1,254	194	Fort Smith, AR–OK	780	241	Danville, VA	290
148	Tyler, TX	1,234	195	Roanoke, VA	763	242	Manchester, NH	276
149	Des Moines, IA	1,214	196	Waterbury, CT	689	243	Altoona, PA	263
150	Amarillo, TX	1,202	197	Medford–Ashland, OR	667	244	Danbury, CT	232
151	Gadsden, AL	1,184	198	Asheville, NC	665	245	Dubuque, IA	219
152	Merced, CA	1,183	199	Bryan–College Station, TX	660	246	Williamsport, PA	214
153	Albany, GA	1,165	200	Bremerton, WA	655	247	Owensboro, KY	199
154	Barnstable–Yarmouth, MA	1,161	201	Richland–Kennewick–Pasco, WA	638	248	Lewiston–Auburn, ME	191
155	Lincoln, NE	1,158	202	Brazoria, TX	635	249	Nashua, NH	175
156	Yuba City, CA	1,131	203	San Angelo, TX	628	250	Cheyenne, WY	162
157	Boise, ID	1,123	204	Fort Collins–Loveland, CO	621	251	Bismarck, ND	151
158	Fitchburg–Leominster, MA	1,122	205	Victoria, TX	612	252	Eau Claire, WI	129
159	San Luis Obispo–Atascadero, CA	1,120	206	Green Bay, WI	585	253	Sheboygan, WI	123
160	Madison, WI	1,112	207	Boulder–Longmont, CO	577	254	Wausau, WI	92
161	Hickory–Morganton, NC	1,109	208	Fort Walton Beach, FL	571	255	Bangor, ME	85
162	Laredo, TX	1,104	209	Binghamton, NY	569	–	Albany, NY**	NA
163	Greenville, NC	1,094	209	Kenosha, WI	569	–	Ann Arbor, MI**	NA
164	Erie, PA	1,086	211	Portland, ME	563	–	Benton Harbor, MI**	NA
165	Dothan, AL	1,061	212	Steubenville–Weirton, OH–WV	549	–	Chicago, IL**	NA
166	Jackson, TN	1,054	213	Lafayette, IN	543	–	Cleveland, OH**	NA
167	Houma, LA	1,046	214	Bloomington, IN	542	–	Detroit, MI**	NA
168	Johnson City–Kingsport–Bristol, TN–VA	1,044	214	Columbia, MO	542	–	Duluth–Superior, MN–WI**	NA
169	Panama City, FL	1,040	216	Sioux Falls, SD	532	–	Fargo–Moorhead, ND–MN**	NA
170	Charleston, WV	1,031	217	Glens Falls, NY	519	–	Flint, MI**	NA
171	Rocky Mount, NC	1,003	218	Waterloo–Cedar Falls, IA	513	–	Grand Forks, ND–MN**	NA
172	Lancaster, PA	981	219	Johnstown, PA	503	–	Grand Rapids–Muskegon–Holland, MI**	NA
172	Texarkana, TX–AR	981	220	Sherman–Denison, TX	466	–	Houston, TX**	NA
174	Stamford–Norwalk, CT	951	221	Kokomo, IN	459	–	Indianapolis, IN**	NA
175	Eugene–Springfield, OR	945	222	Fayetteville–Springdale–Rogers, AR	448	–	Jackson, MI**	NA
176	Athens, GA	923	223	Olympia, WA	427	–	Kalamazoo–Battle Creek, MI**	NA
177	Abilene, TX	915	224	Cumberland, MD–WV	426	–	Kansas City, MO–KS**	NA
178	Pine Bluff, AR	914	224	Jacksonville, NC	426	–	La Crosse, WI–MN**	NA
179	Dutchess County, NY	911	226	Enid, OK	420	–	Lansing–East Lansing, MI**	NA
180	Wichita Falls, TX	902	227	Greeley, CO	418	–	Minneapolis–St. Paul, MN–WI**	NA
181	New London–Norwich, CT–RI	883	228	Pittsfield, MA	406	–	Omaha, NE**	NA
181	Salem, OR	883	229	Provo–Orem, UT	401	–	Rochester, MN**	NA
183	Huntington–Ashland, WV–KY–OH	867	230	Charlottesville, VA	399	–	Saginaw–Bay City–Midland, MI**	NA
184	Goldsboro, NC	861	231	Punta Gorda, FL	385	–	Springfield, MA**	NA
185	Lawton, OK	848	232	St. Joseph, MO	379	–	St. Cloud, MN**	NA
186	Chico–Paradise, CA	836	233	Janesville–Beloit, WI	378	–	St. Louis, MO–IL**	NA
187	Elkhart–Goshen, IN	818	234	Hagerstown, MD	366	–	West Palm Beach–Boca Raton, FL**	NA
188	Lynchburg, VA	806	235	Joplin, MO	363	–	Worcester, MA–CT**	NA

Source: U.S. Department of Justice, Federal Bureau of Investigation
    "Crime in the United States 1993" (Uniform Crime Reports, December 4, 1994)
*Violent crimes are offenses of murder, forcible rape, robbery and aggravated assault.
**Not available.

6. Violent Crime Rate in 1993

National Rate = 746.1 Violent Crimes per 100,000 Population*

RANK	METRO AREA	RATE	RANK	METRO AREA	RATE	RANK	METRO AREA	RATE
97	Abilene, TX	744.3	240	Cheyenne, WY	210.7	72	Fort Worth-Arlington, TX	824.6
164	Akron, OH	466.5	–	Chicago, IL**	NA	32	Fresno, CA	1,084.6
43	Albany, GA	990.0	169	Chico-Paradise, CA	439.3	19	Gadsden, AL	1,177.5
–	Albany, NY**	NA	139	Cincinnati, OH-KY-IN	573.6	11	Gainesville, FL	1,328.6
14	Albuquerque, NM	1,273.6	62	Clarksville-Hopkinsville, TN-KY	869.1	73	Galveston-Texas City, TX	823.0
3	Alexandria, LA	1,833.0	–	Cleveland, OH**	NA	56	Gary-Hammond, IN	894.1
242	Altoona, PA	199.4	167	Colorado Springs, CO	452.9	170	Glens Falls, NY	427.1
130	Amarillo, TX	615.1	166	Columbia, MO	459.9	82	Goldsboro, NC	786.8
57	Anchorage, AK	882.7	25	Columbia, SC	1,129.1	–	Grand Forks, ND-MN**	NA
–	Ann Arbor, MI**	NA	141	Columbus, GA-AL	558.7	–	Grand Rapids-Muskegon-Holland, MI**	NA
17	Anniston, AL	1,183.6	113	Columbus, OH	682.3	207	Greeley, CO	298.9
253	Appleton-Oshkosh-Neenah, WI	106.4	109	Corpus Christi, TX	699.9	217	Green Bay, WI	287.9
200	Asheville, NC	331.5	174	Cumberland, MD-WV	416.0	108	Greensboro-Winston Salem-High Point, NC	703.8
131	Athens, GA	597.5	52	Dallas, TX	946.4	47	Greenville, NC	975.5
55	Atlanta, GA	923.9	248	Danbury, CT	142.7	33	Greenville-Spartanburg-Anderson, SC	1,080.0
69	Atlantic City, NJ	836.6	227	Danville, VA	261.3	215	Hagerstown, MD	288.9
120	Augusta-Aiken, GA-SC	646.7	81	Daytona Beach, FL	791.8	183	Harrisburg-Lebanon-Carlisle, PA	387.5
146	Austin-San Marcos, TX	528.2	143	Dayton-Springfield, OH	550.0	157	Hartford, CT	494.3
59	Bakersfield, CA	879.6	228	Decatur, AL	253.7	192	Hickory-Morganton, NC	364.8
10	Baltimore, MD	1,356.1	101	Denver, CO	731.7	219	Honolulu, HI	285.7
250	Bangor, ME	125.7	208	Des Moines, IA	297.4	141	Houma, LA	558.7
65	Barnstable-Yarmouth, MA	846.7	–	Detroit, MI**	NA	–	Houston, TX**	NA
6	Baton Rouge, LA	1,510.7	83	Dothan, AL	786.7	222	Huntington-Ashland, WV-KY-OH	273.4
66	Beaumont-Port Arthur, TX	845.7	229	Dubuque, IA	250.0	67	Huntsville, AL	841.9
231	Bellingham, WA	244.1	–	Duluth-Superior, MN-WI**	NA	–	Indianapolis, IN**	NA
–	Benton Harbor, MI**	NA	196	Dutchess County, NY	344.9	–	Jackson, MI**	NA
193	Bergen-Passaic, NJ	360.5	254	Eau Claire, WI	91.4	76	Jackson, MS	808.4
239	Binghamton, NY	212.3	38	El Paso, TX	1,031.0	13	Jackson, TN	1,294.7
20	Birmingham, AL	1,146.8	152	Elkhart-Goshen, IN	508.5	8	Jacksonville, FL	1,419.9
246	Bismarck, ND	175.2	99	Enid, OK	739.2	213	Jacksonville, NC	290.1
159	Bloomington, IN	483.1	184	Erie, PA	386.7	225	Janesville-Beloit, WI	262.4
198	Boise, ID	340.7	202	Eugene-Springfield, OR	318.4	21	Jersey City, NJ	1,144.1
87	Boston, MA-NH	777.0	158	Evansville-Henderson, IN-KY	490.2	235	Johnson City-Kingsport-Bristol, TN-VA	231.5
234	Boulder-Longmont, CO	235.4	–	Fargo-Moorhead, ND-MN**	NA	241	Johnstown, PA	208.0
204	Brazoria, TX	305.5	34	Fayetteville, NC	1,076.5	226	Joplin, MO	261.8
206	Bremerton, WA	304.1	243	Fayetteville-Springdale-Rogers, AR	196.0	–	Kalamazoo-Battle Creek, MI**	NA
117	Bridgeport, CT	663.3	75	Fitchburg-Leominster, MA	819.0	–	Kansas City, MO-KS**	NA
100	Brockton, MA	733.0	–	Flint, MI**	NA	173	Kenosha, WI	420.9
111	Brownsville-Harlingen-San Benito, TX	691.5	223	Florence, AL	263.6	115	Killeen-Temple, TX	672.3
151	Bryan-College Station, TX	517.2	37	Florence, SC	1,045.6	165	Kokomo, IN	461.1
93	Buffalo-Niagara Falls, NY	754.8	205	Fort Collins-Loveland, CO	304.6	–	La Crosse, WI-MN**	NA
163	Canton-Massillon, OH	473.6	41	Fort Lauderdale, FL	1,005.4	201	Lafayette, IN	326.2
178	Charleston, WV	405.4	107	Fort Myers-Cape Coral, FL	709.8	136	Lafayette, LA	579.8
53	Charleston-North Charleston, SC	943.8	89	Fort Pierce-Port St. Lucie, FL	774.0	46	Lake Charles, LA	977.7
212	Charlottesville, VA	292.3	171	Fort Smith, AR-OK	427.0	45	Lakeland-Winter Haven, FL	984.3
16	Charlotte-Gastonia-Rock Hill, NC-SC	1,204.4	191	Fort Walton Beach, FL	366.8	236	Lancaster, PA	224.8
70	Chattanooga, TN-GA	833.5	197	Fort Wayne, IN	341.2	–	Lansing-East Lansing, MI**	NA

Source: U.S. Department of Justice, Federal Bureau of Investigation
"Crime in the United States 1993" (Uniform Crime Reports, December 4, 1994)
*Violent crimes are offenses of murder, forcible rape, robbery and aggravated assault.
**Not available.

6. Violent Crime Rate in 1993 (continued)

National Rate = 746.1 Violent Crimes per 100,000 Population*

RANK	METRO AREA	RATE	RANK	METRO AREA	RATE	RANK	METRO AREA	RATE
103	Laredo, TX	729.3	233	Olympia, WA	236.7	134	Seattle-Bellevue-Everett, WA	595.7
49	Las Vegas, NV–AZ	959.5	–	Omaha, NE**	NA	251	Sheboygan, WI	116.1
128	Lawrence, MA–NH	621.1	144	Orange County, CA	536.1	161	Sherman-Denison, TX	480.7
110	Lawton, OK	698.3	26	Orlando, FL	1,118.2	44	Shreveport-Bossier City, LA	987.9
244	Lewiston-Auburn, ME	183.5	237	Owensboro, KY	222.0	24	Sioux City, IA–NE	1,133.8
92	Lexington, KY	759.2	91	Panama City, FL	765.0	194	Sioux Falls, SD	358.6
147	Lincoln, NE	525.4	118	Philadelphia, PA–NJ	662.2	133	South Bend, IN	596.5
7	Little Rock-North Little Rock, AR	1,453.1	77	Phoenix-Mesa, AZ	806.8	156	Spokane, WA	498.3
114	Longview-Marshall, TX	681.9	35	Pine Bluff, AR	1,058.8	–	Springfield, MA**	NA
4	Los Angeles-Long Beach, CA	1,682.4	181	Pittsburgh, PA	393.4	217	Springfield, MO	287.9
124	Louisville, KY–IN	636.1	176	Pittsfield, MA	412.1	216	Stamford-Norwalk, CT	288.5
122	Lubbock, TX	641.8	232	Portland, ME	240.8	185	Steubenville-Weirton, OH–WV	385.5
180	Lynchburg, VA	400.2	106	Portland-Vancouver, OR–WA	711.8	29	Stockton-Lodi, CA	1,091.6
161	Macon, GA	480.7	179	Providence-Fall River-Warwick, RI–MA	402.0	–	St. Cloud, MN**	NA
210	Madison, WI	295.2	249	Provo-Orem, UT	141.9	186	St. Joseph, MO	383.6
247	Manchester, NH	165.4	9	Pueblo, CO	1,403.9	–	St. Louis, MO–IL**	NA
68	Mansfield, OH	840.4	203	Punta Gorda, FL	318.2	18	Sumter, SC	1,179.1
96	McAllen-Edinburg-Mission, TX	749.7	168	Racine, WI	439.5	221	Syracuse, NY	276.1
172	Medford-Ashland, OR	424.3	125	Raleigh-Durham-Chapel Hill, NC	630.7	58	Tacoma, WA	881.3
27	Memphis, TN–AR–MS	1,109.3	175	Rapid City, SD	414.7	5	Tallahassee, FL	1,546.0
129	Merced, CA	619.2	188	Reading, PA	382.1	15	Tampa-St. Petersburg-Clearwater, FL	1,223.4
1	Miami, FL	2,136.2	154	Redding, CA	501.2	80	Texarkana, TX–AR	797.4
214	Middlesex-Sommerset-Hunterdon, NJ	289.2	137	Reno, NV	578.8	132	Toledo, OH	597.2
160	Milwaukee-Waukesha, WI	482.2	182	Richland-Kennewick-Pasco, WA	388.1	121	Trenton, NJ	646.1
–	Minneapolis-St. Paul, MN–WI**	NA	138	Richmond-Petersburg, VA	578.5	94	Tucson, AZ	754.2
64	Mobile, AL	855.3	30	Riverside-San Bernardino, CA	1,089.8	79	Tulsa, OK	801.1
42	Modesto, CA	992.1	199	Roanoke, VA	332.2	40	Tuscaloosa, AL	1,009.3
224	Monmouth-Ocean, NJ	263.4	–	Rochester, MN**	NA	84	Tyler, TX	783.9
48	Monroe, LA	973.5	195	Rochester, NY	351.5	230	Utica-Rome, NY	246.5
74	Montgomery, AL	821.1	105	Rocky Mount, NC	719.5	86	Vallejo-Fairfield-Napa, CA	777.1
60	Myrtle Beach, SC	875.3	78	Sacramento, CA	805.5	155	Ventura, CA	500.4
88	Naples, FL	776.7	–	Saginaw-Bay City-Midland, MI**	NA	85	Victoria, TX	779.1
252	Nashua, NH	109.1	209	Salem, OR	297.1	50	Vineland-Millville-Bridgeton, NJ	953.2
28	Nashville, TN	1,098.7	98	Salinas, CA	741.5	116	Visalia-Tulare-Porterville, CA	664.9
220	Nassau-Suffolk, NY	277.5	189	Salt Lake City-Ogden, UT	378.0	36	Waco, TX	1,052.6
51	New Bedford, MA	950.1	127	San Angelo, TX	621.4	90	Washington, DC-MD-VA-WV	771.4
135	New Haven-Meriden, CT	588.8	126	San Antonio, TX	629.6	190	Waterbury, CT	371.7
211	New London-Norwich, CT–RI	293.1	61	San Diego, CA	873.7	177	Waterloo-Cedar Falls, IA	407.5
12	New Orleans, LA	1,312.6	31	San Francisco, CA	1,088.1	255	Wausau, WI	66.5
2	New York, NY	1,865.5	148	San Jose, CA	524.7	–	West Palm Beach-Boca Raton, FL**	NA
39	Newark, NJ	1,030.9	153	San Luis Obispo-Atascadero, CA	502.7	112	Wichita Falls, TX	690.6
187	Newburgh, NY–PA	382.6	150	Santa Barbara-Santa Maria-Lompoc, CA	520.1	245	Williamsport, PA	176.9
119	Norfolk-Va Beach-Newport News, VA–NC	652.6	102	Santa Cruz-Watsonville, CA	730.2	104	Wilmington, NC	727.0
23	Oakland, CA	1,137.5	149	Santa Rosa, CA	523.1	–	Worcester, MA–CT**	NA
22	Ocala, FL	1,141.7	54	Sarasota-Bradenton, FL	933.9	123	Yakima, WA	639.5
140	Odessa-Midland, TX	562.6	95	Savannah, GA	753.7	145	Yolo, CA	533.9
71	Oklahoma City, OK	828.2	238	Scranton-Wilkes-Barre-Hazleton, PA	214.8	63	Yuba City, CA	859.0

Source: U.S. Department of Justice, Federal Bureau of Investigation
 "Crime in the United States 1993" (Uniform Crime Reports, December 4, 1994)
Violent crimes are offenses of murder, forcible rape, robbery and aggravated assault.
**Not available.*

23

6. Violent Crime Rate in 1993 (continued)

National Rate = 746.1 Violent Crimes per 100,000 Population*

RANK	METRO AREA	RATE	RANK	METRO AREA	RATE	RANK	METRO AREA	RATE
1	Miami, FL	2,136.2	48	Monroe, LA	973.5	95	Savannah, GA	753.7
2	New York, NY	1,865.5	49	Las Vegas, NV–AZ	959.5	96	McAllen–Edinburg–Mission, TX	749.7
3	Alexandria, LA	1,833.0	50	Vineland–Millville–Bridgeton, NJ	953.2	97	Abilene, TX	744.3
4	Los Angeles–Long Beach, CA	1,682.4	51	New Bedford, MA	950.1	98	Salinas, CA	741.5
5	Tallahassee, FL	1,546.0	52	Dallas, TX	946.4	99	Enid, OK	739.2
6	Baton Rouge, LA	1,510.7	53	Charleston–North Charleston, SC	943.8	100	Brockton, MA	733.0
7	Little Rock–North Little Rock, AR	1,453.1	54	Sarasota–Bradenton, FL	933.9	101	Denver, CO	731.7
8	Jacksonville, FL	1,419.9	55	Atlanta, GA	923.9	102	Santa Cruz–Watsonville, CA	730.2
9	Pueblo, CO	1,403.9	56	Gary–Hammond, IN	894.1	103	Laredo, TX	729.3
10	Baltimore, MD	1,356.1	57	Anchorage, AK	882.7	104	Wilmington, NC	727.0
11	Gainesville, FL	1,328.6	58	Tacoma, WA	881.8	105	Rocky Mount, NC	719.5
12	New Orleans, LA	1,312.6	59	Bakersfield, CA	879.6	106	Portland–Vancouver, OR–WA	711.8
13	Jackson, TN	1,294.7	60	Myrtle Beach, SC	875.3	107	Fort Myers–Cape Coral, FL	709.8
14	Albuquerque, NM	1,273.6	61	San Diego, CA	873.7	108	Greensboro–Winston Salem–High Point, NC	703.8
15	Tampa–St. Petersburg–Clearwater, FL	1,223.4	62	Clarksville–Hopkinsville, TN–KY	869.1	109	Corpus Christi, TX	699.9
16	Charlotte–Gastonia–Rock Hill, NC–SC	1,204.4	63	Yuba City, CA	859.0	110	Lawton, OK	698.3
17	Anniston, AL	1,183.6	64	Mobile, AL	855.3	111	Brownsville–Harlingen–San Benito, TX	691.5
18	Sumter, SC	1,179.1	65	Barnstable–Yarmouth, MA	846.7	112	Wichita Falls, TX	690.6
19	Gadsden, AL	1,177.5	66	Beaumont–Port Arthur, TX	845.7	113	Columbus, OH	682.3
20	Birmingham, AL	1,146.8	67	Huntsville, AL	841.9	114	Longview–Marshall, TX	681.9
21	Jersey City, NJ	1,144.1	68	Mansfield, OH	840.4	115	Killeen–Temple, TX	672.3
22	Ocala, FL	1,141.7	69	Atlantic City, NJ	836.6	116	Visalia–Tulare–Porterville, CA	664.9
23	Oakland, CA	1,137.5	70	Chattanooga, TN–GA	833.5	117	Bridgeport, CT	663.3
24	Sioux City, IA–NE	1,133.8	71	Oklahoma City, OK	828.2	118	Philadelphia, PA–NJ	662.2
25	Columbia, SC	1,129.1	72	Fort Worth–Arlington, TX	824.6	119	Norfolk–Va Beach–Newport News, VA–NC	652.6
26	Orlando, FL	1,118.2	73	Galveston–Texas City, TX	823.0	120	Augusta–Aiken, GA–SC	646.7
27	Memphis, TN–AR–MS	1,109.3	74	Montgomery, AL	821.1	121	Trenton, NJ	646.1
28	Nashville, TN	1,098.7	75	Fitchburg–Leominster, MA	819.0	122	Lubbock, TX	641.8
29	Stockton–Lodi, CA	1,091.6	76	Jackson, MS	808.4	123	Yakima, WA	639.5
30	Riverside–San Bernardino, CA	1,089.8	77	Phoenix–Mesa, AZ	806.8	124	Louisville, KY–IN	636.1
31	San Francisco, CA	1,088.1	78	Sacramento, CA	805.5	125	Raleigh–Durham–Chapel Hill, NC	630.7
32	Fresno, CA	1,084.6	79	Tulsa, OK	801.1	126	San Antonio, TX	629.6
33	Greenville–Spartanburg–Anderson, SC	1,080.0	80	Texarkana, TX–AR	797.4	127	San Angelo, TX	621.4
34	Fayetteville, NC	1,076.5	81	Daytona Beach, FL	791.8	128	Lawrence, MA–NH	621.1
35	Pine Bluff, AR	1,058.8	82	Goldsboro, NC	786.8	129	Merced, CA	619.2
36	Waco, TX	1,052.6	83	Dothan, AL	786.7	130	Amarillo, TX	615.1
37	Florence, SC	1,045.8	84	Tyler, TX	783.9	131	Athens, GA	597.5
38	El Paso, TX	1,031.0	85	Victoria, TX	779.1	132	Toledo, OH	597.2
39	Newark, NJ	1,030.9	86	Vallejo–Fairfield–Napa, CA	777.1	133	South Bend, IN	596.5
40	Tuscaloosa, AL	1,009.3	87	Boston, MA–NH	777.0	134	Seattle–Bellevue–Everett, WA	595.7
41	Fort Lauderdale, FL	1,005.4	88	Naples, FL	776.7	135	New Haven–Meriden, CT	588.8
42	Modesto, CA	992.1	89	Fort Pierce–Port St. Lucie, FL	774.0	136	Lafayette, LA	579.8
43	Albany, GA	990.0	90	Washington, DC–MD–VA–WV	771.4	137	Reno, NV	578.8
44	Shreveport–Bossier City, LA	987.9	91	Panama City, FL	765.0	138	Richmond–Petersburg, VA	578.5
45	Lakeland–Winter Haven, FL	984.3	92	Lexington, KY	759.2	139	Cincinnati, OH–KY–IN	573.6
46	Lake Charles, LA	977.7	93	Buffalo–Niagara Falls, NY	754.8	140	Odessa–Midland, TX	562.6
47	Greenville, NC	975.5	94	Tucson, AZ	754.2	141	Columbus, GA–AL	558.7

Source: U.S. Department of Justice, Federal Bureau of Investigation
  "Crime in the United States 1993" (Uniform Crime Reports, December 4, 1994)
*Violent crimes are offenses of murder, forcible rape, robbery and aggravated assault.
**Not available.

6. Violent Crime Rate in 1993 (continued)

National Rate = 746.1 Violent Crimes per 100,000 Population*

RANK	METRO AREA	RATE	RANK	METRO AREA	RATE	RANK	METRO AREA	RATE
141	Houma, LA	558.7	189	Salt Lake City–Ogden, UT	378.0	236	Lancaster, PA	224.8
143	Dayton–Springfield, OH	550.0	190	Waterbury, CT	371.7	237	Owensboro, KY	222.0
144	Orange County, CA	536.1	191	Fort Walton Beach, FL	366.8	238	Scranton–Wilkes-Barre–Hazleton, PA	214.8
145	Yolo, CA	533.9	192	Hickory–Morganton, NC	364.8	239	Binghamton, NY	212.3
146	Austin–San Marcos, TX	528.2	193	Bergen–Passaic, NJ	360.5	240	Cheyenne, WY	210.7
147	Lincoln, NE	525.4	194	Sioux Falls, SD	358.6	241	Johnstown, PA	208.0
148	San Jose, CA	524.7	195	Rochester, NY	351.5	242	Altoona, PA	199.4
149	Santa Rosa, CA	523.1	196	Dutchess County, NY	344.9	243	Fayetteville–Springdale–Rogers, AR	196.0
150	Santa Barbara–Santa Maria–Lompoc, CA	520.1	197	Fort Wayne, IN	341.2	244	Lewiston–Auburn, ME	183.5
151	Bryan–College Station, TX	517.2	198	Boise, ID	340.7	245	Williamsport, PA	176.9
152	Elkhart–Goshen, IN	508.5	199	Roanoke, VA	332.2	246	Bismarck, ND	175.7
153	San Luis Obispo–Atascadero, CA	502.7	200	Asheville, NC	331.5	247	Manchester, NH	165.4
154	Redding, CA	501.2	201	Lafayette, IN	326.2	248	Danbury, CT	142.7
155	Ventura, CA	500.4	202	Eugene–Springfield, OR	318.4	249	Provo–Orem, UT	141.9
156	Spokane, WA	498.3	203	Punta Gorda, FL	318.2	250	Bangor, ME	125.7
157	Hartford, CT	494.3	204	Brazoria, TX	305.5	251	Sheboygan, WI	116.1
158	Evansville–Henderson, IN–KY	490.2	205	Fort Collins–Loveland, CO	304.6	252	Nashua, NH	109.1
159	Bloomington, IN	483.1	206	Bremerton, WA	304.1	253	Appleton–Oshkosh–Neenah, WI	106.4
160	Milwaukee–Waukesha, WI	482.2	207	Greeley, CO	298.9	254	Eau Claire, WI	91.4
161	Macon, GA	480.7	208	Des Moines, IA	297.4	255	Wausau, WI	66.5
161	Sherman–Denison, TX	480.7	209	Salem, OR	297.1	–	Albany, NY**	NA
163	Canton–Massillon, OH	473.6	210	Madison, WI	295.2	–	Ann Arbor, MI**	NA
164	Akron, OH	466.5	211	New London–Norwich, CT–RI	293.1	–	Benton Harbor, MI**	NA
165	Kokomo, IN	461.1	212	Charlottesville, VA	292.3	–	Chicago, IL**	NA
166	Columbia, MO	459.9	213	Jacksonville, NC	290.1	–	Cleveland, OH**	NA
167	Colorado Springs, CO	452.9	214	Middlesex–Somerset–Hunterdon, NJ	289.2	–	Detroit, MI**	NA
168	Racine, WI	439.5	215	Hagerstown, MD	288.9	–	Duluth–Superior, MN–WI**	NA
169	Chico–Paradise, CA	439.3	216	Stamford–Norwalk, CT	288.5	–	Fargo–Moorhead, ND–MN**	NA
170	Glens Falls, NY	427.1	217	Green Bay, WI	287.9	–	Flint, MI**	NA
171	Fort Smith, AR–OK	427.0	217	Springfield, MO	287.9	–	Grand Forks, ND–MN**	NA
172	Medford–Ashland, OR	424.3	219	Honolulu, HI	285.7	–	Grand Rapids–Muskegon–Holland, MI**	NA
173	Kenosha, WI	420.9	220	Nassau–Suffolk, NY	277.5	–	Houston, TX**	NA
174	Cumberland, MD–WV	416.0	221	Syracuse, NY	276.1	–	Indianapolis, IN**	NA
175	Rapid City, SD	414.7	222	Huntington–Ashland, WV–KY–OH	273.4	–	Jackson, MI**	NA
176	Pittsfield, MA	412.1	223	Florence, AL	263.6	–	Kalamazoo–Battle Creek, MI**	NA
177	Waterloo–Cedar Falls, IA	407.5	224	Monmouth–Ocean, NJ	263.4	–	Kansas City, MO–KS**	NA
178	Charleston, WV	405.4	225	Janesville–Beloit, WI	262.4	–	La Crosse, WI–MN**	NA
179	Providence–Fall River–Warwick, RI–MA	402.0	226	Joplin, MO	261.8	–	Lansing–East Lansing, MI**	NA
180	Lynchburg, VA	400.2	227	Danville, VA	261.3	–	Minneapolis–St. Paul, MN–WI**	NA
181	Pittsburgh, PA	393.4	228	Decatur, AL	253.7	–	Omaha, NE**	NA
182	Richland–Kennewick–Pasco, WA	388.1	229	Dubuque, IA	250.0	–	Rochester, MN**	NA
183	Harrisburg–Lebanon–Carlisle, PA	387.5	230	Utica–Rome, NY	246.9	–	Saginaw–Bay City–Midland, MI**	NA
184	Erie, PA	386.7	231	Bellingham, WA	244.1	–	Springfield, MA**	NA
185	Steubenville–Weirton, OH–WV	385.5	232	Portland, ME	240.8	–	St. Cloud, MN**	NA
186	St. Joseph, MO	383.6	233	Olympia, WA	236.7	–	St. Louis, MO–IL**	NA
187	Newburgh, NY–PA	382.6	234	Boulder–Longmont, CO	235.4	–	West Palm Beach–Boca Raton, FL**	NA
188	Reading, PA	382.1	235	Johnson City–Kingsport–Bristol, TN–VA	231.5	–	Worcester, MA–CT**	NA

Source: U.S. Department of Justice, Federal Bureau of Investigation
    "Crime in the United States 1993" (Uniform Crime Reports, December 4, 1994)
*Violent crimes are offenses of murder, forcible rape, robbery and aggravated assault.
**Not available.

7. Percent Change in Violent Crime Rate: 1992 to 1993

National Percent Change = 1.5% Decrease*

RANK	METRO AREA	% CHANGE	RANK	METRO AREA	% CHANGE	RANK	METRO AREA	% CHANGE
60	Abilene, TX	5.31	225	Cheyenne, WY	(20.40)	221	Fort Worth–Arlington, TX	(17.52)
218	Akron, OH	(17.07)	–	Chicago, IL**	NA	97	Fresno, CA	0.77
162	Albany, GA	(4.97)	203	Chico–Paradise, CA	(12.00)	187	Gadsden, AL	(9.11)
–	Albany, NY**	NA	200	Cincinnati, OH–KY–IN	(11.45)	82	Gainesville, FL	2.45
52	Albuquerque, NM	6.45	231	Clarksville–Hopkinsville, TN–KY	(27.50)	74	Galveston–Texas City, TX	3.25
26	Alexandria, LA	13.25	–	Cleveland, OH**	NA	138	Gary–Hammond, IN	(2.80)
6	Altoona, PA	28.98	92	Colorado Springs, CO	1.66	188	Glens Falls, NY	(9.13)
121	Amarillo, TX	(1.39)	177	Columbia, MO	(7.33)	86	Goldsboro, NC	2.18
42	Anchorage, AK	8.19	30	Columbia, SC	10.62	–	Grand Forks, ND–MN**	NA
–	Ann Arbor, MI**	NA	18	Columbus, GA–AL	16.20	–	Grand Rapids–Muskegon–Holland, MI**	NA
32	Anniston, AL	10.26	130	Columbus, OH	(2.05)	109	Greeley, CO	0.00
70	Appleton–Oshkosh–Neenah, WI	3.70	215	Corpus Christi, TX	(15.58)	37	Green Bay, WI	8.81
220	Asheville, NC	(17.35)	49	Cumberland, MD–WV	6.97	88	Greensboro–Winston Salem–High Point, NC	2.00
178	Athens, GA	(7.42)	216	Dallas, TX	(15.84)	17	Greenville, NC	18.06
125	Atlanta, GA	(1.73)	161	Danbury, CT	(4.74)	19	Greenville–Spartanburg–Anderson, SC	15.24
110	Atlantic City, NJ	(0.10)	13	Danville, VA	20.47	180	Hagerstown, MD	(8.17)
159	Augusta–Aiken, GA–SC	(4.62)	169	Daytona Beach, FL	(6.17)	163	Harrisburg–Lebanon–Carlisle, PA	(5.14)
96	Austin–San Marcos, TX	0.96	212	Dayton–Springfield, OH	(15.02)	142	Hartford, CT	(3.08)
213	Bakersfield, CA	(15.20)	205	Decatur, AL	(12.49)	204	Hickory–Morganton, NC	(12.48)
113	Baltimore, MD	(0.24)	139	Denver, CO	(2.92)	61	Honolulu, HI	5.00
179	Bangor, ME	(7.51)	226	Des Moines, IA	(21.59)	111	Houma, LA	(0.13)
24	Barnstable–Yarmouth, MA	13.79	–	Detroit, MI**	NA	–	Houston, TX**	NA
165	Baton Rouge, LA	(5.37)	36	Dothan, AL	9.05	164	Huntington–Ashland, WV–KY–OH	(5.23)
227	Beaumont–Port Arthur, TX	(22.44)	1	Dubuque, IA	58.63	5	Huntsville, AL	29.84
197	Bellingham, WA	(10.55)	–	Duluth–Superior, MN–WI**	NA	–	Indianapolis, IN**	NA
–	Benton Harbor, MI**	NA	–	Dutchess County, NY**	NA	–	Jackson, MI**	NA
–	Bergen–Passaic, NJ**	NA	4	Eau Claire, WI	31.32	58	Jackson, MS	5.67
83	Binghamton, NY	2.41	90	El Paso, TX	1.80	185	Jackson, TN	(8.93)
40	Birmingham, AL	8.28	50	Elkhart–Goshen, IN	6.87	122	Jacksonville, FL	(1.43)
189	Bismarck, ND	(9.18)	10	Enid, OK	23.41	206	Jacksonville, NC	(12.54)
75	Bloomington, IN	3.20	43	Erie, PA	8.14	71	Janesville–Beloit, WI	3.51
78	Boise, ID	2.74	131	Eugene–Springfield, OR	(2.24)	–	Jersey City, NJ**	NA
–	Boston, MA–NH**	NA	210	Evansville–Henderson, IN–KY	(13.82)	196	Johnson City–Kingsport–Bristol, TN–VA	(10.41)
154	Boulder–Longmont, CO	(4.19)	–	Fargo–Moorhead, ND–MN**	NA	107	Johnstown, PA	0.19
53	Brazoria, TX	6.41	20	Fayetteville, NC	14.75	–	Joplin, MO**	NA
175	Bremerton, WA	(6.89)	34	Fayetteville–Springdale–Rogers, AR	9.56	–	Kalamazoo–Battle Creek, MI**	NA
190	Bridgeport, CT	(9.48)	–	Fitchburg–Leominster, MA**	NA	–	Kansas City, MO–KS**	NA
98	Brockton, MA	0.65	–	Flint, MI**	NA	8	Kenosha, WI	25.23
67	Brownsville–Harlingen–San Benito, TX	4.03	184	Florence, AL	(8.69)	16	Killeen–Temple, TX	18.53
168	Bryan–College Station, TX	(6.15)	29	Florence, SC	10.71	14	Kokomo, IN	19.83
–	Buffalo–Niagara Falls, NY**	NA	–	Fort Collins–Loveland, CO**	NA	–	La Crosse, WI–MN**	NA
167	Canton–Massillon, OH	(5.98)	79	Fort Lauderdale, FL	2.71	44	Lafayette, IN	8.08
140	Charleston, WV	(2.99)	173	Fort Myers–Cape Coral, FL	(6.67)	76	Lafayette, LA	3.08
66	Charleston–North Charleston, SC	4.29	38	Fort Pierce–Port St. Lucie, FL	8.45	–	Lake Charles, LA**	NA
151	Charlottesville, VA	(4.13)	22	Fort Smith, AR–OK	14.42	147	Lakeland–Winter Haven, FL	(3.95)
118	Charlotte–Gastonia–Rock Hill, NC–SC	(1.04)	170	Fort Walton Beach, FL	(6.19)	12	Lancaster, PA	20.54
153	Chattanooga, TN–GA	(4.17)	44	Fort Wayne, IN	8.08	–	Lansing–East Lansing, MI**	NA

Source: Morgan Quitno Corporation using data from U.S. Department of Justice, Federal Bureau of Investigation
"Crime in the United States 1993" (Uniform Crime Reports, December 4, 1994)
*Violent crimes are offenses of murder, forcible rape, robbery and aggravated assault.
**Not available.

7. Percent Change in Violent Crime Rate: 1992 to 1993 (continued)

National Percent Change = 1.5% Decrease*

RANK	METRO AREA	% CHANGE	RANK	METRO AREA	% CHANGE	RANK	METRO AREA	CHANGE
57	Laredo, TX	5.76	209	Olympia, WA	(13.20)	72	Seattle-Bellevue-Everett, WA	3.47
7	Las Vegas, NV-AZ	27.25	–	Omaha, NE**	NA	69	Sheboygan, WI	3.75
–	Lawrence, MA-NH**	NA	120	Orange County, CA	(1.13)	47	Sherman-Denison, TX	7.66
207	Lawton, OK	(12.65)	73	Orlando, FL	3.44	55	Shreveport-Bossier City, LA	6.15
2	Lewiston-Auburn, ME	44.94	182	Owensboro, KY	(8.26)	–	Sioux City, IA-NE**	NA
127	Lexington, KY	(1.77)	214	Panama City, FL	(15.32)	51	Sioux Falls, SD	6.54
201	Lincoln, NE	(11.56)	124	Philadelphia, PA-NJ	(1.62)	28	South Bend, IN	10.98
56	Little Rock-North Little Rock, AR	5.85	48	Phoenix-Mesa, AZ	7.59	117	Spokane, WA	(0.82)
129	Longview-Marshall, TX	(1.93)	21	Pine Bluff, AR	14.46	–	Springfield, MA**	NA
166	Los Angeles-Long Beach, CA	(5.41)	150	Pittsburgh, PA	(3.98)	135	Springfield, MO	(2.60)
157	Louisville, KY-IN	(4.46)	64	Pittsfield, MA	4.73	27	Stamford-Norwalk, CT	11.39
95	Lubbock, TX	1.36	198	Portland, ME	(11.27)	33	Steubenville-Weirton, OH-WV	10.02
160	Lynchburg, VA	(4.71)	136	Portland-Vancouver, OR-WA	(2.64)	63	Stockton-Lodi, CA	4.83
230	Macon, GA	(24.33)	102	Providence-Fall River-Warwick, RI-MA	0.47	–	St. Cloud, MN**	NA
181	Madison, WI	(8.18)	39	Provo-Orem, UT	8.40	192	St. Joseph, MO	(9.66)
–	Manchester, NH**	NA	25	Pueblo, CO	13.75	–	St. Louis, MO-IL**	NA
156	Mansfield, OH	(4.38)	–	Punta Gorda, FL**	NA	103	Sumter, SC	0.28
9	McAllen-Edinburg-Mission, TX	24.47	208	Racine, WI	(12.71)	194	Syracuse, NY	(10.18)
23	Medford-Ashland, OR	13.94	191	Raleigh-Durham-Chapel Hill, NC	(9.50)	158	Tacoma, WA	(4.55)
65	Memphis, TN-AR-MS	4.37	211	Rapid City, SD	(14.86)	148	Tallahassee, FL	(3.96)
3	Merced, CA	43.57	172	Reading, PA	(6.65)	145	Tampa-St. Petersburg-Clearwater, FL	(3.54)
62	Miami, FL	4.87	144	Redding, CA	(3.49)	132	Texarkana, TX-AR	(2.29)
–	Middlesex-Sommerset-Hunterdon, NJ**	NA	101	Reno, NV	0.59	100	Toledo, OH	0.61
171	Milwaukee-Waukesha, WI	(6.59)	176	Richland-Kennewick-Pasco, WA	(7.04)	126	Trenton, NJ	(1.76)
–	Minneapolis-St. Paul, MN-WI**	NA	91	Richmond-Petersburg, VA	1.74	104	Tucson, AZ	0.21
–	Mobile, AL**	NA	148	Riverside-San Bernardino, CA	(3.96)	128	Tulsa, OK	(1.92)
15	Modesto, CA	18.66	104	Roanoke, VA	0.21	152	Tuscaloosa, AL	(4.15)
–	Monmouth-Ocean, NJ**	NA	–	Rochester, MN**	NA	112	Tyler, TX	(0.22)
174	Monroe, LA	(6.82)	87	Rochester, NY	2.03	41	Utica-Rome, NY	8.24
68	Montgomery, AL	3.98	141	Rocky Mount, NC	(3.02)	202	Vallejo-Fairfield-Napa, CA	(11.71)
46	Myrtle Beach, SC	7.77	81	Sacramento, CA	2.49	183	Ventura, CA	(8.60)
143	Naples, FL	(3.48)	–	Saginaw-Bay City-Midland, MI**	NA	224	Victoria, TX	(19.61)
134	Nashua, NH	(2.50)	155	Salem, OR	(4.28)	89	Vineland-Millville-Bridgeton, NJ	1.84
59	Nashville, TN	5.54	93	Salinas, CA	1.56	114	Visalia-Tulare-Porterville, CA	(0.37)
–	Nassau-Suffolk, NY**	NA	108	Salt Lake City-Ogden, UT	0.13	11	Waco, TX	21.49
–	New Bedford, MA**	NA	199	San Angelo, TX	(11.43)	115	Washington, DC-MD-VA-WV	(0.45)
223	New Haven-Meriden, CT	(18.55)	146	San Antonio, TX	(3.61)	229	Waterbury, CT	(23.66)
99	New London-Norwich, CT-RI	0.62	193	San Diego, CA	(10.17)	–	Waterloo-Cedar Falls, IA**	NA
119	New Orleans, LA	(1.06)	106	San Francisco, CA	0.20	232	Wausau, WI	(27.95)
–	New York, NY**	NA	94	San Jose, CA	1.41	–	West Palm Beach-Boca Raton, FL**	NA
–	Newark, NJ**	NA	–	San Luis Obispo-Atascadero, CA**	NA	217	Wichita Falls, TX	(16.53)
–	Newburgh, NY-PA**	NA	137	Santa Barbara-Santa Maria-Lompoc, CA	(2.79)	219	Williamsport, PA	(17.10)
85	Norfolk-Va Beach-Newport News, VA-NC	2.32	35	Santa Cruz-Watsonville, CA	9.15	195	Wilmington, NC	(10.27)
84	Oakland, CA	2.35	80	Santa Rosa, CA	2.59	–	Worcester, MA-CT**	NA
123	Ocala, FL	(1.49)	54	Sarasota-Bradenton, FL	6.23	133	Yakima, WA	(2.43)
186	Odessa-Midland, TX	(9.10)	31	Savannah, GA	10.45	222	Yolo, CA	(18.01)
116	Oklahoma City, OK	(0.81)	228	Scranton-Wilkes-Barre-Hazleton, PA	(23.40)	77	Yuba City, CA	2.89

Source: *Morgan Quitno Corporation using data from U.S. Department of Justice, Federal Bureau of Investigation "Crime in the United States 1993" (Uniform Crime Reports, December 4, 1994)*
*Violent crimes are offenses of murder, forcible rape, robbery and aggravated assault.
**Not available.

7. Percent Change in Violent Crime Rate: 1992 to 1993 (continued)

National Percent Change = 1.5% Decrease*

RANK	METRO AREA	% CHANGE	RANK	METRO AREA	% CHANGE	RANK	METRO AREA	% CHANGE
1	Dubuque, IA	58.63	48	Phoenix-Mesa, AZ	7.59	95	Lubbock, TX	1.36
2	Lewiston-Auburn, ME	44.94	49	Cumberland, MD-WV	6.97	96	Austin-San Marcos, TX	0.96
3	Merced, CA	43.57	50	Elkhart-Goshen, IN	6.87	97	Fresno, CA	0.77
4	Eau Claire, WI	31.32	51	Sioux Falls, SD	6.54	98	Brockton, MA	0.65
5	Huntsville, AL	29.84	52	Albuquerque, NM	6.45	99	New London-Norwich, CT-RI	0.62
6	Altoona, PA	28.98	53	Brazoria, TX	6.41	100	Toledo, OH	0.61
7	Las Vegas, NV-AZ	27.25	54	Sarasota-Bradenton, FL	6.23	101	Reno, NV	0.59
8	Kenosha, WI	25.23	55	Shreveport-Bossier City, LA	6.15	102	Providence-Fall River-Warwick, RI-MA	0.47
9	McAllen-Edinburg-Mission, TX	24.47	56	Little Rock-North Little Rock, AR	5.85	103	Sumter, SC	0.28
10	Enid, OK	23.41	57	Laredo, TX	5.76	104	Roanoke, VA	0.21
11	Waco, TX	21.49	58	Jackson, MS	5.67	104	Tucson, AZ	0.21
12	Lancaster, PA	20.54	59	Nashville, TN	5.54	106	San Francisco, CA	0.20
13	Danville, VA	20.47	60	Abilene, TX	5.31	107	Johnstown, PA	0.19
14	Kokomo, IN	19.83	61	Honolulu, HI	5.00	108	Salt Lake City-Ogden, UT	0.13
15	Modesto, CA	18.66	62	Miami, FL	4.87	109	Greeley, CO	0.00
16	Killeen-Temple, TX	18.53	63	Stockton-Lodi, CA	4.83	110	Atlantic City, NJ	(0.10)
17	Greenville, NC	18.06	64	Pittsfield, MA	4.73	111	Houma, LA	(0.13)
18	Columbus, GA-AL	16.20	65	Memphis, TN-AR-MS	4.37	112	Tyler, TX	(0.22)
19	Greenville-Spartanburg-Anderson, SC	15.24	66	Charleston-North Charleston, SC	4.29	113	Baltimore, MD	(0.24)
20	Fayetteville, NC	14.75	67	Brownsville-Harlingen-San Benito, TX	4.03	114	Visalia-Tulare-Porterville, CA	(0.37)
21	Pine Bluff, AR	14.46	68	Montgomery, AL	3.98	115	Washington, DC-MD-VA-WV	(0.45)
22	Fort Smith, AR-OK	14.42	69	Sheboygan, WI	3.75	116	Oklahoma City, OK	(0.81)
23	Medford-Ashland, OR	13.94	70	Appleton-Oshkosh-Neenah, WI	3.70	117	Spokane, WA	(0.82)
24	Barnstable-Yarmouth, MA	13.79	71	Janesville-Beloit, WI	3.51	118	Charlotte-Gastonia-Rock Hill, NC-SC	(1.04)
25	Pueblo, CO	13.75	72	Seattle-Bellevue-Everett, WA	3.47	119	New Orleans, LA	(1.06)
26	Alexandria, LA	13.25	73	Orlando, FL	3.44	120	Orange County, CA	(1.13)
27	Stamford-Norwalk, CT	11.39	74	Galveston-Texas City, TX	3.25	121	Amarillo, TX	(1.39)
28	South Bend, IN	10.98	75	Bloomington, IN	3.20	122	Jacksonville, FL	(1.43)
29	Florence, SC	10.71	76	Lafayette, LA	3.08	123	Ocala, FL	(1.49)
30	Columbia, SC	10.62	77	Yuba City, CA	2.89	124	Philadelphia, PA-NJ	(1.62)
31	Savannah, GA	10.45	78	Boise, ID	2.74	125	Atlanta, GA	(1.73)
32	Anniston, AL	10.26	79	Fort Lauderdale, FL	2.71	126	Trenton, NJ	(1.76)
33	Steubenville-Weirton, OH-WV	10.02	80	Santa Rosa, CA	2.59	127	Lexington, KY	(1.77)
34	Fayetteville-Springdale-Rogers, AR	9.56	81	Sacramento, CA	2.49	128	Tulsa, OK	(1.92)
35	Santa Cruz-Watsonville, CA	9.15	82	Gainesville, FL	2.45	129	Longview-Marshall, TX	(1.93)
36	Dothan, AL	9.05	83	Binghamton, NY	2.41	130	Columbus, OH	(2.05)
37	Green Bay, WI	8.81	84	Oakland, CA	2.35	131	Eugene-Springfield, OR	(2.24)
38	Fort Pierce-Port St. Lucie, FL	8.45	85	Norfolk-Va Beach-Newport News, VA-NC	2.32	132	Texarkana, TX-AR	(2.29)
39	Provo-Orem, UT	8.40	86	Goldsboro, NC	2.18	133	Yakima, WA	(2.43)
40	Birmingham, AL	8.28	87	Rochester, NY	2.03	134	Nashua, NH	(2.50)
41	Utica-Rome, NY	8.24	88	Greensboro-Winston Salem-High Point, NC	2.00	135	Springfield, MO	(2.60)
42	Anchorage, AK	8.19	89	Vineland-Millville-Bridgeton, NJ	1.84	136	Portland-Vancouver, OR-WA	(2.64)
43	Erie, PA	8.14	90	El Paso, TX	1.80	137	Santa Barbara-Santa Maria-Lompoc, CA	(2.79)
44	Fort Wayne, IN	8.08	91	Richmond-Petersburg, VA	1.74	138	Gary-Hammond, IN	(2.80)
44	Lafayette, IN	8.08	92	Colorado Springs, CO	1.66	139	Denver, CO	(2.92)
46	Myrtle Beach, SC	7.77	93	Salinas, CA	1.56	140	Charleston, WV	(2.99)
47	Sherman-Denison, TX	7.66	94	San Jose, CA	1.41	141	Rocky Mount, NC	(3.02)

Source: Morgan Quitno Corporation using data from U.S. Department of Justice, Federal Bureau of Investigation
 "Crime in the United States 1993" (Uniform Crime Reports, December 4, 1994)
*Violent crimes are offenses of murder, forcible rape, robbery and aggravated assault.
**Not available.

7. Percent Change in Violent Crime Rate: 1992 to 1993 (continued)

National Percent Change = 1.5% Decrease*

RANK	METRO AREA	% CHANGE	RANK	METRO AREA	% CHANGE	RANK	METRO AREA	CHANGE
142	Hartford, CT	(3.08)	189	Bismarck, ND	(9.18)	–	Bergen-Passaic, NJ**	NA
143	Naples, FL	(3.48)	190	Bridgeport, CT	(9.48)	–	Boston, MA-NH**	NA
144	Redding, CA	(3.49)	191	Raleigh-Durham-Chapel Hill, NC	(9.50)	–	Buffalo-Niagara Falls, NY**	NA
145	Tampa-St. Petersburg-Clearwater, FL	(3.54)	192	St. Joseph, MO	(9.66)	–	Chicago, IL**	NA
146	San Antonio, TX	(3.61)	193	San Diego, CA	(10.17)	–	Cleveland, OH**	NA
147	Lakeland-Winter Haven, FL	(3.95)	194	Syracuse, NY	(10.18)	–	Detroit, MI**	NA
148	Riverside-San Bernardino, CA	(3.96)	195	Wilmington, NC	(10.27)	–	Duluth-Superior, MN-WI**	NA
148	Tallahassee, FL	(3.96)	196	Johnson City-Kingsport-Bristol, TN-VA	(10.41)	–	Dutchess County, NY**	NA
150	Pittsburgh, PA	(3.98)	197	Bellingham, WA	(10.55)	–	Fargo-Moorhead, ND-MN**	NA
151	Charlottesville, VA	(4.13)	198	Portland, ME	(11.27)	–	Fitchburg-Leominster, MA**	NA
152	Tuscaloosa, AL	(4.15)	199	San Angelo, TX	(11.43)	–	Flint, MI**	NA
153	Chattanooga, TN-GA	(4.17)	200	Cincinnati, OH-KY-IN	(11.45)	–	Fort Collins-Loveland, CO**	NA
154	Boulder-Longmont, CO	(4.19)	201	Lincoln, NE	(11.56)	–	Grand Forks, ND-MN**	NA
155	Salem, OR	(4.28)	202	Vallejo-Fairfield-Napa, CA	(11.71)	–	Grand Rapids-Muskegon-Holland, MI**	NA
156	Mansfield, OH	(4.38)	203	Chico-Paradise, CA	(12.00)	–	Houston, TX**	NA
157	Louisville, KY-IN	(4.46)	204	Hickory-Morganton, NC	(12.48)	–	Indianapolis, IN**	NA
158	Tacoma, WA	(4.55)	205	Decatur, AL	(12.49)	–	Jackson, MI**	NA
159	Augusta-Aiken, GA-SC	(4.62)	206	Jacksonville, NC	(12.54)	–	Jersey City, NJ**	NA
160	Lynchburg, VA	(4.71)	207	Lawton, OK	(12.65)	–	Joplin, MO**	NA
161	Danbury, CT	(4.74)	208	Racine, WI	(12.71)	–	Kalamazoo-Battle Creek, MI**	NA
162	Albany, GA	(4.97)	209	Olympia, WA	(13.20)	–	Kansas City, MO-KS**	NA
163	Harrisburg-Lebanon-Carlisle, PA	(5.14)	210	Evansville-Henderson, IN-KY	(13.82)	–	La Crosse, WI-MN**	NA
164	Huntington-Ashland, WV-KY-OH	(5.23)	211	Rapid City, SD	(14.86)	–	Lake Charles, LA**	NA
165	Baton Rouge, LA	(5.37)	212	Dayton-Springfield, OH	(15.02)	–	Lansing-East Lansing, MI**	NA
166	Los Angeles-Long Beach, CA	(5.41)	213	Bakersfield, CA	(15.20)	–	Lawrence, MA-NH**	NA
167	Canton-Massillon, OH	(5.98)	214	Panama City, FL	(15.32)	–	Manchester, NH**	NA
168	Bryan-College Station, TX	(6.15)	215	Corpus Christi, TX	(15.58)	–	Middlesex-Sommerset-Hunterdon, NJ**	NA
169	Daytona Beach, FL	(6.17)	216	Dallas, TX	(15.84)	–	Minneapolis-St. Paul, MN-WI**	NA
170	Fort Walton Beach, FL	(6.19)	217	Wichita Falls, TX	(16.53)	–	Mobile, AL**	NA
171	Milwaukee-Waukesha, WI	(6.59)	218	Akron, OH	(17.07)	–	Monmouth-Ocean, NJ**	NA
172	Reading, PA	(6.65)	219	Williamsport, PA	(17.10)	–	Nassau-Suffolk, NY**	NA
173	Fort Myers-Cape Coral, FL	(6.67)	220	Asheville, NC	(17.35)	–	New Bedford, MA**	NA
174	Monroe, LA	(6.82)	221	Fort Worth-Arlington, TX	(17.52)	–	New York, NY**	NA
175	Bremerton, WA	(6.89)	222	Yolo, CA	(18.01)	–	Newark, NJ**	NA
176	Richland-Kennewick-Pasco, WA	(7.04)	223	New Haven-Meriden, CT	(18.55)	–	Newburgh, NY-PA**	NA
177	Columbia, MO	(7.33)	224	Victoria, TX	(19.61)	–	Omaha, NE**	NA
178	Athens, GA	(7.42)	225	Cheyenne, WY	(20.40)	–	Punta Gorda, FL**	NA
179	Bangor, ME	(7.51)	226	Des Moines, IA	(21.59)	–	Rochester, MN**	NA
180	Hagerstown, MD	(8.17)	227	Beaumont-Port Arthur, TX	(22.44)	–	Saginaw-Bay City-Midland, MI**	NA
181	Madison, WI	(8.18)	228	Scranton-Wilkes-Barre-Hazleton, PA	(23.40)	–	San Luis Obispo-Atascadero, CA**	NA
182	Owensboro, KY	(8.26)	229	Waterbury, CT	(23.66)	–	Sioux City, IA-NE**	NA
183	Ventura, CA	(8.60)	230	Macon, GA	(24.33)	–	Springfield, MA**	NA
184	Florence, AL	(8.69)	231	Clarksville-Hopkinsville, TN-KY	(27.50)	–	St. Cloud, MN**	NA
185	Jackson, TN	(8.93)	232	Wausau, WI	(27.95)	–	St. Louis, MO-IL**	NA
186	Odessa-Midland, TX	(9.10)	–	Albany, NY**	NA	–	Waterloo-Cedar Falls, IA**	NA
187	Gadsden, AL	(9.11)	–	Ann Arbor, MI**	NA	–	West Palm Beach-Boca Raton, FL**	NA
188	Glens Falls, NY	(9.13)	–	Benton Harbor, MI**	NA	–	Worcester, MA-CT**	NA

Source: Morgan Quitno Corporation using data from U.S. Department of Justice, Federal Bureau of Investigation
"Crime in the United States 1993" (Uniform Crime Reports, December 4, 1994)
*Violent crimes are offenses of murder, forcible rape, robbery and aggravated assault.
**Not available.

8. Percent Change in Violent Crime Rate: 1989 to 1993

National Percent Change = 12.5% Increase*

RANK	METRO AREA	% CHANGE	RANK	METRO AREA	% CHANGE	RANK	METRO AREA	% CHANGE
104	Abilene, TX	18.03	203	Cheyenne, WY	(11.28)	149	Fort Worth–Arlington, TX	7.19
–	Akron, OH**	NA	–	Chicago, IL**	NA	164	Fresno, CA	3.47
143	Albany, GA	8.70	127	Chico–Paradise, CA	10.68	11	Gadsden, AL	78.22
–	Albany, NY**	NA	70	Cincinnati, OH–KY–IN	27.72	107	Gainesville, FL	16.36
71	Albuquerque, NM	27.70	13	Clarksville–Hopkinsville, TN–KY	76.54	32	Galveston–Texas City, TX	46.81
5	Alexandria, LA	116.10	–	Cleveland, OH**	NA	59	Gary–Hammond, IN	31.35
140	Altoona, PA	9.08	123	Colorado Springs, CO	11.06	65	Glens Falls, NY	29.19
91	Amarillo, TX	21.66	126	Columbia, MO	10.71	–	Goldsboro, NC**	NA
14	Anchorage, AK	74.31	150	Columbia, SC	6.87	–	Grand Forks, ND–MN**	NA
–	Ann Arbor, MI**	NA	170	Columbus, GA–AL	2.36	–	Grand Rapids–Muskegon–Holland, MI**	NA
41	Anniston, AL	39.71	154	Columbus, OH	6.48	219	Greeley, CO	(21.77)
205	Appleton–Oshkosh–Neenah, WI	(11.99)	136	Corpus Christi, TX	9.38	19	Green Bay, WI	59.06
120	Asheville, NC	11.77	6	Cumberland, MD–WV	102.73	108	Greensboro–Winston Salem–High Point, NC	16.20
175	Athens, GA	0.20	210	Dallas, TX	(14.32)	–	Greenville, NC**	NA
201	Atlanta, GA	(10.66)	55	Danbury, CT	32.99	83	Greenville–Spartanburg–Anderson, SC	23.71
173	Atlantic City, NJ	1.32	30	Danville, VA	49.91	192	Hagerstown, MD	(5.83)
134	Augusta–Aiken, GA–SC	9.48	169	Daytona Beach, FL	2.45	–	Harrisburg–Lebanon–Carlisle, PA**	NA
128	Austin–San Marcos, TX	10.50	197	Dayton–Springfield, OH	(8.03)	221	Hartford, CT	(25.59)
161	Bakersfield, CA	5.03	212	Decatur, AL	(16.49)	–	Hickory–Morganton, NC**	NA
82	Baltimore, MD	23.75	69	Denver, CO	28.10	159	Honolulu, HI	5.58
29	Bangor, ME	50.54	223	Des Moines, IA	(36.64)	–	Houma, LA**	NA
–	Barnstable–Yarmouth, MA**	NA	–	Detroit, MI**	NA	–	Houston, TX**	NA
21	Baton Rouge, LA	57.00	105	Dothan, AL	17.59	92	Huntington–Ashland, WV–KY–OH	21.46
178	Beaumont–Port Arthur, TX	(0.40)	222	Dubuque, IA	(36.53)	9	Huntsville, AL	91.86
158	Bellingham, WA	5.63	–	Duluth–Superior, MN–WI**	NA	–	Indianapolis, IN**	NA
–	Benton Harbor, MI**	NA	–	Dutchess County, NY**	NA	–	Jackson, MI**	NA
202	Bergen–Passaic, NJ	(11.23)	49	Eau Claire, WI	35.01	15	Jackson, MS	71.74
22	Binghamton, NY	56.91	87	El Paso, TX	22.59	111	Jackson, TN	15.05
33	Birmingham, AL	45.50	23	Elkhart–Goshen, IN	55.27	95	Jacksonville, FL	21.01
2	Bismarck, ND	165.45	56	Enid, OK	32.69	216	Jacksonville, NC	(18.83)
81	Bloomington, IN	23.78	116	Erie, PA	13.47	130	Janesville–Beloit, WI	10.34
156	Boise, ID	6.04	137	Eugene–Springfield, OR	9.30	133	Jersey City, NJ	9.67
–	Boston, MA–NH**	NA	90	Evansville–Henderson, IN–KY	21.97	189	Johnson City–Kingsport–Bristol, TN–VA	(3.70)
220	Boulder–Longmont, CO	(23.42)	–	Fargo–Moorhead, ND–MN**	NA	–	Johnstown, PA**	NA
114	Brazoria, TX	14.04	152	Fayetteville, NC	6.70	113	Joplin, MO	14.07
–	Bremerton, WA**	NA	198	Fayetteville–Springdale–Rogers, AR	(8.11)	–	Kalamazoo–Battle Creek, MI**	NA
192	Bridgeport, CT	(5.83)	27	Fitchburg–Leominster, MA	52.03	–	Kansas City, MO–KS**	NA
–	Brockton, MA**	NA	–	Flint, MI**	NA	4	Kenosha, WI	124.00
51	Brownsville–Harlingen–San Benito, TX	34.06	177	Florence, AL	(0.19)	12	Killeen–Temple, TX	78.05
184	Bryan–College Station, TX	(2.32)	80	Florence, SC	23.94	28	Kokomo, IN	51.48
85	Buffalo–Niagara Falls, NY	22.95	168	Fort Collins–Loveland, CO	2.59	–	La Crosse, WI–MN**	NA
188	Canton–Massillon, OH	(3.11)	167	Fort Lauderdale, FL	2.60	1	Lafayette, IN	237.33
24	Charleston, WV	54.85	7	Fort Myers–Cape Coral, FL	99.44	147	Lafayette, LA	7.73
61	Charleston–North Charleston, SC	30.63	185	Fort Pierce–Port St. Lucie, FL	(2.54)	100	Lake Charles, LA	18.18
174	Charlottesville, VA	1.07	148	Fort Smith, AR–OK	7.45	182	Lakeland–Winter Haven, FL	(1.35)
97	Charlotte–Gastonia–Rock Hill, NC–SC	19.25	109	Fort Walton Beach, FL	15.82	47	Lancaster, PA	35.18
129	Chattanooga, TN–GA	10.44	195	Fort Wayne, IN	(6.98)	–	Lansing–East Lansing, MI**	NA

Source: Morgan Quitno Corporation using data from U.S. Department of Justice, Federal Bureau of Investigation
"Crime in the United States 1993" (Uniform Crime Reports, December 4, 1994)
*Violent crimes are offenses of murder, forcible rape, robbery and aggravated assault.
**Not available.

GAVILAN COLLEGE LIBRARY

8. Percent Change in Violent Crime Rate: 1989 to 1993 (continued)

National Percent Change = 12.5% Increase*

RANK	METRO AREA	% CHANGE	RANK	METRO AREA	% CHANGE	RANK	METRO AREA	CHANGE
217	Laredo, TX	(19.07)	171	Olympia, WA	1.81	144	Seattle–Bellevue–Everett, WA	8.13
36	Las Vegas, NV–AZ	42.87	–	Omaha, NE**	NA	226	Sheboygan, WI	(46.00)
39	Lawrence, MA–NH	41.77	124	Orange County, CA	10.92	102	Sherman–Denison, TX	18.14
50	Lawton, OK	34.94	119	Orlando, FL	12.15	106	Shreveport–Bossier City, LA	16.81
163	Lewiston–Auburn, ME	4.98	64	Owensboro, KY	29.22	3	Sioux City, IA–NE	157.39
45	Lexington, KY	37.74	25	Panama City, FL	52.91	57	Sioux Falls, SD	32.32
93	Lincoln, NE	21.26	141	Philadelphia, PA–NJ	8.82	–	South Bend, IN**	NA
37	Little Rock–North Little Rock, AR	42.46	63	Phoenix–Mesa, AZ	30.13	73	Spokane, WA	26.76
54	Longview–Marshall, TX	33.73	121	Pine Bluff, AR	11.53	–	Springfield, MA**	NA
160	Los Angeles–Long Beach, CA	5.08	166	Pittsburgh, PA	2.77	199	Springfield, MO	(9.15)
44	Louisville, KY–IN	38.28	–	Pittsfield, MA**	NA	183	Stamford–Norwalk, CT	(2.14)
60	Lubbock, TX	31.17	200	Portland, ME	(9.20)	–	Steubenville–Weirton, OH–WV**	NA
181	Lynchburg, VA	(0.79)	208	Portland–Vancouver, OR–WA	(12.81)	42	Stockton–Lodi, CA	39.16
209	Macon, GA	(13.98)	194	Providence–Fall River–Warwick, RI–MA	(6.34)	–	St. Cloud, MN**	NA
72	Madison, WI	27.19	–	Provo–Orem, UT**	NA	224	St. Joseph, MO	(39.25)
213	Manchester, NH	(16.55)	38	Pueblo, CO	41.97	–	St. Louis, MO–IL**	NA
131	Mansfield, OH	10.14	–	Punta Gorda, FL**	NA	–	Sumter, SC**	NA
10	McAllen–Edinburg–Mission, TX	79.05	206	Racine, WI	(12.08)	190	Syracuse, NY	(4.86)
77	Medford–Ashland, OR	25.20	34	Raleigh–Durham–Chapel Hill, NC	43.83	162	Tacoma, WA	4.99
112	Memphis, TN–AR–MS	14.57	66	Rapid City, SD	28.67	89	Tallahassee, FL	22.32
18	Merced, CA	61.76	–	Reading, PA**	NA	132	Tampa–St. Petersburg–Clearwater, FL	9.69
187	Miami, FL	(3.08)	146	Redding, CA	7.92	26	Texarkana, TX–AR	52.18
67	Middlesex–Sommerset–Hunterdon, NJ	28.36	218	Reno, NV	(20.01)	191	Toledo, OH	(5.82)
74	Milwaukee–Waukesha, WI	26.56	145	Richland–Kennewick–Pasco, WA	7.99	180	Trenton, NJ	(0.71)
–	Minneapolis–St. Paul, MN–WI**	NA	157	Richmond–Petersburg, VA	5.82	–	Tucson, AZ**	NA
211	Mobile, AL	(15.58)	–	Riverside–San Bernardino, CA**	NA	153	Tulsa, OK	6.63
101	Modesto, CA	18.15	99	Roanoke, VA	18.47	68	Tuscaloosa, AL	28.33
176	Monmouth–Ocean, NJ	0.08	–	Rochester, MN**	NA	35	Tyler, TX	43.31
96	Monroe, LA	20.98	172	Rochester, NY	1.44	17	Utica–Rome, NY	64.27
8	Montgomery, AL	96.15	–	Rocky Mount, NC**	NA	204	Vallejo–Fairfield–Napa, CA	(11.69)
–	Myrtle Beach, SC**	NA	86	Sacramento, CA	22.88	76	Ventura, CA	25.48
117	Naples, FL	12.53	–	Saginaw–Bay City–Midland, MI**	NA	52	Victoria, TX	33.98
225	Nashua, NH	(43.09)	215	Salem, OR	(18.15)	78	Vineland–Millville–Bridgeton, NJ	25.04
20	Nashville, TN	58.15	103	Salinas, CA	18.09	179	Visalia–Tulare–Porterville, CA	(0.48)
118	Nassau–Suffolk, NY	12.26	98	Salt Lake City–Ogden, UT	19.13	31	Waco, TX	48.80
46	New Bedford, MA	36.57	125	San Angelo, TX	10.79	151	Washington, DC–MD–VA–WV	6.81
214	New Haven–Meriden, CT	(17.98)	84	San Antonio, TX	23.06	165	Waterbury, CT	3.42
207	New London–Norwich, CT–RI	(12.22)	110	San Diego, CA	15.54	53	Waterloo–Cedar Falls, IA	33.83
142	New Orleans, LA	8.75	75	San Francisco, CA	26.42	227	Wausau, WI	(46.07)
196	New York, NY	(7.70)	139	San Jose, CA	9.15	–	West Palm Beach–Boca Raton, FL**	NA
186	Newark, NJ	(3.01)	–	San Luis Obispo–Atascadero, CA**	NA	155	Wichita Falls, TX	6.15
–	Newburgh, NY–PA**	NA	122	Santa Barbara–Santa Maria–Lompoc, CA	11.09	–	Williamsport, PA**	NA
40	Norfolk–Va Beach–Newport News, VA–NC	39.86	16	Santa Cruz–Watsonville, CA	66.11	115	Wilmington, NC	13.51
43	Oakland, CA	39.02	48	Santa Rosa, CA	35.17	–	Worcester, MA–CT**	NA
79	Ocala, FL	24.07	88	Sarasota–Bradenton, FL	22.33	135	Yakima, WA	9.47
62	Odessa–Midland, TX	30.14	94	Savannah, GA	21.08	–	Yolo, CA**	NA
57	Oklahoma City, OK	32.32	–	Scranton–Wilkes-Barre–Hazleton, PA**	NA	138	Yuba City, CA	9.18

Source: Morgan Quitno Corporation using data from U.S. Department of Justice, Federal Bureau of Investigation
   "Crime in the United States 1993" (Uniform Crime Reports, December 4, 1994)
*Violent crimes are offenses of murder, forcible rape, robbery and aggravated assault.
**Not available.

REF
HV
6787 City crime rankings
C57
1995
44785

8. Percent Change in Violent Crime Rate: 1989 to 1993 (continued)

National Percent Change = 12.5% Increase*

RANK	METRO AREA	% CHANGE	RANK	METRO AREA	% CHANGE	RANK	METRO AREA	% CHANGE
1	Lafayette, IN	237.33	48	Santa Rosa, CA	35.17	95	Jacksonville, FL	21.01
2	Bismarck, ND	165.45	49	Eau Claire, WI	35.01	96	Monroe, LA	20.98
3	Sioux City, IA–NE	157.39	50	Lawton, OK	34.94	97	Charlotte-Gastonia-Rock Hill, NC–SC	19.25
4	Kenosha, WI	124.00	51	Brownsville-Harlingen-San Benito, TX	34.06	98	Salt Lake City-Ogden, UT	19.13
5	Alexandria, LA	116.10	52	Victoria, TX	33.98	99	Roanoke, VA	18.47
6	Cumberland, MD–WV	102.73	53	Waterloo-Cedar Falls, IA	33.83	100	Lake Charles, LA	18.18
7	Fort Myers-Cape Coral, FL	99.44	54	Longview-Marshall, TX	33.73	101	Modesto, CA	18.15
8	Montgomery, AL	96.15	55	Danbury, CT	32.99	102	Sherman-Denison, TX	18.14
9	Huntsville, AL	91.86	56	Enid, OK	32.69	103	Salinas, CA	18.09
10	McAllen-Edinburg-Mission, TX	79.05	57	Oklahoma City, OK	32.32	104	Abilene, TX	18.03
11	Gadsden, AL	78.22	57	Sioux Falls, SD	32.32	105	Dothan, AL	17.59
12	Killeen-Temple, TX	78.05	59	Gary-Hammond, IN	31.35	106	Shreveport-Bossier City, LA	16.81
13	Clarksville-Hopkinsville, TN–KY	76.54	60	Lubbock, TX	31.17	107	Gainesville, FL	16.36
14	Anchorage, AK	74.31	61	Charleston-North Charleston, SC	30.63	108	Greensboro-Winston Salem-High Point, NC	16.20
15	Jackson, MS	71.74	62	Odessa-Midland, TX	30.14	109	Fort Walton Beach, FL	15.82
16	Santa Cruz-Watsonville, CA	66.11	63	Phoenix-Mesa, AZ	30.13	110	San Diego, CA	15.54
17	Utica-Rome, NY	64.27	64	Owensboro, KY	29.22	111	Jackson, TN	15.05
18	Merced, CA	61.76	65	Glens Falls, NY	29.19	112	Memphis, TN–AR–MS	14.57
19	Green Bay, WI	59.06	66	Rapid City, SD	28.67	113	Joplin, MO	14.07
20	Nashville, TN	58.15	67	Middlesex-Sommerset-Hunterdon, NJ	28.36	114	Brazoria, TX	14.04
21	Baton Rouge, LA	57.00	68	Tuscaloosa, AL	28.33	115	Wilmington, NC	13.51
22	Binghamton, NY	56.91	69	Denver, CO	28.10	116	Erie, PA	13.47
23	Elkhart-Goshen, IN	55.27	70	Cincinnati, OH–KY–IN	27.72	117	Naples, FL	12.53
24	Charleston, WV	54.85	71	Albuquerque, NM	27.70	118	Nassau-Suffolk, NY	12.26
25	Panama City, FL	52.91	72	Madison, WI	27.19	119	Orlando, FL	12.15
26	Texarkana, TX–AR	52.18	73	Spokane, WA	26.76	120	Asheville, NC	11.77
27	Fitchburg-Leominster, MA	52.03	74	Milwaukee-Waukesha, WI	26.56	121	Pine Bluff, AR	11.53
28	Kokomo, IN	51.48	75	San Francisco, CA	26.42	122	Santa Barbara-Santa Maria-Lompoc, CA	11.09
29	Bangor, ME	50.54	76	Ventura, CA	25.48	123	Colorado Springs, CO	11.06
30	Danville, VA	49.91	77	Medford-Ashland, OR	25.20	124	Orange County, CA	10.92
31	Waco, TX	48.80	78	Vineland-Millville-Bridgeton, NJ	25.04	125	San Angelo, TX	10.79
32	Galveston-Texas City, TX	46.81	79	Ocala, FL	24.07	126	Columbia, MO	10.71
33	Birmingham, AL	45.50	80	Florence, SC	23.94	127	Chico-Paradise, CA	10.68
34	Raleigh-Durham-Chapel Hill, NC	43.83	81	Bloomington, IN	23.78	128	Austin-San Marcos, TX	10.50
35	Tyler, TX	43.31	82	Baltimore, MD	23.75	129	Chattanooga, TN–GA	10.44
36	Las Vegas, NV–AZ	42.87	83	Greenville-Spartanburg-Anderson, SC	23.71	130	Janesville-Beloit, WI	10.34
37	Little Rock-North Little Rock, AR	42.46	84	San Antonio, TX	23.06	131	Mansfield, OH	10.14
38	Pueblo, CO	41.97	85	Buffalo-Niagara Falls, NY	22.95	132	Tampa-St. Petersburg-Clearwater, FL	9.69
39	Lawrence, MA–NH	41.77	86	Sacramento, CA	22.88	133	Jersey City, NJ	9.67
40	Norfolk-Va Beach-Newport News, VA–NC	39.86	87	El Paso, TX	22.59	134	Augusta-Aiken, GA–SC	9.48
41	Anniston, AL	39.71	88	Sarasota-Bradenton, FL	22.33	135	Yakima, WA	9.47
42	Stockton-Lodi, CA	39.16	89	Tallahassee, FL	22.32	136	Corpus Christi, TX	9.38
43	Oakland, CA	39.02	90	Evansville-Henderson, IN–KY	21.97	137	Eugene-Springfield, OR	9.30
44	Louisville, KY–IN	38.28	91	Amarillo, TX	21.66	138	Yuba City, CA	9.18
45	Lexington, KY	37.74	92	Huntington-Ashland, WV–KY–OH	21.46	139	San Jose, CA	9.15
46	New Bedford, MA	36.57	93	Lincoln, NE	21.26	140	Altoona, PA	9.08
47	Lancaster, PA	35.18	94	Savannah, GA	21.08	141	Philadelphia, PA–NJ	8.82

Source: Morgan Quitno Corporation using data from U.S. Department of Justice, Federal Bureau of Investigation
   "Crime in the United States 1993" (Uniform Crime Reports, December 4, 1994)
*Violent crimes are offenses of murder, forcible rape, robbery and aggravated assault.
**Not available.

8. Percent Change in Violent Crime Rate: 1989 to 1993 (continued)

National Percent Change = 12.5% Increase*

RANK	METRO AREA	% CHANGE	RANK	METRO AREA	% CHANGE	RANK	METRO AREA	CHANGE
142	New Orleans, LA	8.75	189	Johnson City-Kingsport-Bristol, TN-VA	(3.70)	–	Chicago, IL**	NA
143	Albany, GA	8.70	190	Syracuse, NY	(4.86)	–	Cleveland, OH**	NA
144	Seattle-Bellevue-Everett, WA	8.13	191	Toledo, OH	(5.82)	–	Detroit, MI**	NA
145	Richland-Kennewick-Pasco, WA	7.99	192	Bridgeport, CT	(5.83)	–	Duluth-Superior, MN-WI**	NA
146	Redding, CA	7.92	192	Hagerstown, MD	(5.83)	–	Dutchess County, NY**	NA
147	Lafayette, LA	7.73	194	Providence-Fall River-Warwick, RI-MA	(6.34)	–	Fargo-Moorhead, ND-MN**	NA
148	Fort Smith, AR-OK	7.45	195	Fort Wayne, IN	(6.98)	–	Flint, MI**	NA
149	Fort Worth-Arlington, TX	7.19	196	New York, NY	(7.70)	–	Goldsboro, NC**	NA
150	Columbia, SC	6.87	197	Dayton-Springfield, OH	(8.03)	–	Grand Forks, ND-MN**	NA
151	Washington, DC-MD-VA-WV	6.81	198	Fayetteville-Springdale-Rogers, AR	(8.11)	–	Grand Rapids-Muskegon-Holland, MI**	NA
152	Fayetteville, NC	6.70	199	Springfield, MO	(9.15)	–	Greenville, NC**	NA
153	Tulsa, OK	6.63	200	Portland, ME	(9.20)	–	Harrisburg-Lebanon-Carlisle, PA**	NA
154	Columbus, OH	6.48	201	Atlanta, GA	(10.66)	–	Hickory-Morganton, NC**	NA
155	Wichita Falls, TX	6.15	202	Bergen-Passaic, NJ	(11.23)	–	Houma, LA**	NA
156	Boise, ID	6.04	203	Cheyenne, WY	(11.28)	–	Houston, TX**	NA
157	Richmond-Petersburg, VA	5.82	204	Vallejo-Fairfield-Napa, CA	(11.69)	–	Indianapolis, IN**	NA
158	Bellingham, WA	5.63	205	Appleton-Oshkosh-Neenah, WI	(11.99)	–	Jackson, MI**	NA
159	Honolulu, HI	5.58	206	Racine, WI	(12.08)	–	Johnstown, PA**	NA
160	Los Angeles-Long Beach, CA	5.08	207	New London-Norwich, CT-RI	(12.22)	–	Kalamazoo-Battle Creek, MI**	NA
161	Bakersfield, CA	5.03	208	Portland-Vancouver, OR-WA	(12.81)	–	Kansas City, MO-KS**	NA
162	Tacoma, WA	4.99	209	Macon, GA	(13.98)	–	La Crosse, WI-MN**	NA
163	Lewiston-Auburn, ME	4.98	210	Dallas, TX	(14.32)	–	Lansing-East Lansing, MI**	NA
164	Fresno, CA	3.47	211	Mobile, AL	(15.58)	–	Minneapolis-St. Paul, MN-WI**	NA
165	Waterbury, CT	3.42	212	Decatur, AL	(16.49)	–	Myrtle Beach, SC**	NA
166	Pittsburgh, PA	2.77	213	Manchester, NH	(16.55)	–	Newburgh, NY-PA**	NA
167	Fort Lauderdale, FL	2.60	214	New Haven-Meriden, CT	(17.98)	–	Omaha, NE**	NA
168	Fort Collins-Loveland, CO	2.59	215	Salem, OR	(18.15)	–	Pittsfield, MA**	NA
169	Daytona Beach, FL	2.45	216	Jacksonville, NC	(18.83)	–	Provo-Orem, UT**	NA
170	Columbus, GA-AL	2.36	217	Laredo, TX	(19.07)	–	Punta Gorda, FL**	NA
171	Olympia, WA	1.81	218	Reno, NV	(20.01)	–	Reading, PA**	NA
172	Rochester, NY	1.44	219	Greeley, CO	(21.77)	–	Riverside-San Bernardino, CA**	NA
173	Atlantic City, NJ	1.32	220	Boulder-Longmont, CO	(23.42)	–	Rochester, MN**	NA
174	Charlottesville, VA	1.07	221	Hartford, CT	(25.59)	–	Rocky Mount, NC**	NA
175	Athens, GA	0.20	222	Dubuque, IA	(36.53)	–	Saginaw-Bay City-Midland, MI**	NA
176	Monmouth-Ocean, NJ	0.08	223	Des Moines, IA	(36.64)	–	San Luis Obispo-Atascadero, CA**	NA
177	Florence, AL	(0.19)	224	St. Joseph, MO	(39.25)	–	Scranton-Wilkes-Barre-Hazleton, PA**	NA
178	Beaumont-Port Arthur, TX	(0.40)	225	Nashua, NH	(43.09)	–	South Bend, IN**	NA
179	Visalia-Tulare-Porterville, CA	(0.48)	226	Sheboygan, WI	(46.00)	–	Springfield, MA**	NA
180	Trenton, NJ	(0.71)	227	Wausau, WI	(46.07)	–	Steubenville-Weirton, OH-WV**	NA
181	Lynchburg, VA	(0.79)	–	Akron, OH**	NA	–	St. Cloud, MN**	NA
182	Lakeland-Winter Haven, FL	(1.35)	–	Albany, NY**	NA	–	St. Louis, MO-IL**	NA
183	Stamford-Norwalk, CT	(2.14)	–	Ann Arbor, MI**	NA	–	Sumter, SC**	NA
184	Bryan-College Station, TX	(2.32)	–	Barnstable-Yarmouth, MA**	NA	–	Tucson, AZ**	NA
185	Fort Pierce-Port St. Lucie, FL	(2.54)	–	Benton Harbor, MI**	NA	–	West Palm Beach-Boca Raton, FL**	NA
186	Newark, NJ	(3.01)	–	Boston, MA-NH**	NA	–	Williamsport, PA**	NA
187	Miami, FL	(3.08)	–	Bremerton, WA**	NA	–	Worcester, MA-CT**	NA
188	Canton-Massillon, OH	(3.11)	–	Brockton, MA**	NA	–	Yolo, CA**	NA

Source: Morgan Quitno Corporation using data from U.S. Department of Justice, Federal Bureau of Investigation "Crime in the United States 1993" (Uniform Crime Reports, December 4, 1994)
*Violent crimes are offenses of murder, forcible rape, robbery and aggravated assault.
**Not available.

9. Murders in 1993

National Total = 24,526 Murders*

RANK	METRO AREA	MURDERS	RANK	METRO AREA	MURDERS	RANK	METRO AREA	MURDERS
199	Abilene, TX	8	267	Cheyenne, WY	0	21	Fort Worth-Arlington, TX	180
108	Akron, OH	24	–	Chicago, IL**	NA	30	Fresno, CA	137
118	Albany, GA	22	214	Chico-Paradise, CA	6	163	Gadsden, AL	13
–	Albany, NY**	NA	63	Cincinnati, OH-KY-IN	59	174	Gainesville, FL	11
66	Albuquerque, NM	57	206	Clarksville-Hopkinsville, TN-KY	7	89	Galveston-Texas City, TX	36
105	Alexandria, LA	26	–	Cleveland, OH**	NA	35	Gary-Hammond, IN	126
258	Altoona, PA	1	108	Colorado Springs, CO	24	246	Glens Falls, NY	2
168	Amarillo, TX	12	246	Columbia, MO	2	181	Goldsboro, NC	10
112	Anchorage, AK	23	73	Columbia, SC	50	258	Grand Forks, ND-MN	1
149	Ann Arbor, MI	16	87	Columbus, GA-AL	38	71	Grand Rapids-Muskegon-Holland, MI	52
142	Anniston, AL	17	36	Columbus, OH	117	214	Greeley, CO	6
206	Appleton-Oshkosh-Neenah, WI	7	78	Corpus Christi, TX	44	234	Green Bay, WI	3
149	Asheville, NC	16	246	Cumberland, MD-WV	2	37	Greensboro-Winston Salem-High Point, NC	116
142	Athens, GA	17	10	Dallas, TX	403	168	Greenville, NC	12
11	Atlanta, GA	394	234	Danbury, CT	3	50	Greenville-Spartanburg-Anderson, SC	87
118	Atlantic City, NJ	22	142	Danville, VA	17	221	Hagerstown, MD	5
64	Augusta-Aiken, GA-SC	58	118	Daytona Beach, FL	22	84	Harrisburg-Lebanon-Carlisle, PA	40
68	Austin-San Marcos, TX	55	53	Dayton-Springfield, OH	76	71	Hartford, CT	52
54	Bakersfield, CA	74	160	Decatur, AL	14	149	Hickory-Morganton, NC	16
8	Baltimore, MD	423	31	Denver, CO	132	96	Honolulu, HI	31
246	Bangor, ME	2	181	Des Moines, IA	10	174	Houma, LA	11
246	Barnstable-Yarmouth, MA	2	4	Detroit, MI	686	6	Houston, TX	571
42	Baton Rouge, LA	105	199	Dothan, AL	8	135	Huntington-Ashland, WV-KY-OH	18
81	Beaumont-Port Arthur, TX	42	267	Dubuque, IA	0	118	Huntsville, AL	22
234	Bellingham, WA	3	174	Duluth-Superior, MN-WI	11	–	Indianapolis, IN**	NA
174	Benton Harbor, MI	11	160	Dutchess County, NY	14	206	Jackson, MI	7
79	Bergen-Passaic, NJ	43	267	Eau Claire, WI	0	44	Jackson, MS	103
214	Binghamton, NY	6	68	El Paso, TX	55	131	Jackson, TN	19
23	Birmingham, AL	168	225	Elkhart-Goshen, IN	4	28	Jacksonville, FL	146
258	Bismarck, ND	1	246	Enid, OK	2	221	Jacksonville, NC	5
267	Bloomington, IN	0	199	Erie, PA	8	267	Janesville-Beloit, WI	0
199	Boise, ID	8	214	Eugene-Springfield, OR	6	99	Jersey City, NJ	29
29	Boston, MA-NH	145	181	Evansville-Henderson, IN-KY	10	163	Johnson City-Kingsport-Bristol, TN-VA	13
214	Boulder-Longmont, CO	6	258	Fargo-Moorhead, ND-MN	1	225	Johnstown, PA	4
206	Brazoria, TX	7	61	Fayetteville, NC	61	188	Joplin, MO	9
234	Bremerton, WA	3	188	Fayetteville-Springdale-Rogers, AR	9	105	Kalamazoo-Battle Creek, MI	26
56	Bridgeport, CT	67	221	Fitchburg-Leominster, MA	5	–	Kansas City, MO-KS**	NA
149	Brockton, MA	16	70	Flint, MI	54	188	Kenosha, WI	9
96	Brownsville-Harlingen-San Benito, TX	31	168	Florence, AL	12	135	Killeen-Temple, TX	18
234	Bryan-College Station, TX	3	142	Florence, SC	17	246	Kokomo, IN	2
49	Buffalo-Niagara Falls, NY	88	246	Fort Collins-Loveland, CO	2	267	La Crosse, WI-MN	0
135	Canton-Massillon, OH	18	43	Fort Lauderdale, FL	104	246	Lafayette, IN	2
105	Charleston, WV	26	131	Fort Myers-Cape Coral, FL	19	92	Lafayette, LA	32
79	Charleston-North Charleston, SC	43	104	Fort Pierce-Port St. Lucie, FL	27	135	Lake Charles, LA	18
234	Charlottesville, VA	3	188	Fort Smith, AR-OK	9	90	Lakeland-Winter Haven, FL	35
18	Charlotte-Gastonia-Rock Hill, NC-SC	204	206	Fort Walton Beach, FL	7	155	Lancaster, PA	15
76	Chattanooga, TN-GA	45	83	Fort Wayne, IN	41	124	Lansing-East Lansing, MI	21

Source: U.S. Department of Justice, Federal Bureau of Investigation
   "Crime in the United States 1993" (Uniform Crime Reports, December 4, 1994)
*Includes nonnegligent manslaughter.
**Not available.

9. Murders in 1993 (continued)

National Total = 24,526 Murders*

RANK	METRO AREA	MURDERS	RANK	METRO AREA	MURDERS	RANK	METRO AREA	MURDERS
124	Laredo, TX	21	258	Olympia, WA	1	39	Seattle–Bellevue–Everett, WA	114
31	Las Vegas, NV–AZ	132	–	Omaha, NE**	NA	258	Sheboygan, WI	1
206	Lawrence, MA–NH	7	19	Orange County, CA	196	225	Sherman–Denison, TX	4
160	Lawton, OK	14	55	Orlando, FL	69	46	Shreveport–Bossier City, LA	97
258	Lewiston–Auburn, ME	1	225	Owensboro, KY	4	225	Sioux City, IA–NE	4
174	Lexington, KY	11	181	Panama City, FL	10	246	Sioux Falls, SD	2
206	Lincoln, NE	7	5	Philadelphia, PA–NJ	596	108	South Bend, IN	24
40	Little Rock–North Little Rock, AR	107	17	Phoenix–Mesa, AZ	229	142	Spokane, WA	17
112	Longview–Marshall, TX	23	142	Pine Bluff, AR	17	99	Springfield, MA	29
2	Los Angeles–Long Beach, CA	1,944	34	Pittsburgh, PA	128	199	Springfield, MO	8
64	Louisville, KY–IN	58	267	Pittsfield, MA	0	135	Stamford–Norwalk, CT	18
131	Lubbock, TX	19	246	Portland, ME	2	214	Steubenville–Weirton, OH–WV	6
188	Lynchburg, VA	9	47	Portland–Vancouver, OR–WA	93	57	Stockton–Lodi, CA	65
91	Macon, GA	34	88	Providence–Fall River–Warwick, RI–MA	37	258	St. Cloud, MN	1
234	Madison, WI	3	234	Provo–Orem, UT	3	225	St. Joseph, MO	4
206	Manchester, NH	7	188	Pueblo, CO	9	–	St. Louis, MO–IL**	NA
234	Mansfield, OH	3	214	Punta Gorda, FL	6	181	Sumter, SC	10
84	McAllen–Edinburg–Mission, TX	40	188	Racine, WI	9	92	Syracuse, NY	32
225	Medford–Ashland, OR	4	51	Raleigh–Durham–Chapel Hill, NC	86	66	Tacoma, WA	57
16	Memphis, TN–AR–MS	230	225	Rapid City, SD	4	135	Tallahassee, FL	18
124	Merced, CA	21	174	Reading, PA	11	33	Tampa–St. Petersburg–Clearwater, FL	130
12	Miami, FL	368	168	Redding, CA	12	124	Texarkana, TX–AR	21
149	Middlesex–Sommerset–Hunterdon, NJ	16	112	Reno, NV	23	74	Toledo, OH	49
24	Milwaukee–Waukesha, WI	166	188	Richland–Kennewick–Pasco, WA	9	131	Trenton, NJ	19
37	Minneapolis–St. Paul, MN–WI	116	27	Richmond–Petersburg, VA	158	57	Tucson, AZ	65
57	Mobile, AL	65	9	Riverside–San Bernardino, CA	414	60	Tulsa, OK	63
112	Modesto, CA	23	155	Roanoke, VA	15	181	Tuscaloosa, AL	10
112	Monmouth–Ocean, NJ	23	234	Rochester, MN	3	142	Tyler, TX	17
112	Monroe, LA	23	52	Rochester, NY	79	135	Utica–Rome, NY	18
75	Montgomery, AL	46	118	Rocky Mount, NC	22	96	Vallejo–Fairfield–Napa, CA	31
163	Myrtle Beach, SC	13	26	Sacramento, CA	159	81	Ventura, CA	42
174	Naples, FL	11	99	Saginaw–Bay City–Midland, MI	29	225	Victoria, TX	4
234	Nashua, NH	3	155	Salem, OR	15	124	Vineland–Millville–Bridgeton, NJ	21
40	Nashville, TN	107	92	Salinas, CA	32	102	Visalia–Tulare–Porterville, CA	28
48	Nassau–Suffolk, NY	92	76	Salt Lake City–Ogden, UT	45	92	Waco, TX	32
234	New Bedford, MA	3	199	San Angelo, TX	8	3	Washington, DC–MD–VA–WV	696
102	New Haven–Meriden, CT	28	14	San Antonio, TX	261	129	Waterbury, CT	20
149	New London–Norwich, CT–RI	16	15	San Diego, CA	245	188	Waterloo–Cedar Falls, IA	9
7	New Orleans, LA	475	24	San Francisco, CA	166	258	Wausau, WI	1
1	New York, NY	2,001	61	San Jose, CA	61	–	West Palm Beach–Boca Raton, FL**	NA
22	Newark, NJ	172	267	San Luis Obispo–Atascadero, CA	0	188	Wichita Falls, TX	9
163	Newburgh, NY–PA	13	168	Santa Barbara–Santa Maria–Lompoc, CA	12	246	Williamsport, PA	2
20	Norfolk–Va Beach–Newport News, VA–NC	184	188	Santa Cruz–Watsonville, CA	9	163	Wilmington, NC	13
13	Oakland, CA	312	108	Santa Rosa, CA	24	155	Worcester, MA–CT	15
199	Ocala, FL	8	129	Sarasota–Bradenton, FL	20	155	Yakima, WA	15
118	Odessa–Midland, TX	22	84	Savannah, GA	40	181	Yolo, CA	10
44	Oklahoma City, OK	103	168	Scranton–Wilkes-Barre–Hazleton, PA	12	221	Yuba City, CA	5

Source: U.S. Department of Justice, Federal Bureau of Investigation
   "Crime in the United States 1993" (Uniform Crime Reports, December 4, 1994)
*Includes nonnegligent manslaughter.
**Not available.

9. Murders in 1993 (continued)

National Total = 24,526 Murders*

RANK	METRO AREA	MURDERS	RANK	METRO AREA	MURDERS	RANK	METRO AREA	MURDERS
1	New York, NY	2,001	48	Nassau–Suffolk, NY	92	92	Waco, TX	32
2	Los Angeles–Long Beach, CA	1,944	49	Buffalo–Niagara Falls, NY	88	96	Brownsville–Harlingen–San Benito, TX	31
3	Washington, DC–MD–VA–WV	696	50	Greenville–Spartanburg–Anderson, SC	87	96	Honolulu, HI	31
4	Detroit, MI	686	51	Raleigh–Durham–Chapel Hill, NC	86	96	Vallejo–Fairfield–Napa, CA	31
5	Philadelphia, PA–NJ	596	52	Rochester, NY	79	99	Jersey City, NJ	29
6	Houston, TX	571	53	Dayton–Springfield, OH	76	99	Saginaw–Bay City–Midland, MI	29
7	New Orleans, LA	475	54	Bakersfield, CA	74	99	Springfield, MA	29
8	Baltimore, MD	423	55	Orlando, FL	69	102	New Haven–Meriden, CT	28
9	Riverside–San Bernardino, CA	414	56	Bridgeport, CT	67	102	Visalia–Tulare–Porterville, CA	28
10	Dallas, TX	403	57	Mobile, AL	65	104	Fort Pierce–Port St. Lucie, FL	27
11	Atlanta, GA	394	57	Stockton–Lodi, CA	65	105	Alexandria, LA	26
12	Miami, FL	368	57	Tucson, AZ	65	105	Charleston, WV	26
13	Oakland, CA	312	60	Tulsa, OK	63	105	Kalamazoo–Battle Creek, MI	26
14	San Antonio, TX	261	61	Fayetteville, NC	61	108	Akron, OH	24
15	San Diego, CA	245	61	San Jose, CA	61	108	Colorado Springs, CO	24
16	Memphis, TN–AR–MS	230	63	Cincinnati, OH–KY–IN	59	108	Santa Rosa, CA	24
17	Phoenix–Mesa, AZ	229	64	Augusta–Aiken, GA–SC	58	108	South Bend, IN	24
18	Charlotte–Gastonia–Rock Hill, NC–SC	204	64	Louisville, KY–IN	58	112	Anchorage, AK	23
19	Orange County, CA	196	66	Albuquerque, NM	57	112	Longview–Marshall, TX	23
20	Norfolk–Va Beach–Newport News, VA–NC	184	66	Tacoma, WA	57	112	Modesto, CA	23
21	Fort Worth–Arlington, TX	180	68	Austin–San Marcos, TX	55	112	Monmouth–Ocean, NJ	23
22	Newark, NJ	172	68	El Paso, TX	55	112	Monroe, LA	23
23	Birmingham, AL	168	70	Flint, MI	54	112	Reno, NV	23
24	Milwaukee–Waukesha, WI	166	71	Grand Rapids–Muskegon–Holland, MI	52	118	Albany, GA	22
24	San Francisco, CA	166	71	Hartford, CT	52	118	Atlantic City, NJ	22
26	Sacramento, CA	159	73	Columbia, SC	50	118	Daytona Beach, FL	22
27	Richmond–Petersburg, VA	158	74	Toledo, OH	49	118	Huntsville, AL	22
28	Jacksonville, FL	146	75	Montgomery, AL	46	118	Odessa–Midland, TX	22
29	Boston, MA–NH	145	76	Chattanooga, TN–GA	45	118	Rocky Mount, NC	22
30	Fresno, CA	137	76	Salt Lake City–Ogden, UT	45	124	Lansing–East Lansing, MI	21
31	Denver, CO	132	78	Corpus Christi, TX	44	124	Laredo, TX	21
31	Las Vegas, NV–AZ	132	79	Bergen–Passaic, NJ	43	124	Merced, CA	21
33	Tampa–St. Petersburg–Clearwater, FL	130	79	Charleston–North Charleston, SC	43	124	Texarkana, TX–AR	21
34	Pittsburgh, PA	128	81	Beaumont–Port Arthur, TX	42	124	Vineland–Millville–Bridgeton, NJ	21
35	Gary–Hammond, IN	126	81	Ventura, CA	42	129	Sarasota–Bradenton, FL	20
36	Columbus, OH	117	83	Fort Wayne, IN	41	129	Waterbury, CT	20
37	Greensboro–Winston Salem–High Point, NC	116	84	Harrisburg–Lebanon–Carlisle, PA	40	131	Fort Myers–Cape Coral, FL	19
37	Minneapolis–St. Paul, MN–WI	116	84	McAllen–Edinburg–Mission, TX	40	131	Jackson, TN	19
39	Seattle–Bellevue–Everett, WA	114	84	Savannah, GA	40	131	Lubbock, TX	19
40	Little Rock–North Little Rock, AR	107	87	Columbus, GA–AL	38	131	Trenton, NJ	19
40	Nashville, TN	107	88	Providence–Fall River–Warwick, RI–MA	37	135	Canton–Massillon, OH	18
42	Baton Rouge, LA	105	89	Galveston–Texas City, TX	36	135	Huntington–Ashland, WV–KY–OH	18
43	Fort Lauderdale, FL	104	90	Lakeland–Winter Haven, FL	35	135	Killeen–Temple, TX	18
44	Jackson, MS	103	91	Macon, GA	34	135	Lake Charles, LA	18
44	Oklahoma City, OK	103	92	Lafayette, LA	32	135	Stamford–Norwalk, CT	18
46	Shreveport–Bossier City, LA	97	92	Salinas, CA	32	135	Tallahassee, FL	18
47	Portland–Vancouver, OR–WA	93	92	Syracuse, NY	32	135	Utica–Rome, NY	18

Source: U.S. Department of Justice, Federal Bureau of Investigation
  "Crime in the United States 1993" (Uniform Crime Reports, December 4, 1994)
*Includes nonnegligent manslaughter.
**Not available.

9. Murders in 1993 (continued)

National Total = 24,526 Murders*

RANK	METRO AREA	MURDERS	RANK	METRO AREA	MURDERS	RANK	METRO AREA	MURDERS
142	Anniston, AL	17	188	Fort Smith, AR–OK	9	234	Bryan–College Station, TX	3
142	Athens, GA	17	188	Joplin, MO	9	234	Charlottesville, VA	3
142	Danville, VA	17	188	Kenosha, WI	9	234	Danbury, CT	3
142	Florence, SC	17	188	Lynchburg, VA	9	234	Green Bay, WI	3
142	Pine Bluff, AR	17	188	Pueblo, CO	9	234	Madison, WI	3
142	Spokane, WA	17	188	Racine, WI	9	234	Mansfield, OH	3
142	Tyler, TX	17	188	Richland–Kennewick–Pasco, WA	9	234	Nashua, NH	3
149	Ann Arbor, MI	16	188	Santa Cruz–Watsonville, CA	9	234	New Bedford, MA	3
149	Asheville, NC	16	188	Waterloo–Cedar Falls, IA	9	234	Provo–Orem, UT	3
149	Brockton, MA	16	188	Wichita Falls, TX	9	234	Rochester, MN	3
149	Hickory–Morganton, NC	16	199	Abilene, TX	8	246	Bangor, ME	2
149	Middlesex–Somerset–Hunterdon, NJ	16	199	Boise, ID	8	246	Barnstable–Yarmouth, MA	2
149	New London–Norwich, CT–RI	16	199	Dothan, AL	8	246	Columbia, MO	2
155	Lancaster, PA	15	199	Erie, PA	8	246	Cumberland, MD–WV	2
155	Roanoke, VA	15	199	Ocala, FL	8	246	Enid, OK	2
155	Salem, OR	15	199	San Angelo, TX	8	246	Fort Collins–Loveland, CO	2
155	Worcester, MA–CT	15	199	Springfield, MO	8	246	Glens Falls, NY	2
155	Yakima, WA	15	206	Appleton–Oshkosh–Neenah, WI	7	246	Kokomo, IN	2
160	Decatur, AL	14	206	Brazoria, TX	7	246	Lafayette, IN	2
160	Dutchess County, NY	14	206	Clarksville–Hopkinsville, TN–KY	7	246	Portland, ME	2
160	Lawton, OK	14	206	Fort Walton Beach, FL	7	246	Sioux Falls, SD	2
163	Gadsden, AL	13	206	Jackson, MI	7	246	Williamsport, PA	2
163	Johnson City–Kingsport–Bristol, TN–VA	13	206	Lawrence, MA–NH	7	258	Altoona, PA	1
163	Myrtle Beach, SC	13	206	Lincoln, NE	7	258	Bismarck, ND	1
163	Newburgh, NY–PA	13	206	Manchester, NH	7	258	Fargo–Moorhead, ND–MN	1
163	Wilmington, NC	13	214	Binghamton, NY	6	258	Grand Forks, ND–MN	1
168	Amarillo, TX	12	214	Boulder–Longmont, CO	6	258	Lewiston–Auburn, ME	1
168	Florence, AL	12	214	Chico–Paradise, CA	6	258	Olympia, WA	1
168	Greenville, NC	12	214	Eugene–Springfield, OR	6	258	Sheboygan, WI	1
168	Redding, CA	12	214	Greeley, CO	6	258	St. Cloud, MN	1
168	Santa Barbara–Santa Maria–Lompoc, CA	12	214	Punta Gorda, FL	6	258	Wausau, WI	1
168	Scranton–Wilkes-Barre–Hazleton, PA	12	214	Steubenville–Weirton, OH–WV	6	267	Bloomington, IN	0
174	Benton Harbor, MI	11	221	Fitchburg–Leominster, MA	5	267	Cheyenne, WY	0
174	Duluth–Superior, MN–WI	11	221	Hagerstown, MD	5	267	Dubuque, IA	0
174	Gainesville, FL	11	221	Jacksonville, NC	5	267	Eau Claire, WI	0
174	Houma, LA	11	221	Yuba City, CA	5	267	Janesville–Beloit, WI	0
174	Lexington, KY	11	225	Elkhart–Goshen, IN	4	267	La Crosse, WI–MN	0
174	Naples, FL	11	225	Johnstown, PA	4	267	Pittsfield, MA	0
174	Reading, PA	11	225	Medford–Ashland, OR	4	267	San Luis Obispo–Atascadero, CA	0
181	Des Moines, IA	10	225	Owensboro, KY	4	–	Albany, NY**	NA
181	Evansville–Henderson, IN–KY	10	225	Rapid City, SD	4	–	Chicago, IL**	NA
181	Goldsboro, NC	10	225	Sherman–Denison, TX	4	–	Cleveland, OH**	NA
181	Panama City, FL	10	225	Sioux City, IA–NE	4	–	Indianapolis, IN**	NA
181	Sumter, SC	10	225	St. Joseph, MO	4	–	Kansas City, MO–KS**	NA
181	Tuscaloosa, AL	10	225	Victoria, TX	4	–	Omaha, NE**	NA
181	Yolo, CA	10	234	Bellingham, WA	3	–	St. Louis, MO–IL**	NA
188	Fayetteville–Springdale–Rogers, AR	9	234	Bremerton, WA	3	–	West Palm Beach–Boca Raton, FL**	NA

Source: U.S. Department of Justice, Federal Bureau of Investigation
"Crime in the United States 1993" (Uniform Crime Reports, December 4, 1994)
*Includes nonnegligent manslaughter.
**Not available.

10. Murder Rate in 1993

National Rate = 9.5 Murders per 100,000 Population*

RANK	METRO AREA	RATE	RANK	METRO AREA	RATE	RANK	METRO AREA	RATE
130	Abilene, TX	6.5	267	Cheyenne, WY	0.0	54	Fort Worth–Arlington, TX	11.7
201	Akron, OH	3.6	–	Chicago, IL**	NA	21	Fresno, CA	16.9
15	Albany, GA	18.7	212	Chico–Paradise, CA	3.2	45	Gadsden, AL	12.9
–	Albany, NY**	NA	197	Cincinnati, OH–KY–IN	3.8	147	Gainesville, FL	5.7
87	Albuquerque, NM	9.1	191	Clarksville–Hopkinsville, TN–KY	3.9	29	Galveston–Texas City, TX	15.5
11	Alexandria, LA	19.8	–	Cleveland, OH**	NA	9	Gary–Hammond, IN	20.2
261	Altoona, PA	0.8	151	Colorado Springs, CO	5.5	247	Glens Falls, NY	1.6
136	Amarillo, TX	6.1	242	Columbia, MO	1.7	87	Goldsboro, NC	9.1
84	Anchorage, AK	9.2	68	Columbia, SC	10.5	256	Grand Forks, ND–MN	1.0
212	Ann Arbor, MI	3.2	42	Columbus, GA–AL	13.7	155	Grand Rapids–Muskegon–Holland, MI	5.4
38	Anniston, AL	14.4	99	Columbus, OH	8.3	182	Greeley, CO	4.3
234	Appleton–Oshkosh–Neenah, WI	2.1	53	Corpus Christi, TX	11.9	248	Green Bay, WI	1.5
103	Asheville, NC	8.0	236	Cumberland, MD–WV	2.0	67	Greensboro–Winston Salem–High Point, NC	10.6
61	Athens, GA	11.0	35	Dallas, TX	14.6	66	Greenville, NC	10.7
50	Atlanta, GA	12.2	241	Danbury, CT	1.8	75	Greenville–Spartanburg–Anderson, SC	10.1
126	Atlantic City, NJ	6.7	30	Danville, VA	15.3	191	Hagerstown, MD	3.9
46	Augusta–Aiken, GA–SC	12.8	164	Daytona Beach, FL	5.1	128	Harrisburg–Lebanon–Carlisle, PA	6.6
139	Austin–San Marcos, TX	6.0	108	Dayton–Springfield, OH	7.8	170	Hartford, CT	4.9
48	Bakersfield, CA	12.5	73	Decatur, AL	10.2	157	Hickory–Morganton, NC	5.3
19	Baltimore, MD	17.2	110	Denver, CO	7.5	203	Honolulu, HI	3.5
218	Bangor, ME	3.0	226	Des Moines, IA	2.4	140	Houma, LA	5.9
248	Barnstable–Yarmouth, MA	1.5	25	Detroit, MI	15.8	24	Houston, TX	15.9
14	Baton Rouge, LA	19.1	140	Dothan, AL	5.9	147	Huntington–Ashland, WV–KY–OH	5.7
58	Beaumont–Port Arthur, TX	11.1	267	Dubuque, IA	0.0	118	Huntsville, AL	7.1
234	Bellingham, WA	2.1	175	Duluth–Superior, MN–WI	4.5	–	Indianapolis, IN**	NA
124	Benton Harbor, MI	6.8	157	Dutchess County, NY	5.3	174	Jackson, MI	4.6
211	Bergen–Passaic, NJ	3.3	267	Eau Claire, WI	0.0	3	Jackson, MS	25.2
232	Binghamton, NY	2.2	94	El Paso, TX	8.6	4	Jackson, TN	23.3
13	Birmingham, AL	19.3	224	Elkhart–Goshen, IN	2.5	31	Jacksonville, FL	15.1
253	Bismarck, ND	1.2	203	Enid, OK	3.5	207	Jacksonville, NC	3.4
267	Bloomington, IN	0.0	222	Erie, PA	2.8	267	Janesville–Beloit, WI	0.0
226	Boise, ID	2.4	236	Eugene–Springfield, OR	2.0	162	Jersey City, NJ	5.2
182	Boston, MA–NH	4.3	203	Evansville–Henderson, IN–KY	3.5	220	Johnson City–Kingsport–Bristol, TN–VA	2.9
226	Boulder–Longmont, CO	2.4	264	Fargo–Moorhead, ND–MN	0.6	242	Johnstown, PA	1.7
207	Brazoria, TX	3.4	7	Fayetteville, NC	21.7	130	Joplin, MO	6.5
251	Bremerton, WA	1.4	191	Fayetteville–Springdale–Rogers, AR	3.9	140	Kalamazoo–Battle Creek, MI	5.9
34	Bridgeport, CT	14.8	201	Fitchburg–Leominster, MA	3.6	–	Kansas City, MO–KS**	NA
130	Brockton, MA	6.5	49	Flint, MI	12.4	126	Kenosha, WI	6.7
63	Brownsville–Harlingen–San Benito, TX	10.9	92	Florence, AL	8.8	122	Killeen–Temple, TX	6.9
226	Bryan–College Station, TX	2.4	40	Florence, SC	14.2	236	Kokomo, IN	2.0
114	Buffalo–Niagara Falls, NY	7.3	256	Fort Collins–Loveland, CO	1.0	267	La Crosse, WI–MN	0.0
175	Canton–Massillon, OH	4.5	105	Fort Lauderdale, FL	7.9	253	Lafayette, IN	1.2
73	Charleston, WV	10.2	157	Fort Myers–Cape Coral, FL	5.3	89	Lafayette, LA	9.0
103	Charleston–North Charleston, SC	8.0	77	Fort Pierce–Port St. Lucie, FL	10.0	68	Lake Charles, LA	10.5
232	Charlottesville, VA	2.2	170	Fort Smith, AR–OK	4.9	101	Lakeland–Winter Haven, FL	8.2
22	Charlotte–Gastonia–Rock Hill, NC–SC	16.6	175	Fort Walton Beach, FL	4.5	207	Lancaster, PA	3.4
71	Chattanooga, TN–GA	10.3	92	Fort Wayne, IN	8.8	172	Lansing–East Lansing, MI	4.8

Source: U.S. Department of Justice, Federal Bureau of Investigation
  "Crime in the United States 1993" (Uniform Crime Reports, December 4, 1994)
*Includes nonnegligent manslaughter.
**Not available.

10. Murder Rate in 1993 (continued)

National Rate = 9.5 Murders per 100,000 Population*

RANK	METRO AREA	RATE	RANK	METRO AREA	RATE	RANK	METRO AREA	RATE
41	Laredo, TX	13.9	264	Olympia, WA	0.6	151	Seattle–Bellevue–Everett, WA	5.5
43	Las Vegas, NV–AZ	13.1	–	Omaha, NE**	NA	259	Sheboygan, WI	0.9
226	Lawrence, MA–NH	2.4	108	Orange County, CA	7.8	187	Sherman–Denison, TX	4.1
55	Lawton, OK	11.5	162	Orlando, FL	5.2	2	Shreveport–Bossier City, LA	25.8
256	Lewiston–Auburn, ME	1.0	175	Owensboro, KY	4.5	207	Sioux City, IA–NE	3.4
218	Lexington, KY	3.0	112	Panama City, FL	7.4	252	Sioux Falls, SD	1.3
212	Lincoln, NE	3.2	52	Philadelphia, PA–NJ	12.0	79	South Bend, IN	9.5
10	Little Rock–North Little Rock, AR	20.1	78	Phoenix–Mesa, AZ	9.6	180	Spokane, WA	4.4
57	Longview–Marshall, TX	11.3	12	Pine Bluff, AR	19.7	155	Springfield, MA	5.4
8	Los Angeles–Long Beach, CA	21.3	157	Pittsburgh, PA	5.3	220	Springfield, MO	2.9
140	Louisville, KY–IN	5.9	267	Pittsfield, MA	0.0	151	Stamford–Norwalk, CT	5.5
99	Lubbock, TX	8.3	259	Portland, ME	0.9	184	Steubenville–Weirton, OH–WV	4.2
175	Lynchburg, VA	4.5	147	Portland–Vancouver, OR–WA	5.7	46	Stockton–Lodi, CA	12.8
58	Macon, GA	11.1	191	Providence–Fall River–Warwick, RI–MA	3.9	264	St. Cloud, MN	0.6
261	Madison, WI	0.8	255	Provo–Orem, UT	1.1	188	St. Joseph, MO	4.0
184	Manchester, NH	4.2	118	Pueblo, CO	7.1	–	St. Louis, MO–IL**	NA
242	Mansfield, OH	1.7	166	Punta Gorda, FL	5.0	80	Sumter, SC	9.4
81	McAllen–Edinburg–Mission, TX	9.3	166	Racine, WI	5.0	184	Syracuse, NY	4.2
224	Medford–Ashland, OR	2.5	81	Raleigh–Durham–Chapel Hill, NC	9.3	89	Tacoma, WA	9.0
6	Memphis, TN–AR–MS	21.9	173	Rapid City, SD	4.7	116	Tallahassee, FL	7.2
61	Merced, CA	11.0	212	Reading, PA	3.2	136	Tampa–St. Petersburg–Clearwater, FL	6.1
17	Miami, FL	18.1	110	Redding, CA	7.5	20	Texarkana, TX–AR	17.1
248	Middlesex–Sommerset–Hunterdon, NJ	1.5	101	Reno, NV	8.2	105	Toledo, OH	7.9
56	Milwaukee–Waukesha, WI	11.4	151	Richland–Kennewick–Pasco, WA	5.5	145	Trenton, NJ	5.8
180	Minneapolis–St. Paul, MN–WI	4.4	18	Richmond–Petersburg, VA	17.4	84	Tucson, AZ	9.2
44	Mobile, AL	13.0	35	Riverside–San Bernardino, CA	14.6	96	Tulsa, OK	8.5
145	Modesto, CA	5.8	130	Roanoke, VA	6.5	135	Tuscaloosa, AL	6.4
231	Monmouth–Ocean, NJ	2.3	223	Rochester, MN	2.7	64	Tyler, TX	10.8
25	Monroe, LA	15.8	114	Rochester, NY	7.3	147	Utica–Rome, NY	5.7
33	Montgomery, AL	14.9	25	Rocky Mount, NC	15.8	130	Vallejo–Fairfield–Napa, CA	6.5
97	Myrtle Beach, SC	8.4	58	Sacramento, CA	11.1	136	Ventura, CA	6.1
128	Naples, FL	6.6	116	Saginaw–Bay City–Midland, MI	7.2	164	Victoria, TX	5.1
239	Nashua, NH	1.9	166	Salem, OR	5.0	32	Vineland–Millville–Bridgeton, NJ	15.0
71	Nashville, TN	10.3	94	Salinas, CA	8.6	97	Visalia–Tulare–Porterville, CA	8.4
203	Nassau–Suffolk, NY	3.5	191	Salt Lake City–Ogden, UT	3.9	23	Waco, TX	16.4
242	New Bedford, MA	1.7	105	San Angelo, TX	7.9	25	Washington, DC–MD–VA–WV	15.8
166	New Haven–Meriden, CT	5.0	16	San Antonio, TX	18.6	64	Waterbury, CT	10.8
157	New London–Norwich, CT–RI	5.3	81	San Diego, CA	9.3	118	Waterloo–Cedar Falls, IA	7.1
1	New Orleans, LA	37.7	75	San Francisco, CA	10.1	263	Wausau, WI	0.7
5	New York, NY	23.2	188	San Jose, CA	4.0	–	West Palm Beach–Boca Raton, FL**	NA
91	Newark, NJ	8.9	267	San Luis Obispo–Atascadero, CA	0.0	122	Wichita Falls, TX	6.9
200	Newburgh, NY–PA	3.7	212	Santa Barbara–Santa Maria–Lompoc, CA	3.2	242	Williamsport, PA	1.7
51	Norfolk–Va Beach–Newport News, VA–NC	12.1	191	Santa Cruz–Watsonville, CA	3.9	121	Wilmington, NC	7.0
38	Oakland, CA	14.4	140	Santa Rosa, CA	5.9	212	Worcester, MA–CT	3.2
197	Ocala, FL	3.8	188	Sarasota–Bradenton, FL	4.0	112	Yakima, WA	7.4
84	Odessa–Midland, TX	9.2	35	Savannah, GA	14.6	124	Yolo, CA	6.8
70	Oklahoma City, OK	10.4	239	Scranton–Wilkes-Barre–Hazleton, PA	1.9	197	Yuba City, CA	3.8

Source: U.S. Department of Justice, Federal Bureau of Investigation
    "Crime in the United States 1993" (Uniform Crime Reports, December 4, 1994)
*Includes nonnegligent manslaughter.
**Not available.

10. Murder Rate in 1993 (continued)

National Rate = 9.5 Murders per 100,000 Population*

RANK	METRO AREA	RATE	RANK	METRO AREA	RATE	RANK	METRO AREA	RATE
1	New Orleans, LA	37.7	48	Bakersfield, CA	12.5	94	Salinas, CA	8.6
2	Shreveport–Bossier City, LA	25.8	49	Flint, MI	12.4	96	Tulsa, OK	8.5
3	Jackson, MS	25.2	50	Atlanta, GA	12.2	97	Myrtle Beach, SC	8.4
4	Jackson, TN	23.3	51	Norfolk–Va Beach–Newport News, VA–NC	12.1	97	Visalia–Tulare–Porterville, CA	8.4
5	New York, NY	23.2	52	Philadelphia, PA–NJ	12.0	99	Columbus, OH	8.3
6	Memphis, TN–AR–MS	21.9	53	Corpus Christi, TX	11.9	99	Lubbock, TX	8.3
7	Fayetteville, NC	21.7	54	Fort Worth–Arlington, TX	11.7	101	Lakeland–Winter Haven, FL	8.2
8	Los Angeles–Long Beach, CA	21.3	55	Lawton, OK	11.5	101	Reno, NV	8.2
9	Gary–Hammond, IN	20.2	56	Milwaukee–Waukesha, WI	11.4	103	Asheville, NC	8.0
10	Little Rock–North Little Rock, AR	20.1	57	Longview–Marshall, TX	11.3	103	Charleston–North Charleston, SC	8.0
11	Alexandria, LA	19.8	58	Beaumont–Port Arthur, TX	11.1	105	Fort Lauderdale, FL	7.9
12	Pine Bluff, AR	19.7	58	Macon, GA	11.1	105	San Angelo, TX	7.9
13	Birmingham, AL	19.3	58	Sacramento, CA	11.1	105	Toledo, OH	7.9
14	Baton Rouge, LA	19.1	61	Athens, GA	11.0	108	Dayton–Springfield, OH	7.8
15	Albany, GA	18.7	61	Merced, CA	11.0	108	Orange County, CA	7.8
16	San Antonio, TX	18.6	63	Brownsville–Harlingen–San Benito, TX	10.9	110	Denver, CO	7.5
17	Miami, FL	18.1	64	Tyler, TX	10.8	110	Redding, CA	7.5
18	Richmond–Petersburg, VA	17.4	64	Waterbury, CT	10.8	112	Panama City, FL	7.4
19	Baltimore, MD	17.2	66	Greenville, NC	10.7	112	Yakima, WA	7.4
20	Texarkana, TX–AR	17.1	67	Greensboro–Winston Salem–High Point, NC	10.6	114	Buffalo–Niagara Falls, NY	7.3
21	Fresno, CA	16.9	68	Columbia, SC	10.5	114	Rochester, NY	7.3
22	Charlotte–Gastonia–Rock Hill, NC–SC	16.6	68	Lake Charles, LA	10.5	116	Saginaw–Bay City–Midland, MI	7.2
23	Waco, TX	16.4	70	Oklahoma City, OK	10.4	116	Tallahassee, FL	7.2
24	Houston, TX	15.9	71	Chattanooga, TN–GA	10.3	118	Huntsville, AL	7.1
25	Detroit, MI	15.8	71	Nashville, TN	10.3	118	Pueblo, CO	7.1
25	Monroe, LA	15.8	73	Charleston, WV	10.2	118	Waterloo–Cedar Falls, IA	7.1
25	Rocky Mount, NC	15.8	73	Decatur, AL	10.2	121	Wilmington, NC	7.0
25	Washington, DC–MD–VA–WV	15.8	75	Greenville–Spartanburg–Anderson, SC	10.1	122	Killeen–Temple, TX	6.9
29	Galveston–Texas City, TX	15.5	75	San Francisco, CA	10.1	122	Wichita Falls, TX	6.9
30	Danville, VA	15.3	77	Fort Pierce–Port St. Lucie, FL	10.0	124	Benton Harbor, MI	6.8
31	Jacksonville, FL	15.1	78	Phoenix–Mesa, AZ	9.6	124	Yolo, CA	6.8
32	Vineland–Millville–Bridgeton, NJ	15.0	79	South Bend, IN	9.5	126	Atlantic City, NJ	6.7
33	Montgomery, AL	14.9	80	Sumter, SC	9.4	126	Kenosha, WI	6.7
34	Bridgeport, CT	14.8	81	McAllen–Edinburg–Mission, TX	9.3	128	Harrisburg–Lebanon–Carlisle, PA	6.6
35	Dallas, TX	14.6	81	Raleigh–Durham–Chapel Hill, NC	9.3	128	Naples, FL	6.6
35	Riverside–San Bernardino, CA	14.6	81	San Diego, CA	9.3	130	Abilene, TX	6.5
35	Savannah, GA	14.6	84	Anchorage, AK	9.2	130	Brockton, MA	6.5
38	Anniston, AL	14.4	84	Odessa–Midland, TX	9.2	130	Joplin, MO	6.5
38	Oakland, CA	14.4	84	Tucson, AZ	9.2	130	Roanoke, VA	6.5
40	Florence, SC	14.2	87	Albuquerque, NM	9.1	130	Vallejo–Fairfield–Napa, CA	6.5
41	Laredo, TX	13.9	87	Goldsboro, NC	9.1	135	Tuscaloosa, AL	6.4
42	Columbus, GA–AL	13.7	89	Lafayette, LA	9.0	136	Amarillo, TX	6.1
43	Las Vegas, NV–AZ	13.1	89	Tacoma, WA	9.0	136	Tampa–St. Petersburg–Clearwater, FL	6.1
44	Mobile, AL	13.0	91	Newark, NJ	8.9	136	Ventura, CA	6.1
45	Gadsden, AL	12.9	92	Florence, AL	8.8	139	Austin–San Marcos, TX	6.0
46	Augusta–Aiken, GA–SC	12.8	92	Fort Wayne, IN	8.8	140	Dothan, AL	5.9
46	Stockton–Lodi, CA	12.8	94	El Paso, TX	8.6	140	Houma, LA	5.9

Source: U.S. Department of Justice, Federal Bureau of Investigation
  "Crime in the United States 1993" (Uniform Crime Reports, December 4, 1994)
*Includes nonnegligent manslaughter.
**Not available.

10. Murder Rate in 1993 (continued)

National Rate = 9.5 Murders per 100,000 Population*

RANK	METRO AREA	RATE	RANK	METRO AREA	RATE	RANK	METRO AREA	RATE
140	Kalamazoo–Battle Creek, MI	5.9	188	Sarasota–Bradenton, FL	4.0	236	Cumberland, MD–WV	2.0
140	Louisville, KY–IN	5.9	188	St. Joseph, MO	4.0	236	Eugene–Springfield, OR	2.0
140	Santa Rosa, CA	5.9	191	Clarksville–Hopkinsville, TN–KY	3.9	236	Kokomo, IN	2.0
145	Modesto, CA	5.8	191	Fayetteville–Springdale–Rogers, AR	3.9	239	Nashua, NH	1.9
145	Trenton, NJ	5.8	191	Hagerstown, MD	3.9	239	Scranton–Wilkes-Barre–Hazleton, PA	1.9
147	Gainesville, FL	5.7	191	Providence–Fall River–Warwick, RI–MA	3.9	241	Danbury, CT	1.8
147	Huntington–Ashland, WV–KY–OH	5.7	191	Salt Lake City–Ogden, UT	3.9	242	Columbia, MO	1.7
147	Portland–Vancouver, OR–WA	5.7	191	Santa Cruz–Watsonville, CA	3.9	242	Johnstown, PA	1.7
147	Utica–Rome, NY	5.7	197	Cincinnati, OH–KY–IN	3.8	242	Mansfield, OH	1.7
151	Colorado Springs, CO	5.5	197	Ocala, FL	3.8	242	New Bedford, MA	1.7
151	Richland–Kennewick–Pasco, WA	5.5	197	Yuba City, CA	3.8	242	Williamsport, PA	1.7
151	Seattle–Bellevue–Everett, WA	5.5	200	Newburgh, NY–PA	3.7	247	Glens Falls, NY	1.6
151	Stamford–Norwalk, CT	5.5	201	Akron, OH	3.6	248	Barnstable–Yarmouth, MA	1.5
155	Grand Rapids–Muskegon–Holland, MI	5.4	201	Fitchburg–Leominster, MA	3.6	248	Green Bay, WI	1.5
155	Springfield, MA	5.4	203	Enid, OK	3.5	248	Middlesex–Sommerset–Hunterdon, NJ	1.5
157	Dutchess County, NY	5.3	203	Evansville–Henderson, IN–KY	3.5	251	Bremerton, WA	1.4
157	Fort Myers–Cape Coral, FL	5.3	203	Honolulu, HI	3.5	252	Sioux Falls, SD	1.3
157	Hickory–Morganton, NC	5.3	203	Nassau–Suffolk, NY	3.5	253	Bismarck, ND	1.2
157	New London–Norwich, CT–RI	5.3	207	Brazoria, TX	3.4	253	Lafayette, IN	1.2
157	Pittsburgh, PA	5.3	207	Jacksonville, NC	3.4	255	Provo–Orem, UT	1.1
162	Jersey City, NJ	5.2	207	Lancaster, PA	3.4	256	Fort Collins–Loveland, CO	1.0
162	Orlando, FL	5.2	207	Sioux City, IA–NE	3.4	256	Grand Forks, ND–MN	1.0
164	Daytona Beach, FL	5.1	211	Bergen–Passaic, NJ	3.3	256	Lewiston–Auburn, ME	1.0
164	Victoria, TX	5.1	212	Ann Arbor, MI	3.2	259	Portland, ME	0.9
166	New Haven–Meriden, CT	5.0	212	Chico–Paradise, CA	3.2	259	Sheboygan, WI	0.9
166	Punta Gorda, FL	5.0	212	Lincoln, NE	3.2	261	Altoona, PA	0.8
166	Racine, WI	5.0	212	Reading, PA	3.2	261	Madison, WI	0.8
166	Salem, OR	5.0	212	Santa Barbara–Santa Maria–Lompoc, CA	3.2	263	Wausau, WI	0.7
170	Fort Smith, AR–OK	4.9	212	Worcester, MA–CT	3.2	264	Fargo–Moorhead, ND–MN	0.6
170	Hartford, CT	4.9	218	Bangor, ME	3.0	264	Olympia, WA	0.6
172	Lansing–East Lansing, MI	4.8	218	Lexington, KY	3.0	264	St. Cloud, MN	0.6
173	Rapid City, SD	4.7	220	Johnson City–Kingsport–Bristol, TN–VA	2.9	267	Bloomington, IN	0.0
174	Jackson, MI	4.6	220	Springfield, MO	2.9	267	Cheyenne, WY	0.0
175	Canton–Massillon, OH	4.5	222	Erie, PA	2.8	267	Dubuque, IA	0.0
175	Duluth–Superior, MN–WI	4.5	223	Rochester, MN	2.7	267	Eau Claire, WI	0.0
175	Fort Walton Beach, FL	4.5	224	Elkhart–Goshen, IN	2.5	267	Janesville–Beloit, WI	0.0
175	Lynchburg, VA	4.5	224	Medford–Ashland, OR	2.5	267	La Crosse, WI–MN	0.0
175	Owensboro, KY	4.5	226	Boise, ID	2.4	267	Pittsfield, MA	0.0
180	Minneapolis–St. Paul, MN–WI	4.4	226	Boulder–Longmont, CO	2.4	267	San Luis Obispo–Atascadero, CA	0.0
180	Spokane, WA	4.4	226	Bryan–College Station, TX	2.4	–	Albany, NY**	NA
182	Boston, MA–NH	4.3	226	Des Moines, IA	2.4	–	Chicago, IL**	NA
182	Greeley, CO	4.3	226	Lawrence, MA–NH	2.4	–	Cleveland, OH**	NA
184	Manchester, NH	4.2	231	Monmouth–Ocean, NJ	2.3	–	Indianapolis, IN**	NA
184	Steubenville–Weirton, OH–WV	4.2	232	Binghamton, NY	2.2	–	Kansas City, MO–KS**	NA
184	Syracuse, NY	4.2	232	Charlottesville, VA	2.2	–	Omaha, NE**	NA
187	Sherman–Denison, TX	4.1	234	Appleton–Oshkosh–Neenah, WI	2.1	–	St. Louis, MO–IL**	NA
188	San Jose, CA	4.0	234	Bellingham, WA	2.1	–	West Palm Beach–Boca Raton, FL**	NA

Source: U.S. Department of Justice, Federal Bureau of Investigation
"Crime in the United States 1993" (Uniform Crime Reports, December 4, 1994)
*Includes nonnegligent manslaughter.
**Not available.

11. Percent Change in Murder Rate: 1992 to 1993

National Percent Change = 2.2% Increase*

RANK	METRO AREA	% CHANGE	RANK	METRO AREA	% CHANGE	RANK	METRO AREA	% CHANGE
50	Abilene, TX	35.42	238	Cheyenne, WY	(100.00)	165	Fort Worth–Arlington, TX	(10.69)
184	Akron, OH	(20.00)	–	Chicago, IL**	NA	145	Fresno, CA	(3.43)
109	Albany, GA	4.47	227	Chico–Paradise, CA	(56.76)	209	Gadsden, AL	(34.52)
–	Albany, NY**	NA	176	Cincinnati, OH–KY–IN	(15.56)	208	Gainesville, FL	(32.94)
113	Albuquerque, NM	3.41	214	Clarksville–Hopkinsville, TN–KY	(38.10)	164	Galveston–Texas City, TX	(10.40)
18	Alexandria, LA	104.12	–	Cleveland, OH**	NA	75	Gary–Hammond, IN	17.44
–	Altoona, PA**	NA	96	Colorado Springs, CO	10.00	–	Glens Falls, NY**	NA
203	Amarillo, TX	(29.89)	224	Columbia, MO	(51.43)	204	Goldsboro, NC	(30.00)
57	Anchorage, AK	31.43	181	Columbia, SC	(17.97)	–	Grand Forks, ND–MN**	NA
41	Ann Arbor, MI	45.45	53	Columbus, GA–AL	34.31	46	Grand Rapids–Muskegon–Holland, MI	42.11
70	Anniston, AL	22.03	170	Columbus, OH	(12.63)	173	Greeley, CO	(14.00)
4	Appleton–Oshkosh–Neenah, WI	250.00	51	Corpus Christi, TX	35.23	6	Green Bay, WI	200.00
25	Asheville, NC	77.78	19	Cumberland, MD–WV	100.00	107	Greensboro–Winston Salem–High Point, NC	4.95
73	Athens, GA	20.88	178	Dallas, TX	(16.57)	216	Greenville, NC	(41.53)
146	Atlanta, GA	(3.94)	223	Danbury, CT	(51.35)	61	Greenville–Spartanburg–Anderson, SC	27.85
83	Atlantic City, NJ	13.56	102	Danville, VA	6.99	8	Hagerstown, MD	143.75
174	Augusta–Aiken, GA–SC	(14.09)	215	Daytona Beach, FL	(40.70)	28	Harrisburg–Lebanon–Carlisle, PA	65.00
122	Austin–San Marcos, TX	1.69	160	Dayton–Springfield, OH	(9.30)	14	Hartford, CT	122.73
47	Bakersfield, CA	40.45	10	Decatur, AL	126.67	211	Hickory–Morganton, NC	(36.14)
114	Baltimore, MD	2.99	155	Denver, CO	(8.54)	127	Honolulu, HI	0.00
127	Bangor, ME	0.00	110	Des Moines, IA	4.35	220	Houma, LA	(45.37)
127	Barnstable–Yarmouth, MA	0.00	148	Detroit, MI	(4.24)	162	Houston, TX	(9.66)
82	Baton Rouge, LA	13.69	84	Dothan, AL	13.46	92	Huntington–Ashland, WV–KY–OH	11.76
183	Beaumont–Port Arthur, TX	(18.38)	238	Dubuque, IA	(100.00)	152	Huntsville, AL	(7.79)
204	Bellingham, WA	(30.00)	7	Duluth–Superior, MN–WI	181.25	–	Indianapolis, IN**	NA
172	Benton Harbor, MI	(13.92)	–	Dutchess County, NY**	NA	49	Jackson, MI	39.39
–	Bergen–Passaic, NJ**	NA	127	Eau Claire, WI	0.00	52	Jackson, MS	34.76
77	Binghamton, NY	15.79	85	El Paso, TX	13.16	54	Jackson, TN	33.91
147	Birmingham, AL	(3.98)	127	Elkhart–Goshen, IN	0.00	125	Jacksonville, FL	0.67
236	Bismarck, ND	(85.71)	17	Enid, OK	105.88	222	Jacksonville, NC	(47.69)
238	Bloomington, IN	(100.00)	90	Erie, PA	12.00	238	Janesville–Beloit, WI	(100.00)
196	Boise, ID	(25.00)	221	Eugene–Springfield, OR	(45.95)	–	Jersey City, NJ**	NA
–	Boston, MA–NH**	NA	163	Evansville–Henderson, IN–KY	(10.26)	168	Johnson City–Kingsport–Bristol, TN–VA	(12.12)
–	Boulder–Longmont, CO**	NA	233	Fargo–Moorhead, ND–MN	(68.42)	226	Johnstown, PA	(54.05)
206	Brazoria, TX	(32.00)	22	Fayetteville, NC	99.08	–	Joplin, MO**	NA
229	Bremerton, WA	(60.00)	27	Fayetteville–Springdale–Rogers, AR	69.57	45	Kalamazoo–Battle Creek, MI	43.90
104	Bridgeport, CT	6.47	–	Fitchburg–Leominster, MA**	NA	–	Kansas City, MO–KS**	NA
12	Brockton, MA	124.14	149	Flint, MI	(4.62)	13	Kenosha, WI	123.33
151	Brownsville–Harlingen–San Benito, TX	(5.22)	9	Florence, AL	137.84	101	Killeen–Temple, TX	7.81
127	Bryan–College Station, TX	0.00	91	Florence, SC	11.81	127	Kokomo, IN	0.00
–	Buffalo–Niagara Falls, NY**	NA	–	Fort Collins–Loveland, CO**	NA	238	La Crosse, WI–MN	(100.00)
171	Canton–Massillon, OH	(13.46)	71	Fort Lauderdale, FL	21.54	231	Lafayette, IN	(66.67)
68	Charleston, WV	22.89	219	Fort Myers–Cape Coral, FL	(45.36)	118	Lafayette, LA	2.27
158	Charleston–North Charleston, SC	(9.09)	29	Fort Pierce–Port St. Lucie, FL	63.93	–	Lake Charles, LA**	NA
232	Charlottesville, VA	(67.16)	26	Fort Smith, AR–OK	75.00	166	Lakeland–Winter Haven, FL	(10.87)
65	Charlotte–Gastonia–Rock Hill, NC–SC	23.88	11	Fort Walton Beach, FL	125.00	72	Lancaster, PA	21.43
74	Chattanooga, TN–GA	18.39	40	Fort Wayne, IN	46.67	23	Lansing–East Lansing, MI	92.00

Source: Morgan Quitno Corporation using data from U.S. Department of Justice, Federal Bureau of Investigation "Crime in the United States 1993" (Uniform Crime Reports, December 4, 1994)
Includes nonnegligent manslaughter.
**Not available. The metro areas of Altoona, PA; Boulder–Longmont CO; Glens Falls, NY; Grand Forks, ND–MN; Owensboro, KY; Rapid City, SD and Sioux Falls, SD had murder rates of 0 in 1992 but had at least one murder in 1993. Calculating percent increase from zero results in an infinite number. These are shown as "NA."*

11. Percent Change in Murder Rate: 1992 to 1993 (continued)

National Percent Change = 2.2% Increase*

RANK	METRO AREA	% CHANGE	RANK	METRO AREA	% CHANGE	RANK	METRO AREA	CHANGE
156	Laredo, TX	(8.55)	237	Olympia, WA	(87.23)	88	Seattle-Bellevue-Everett, WA	12.24
150	Las Vegas, NV-AZ	(5.07)	–	Omaha, NE**	NA	127	Sheboygan, WI	0.00
–	Lawrence, MA-NH**	NA	86	Orange County, CA	13.04	207	Sherman-Denison, TX	(32.79)
15	Lawton, OK	116.98	127	Orlando, FL	0.00	39	Shreveport-Bossier City, LA	49.13
95	Lewiston-Auburn, ME	11.11	–	Owensboro, KY**	NA	–	Sioux City, IA-NE**	NA
230	Lexington, KY	(62.03)	66	Panama City, FL	23.33	–	Sioux Falls, SD**	NA
212	Lincoln, NE	(37.25)	98	Philadelphia, PA-NJ	9.09	127	South Bend, IN	0.00
58	Little Rock-North Little Rock, AR	31.37	98	Phoenix-Mesa, AZ	9.09	184	Spokane, WA	(20.00)
80	Longview-Marshall, TX	15.31	161	Pine Bluff, AR	(9.63)	69	Springfield, MA	22.73
121	Los Angeles-Long Beach, CA	1.91	67	Pittsburgh, PA	23.26	189	Springfield, MO	(21.62)
167	Louisville, KY-IN	(11.94)	238	Pittsfield, MA	(100.00)	60	Stamford-Norwalk, CT	27.91
89	Lubbock, TX	12.16	235	Portland, ME	(70.00)	35	Steubenville-Weirton, OH-WV	50.00
182	Lynchburg, VA	(18.18)	64	Portland-Vancouver, OR-WA	23.91	157	Stockton-Lodi, CA	(8.57)
190	Macon, GA	(23.45)	106	Providence-Fall River-Warwick, RI-MA	5.41	225	St. Cloud, MN	(53.85)
199	Madison, WI	(27.27)	127	Provo-Orem, UT	0.00	19	St. Joseph, MO	100.00
–	Manchester, NH**	NA	115	Pueblo, CO	2.90	–	St. Louis, MO-IL**	NA
198	Mansfield, OH	(26.09)	–	Punta Gorda, FL**	NA	191	Sumter, SC	(23.58)
30	McAllen-Edinburg-Mission, TX	60.34	197	Racine, WI	(25.37)	35	Syracuse, NY	50.00
195	Medford-Ashland, OR	(24.24)	120	Raleigh-Durham-Chapel Hill, NC	2.20	127	Tacoma, WA	0.00
87	Memphis, TN-AR-MS	12.89	–	Rapid City, SD**	NA	184	Tallahassee, FL	(20.00)
24	Merced, CA	86.44	127	Reading, PA	0.00	177	Tampa-St. Petersburg-Clearwater, FL	(16.44)
104	Miami, FL	6.47	62	Redding, CA	27.12	56	Texarkana, TX-AR	32.56
–	Middlesex-Sommerset-Hunterdon, NJ**	NA	78	Reno, NV	15.49	116	Toledo, OH	2.60
108	Milwaukee-Waukesha, WI	4.59	43	Richland-Kennewick-Pasco, WA	44.74	93	Trenton, NJ	11.54
117	Minneapolis-St. Paul, MN-WI	2.33	111	Richmond-Petersburg, VA	4.19	103	Tucson, AZ	6.98
–	Mobile, AL**	NA	100	Riverside-San Bernardino, CA	8.96	44	Tulsa, OK	44.07
218	Modesto, CA	(42.57)	127	Roanoke, VA	0.00	180	Tuscaloosa, AL	(17.95)
–	Monmouth-Ocean, NJ**	NA	35	Rochester, MN	50.00	32	Tyler, TX	54.29
169	Monroe, LA	(12.22)	59	Rochester, NY	28.07	3	Utica-Rome, NY	256.25
97	Montgomery, AL	9.56	81	Rocky Mount, NC	14.49	123	Vallejo-Fairfield-Napa, CA	1.56
188	Myrtle Beach, SC	(21.50)	34	Sacramento, CA	52.05	42	Ventura, CA	45.24
35	Naples, FL	50.00	187	Saginaw-Bay City-Midland, MI	(20.88)	210	Victoria, TX	(34.62)
193	Nashua, NH	(24.00)	200	Salem, OR	(27.54)	5	Vineland-Millville-Bridgeton, NJ	248.84
153	Nashville, TN	(8.04)	144	Salinas, CA	(3.37)	179	Visalia-Tulare-Porterville, CA	(17.65)
–	Nassau-Suffolk, NY**	NA	94	Salt Lake City-Ogden, UT	11.43	78	Waco, TX	15.49
–	New Bedford, MA**	NA	76	San Angelo, TX	16.18	126	Washington, DC-MD-VA-WV	0.64
200	New Haven-Meriden, CT	(27.54)	124	San Antonio, TX	1.09	32	Waterbury, CT	54.29
1	New London-Norwich, CT-RI	657.14	143	San Diego, CA	(2.11)	–	Waterloo-Cedar Falls, IA**	NA
55	New Orleans, LA	33.22	154	San Francisco, CA	(8.18)	127	Wausau, WI	0.00
–	New York, NY**	NA	158	San Jose, CA	(9.09)	–	West Palm Beach-Boca Raton, FL**	NA
–	Newark, NJ**	NA	–	San Luis Obispo-Atascadero, CA**	NA	213	Wichita Falls, TX	(37.84)
–	Newburgh, NY-PA**	NA	192	Santa Barbara-Santa Maria-Lompoc, CA	(23.81)	127	Williamsport, PA	0.00
175	Norfolk-Va Beach-Newport News, VA-NC	(15.38)	31	Santa Cruz-Watsonville, CA	56.00	217	Wilmington, NC	(42.15)
112	Oakland, CA	3.60	2	Santa Rosa, CA	293.33	–	Worcester, MA-CT**	NA
234	Ocala, FL	(69.11)	202	Sarasota-Bradenton, FL	(29.82)	16	Yakima, WA	111.43
119	Odessa-Midland, TX	2.22	48	Savannah, GA	40.38	19	Yolo, CA	100.00
63	Oklahoma City, OK	26.83	193	Scranton-Wilkes-Barre-Hazleton, PA	(24.00)	228	Yuba City, CA	(59.57)

Source: Morgan Quitno Corporation using data from U.S. Department of Justice, Federal Bureau of Investigation
    "Crime in the United States 1993" (Uniform Crime Reports, December 4, 1994)
Includes nonnegligent manslaughter.
**Not available. The metro areas of Altoona, PA; Boulder-Longmont CO; Glens Falls, NY; Grand Forks, ND-MN; Owensboro, KY; Rapid City, SD and Sioux Falls, SD had murder rates of 0 in 1992 but had at least one murder in 1993. Calculating percent increase from zero results in an infinite number. These are shown as "NA."*

11. Percent Change in Murder Rate: 1992 to 1993 (continued)

National Percent Change = 2.2% Increase*

RANK	METRO AREA	% CHANGE	RANK	METRO AREA	% CHANGE	RANK	METRO AREA	% CHANGE
1	New London–Norwich, CT–RI	657.14	48	Savannah, GA	40.38	95	Lewiston–Auburn, ME	11.11
2	Santa Rosa, CA	293.33	49	Jackson, MI	39.39	96	Colorado Springs, CO	10.00
3	Utica–Rome, NY	256.25	50	Abilene, TX	35.42	97	Montgomery, AL	9.56
4	Appleton–Oshkosh–Neenah, WI	250.00	51	Corpus Christi, TX	35.23	98	Philadelphia, PA–NJ	9.09
5	Vineland–Millville–Bridgeton, NJ	248.84	52	Jackson, MS	34.76	98	Phoenix–Mesa, AZ	9.09
6	Green Bay, WI	200.00	53	Columbus, GA–AL	34.31	100	Riverside–San Bernardino, CA	8.96
7	Duluth–Superior, MN–WI	181.25	54	Jackson, TN	33.91	101	Killeen–Temple, TX	7.81
8	Hagerstown, MD	143.75	55	New Orleans, LA	33.22	102	Danville, VA	6.99
9	Florence, AL	137.84	56	Texarkana, TX–AR	32.56	103	Tucson, AZ	6.98
10	Decatur, AL	126.67	57	Anchorage, AK	31.43	104	Bridgeport, CT	6.47
11	Fort Walton Beach, FL	125.00	58	Little Rock–North Little Rock, AR	31.37	104	Miami, FL	6.47
12	Brockton, MA	124.14	59	Rochester, NY	28.07	106	Providence–Fall River–Warwick, RI–MA	5.41
13	Kenosha, WI	123.33	60	Stamford–Norwalk, CT	27.91	107	Greensboro–Winston Salem–High Point, NC	4.95
14	Hartford, CT	122.73	61	Greenville–Spartanburg–Anderson, SC	27.85	108	Milwaukee–Waukesha, WI	4.59
15	Lawton, OK	116.98	62	Redding, CA	27.12	109	Albany, GA	4.47
16	Yakima, WA	111.43	63	Oklahoma City, OK	26.83	110	Des Moines, IA	4.35
17	Enid, OK	105.88	64	Portland–Vancouver, OR–WA	23.91	111	Richmond–Petersburg, VA	4.19
18	Alexandria, LA	104.12	65	Charlotte–Gastonia–Rock Hill, NC–SC	23.88	112	Oakland, CA	3.60
19	Cumberland, MD–WV	100.00	66	Panama City, FL	23.33	113	Albuquerque, NM	3.41
19	St. Joseph, MO	100.00	67	Pittsburgh, PA	23.26	114	Baltimore, MD	2.99
19	Yolo, CA	100.00	68	Charleston, WV	22.89	115	Pueblo, CO	2.90
22	Fayetteville, NC	99.08	69	Springfield, MA	22.73	116	Toledo, OH	2.60
23	Lansing–East Lansing, MI	92.00	70	Anniston, AL	22.03	117	Minneapolis–St. Paul, MN–WI	2.33
24	Merced, CA	86.44	71	Fort Lauderdale, FL	21.54	118	Lafayette, LA	2.27
25	Asheville, NC	77.78	72	Lancaster, PA	21.43	119	Odessa–Midland, TX	2.22
26	Fort Smith, AR–OK	75.00	73	Athens, GA	20.88	120	Raleigh–Durham–Chapel Hill, NC	2.20
27	Fayetteville–Springdale–Rogers, AR	69.57	74	Chattanooga, TN–GA	18.39	121	Los Angeles–Long Beach, CA	1.91
28	Harrisburg–Lebanon–Carlisle, PA	65.00	75	Gary–Hammond, IN	17.44	122	Austin–San Marcos, TX	1.69
29	Fort Pierce–Port St. Lucie, FL	63.93	76	San Angelo, TX	16.18	123	Vallejo–Fairfield–Napa, CA	1.56
30	McAllen–Edinburg–Mission, TX	60.34	77	Binghamton, NY	15.79	124	San Antonio, TX	1.09
31	Santa Cruz–Watsonville, CA	56.00	78	Reno, NV	15.49	125	Jacksonville, FL	0.67
32	Tyler, TX	54.29	78	Waco, TX	15.49	126	Washington, DC–MD–VA–WV	0.64
32	Waterbury, CT	54.29	80	Longview–Marshall, TX	15.31	127	Bangor, ME	0.00
34	Sacramento, CA	52.05	81	Rocky Mount, NC	14.49	127	Barnstable–Yarmouth, MA	0.00
35	Naples, FL	50.00	82	Baton Rouge, LA	13.69	127	Bryan–College Station, TX	0.00
35	Rochester, MN	50.00	83	Atlantic City, NJ	13.56	127	Eau Claire, WI	0.00
35	Steubenville–Weirton, OH–WV	50.00	84	Dothan, AL	13.46	127	Elkhart–Goshen, IN	0.00
35	Syracuse, NY	50.00	85	El Paso, TX	13.16	127	Honolulu, HI	0.00
39	Shreveport–Bossier City, LA	49.13	86	Orange County, CA	13.04	127	Kokomo, IN	0.00
40	Fort Wayne, IN	46.67	87	Memphis, TN–AR–MS	12.89	127	Orlando, FL	0.00
41	Ann Arbor, MI	45.45	88	Seattle–Bellevue–Everett, WA	12.24	127	Provo–Orem, UT	0.00
42	Ventura, CA	45.24	89	Lubbock, TX	12.16	127	Reading, PA	0.00
43	Richland–Kennewick–Pasco, WA	44.74	90	Erie, PA	12.00	127	Roanoke, VA	0.00
44	Tulsa, OK	44.07	91	Florence, SC	11.81	127	Sheboygan, WI	0.00
45	Kalamazoo–Battle Creek, MI	43.90	92	Huntington–Ashland, WV–KY–OH	11.76	127	South Bend, IN	0.00
46	Grand Rapids–Muskegon–Holland, MI	42.11	93	Trenton, NJ	11.54	127	Tacoma, WA	0.00
47	Bakersfield, CA	40.45	94	Salt Lake City–Ogden, UT	11.43	127	Wausau, WI	0.00

Source: Morgan Quitno Corporation using data from U.S. Department of Justice, Federal Bureau of Investigation
"Crime in the United States 1993" (Uniform Crime Reports, December 4, 1994)
*Includes nonnegligent manslaughter.
**Not available. The metro areas of Altoona, PA; Boulder-Longmont CO; Glens Falls, NY; Grand Forks, ND-MN; Owensboro, KY; Rapid City, SD and Sioux Falls, SD had murder rates of 0 in 1992 but had at least one murder in 1993. Calculating percent increase from zero results in an infinite number. These are shown as "NA."*

11. Percent Change in Murder Rate: 1992 to 1993 (continued)

National Percent Change = 2.2% Increase*

RANK	METRO AREA	% CHANGE	RANK	METRO AREA	% CHANGE	RANK	METRO AREA	CHANGE
127	Williamsport, PA	0.00	189	Springfield, MO	(21.62)	236	Bismarck, ND	(85.71)
143	San Diego, CA	(2.11)	190	Macon, GA	(23.45)	237	Olympia, WA	(87.23)
144	Salinas, CA	(3.37)	191	Sumter, SC	(23.58)	238	Bloomington, IN	(100.00)
145	Fresno, CA	(3.43)	192	Santa Barbara–Santa Maria–Lompoc, CA	(23.81)	238	Cheyenne, WY	(100.00)
146	Atlanta, GA	(3.94)	193	Nashua, NH	(24.00)	238	Dubuque, IA	(100.00)
147	Birmingham, AL	(3.98)	193	Scranton–Wilkes-Barre–Hazleton, PA	(24.00)	238	Janesville–Beloit, WI	(100.00)
148	Detroit, MI	(4.24)	195	Medford–Ashland, OR	(24.24)	238	La Crosse, WI–MN	(100.00)
149	Flint, MI	(4.62)	196	Boise, ID	(25.00)	238	Pittsfield, MA	(100.00)
150	Las Vegas, NV–AZ	(5.07)	197	Racine, WI	(25.37)	–	Albany, NY**	NA
151	Brownsville–Harlingen–San Benito, TX	(5.22)	198	Mansfield, OH	(26.09)	–	Altoona, PA**	NA
152	Huntsville, AL	(7.79)	199	Madison, WI	(27.27)	–	Bergen–Passaic, NJ**	NA
153	Nashville, TN	(8.04)	200	New Haven–Meriden, CT	(27.54)	–	Boston, MA–NH**	NA
154	San Francisco, CA	(8.18)	200	Salem, OR	(27.54)	–	Boulder–Longmont, CO**	NA
155	Denver, CO	(8.54)	202	Sarasota–Bradenton, FL	(29.82)	–	Buffalo–Niagara Falls, NY**	NA
156	Laredo, TX	(8.55)	203	Amarillo, TX	(29.89)	–	Chicago, IL**	NA
157	Stockton–Lodi, CA	(8.57)	204	Bellingham, WA	(30.00)	–	Cleveland, OH**	NA
158	Charleston–North Charleston, SC	(9.09)	204	Goldsboro, NC	(30.00)	–	Dutchess County, NY**	NA
158	San Jose, CA	(9.09)	206	Brazoria, TX	(32.00)	–	Fitchburg–Leominster, MA**	NA
160	Dayton–Springfield, OH	(9.30)	207	Sherman–Denison, TX	(32.79)	–	Fort Collins–Loveland, CO**	NA
161	Pine Bluff, AR	(9.63)	208	Gainesville, FL	(32.94)	–	Glens Falls, NY**	NA
162	Houston, TX	(9.66)	209	Gadsden, AL	(34.52)	–	Grand Forks, ND–MN**	NA
163	Evansville–Henderson, IN–KY	(10.26)	210	Victoria, TX	(34.62)	–	Indianapolis, IN**	NA
164	Galveston–Texas City, TX	(10.40)	211	Hickory–Morganton, NC	(36.14)	–	Jersey City, NJ**	NA
165	Fort Worth–Arlington, TX	(10.69)	212	Lincoln, NE	(37.25)	–	Joplin, MO**	NA
166	Lakeland–Winter Haven, FL	(10.87)	213	Wichita Falls, TX	(37.84)	–	Kansas City, MO–KS**	NA
167	Louisville, KY–IN	(11.94)	214	Clarksville–Hopkinsville, TN–KY	(38.10)	–	Lake Charles, LA**	NA
168	Johnson City–Kingsport–Bristol, TN–VA	(12.12)	215	Daytona Beach, FL	(40.70)	–	Lawrence, MA–NH**	NA
169	Monroe, LA	(12.22)	216	Greenville, NC	(41.53)	–	Manchester, NH**	NA
170	Columbus, OH	(12.63)	217	Wilmington, NC	(42.15)	–	Middlesex–Sommerset–Hunterdon, NJ**	NA
171	Canton–Massillon, OH	(13.46)	218	Modesto, CA	(42.57)	–	Mobile, AL**	NA
172	Benton Harbor, MI	(13.92)	219	Fort Myers–Cape Coral, FL	(45.36)	–	Monmouth–Ocean, NJ**	NA
173	Greeley, CO	(14.00)	220	Houma, LA	(45.37)	–	Nassau–Suffolk, NY**	NA
174	Augusta–Aiken, GA–SC	(14.09)	221	Eugene–Springfield, OR	(45.95)	–	New Bedford, MA**	NA
175	Norfolk–Va Beach–Newport News, VA–NC	(15.38)	222	Jacksonville, NC	(47.69)	–	New York, NY**	NA
176	Cincinnati, OH–KY–IN	(15.56)	223	Danbury, CT	(51.35)	–	Newark, NJ**	NA
177	Tampa–St. Petersburg–Clearwater, FL	(16.44)	224	Columbia, MO	(51.43)	–	Newburgh, NY–PA**	NA
178	Dallas, TX	(16.57)	225	St. Cloud, MN	(53.85)	–	Omaha, NE**	NA
179	Visalia–Tulare–Porterville, CA	(17.65)	226	Johnstown, PA	(54.05)	–	Owensboro, KY**	NA
180	Tuscaloosa, AL	(17.95)	227	Chico–Paradise, CA	(56.76)	–	Punta Gorda, FL**	NA
181	Columbia, SC	(17.97)	228	Yuba City, CA	(59.57)	–	Rapid City, SD**	NA
182	Lynchburg, VA	(18.18)	229	Bremerton, WA	(60.00)	–	San Luis Obispo–Atascadero, CA**	NA
183	Beaumont–Port Arthur, TX	(18.38)	230	Lexington, KY	(62.03)	–	Sioux City, IA–NE**	NA
184	Akron, OH	(20.00)	231	Lafayette, IN	(66.67)	–	Sioux Falls, SD**	NA
184	Spokane, WA	(20.00)	232	Charlottesville, VA	(67.16)	–	St. Louis, MO–IL**	NA
184	Tallahassee, FL	(20.00)	233	Fargo–Moorhead, ND–MN	(68.42)	–	Waterloo–Cedar Falls, IA**	NA
187	Saginaw–Bay City–Midland, MI	(20.88)	234	Ocala, FL	(69.11)	–	West Palm Beach–Boca Raton, FL**	NA
188	Myrtle Beach, SC	(21.50)	235	Portland, ME	(70.00)	–	Worcester, MA–CT**	NA

Source: Morgan Quitno Corporation using data from U.S. Department of Justice, Federal Bureau of Investigation
    "Crime in the United States 1993" (Uniform Crime Reports, December 4, 1994)
*Includes nonnegligent manslaughter.
**Not available. The metro areas of Altoona, PA; Boulder-Longmont CO; Glens Falls, NY; Grand Forks, ND-MN; Owensboro, KY; Rapid City, SD and Sioux Falls, SD had murder rates of 0 in 1992 but had at least one murder in 1993. Calculating percent increase from zero results in an infinite number. These are shown as "NA."

12. Percent Change in Murder Rate: 1989 to 1993

National Percent Change = 9.2% Increase*

RANK	METRO AREA	% CHANGE	RANK	METRO AREA	% CHANGE	RANK	METRO AREA	% CHANGE
145	Abilene, TX	0.00	145	Cheyenne, WY	0.00	140	Fort Worth-Arlington, TX	1.74
–	Akron, OH**	NA	–	Chicago, IL**	NA	48	Fresno, CA	59.43
133	Albany, GA	5.06	227	Chico-Paradise, CA	(52.24)	43	Gadsden, AL	65.38
–	Albany, NY**	NA	206	Cincinnati, OH-KY-IN	(32.14)	122	Gainesville, FL	9.62
171	Albuquerque, NM	(10.78)	173	Clarksville-Hopkinsville, TN-KY	(11.36)	44	Galveston-Texas City, TX	64.89
20	Alexandria, LA	108.42	–	Cleveland, OH**	NA	52	Gary-Hammond, IN	54.20
–	Altoona, PA**	NA	49	Colorado Springs, CO	57.14	34	Glens Falls, NY	77.78
200	Amarillo, TX	(29.07)	231	Columbia, MO	(55.26)	–	Goldsboro, NC**	NA
28	Anchorage, AK	87.76	126	Columbia, SC	8.25	235	Grand Forks, ND-MN	(65.52)
90	Ann Arbor, MI	23.08	103	Columbus, GA-AL	18.10	75	Grand Rapids-Muskegon-Holland, MI	31.71
69	Anniston, AL	37.14	143	Columbus, OH	1.22	26	Greeley, CO	95.45
8	Appleton-Oshkosh-Neenah, WI	250.00	31	Corpus Christi, TX	80.30	56	Green Bay, WI	50.00
106	Asheville, NC	17.65	131	Cumberland, MD-WV	5.26	110	Greensboro-Winston Salem-High Point, NC	16.48
112	Athens, GA	15.79	181	Dallas, TX	(15.61)	–	Greenville, NC**	NA
186	Atlanta, GA	(18.12)	199	Danbury, CT	(28.00)	107	Greenville-Spartanburg-Anderson, SC	17.44
176	Atlantic City, NJ	(12.99)	41	Danville, VA	68.13	229	Hagerstown, MD	(53.57)
168	Augusta-Aiken, GA-SC	(9.86)	220	Daytona Beach, FL	(46.32)	–	Harrisburg-Lebanon-Carlisle, PA**	NA
174	Austin-San Marcos, TX	(11.76)	156	Dayton-Springfield, OH	(1.27)	172	Hartford, CT	(10.91)
61	Bakersfield, CA	45.35	39	Decatur, AL	70.00	–	Hickory-Morganton, NC**	NA
92	Baltimore, MD	21.13	60	Denver, CO	47.06	204	Honolulu, HI	(31.37)
23	Bangor, ME	100.00	221	Des Moines, IA	(47.83)	–	Houma, LA**	NA
–	Barnstable-Yarmouth, MA**	NA	167	Detroit, MI	(9.71)	166	Houston, TX	(8.62)
53	Baton Rouge, LA	54.03	215	Dothan, AL	(40.40)	159	Huntington-Ashland, WV-KY-OH	(3.39)
191	Beaumont-Port Arthur, TX	(21.83)	145	Dubuque, IA	0.00	130	Huntsville, AL	5.97
223	Bellingham, WA	(48.78)	6	Duluth-Superior, MN-WI	275.00	–	Indianapolis, IN**	NA
136	Benton Harbor, MI	3.03	–	Dutchess County, NY**	NA	177	Jackson, MI	(13.21)
104	Bergen-Passaic, NJ	17.86	242	Eau Claire, WI	(100.00)	32	Jackson, MS	78.72
187	Binghamton, NY	(18.52)	117	El Paso, TX	13.16	3	Jackson, TN	356.86
86	Birmingham, AL	24.52	195	Elkhart-Goshen, IN	(24.24)	190	Jacksonville, FL	(21.35)
145	Bismarck, ND	0.00	21	Enid, OK	105.88	59	Jacksonville, NC	47.83
145	Bloomington, IN	0.00	50	Erie, PA	55.56	242	Janesville-Beloit, WI	(100.00)
2	Boise, ID	380.00	224	Eugene-Springfield, OR	(50.00)	222	Jersey City, NJ	(48.51)
–	Boston, MA-NH**	NA	213	Evansville-Henderson, IN-KY	(38.60)	216	Johnson City-Kingsport-Bristol, TN-VA	(40.82)
11	Boulder-Longmont, CO	166.67	–	Fargo-Moorhead, ND-MN**	NA	–	Johnstown, PA**	NA
201	Brazoria, TX	(29.17)	38	Fayetteville, NC	70.87	10	Joplin, MO	195.45
–	Bremerton, WA**	NA	125	Fayetteville-Springdale-Rogers, AR	8.33	175	Kalamazoo-Battle Creek, MI	(11.94)
58	Bridgeport, CT	49.49	94	Fitchburg-Leominster, MA	20.00	–	Kansas City, MO-KS**	NA
–	Brockton, MA**	NA	183	Flint, MI	(16.22)	70	Kenosha, WI	36.73
163	Brownsville-Harlingen-San Benito, TX	(6.03)	5	Florence, AL	300.00	99	Killeen-Temple, TX	18.97
232	Bryan-College Station, TX	(59.32)	162	Florence, SC	(5.96)	224	Kokomo, IN	(50.00)
33	Buffalo-Niagara Falls, NY	78.05	234	Fort Collins-Loveland, CO	(62.96)	145	La Crosse, WI-MN	0.00
145	Canton-Massillon, OH	0.00	182	Fort Lauderdale, FL	(15.96)	56	Lafayette, IN	50.00
144	Charleston, WV	0.99	189	Fort Myers-Cape Coral, FL	(19.70)	72	Lafayette, LA	34.33
83	Charleston-North Charleston, SC	25.00	192	Fort Pierce-Port St. Lucie, FL	(23.08)	129	Lake Charles, LA	6.06
233	Charlottesville, VA	(60.71)	158	Fort Smith, AR-OK	(2.00)	209	Lakeland-Winter Haven, FL	(35.94)
68	Charlotte-Gastonia-Rock Hill, NC-SC	37.19	16	Fort Walton Beach, FL	136.84	78	Lancaster, PA	30.77
27	Chattanooga, TN-GA	90.74	64	Fort Wayne, IN	41.94	161	Lansing-East Lansing, MI	(5.88)

Source: Morgan Quitno Corporation using data from U.S. Department of Justice, Federal Bureau of Investigation

"Crime in the United States 1993" (Uniform Crime Reports, December 4, 1994)

*Includes nonnegligent manslaughter.

**Not available. The metro areas of Altoona, PA and Fargo-Moorhead, ND-MN had murder rates of 0 in 1989 but had at least one murder in 1993. Calculating percent increase from zero results in an infinite number. These are shown as "NA."

12. Percent Change in Murder Rate: 1989 to 1993 (continued)

National Percent Change = 9.2% Increase*

RANK	METRO AREA	% CHANGE	RANK	METRO AREA	% CHANGE	RANK	METRO AREA	CHANGE
55	Laredo, TX	51.09	237	Olympia, WA	(68.42)	62	Seattle–Bellevue–Everett, WA	44.74
85	Las Vegas, NV–AZ	24.76	–	Omaha, NE**	NA	169	Sheboygan, WI	(10.00)
205	Lawrence, MA–NH	(31.43)	87	Orange County, CA	23.81	236	Sherman–Denison, TX	(66.12)
9	Lawton, OK	238.24	193	Orlando, FL	(23.53)	77	Shreveport–Bossier City, LA	31.63
241	Lewiston–Auburn, ME	(79.17)	25	Owensboro, KY	95.65	208	Sioux City, IA–NE	(34.62)
214	Lexington, KY	(38.78)	210	Panama City, FL	(36.21)	188	Sioux Falls, SD	(18.75)
40	Lincoln, NE	68.42	141	Philadelphia, PA–NJ	1.69	–	South Bend, IN**	NA
47	Little Rock–North Little Rock, AR	59.52	108	Phoenix–Mesa, AZ	17.07	45	Spokane, WA	62.96
180	Longview–Marshall, TX	(15.04)	93	Pine Bluff, AR	20.12	13	Springfield, MA	157.14
102	Los Angeles–Long Beach, CA	18.33	29	Pittsburgh, PA	82.76	179	Springfield, MO	(14.71)
170	Louisville, KY–IN	(10.61)	–	Pittsfield, MA**	NA	135	Stamford–Norwalk, CT	3.77
101	Lubbock, TX	18.57	238	Portland, ME	(76.92)	–	Steubenville–Weirton, OH–WV**	NA
228	Lynchburg, VA	(52.63)	127	Portland–Vancouver, OR–WA	7.55	145	Stockton–Lodi, CA	0.00
157	Macon, GA	(1.77)	202	Providence–Fall River–Warwick, RI–MA	(30.36)	94	St. Cloud, MN	20.00
239	Madison, WI	(77.14)	–	Provo–Orem, UT**	NA	36	St. Joseph, MO	73.91
88	Manchester, NH	23.53	142	Pueblo, CO	1.43	–	St. Louis, MO–IL**	NA
218	Mansfield, OH	(45.16)	–	Punta Gorda, FL**	NA	–	Sumter, SC**	NA
30	McAllen–Edinburg–Mission, TX	82.35	83	Racine, WI	25.00	46	Syracuse, NY	61.54
198	Medford–Ashland, OR	(26.47)	67	Raleigh–Durham–Chapel Hill, NC	38.81	119	Tacoma, WA	12.50
81	Memphis, TN–AR–MS	29.59	24	Rapid City, SD	95.83	145	Tallahassee, FL	0.00
19	Merced, CA	111.54	–	Reading, PA**	NA	203	Tampa–St. Petersburg–Clearwater, FL	(30.68)
184	Miami, FL	(16.97)	7	Redding, CA	257.14	37	Texarkana, TX–AR	71.00
114	Middlesex–Sommerset–Hunterdon, NJ	15.38	79	Reno, NV	30.16	128	Toledo, OH	6.76
73	Milwaukee–Waukesha, WI	34.12	109	Richland–Kennewick–Pasco, WA	17.02	197	Trenton, NJ	(25.64)
82	Minneapolis–St. Paul, MN–WI	25.71	121	Richmond–Petersburg, VA	10.13	–	Tucson, AZ**	NA
123	Mobile, AL	9.24	–	Riverside–San Bernardino, CA**	NA	89	Tulsa, OK	23.19
139	Modesto, CA	1.75	178	Roanoke, VA	(14.47)	111	Tuscaloosa, AL	16.36
17	Monmouth–Ocean, NJ	130.00	71	Rochester, MN	35.00	100	Tyler, TX	18.68
14	Monroe, LA	150.79	51	Rochester, NY	55.32	4	Utica–Rome, NY	338.46
120	Montgomery, AL	10.37	–	Rocky Mount, NC**	NA	145	Vallejo–Fairfield–Napa, CA	0.00
–	Myrtle Beach, SC**	NA	35	Sacramento, CA	76.19	22	Ventura, CA	103.33
212	Naples, FL	(37.14)	91	Saginaw–Bay City–Midland, MI	22.03	194	Victoria, TX	(23.88)
217	Nashua, NH	(44.12)	66	Salem, OR	38.89	1	Vineland–Millville–Bridgeton, NJ	581.82
124	Nashville, TN	8.42	105	Salinas, CA	17.81	137	Visalia–Tulare–Porterville, CA	2.44
80	Nassau–Suffolk, NY	29.63	115	Salt Lake City–Ogden, UT	14.71	185	Waco, TX	(18.00)
226	New Bedford, MA	(51.43)	118	San Angelo, TX	12.86	165	Washington, DC–MD–VA–WV	(7.06)
207	New Haven–Meriden, CT	(33.33)	74	San Antonio, TX	33.81	15	Waterbury, CT	145.45
134	New London–Norwich, CT–RI	3.92	97	San Diego, CA	19.23	12	Waterloo–Cedar Falls, IA	162.96
54	New Orleans, LA	52.63	63	San Francisco, CA	44.29	145	Wausau, WI	0.00
138	New York, NY	2.20	131	San Jose, CA	5.26	–	West Palm Beach–Boca Raton, FL**	NA
164	Newark, NJ	(6.32)	–	San Luis Obispo–Atascadero, CA**	NA	219	Wichita Falls, TX	(45.67)
–	Newburgh, NY–PA**	NA	18	Santa Barbara–Santa Maria–Lompoc, CA	128.57	–	Williamsport, PA**	NA
96	Norfolk–Va Beach–Newport News, VA–NC	19.80	196	Santa Cruz–Watsonville, CA	(25.00)	42	Wilmington, NC	66.67
98	Oakland, CA	19.01	113	Santa Rosa, CA	15.69	–	Worcester, MA–CT**	NA
230	Ocala, FL	(53.66)	160	Sarasota–Bradenton, FL	(4.76)	210	Yakima, WA	(36.21)
116	Odessa–Midland, TX	13.58	65	Savannah, GA	39.05	–	Yolo, CA**	NA
76	Oklahoma City, OK	31.65	–	Scranton–Wilkes-Barre–Hazleton, PA**	NA	240	Yuba City, CA	(78.03)

Source: Morgan Quitno Corporation using data from U.S. Department of Justice, Federal Bureau of Investigation
   "Crime in the United States 1993" (Uniform Crime Reports, December 4, 1994)
*Includes nonnegligent manslaughter.
**Not available. The metro areas of Altoona, PA and Fargo-Moorhead, ND-MN had murder rates of 0 in 1989 but had at least one murder in 1993. Calculating percent increase from zero results in an infinite number. These are shown as "NA."

12. Percent Change in Murder Rate: 1989 to 1993 (continued)

National Percent Change = 9.2% Increase*

RANK	METRO AREA	% CHANGE	RANK	METRO AREA	% CHANGE	RANK	METRO AREA	% CHANGE
1	Vineland–Millville–Bridgeton, NJ	581.82	48	Fresno, CA	59.43	94	St. Cloud, MN	20.00
2	Boise, ID	380.00	49	Colorado Springs, CO	57.14	96	Norfolk–Va Beach–Newport News, VA–NC	19.80
3	Jackson, TN	356.86	50	Erie, PA	55.56	97	San Diego, CA	19.23
4	Utica–Rome, NY	338.46	51	Rochester, NY	55.32	98	Oakland, CA	19.01
5	Florence, AL	300.00	52	Gary–Hammond, IN	54.20	99	Killeen–Temple, TX	18.97
6	Duluth–Superior, MN–WI	275.00	53	Baton Rouge, LA	54.03	100	Tyler, TX	18.68
7	Redding, CA	257.14	54	New Orleans, LA	52.63	101	Lubbock, TX	18.57
8	Appleton–Oshkosh–Neenah, WI	250.00	55	Laredo, TX	51.09	102	Los Angeles–Long Beach, CA	18.33
9	Lawton, OK	238.24	56	Green Bay, WI	50.00	103	Columbus, GA–AL	18.10
10	Joplin, MO	195.45	56	Lafayette, IN	50.00	104	Bergen–Passaic, NJ	17.86
11	Boulder–Longmont, CO	166.67	58	Bridgeport, CT	49.49	105	Salinas, CA	17.81
12	Waterloo–Cedar Falls, IA	162.96	59	Jacksonville, NC	47.83	106	Asheville, NC	17.65
13	Springfield, MA	157.14	60	Denver, CO	47.06	107	Greenville–Spartanburg–Anderson, SC	17.44
14	Monroe, LA	150.79	61	Bakersfield, CA	45.35	108	Phoenix–Mesa, AZ	17.07
15	Waterbury, CT	145.45	62	Seattle–Bellevue–Everett, WA	44.74	109	Richland–Kennewick–Pasco, WA	17.02
16	Fort Walton Beach, FL	136.84	63	San Francisco, CA	44.29	110	Greensboro–Winston Salem–High Point, NC	16.48
17	Monmouth–Ocean, NJ	130.00	64	Fort Wayne, IN	41.94	111	Tuscaloosa, AL	16.36
18	Santa Barbara–Santa Maria–Lompoc, CA	128.57	65	Savannah, GA	39.05	112	Athens, GA	15.79
19	Merced, CA	111.54	66	Salem, OR	38.89	113	Santa Rosa, CA	15.69
20	Alexandria, LA	108.42	67	Raleigh–Durham–Chapel Hill, NC	38.81	114	Middlesex–Somerset–Hunterdon, NJ	15.38
21	Enid, OK	105.88	68	Charlotte–Gastonia–Rock Hill, NC–SC	37.19	115	Salt Lake City–Ogden, UT	14.71
22	Ventura, CA	103.33	69	Anniston, AL	37.14	116	Odessa–Midland, TX	13.58
23	Bangor, ME	100.00	70	Kenosha, WI	36.73	117	El Paso, TX	13.16
24	Rapid City, SD	95.83	71	Rochester, MN	35.00	118	San Angelo, TX	12.86
25	Owensboro, KY	95.65	72	Lafayette, LA	34.33	119	Tacoma, WA	12.50
26	Greeley, CO	95.45	73	Milwaukee–Waukesha, WI	34.12	120	Montgomery, AL	10.37
27	Chattanooga, TN–GA	90.74	74	San Antonio, TX	33.81	121	Richmond–Petersburg, VA	10.13
28	Anchorage, AK	87.76	75	Grand Rapids–Muskegon–Holland, MI	31.71	122	Gainesville, FL	9.62
29	Pittsburgh, PA	82.76	76	Oklahoma City, OK	31.65	123	Mobile, AL	9.24
30	McAllen–Edinburg–Mission, TX	82.35	77	Shreveport–Bossier City, LA	31.63	124	Nashville, TN	8.42
31	Corpus Christi, TX	80.30	78	Lancaster, PA	30.77	125	Fayetteville–Springdale–Rogers, AR	8.33
32	Jackson, MS	78.72	79	Reno, NV	30.16	126	Columbia, SC	8.25
33	Buffalo–Niagara Falls, NY	78.05	80	Nassau–Suffolk, NY	29.63	127	Portland–Vancouver, OR–WA	7.55
34	Glens Falls, NY	77.78	81	Memphis, TN–AR–MS	29.59	128	Toledo, OH	6.76
35	Sacramento, CA	76.19	82	Minneapolis–St. Paul, MN–WI	25.71	129	Lake Charles, LA	6.06
36	St. Joseph, MO	73.91	83	Charleston–North Charleston, SC	25.00	130	Huntsville, AL	5.97
37	Texarkana, TX–AR	71.00	83	Racine, WI	25.00	131	Cumberland, MD–WV	5.26
38	Fayetteville, NC	70.87	85	Las Vegas, NV–AZ	24.76	131	San Jose, CA	5.26
39	Decatur, AL	70.00	86	Birmingham, AL	24.52	133	Albany, GA	5.06
40	Lincoln, NE	68.42	87	Orange County, CA	23.81	134	New London–Norwich, CT–RI	3.92
41	Danville, VA	68.13	88	Manchester, NH	23.53	135	Stamford–Norwalk, CT	3.77
42	Wilmington, NC	66.67	89	Tulsa, OK	23.19	136	Benton Harbor, MI	3.03
43	Gadsden, AL	65.38	90	Ann Arbor, MI	23.08	137	Visalia–Tulare–Porterville, CA	2.44
44	Galveston–Texas City, TX	64.89	91	Saginaw–Bay City–Midland, MI	22.03	138	New York, NY	2.20
45	Spokane, WA	62.96	92	Baltimore, MD	21.13	139	Modesto, CA	1.75
46	Syracuse, NY	61.54	93	Pine Bluff, AR	20.12	140	Fort Worth–Arlington, TX	1.74
47	Little Rock–North Little Rock, AR	59.52	94	Fitchburg–Leominster, MA	20.00	141	Philadelphia, PA–NJ	1.69

Source: Morgan Quitno Corporation using data from U.S. Department of Justice, Federal Bureau of Investigation
"Crime in the United States 1993" (Uniform Crime Reports, December 4, 1994)
*Includes nonnegligent manslaughter.
**Not available. The metro areas of Altoona, PA and Fargo-Moorhead, ND-MN had murder rates of 0 in 1989 but had at least one murder in 1993. Calculating percent increase from zero results in an infinite number. These are shown as "NA."

12. Percent Change in Murder Rate: 1989 to 1993 (continued)

National Percent Change = 9.2% Increase*

RANK	METRO AREA	% CHANGE	RANK	METRO AREA	% CHANGE	RANK	METRO AREA	CHANGE
142	Pueblo, CO	1.43	189	Fort Myers–Cape Coral, FL	(19.70)	236	Sherman–Denison, TX	(66.12)
143	Columbus, OH	1.22	190	Jacksonville, FL	(21.35)	237	Olympia, WA	(68.42)
144	Charleston, WV	0.99	191	Beaumont–Port Arthur, TX	(21.83)	238	Portland, ME	(76.92)
145	Abilene, TX	0.00	192	Fort Pierce–Port St. Lucie, FL	(23.08)	239	Madison, WI	(77.14)
145	Bismarck, ND	0.00	193	Orlando, FL	(23.53)	240	Yuba City, CA	(78.03)
145	Bloomington, IN	0.00	194	Victoria, TX	(23.88)	241	Lewiston–Auburn, ME	(79.17)
145	Canton–Massillon, OH	0.00	195	Elkhart–Goshen, IN	(24.24)	242	Eau Claire, WI	(100.00)
145	Cheyenne, WY	0.00	196	Santa Cruz–Watsonville, CA	(25.00)	242	Janesville–Beloit, WI	(100.00)
145	Dubuque, IA	0.00	197	Trenton, NJ	(25.64)	–	Akron, OH**	NA
145	La Crosse, WI–MN	0.00	198	Medford–Ashland, OR	(26.47)	–	Albany, NY**	NA
145	Stockton–Lodi, CA	0.00	199	Danbury, CT	(28.00)	–	Altoona, PA**	NA
145	Tallahassee, FL	0.00	200	Amarillo, TX	(29.07)	–	Barnstable–Yarmouth, MA**	NA
145	Vallejo–Fairfield–Napa, CA	0.00	201	Brazoria, TX	(29.17)	–	Boston, MA–NH**	NA
145	Wausau, WI	0.00	202	Providence–Fall River–Warwick, RI–MA	(30.36)	–	Bremerton, WA**	NA
156	Dayton–Springfield, OH	(1.27)	203	Tampa–St. Petersburg–Clearwater, FL	(30.68)	–	Brockton, MA**	NA
157	Macon, GA	(1.77)	204	Honolulu, HI	(31.37)	–	Chicago, IL**	NA
158	Fort Smith, AR–OK	(2.00)	205	Lawrence, MA–NH	(31.43)	–	Cleveland, OH**	NA
159	Huntington–Ashland, WV–KY–OH	(3.39)	206	Cincinnati, OH–KY–IN	(32.14)	–	Dutchess County, NY**	NA
160	Sarasota–Bradenton, FL	(4.76)	207	New Haven–Meriden, CT	(33.33)	–	Fargo–Moorhead, ND–MN**	NA
161	Lansing–East Lansing, MI	(5.88)	208	Sioux City, IA–NE	(34.62)	–	Goldsboro, NC**	NA
162	Florence, SC	(5.96)	209	Lakeland–Winter Haven, FL	(35.94)	–	Greenville, NC**	NA
163	Brownsville–Harlingen–San Benito, TX	(6.03)	210	Panama City, FL	(36.21)	–	Harrisburg–Lebanon–Carlisle, PA**	NA
164	Newark, NJ	(6.32)	210	Yakima, WA	(36.21)	–	Hickory–Morganton, NC**	NA
165	Washington, DC–MD–VA–WV	(7.06)	212	Naples, FL	(37.14)	–	Houma, LA**	NA
166	Houston, TX	(8.62)	213	Evansville–Henderson, IN–KY	(38.60)	–	Indianapolis, IN**	NA
167	Detroit, MI	(9.71)	214	Lexington, KY	(38.78)	–	Johnstown, PA**	NA
168	Augusta–Aiken, GA–SC	(9.86)	215	Dothan, AL	(40.40)	–	Kansas City, MO–KS**	NA
169	Sheboygan, WI	(10.00)	216	Johnson City–Kingsport–Bristol, TN–VA	(40.82)	–	Myrtle Beach, SC**	NA
170	Louisville, KY–IN	(10.61)	217	Nashua, NH	(44.12)	–	Newburgh, NY–PA**	NA
171	Albuquerque, NM	(10.78)	218	Mansfield, OH	(45.16)	–	Omaha, NE**	NA
172	Hartford, CT	(10.91)	219	Wichita Falls, TX	(45.67)	–	Pittsfield, MA**	NA
173	Clarksville–Hopkinsville, TN–KY	(11.36)	220	Daytona Beach, FL	(46.32)	–	Provo–Orem, UT**	NA
174	Austin–San Marcos, TX	(11.76)	221	Des Moines, IA	(47.83)	–	Punta Gorda, FL**	NA
175	Kalamazoo–Battle Creek, MI	(11.94)	222	Jersey City, NJ	(48.51)	–	Reading, PA**	NA
176	Atlantic City, NJ	(12.99)	223	Bellingham, WA	(48.78)	–	Riverside–San Bernardino, CA**	NA
177	Jackson, MI	(13.21)	224	Eugene–Springfield, OR	(50.00)	–	Rocky Mount, NC**	NA
178	Roanoke, VA	(14.47)	224	Kokomo, IN	(50.00)	–	San Luis Obispo–Atascadero, CA**	NA
179	Springfield, MO	(14.71)	226	New Bedford, MA	(51.43)	–	Scranton–Wilkes-Barre–Hazleton, PA**	NA
180	Longview–Marshall, TX	(15.04)	227	Chico–Paradise, CA	(52.24)	–	South Bend, IN**	NA
181	Dallas, TX	(15.61)	228	Lynchburg, VA	(52.63)	–	Steubenville–Weirton, OH–WV**	NA
182	Fort Lauderdale, FL	(15.96)	229	Hagerstown, MD	(53.57)	–	St. Louis, MO–IL**	NA
183	Flint, MI	(16.22)	230	Ocala, FL	(53.66)	–	Sumter, SC**	NA
184	Miami, FL	(16.97)	231	Columbia, MO	(55.26)	–	Tucson, AZ**	NA
185	Waco, TX	(18.00)	232	Bryan–College Station, TX	(59.32)	–	West Palm Beach–Boca Raton, FL**	NA
186	Atlanta, GA	(18.12)	233	Charlottesville, VA	(60.71)	–	Williamsport, PA**	NA
187	Binghamton, NY	(18.52)	234	Fort Collins–Loveland, CO	(62.96)	–	Worcester, MA–CT**	NA
188	Sioux Falls, SD	(18.75)	235	Grand Forks, ND–MN	(65.52)	–	Yolo, CA**	NA

Source: Morgan Quitno Corporation using data from U.S. Department of Justice, Federal Bureau of Investigation
"Crime in the United States 1993" (Uniform Crime Reports, December 4, 1994)
*Includes nonnegligent manslaughter.
**Not available. The metro areas of Altoona, PA and Fargo-Moorhead, ND-MN had murder rates of 0 in 1989 but had at least one murder in 1993. Calculating percent increase from zero results in an infinite number. These are shown as "NA."

13. Rapes in 1993

National Total = 104,806 Rapes*

RANK	METRO AREA	RAPES	RANK	METRO AREA	RAPES	RANK	METRO AREA	RAPES
173	Abilene, TX	80	227	Cheyenne, WY	40	14	Fort Worth-Arlington, TX	987
58	Akron, OH	307	–	Chicago, IL**	NA	48	Fresno, CA	424
205	Albany, GA	56	168	Chico-Paradise, CA	82	212	Gadsden, AL	51
–	Albany, NY**	NA	20	Cincinnati, OH-KY-IN	840	100	Gainesville, FL	173
54	Albuquerque, NM	378	128	Clarksville-Hopkinsville, TN-KY	115	107	Galveston-Texas City, TX	156
200	Alexandria, LA	59	–	Cleveland, OH**	NA	59	Gary-Hammond, IN	306
246	Altoona, PA	26	63	Colorado Springs, CO	288	229	Glens Falls, NY	39
139	Amarillo, TX	104	222	Columbia, MO	43	241	Goldsboro, NC	30
77	Anchorage, AK	212	56	Columbia, SC	321	–	Grand Forks, ND-MN**	NA
–	Ann Arbor, MI**	NA	158	Columbus, GA-AL	87	–	Grand Rapids-Muskegon-Holland, MI**	NA
199	Anniston, AL	60	18	Columbus, OH	887	211	Greeley, CO	52
218	Appleton-Oshkosh-Neenah, WI	46	71	Corpus Christi, TX	248	164	Green Bay, WI	85
202	Asheville, NC	58	253	Cumberland, MD-WV	15	45	Greensboro-Winston Salem-High Point, NC	438
195	Athens, GA	65	4	Dallas, TX	1,623	181	Greenville, NC	72
8	Atlanta, GA	1,367	251	Danbury, CT	17	46	Greenville-Spartanburg-Anderson, SC	428
94	Atlantic City, NJ	184	212	Danville, VA	51	244	Hagerstown, MD	27
89	Augusta-Aiken, GA-SC	192	73	Daytona Beach, FL	240	105	Harrisburg-Lebanon-Carlisle, PA	163
42	Austin-San Marcos, TX	502	36	Dayton-Springfield, OH	571	69	Hartford, CT	253
98	Bakersfield, CA	177	237	Decatur, AL	31	166	Hickory-Morganton, NC	83
9	Baltimore, MD	1,221	23	Denver, CO	800	64	Honolulu, HI	286
247	Bangor, ME	22	132	Des Moines, IA	113	216	Houma, LA	49
226	Barnstable-Yarmouth, MA	41	–	Detroit, MI**	NA	3	Houston, TX	2,455
65	Baton Rouge, LA	274	222	Dothan, AL	43	138	Huntington-Ashland, WV-KY-OH	106
61	Beaumont-Port Arthur, TX	300	197	Dubuque, IA	62	142	Huntsville, AL	102
168	Bellingham, WA	82	–	Duluth-Superior, MN-WI**	NA	–	Indianapolis, IN**	NA
–	Benton Harbor, MI**	NA	231	Dutchess County, NY	38	–	Jackson, MI**	NA
79	Bergen-Passaic, NJ	207	256	Eau Claire, WI	11	74	Jackson, MS	228
198	Binghamton, NY	61	55	El Paso, TX	340	220	Jackson, TN	45
43	Birmingham, AL	452	156	Elkhart-Goshen, IN	90	21	Jacksonville, FL	824
242	Bismarck, ND	29	237	Enid, OK	31	220	Jacksonville, NC	45
244	Bloomington, IN	27	139	Erie, PA	104	222	Janesville-Beloit, WI	43
122	Boise, ID	126	116	Eugene-Springfield, OR	134	104	Jersey City, NJ	164
13	Boston, MA-NH	1,061	160	Evansville-Henderson, IN-KY	86	142	Johnson City-Kingsport-Bristol, TN-VA	102
149	Boulder-Longmont, CO	98	–	Fargo-Moorhead, ND-MN**	NA	210	Johnstown, PA	54
158	Brazoria, TX	87	86	Fayetteville, NC	195	218	Joplin, MO	46
139	Bremerton, WA	104	181	Fayetteville-Springdale-Rogers, AR	72	–	Kalamazoo-Battle Creek, MI**	NA
144	Bridgeport, CT	101	180	Fitchburg-Leominster, MA	73	–	Kansas City, MO-KS**	NA
185	Brockton, MA	70	–	Flint, MI**	NA	189	Kenosha, WI	69
207	Brownsville-Harlingen-San Benito, TX	55	254	Florence, AL	14	70	Killeen-Temple, TX	249
175	Bryan-College Station, TX	77	178	Florence, SC	76	229	Kokomo, IN	39
44	Buffalo-Niagara Falls, NY	445	135	Fort Collins-Loveland, CO	108	–	La Crosse, WI-MN**	NA
95	Canton-Massillon, OH	183	40	Fort Lauderdale, FL	533	215	Lafayette, IN	50
173	Charleston, WV	80	92	Fort Myers-Cape Coral, FL	187	144	Lafayette, LA	101
59	Charleston-North Charleston, SC	306	121	Fort Pierce-Port St. Lucie, FL	128	150	Lake Charles, LA	96
212	Charlottesville, VA	51	160	Fort Smith, AR-OK	86	97	Lakeland-Winter Haven, FL	180
35	Charlotte-Gastonia-Rock Hill, NC-SC	575	234	Fort Walton Beach, FL	36	146	Lancaster, PA	99
85	Chattanooga, TN-GA	197	103	Fort Wayne, IN	166	–	Lansing-East Lansing, MI**	NA

Source: U.S. Department of Justice, Federal Bureau of Investigation
   "Crime in the United States 1993" (Uniform Crime Reports, December 4, 1994)
*Forcible rape is the carnal knowledge of a female forcibly and against her will. Assaults or attempts to commit rape by force or threat of force are included. However, statutory rape without force and other sex offenses are excluded.
**Not available.

13. Rapes in 1993 (continued)

National Total = 104,806 Rapes*

RANK	METRO AREA	RAPES	RANK	METRO AREA	RAPES	RANK	METRO AREA	RAPES
257	Laredo, TX	10	133	Olympia, WA	112	6	Seattle–Bellevue–Everett, WA	1,514
32	Las Vegas, NV–AZ	603	–	Omaha, NE**	NA	242	Sheboygan, WI	29
124	Lawrence, MA–NH	124	39	Orange County, CA	546	217	Sherman–Denison, TX	48
195	Lawton, OK	65	25	Orlando, FL	749	106	Shreveport–Bossier City, LA	160
250	Lewiston–Auburn, ME	19	234	Owensboro, KY	36	185	Sioux City, IA–NE	70
78	Lexington, KY	208	168	Panama City, FL	82	128	Sioux Falls, SD	115
157	Lincoln, NE	89	5	Philadelphia, PA–NJ	1,539	111	South Bend, IN	145
52	Little Rock–North Little Rock, AR	390	19	Phoenix–Mesa, AZ	881	96	Spokane, WA	182
116	Longview–Marshall, TX	134	189	Pine Bluff, AR	69	72	Springfield, MA	244
1	Los Angeles–Long Beach, CA	3,688	30	Pittsburgh, PA	659	150	Springfield, MO	96
62	Louisville, KY–IN	296	251	Pittsfield, MA	17	236	Stamford–Norwalk, CT	35
108	Lubbock, TX	155	146	Portland, ME	99	255	Steubenville–Weirton, OH–WV	13
168	Lynchburg, VA	82	16	Portland–Vancouver, OR–WA	928	68	Stockton–Lodi, CA	266
123	Macon, GA	125	65	Providence–Fall River–Warwick, RI–MA	274	–	St. Cloud, MN**	NA
127	Madison, WI	117	153	Provo–Orem, UT	94	233	St. Joseph, MO	37
227	Manchester, NH	40	154	Pueblo, CO	92	–	St. Louis, MO–IL**	NA
192	Mansfield, OH	67	249	Punta Gorda, FL	20	200	Sumter, SC	59
126	McAllen–Edinburg–Mission, TX	119	237	Racine, WI	31	87	Syracuse, NY	193
160	Medford–Ashland, OR	86	57	Raleigh–Durham–Chapel Hill, NC	317	51	Tacoma, WA	415
17	Memphis, TN–AR–MS	899	164	Rapid City, SD	85	75	Tallahassee, FL	219
185	Merced, CA	70	181	Reading, PA	72	11	Tampa–St. Petersburg–Clearwater, FL	1,144
12	Miami, FL	1,080	155	Redding, CA	91	193	Texarkana, TX–AR	66
113	Middlesex–Sommerset–Hunterdon, NJ	144	90	Reno, NV	191	49	Toledo, OH	421
41	Milwaukee–Waukesha, WI	515	136	Richland–Kennewick–Pasco, WA	107	114	Trenton, NJ	136
–	Minneapolis–St. Paul, MN–WI**	NA	53	Richmond–Petersburg, VA	381	47	Tucson, AZ	427
84	Mobile, AL	200	10	Riverside–San Bernardino, CA	1,170	49	Tulsa, OK	421
87	Modesto, CA	193	207	Roanoke, VA	55	175	Tuscaloosa, AL	77
80	Monmouth–Ocean, NJ	206	–	Rochester, MN**	NA	125	Tyler, TX	123
225	Monroe, LA	42	67	Rochester, NY	272	160	Utica–Rome, NY	86
131	Montgomery, AL	114	231	Rocky Mount, NC	38	83	Vallejo–Fairfield–Napa, CA	201
152	Myrtle Beach, SC	95	38	Sacramento, CA	550	93	Ventura, CA	185
136	Naples, FL	107	–	Saginaw–Bay City–Midland, MI**	NA	237	Victoria, TX	31
184	Nashua, NH	71	118	Salem, OR	132	133	Vineland–Millville–Bridgeton, NJ	112
24	Nashville, TN	769	128	Salinas, CA	115	118	Visalia–Tulare–Porterville, CA	132
82	Nassau–Suffolk, NY	203	34	Salt Lake City–Ogden, UT	586	102	Waco, TX	168
189	New Bedford, MA	69	207	San Angelo, TX	55	7	Washington, DC–MD–VA–WV	1,469
99	New Haven–Meriden, CT	174	29	San Antonio, TX	687	205	Waterbury, CT	56
146	New London–Norwich, CT–RI	99	22	San Diego, CA	803	202	Waterloo–Cedar Falls, IA	58
30	New Orleans, LA	659	37	San Francisco, CA	559	258	Wausau, WI	9
2	New York, NY	2,996	33	San Jose, CA	590	–	West Palm Beach–Boca Raton, FL**	NA
28	Newark, NJ	704	166	San Luis Obispo–Atascadero, CA	83	175	Wichita Falls, TX	77
172	Newburgh, NY–PA	81	109	Santa Barbara–Santa Maria–Lompoc, CA	149	247	Williamsport, PA	22
27	Norfolk–Va Beach–Newport News, VA–NC	728	204	Santa Cruz–Watsonville, CA	57	185	Wilmington, NC	70
15	Oakland, CA	934	80	Santa Rosa, CA	206	111	Worcester, MA–CT	145
90	Ocala, FL	191	76	Sarasota–Bradenton, FL	213	101	Yakima, WA	170
110	Odessa–Midland, TX	146	120	Savannah, GA	130	178	Yolo, CA	76
26	Oklahoma City, OK	733	114	Scranton–Wilkes-Barre–Hazleton, PA	136	193	Yuba City, CA	66

Source: U.S. Department of Justice, Federal Bureau of Investigation
      "Crime in the United States 1993" (Uniform Crime Reports, December 4, 1994)
*Forcible rape is the carnal knowledge of a female forcibly and against her will. Assaults or attempts to commit rape by force or threat of force are included. However, statutory rape without force and other sex offenses are excluded.
**Not available.

13. Rapes in 1993 (continued)

National Total = 104,806 Rapes*

RANK	METRO AREA	RAPES	RANK	METRO AREA	RAPES	RANK	METRO AREA	RAPES
1	Los Angeles–Long Beach, CA	3,688	48	Fresno, CA	424	95	Canton–Massillon, OH	183
2	New York, NY	2,996	49	Toledo, OH	421	96	Spokane, WA	182
3	Houston, TX	2,455	49	Tulsa, OK	421	97	Lakeland–Winter Haven, FL	180
4	Dallas, TX	1,623	51	Tacoma, WA	415	98	Bakersfield, CA	177
5	Philadelphia, PA–NJ	1,539	52	Little Rock–North Little Rock, AR	390	99	New Haven–Meriden, CT	174
6	Seattle–Bellevue–Everett, WA	1,514	53	Richmond–Petersburg, VA	381	100	Gainesville, FL	173
7	Washington, DC–MD–VA–WV	1,469	54	Albuquerque, NM	378	101	Yakima, WA	170
8	Atlanta, GA	1,367	55	El Paso, TX	340	102	Waco, TX	168
9	Baltimore, MD	1,221	56	Columbia, SC	321	103	Fort Wayne, IN	166
10	Riverside–San Bernardino, CA	1,170	57	Raleigh–Durham–Chapel Hill, NC	317	104	Jersey City, NJ	164
11	Tampa–St. Petersburg–Clearwater, FL	1,144	58	Akron, OH	307	105	Harrisburg–Lebanon–Carlisle, PA	163
12	Miami, FL	1,080	59	Charleston–North Charleston, SC	306	106	Shreveport–Bossier City, LA	160
13	Boston, MA–NH	1,061	59	Gary–Hammond, IN	306	107	Galveston–Texas City, TX	156
14	Fort Worth–Arlington, TX	987	61	Beaumont–Port Arthur, TX	300	108	Lubbock, TX	155
15	Oakland, CA	934	62	Louisville, KY–IN	296	109	Santa Barbara–Santa Maria–Lompoc, CA	149
16	Portland–Vancouver, OR–WA	928	63	Colorado Springs, CO	288	110	Odessa–Midland, TX	146
17	Memphis, TN–AR–MS	899	64	Honolulu, HI	286	111	South Bend, IN	145
18	Columbus, OH	887	65	Baton Rouge, LA	274	111	Worcester, MA–CT	145
19	Phoenix–Mesa, AZ	881	65	Providence–Fall River–Warwick, RI–MA	274	113	Middlesex–Sommerset–Hunterdon, NJ	144
20	Cincinnati, OH–KY–IN	840	67	Rochester, NY	272	114	Scranton–Wilkes-Barre–Hazleton, PA	136
21	Jacksonville, FL	824	68	Stockton–Lodi, CA	266	114	Trenton, NJ	136
22	San Diego, CA	803	69	Hartford, CT	253	116	Eugene–Springfield, OR	134
23	Denver, CO	800	70	Killeen–Temple, TX	249	116	Longview–Marshall, TX	134
24	Nashville, TN	769	71	Corpus Christi, TX	248	118	Salem, OR	132
25	Orlando, FL	749	72	Springfield, MA	244	118	Visalia–Tulare–Porterville, CA	132
26	Oklahoma City, OK	733	73	Daytona Beach, FL	240	120	Savannah, GA	130
27	Norfolk–Va Beach–Newport News, VA–NC	728	74	Jackson, MS	228	121	Fort Pierce–Port St. Lucie, FL	128
28	Newark, NJ	704	75	Tallahassee, FL	219	122	Boise, ID	126
29	San Antonio, TX	687	76	Sarasota–Bradenton, FL	213	123	Macon, GA	125
30	New Orleans, LA	659	77	Anchorage, AK	212	124	Lawrence, MA–NH	124
30	Pittsburgh, PA	659	78	Lexington, KY	208	125	Tyler, TX	123
32	Las Vegas, NV–AZ	603	79	Bergen–Passaic, NJ	207	126	McAllen–Edinburg–Mission, TX	119
33	San Jose, CA	590	80	Monmouth–Ocean, NJ	206	127	Madison, WI	117
34	Salt Lake City–Ogden, UT	586	80	Santa Rosa, CA	206	128	Clarksville–Hopkinsville, TN–KY	115
35	Charlotte–Gastonia–Rock Hill, NC–SC	575	82	Nassau–Suffolk, NY	203	128	Salinas, CA	115
36	Dayton–Springfield, OH	571	83	Vallejo–Fairfield–Napa, CA	201	128	Sioux Falls, SD	115
37	San Francisco, CA	559	84	Mobile, AL	200	131	Montgomery, AL	114
38	Sacramento, CA	550	85	Chattanooga, TN–GA	197	132	Des Moines, IA	113
39	Orange County, CA	546	86	Fayetteville, NC	195	133	Olympia, WA	112
40	Fort Lauderdale, FL	533	87	Modesto, CA	193	133	Vineland–Millville–Bridgeton, NJ	112
41	Milwaukee–Waukesha, WI	515	87	Syracuse, NY	193	135	Fort Collins–Loveland, CO	108
42	Austin–San Marcos, TX	502	89	Augusta–Aiken, GA–SC	192	136	Naples, FL	107
43	Birmingham, AL	452	90	Ocala, FL	191	136	Richland–Kennewick–Pasco, WA	107
44	Buffalo–Niagara Falls, NY	445	90	Reno, NV	191	138	Huntington–Ashland, WV–KY–OH	106
45	Greensboro–Winston Salem–High Point, NC	438	92	Fort Myers–Cape Coral, FL	187	139	Amarillo, TX	104
46	Greenville–Spartanburg–Anderson, SC	428	93	Ventura, CA	185	139	Bremerton, WA	104
47	Tucson, AZ	427	94	Atlantic City, NJ	184	139	Erie, PA	104

Source: U.S. Department of Justice, Federal Bureau of Investigation
  "Crime in the United States 1993" (Uniform Crime Reports, December 4, 1994)
Forcible rape is the carnal knowledge of a female forcibly and against her will. Assaults or attempts to commit rape by force or threat of force are included. However, statutory rape without force and other sex offenses are excluded.
**Not available.*

13. Rapes in 1993 (continued)

National Total = 104,806 Rapes*

RANK	METRO AREA	RAPES	RANK	METRO AREA	RAPES	RANK	METRO AREA	RAPES
142	Huntsville, AL	102	189	Kenosha, WI	69	236	Stamford–Norwalk, CT	35
142	Johnson City–Kingsport–Bristol, TN–VA	102	189	New Bedford, MA	69	237	Decatur, AL	31
144	Bridgeport, CT	101	189	Pine Bluff, AR	69	237	Enid, OK	31
144	Lafayette, LA	101	192	Mansfield, OH	67	237	Racine, WI	31
146	Lancaster, PA	99	193	Texarkana, TX–AR	66	237	Victoria, TX	31
146	New London–Norwich, CT–RI	99	193	Yuba City, CA	66	241	Goldsboro, NC	30
146	Portland, ME	99	195	Athens, GA	65	242	Bismarck, ND	29
149	Boulder–Longmont, CO	98	195	Lawton, OK	65	242	Sheboygan, WI	29
150	Lake Charles, LA	96	197	Dubuque, IA	62	244	Bloomington, IN	27
150	Springfield, MO	96	198	Binghamton, NY	61	244	Hagerstown, MD	27
152	Myrtle Beach, SC	95	199	Anniston, AL	60	246	Altoona, PA	26
153	Provo–Orem, UT	94	200	Alexandria, LA	59	247	Bangor, ME	22
154	Pueblo, CO	92	200	Sumter, SC	59	247	Williamsport, PA	22
155	Redding, CA	91	202	Asheville, NC	58	249	Punta Gorda, FL	20
156	Elkhart–Goshen, IN	90	202	Waterloo–Cedar Falls, IA	58	250	Lewiston–Auburn, ME	19
157	Lincoln, NE	89	204	Santa Cruz–Watsonville, CA	57	251	Danbury, CT	17
158	Brazoria, TX	87	205	Albany, GA	56	251	Pittsfield, MA	17
158	Columbus, GA–AL	87	205	Waterbury, CT	56	253	Cumberland, MD–WV	15
160	Evansville–Henderson, IN–KY	86	207	Brownsville–Harlingen–San Benito, TX	55	254	Florence, AL	14
160	Fort Smith, AR–OK	86	207	Roanoke, VA	55	255	Steubenville–Weirton, OH–WV	13
160	Medford–Ashland, OR	86	207	San Angelo, TX	55	256	Eau Claire, WI	11
160	Utica–Rome, NY	86	210	Johnstown, PA	54	257	Laredo, TX	10
164	Green Bay, WI	85	211	Greeley, CO	52	258	Wausau, WI	9
164	Rapid City, SD	85	212	Charlottesville, VA	51	–	Albany, NY**	NA
166	Hickory–Morganton, NC	83	212	Danville, VA	51	–	Ann Arbor, MI**	NA
166	San Luis Obispo–Atascadero, CA	83	212	Gadsden, AL	51	–	Benton Harbor, MI**	NA
168	Bellingham, WA	82	215	Lafayette, IN	50	–	Chicago, IL**	NA
168	Chico–Paradise, CA	82	216	Houma, LA	49	–	Cleveland, OH**	NA
168	Lynchburg, VA	82	217	Sherman–Denison, TX	48	–	Detroit, MI**	NA
168	Panama City, FL	82	218	Appleton–Oshkosh–Neenah, WI	46	–	Duluth–Superior, MN–WI**	NA
172	Newburgh, NY–PA	81	218	Joplin, MO	46	–	Fargo–Moorhead, ND–MN**	NA
173	Abilene, TX	80	220	Jackson, TN	45	–	Flint, MI**	NA
173	Charleston, WV	80	220	Jacksonville, NC	45	–	Grand Forks, ND–MN**	NA
175	Bryan–College Station, TX	77	222	Columbia, MO	43	–	Grand Rapids–Muskegon–Holland, MI**	NA
175	Tuscaloosa, AL	77	222	Dothan, AL	43	–	Indianapolis, IN**	NA
175	Wichita Falls, TX	77	222	Janesville–Beloit, WI	43	–	Jackson, MI**	NA
178	Florence, SC	76	225	Monroe, LA	42	–	Kalamazoo–Battle Creek, MI**	NA
178	Yolo, CA	76	226	Barnstable–Yarmouth, MA	41	–	Kansas City, MO–KS**	NA
180	Fitchburg–Leominster, MA	73	227	Cheyenne, WY	40	–	La Crosse, WI–MN**	NA
181	Fayetteville–Springdale–Rogers, AR	72	227	Manchester, NH	40	–	Lansing–East Lansing, MI**	NA
181	Greenville, NC	72	229	Glens Falls, NY	39	–	Minneapolis–St. Paul, MN–WI**	NA
181	Reading, PA	72	229	Kokomo, IN	39	–	Omaha, NE**	NA
184	Nashua, NH	71	231	Dutchess County, NY	38	–	Rochester, MN**	NA
185	Brockton, MA	70	231	Rocky Mount, NC	38	–	Saginaw–Bay City–Midland, MI**	NA
185	Merced, CA	70	233	St. Joseph, MO	37	–	St. Cloud, MN**	NA
185	Sioux City, IA–NE	70	234	Fort Walton Beach, FL	36	–	St. Louis, MO–IL**	NA
185	Wilmington, NC	70	234	Owensboro, KY	36	–	West Palm Beach–Boca Raton, FL**	NA

Source: U.S. Department of Justice, Federal Bureau of Investigation
    "Crime in the United States 1993" (Uniform Crime Reports, December 4, 1994)
*Forcible rape is the carnal knowledge of a female forcibly and against her will. Assaults or attempts to commit rape by force or threat of force are included. However, statutory rape without force and other sex offenses are excluded.
**Not available.

14. Rape Rate in 1993

National Rate = 40.6 Rapes per 100,000 Population*

RANK	METRO AREA	RATE	RANK	METRO AREA	RATE	RANK	METRO AREA	RATE
33	Abilene, TX	65.1	85	Cheyenne, WY	52.0	36	Fort Worth-Arlington, TX	64.1
111	Akron, OH	46.0	–	Chicago, IL**	NA	83	Fresno, CA	52.2
104	Albany, GA	47.6	121	Chico-Paradise, CA	43.1	91	Gadsden, AL	50.7
–	Albany, NY**	NA	73	Cincinnati, OH-KY-IN	53.5	4	Gainesville, FL	90.0
47	Albuquerque, NM	60.0	38	Clarksville-Hopkinsville, TN-KY	63.7	28	Galveston-Texas City, TX	67.1
117	Alexandria, LA	45.0	–	Cleveland, OH**	NA	99	Gary-Hammond, IN	49.1
239	Altoona, PA	19.7	30	Colorado Springs, CO	66.4	182	Glens Falls, NY	32.1
77	Amarillo, TX	53.2	165	Columbia, MO	36.5	210	Goldsboro, NC	27.4
9	Anchorage, AK	84.6	27	Columbia, SC	67.2	–	Grand Forks, ND-MN**	NA
–	Ann Arbor, MI**	NA	186	Columbus, GA-AL	31.3	–	Grand Rapids-Muskegon-Holland, MI**	NA
89	Anniston, AL	50.9	40	Columbus, OH	63.3	159	Greeley, CO	37.2
249	Appleton-Oshkosh-Neenah, WI	13.9	28	Corpus Christi, TX	67.1	134	Green Bay, WI	41.8
203	Asheville, NC	28.9	247	Cumberland, MD-WV	14.6	143	Greensboro-Winston Salem-High Point, NC	40.0
128	Athens, GA	42.1	50	Dallas, TX	59.0	35	Greenville, NC	64.2
125	Atlanta, GA	42.4	252	Danbury, CT	10.5	96	Greenville-Spartanburg-Anderson, SC	49.6
62	Atlantic City, NJ	56.0	111	Danville, VA	46.0	235	Hagerstown, MD	21.3
124	Augusta-Aiken, GA-SC	42.5	61	Daytona Beach, FL	56.1	216	Harrisburg-Lebanon-Carlisle, PA	26.9
69	Austin-San Marcos, TX	54.6	50	Dayton-Springfield, OH	59.0	223	Hartford, CT	24.0
201	Bakersfield, CA	29.8	229	Decatur, AL	22.7	212	Hickory-Morganton, NC	27.3
95	Baltimore, MD	49.7	113	Denver, CO	45.5	179	Honolulu, HI	32.7
181	Bangor, ME	32.5	208	Des Moines, IA	27.7	218	Houma, LA	26.2
199	Barnstable-Yarmouth, MA	29.9	–	Detroit, MI**	NA	24	Houston, TX	68.2
94	Baton Rouge, LA	50.0	183	Dothan, AL	31.9	174	Huntington-Ashland, WV-KY-OH	33.4
13	Beaumont-Port Arthur, TX	79.6	21	Dubuque, IA	70.8	179	Huntsville, AL	32.7
53	Bellingham, WA	58.2	–	Duluth-Superior, MN-WI**	NA	–	Indianapolis, IN**	NA
–	Benton Harbor, MI**	NA	248	Dutchess County, NY	14.4	–	Jackson, MI**	NA
246	Bergen-Passaic, NJ	15.9	255	Eau Claire, WI	7.8	65	Jackson, MS	55.7
228	Binghamton, NY	22.8	78	El Paso, TX	53.1	67	Jackson, TN	55.3
85	Birmingham, AL	52.0	63	Elkhart-Goshen, IN	55.9	8	Jacksonville, FL	85.3
173	Bismarck, ND	33.6	69	Enid, OK	54.6	193	Jacksonville, NC	30.6
222	Bloomington, IN	24.1	160	Erie, PA	37.0	199	Janesville-Beloit, WI	29.9
152	Boise, ID	38.2	116	Eugene-Springfield, OR	45.1	202	Jersey City, NJ	29.3
186	Boston, MA-NH	31.3	197	Evansville-Henderson, IN-KY	30.1	231	Johnson City-Kingsport-Bristol, TN-VA	22.6
143	Boulder-Longmont, CO	40.0	–	Fargo-Moorhead, ND-MN**	NA	232	Johnstown, PA	22.3
130	Brazoria, TX	41.9	22	Fayetteville, NC	69.2	177	Joplin, MO	33.2
101	Bremerton, WA	48.3	184	Fayetteville-Springdale-Rogers, AR	31.5	–	Kalamazoo-Battle Creek, MI**	NA
232	Bridgeport, CT	22.3	76	Fitchburg-Leominster, MA	53.3	–	Kansas City, MO-KS**	NA
207	Brockton, MA	28.4	–	Flint, MI**	NA	88	Kenosha, WI	51.0
240	Brownsville-Harlingen-San Benito, TX	19.4	253	Florence, AL	10.3	2	Killeen-Temple, TX	95.8
44	Bryan-College Station, TX	60.3	39	Florence, SC	63.4	150	Kokomo, IN	39.2
160	Buffalo-Niagara Falls, NY	37.0	79	Fort Collins-Loveland, CO	53.0	–	La Crosse, WI-MN**	NA
113	Canton-Massillon, OH	45.5	139	Fort Lauderdale, FL	40.4	198	Lafayette, IN	30.0
184	Charleston, WV	31.5	81	Fort Myers-Cape Coral, FL	52.4	206	Lafayette, LA	28.5
54	Charleston-North Charleston, SC	57.3	106	Fort Pierce-Port St. Lucie, FL	47.5	64	Lake Charles, LA	55.8
157	Charlottesville, VA	37.4	107	Fort Smith, AR-OK	47.1	126	Lakeland-Winter Haven, FL	42.3
108	Charlotte-Gastonia-Rock Hill, NC-SC	46.7	226	Fort Walton Beach, FL	23.1	229	Lancaster, PA	22.7
117	Chattanooga, TN-GA	45.0	167	Fort Wayne, IN	35.5	–	Lansing-East Lansing, MI**	NA

Source: U.S. Department of Justice, Federal Bureau of Investigation
   "Crime in the United States 1993" (Uniform Crime Reports, December 4, 1994)
*Forcible rape is the carnal knowledge of a female forcibly and against her will. Assaults or attempts to commit rape by force or threat of force are included. However, statutory rape without force and other sex offenses are excluded.
**Not available.

14. Rape Rate in 1993 (continued)

National Rate = 40.6 Rapes per 100,000 Population*

RANK	METRO AREA	RATE	RANK	METRO AREA	RATE	RANK	METRO AREA	RATE
257	Laredo, TX	6.6	41	Olympia, WA	62.1	19	Seattle–Bellevue–Everett, WA	72.9
48	Las Vegas, NV–AZ	59.8	–	Omaha, NE**	NA	210	Sheboygan, WI	27.4
130	Lawrence, MA–NH	41.9	234	Orange County, CA	21.8	97	Sherman–Denison, TX	49.5
73	Lawton, OK	53.5	59	Orlando, FL	56.6	123	Shreveport–Bossier City, LA	42.6
241	Lewiston–Auburn, ME	18.3	142	Owensboro, KY	40.2	49	Sioux City, IA–NE	59.5
57	Lexington, KY	57.1	44	Panama City, FL	60.3	15	Sioux Falls, SD	77.5
139	Lincoln, NE	40.4	189	Philadelphia, PA–NJ	31.0	54	South Bend, IN	57.3
18	Little Rock–North Little Rock, AR	73.3	162	Phoenix–Mesa, AZ	36.8	108	Spokane, WA	46.7
31	Longview–Marshall, TX	65.7	12	Pine Bluff, AR	79.9	115	Springfield, MA	45.2
141	Los Angeles–Long Beach, CA	40.3	214	Pittsburgh, PA	27.2	170	Springfield, MO	34.5
195	Louisville, KY–IN	30.3	243	Pittsfield, MA	17.3	251	Stamford–Norwalk, CT	10.6
26	Lubbock, TX	67.9	126	Portland, ME	42.3	254	Steubenville–Weirton, OH–WV	9.1
138	Lynchburg, VA	40.7	59	Portland–Vancouver, OR–WA	56.6	83	Stockton–Lodi, CA	52.2
137	Macon, GA	41.0	205	Providence–Fall River–Warwick, RI–MA	28.6	–	St. Cloud, MN**	NA
188	Madison, WI	31.1	176	Provo–Orem, UT	33.3	156	St. Joseph, MO	37.5
223	Manchester, NH	24.0	20	Pueblo, CO	72.2	–	St. Louis, MO–IL**	NA
154	Mansfield, OH	37.9	245	Punta Gorda, FL	16.5	66	Sumter, SC	55.4
208	McAllen–Edinburg–Mission, TX	27.7	244	Racine, WI	17.1	219	Syracuse, NY	25.5
68	Medford–Ashland, OR	54.7	171	Raleigh–Durham–Chapel Hill, NC	34.3	32	Tacoma, WA	65.5
7	Memphis, TN–AR–MS	85.8	1	Rapid City, SD	99.0	5	Tallahassee, FL	88.0
164	Merced, CA	36.6	237	Reading, PA	20.9	73	Tampa–St. Petersburg–Clearwater, FL	53.5
79	Miami, FL	53.0	56	Redding, CA	57.2	72	Texarkana, TX–AR	53.6
250	Middlesex–Sommerset–Hunterdon, NJ	13.7	23	Reno, NV	68.4	25	Toledo, OH	68.0
168	Milwaukee–Waukesha, WI	35.4	33	Richland–Kennewick–Pasco, WA	65.1	135	Trenton, NJ	41.2
–	Minneapolis–St. Paul, MN–WI**	NA	130	Richmond–Petersburg, VA	41.9	46	Tucson, AZ	60.2
145	Mobile, AL	39.9	135	Riverside–San Bernardino, CA	41.2	57	Tulsa, OK	57.1
101	Modesto, CA	48.3	225	Roanoke, VA	23.9	97	Tuscaloosa, AL	49.5
238	Monmouth–Ocean, NJ	20.4	–	Rochester, MN**	NA	14	Tyler, TX	78.1
203	Monroe, LA	28.9	220	Rochester, NY	25.0	215	Utica–Rome, NY	27.1
162	Montgomery, AL	36.8	212	Rocky Mount, NC	27.3	130	Vallejo–Fairfield–Napa, CA	41.9
42	Myrtle Beach, SC	61.7	151	Sacramento, CA	38.4	217	Ventura, CA	26.7
37	Naples, FL	64.0	–	Saginaw–Bay City–Midland, MI**	NA	146	Victoria, TX	39.5
120	Nashua, NH	44.3	119	Salem, OR	44.4	11	Vineland–Millville–Bridgeton, NJ	80.3
16	Nashville, TN	74.0	190	Salinas, CA	30.9	146	Visalia–Tulare–Porterville, CA	39.5
256	Nassau–Suffolk, NY	7.7	92	Salt Lake City–Ogden, UT	50.6	6	Waco, TX	86.0
146	New Bedford, MA	39.5	71	San Angelo, TX	54.4	174	Washington, DC–MD–VA–WV	33.4
190	New Haven–Meriden, CT	30.9	100	San Antonio, TX	48.9	196	Waterbury, CT	30.2
178	New London–Norwich, CT–RI	32.9	193	San Diego, CA	30.6	110	Waterloo–Cedar Falls, IA	46.1
82	New Orleans, LA	52.3	172	San Francisco, CA	34.0	258	Wausau, WI	6.5
169	New York, NY	34.8	152	San Jose, CA	38.2	–	West Palm Beach–Boca Raton, FL**	NA
166	Newark, NJ	36.3	158	San Luis Obispo–Atascadero, CA	37.3	50	Wichita Falls, TX	59.0
226	Newburgh, NY–PA	23.1	149	Santa Barbara–Santa Maria–Lompoc, CA	39.3	242	Williamsport, PA	18.2
103	Norfolk–Va Beach–Newport News, VA–NC	47.9	221	Santa Cruz–Watsonville, CA	24.4	155	Wilmington, NC	37.8
122	Oakland, CA	43.0	89	Santa Rosa, CA	50.9	192	Worcester, MA–CT	30.8
3	Ocala, FL	90.5	128	Sarasota–Bradenton, FL	42.1	10	Yakima, WA	84.0
43	Odessa–Midland, TX	61.2	104	Savannah, GA	47.6	85	Yolo, CA	52.0
17	Oklahoma City, OK	73.9	236	Scranton–Wilkes-Barre–Hazleton, PA	21.2	93	Yuba City, CA	50.1

Source: U.S. Department of Justice, Federal Bureau of Investigation
"Crime in the United States 1993" (Uniform Crime Reports, December 4, 1994)
*Forcible rape is the carnal knowledge of a female forcibly and against her will. Assaults or attempts to commit rape by force or threat of force are included. However, statutory rape without force and other sex offenses are excluded.
**Not available.

14. Rape Rate in 1993 (continued)

National Rate = 40.6 Rapes per 100,000 Population*

RANK	METRO AREA	RATE	RANK	METRO AREA	RATE	RANK	METRO AREA	RATE
1	Rapid City, SD	99.0	48	Las Vegas, NV–AZ	59.8	95	Baltimore, MD	49.7
2	Killeen-Temple, TX	95.8	49	Sioux City, IA–NE	59.5	96	Greenville-Spartanburg-Anderson, SC	49.6
3	Ocala, FL	90.5	50	Dallas, TX	59.0	97	Sherman-Denison, TX	49.5
4	Gainesville, FL	90.0	50	Dayton-Springfield, OH	59.0	97	Tuscaloosa, AL	49.5
5	Tallahassee, FL	88.0	50	Wichita Falls, TX	59.0	99	Gary-Hammond, IN	49.1
6	Waco, TX	86.0	53	Bellingham, WA	58.2	100	San Antonio, TX	48.9
7	Memphis, TN–AR–MS	85.8	54	Charleston-North Charleston, SC	57.3	101	Bremerton, WA	48.3
8	Jacksonville, FL	85.3	54	South Bend, IN	57.3	101	Modesto, CA	48.3
9	Anchorage, AK	84.6	56	Redding, CA	57.2	103	Norfolk-Va Beach-Newport News, VA–NC	47.9
10	Yakima, WA	84.0	57	Lexington, KY	57.1	104	Albany, GA	47.6
11	Vineland-Millville-Bridgeton, NJ	80.3	57	Tulsa, OK	57.1	104	Savannah, GA	47.6
12	Pine Bluff, AR	79.9	59	Orlando, FL	56.6	106	Fort Pierce-Port St. Lucie, FL	47.5
13	Beaumont-Port Arthur, TX	79.6	59	Portland-Vancouver, OR–WA	56.6	107	Fort Smith, AR–OK	47.1
14	Tyler, TX	78.1	61	Daytona Beach, FL	56.1	108	Charlotte-Gastonia-Rock Hill, NC–SC	46.7
15	Sioux Falls, SD	77.5	62	Atlantic City, NJ	56.0	108	Spokane, WA	46.7
16	Nashville, TN	74.0	63	Elkhart-Goshen, IN	55.9	110	Waterloo-Cedar Falls, IA	46.1
17	Oklahoma City, OK	73.9	64	Lake Charles, LA	55.8	111	Akron, OH	46.0
18	Little Rock-North Little Rock, AR	73.3	65	Jackson, MS	55.7	111	Danville, VA	46.0
19	Seattle-Bellevue-Everett, WA	72.9	66	Sumter, SC	55.4	113	Canton-Massillon, OH	45.5
20	Pueblo, CO	72.2	67	Jackson, TN	55.3	113	Denver, CO	45.5
21	Dubuque, IA	70.8	68	Medford-Ashland, OR	54.7	115	Springfield, MA	45.2
22	Fayetteville, NC	69.2	69	Austin-San Marcos, TX	54.6	116	Eugene-Springfield, OR	45.1
23	Reno, NV	68.4	69	Enid, OK	54.6	117	Alexandria, LA	45.0
24	Houston, TX	68.2	71	San Angelo, TX	54.4	117	Chattanooga, TN–GA	45.0
25	Toledo, OH	68.0	72	Texarkana, TX–AR	53.6	119	Salem, OR	44.4
26	Lubbock, TX	67.9	73	Cincinnati, OH–KY–IN	53.5	120	Nashua, NH	44.3
27	Columbia, SC	67.2	73	Lawton, OK	53.5	121	Chico-Paradise, CA	43.1
28	Corpus Christi, TX	67.1	73	Tampa-St. Petersburg-Clearwater, FL	53.5	122	Oakland, CA	43.0
28	Galveston-Texas City, TX	67.1	76	Fitchburg-Leominster, MA	53.3	123	Shreveport-Bossier City, LA	42.6
30	Colorado Springs, CO	66.4	77	Amarillo, TX	53.2	124	Augusta-Aiken, GA–SC	42.5
31	Longview-Marshall, TX	65.7	78	El Paso, TX	53.1	125	Atlanta, GA	42.4
32	Tacoma, WA	65.5	79	Fort Collins-Loveland, CO	53.0	126	Lakeland-Winter Haven, FL	42.3
33	Abilene, TX	65.1	79	Miami, FL	53.0	126	Portland, ME	42.3
33	Richland-Kennewick-Pasco, WA	65.1	81	Fort Myers-Cape Coral, FL	52.4	128	Athens, GA	42.1
35	Greenville, NC	64.2	82	New Orleans, LA	52.3	128	Sarasota-Bradenton, FL	42.1
36	Fort Worth-Arlington, TX	64.1	83	Fresno, CA	52.2	130	Brazoria, TX	41.9
37	Naples, FL	64.0	83	Stockton-Lodi, CA	52.2	130	Lawrence, MA–NH	41.9
38	Clarksville-Hopkinsville, TN–KY	63.7	85	Birmingham, AL	52.0	130	Richmond-Petersburg, VA	41.9
39	Florence, SC	63.4	85	Cheyenne, WY	52.0	130	Vallejo-Fairfield-Napa, CA	41.9
40	Columbus, OH	63.3	85	Yolo, CA	52.0	134	Green Bay, WI	41.8
41	Olympia, WA	62.1	88	Kenosha, WI	51.0	135	Riverside-San Bernardino, CA	41.2
42	Myrtle Beach, SC	61.7	89	Anniston, AL	50.9	135	Trenton, NJ	41.2
43	Odessa-Midland, TX	61.2	89	Santa Rosa, CA	50.9	137	Macon, GA	41.0
44	Bryan-College Station, TX	60.3	91	Gadsden, AL	50.7	138	Lynchburg, VA	40.7
44	Panama City, FL	60.3	92	Salt Lake City-Ogden, UT	50.6	139	Fort Lauderdale, FL	40.4
46	Tucson, AZ	60.2	93	Yuba City, CA	50.1	139	Lincoln, NE	40.4
47	Albuquerque, NM	60.0	94	Baton Rouge, LA	50.0	141	Los Angeles-Long Beach, CA	40.3

Source: U.S. Department of Justice, Federal Bureau of Investigation
"Crime in the United States 1993" (Uniform Crime Reports, December 4, 1994)
*Forcible rape is the carnal knowledge of a female forcibly and against her will. Assaults or attempts to commit rape by force or threat of force are included. However, statutory rape without force and other sex offenses are excluded.
**Not available.*

14. Rape Rate in 1993 (continued)

National Rate = 40.6 Rapes per 100,000 Population*

RANK	METRO AREA	RATE	RANK	METRO AREA	RATE	RANK	METRO AREA	RATE
142	Owensboro, KY	40.2	189	Philadelphia, PA–NJ	31.0	236	Scranton–Wilkes-Barre–Hazleton, PA	21.2
143	Boulder–Longmont, CO	40.0	190	New Haven–Meriden, CT	30.9	237	Reading, PA	20.9
143	Greensboro–Winston Salem–High Point, NC	40.0	190	Salinas, CA	30.9	238	Monmouth–Ocean, NJ	20.4
145	Mobile, AL	39.9	192	Worcester, MA–CT	30.8	239	Altoona, PA	19.7
146	New Bedford, MA	39.5	193	Jacksonville, NC	30.6	240	Brownsville–Harlingen–San Benito, TX	19.4
146	Victoria, TX	39.5	193	San Diego, CA	30.6	241	Lewiston–Auburn, ME	18.3
146	Visalia–Tulare–Porterville, CA	39.5	195	Louisville, KY–IN	30.3	242	Williamsport, PA	18.2
149	Santa Barbara–Santa Maria–Lompoc, CA	39.3	196	Waterbury, CT	30.2	243	Pittsfield, MA	17.3
150	Kokomo, IN	39.2	197	Evansville–Henderson, IN–KY	30.1	244	Racine, WI	17.1
151	Sacramento, CA	38.4	198	Lafayette, IN	30.0	245	Punta Gorda, FL	16.5
152	Boise, ID	38.2	199	Barnstable–Yarmouth, MA	29.9	246	Bergen–Passaic, NJ	15.9
152	San Jose, CA	38.2	199	Janesville–Beloit, WI	29.9	247	Cumberland, MD–WV	14.6
154	Mansfield, OH	37.9	201	Bakersfield, CA	29.8	248	Dutchess County, NY	14.4
155	Wilmington, NC	37.8	202	Jersey City, NJ	29.3	249	Appleton–Oshkosh–Neenah, WI	13.9
156	St. Joseph, MO	37.5	203	Asheville, NC	28.9	250	Middlesex–Sommerset–Hunterdon, NJ	13.7
157	Charlottesville, VA	37.4	203	Monroe, LA	28.9	251	Stamford–Norwalk, CT	10.6
158	San Luis Obispo–Atascadero, CA	37.3	205	Providence–Fall River–Warwick, RI–MA	28.6	252	Danbury, CT	10.5
159	Greeley, CO	37.2	206	Lafayette, LA	28.5	253	Florence, AL	10.3
160	Buffalo–Niagara Falls, NY	37.0	207	Brockton, MA	28.4	254	Steubenville–Weirton, OH–WV	9.1
160	Erie, PA	37.0	208	Des Moines, IA	27.7	255	Eau Claire, WI	7.8
162	Montgomery, AL	36.8	208	McAllen–Edinburg–Mission, TX	27.7	256	Nassau–Suffolk, NY	7.7
162	Phoenix–Mesa, AZ	36.8	210	Goldsboro, NC	27.4	257	Laredo, TX	6.6
164	Merced, CA	36.6	210	Sheboygan, WI	27.4	258	Wausau, WI	6.5
165	Columbia, MO	36.5	212	Hickory–Morganton, NC	27.3	–	Albany, NY**	NA
166	Newark, NJ	36.3	212	Rocky Mount, NC	27.3	–	Ann Arbor, MI**	NA
167	Fort Wayne, IN	35.5	214	Pittsburgh, PA	27.2	–	Benton Harbor, MI**	NA
168	Milwaukee–Waukesha, WI	35.4	215	Utica–Rome, NY	27.1	–	Chicago, IL**	NA
169	New York, NY	34.8	216	Harrisburg–Lebanon–Carlisle, PA	26.9	–	Cleveland, OH**	NA
170	Springfield, MO	34.5	217	Ventura, CA	26.7	–	Detroit, MI**	NA
171	Raleigh–Durham–Chapel Hill, NC	34.3	218	Houma, LA	26.2	–	Duluth–Superior, MN–WI**	NA
172	San Francisco, CA	34.0	219	Syracuse, NY	25.5	–	Fargo–Moorhead, ND–MN**	NA
173	Bismarck, ND	33.6	220	Rochester, NY	25.0	–	Flint, MI**	NA
174	Huntington–Ashland, WV–KY–OH	33.4	221	Santa Cruz–Watsonville, CA	24.4	–	Grand Forks, ND–MN**	NA
174	Washington, DC–MD–VA–WV	33.4	222	Bloomington, IN	24.1	–	Grand Rapids–Muskegon–Holland, MI**	NA
176	Provo–Orem, UT	33.3	223	Hartford, CT	24.0	–	Indianapolis, IN**	NA
177	Joplin, MO	33.2	223	Manchester, NH	24.0	–	Jackson, MI**	NA
178	New London–Norwich, CT–RI	32.9	225	Roanoke, VA	23.9	–	Kalamazoo–Battle Creek, MI**	NA
179	Honolulu, HI	32.7	226	Fort Walton Beach, FL	23.1	–	Kansas City, MO–KS**	NA
179	Huntsville, AL	32.7	226	Newburgh, NY–PA	23.1	–	La Crosse, WI–MN**	NA
181	Bangor, ME	32.5	228	Binghamton, NY	22.8	–	Lansing–East Lansing, MI**	NA
182	Glens Falls, NY	32.1	229	Decatur, AL	22.7	–	Minneapolis–St. Paul, MN–WI**	NA
183	Dothan, AL	31.9	229	Lancaster, PA	22.7	–	Omaha, NE**	NA
184	Charleston, WV	31.5	231	Johnson City–Kingsport–Bristol, TN–VA	22.6	–	Rochester, MN**	NA
184	Fayetteville–Springdale–Rogers, AR	31.5	232	Bridgeport, CT	22.3	–	Saginaw–Bay City–Midland, MI**	NA
186	Boston, MA–NH	31.3	232	Johnstown, PA	22.3	–	St. Cloud, MN**	NA
186	Columbus, GA–AL	31.3	234	Orange County, CA	21.8	–	St. Louis, MO–IL**	NA
188	Madison, WI	31.1	235	Hagerstown, MD	21.3	–	West Palm Beach–Boca Raton, FL**	NA

Source: U.S. Department of Justice, Federal Bureau of Investigation
   "Crime in the United States 1993" (Uniform Crime Reports, December 4, 1994)
Forcible rape is the carnal knowledge of a female forcibly and against her will. Assaults or attempts to commit rape by force or threat of force are included. However, statutory rape without force and other sex offenses are excluded.
**Not available.*

Alpha Order – Metro

15. Percent Change in Rape Rate: 1992 to 1993

National Percent Change = 5.1% Decrease*

RANK	METRO AREA	% CHANGE	RANK	METRO AREA	% CHANGE	RANK	METRO AREA	% CHANGE
138	Abilene, TX	(9.08)	156	Cheyenne, WY	(11.11)	117	Fort Worth–Arlington, TX	(5.18)
116	Akron, OH	(5.15)	–	Chicago, IL**	NA	95	Fresno, CA	(2.43)
230	Albany, GA	(39.97)	181	Chico–Paradise, CA	(15.16)	15	Gadsden, AL	35.56
–	Albany, NY**	NA	139	Cincinnati, OH–KY–IN	(9.17)	23	Gainesville, FL	29.12
71	Albuquerque, NM	1.35	6	Clarksville–Hopkinsville, TN–KY	65.03	98	Galveston–Texas City, TX	(2.75)
158	Alexandria, LA	(11.59)	–	Cleveland, OH**	NA	103	Gary–Hammond, IN	(3.16)
232	Altoona, PA	(42.23)	53	Colorado Springs, CO	9.75	13	Glens Falls, NY	36.60
114	Amarillo, TX	(4.83)	194	Columbia, MO	(18.34)	69	Goldsboro, NC	2.24
198	Anchorage, AK	(19.20)	185	Columbia, SC	(16.42)	–	Grand Forks, ND–MN**	NA
–	Ann Arbor, MI**	NA	105	Columbus, GA–AL	(3.69)	–	Grand Rapids–Muskegon–Holland, MI**	NA
108	Anniston, AL	(3.96)	149	Columbus, OH	(10.85)	187	Greeley, CO	(16.78)
64	Appleton–Oshkosh–Neenah, WI	3.73	8	Corpus Christi, TX	48.12	19	Green Bay, WI	32.28
51	Asheville, NC	10.31	152	Cumberland, MD–WV	(10.98)	99	Greensboro–Winston Salem–High Point, NC	(2.91)
41	Athens, GA	13.48	132	Dallas, TX	(7.96)	16	Greenville, NC	35.16
224	Atlanta, GA	(28.86)	75	Danbury, CT	0.00	83	Greenville–Spartanburg–Anderson, SC	(1.39)
91	Atlantic City, NJ	(2.10)	2	Danville, VA	156.98	161	Hagerstown, MD	(11.62)
140	Augusta–Aiken, GA–SC	(9.19)	148	Daytona Beach, FL	(10.81)	80	Harrisburg–Lebanon–Carlisle, PA	(0.74)
107	Austin–San Marcos, TX	(3.87)	141	Dayton–Springfield, OH	(9.37)	195	Hartford, CT	(18.64)
199	Bakersfield, CA	(21.78)	31	Decatur, AL	21.39	111	Hickory–Morganton, NC	(4.21)
130	Baltimore, MD	(7.79)	166	Denver, CO	(12.33)	165	Honolulu, HI	(12.10)
14	Bangor, ME	35.98	150	Des Moines, IA	(10.93)	223	Houma, LA	(28.42)
90	Barnstable–Yarmouth, MA	(1.97)	–	Detroit, MI**	NA	33	Houston, TX	18.40
125	Baton Rouge, LA	(6.72)	208	Dothan, AL	(23.68)	229	Huntington–Ashland, WV–KY–OH	(38.60)
20	Beaumont–Port Arthur, TX	31.14	1	Dubuque, IA	264.95	121	Huntsville, AL	(5.76)
209	Bellingham, WA	(23.82)	–	Duluth–Superior, MN–WI**	NA	–	Indianapolis, IN**	NA
–	Benton Harbor, MI**	NA	–	Dutchess County, NY**	NA	–	Jackson, MI**	NA
–	Bergen–Passaic, NJ**	NA	52	Eau Claire, WI	9.86	158	Jackson, MS	(11.59)
57	Binghamton, NY	7.04	65	El Paso, TX	3.71	215	Jackson, TN	(25.97)
179	Birmingham, AL	(14.75)	29	Elkhart–Goshen, IN	23.95	109	Jacksonville, FL	(4.05)
18	Bismarck, ND	33.33	82	Enid, OK	(1.09)	47	Jacksonville, NC	12.50
197	Bloomington, IN	(18.86)	155	Erie, PA	(11.06)	38	Janesville–Beloit, WI	15.44
187	Boise, ID	(16.78)	55	Eugene–Springfield, OR	8.67	–	Jersey City, NJ**	NA
–	Boston, MA–NH**	NA	124	Evansville–Henderson, IN–KY	(5.94)	154	Johnson City–Kingsport–Bristol, TN–VA	(11.02)
75	Boulder–Longmont, CO	0.00	–	Fargo–Moorhead, ND–MN**	NA	43	Johnstown, PA	13.20
17	Brazoria, TX	34.73	104	Fayetteville, NC	(3.35)	–	Joplin, MO**	NA
210	Bremerton, WA	(24.41)	5	Fayetteville–Springdale–Rogers, AR	83.14	–	Kalamazoo–Battle Creek, MI**	NA
81	Bridgeport, CT	(0.89)	–	Fitchburg–Leominster, MA**	NA	–	Kansas City, MO–KS**	NA
164	Brockton, MA	(12.07)	–	Flint, MI**	NA	42	Kenosha, WI	13.33
184	Brownsville–Harlingen–San Benito, TX	(15.28)	218	Florence, AL	(26.95)	56	Killeen–Temple, TX	8.62
120	Bryan–College Station, TX	(5.63)	201	Florence, SC	(22.02)	35	Kokomo, IN	17.72
–	Buffalo–Niagara Falls, NY**	NA	–	Fort Collins–Loveland, CO**	NA	–	La Crosse, WI–MN**	NA
72	Canton–Massillon, OH	1.11	67	Fort Lauderdale, FL	3.32	28	Lafayette, IN	23.97
48	Charleston, WV	12.10	45	Fort Myers–Cape Coral, FL	12.93	202	Lafayette, LA	(22.55)
118	Charleston–North Charleston, SC	(5.29)	21	Fort Pierce–Port St. Lucie, FL	29.43	–	Lake Charles, LA**	NA
30	Charlottesville, VA	23.43	27	Fort Smith, AR–OK	24.27	182	Lakeland–Winter Haven, FL	(15.23)
113	Charlotte–Gastonia–Rock Hill, NC–SC	(4.69)	4	Fort Walton Beach, FL	104.42	25	Lancaster, PA	27.53
87	Chattanooga, TN–GA	(1.75)	97	Fort Wayne, IN	(2.74)	–	Lansing–East Lansing, MI**	NA

Source: Morgan Quitno Corporation using data from U.S. Department of Justice, Federal Bureau of Investigation
"Crime in the United States 1993" (Uniform Crime Reports, December 4, 1994)
*Forcible rape is the carnal knowledge of a female forcibly and against her will. Assaults or attempts to commit rape by force or threat of force are included. However, statutory rape without force and other sex offenses are excluded.
**Not available.

58

15. Percent Change in Rape Rate: 1992 to 1993 (continued)

National Percent Change = 5.1% Decrease*

RANK	METRO AREA	% CHANGE	RANK	METRO AREA	% CHANGE	RANK	METRO AREA	CHANGE
234	Laredo, TX	(56.58)	180	Olympia, WA	(14.81)	43	Seattle–Bellevue–Everett, WA	13.20
77	Las Vegas, NV–AZ	(0.17)	–	Omaha, NE**	NA	10	Sheboygan, WI	45.74
–	Lawrence, MA–NH**	NA	174	Orange County, CA	(13.49)	207	Sherman–Denison, TX	(23.61)
68	Lawton, OK	3.28	58	Orlando, FL	6.59	211	Shreveport–Bossier City, LA	(24.60)
226	Lewiston–Auburn, ME	(33.21)	3	Owensboro, KY	110.47	–	Sioux City, IA–NE**	NA
101	Lexington, KY	(3.06)	205	Panama City, FL	(23.28)	59	Sioux Falls, SD	5.16
214	Lincoln, NE	(24.91)	129	Philadelphia, PA–NJ	(7.74)	145	South Bend, IN	(10.19)
115	Little Rock–North Little Rock, AR	(4.93)	162	Phoenix–Mesa, AZ	(11.75)	32	Spokane, WA	20.36
100	Longview–Marshall, TX	(2.95)	170	Pine Bluff, AR	(12.87)	178	Springfield, MA	(14.56)
109	Los Angeles–Long Beach, CA	(4.05)	126	Pittsburgh, PA	(7.17)	46	Springfield, MO	12.75
89	Louisville, KY–IN	(1.94)	231	Pittsfield, MA	(40.55)	168	Stamford–Norwalk, CT	(12.40)
131	Lubbock, TX	(7.87)	37	Portland, ME	16.21	9	Steubenville–Weirton, OH–WV	46.77
22	Lynchburg, VA	29.21	134	Portland–Vancouver, OR–WA	(8.27)	196	Stockton–Lodi, CA	(18.69)
157	Macon, GA	(11.26)	144	Providence–Fall River–Warwick, RI–MA	(10.06)	–	St. Cloud, MN**	NA
62	Madison, WI	4.36	63	Provo–Orem, UT	3.74	11	St. Joseph, MO	43.13
–	Manchester, NH**	NA	79	Pueblo, CO	(0.41)	–	St. Louis, MO–IL**	NA
176	Mansfield, OH	(14.06)	–	Punta Gorda, FL**	NA	150	Sumter, SC	(10.93)
12	McAllen–Edinburg–Mission, TX	37.81	206	Racine, WI	(23.32)	86	Syracuse, NY	(1.54)
39	Medford–Ashland, OR	14.92	204	Raleigh–Durham–Chapel Hill, NC	(23.09)	228	Tacoma, WA	(38.44)
66	Memphis, TN–AR–MS	3.62	221	Rapid City, SD	(27.79)	147	Tallahassee, FL	(10.30)
216	Merced, CA	(26.36)	220	Reading, PA	(27.43)	112	Tampa–St. Petersburg–Clearwater, FL	(4.46)
92	Miami, FL	(2.21)	163	Redding, CA	(11.86)	175	Texarkana, TX–AR	(13.55)
–	Middlesex–Sommerset–Hunterdon, NJ**	NA	173	Reno, NV	(13.42)	102	Toledo, OH	(3.13)
191	Milwaukee–Waukesha, WI	(17.29)	193	Richland–Kennewick–Pasco, WA	(18.22)	128	Trenton, NJ	(7.42)
–	Minneapolis–St. Paul, MN–WI**	NA	84	Richmond–Petersburg, VA	(1.41)	169	Tucson, AZ	(12.75)
–	Mobile, AL**	NA	158	Riverside–San Bernardino, CA	(11.59)	137	Tulsa, OK	(8.93)
93	Modesto, CA	(2.23)	142	Roanoke, VA	(9.47)	192	Tuscaloosa, AL	(18.05)
–	Monmouth–Ocean, NJ**	NA	–	Rochester, MN**	NA	167	Tyler, TX	(12.35)
222	Monroe, LA	(28.11)	135	Rochester, NY	(8.42)	36	Utica–Rome, NY	17.32
217	Montgomery, AL	(26.55)	225	Rocky Mount, NC	(31.41)	171	Vallejo–Fairfield–Napa, CA	(12.89)
34	Myrtle Beach, SC	17.75	182	Sacramento, CA	(15.23)	88	Ventura, CA	(1.84)
219	Naples, FL	(27.02)	–	Saginaw–Bay City–Midland, MI**	NA	85	Victoria, TX	(1.50)
70	Nashua, NH	2.07	186	Salem, OR	(16.70)	24	Vineland–Millville–Bridgeton, NJ	28.48
78	Nashville, TN	(0.27)	123	Salinas, CA	(5.79)	172	Visalia–Tulare–Porterville, CA	(13.00)
–	Nassau–Suffolk, NY**	NA	127	Salt Lake City–Ogden, UT	(7.33)	50	Waco, TX	10.54
–	New Bedford, MA**	NA	212	San Angelo, TX	(24.76)	54	Washington, DC–MD–VA–WV	8.79
177	New Haven–Meriden, CT	(14.17)	133	San Antonio, TX	(8.08)	213	Waterbury, CT	(24.88)
40	New London–Norwich, CT–RI	14.63	190	San Diego, CA	(17.07)	–	Waterloo–Cedar Falls, IA**	NA
60	New Orleans, LA	4.60	153	San Francisco, CA	(10.99)	233	Wausau, WI	(47.58)
–	New York, NY**	NA	143	San Jose, CA	(9.91)	–	West Palm Beach–Boca Raton, FL**	NA
–	Newark, NJ**	NA	–	San Luis Obispo–Atascadero, CA**	NA	187	Wichita Falls, TX	(16.78)
–	Newburgh, NY–PA**	NA	61	Santa Barbara–Santa Maria–Lompoc, CA	4.52	200	Williamsport, PA	(21.89)
136	Norfolk–Va Beach–Newport News, VA–NC	(8.76)	227	Santa Cruz–Watsonville, CA	(34.76)	203	Wilmington, NC	(23.01)
118	Oakland, CA	(5.29)	96	Santa Rosa, CA	(2.49)	–	Worcester, MA–CT**	NA
7	Ocala, FL	54.44	73	Sarasota–Bradenton, FL	0.48	106	Yakima, WA	(3.78)
94	Odessa–Midland, TX	(2.39)	26	Savannah, GA	25.59	74	Yolo, CA	0.19
49	Oklahoma City, OK	11.30	122	Scranton–Wilkes-Barre–Hazleton, PA	(5.78)	146	Yuba City, CA	(10.22)

Source: Morgan Quitno Corporation using data from U.S. Department of Justice, Federal Bureau of Investigation
"Crime in the United States 1993" (Uniform Crime Reports, December 4, 1994)
*Forcible rape is the carnal knowledge of a female forcibly and against her will. Assaults or attempts to commit rape by force or threat of force are included. However, statutory rape without force and other sex offenses are excluded.
**Not available.

15. Percent Change in Rape Rate: 1992 to 1993 (continued)

National Percent Change = 5.1% Decrease*

RANK	METRO AREA	% CHANGE	RANK	METRO AREA	% CHANGE	RANK	METRO AREA	% CHANGE
1	Dubuque, IA	264.95	48	Charleston, WV	12.10	95	Fresno, CA	(2.43)
2	Danville, VA	156.98	49	Oklahoma City, OK	11.30	96	Santa Rosa, CA	(2.49)
3	Owensboro, KY	110.47	50	Waco, TX	10.54	97	Fort Wayne, IN	(2.74)
4	Fort Walton Beach, FL	104.42	51	Asheville, NC	10.31	98	Galveston-Texas City, TX	(2.75)
5	Fayetteville-Springdale-Rogers, AR	83.14	52	Eau Claire, WI	9.86	99	Greensboro-Winston Salem-High Point, NC	(2.91)
6	Clarksville-Hopkinsville, TN-KY	65.03	53	Colorado Springs, CO	9.75	100	Longview-Marshall, TX	(2.95)
7	Ocala, FL	54.44	54	Washington, DC-MD-VA-WV	8.79	101	Lexington, KY	(3.06)
8	Corpus Christi, TX	48.12	55	Eugene-Springfield, OR	8.67	102	Toledo, OH	(3.13)
9	Steubenville-Weirton, OH-WV	46.77	56	Killeen-Temple, TX	8.62	103	Gary-Hammond, IN	(3.16)
10	Sheboygan, WI	45.74	57	Binghamton, NY	7.04	104	Fayetteville, NC	(3.35)
11	St. Joseph, MO	43.13	58	Orlando, FL	6.59	105	Columbus, GA-AL	(3.69)
12	McAllen-Edinburg-Mission, TX	37.81	59	Sioux Falls, SD	5.16	106	Yakima, WA	(3.78)
13	Glens Falls, NY	36.60	60	New Orleans, LA	4.60	107	Austin-San Marcos, TX	(3.87)
14	Bangor, ME	35.98	61	Santa Barbara-Santa Maria-Lompoc, CA	4.52	108	Anniston, AL	(3.96)
15	Gadsden, AL	35.56	62	Madison, WI	4.36	109	Jacksonville, FL	(4.05)
16	Greenville, NC	35.16	63	Provo-Orem, UT	3.74	109	Los Angeles-Long Beach, CA	(4.05)
17	Brazoria, TX	34.73	64	Appleton-Oshkosh-Neenah, WI	3.73	111	Hickory-Morganton, NC	(4.21)
18	Bismarck, ND	33.33	65	El Paso, TX	3.71	112	Tampa-St. Petersburg-Clearwater, FL	(4.46)
19	Green Bay, WI	32.28	66	Memphis, TN-AR-MS	3.62	113	Charlotte-Gastonia-Rock Hill, NC-SC	(4.69)
20	Beaumont-Port Arthur, TX	31.14	67	Fort Lauderdale, FL	3.32	114	Amarillo, TX	(4.83)
21	Fort Pierce-Port St. Lucie, FL	29.43	68	Lawton, OK	3.28	115	Little Rock-North Little Rock, AR	(4.93)
22	Lynchburg, VA	29.21	69	Goldsboro, NC	2.24	116	Akron, OH	(5.15)
23	Gainesville, FL	29.12	70	Nashua, NH	2.07	117	Fort Worth-Arlington, TX	(5.18)
24	Vineland-Millville-Bridgeton, NJ	28.48	71	Albuquerque, NM	1.35	118	Charleston-North Charleston, SC	(5.29)
25	Lancaster, PA	27.53	72	Canton-Massillon, OH	1.11	118	Oakland, CA	(5.29)
26	Savannah, GA	25.59	73	Sarasota-Bradenton, FL	0.48	120	Bryan-College Station, TX	(5.63)
27	Fort Smith, AR-OK	24.27	74	Yolo, CA	0.19	121	Huntsville, AL	(5.76)
28	Lafayette, IN	23.97	75	Boulder-Longmont, CO	0.00	122	Scranton-Wilkes-Barre-Hazleton, PA	(5.78)
29	Elkhart-Goshen, IN	23.95	75	Danbury, CT	0.00	123	Salinas, CA	(5.79)
30	Charlottesville, VA	23.43	77	Las Vegas, NV-AZ	(0.17)	124	Evansville-Henderson, IN-KY	(5.94)
31	Decatur, AL	21.39	78	Nashville, TN	(0.27)	125	Baton Rouge, LA	(6.72)
32	Spokane, WA	20.36	79	Pueblo, CO	(0.41)	126	Pittsburgh, PA	(7.17)
33	Houston, TX	18.40	80	Harrisburg-Lebanon-Carlisle, PA	(0.74)	127	Salt Lake City-Ogden, UT	(7.33)
34	Myrtle Beach, SC	17.75	81	Bridgeport, CT	(0.89)	128	Trenton, NJ	(7.42)
35	Kokomo, IN	17.72	82	Enid, OK	(1.09)	129	Philadelphia, PA-NJ	(7.74)
36	Utica-Rome, NY	17.32	83	Greenville-Spartanburg-Anderson, SC	(1.39)	130	Baltimore, MD	(7.79)
37	Portland, ME	16.21	84	Richmond-Petersburg, VA	(1.41)	131	Lubbock, TX	(7.87)
38	Janesville-Beloit, WI	15.44	85	Victoria, TX	(1.50)	132	Dallas, TX	(7.96)
39	Medford-Ashland, OR	14.92	86	Syracuse, NY	(1.54)	133	San Antonio, TX	(8.08)
40	New London-Norwich, CT-RI	14.63	87	Chattanooga, TN-GA	(1.75)	134	Portland-Vancouver, OR-WA	(8.27)
41	Athens, GA	13.48	88	Ventura, CA	(1.84)	135	Rochester, NY	(8.42)
42	Kenosha, WI	13.33	89	Louisville, KY-IN	(1.94)	136	Norfolk-Va Beach-Newport News, VA-NC	(8.76)
43	Johnstown, PA	13.20	90	Barnstable-Yarmouth, MA	(1.97)	137	Tulsa, OK	(8.93)
43	Seattle-Bellevue-Everett, WA	13.20	91	Atlantic City, NJ	(2.10)	138	Abilene, TX	(9.08)
45	Fort Myers-Cape Coral, FL	12.93	92	Miami, FL	(2.21)	139	Cincinnati, OH-KY-IN	(9.17)
46	Springfield, MO	12.75	93	Modesto, CA	(2.23)	140	Augusta-Aiken, GA-SC	(9.19)
47	Jacksonville, NC	12.50	94	Odessa-Midland, TX	(2.39)	141	Dayton-Springfield, OH	(9.37)

Source: Morgan Quitno Corporation using data from U.S. Department of Justice, Federal Bureau of Investigation
"Crime in the United States 1993" (Uniform Crime Reports, December 4, 1994)
*Forcible rape is the carnal knowledge of a female forcibly and against her will. Assaults or attempts to commit rape by force or threat of force are included. However, statutory rape without force and other sex offenses are excluded.
**Not available.

15. Percent Change in Rape Rate: 1992 to 1993 (continued)

National Percent Change = 5.1% Decrease*

RANK	METRO AREA	% CHANGE	RANK	METRO AREA	% CHANGE	RANK	METRO AREA	CHANGE
142	Roanoke, VA	(9.47)	187	Wichita Falls, TX	(16.78)	–	Ann Arbor, MI**	NA
143	San Jose, CA	(9.91)	190	San Diego, CA	(17.07)	–	Benton Harbor, MI**	NA
144	Providence–Fall River–Warwick, RI–MA	(10.06)	191	Milwaukee–Waukesha, WI	(17.29)	–	Bergen–Passaic, NJ**	NA
145	South Bend, IN	(10.19)	192	Tuscaloosa, AL	(18.05)	–	Boston, MA–NH**	NA
146	Yuba City, CA	(10.22)	193	Richland–Kennewick–Pasco, WA	(18.22)	–	Buffalo–Niagara Falls, NY**	NA
147	Tallahassee, FL	(10.30)	194	Columbia, MO	(18.34)	–	Chicago, IL**	NA
148	Daytona Beach, FL	(10.81)	195	Hartford, CT	(18.64)	–	Cleveland, OH**	NA
149	Columbus, OH	(10.85)	196	Stockton–Lodi, CA	(18.69)	–	Detroit, MI**	NA
150	Des Moines, IA	(10.93)	197	Bloomington, IN	(18.86)	–	Duluth–Superior, MN–WI**	NA
150	Sumter, SC	(10.93)	198	Anchorage, AK	(19.20)	–	Dutchess County, NY**	NA
152	Cumberland, MD–WV	(10.98)	199	Bakersfield, CA	(21.78)	–	Fargo–Moorhead, ND–MN**	NA
153	San Francisco, CA	(10.99)	200	Williamsport, PA	(21.89)	–	Fitchburg–Leominster, MA**	NA
154	Johnson City–Kingsport–Bristol, TN–VA	(11.02)	201	Florence, SC	(22.02)	–	Flint, MI**	NA
155	Erie, PA	(11.06)	202	Lafayette, LA	(22.55)	–	Fort Collins–Loveland, CO**	NA
156	Cheyenne, WY	(11.11)	203	Wilmington, NC	(23.01)	–	Grand Forks, ND–MN**	NA
157	Macon, GA	(11.26)	204	Raleigh–Durham–Chapel Hill, NC	(23.09)	–	Grand Rapids–Muskegon–Holland, MI**	NA
158	Alexandria, LA	(11.59)	205	Panama City, FL	(23.28)	–	Indianapolis, IN**	NA
158	Jackson, MS	(11.59)	206	Racine, WI	(23.32)	–	Jackson, MI**	NA
158	Riverside–San Bernardino, CA	(11.59)	207	Sherman–Denison, TX	(23.61)	–	Jersey City, NJ**	NA
161	Hagerstown, MD	(11.62)	208	Dothan, AL	(23.68)	–	Joplin, MO**	NA
162	Phoenix–Mesa, AZ	(11.75)	209	Bellingham, WA	(23.82)	–	Kalamazoo–Battle Creek, MI**	NA
163	Redding, CA	(11.86)	210	Bremerton, WA	(24.41)	–	Kansas City, MO–KS**	NA
164	Brockton, MA	(12.07)	211	Shreveport–Bossier City, LA	(24.60)	–	La Crosse, WI–MN**	NA
165	Honolulu, HI	(12.10)	212	San Angelo, TX	(24.76)	–	Lake Charles, LA**	NA
166	Denver, CO	(12.33)	213	Waterbury, CT	(24.88)	–	Lansing–East Lansing, MI**	NA
167	Tyler, TX	(12.35)	214	Lincoln, NE	(24.91)	–	Lawrence, MA–NH**	NA
168	Stamford–Norwalk, CT	(12.40)	215	Jackson, TN	(25.97)	–	Manchester, NH**	NA
169	Tucson, AZ	(12.75)	216	Merced, CA	(26.36)	–	Middlesex–Sommerset–Hunterdon, NJ**	NA
170	Pine Bluff, AR	(12.87)	217	Montgomery, AL	(26.55)	–	Minneapolis–St. Paul, MN–WI**	NA
171	Vallejo–Fairfield–Napa, CA	(12.89)	218	Florence, AL	(26.95)	–	Mobile, AL**	NA
172	Visalia–Tulare–Porterville, CA	(13.00)	219	Naples, FL	(27.02)	–	Monmouth–Ocean, NJ**	NA
173	Reno, NV	(13.42)	220	Reading, PA	(27.43)	–	Nassau–Suffolk, NY**	NA
174	Orange County, CA	(13.49)	221	Rapid City, SD	(27.79)	–	New Bedford, MA**	NA
175	Texarkana, TX–AR	(13.55)	222	Monroe, LA	(28.11)	–	New York, NY**	NA
176	Mansfield, OH	(14.06)	223	Houma, LA	(28.42)	–	Newark, NJ**	NA
177	New Haven–Meriden, CT	(14.17)	224	Atlanta, GA	(28.86)	–	Newburgh, NY–PA**	NA
178	Springfield, MA	(14.56)	225	Rocky Mount, NC	(31.41)	–	Omaha, NE**	NA
179	Birmingham, AL	(14.75)	226	Lewiston–Auburn, ME	(33.21)	–	Punta Gorda, FL**	NA
180	Olympia, WA	(14.81)	227	Santa Cruz–Watsonville, CA	(34.76)	–	Rochester, MN**	NA
181	Chico–Paradise, CA	(15.16)	228	Tacoma, WA	(38.44)	–	Saginaw–Bay City–Midland, MI**	NA
182	Lakeland–Winter Haven, FL	(15.23)	229	Huntington–Ashland, WV–KY–OH	(38.60)	–	San Luis Obispo–Atascadero, CA**	NA
182	Sacramento, CA	(15.23)	230	Albany, GA	(39.97)	–	Sioux City, IA–NE**	NA
184	Brownsville–Harlingen–San Benito, TX	(15.28)	231	Pittsfield, MA	(40.55)	–	St. Cloud, MN**	NA
185	Columbia, SC	(16.42)	232	Altoona, PA	(42.23)	–	St. Louis, MO–IL**	NA
186	Salem, OR	(16.70)	233	Wausau, WI	(47.58)	–	Waterloo–Cedar Falls, IA**	NA
187	Boise, ID	(16.78)	234	Laredo, TX	(56.58)	–	West Palm Beach–Boca Raton, FL**	NA
187	Greeley, CO	(16.78)	–	Albany, NY**	NA	–	Worcester, MA–CT**	NA

Source: Morgan Quitno Corporation using data from U.S. Department of Justice, Federal Bureau of Investigation
    "Crime in the United States 1993" (Uniform Crime Reports, December 4, 1994)
Forcible rape is the carnal knowledge of a female forcibly and against her will. Assaults or attempts to commit rape by force or threat of force are included. However, statutory rape without force and other sex offenses are excluded.
**Not available.*

61

16. Percent Change in Rape Rate: 1989 to 1993

National Percent Change = 6.6% Increase*

RANK	METRO AREA	% CHANGE	RANK	METRO AREA	% CHANGE	RANK	METRO AREA	% CHANGE
110	Abilene, TX	12.63	52	Cheyenne, WY	38.30	105	Fort Worth-Arlington, TX	12.85
–	Akron, OH**	NA	–	Chicago, IL**	NA	205	Fresno, CA	(18.69)
223	Albany, GA	(36.19)	54	Chico-Paradise, CA	37.70	36	Gadsden, AL	53.17
–	Albany, NY**	NA	76	Cincinnati, OH-KY-IN	23.27	64	Gainesville, FL	30.62
71	Albuquerque, NM	26.32	32	Clarksville-Hopkinsville, TN-KY	56.51	151	Galveston-Texas City, TX	(1.32)
16	Alexandria, LA	92.31	–	Cleveland, OH**	NA	40	Gary-Hammond, IN	45.27
175	Altoona, PA	(6.64)	78	Colorado Springs, CO	21.61	43	Glens Falls, NY	43.95
86	Amarillo, TX	18.49	4	Columbia, MO	158.87	–	Goldsboro, NC**	NA
56	Anchorage, AK	36.01	100	Columbia, SC	13.51	–	Grand Forks, ND-MN**	NA
–	Ann Arbor, MI**	NA	216	Columbus, GA-AL	(29.50)	–	Grand Rapids-Muskegon-Holland, MI**	NA
17	Anniston, AL	90.64	112	Columbus, OH	12.43	104	Greeley, CO	13.07
23	Appleton-Oshkosh-Neenah, WI	73.75	95	Corpus Christi, TX	15.69	5	Green Bay, WI	143.02
180	Asheville, NC	(7.96)	226	Cumberland, MD-WV	(42.06)	101	Greensboro-Winston Salem-High Point, NC	13.31
210	Athens, GA	(20.86)	201	Dallas, TX	(17.13)	–	Greenville, NC**	NA
217	Atlanta, GA	(30.26)	224	Danbury, CT	(38.95)	159	Greenville-Spartanburg-Anderson, SC	(3.31)
206	Atlantic City, NJ	(19.66)	15	Danville, VA	94.09	13	Hagerstown, MD	113.00
84	Augusta-Aiken, GA-SC	19.38	188	Daytona Beach, FL	(11.93)	–	Harrisburg-Lebanon-Carlisle, PA**	NA
128	Austin-San Marcos, TX	6.64	139	Dayton-Springfield, OH	1.72	222	Hartford, CT	(35.14)
221	Bakersfield, CA	(34.79)	26	Decatur, AL	68.15	–	Hickory-Morganton, NC**	NA
87	Baltimore, MD	18.33	113	Denver, CO	12.35	219	Honolulu, HI	(32.58)
6	Bangor, ME	137.23	121	Des Moines, IA	8.63	–	Houma, LA**	NA
–	Barnstable-Yarmouth, MA**	NA	–	Detroit, MI**	NA	44	Houston, TX	41.79
34	Baton Rouge, LA	53.37	116	Dothan, AL	10.38	69	Huntington-Ashland, WV-KY-OH	27.48
51	Beaumont-Port Arthur, TX	39.89	1	Dubuque, IA	819.48	197	Huntsville, AL	(15.50)
152	Bellingham, WA	(1.69)	–	Duluth-Superior, MN-WI**	NA	–	Indianapolis, IN**	NA
–	Benton Harbor, MI**	NA	–	Dutchess County, NY**	NA	–	Jackson, MI**	NA
155	Bergen-Passaic, NJ	(2.45)	3	Eau Claire, WI	168.97	181	Jackson, MS	(8.39)
41	Binghamton, NY	45.22	90	El Paso, TX	18.00	49	Jackson, TN	40.71
93	Birmingham, AL	17.38	18	Elkhart-Goshen, IN	85.10	98	Jacksonville, FL	14.19
2	Bismarck, ND	373.24	70	Enid, OK	26.68	204	Jacksonville, NC	(18.40)
85	Bloomington, IN	19.31	123	Erie, PA	8.19	21	Janesville-Beloit, WI	77.98
91	Boise, ID	17.54	107	Eugene-Springfield, OR	12.75	108	Jersey City, NJ	12.69
–	Boston, MA-NH**	NA	59	Evansville-Henderson, IN-KY	33.19	194	Johnson City-Kingsport-Bristol, TN-VA	(15.36)
75	Boulder-Longmont, CO	23.46	–	Fargo-Moorhead, ND-MN**	NA	–	Johnstown, PA**	NA
19	Brazoria, TX	81.39	162	Fayetteville, NC	(3.62)	14	Joplin, MO	96.45
–	Bremerton, WA**	NA	178	Fayetteville-Springdale-Rogers, AR	(7.89)	–	Kalamazoo-Battle Creek, MI**	NA
191	Bridgeport, CT	(12.55)	77	Fitchburg-Leominster, MA	22.53	–	Kansas City, MO-KS**	NA
–	Brockton, MA**	NA	–	Flint, MI**	NA	87	Kenosha, WI	18.33
213	Brownsville-Harlingen-San Benito, TX	(25.10)	227	Florence, AL	(46.07)	74	Killeen-Temple, TX	23.93
80	Bryan-College Station, TX	20.36	57	Florence, SC	35.18	11	Kokomo, IN	116.57
120	Buffalo-Niagara Falls, NY	8.82	25	Fort Collins-Loveland, CO	69.87	–	La Crosse, WI-MN**	NA
103	Canton-Massillon, OH	13.18	92	Fort Lauderdale, FL	17.44	24	Lafayette, IN	72.41
145	Charleston, WV	0.00	9	Fort Myers-Cape Coral, FL	130.84	215	Lafayette, LA	(26.74)
94	Charleston-North Charleston, SC	16.23	198	Fort Pierce-Port St. Lucie, FL	(15.63)	146	Lake Charles, LA	(0.36)
58	Charlottesville, VA	34.05	31	Fort Smith, AR-OK	60.75	154	Lakeland-Winter Haven, FL	(2.31)
131	Charlotte-Gastonia-Rock Hill, NC-SC	6.38	62	Fort Walton Beach, FL	32.00	67	Lancaster, PA	27.53
208	Chattanooga, TN-GA	(19.79)	132	Fort Wayne, IN	5.97	–	Lansing-East Lansing, MI**	NA

Source: Morgan Quitno Corporation using data from U.S. Department of Justice, Federal Bureau of Investigation
    "Crime in the United States 1993" (Uniform Crime Reports, December 4, 1994)
*Forcible rape is the carnal knowledge of a female forcibly and against her will. Assaults or attempts to commit rape by force or threat of force are included. However, statutory rape without force and other sex offenses are excluded.
**Not available.

16. Percent Change in Rape Rate: 1989 to 1993 (continued)

National Percent Change = 6.6% Increase*

RANK	METRO AREA	% CHANGE	RANK	METRO AREA	% CHANGE	RANK	METRO AREA	CHANGE
167	Laredo, TX	(4.35)	126	Olympia, WA	7.07	105	Seattle–Bellevue–Everett, WA	12.85
129	Las Vegas, NV–AZ	6.60	–	Omaha, NE**	NA	22	Sheboygan, WI	76.77
7	Lawrence, MA–NH	136.72	200	Orange County, CA	(17.11)	8	Sherman–Denison, TX	132.39
46	Lawton, OK	41.16	117	Orlando, FL	9.90	176	Shreveport–Bossier City, LA	(6.78)
130	Lewiston–Auburn, ME	6.40	72	Owensboro, KY	26.02	48	Sioux City, IA–NE	41.00
38	Lexington, KY	49.48	134	Panama City, FL	5.05	141	Sioux Falls, SD	1.57
138	Lincoln, NE	2.28	160	Philadelphia, PA–NJ	(3.43)	–	South Bend, IN**	NA
157	Little Rock–North Little Rock, AR	(2.91)	135	Phoenix–Mesa, AZ	4.55	166	Spokane, WA	(4.30)
164	Longview–Marshall, TX	(4.23)	170	Pine Bluff, AR	(5.33)	179	Springfield, MA	(7.94)
187	Los Angeles–Long Beach, CA	(11.23)	142	Pittsburgh, PA	1.49	119	Springfield, MO	9.52
143	Louisville, KY–IN	1.34	–	Pittsfield, MA**	NA	207	Stamford–Norwalk, CT	(19.70)
150	Lubbock, TX	(1.31)	28	Portland, ME	65.23	–	Steubenville–Weirton, OH–WV**	NA
96	Lynchburg, VA	15.30	127	Portland–Vancouver, OR–WA	6.79	193	Stockton–Lodi, CA	(13.72)
196	Macon, GA	(15.46)	169	Providence–Fall River–Warwick, RI–MA	(4.67)	–	St. Cloud, MN**	NA
27	Madison, WI	66.31	–	Provo–Orem, UT**	NA	12	St. Joseph, MO	114.29
99	Manchester, NH	13.74	65	Pueblo, CO	30.32	–	St. Louis, MO–IL**	NA
161	Mansfield, OH	(3.56)	–	Punta Gorda, FL**	NA	–	Sumter, SC**	NA
61	McAllen–Edinburg–Mission, TX	32.54	229	Racine, WI	(51.14)	174	Syracuse, NY	(6.59)
82	Medford–Ashland, OR	19.69	144	Raleigh–Durham–Chapel Hill, NC	0.59	220	Tacoma, WA	(33.43)
192	Memphis, TN–AR–MS	(12.72)	73	Rapid City, SD	25.16	124	Tallahassee, FL	7.58
67	Merced, CA	27.53	–	Reading, PA**	NA	81	Tampa–St. Petersburg–Clearwater, FL	19.96
202	Miami, FL	(17.96)	29	Redding, CA	63.90	39	Texarkana, TX–AR	46.85
211	Middlesex–Sommerset–Hunterdon, NJ	(21.26)	218	Reno, NV	(30.91)	168	Toledo, OH	(4.63)
171	Milwaukee–Waukesha, WI	(5.60)	137	Richland–Kennewick–Pasco, WA	2.68	133	Trenton, NJ	5.10
–	Minneapolis–St. Paul, MN–WI**	NA	136	Richmond–Petersburg, VA	3.71	–	Tucson, AZ**	NA
153	Mobile, AL	(2.21)	–	Riverside–San Bernardino, CA**	NA	125	Tulsa, OK	7.13
111	Modesto, CA	12.59	42	Roanoke, VA	44.85	20	Tuscaloosa, AL	80.66
186	Monmouth–Ocean, NJ	(10.92)	–	Rochester, MN**	NA	66	Tyler, TX	29.30
225	Monroe, LA	(41.73)	177	Rochester, NY	(7.75)	53	Utica–Rome, NY	38.27
118	Montgomery, AL	9.85	–	Rocky Mount, NC**	NA	158	Vallejo–Fairfield–Napa, CA	(3.23)
–	Myrtle Beach, SC**	NA	173	Sacramento, CA	(6.34)	147	Ventura, CA	(0.37)
115	Naples, FL	11.11	–	Saginaw–Bay City–Midland, MI**	NA	47	Victoria, TX	41.07
214	Nashua, NH	(26.41)	108	Salem, OR	12.69	30	Vineland–Millville–Bridgeton, NJ	63.88
83	Nashville, TN	19.55	203	Salinas, CA	(18.04)	114	Visalia–Tulare–Porterville, CA	11.90
195	Nassau–Suffolk, NY	(15.38)	33	Salt Lake City–Ogden, UT	54.27	60	Waco, TX	32.72
199	New Bedford, MA	(16.31)	172	San Angelo, TX	(6.04)	79	Washington, DC–MD–VA–WV	20.58
149	New Haven–Meriden, CT	(0.96)	102	San Antonio, TX	13.19	35	Waterbury, CT	53.30
190	New London–Norwich, CT–RI	(12.27)	185	San Diego, CA	(10.79)	10	Waterloo–Cedar Falls, IA	127.09
163	New Orleans, LA	(3.68)	164	San Francisco, CA	(4.23)	122	Wausau, WI	8.33
189	New York, NY	(12.12)	184	San Jose, CA	(10.12)	–	West Palm Beach–Boca Raton, FL**	NA
209	Newark, NJ	(20.57)	–	San Luis Obispo–Atascadero, CA**	NA	181	Wichita Falls, TX	(8.39)
–	Newburgh, NY–PA**	NA	148	Santa Barbara–Santa Maria–Lompoc, CA	(0.51)	–	Williamsport, PA**	NA
97	Norfolk–Va Beach–Newport News, VA–NC	15.14	228	Santa Cruz–Watsonville, CA	(46.49)	89	Wilmington, NC	18.12
183	Oakland, CA	(9.09)	50	Santa Rosa, CA	40.61	–	Worcester, MA–CT**	NA
37	Ocala, FL	52.10	156	Sarasota–Bradenton, FL	(2.55)	55	Yakima, WA	36.36
140	Odessa–Midland, TX	1.66	212	Savannah, GA	(22.35)	–	Yolo, CA**	NA
63	Oklahoma City, OK	31.96	–	Scranton–Wilkes-Barre–Hazleton, PA**	NA	45	Yuba City, CA	41.53

Source: Morgan Quitno Corporation using data from U.S. Department of Justice, Federal Bureau of Investigation
"Crime in the United States 1993" (Uniform Crime Reports, December 4, 1994)
Forcible rape is the carnal knowledge of a female forcibly and against her will. Assaults or attempts to commit rape by force or threat of force are included. However, statutory rape without force and other sex offenses are excluded.
**Not available.*

16. Percent Change in Rape Rate: 1989 to 1993 (continued)

National Percent Change = 6.6% Increase*

RANK	METRO AREA	% CHANGE	RANK	METRO AREA	% CHANGE	RANK	METRO AREA	% CHANGE
1	Dubuque, IA	819.48	48	Sioux City, IA–NE	41.00	95	Corpus Christi, TX	15.69
2	Bismarck, ND	373.24	49	Jackson, TN	40.71	96	Lynchburg, VA	15.30
3	Eau Claire, WI	168.97	50	Santa Rosa, CA	40.61	97	Norfolk-Va Beach-Newport News, VA–NC	15.14
4	Columbia, MO	158.87	51	Beaumont-Port Arthur, TX	39.89	98	Jacksonville, FL	14.19
5	Green Bay, WI	143.02	52	Cheyenne, WY	38.30	99	Manchester, NH	13.74
6	Bangor, ME	137.23	53	Utica-Rome, NY	38.27	100	Columbia, SC	13.51
7	Lawrence, MA–NH	136.72	54	Chico-Paradise, CA	37.70	101	Greensboro-Winston Salem-High Point, NC	13.31
8	Sherman-Denison, TX	132.39	55	Yakima, WA	36.36	102	San Antonio, TX	13.19
9	Fort Myers-Cape Coral, FL	130.84	56	Anchorage, AK	36.01	103	Canton-Massillon, OH	13.18
10	Waterloo-Cedar Falls, IA	127.09	57	Florence, SC	35.18	104	Greeley, CO	13.07
11	Kokomo, IN	116.57	58	Charlottesville, VA	34.05	105	Fort Worth-Arlington, TX	12.85
12	St. Joseph, MO	114.29	59	Evansville-Henderson, IN–KY	33.19	105	Seattle-Bellevue-Everett, WA	12.85
13	Hagerstown, MD	113.00	60	Waco, TX	32.72	107	Eugene-Springfield, OR	12.75
14	Joplin, MO	96.45	61	McAllen-Edinburg-Mission, TX	32.54	108	Jersey City, NJ	12.69
15	Danville, VA	94.09	62	Fort Walton Beach, FL	32.00	108	Salem, OR	12.69
16	Alexandria, LA	92.31	63	Oklahoma City, OK	31.96	110	Abilene, TX	12.63
17	Anniston, AL	90.64	64	Gainesville, FL	30.62	111	Modesto, CA	12.59
18	Elkhart-Goshen, IN	85.10	65	Pueblo, CO	30.32	112	Columbus, OH	12.43
19	Brazoria, TX	81.39	66	Tyler, TX	29.30	113	Denver, CO	12.35
20	Tuscaloosa, AL	80.66	67	Lancaster, PA	27.53	114	Visalia-Tulare-Porterville, CA	11.90
21	Janesville-Beloit, WI	77.98	67	Merced, CA	27.53	115	Naples, FL	11.11
22	Sheboygan, WI	76.77	69	Huntington-Ashland, WV–KY–OH	27.48	116	Dothan, AL	10.38
23	Appleton-Oshkosh-Neenah, WI	73.75	70	Enid, OK	26.68	117	Orlando, FL	9.90
24	Lafayette, IN	72.41	71	Albuquerque, NM	26.32	118	Montgomery, AL	9.85
25	Fort Collins-Loveland, CO	69.87	72	Owensboro, KY	26.02	119	Springfield, MO	9.52
26	Decatur, AL	68.15	73	Rapid City, SD	25.16	120	Buffalo-Niagara Falls, NY	8.82
27	Madison, WI	66.31	74	Killeen-Temple, TX	23.93	121	Des Moines, IA	8.63
28	Portland, ME	65.23	75	Boulder-Longmont, CO	23.46	122	Wausau, WI	8.33
29	Redding, CA	63.90	76	Cincinnati, OH–KY–IN	23.27	123	Erie, PA	8.19
30	Vineland-Millville-Bridgeton, NJ	63.88	77	Fitchburg-Leominster, MA	22.53	124	Tallahassee, FL	7.58
31	Fort Smith, AR–OK	60.75	78	Colorado Springs, CO	21.61	125	Tulsa, OK	7.13
32	Clarksville-Hopkinsville, TN–KY	56.51	79	Washington, DC–MD–VA–WV	20.58	126	Olympia, WA	7.07
33	Salt Lake City-Ogden, UT	54.27	80	Bryan-College Station, TX	20.36	127	Portland-Vancouver, OR–WA	6.79
34	Baton Rouge, LA	53.37	81	Tampa-St. Petersburg-Clearwater, FL	19.96	128	Austin-San Marcos, TX	6.64
35	Waterbury, CT	53.30	82	Medford-Ashland, OR	19.69	129	Las Vegas, NV–AZ	6.60
36	Gadsden, AL	53.17	83	Nashville, TN	19.55	130	Lewiston-Auburn, ME	6.40
37	Ocala, FL	52.10	84	Augusta-Aiken, GA–SC	19.38	131	Charlotte-Gastonia-Rock Hill, NC–SC	6.38
38	Lexington, KY	49.48	85	Bloomington, IN	19.31	132	Fort Wayne, IN	5.97
39	Texarkana, TX–AR	46.85	86	Amarillo, TX	18.49	133	Trenton, NJ	5.10
40	Gary-Hammond, IN	45.27	87	Baltimore, MD	18.33	134	Panama City, FL	5.05
41	Binghamton, NY	45.22	87	Kenosha, WI	18.33	135	Phoenix-Mesa, AZ	4.55
42	Roanoke, VA	44.85	89	Wilmington, NC	18.12	136	Richmond-Petersburg, VA	3.71
43	Glens Falls, NY	43.95	90	El Paso, TX	18.00	137	Richland-Kennewick-Pasco, WA	2.68
44	Houston, TX	41.79	91	Boise, ID	17.54	138	Lincoln, NE	2.28
45	Yuba City, CA	41.53	92	Fort Lauderdale, FL	17.44	139	Dayton-Springfield, OH	1.72
46	Lawton, OK	41.16	93	Birmingham, AL	17.38	140	Odessa-Midland, TX	1.66
47	Victoria, TX	41.07	94	Charleston-North Charleston, SC	16.23	141	Sioux Falls, SD	1.57

Source: Morgan Quitno Corporation using data from U.S. Department of Justice, Federal Bureau of Investigation
    "Crime in the United States 1993" (Uniform Crime Reports, December 4, 1994)
*Forcible rape is the carnal knowledge of a female forcibly and against her will. Assaults or attempts to commit rape by force or threat of force are included. However, statutory rape without force and other sex offenses are excluded.
**Not available.

16. Percent Change in Rape Rate: 1989 to 1993 (continued)

National Percent Change = 6.6% Increase*

RANK	METRO AREA	% CHANGE	RANK	METRO AREA	% CHANGE	RANK	METRO AREA	CHANGE
142	Pittsburgh, PA	1.49	189	New York, NY	(12.12)	–	Bremerton, WA**	NA
143	Louisville, KY-IN	1.34	190	New London-Norwich, CT-RI	(12.27)	–	Brockton, MA**	NA
144	Raleigh-Durham-Chapel Hill, NC	0.59	191	Bridgeport, CT	(12.55)	–	Chicago, IL**	NA
145	Charleston, WV	0.00	192	Memphis, TN-AR-MS	(12.72)	–	Cleveland, OH**	NA
146	Lake Charles, LA	(0.36)	193	Stockton-Lodi, CA	(13.72)	–	Detroit, MI**	NA
147	Ventura, CA	(0.37)	194	Johnson City-Kingsport-Bristol, TN-VA	(15.36)	–	Duluth-Superior, MN-WI**	NA
148	Santa Barbara-Santa Maria-Lompoc, CA	(0.51)	195	Nassau-Suffolk, NY	(15.38)	–	Dutchess County, NY**	NA
149	New Haven-Meriden, CT	(0.96)	196	Macon, GA	(15.46)	–	Fargo-Moorhead, ND-MN**	NA
150	Lubbock, TX	(1.31)	197	Huntsville, AL	(15.50)	–	Flint, MI**	NA
151	Galveston-Texas City, TX	(1.32)	198	Fort Pierce-Port St. Lucie, FL	(15.63)	–	Goldsboro, NC**	NA
152	Bellingham, WA	(1.69)	199	New Bedford, MA	(16.31)	–	Grand Forks, ND-MN**	NA
153	Mobile, AL	(2.21)	200	Orange County, CA	(17.11)	–	Grand Rapids-Muskegon-Holland, MI**	NA
154	Lakeland-Winter Haven, FL	(2.31)	201	Dallas, TX	(17.13)	–	Greenville, NC**	NA
155	Bergen-Passaic, NJ	(2.45)	202	Miami, FL	(17.96)	–	Harrisburg-Lebanon-Carlisle, PA**	NA
156	Sarasota-Bradenton, FL	(2.55)	203	Salinas, CA	(18.04)	–	Hickory-Morganton, NC**	NA
157	Little Rock-North Little Rock, AR	(2.91)	204	Jacksonville, NC	(18.40)	–	Houma, LA**	NA
158	Vallejo-Fairfield-Napa, CA	(3.23)	205	Fresno, CA	(18.69)	–	Indianapolis, IN**	NA
159	Greenville-Spartanburg-Anderson, SC	(3.31)	206	Atlantic City, NJ	(19.66)	–	Jackson, MI**	NA
160	Philadelphia, PA-NJ	(3.43)	207	Stamford-Norwalk, CT	(19.70)	–	Johnstown, PA**	NA
161	Mansfield, OH	(3.56)	208	Chattanooga, TN-GA	(19.79)	–	Kalamazoo-Battle Creek, MI**	NA
162	Fayetteville, NC	(3.62)	209	Newark, NJ	(20.57)	–	Kansas City, MO-KS**	NA
163	New Orleans, LA	(3.68)	210	Athens, GA	(20.86)	–	La Crosse, WI-MN**	NA
164	Longview-Marshall, TX	(4.23)	211	Middlesex-Sommerset-Hunterdon, NJ	(21.26)	–	Lansing-East Lansing, MI**	NA
164	San Francisco, CA	(4.23)	212	Savannah, GA	(22.35)	–	Minneapolis-St. Paul, MN-WI**	NA
166	Spokane, WA	(4.30)	213	Brownsville-Harlingen-San Benito, TX	(25.10)	–	Myrtle Beach, SC**	NA
167	Laredo, TX	(4.35)	214	Nashua, NH	(26.41)	–	Newburgh, NY-PA**	NA
168	Toledo, OH	(4.63)	215	Lafayette, LA	(26.74)	–	Omaha, NE**	NA
169	Providence-Fall River-Warwick, RI-MA	(4.67)	216	Columbus, GA-AL	(29.50)	–	Pittsfield, MA**	NA
170	Pine Bluff, AR	(5.33)	217	Atlanta, GA	(30.26)	–	Provo-Orem, UT**	NA
171	Milwaukee-Waukesha, WI	(5.60)	218	Reno, NV	(30.91)	–	Punta Gorda, FL**	NA
172	San Angelo, TX	(6.04)	219	Honolulu, HI	(32.58)	–	Reading, PA**	NA
173	Sacramento, CA	(6.34)	220	Tacoma, WA	(33.43)	–	Riverside-San Bernardino, CA**	NA
174	Syracuse, NY	(6.59)	221	Bakersfield, CA	(34.79)	–	Rochester, MN**	NA
175	Altoona, PA	(6.64)	222	Hartford, CT	(35.14)	–	Rocky Mount, NC**	NA
176	Shreveport-Bossier City, LA	(6.78)	223	Albany, GA	(36.19)	–	Saginaw-Bay City-Midland, MI**	NA
177	Rochester, NY	(7.75)	224	Danbury, CT	(38.95)	–	San Luis Obispo-Atascadero, CA**	NA
178	Fayetteville-Springdale-Rogers, AR	(7.89)	225	Monroe, LA	(41.73)	–	Scranton-Wilkes-Barre-Hazleton, PA**	NA
179	Springfield, MA	(7.94)	226	Cumberland, MD-WV	(42.06)	–	South Bend, IN**	NA
180	Asheville, NC	(7.96)	227	Florence, AL	(46.07)	–	Steubenville-Weirton, OH-WV**	NA
181	Jackson, MS	(8.39)	228	Santa Cruz-Watsonville, CA	(46.49)	–	St. Cloud, MN**	NA
181	Wichita Falls, TX	(8.39)	229	Racine, WI	(51.14)	–	St. Louis, MO-IL**	NA
183	Oakland, CA	(9.09)	–	Akron, OH**	NA	–	Sumter, SC**	NA
184	San Jose, CA	(10.12)	–	Albany, NY**	NA	–	Tucson, AZ**	NA
185	San Diego, CA	(10.79)	–	Ann Arbor, MI**	NA	–	West Palm Beach-Boca Raton, FL**	NA
186	Monmouth-Ocean, NJ	(10.92)	–	Barnstable-Yarmouth, MA**	NA	–	Williamsport, PA**	NA
187	Los Angeles-Long Beach, CA	(11.23)	–	Benton Harbor, MI**	NA	–	Worcester, MA-CT**	NA
188	Daytona Beach, FL	(11.93)	–	Boston, MA-NH**	NA	–	Yolo, CA**	NA

Source: Morgan Quitno Corporation using data from U.S. Department of Justice, Federal Bureau of Investigation
"Crime in the United States 1993" (Uniform Crime Reports, December 4, 1994)
*Forcible rape is the carnal knowledge of a female forcibly and against her will. Assaults or attempts to commit rape by force or threat of force are included. However, statutory rape without force and other sex offenses are excluded.
**Not available.

17. Robberies in 1993

National Total = 659,757 Robberies*

RANK	METRO AREA	ROBBERY	RANK	METRO AREA	ROBBERY	RANK	METRO AREA	ROBBERY
198	Abilene, TX	137	259	Cheyenne, WY	24	30	Fort Worth–Arlington, TX	4,062
79	Akron, OH	1,069	–	Chicago, IL**	NA	35	Fresno, CA	3,477
120	Albany, GA	485	200	Chico–Paradise, CA	135	174	Gadsden, AL	206
–	Albany, NY**	NA	41	Cincinnati, OH–KY–IN	3,175	109	Gainesville, FL	578
62	Albuquerque, NM	1,631	180	Clarksville–Hopkinsville, TN–KY	186	118	Galveston–Texas City, TX	490
204	Alexandria, LA	131	–	Cleveland, OH**	NA	66	Gary–Hammond, IN	1,530
246	Altoona, PA	47	128	Colorado Springs, CO	425	262	Glens Falls, NY	22
172	Amarillo, TX	213	209	Columbia, MO	120	169	Goldsboro, NC	243
110	Anchorage, AK	568	68	Columbia, SC	1,441	266	Grand Forks, ND–MN	16
125	Ann Arbor, MI	436	115	Columbus, GA–AL	507	69	Grand Rapids–Muskegon–Holland, MI	1,293
185	Anniston, AL	171	24	Columbus, OH	4,458	250	Greeley, CO	42
256	Appleton–Oshkosh–Neenah, WI	34	113	Corpus Christi, TX	527	242	Green Bay, WI	56
181	Asheville, NC	175	258	Cumberland, MD–WV	26	43	Greensboro–Winston Salem–High Point, NC	2,539
156	Athens, GA	283	12	Dallas, TX	8,979	155	Greenville, NC	285
8	Atlanta, GA	11,907	225	Danbury, CT	79	64	Greenville–Spartanburg–Anderson, SC	1,576
80	Atlantic City, NJ	1,022	218	Danville, VA	95	233	Hagerstown, MD	70
96	Augusta–Aiken, GA–SC	794	102	Daytona Beach, FL	644	95	Harrisburg–Lebanon–Carlisle, PA	798
57	Austin–San Marcos, TX	1,748	48	Dayton–Springfield, OH	2,132	51	Hartford, CT	1,972
72	Bakersfield, CA	1,182	216	Decatur, AL	96	162	Hickory–Morganton, NC	264
6	Baltimore, MD	15,632	37	Denver, CO	3,278	77	Honolulu, HI	1,085
259	Bangor, ME	24	151	Des Moines, IA	292	181	Houma, LA	175
243	Barnstable–Yarmouth, MA	55	4	Detroit, MI	17,332	–	Houston, TX**	NA
46	Baton Rouge, LA	2,210	195	Dothan, AL	144	192	Huntington–Ashland, WV–KY–OH	151
76	Beaumont–Port Arthur, TX	1,095	271	Dubuque, IA	14	138	Huntsville, AL	361
237	Bellingham, WA	61	229	Duluth–Superior, MN–WI	77	–	Indianapolis, IN**	NA
154	Benton Harbor, MI	286	164	Dutchess County, NY	260	213	Jackson, MI	107
49	Bergen–Passaic, NJ	2,083	268	Eau Claire, WI	15	59	Jackson, MS	1,665
219	Binghamton, NY	92	63	El Paso, TX	1,629	163	Jackson, TN	262
44	Birmingham, AL	2,370	195	Elkhart–Goshen, IN	144	32	Jacksonville, FL	3,924
273	Bismarck, ND	5	254	Enid, OK	37	198	Jacksonville, NC	137
268	Bloomington, IN	15	121	Erie, PA	458	215	Janesville–Beloit, WI	104
222	Boise, ID	87	166	Eugene–Springfield, OR	253	36	Jersey City, NJ	3,345
16	Boston, MA–NH	6,871	179	Evansville–Henderson, IN–KY	187	208	Johnson City–Kingsport–Bristol, TN–VA	121
225	Boulder–Longmont, CO	79	265	Fargo–Moorhead, ND–MN	21	235	Johnstown, PA	68
222	Brazoria, TX	87	87	Fayetteville, NC	987	228	Joplin, MO	78
203	Bremerton, WA	132	240	Fayetteville–Springdale–Rogers, AR	58	108	Kalamazoo–Battle Creek, MI	588
56	Bridgeport, CT	1,778	201	Fitchburg–Leominster, MA	133	–	Kansas City, MO–KS**	NA
132	Brockton, MA	403	70	Flint, MI	1,284	197	Kenosha, WI	143
134	Brownsville–Harlingen–San Benito, TX	388	255	Florence, AL	36	140	Killeen–Temple, TX	359
212	Bryan–College Station, TX	113	159	Florence, SC	277	248	Kokomo, IN	46
34	Buffalo–Niagara Falls, NY	3,521	251	Fort Collins–Loveland, CO	41	268	La Crosse, WI–MN	15
93	Canton–Massillon, OH	848	22	Fort Lauderdale, FL	4,839	244	Lafayette, IN	53
145	Charleston, WV	326	99	Fort Myers–Cape Coral, FL	698	133	Lafayette, LA	397
73	Charleston–North Charleston, SC	1,159	122	Fort Pierce–Port St. Lucie, FL	453	150	Lake Charles, LA	300
216	Charlottesville, VA	96	233	Fort Smith, AR–OK	70	89	Lakeland–Winter Haven, FL	964
26	Charlotte–Gastonia–Rock Hill, NC–SC	4,222	221	Fort Walton Beach, FL	91	138	Lancaster, PA	361
94	Chattanooga, TN–GA	802	106	Fort Wayne, IN	609	127	Lansing–East Lansing, MI	426

Source: U.S. Department of Justice, Federal Bureau of Investigation

"Crime in the United States 1993" (Uniform Crime Reports, December 4, 1994)

*Robbery is the taking or attempting to take anything of value by force or threat of force.

**Not available.

17. Robberies in 1993 (continued)

National Total = 659,757 Robberies*

RANK	METRO AREA	ROBBERY	RANK	METRO AREA	ROBBERY	RANK	METRO AREA	ROBBERY
186	Laredo, TX	166	230	Olympia, WA	75	28	Seattle-Bellevue-Everett, WA	4,155
27	Las Vegas, NV–AZ	4,172	–	Omaha, NE**	NA	259	Sheboygan, WI	24
117	Lawrence, MA–NH	502	19	Orange County, CA	5,567	214	Sherman-Denison, TX	105
188	Lawton, OK	165	39	Orlando, FL	3,240	84	Shreveport-Bossier City, LA	1,002
239	Lewiston-Auburn, ME	60	241	Owensboro, KY	57	206	Sioux City, IA–NE	127
107	Lexington, KY	606	189	Panama City, FL	161	246	Sioux Falls, SD	47
201	Lincoln, NE	133	5	Philadelphia, PA–NJ	16,261	112	South Bend, IN	534
60	Little Rock-North Little Rock, AR	1,647	20	Phoenix-Mesa, AZ	4,908	123	Spokane, WA	445
152	Longview-Marshall, TX	287	160	Pine Bluff, AR	272	81	Springfield, MA	1,019
2	Los Angeles-Long Beach, CA	65,994	31	Pittsburgh, PA	4,053	190	Springfield, MO	160
52	Louisville, KY–IN	1,939	253	Pittsfield, MA	38	115	Stamford-Norwalk, CT	507
152	Lubbock, TX	287	211	Portland, ME	114	245	Steubenville-Weirton, OH–WV	52
207	Lynchburg, VA	124	40	Portland-Vancouver, OR–WA	3,218	53	Stockton-Lodi, CA	1,932
119	Macon, GA	487	86	Providence-Fall River-Warwick, RI–MA	991	266	St. Cloud, MN	16
135	Madison, WI	366	249	Provo-Orem, UT	45	236	St. Joseph, MO	64
191	Manchester, NH	153	184	Pueblo, CO	172	–	St. Louis, MO–IL**	NA
186	Mansfield, OH	166	225	Punta Gorda, FL	79	168	Sumter, SC	246
128	McAllen-Edinburg-Mission, TX	425	135	Racine, WI	366	100	Syracuse, NY	692
232	Medford-Ashland, OR	73	47	Raleigh-Durham-Chapel Hill, NC	2,137	67	Tacoma, WA	1,446
18	Memphis, TN–AR–MS	5,754	257	Rapid City, SD	28	82	Tallahassee, FL	1,017
172	Merced, CA	213	104	Reading, PA	614	17	Tampa-St. Petersburg-Clearwater, FL	6,622
3	Miami, FL	18,610	193	Redding, CA	149	178	Texarkana, TX–AR	190
75	Middlesex-Sommerset-Hunterdon, NJ	1,122	111	Reno, NV	554	58	Toledo, OH	1,709
25	Milwaukee-Waukesha, WI	4,377	230	Richland-Kennewick-Pasco, WA	75	92	Trenton, NJ	874
21	Minneapolis-St. Paul, MN–WI	4,881	45	Richmond-Petersburg, VA	2,282	78	Tucson, AZ	1,084
61	Mobile, AL	1,646	13	Riverside-San Bernardino, CA	8,753	71	Tulsa, OK	1,254
105	Modesto, CA	612	169	Roanoke, VA	243	142	Tuscaloosa, AL	345
97	Monmouth-Ocean, NJ	753	262	Rochester, MN	22	161	Tyler, TX	266
194	Monroe, LA	147	54	Rochester, NY	1,906	175	Utica-Rome, NY	204
103	Montgomery, AL	637	157	Rocky Mount, NC	280	83	Vallejo-Fairfield-Napa, CA	1,016
146	Myrtle Beach, SC	322	29	Sacramento, CA	4,101	90	Ventura, CA	921
148	Naples, FL	305	101	Saginaw-Bay City-Midland, MI	678	224	Victoria, TX	86
262	Nashua, NH	22	147	Salem, OR	310	130	Vineland-Millville-Bridgeton, NJ	417
42	Nashville, TN	3,042	91	Salinas, CA	910	131	Visalia-Tulare-Porterville, CA	408
33	Nassau-Suffolk, NY	3,527	85	Salt Lake City-Ogden, UT	997	114	Waco, TX	509
137	New Bedford, MA	363	251	San Angelo, TX	41	7	Washington, DC-MD-VA-WV	14,251
65	New Haven-Meriden, CT	1,547	38	San Antonio, TX	3,274	149	Waterbury, CT	303
176	New London-Norwich, CT–RI	198	14	San Diego, CA	7,494	205	Waterloo-Cedar Falls, IA	130
15	New Orleans, LA	7,047	11	San Francisco, CA	9,755	271	Wausau, WI	14
1	New York, NY	90,310	55	San Jose, CA	1,802	–	West Palm Beach-Boca Raton, FL**	NA
9	Newark, NJ	10,945	219	San Luis Obispo-Atascadero, CA	92	177	Wichita Falls, TX	192
165	Newburgh, NY–PA	256	124	Santa Barbara-Santa Maria-Lompoc, CA	444	237	Williamsport, PA	61
23	Norfolk-Va Beach-Newport News, VA–NC	4,460	143	Santa Cruz-Watsonville, CA	334	144	Wilmington, NC	333
10	Oakland, CA	9,832	141	Santa Rosa, CA	347	98	Worcester, MA–CT	713
126	Ocala, FL	432	74	Sarasota-Bradenton, FL	1,127	171	Yakima, WA	233
166	Odessa-Midland, TX	253	88	Savannah, GA	982	183	Yolo, CA	173
50	Oklahoma City, OK	2,021	157	Scranton-Wilkes-Barre-Hazleton, PA	280	210	Yuba City, CA	116

Source: U.S. Department of Justice, Federal Bureau of Investigation
"Crime in the United States 1993" (Uniform Crime Reports, December 4, 1994)
*Robbery is the taking or attempting to take anything of value by force or threat of force.
**Not available.

17. Robberies in 1993 (continued)

National Total = 659,757 Robberies*

RANK	METRO AREA	ROBBERY	RANK	METRO AREA	ROBBERY	RANK	METRO AREA	ROBBERY
1	New York, NY	90,310	48	Dayton–Springfield, OH	2,132	95	Harrisburg–Lebanon–Carlisle, PA	798
2	Los Angeles–Long Beach, CA	65,994	49	Bergen–Passaic, NJ	2,083	96	Augusta–Aiken, GA–SC	794
3	Miami, FL	18,610	50	Oklahoma City, OK	2,021	97	Monmouth–Ocean, NJ	753
4	Detroit, MI	17,332	51	Hartford, CT	1,972	98	Worcester, MA–CT	713
5	Philadelphia, PA–NJ	16,261	52	Louisville, KY–IN	1,939	99	Fort Myers–Cape Coral, FL	698
6	Baltimore, MD	15,632	53	Stockton–Lodi, CA	1,932	100	Syracuse, NY	692
7	Washington, DC–MD–VA–WV	14,251	54	Rochester, NY	1,906	101	Saginaw–Bay City–Midland, MI	678
8	Atlanta, GA	11,907	55	San Jose, CA	1,802	102	Daytona Beach, FL	644
9	Newark, NJ	10,945	56	Bridgeport, CT	1,778	103	Montgomery, AL	637
10	Oakland, CA	9,832	57	Austin–San Marcos, TX	1,748	104	Reading, PA	614
11	San Francisco, CA	9,755	58	Toledo, OH	1,709	105	Modesto, CA	612
12	Dallas, TX	8,979	59	Jackson, MS	1,665	106	Fort Wayne, IN	609
13	Riverside–San Bernardino, CA	8,753	60	Little Rock–North Little Rock, AR	1,647	107	Lexington, KY	606
14	San Diego, CA	7,494	61	Mobile, AL	1,646	108	Kalamazoo–Battle Creek, MI	588
15	New Orleans, LA	7,047	62	Albuquerque, NM	1,631	109	Gainesville, FL	578
16	Boston, MA–NH	6,871	63	El Paso, TX	1,629	110	Anchorage, AK	568
17	Tampa–St. Petersburg–Clearwater, FL	6,622	64	Greenville–Spartanburg–Anderson, SC	1,576	111	Reno, NV	554
18	Memphis, TN–AR–MS	5,754	65	New Haven–Meriden, CT	1,547	112	South Bend, IN	534
19	Orange County, CA	5,567	66	Gary–Hammond, IN	1,530	113	Corpus Christi, TX	527
20	Phoenix–Mesa, AZ	4,908	67	Tacoma, WA	1,446	114	Waco, TX	509
21	Minneapolis–St. Paul, MN–WI	4,881	68	Columbia, SC	1,441	115	Columbus, GA–AL	507
22	Fort Lauderdale, FL	4,839	69	Grand Rapids–Muskegon–Holland, MI	1,293	115	Stamford–Norwalk, CT	507
23	Norfolk–Va Beach–Newport News, VA–NC	4,460	70	Flint, MI	1,284	117	Lawrence, MA–NH	502
24	Columbus, OH	4,458	71	Tulsa, OK	1,254	118	Galveston–Texas City, TX	490
25	Milwaukee–Waukesha, WI	4,377	72	Bakersfield, CA	1,182	119	Macon, GA	487
26	Charlotte–Gastonia–Rock Hill, NC–SC	4,222	73	Charleston–North Charleston, SC	1,159	120	Albany, GA	485
27	Las Vegas, NV–AZ	4,172	74	Sarasota–Bradenton, FL	1,127	121	Erie, PA	458
28	Seattle–Bellevue–Everett, WA	4,155	75	Middlesex–Somerset–Hunterdon, NJ	1,122	122	Fort Pierce–Port St. Lucie, FL	453
29	Sacramento, CA	4,101	76	Beaumont–Port Arthur, TX	1,095	123	Spokane, WA	445
30	Fort Worth–Arlington, TX	4,062	77	Honolulu, HI	1,085	124	Santa Barbara–Santa Maria–Lompoc, CA	444
31	Pittsburgh, PA	4,053	78	Tucson, AZ	1,084	125	Ann Arbor, MI	436
32	Jacksonville, FL	3,924	79	Akron, OH	1,069	126	Ocala, FL	432
33	Nassau–Suffolk, NY	3,527	80	Atlantic City, NJ	1,022	127	Lansing–East Lansing, MI	426
34	Buffalo–Niagara Falls, NY	3,521	81	Springfield, MA	1,019	128	Colorado Springs, CO	425
35	Fresno, CA	3,477	82	Tallahassee, FL	1,017	128	McAllen–Edinburg–Mission, TX	425
36	Jersey City, NJ	3,345	83	Vallejo–Fairfield–Napa, CA	1,016	130	Vineland–Millville–Bridgeton, NJ	417
37	Denver, CO	3,278	84	Shreveport–Bossier City, LA	1,002	131	Visalia–Tulare–Porterville, CA	408
38	San Antonio, TX	3,274	85	Salt Lake City–Ogden, UT	997	132	Brockton, MA	403
39	Orlando, FL	3,240	86	Providence–Fall River–Warwick, RI–MA	991	133	Lafayette, LA	397
40	Portland–Vancouver, OR–WA	3,218	87	Fayetteville, NC	987	134	Brownsville–Harlingen–San Benito, TX	388
41	Cincinnati, OH–KY–IN	3,175	88	Savannah, GA	982	135	Madison, WI	366
42	Nashville, TN	3,042	89	Lakeland–Winter Haven, FL	964	135	Racine, WI	366
43	Greensboro–Winston Salem–High Point, NC	2,539	90	Ventura, CA	921	137	New Bedford, MA	363
44	Birmingham, AL	2,370	91	Salinas, CA	910	138	Huntsville, AL	361
45	Richmond–Petersburg, VA	2,282	92	Trenton, NJ	874	138	Lancaster, PA	361
46	Baton Rouge, LA	2,210	93	Canton–Massillon, OH	848	140	Killeen–Temple, TX	359
47	Raleigh–Durham–Chapel Hill, NC	2,137	94	Chattanooga, TN–GA	802	141	Santa Rosa, CA	347

Source: U.S. Department of Justice, Federal Bureau of Investigation
  "Crime in the United States 1993" (Uniform Crime Reports, December 4, 1994)
Robbery is the taking or attempting to take anything of value by force or threat of force.
**Not available.*

17. Robberies in 1993 (continued)

National Total = 659,757 Robberies*

RANK	METRO AREA	ROBBERY	RANK	METRO AREA	ROBBERY	RANK	METRO AREA	ROBBERY
142	Tuscaloosa, AL	345	189	Panama City, FL	161	236	St. Joseph, MO	64
143	Santa Cruz-Watsonville, CA	334	190	Springfield, MO	160	237	Bellingham, WA	61
144	Wilmington, NC	333	191	Manchester, NH	153	237	Williamsport, PA	61
145	Charleston, WV	326	192	Huntington-Ashland, WV-KY-OH	151	239	Lewiston-Auburn, ME	60
146	Myrtle Beach, SC	322	193	Redding, CA	149	240	Fayetteville-Springdale-Rogers, AR	58
147	Salem, OR	310	194	Monroe, LA	147	241	Owensboro, KY	57
148	Naples, FL	305	195	Dothan, AL	144	242	Green Bay, WI	56
149	Waterbury, CT	303	195	Elkhart-Goshen, IN	144	243	Barnstable-Yarmouth, MA	55
150	Lake Charles, LA	300	197	Kenosha, WI	143	244	Lafayette, IN	53
151	Des Moines, IA	292	198	Abilene, TX	137	245	Steubenville-Weirton, OH-WV	52
152	Longview-Marshall, TX	287	198	Jacksonville, NC	137	246	Altoona, PA	47
152	Lubbock, TX	287	200	Chico-Paradise, CA	135	246	Sioux Falls, SD	47
154	Benton Harbor, MI	286	201	Fitchburg-Leominster, MA	133	248	Kokomo, IN	46
155	Greenville, NC	285	201	Lincoln, NE	133	249	Provo-Orem, UT	45
156	Athens, GA	283	203	Bremerton, WA	132	250	Greeley, CO	42
157	Rocky Mount, NC	280	204	Alexandria, LA	131	251	Fort Collins-Loveland, CO	41
157	Scranton-Wilkes-Barre-Hazleton, PA	280	205	Waterloo-Cedar Falls, IA	130	251	San Angelo, TX	41
159	Florence, SC	277	206	Sioux City, IA-NE	127	253	Pittsfield, MA	38
160	Pine Bluff, AR	272	207	Lynchburg, VA	124	254	Enid, OK	37
161	Tyler, TX	266	208	Johnson City-Kingsport-Bristol, TN-VA	121	255	Florence, AL	36
162	Hickory-Morganton, NC	264	209	Columbia, MO	120	256	Appleton-Oshkosh-Neenah, WI	34
163	Jackson, TN	262	210	Yuba City, CA	116	257	Rapid City, SD	28
164	Dutchess County, NY	260	211	Portland, ME	114	258	Cumberland, MD-WV	26
165	Newburgh, NY-PA	256	212	Bryan-College Station, TX	113	259	Bangor, ME	24
166	Eugene-Springfield, OR	253	213	Jackson, MI	107	259	Cheyenne, WY	24
166	Odessa-Midland, TX	253	214	Sherman-Denison, TX	105	259	Sheboygan, WI	24
168	Sumter, SC	246	215	Janesville-Beloit, WI	104	262	Glens Falls, NY	22
169	Goldsboro, NC	243	216	Charlottesville, VA	96	262	Nashua, NH	22
169	Roanoke, VA	243	216	Decatur, AL	96	262	Rochester, MN	22
171	Yakima, WA	233	218	Danville, VA	95	265	Fargo-Moorhead, ND-MN	21
172	Amarillo, TX	213	219	Binghamton, NY	92	266	Grand Forks, ND-MN	16
172	Merced, CA	213	219	San Luis Obispo-Atascadero, CA	92	266	St. Cloud, MN	16
174	Gadsden, AL	206	221	Fort Walton Beach, FL	91	268	Bloomington, IN	15
175	Utica-Rome, NY	204	222	Boise, ID	87	268	Eau Claire, WI	15
176	New London-Norwich, CT-RI	198	222	Brazoria, TX	87	268	La Crosse, WI-MN	15
177	Wichita Falls, TX	192	224	Victoria, TX	86	271	Dubuque, IA	14
178	Texarkana, TX-AR	190	225	Boulder-Longmont, CO	79	271	Wausau, WI	14
179	Evansville-Henderson, IN-KY	187	225	Danbury, CT	79	273	Bismarck, ND	5
180	Clarksville-Hopkinsville, TN-KY	186	225	Punta Gorda, FL	79	–	Albany, NY**	NA
181	Asheville, NC	175	228	Joplin, MO	78	–	Chicago, IL**	NA
181	Houma, LA	175	229	Duluth-Superior, MN-WI	77	–	Cleveland, OH**	NA
183	Yolo, CA	173	230	Olympia, WA	75	–	Houston, TX**	NA
184	Pueblo, CO	172	230	Richland-Kennewick-Pasco, WA	75	–	Indianapolis, IN**	NA
185	Anniston, AL	171	232	Medford-Ashland, OR	73	–	Kansas City, MO-KS**	NA
186	Laredo, TX	166	233	Fort Smith, AR-OK	70	–	Omaha, NE**	NA
186	Mansfield, OH	166	233	Hagerstown, MD	70	–	St. Louis, MO-IL**	NA
188	Lawton, OK	165	235	Johnstown, PA	68	–	West Palm Beach-Boca Raton, FL**	NA

Source: U.S. Department of Justice, Federal Bureau of Investigation
    "Crime in the United States 1993" (Uniform Crime Reports, December 4, 1994)
*Robbery is the taking or attempting to take anything of value by force or threat of force.
**Not available.

18. Robbery Rate in 1993

National Rate = 255.8 Robberies per 100,000 Population*

RANK	METRO AREA	RATE	RANK	METRO AREA	RATE	RANK	METRO AREA	RATE
160	Abilene, TX	111.4	249	Cheyenne, WY	31.2	53	Fort Worth–Arlington, TX	264.0
124	Akron, OH	160.0	–	Chicago, IL**	NA	11	Fresno, CA	427.7
13	Albany, GA	412.1	205	Chico–Paradise, CA	70.9	84	Gadsden, AL	204.9
–	Albany, NY**	NA	88	Cincinnati, OH–KY–IN	202.1	39	Gainesville, FL	300.8
55	Albuquerque, NM	259.0	174	Clarksville–Hopkinsville, TN–KY	103.1	79	Galveston–Texas City, TX	210.7
177	Alexandria, LA	100.0	–	Cleveland, OH**	NA	59	Gary–Hammond, IN	245.7
241	Altoona, PA	35.6	180	Colorado Springs, CO	98.0	261	Glens Falls, NY	18.1
163	Amarillo, TX	109.0	175	Columbia, MO	101.8	71	Goldsboro, NC	222.1
69	Anchorage, AK	226.5	37	Columbia, SC	301.7	264	Grand Forks, ND–MN	15.4
195	Ann Arbor, MI	86.5	106	Columbus, GA–AL	182.2	143	Grand Rapids–Muskegon–Holland, MI	133.5
133	Anniston, AL	145.2	31	Columbus, OH	318.1	250	Greeley, CO	30.0
271	Appleton–Oshkosh–Neenah, WI	10.3	135	Corpus Christi, TX	142.6	252	Green Bay, WI	27.6
193	Asheville, NC	87.2	256	Cumberland, MD–WV	25.4	63	Greensboro–Winston Salem–High Point, NC	231.6
102	Athens, GA	183.2	28	Dallas, TX	326.4	57	Greenville, NC	254.1
21	Atlanta, GA	369.1	226	Danbury, CT	48.6	104	Greenville–Spartanburg–Anderson, SC	182.5
33	Atlantic City, NJ	310.9	198	Danville, VA	85.6	223	Hagerstown, MD	55.2
110	Augusta–Aiken, GA–SC	175.9	131	Daytona Beach, FL	150.5	145	Harrisburg–Lebanon–Carlisle, PA	131.9
97	Austin–San Marcos, TX	190.3	74	Dayton–Springfield, OH	220.2	99	Hartford, CT	187.1
92	Bakersfield, CA	199.1	207	Decatur, AL	70.2	194	Hickory–Morganton, NC	86.8
4	Baltimore, MD	636.2	100	Denver, CO	186.5	149	Honolulu, HI	123.9
242	Bangor, ME	35.5	204	Des Moines, IA	71.5	186	Houma, LA	93.5
237	Barnstable–Yarmouth, MA	40.1	18	Detroit, MI	400.2	–	Houston, TX**	NA
17	Baton Rouge, LA	403.0	166	Dothan, AL	106.8	227	Huntington–Ashland, WV–KY–OH	47.6
45	Beaumont–Port Arthur, TX	290.4	262	Dubuque, IA	16.0	155	Huntsville, AL	115.8
232	Bellingham, WA	43.3	248	Duluth–Superior, MN–WI	31.6	–	Indianapolis, IN**	NA
109	Benton Harbor, MI	176.3	179	Dutchess County, NY	98.4	207	Jackson, MI	70.2
123	Bergen–Passaic, NJ	160.1	269	Eau Claire, WI	10.6	15	Jackson, MS	406.9
243	Binghamton, NY	34.3	56	El Paso, TX	254.2	30	Jackson, TN	321.8
50	Birmingham, AL	272.6	190	Elkhart–Goshen, IN	89.5	16	Jacksonville, FL	406.0
273	Bismarck, ND	5.8	212	Enid, OK	65.1	187	Jacksonville, NC	93.3
266	Bloomington, IN	13.4	122	Erie, PA	163.1	203	Janesville–Beloit, WI	72.2
255	Boise, ID	26.4	199	Eugene–Springfield, OR	85.2	5	Jersey City, NJ	598.3
87	Boston, MA–NH	202.5	210	Evansville–Henderson, IN–KY	65.5	253	Johnson City–Kingsport–Bristol, TN–VA	26.8
245	Boulder–Longmont, CO	32.2	267	Fargo–Moorhead, ND–MN	13.3	251	Johnstown, PA	28.1
233	Brazoria, TX	41.9	24	Fayetteville, NC	350.3	222	Joplin, MO	56.3
217	Bremerton, WA	61.3	256	Fayetteville–Springdale–Rogers, AR	25.4	142	Kalamazoo–Battle Creek, MI	134.1
19	Bridgeport, CT	392.6	183	Fitchburg–Leominster, MA	97.1	–	Kansas City, MO–KS**	NA
120	Brockton, MA	163.7	41	Flint, MI	294.9	169	Kenosha, WI	105.8
138	Brownsville–Harlingen–San Benito, TX	136.5	254	Florence, AL	26.5	137	Killeen–Temple, TX	138.1
191	Bryan–College Station, TX	88.5	65	Florence, SC	231.0	229	Kokomo, IN	46.2
43	Buffalo–Niagara Falls, NY	293.0	259	Fort Collins–Loveland, CO	20.1	268	La Crosse, WI–MN	12.6
78	Canton–Massillon, OH	211.0	22	Fort Lauderdale, FL	366.5	246	Lafayette, IN	31.8
147	Charleston, WV	128.2	96	Fort Myers–Cape Coral, FL	195.4	158	Lafayette, LA	112.0
75	Charleston–North Charleston, SC	216.9	116	Fort Pierce–Port St. Lucie, FL	168.2	112	Lake Charles, LA	174.3
206	Charlottesville, VA	70.3	239	Fort Smith, AR–OK	38.3	68	Lakeland–Winter Haven, FL	226.8
25	Charlotte–Gastonia–Rock Hill, NC–SC	343.0	219	Fort Walton Beach, FL	58.5	200	Lancaster, PA	82.7
103	Chattanooga, TN–GA	183.0	146	Fort Wayne, IN	130.2	181	Lansing–East Lansing, MI	97.2

Source: U.S. Department of Justice, Federal Bureau of Investigation
   "Crime in the United States 1993" (Uniform Crime Reports, December 4, 1994)
*Robbery is the taking or attempting to take anything of value by force or threat of force.
**Not available.

18. Robbery Rate in 1993 (continued)

National Rate = 255.8 Robberies per 100,000 Population*

RANK	METRO AREA	RATE	RANK	METRO AREA	RATE	RANK	METRO AREA	RATE
161	Laredo, TX	109.7	234	Olympia, WA	41.6	91	Seattle–Bellevue–Everett, WA	200.2
12	Las Vegas, NV–AZ	413.9	–	Omaha, NE**	NA	258	Sheboygan, WI	22.6
114	Lawrence, MA–NH	169.6	73	Orange County, CA	221.8	164	Sherman–Denison, TX	108.3
139	Lawton, OK	135.9	60	Orlando, FL	244.8	51	Shreveport–Bossier City, LA	266.8
220	Lewiston–Auburn, ME	57.6	215	Owensboro, KY	63.6	165	Sioux City, IA–NE	108.0
119	Lexington, KY	166.4	151	Panama City, FL	118.4	247	Sioux Falls, SD	31.7
218	Lincoln, NE	60.3	27	Philadelphia, PA–NJ	327.2	77	South Bend, IN	211.1
35	Little Rock–North Little Rock, AR	309.5	83	Phoenix–Mesa, AZ	205.1	157	Spokane, WA	114.3
136	Longview–Marshall, TX	140.8	32	Pine Bluff, AR	315.1	98	Springfield, MA	188.8
3	Los Angeles–Long Beach, CA	721.6	118	Pittsburgh, PA	167.2	220	Springfield, MO	57.6
93	Louisville, KY–IN	198.5	238	Pittsfield, MA	38.6	127	Stamford–Norwalk, CT	153.8
148	Lubbock, TX	125.7	225	Portland, ME	48.8	240	Steubenville–Weirton, OH–WV	36.5
216	Lynchburg, VA	61.6	95	Portland–Vancouver, OR–WA	196.1	20	Stockton–Lodi, CA	379.4
125	Macon, GA	159.7	172	Providence–Fall River–Warwick, RI–MA	103.6	270	St. Cloud, MN	10.4
181	Madison, WI	97.2	263	Provo–Orem, UT	15.9	213	St. Joseph, MO	64.8
188	Manchester, NH	91.7	140	Pueblo, CO	135.0	–	St. Louis, MO–IL**	NA
184	Mansfield, OH	94.0	211	Punta Gorda, FL	65.3	66	Sumter, SC	230.9
178	McAllen–Edinburg–Mission, TX	99.0	88	Racine, WI	202.1	189	Syracuse, NY	91.4
228	Medford–Ashland, OR	46.4	64	Raleigh–Durham–Chapel Hill, NC	231.5	67	Tacoma, WA	228.1
9	Memphis, TN–AR–MS	548.9	244	Rapid City, SD	32.6	14	Tallahassee, FL	408.7
159	Merced, CA	111.5	108	Reading, PA	178.2	34	Tampa–St. Petersburg–Clearwater, FL	309.7
2	Miami, FL	913.3	185	Redding, CA	93.6	126	Texarkana, TX–AR	154.4
167	Middlesex–Sommerset–Hunterdon, NJ	106.4	94	Reno, NV	198.4	48	Toledo, OH	276.0
38	Milwaukee–Waukesha, WI	301.1	230	Richland–Kennewick–Pasco, WA	45.6	52	Trenton, NJ	264.7
101	Minneapolis–St. Paul, MN–WI	184.3	58	Richmond–Petersburg, VA	250.9	129	Tucson, AZ	152.9
26	Mobile, AL	328.3	36	Riverside–San Bernardino, CA	308.5	113	Tulsa, OK	170.0
128	Modesto, CA	153.3	169	Roanoke, VA	105.8	72	Tuscaloosa, AL	221.9
201	Monmouth–Ocean, NJ	74.5	260	Rochester, MN	19.7	115	Tyler, TX	169.0
176	Monroe, LA	101.1	111	Rochester, NY	175.4	214	Utica–Rome, NY	64.2
82	Montgomery, AL	205.8	90	Rocky Mount, NC	200.9	76	Vallejo–Fairfield–Napa, CA	211.7
80	Myrtle Beach, SC	209.1	46	Sacramento, CA	286.2	144	Ventura, CA	132.8
104	Naples, FL	182.5	117	Saginaw–Bay City–Midland, MI	167.6	162	Victoria, TX	109.5
265	Nashua, NH	13.7	171	Salem, OR	104.3	40	Vineland–Millville–Bridgeton, NJ	298.8
44	Nashville, TN	292.9	61	Salinas, CA	244.6	150	Visalia–Tulare–Porterville, CA	122.0
141	Nassau–Suffolk, NY	134.2	196	Salt Lake City–Ogden, UT	86.1	54	Waco, TX	260.6
81	New Bedford, MA	207.9	236	San Angelo, TX	40.6	29	Washington, DC–MD–VA–WV	324.0
49	New Haven–Meriden, CT	274.9	62	San Antonio, TX	232.9	121	Waterbury, CT	163.5
209	New London–Norwich, CT–RI	65.7	47	San Diego, CA	285.2	173	Waterloo–Cedar Falls, IA	103.3
8	New Orleans, LA	558.9	6	San Francisco, CA	593.8	272	Wausau, WI	10.1
1	New York, NY	1,047.7	154	San Jose, CA	116.7	–	West Palm Beach–Boca Raton, FL**	NA
7	Newark, NJ	564.8	235	San Luis Obispo–Atascadero, CA	41.3	132	Wichita Falls, TX	147.0
202	Newburgh, NY–PA	73.1	153	Santa Barbara–Santa Maria–Lompoc, CA	117.0	224	Williamsport, PA	50.4
42	Norfolk–Va Beach–Newport News, VA–NC	293.5	134	Santa Cruz–Watsonville, CA	143.1	107	Wilmington, NC	179.9
10	Oakland, CA	453.1	197	Santa Rosa, CA	85.7	130	Worcester, MA–CT	151.5
85	Ocala, FL	204.7	70	Sarasota–Bradenton, FL	222.7	156	Yakima, WA	115.2
168	Odessa–Midland, TX	106.1	23	Savannah, GA	359.7	152	Yolo, CA	118.3
86	Oklahoma City, OK	203.8	231	Scranton–Wilkes-Barre–Hazleton, PA	43.7	192	Yuba City, CA	88.1

Source: U.S. Department of Justice, Federal Bureau of Investigation
   "Crime in the United States 1993" (Uniform Crime Reports, December 4, 1994)
*Robbery is the taking or attempting to take anything of value by force or threat of force.
**Not available.

18. Robbery Rate in 1993 (continued)

National Rate = 255.8 Robberies per 100,000 Population*

RANK	METRO AREA	RATE	RANK	METRO AREA	RATE	RANK	METRO AREA	RATE
1	New York, NY	1,047.7	48	Toledo, OH	276.0	95	Portland-Vancouver, OR-WA	196.1
2	Miami, FL	913.3	49	New Haven-Meriden, CT	274.9	96	Fort Myers-Cape Coral, FL	195.4
3	Los Angeles-Long Beach, CA	721.6	50	Birmingham, AL	272.6	97	Austin-San Marcos, TX	190.3
4	Baltimore, MD	636.2	51	Shreveport-Bossier City, LA	266.8	98	Springfield, MA	188.8
5	Jersey City, NJ	598.3	52	Trenton, NJ	264.7	99	Hartford, CT	187.1
6	San Francisco, CA	593.8	53	Fort Worth-Arlington, TX	264.0	100	Denver, CO	186.5
7	Newark, NJ	564.8	54	Waco, TX	260.6	101	Minneapolis-St. Paul, MN-WI	184.3
8	New Orleans, LA	558.9	55	Albuquerque, NM	259.0	102	Athens, GA	183.2
9	Memphis, TN-AR-MS	548.9	56	El Paso, TX	254.2	103	Chattanooga, TN-GA	183.0
10	Oakland, CA	453.1	57	Greenville, NC	254.1	104	Greenville-Spartanburg-Anderson, SC	182.5
11	Fresno, CA	427.7	58	Richmond-Petersburg, VA	250.9	104	Naples, FL	182.5
12	Las Vegas, NV-AZ	413.9	59	Gary-Hammond, IN	245.7	106	Columbus, GA-AL	182.2
13	Albany, GA	412.1	60	Orlando, FL	244.8	107	Wilmington, NC	179.9
14	Tallahassee, FL	408.7	61	Salinas, CA	244.6	108	Reading, PA	178.2
15	Jackson, MS	406.9	62	San Antonio, TX	232.9	109	Benton Harbor, MI	176.3
16	Jacksonville, FL	406.0	63	Greensboro-Winston Salem-High Point, NC	231.6	110	Augusta-Aiken, GA-SC	175.9
17	Baton Rouge, LA	403.0	64	Raleigh-Durham-Chapel Hill, NC	231.5	111	Rochester, NY	175.4
18	Detroit, MI	400.2	65	Florence, SC	231.0	112	Lake Charles, LA	174.3
19	Bridgeport, CT	392.6	66	Sumter, SC	230.9	113	Tulsa, OK	170.0
20	Stockton-Lodi, CA	379.4	67	Tacoma, WA	228.1	114	Lawrence, MA-NH	169.6
21	Atlanta, GA	369.1	68	Lakeland-Winter Haven, FL	226.8	115	Tyler, TX	169.0
22	Fort Lauderdale, FL	366.5	69	Anchorage, AK	226.5	116	Fort Pierce-Port St. Lucie, FL	168.2
23	Savannah, GA	359.7	70	Sarasota-Bradenton, FL	222.7	117	Saginaw-Bay City-Midland, MI	167.6
24	Fayetteville, NC	350.3	71	Goldsboro, NC	222.1	118	Pittsburgh, PA	167.2
25	Charlotte-Gastonia-Rock Hill, NC-SC	343.0	72	Tuscaloosa, AL	221.9	119	Lexington, KY	166.4
26	Mobile, AL	328.3	73	Orange County, CA	221.8	120	Brockton, MA	163.7
27	Philadelphia, PA-NJ	327.2	74	Dayton-Springfield, OH	220.2	121	Waterbury, CT	163.5
28	Dallas, TX	326.4	75	Charleston-North Charleston, SC	216.9	122	Erie, PA	163.1
29	Washington, DC-MD-VA-WV	324.0	76	Vallejo-Fairfield-Napa, CA	211.7	123	Bergen-Passaic, NJ	160.1
30	Jackson, TN	321.8	77	South Bend, IN	211.1	124	Akron, OH	160.0
31	Columbus, OH	318.1	78	Canton-Massillon, OH	211.0	125	Macon, GA	159.7
32	Pine Bluff, AR	315.1	79	Galveston-Texas City, TX	210.7	126	Texarkana, TX-AR	154.4
33	Atlantic City, NJ	310.9	80	Myrtle Beach, SC	209.1	127	Stamford-Norwalk, CT	153.8
34	Tampa-St. Petersburg-Clearwater, FL	309.7	81	New Bedford, MA	207.9	128	Modesto, CA	153.3
35	Little Rock-North Little Rock, AR	309.5	82	Montgomery, AL	205.8	129	Tucson, AZ	152.9
36	Riverside-San Bernardino, CA	308.5	83	Phoenix-Mesa, AZ	205.1	130	Worcester, MA-CT	151.5
37	Columbia, SC	301.7	84	Gadsden, AL	204.9	131	Daytona Beach, FL	150.5
38	Milwaukee-Waukesha, WI	301.1	85	Ocala, FL	204.7	132	Wichita Falls, TX	147.0
39	Gainesville, FL	300.8	86	Oklahoma City, OK	203.8	133	Anniston, AL	145.2
40	Vineland-Millville-Bridgeton, NJ	298.8	87	Boston, MA-NH	202.5	134	Santa Cruz-Watsonville, CA	143.1
41	Flint, MI	294.9	88	Cincinnati, OH-KY-IN	202.1	135	Corpus Christi, TX	142.6
42	Norfolk-Va Beach-Newport News, VA-NC	293.5	88	Racine, WI	202.1	136	Longview-Marshall, TX	140.8
43	Buffalo-Niagara Falls, NY	293.0	90	Rocky Mount, NC	200.9	137	Killeen-Temple, TX	138.1
44	Nashville, TN	292.9	91	Seattle-Bellevue-Everett, WA	200.2	138	Brownsville-Harlingen-San Benito, TX	136.5
45	Beaumont-Port Arthur, TX	290.4	92	Bakersfield, CA	199.1	139	Lawton, OK	135.9
46	Sacramento, CA	286.2	93	Louisville, KY-IN	198.5	140	Pueblo, CO	135.0
47	San Diego, CA	285.2	94	Reno, NV	198.4	141	Nassau-Suffolk, NY	134.2

Source: U.S. Department of Justice, Federal Bureau of Investigation
    "Crime in the United States 1993" (Uniform Crime Reports, December 4, 1994)
*Robbery is the taking or attempting to take anything of value by force or threat of force.
**Not available.

18. Robbery Rate in 1993 (continued)

National Rate = 255.8 Robberies per 100,000 Population*

RANK	METRO AREA	RATE	RANK	METRO AREA	RATE	RANK	METRO AREA	RATE
142	Kalamazoo–Battle Creek, MI	134.1	189	Syracuse, NY	91.4	236	San Angelo, TX	40.6
143	Grand Rapids–Muskegon–Holland, MI	133.5	190	Elkhart–Goshen, IN	89.5	237	Barnstable–Yarmouth, MA	40.1
144	Ventura, CA	132.8	191	Bryan–College Station, TX	88.5	238	Pittsfield, MA	38.6
145	Harrisburg–Lebanon–Carlisle, PA	131.9	192	Yuba City, CA	88.1	239	Fort Smith, AR–OK	38.3
146	Fort Wayne, IN	130.2	193	Asheville, NC	87.2	240	Steubenville–Weirton, OH–WV	36.5
147	Charleston, WV	128.2	194	Hickory–Morganton, NC	86.8	241	Altoona, PA	35.6
148	Lubbock, TX	125.7	195	Ann Arbor, MI	86.5	242	Bangor, ME	35.5
149	Honolulu, HI	123.9	196	Salt Lake City–Ogden, UT	86.1	243	Binghamton, NY	34.3
150	Visalia–Tulare–Porterville, CA	122.0	197	Santa Rosa, CA	85.7	244	Rapid City, SD	32.6
151	Panama City, FL	118.4	198	Danville, VA	85.6	245	Boulder–Longmont, CO	32.2
152	Yolo, CA	118.3	199	Eugene–Springfield, OR	85.2	246	Lafayette, IN	31.8
153	Santa Barbara–Santa Maria–Lompoc, CA	117.0	200	Lancaster, PA	82.7	247	Sioux Falls, SD	31.7
154	San Jose, CA	116.7	201	Monmouth–Ocean, NJ	74.5	248	Duluth–Superior, MN–WI	31.6
155	Huntsville, AL	115.8	202	Newburgh, NY–PA	73.1	249	Cheyenne, WY	31.2
156	Yakima, WA	115.2	203	Janesville–Beloit, WI	72.2	250	Greeley, CO	30.0
157	Spokane, WA	114.3	204	Des Moines, IA	71.5	251	Johnstown, PA	28.1
158	Lafayette, LA	112.0	205	Chico–Paradise, CA	70.9	252	Green Bay, WI	27.6
159	Merced, CA	111.5	206	Charlottesville, VA	70.3	253	Johnson City–Kingsport–Bristol, TN–VA	26.8
160	Abilene, TX	111.4	207	Decatur, AL	70.2	254	Florence, AL	26.5
161	Laredo, TX	109.7	207	Jackson, MI	70.2	255	Boise, ID	26.4
162	Victoria, TX	109.5	209	New London–Norwich, CT–RI	65.7	256	Cumberland, MD–WV	25.4
163	Amarillo, TX	109.0	210	Evansville–Henderson, IN–KY	65.5	256	Fayetteville–Springdale–Rogers, AR	25.4
164	Sherman–Denison, TX	108.3	211	Punta Gorda, FL	65.3	258	Sheboygan, WI	22.6
165	Sioux City, IA–NE	108.0	212	Enid, OK	65.1	259	Fort Collins–Loveland, CO	20.1
166	Dothan, AL	106.8	213	St. Joseph, MO	64.8	260	Rochester, MN	19.7
167	Middlesex–Sommerset–Hunterdon, NJ	106.4	214	Utica–Rome, NY	64.2	261	Glens Falls, NY	18.1
168	Odessa–Midland, TX	106.1	215	Owensboro, KY	63.6	262	Dubuque, IA	16.0
169	Kenosha, WI	105.8	216	Lynchburg, VA	61.6	263	Provo–Orem, UT	15.9
169	Roanoke, VA	105.8	217	Bremerton, WA	61.3	264	Grand Forks, ND–MN	15.4
171	Salem, OR	104.3	218	Lincoln, NE	60.3	265	Nashua, NH	13.7
172	Providence–Fall River–Warwick, RI–MA	103.6	219	Fort Walton Beach, FL	58.5	266	Bloomington, IN	13.4
173	Waterloo–Cedar Falls, IA	103.3	220	Lewiston–Auburn, ME	57.6	267	Fargo–Moorhead, ND–MN	13.3
174	Clarksville–Hopkinsville, TN–KY	103.1	220	Springfield, MO	57.6	268	La Crosse, WI–MN	12.6
175	Columbia, MO	101.8	222	Joplin, MO	56.3	269	Eau Claire, WI	10.6
176	Monroe, LA	101.1	223	Hagerstown, MD	55.2	270	St. Cloud, MN	10.4
177	Alexandria, LA	100.0	224	Williamsport, PA	50.4	271	Appleton–Oshkosh–Neenah, WI	10.3
178	McAllen–Edinburg–Mission, TX	99.0	225	Portland, ME	48.8	272	Wausau, WI	10.1
179	Dutchess County, NY	98.4	226	Danbury, CT	48.6	273	Bismarck, ND	5.8
180	Colorado Springs, CO	98.0	227	Huntington–Ashland, WV–KY–OH	47.6	–	Albany, NY**	NA
181	Lansing–East Lansing, MI	97.2	228	Medford–Ashland, OR	46.4	–	Chicago, IL**	NA
181	Madison, WI	97.2	229	Kokomo, IN	46.2	–	Cleveland, OH**	NA
183	Fitchburg–Leominster, MA	97.1	230	Richland–Kennewick–Pasco, WA	45.6	–	Houston, TX**	NA
184	Mansfield, OH	94.0	231	Scranton–Wilkes-Barre–Hazleton, PA	43.7	–	Indianapolis, IN**	NA
185	Redding, CA	93.6	232	Bellingham, WA	43.3	–	Kansas City, MO–KS**	NA
186	Houma, LA	93.5	233	Brazoria, TX	41.9	–	Omaha, NE**	NA
187	Jacksonville, NC	93.3	234	Olympia, WA	41.6	–	St. Louis, MO–IL**	NA
188	Manchester, NH	91.7	235	San Luis Obispo–Atascadero, CA	41.3	–	West Palm Beach–Boca Raton, FL**	NA

Source: U.S. Department of Justice, Federal Bureau of Investigation
    "Crime in the United States 1993" (Uniform Crime Reports, December 4, 1994)
*Robbery is the taking or attempting to take anything of value by force or threat of force.
**Not available.

19. Percent Change in Robbery Rate: 1992 to 1993

National Percent Change = 3.0% Decrease*

RANK	METRO AREA	% CHANGE	RANK	METRO AREA	% CHANGE	RANK	METRO AREA	% CHANGE
99	Abilene, TX	1.83	1	Cheyenne, WY	95.00	217	Fort Worth-Arlington, TX	(19.04)
201	Akron, OH	(15.34)	–	Chicago, IL**	NA	176	Fresno, CA	(10.54)
148	Albany, GA	(4.27)	80	Chico-Paradise, CA	5.51	31	Gadsden, AL	18.44
–	Albany, NY**	NA	126	Cincinnati, OH-KY-IN	(1.56)	124	Gainesville, FL	(1.31)
84	Albuquerque, NM	4.23	8	Clarksville-Hopkinsville, TN-KY	39.89	180	Galveston-Texas City, TX	(11.17)
81	Alexandria, LA	5.26	–	Cleveland, OH**	NA	77	Gary-Hammond, IN	6.09
46	Altoona, PA	11.95	193	Colorado Springs, CO	(13.35)	17	Glens Falls, NY	27.46
231	Amarillo, TX	(24.67)	221	Columbia, MO	(19.91)	179	Goldsboro, NC	(11.12)
42	Anchorage, AK	13.02	67	Columbia, SC	7.10	41	Grand Forks, ND-MN	14.07
142	Ann Arbor, MI	(3.67)	15	Columbus, GA-AL	30.52	48	Grand Rapids-Muskegon-Holland, MI	11.62
203	Anniston, AL	(15.48)	105	Columbus, OH	1.21	234	Greeley, CO	(27.01)
215	Appleton-Oshkosh-Neenah, WI	(17.60)	155	Corpus Christi, TX	(6.00)	26	Green Bay, WI	22.12
232	Asheville, NC	(25.79)	9	Cumberland, MD-WV	38.80	74	Greensboro-Winston Salem-High Point, NC	6.34
169	Athens, GA	(8.67)	225	Dallas, TX	(22.78)	47	Greenville, NC	11.64
119	Atlanta, GA	(0.27)	96	Danbury, CT	2.32	61	Greenville-Spartanburg-Anderson, SC	8.44
60	Atlantic City, NJ	8.52	32	Danville, VA	18.40	138	Hagerstown, MD	(3.16)
209	Augusta-Aiken, GA-SC	(16.32)	229	Daytona Beach, FL	(23.68)	127	Harrisburg-Lebanon-Carlisle, PA	(1.64)
94	Austin-San Marcos, TX	2.64	196	Dayton-Springfield, OH	(13.95)	181	Hartford, CT	(11.41)
129	Bakersfield, CA	(1.73)	187	Decatur, AL	(12.25)	92	Hickory-Morganton, NC	2.72
116	Baltimore, MD	(0.14)	115	Denver, CO	(0.05)	68	Honolulu, HI	7.09
226	Bangor, ME	(23.33)	165	Des Moines, IA	(7.86)	230	Houma, LA	(24.47)
18	Barnstable-Yarmouth, MA	25.31	56	Detroit, MI	9.31	–	Houston, TX**	NA
130	Baton Rouge, LA	(1.92)	36	Dothan, AL	17.36	241	Huntington-Ashland, WV-KY-OH	(34.07)
183	Beaumont-Port Arthur, TX	(11.65)	191	Dubuque, IA	(12.57)	227	Huntsville, AL	(23.51)
4	Bellingham, WA	49.83	211	Duluth-Superior, MN-WI	(16.40)	–	Indianapolis, IN**	NA
20	Benton Harbor, MI	24.51	–	Dutchess County, NY**	NA	52	Jackson, MI	10.03
–	Bergen-Passaic, NJ**	NA	69	Eau Claire, WI	7.07	35	Jackson, MS	17.40
6	Binghamton, NY	43.51	153	El Paso, TX	(5.43)	53	Jackson, TN	9.98
151	Birmingham, AL	(4.62)	65	Elkhart-Goshen, IN	7.31	139	Jacksonville, FL	(3.31)
248	Bismarck, ND	(51.67)	167	Enid, OK	(8.05)	109	Jacksonville, NC	0.86
246	Bloomington, IN	(40.44)	27	Erie, PA	22.08	2	Janesville-Beloit, WI	53.94
242	Boise, ID	(34.33)	222	Eugene-Springfield, OR	(20.08)	–	Jersey City, NJ**	NA
–	Boston, MA-NH**	NA	140	Evansville-Henderson, IN-KY	(3.39)	178	Johnson City-Kingsport-Bristol, TN-VA	(10.96)
43	Boulder-Longmont, CO	12.20	199	Fargo-Moorhead, ND-MN	(14.74)	210	Johnstown, PA	(16.37)
175	Brazoria, TX	(10.28)	29	Fayetteville, NC	21.84	–	Joplin, MO**	NA
188	Bremerton, WA	(12.30)	198	Fayetteville-Springdale-Rogers, AR	(14.48)	173	Kalamazoo-Battle Creek, MI	(10.06)
189	Bridgeport, CT	(12.46)	–	Fitchburg-Leominster, MA**	NA	–	Kansas City, MO-KS**	NA
184	Brockton, MA	(11.89)	66	Flint, MI	7.28	135	Kenosha, WI	(2.22)
30	Brownsville-Harlingen-San Benito, TX	21.01	235	Florence, AL	(27.40)	5	Killeen-Temple, TX	45.37
189	Bryan-College Station, TX	(12.46)	3	Florence, SC	51.67	185	Kokomo, IN	(12.00)
–	Buffalo-Niagara Falls, NY**	NA	–	Fort Collins-Loveland, CO**	NA	114	La Crosse, WI-MN	0.00
91	Canton-Massillon, OH	2.73	82	Fort Lauderdale, FL	4.62	57	Lafayette, IN	9.28
63	Charleston, WV	7.91	236	Fort Myers-Cape Coral, FL	(28.29)	103	Lafayette, LA	1.45
55	Charleston-North Charleston, SC	9.43	121	Fort Pierce-Port St. Lucie, FL	(0.41)	–	Lake Charles, LA**	NA
219	Charlottesville, VA	(19.47)	238	Fort Smith, AR-OK	(31.24)	206	Lakeland-Winter Haven, FL	(16.06)
101	Charlotte-Gastonia-Rock Hill, NC-SC	1.69	224	Fort Walton Beach, FL	(21.05)	22	Lancaster, PA	24.36
152	Chattanooga, TN-GA	(5.08)	87	Fort Wayne, IN	3.91	79	Lansing-East Lansing, MI	5.65

Source: Morgan Quitno Corporation using data from U.S. Department of Justice, Federal Bureau of Investigation
    "Crime in the United States 1993" (Uniform Crime Reports, December 4, 1994)
Robbery is the taking or attempting to take anything of value by force or threat of force.
**Not available.*

19. Percent Change in Robbery Rate: 1992 to 1993 (continued)

National Percent Change = 3.0% Decrease*

RANK	METRO AREA	% CHANGE	RANK	METRO AREA	% CHANGE	RANK	METRO AREA	CHANGE
156	Laredo, TX	(6.24)	118	Olympia, WA	(0.24)	75	Seattle–Bellevue–Everett, WA	6.26
107	Las Vegas, NV–AZ	1.12	–	Omaha, NE**	NA	40	Sheboygan, WI	14.14
–	Lawrence, MA–NH**	NA	145	Orange County, CA	(3.98)	70	Sherman–Denison, TX	6.91
125	Lawton, OK	(1.45)	137	Orlando, FL	(2.97)	45	Shreveport–Bossier City, LA	11.96
21	Lewiston–Auburn, ME	24.41	7	Owensboro, KY	41.33	–	Sioux City, IA–NE**	NA
85	Lexington, KY	4.20	34	Panama City, FL	17.81	13	Sioux Falls, SD	34.32
163	Lincoln, NE	(7.66)	122	Philadelphia, PA–NJ	(0.73)	83	South Bend, IN	4.25
141	Little Rock–North Little Rock, AR	(3.49)	50	Phoenix–Mesa, AZ	10.80	149	Spokane, WA	(4.43)
120	Longview–Marshall, TX	(0.28)	11	Pine Bluff, AR	35.41	197	Springfield, MA	(14.06)
143	Los Angeles–Long Beach, CA	(3.80)	159	Pittsburgh, PA	(6.64)	205	Springfield, MO	(16.03)
72	Louisville, KY–IN	6.84	104	Pittsfield, MA	1.31	23	Stamford–Norwalk, CT	23.24
223	Lubbock, TX	(20.14)	168	Portland, ME	(8.10)	12	Steubenville–Weirton, OH–WV	35.19
192	Lynchburg, VA	(13.24)	195	Portland–Vancouver, OR–WA	(13.80)	110	Stockton–Lodi, CA	0.82
157	Macon, GA	(6.33)	78	Providence–Fall River–Warwick, RI–MA	5.93	244	St. Cloud, MN	(38.82)
49	Madison, WI	10.96	147	Provo–Orem, UT	(4.22)	38	St. Joseph, MO	14.69
–	Manchester, NH**	NA	33	Pueblo, CO	18.32	–	St. Louis, MO–IL**	NA
220	Mansfield, OH	(19.73)	–	Punta Gorda, FL**	NA	59	Sumter, SC	8.86
51	McAllen–Edinburg–Mission, TX	10.24	150	Racine, WI	(4.49)	204	Syracuse, NY	(15.68)
63	Medford–Ashland, OR	7.91	160	Raleigh–Durham–Chapel Hill, NC	(6.80)	170	Tacoma, WA	(8.91)
100	Memphis, TN–AR–MS	1.74	247	Rapid City, SD	(45.76)	24	Tallahassee, FL	22.73
37	Merced, CA	16.51	108	Reading, PA	1.02	134	Tampa–St. Petersburg–Clearwater, FL	(2.18)
106	Miami, FL	1.20	19	Redding, CA	25.13	233	Texarkana, TX–AR	(25.98)
–	Middlesex–Sommerset–Hunterdon, NJ**	NA	90	Reno, NV	2.90	86	Toledo, OH	3.95
164	Milwaukee–Waukesha, WI	(7.75)	177	Richland–Kennewick–Pasco, WA	(10.94)	89	Trenton, NJ	3.08
97	Minneapolis–St. Paul, MN–WI	2.16	102	Richmond–Petersburg, VA	1.46	172	Tucson, AZ	(8.99)
–	Mobile, AL**	NA	162	Riverside–San Bernardino, CA	(7.63)	212	Tulsa, OK	(16.50)
171	Modesto, CA	(8.97)	133	Roanoke, VA	(2.13)	76	Tuscaloosa, AL	6.17
–	Monmouth–Ocean, NJ**	NA	239	Rochester, MN	(32.99)	146	Tyler, TX	(4.09)
182	Monroe, LA	(11.47)	88	Rochester, NY	3.48	166	Utica–Rome, NY	(8.02)
132	Montgomery, AL	(2.09)	186	Rocky Mount, NC	(12.23)	202	Vallejo–Fairfield–Napa, CA	(15.39)
10	Myrtle Beach, SC	35.96	136	Sacramento, CA	(2.69)	214	Ventura, CA	(17.16)
28	Naples, FL	22.07	98	Saginaw–Bay City–Midland, MI	1.88	245	Victoria, TX	(40.39)
249	Nashua, NH	(53.72)	208	Salem, OR	(16.29)	58	Vineland–Millville–Bridgeton, NJ	9.09
95	Nashville, TN	2.38	25	Salinas, CA	22.42	112	Visalia–Tulare–Porterville, CA	0.41
–	Nassau–Suffolk, NY**	NA	73	Salt Lake City–Ogden, UT	6.43	14	Waco, TX	32.35
–	New Bedford, MA**	NA	213	San Angelo, TX	(16.97)	123	Washington, DC–MD–VA–WV	(1.25)
117	New Haven–Meriden, CT	(0.15)	200	San Antonio, TX	(15.12)	216	Waterbury, CT	(18.70)
44	New London–Norwich, CT–RI	12.12	194	San Diego, CA	(13.63)	–	Waterloo–Cedar Falls, IA**	NA
128	New Orleans, LA	(1.65)	92	San Francisco, CA	2.72	237	Wausau, WI	(30.34)
–	New York, NY**	NA	154	San Jose, CA	(5.51)	–	West Palm Beach–Boca Raton, FL**	NA
–	Newark, NJ**	NA	–	San Luis Obispo–Atascadero, CA**	NA	243	Wichita Falls, TX	(35.33)
–	Newburgh, NY–PA**	NA	111	Santa Barbara–Santa Maria–Lompoc, CA	0.78	240	Williamsport, PA	(33.60)
62	Norfolk–Va Beach–Newport News, VA–NC	8.26	16	Santa Cruz–Watsonville, CA	27.65	227	Wilmington, NC	(23.51)
113	Oakland, CA	0.07	144	Santa Rosa, CA	(3.92)	–	Worcester, MA–CT**	NA
218	Ocala, FL	(19.41)	39	Sarasota–Bradenton, FL	14.21	161	Yakima, WA	(7.47)
207	Odessa–Midland, TX	(16.26)	131	Savannah, GA	(1.99)	71	Yolo, CA	6.87
174	Oklahoma City, OK	(10.22)	158	Scranton–Wilkes-Barre–Hazleton, PA	(6.62)	54	Yuba City, CA	9.85

Source: Morgan Quitno Corporation using data from U.S. Department of Justice, Federal Bureau of Investigation
"Crime in the United States 1993" (Uniform Crime Reports, December 4, 1994)
Robbery is the taking or attempting to take anything of value by force or threat of force.
**Not available.*

19. Percent Change in Robbery Rate: 1992 to 1993 (continued)

National Percent Change = 3.0% Decrease*

RANK	METRO AREA	% CHANGE	RANK	METRO AREA	% CHANGE	RANK	METRO AREA	% CHANGE
1	Cheyenne, WY	95.00	48	Grand Rapids–Muskegon–Holland, MI	11.62	95	Nashville, TN	2.38
2	Janesville–Beloit, WI	53.94	49	Madison, WI	10.96	96	Danbury, CT	2.32
3	Florence, SC	51.67	50	Phoenix–Mesa, AZ	10.80	97	Minneapolis–St. Paul, MN–WI	2.16
4	Bellingham, WA	49.83	51	McAllen–Edinburg–Mission, TX	10.24	98	Saginaw–Bay City–Midland, MI	1.88
5	Killeen–Temple, TX	45.37	52	Jackson, MI	10.03	99	Abilene, TX	1.83
6	Binghamton, NY	43.51	53	Jackson, TN	9.98	100	Memphis, TN–AR–MS	1.74
7	Owensboro, KY	41.33	54	Yuba City, CA	9.85	101	Charlotte–Gastonia–Rock Hill, NC–SC	1.69
8	Clarksville–Hopkinsville, TN–KY	39.89	55	Charleston–North Charleston, SC	9.43	102	Richmond–Petersburg, VA	1.46
9	Cumberland, MD–WV	38.80	56	Detroit, MI	9.31	103	Lafayette, LA	1.45
10	Myrtle Beach, SC	35.96	57	Lafayette, IN	9.28	104	Pittsfield, MA	1.31
11	Pine Bluff, AR	35.41	58	Vineland–Millville–Bridgeton, NJ	9.09	105	Columbus, OH	1.21
12	Steubenville–Weirton, OH–WV	35.19	59	Sumter, SC	8.86	106	Miami, FL	1.20
13	Sioux Falls, SD	34.32	60	Atlantic City, NJ	8.52	107	Las Vegas, NV–AZ	1.12
14	Waco, TX	32.35	61	Greenville–Spartanburg–Anderson, SC	8.44	108	Reading, PA	1.02
15	Columbus, GA–AL	30.52	62	Norfolk–Va Beach–Newport News, VA–NC	8.26	109	Jacksonville, NC	0.86
16	Santa Cruz–Watsonville, CA	27.65	63	Charleston, WV	7.91	110	Stockton–Lodi, CA	0.82
17	Glens Falls, NY	27.46	63	Medford–Ashland, OR	7.91	111	Santa Barbara–Santa Maria–Lompoc, CA	0.78
18	Barnstable–Yarmouth, MA	25.31	65	Elkhart–Goshen, IN	7.31	112	Visalia–Tulare–Porterville, CA	0.41
19	Redding, CA	25.13	66	Flint, MI	7.28	113	Oakland, CA	0.07
20	Benton Harbor, MI	24.51	67	Columbia, SC	7.10	114	La Crosse, WI–MN	0.00
21	Lewiston–Auburn, ME	24.41	68	Honolulu, HI	7.09	115	Denver, CO	(0.05)
22	Lancaster, PA	24.36	69	Eau Claire, WI	7.07	116	Baltimore, MD	(0.14)
23	Stamford–Norwalk, CT	23.24	70	Sherman–Denison, TX	6.91	117	New Haven–Meriden, CT	(0.15)
24	Tallahassee, FL	22.73	71	Yolo, CA	6.87	118	Olympia, WA	(0.24)
25	Salinas, CA	22.42	72	Louisville, KY–IN	6.84	119	Atlanta, GA	(0.27)
26	Green Bay, WI	22.12	73	Salt Lake City–Ogden, UT	6.43	120	Longview–Marshall, TX	(0.28)
27	Erie, PA	22.08	74	Greensboro–Winston Salem–High Point, NC	6.34	121	Fort Pierce–Port St. Lucie, FL	(0.41)
28	Naples, FL	22.07	75	Seattle–Bellevue–Everett, WA	6.26	122	Philadelphia, PA–NJ	(0.73)
29	Fayetteville, NC	21.84	76	Tuscaloosa, AL	6.17	123	Washington, DC–MD–VA–WV	(1.25)
30	Brownsville–Harlingen–San Benito, TX	21.01	77	Gary–Hammond, IN	6.09	124	Gainesville, FL	(1.31)
31	Gadsden, AL	18.44	78	Providence–Fall River–Warwick, RI–MA	5.93	125	Lawton, OK	(1.45)
32	Danville, VA	18.40	79	Lansing–East Lansing, MI	5.65	126	Cincinnati, OH–KY–IN	(1.56)
33	Pueblo, CO	18.32	80	Chico–Paradise, CA	5.51	127	Harrisburg–Lebanon–Carlisle, PA	(1.64)
34	Panama City, FL	17.81	81	Alexandria, LA	5.26	128	New Orleans, LA	(1.65)
35	Jackson, MS	17.40	82	Fort Lauderdale, FL	4.62	129	Bakersfield, CA	(1.73)
36	Dothan, AL	17.36	83	South Bend, IN	4.25	130	Baton Rouge, LA	(1.92)
37	Merced, CA	16.51	84	Albuquerque, NM	4.23	131	Savannah, GA	(1.99)
38	St. Joseph, MO	14.69	85	Lexington, KY	4.20	132	Montgomery, AL	(2.09)
39	Sarasota–Bradenton, FL	14.21	86	Toledo, OH	3.95	133	Roanoke, VA	(2.13)
40	Sheboygan, WI	14.14	87	Fort Wayne, IN	3.91	134	Tampa–St. Petersburg–Clearwater, FL	(2.18)
41	Grand Forks, ND–MN	14.07	88	Rochester, NY	3.48	135	Kenosha, WI	(2.22)
42	Anchorage, AK	13.02	89	Trenton, NJ	3.08	136	Sacramento, CA	(2.69)
43	Boulder–Longmont, CO	12.20	90	Reno, NV	2.90	137	Orlando, FL	(2.97)
44	New London–Norwich, CT–RI	12.12	91	Canton–Massillon, OH	2.73	138	Hagerstown, MD	(3.16)
45	Shreveport–Bossier City, LA	11.96	92	Hickory–Morganton, NC	2.72	139	Jacksonville, FL	(3.31)
46	Altoona, PA	11.95	92	San Francisco, CA	2.72	140	Evansville–Henderson, IN–KY	(3.39)
47	Greenville, NC	11.64	94	Austin–San Marcos, TX	2.64	141	Little Rock–North Little Rock, AR	(3.49)

Source: Morgan Quitno Corporation using data from U.S. Department of Justice, Federal Bureau of Investigation
"Crime in the United States 1993" (Uniform Crime Reports, December 4, 1994)
Robbery is the taking or attempting to take anything of value by force or threat of force.
**Not available.*

19. Percent Change in Robbery Rate: 1992 to 1993 (continued)

National Percent Change = 3.0% Decrease*

RANK	METRO AREA	% CHANGE	RANK	METRO AREA	% CHANGE	RANK	METRO AREA	CHANGE
142	Ann Arbor, MI	(3.67)	189	Bridgeport, CT	(12.46)	236	Fort Myers–Cape Coral, FL	(28.29)
143	Los Angeles–Long Beach, CA	(3.80)	189	Bryan–College Station, TX	(12.46)	237	Wausau, WI	(30.34)
144	Santa Rosa, CA	(3.92)	191	Dubuque, IA	(12.57)	238	Fort Smith, AR–OK	(31.24)
145	Orange County, CA	(3.98)	192	Lynchburg, VA	(13.24)	239	Rochester, MN	(32.99)
146	Tyler, TX	(4.09)	193	Colorado Springs, CO	(13.35)	240	Williamsport, PA	(33.60)
147	Provo–Orem, UT	(4.22)	194	San Diego, CA	(13.63)	241	Huntington–Ashland, WV–KY–OH	(34.07)
148	Albany, GA	(4.27)	195	Portland–Vancouver, OR–WA	(13.80)	242	Boise, ID	(34.33)
149	Spokane, WA	(4.43)	196	Dayton–Springfield, OH	(13.95)	243	Wichita Falls, TX	(35.33)
150	Racine, WI	(4.49)	197	Springfield, MA	(14.06)	244	St. Cloud, MN	(38.82)
151	Birmingham, AL	(4.62)	198	Fayetteville–Springdale–Rogers, AR	(14.48)	245	Victoria, TX	(40.39)
152	Chattanooga, TN–GA	(5.08)	199	Fargo–Moorhead, ND–MN	(14.74)	246	Bloomington, IN	(40.44)
153	El Paso, TX	(5.43)	200	San Antonio, TX	(15.12)	247	Rapid City, SD	(45.76)
154	San Jose, CA	(5.51)	201	Akron, OH	(15.34)	248	Bismarck, ND	(51.67)
155	Corpus Christi, TX	(6.00)	202	Vallejo–Fairfield–Napa, CA	(15.39)	249	Nashua, NH	(53.72)
156	Laredo, TX	(6.24)	203	Anniston, AL	(15.48)	–	Albany, NY**	NA
157	Macon, GA	(6.33)	204	Syracuse, NY	(15.68)	–	Bergen–Passaic, NJ**	NA
158	Scranton–Wilkes-Barre–Hazleton, PA	(6.62)	205	Springfield, MO	(16.03)	–	Boston, MA–NH**	NA
159	Pittsburgh, PA	(6.64)	206	Lakeland–Winter Haven, FL	(16.06)	–	Buffalo–Niagara Falls, NY**	NA
160	Raleigh–Durham–Chapel Hill, NC	(6.80)	207	Odessa–Midland, TX	(16.26)	–	Chicago, IL**	NA
161	Yakima, WA	(7.47)	208	Salem, OR	(16.29)	–	Cleveland, OH**	NA
162	Riverside–San Bernardino, CA	(7.63)	209	Augusta–Aiken, GA–SC	(16.32)	–	Dutchess County, NY**	NA
163	Lincoln, NE	(7.66)	210	Johnstown, PA	(16.37)	–	Fitchburg–Leominster, MA**	NA
164	Milwaukee–Waukesha, WI	(7.75)	211	Duluth–Superior, MN–WI	(16.40)	–	Fort Collins–Loveland, CO**	NA
165	Des Moines, IA	(7.86)	212	Tulsa, OK	(16.50)	–	Houston, TX**	NA
166	Utica–Rome, NY	(8.02)	213	San Angelo, TX	(16.97)	–	Indianapolis, IN**	NA
167	Enid, OK	(8.05)	214	Ventura, CA	(17.16)	–	Jersey City, NJ**	NA
168	Portland, ME	(8.10)	215	Appleton–Oshkosh–Neenah, WI	(17.60)	–	Joplin, MO**	NA
169	Athens, GA	(8.67)	216	Waterbury, CT	(18.70)	–	Kansas City, MO–KS**	NA
170	Tacoma, WA	(8.91)	217	Fort Worth–Arlington, TX	(19.04)	–	Lake Charles, LA**	NA
171	Modesto, CA	(8.97)	218	Ocala, FL	(19.41)	–	Lawrence, MA–NH**	NA
172	Tucson, AZ	(8.99)	219	Charlottesville, VA	(19.47)	–	Manchester, NH**	NA
173	Kalamazoo–Battle Creek, MI	(10.06)	220	Mansfield, OH	(19.73)	–	Middlesex–Sommerset–Hunterdon, NJ**	NA
174	Oklahoma City, OK	(10.22)	221	Columbia, MO	(19.91)	–	Mobile, AL**	NA
175	Brazoria, TX	(10.28)	222	Eugene–Springfield, OR	(20.08)	–	Monmouth–Ocean, NJ**	NA
176	Fresno, CA	(10.54)	223	Lubbock, TX	(20.14)	–	Nassau–Suffolk, NY**	NA
177	Richland–Kennewick–Pasco, WA	(10.94)	224	Fort Walton Beach, FL	(21.05)	–	New Bedford, MA**	NA
178	Johnson City–Kingsport–Bristol, TN–VA	(10.96)	225	Dallas, TX	(22.78)	–	New York, NY**	NA
179	Goldsboro, NC	(11.12)	226	Bangor, ME	(23.33)	–	Newark, NJ**	NA
180	Galveston–Texas City, TX	(11.17)	227	Huntsville, AL	(23.51)	–	Newburgh, NY–PA**	NA
181	Hartford, CT	(11.41)	227	Wilmington, NC	(23.51)	–	Omaha, NE**	NA
182	Monroe, LA	(11.47)	229	Daytona Beach, FL	(23.68)	–	Punta Gorda, FL**	NA
183	Beaumont–Port Arthur, TX	(11.65)	230	Houma, LA	(24.47)	–	San Luis Obispo–Atascadero, CA**	NA
184	Brockton, MA	(11.89)	231	Amarillo, TX	(24.67)	–	Sioux City, IA–NE**	NA
185	Kokomo, IN	(12.00)	232	Asheville, NC	(25.79)	–	St. Louis, MO–IL**	NA
186	Rocky Mount, NC	(12.23)	233	Texarkana, TX–AR	(25.98)	–	Waterloo–Cedar Falls, IA**	NA
187	Decatur, AL	(12.25)	234	Greeley, CO	(27.01)	–	West Palm Beach–Boca Raton, FL**	NA
188	Bremerton, WA	(12.30)	235	Florence, AL	(27.40)	–	Worcester, MA–CT**	NA

Source: Morgan Quitno Corporation using data from U.S. Department of Justice, Federal Bureau of Investigation
"Crime in the United States 1993" (Uniform Crime Reports, December 4, 1994)
*Robbery is the taking or attempting to take anything of value by force or threat of force.
**Not available.

Alpha Order – Metro

20. Percent Change in Robbery Rate: 1989 to 1993

National Percent Change = 9.8% Increase*

RANK	METRO AREA	% CHANGE	RANK	METRO AREA	% CHANGE	RANK	METRO AREA	% CHANGE
219	Abilene, TX	(22.21)	197	Cheyenne, WY	(13.81)	158	Fort Worth–Arlington, TX	0.27
–	Akron, OH**	NA	–	Chicago, IL**	NA	34	Fresno, CA	49.86
161	Albany, GA	(0.12)	28	Chico–Paradise, CA	56.86	7	Gadsden, AL	100.49
–	Albany, NY**	NA	51	Cincinnati, OH–KY–IN	38.42	116	Gainesville, FL	11.74
92	Albuquerque, NM	22.17	48	Clarksville–Hopkinsville, TN–KY	39.70	151	Galveston–Texas City, TX	2.38
139	Alexandria, LA	6.16	–	Cleveland, OH**	NA	22	Gary–Hammond, IN	61.54
133	Altoona, PA	7.55	143	Colorado Springs, CO	4.26	120	Glens Falls, NY	11.04
218	Amarillo, TX	(21.19)	100	Columbia, MO	18.79	–	Goldsboro, NC**	NA
10	Anchorage, AK	85.96	66	Columbia, SC	31.80	171	Grand Forks, ND–MN	(2.53)
243	Ann Arbor, MI	(45.32)	167	Columbus, GA–AL	(1.25)	106	Grand Rapids–Muskegon–Holland, MI	16.39
210	Anniston, AL	(18.70)	111	Columbus, OH	13.49	132	Greeley, CO	7.91
189	Appleton–Oshkosh–Neenah, WI	(10.43)	200	Corpus Christi, TX	(14.35)	33	Green Bay, WI	50.82
191	Asheville, NC	(11.65)	83	Cumberland, MD–WV	25.12	75	Greensboro–Winston Salem–High Point, NC	27.60
179	Athens, GA	(6.34)	229	Dallas, TX	(27.93)	–	Greenville, NC**	NA
198	Atlanta, GA	(13.90)	69	Danbury, CT	29.95	126	Greenville–Spartanburg–Anderson, SC	8.63
98	Atlantic City, NJ	19.07	1	Danville, VA	184.39	84	Hagerstown, MD	24.60
225	Augusta–Aiken, GA–SC	(24.15)	241	Daytona Beach, FL	(37.94)	–	Harrisburg–Lebanon–Carlisle, PA**	NA
82	Austin–San Marcos, TX	25.44	170	Dayton–Springfield, OH	(2.26)	230	Hartford, CT	(28.70)
168	Bakersfield, CA	(1.34)	53	Decatur, AL	37.92	–	Hickory–Morganton, NC**	NA
41	Baltimore, MD	42.97	50	Denver, CO	38.46	70	Honolulu, HI	29.06
89	Bangor, ME	22.84	235	Des Moines, IA	(31.51)	–	Houma, LA**	NA
–	Barnstable–Yarmouth, MA**	NA	113	Detroit, MI	12.29	–	Houston, TX**	NA
2	Baton Rouge, LA	133.89	63	Dothan, AL	32.51	202	Huntington–Ashland, WV–KY–OH	(14.54)
131	Beaumont–Port Arthur, TX	8.04	115	Dubuque, IA	11.89	121	Huntsville, AL	10.92
97	Bellingham, WA	19.61	47	Duluth–Superior, MN–WI	39.82	–	Indianapolis, IN**	NA
21	Benton Harbor, MI	64.61	–	Dutchess County, NY**	NA	206	Jackson, MI	(17.02)
195	Bergen–Passaic, NJ	(13.18)	169	Eau Claire, WI	(1.85)	4	Jackson, MS	118.53
77	Binghamton, NY	26.57	74	El Paso, TX	28.25	58	Jackson, TN	34.36
164	Birmingham, AL	(0.73)	117	Elkhart–Goshen, IN	11.60	192	Jacksonville, FL	(11.85)
242	Bismarck, ND	(38.30)	163	Enid, OK	(0.61)	40	Jacksonville, NC	43.98
240	Bloomington, IN	(36.79)	61	Erie, PA	33.25	38	Janesville–Beloit, WI	47.35
134	Boise, ID	7.32	154	Eugene–Springfield, OR	1.55	127	Jersey City, NJ	8.56
–	Boston, MA–NH**	NA	159	Evansville–Henderson, IN–KY	0.15	236	Johnson City–Kingsport–Bristol, TN–VA	(31.98)
222	Boulder–Longmont, CO	(22.60)	244	Fargo–Moorhead, ND–MN	(49.62)	–	Johnstown, PA**	NA
80	Brazoria, TX	25.83	62	Fayetteville, NC	32.64	93	Joplin, MO	21.86
–	Bremerton, WA**	NA	141	Fayetteville–Springdale–Rogers, AR	4.53	234	Kalamazoo–Battle Creek, MI	(31.44)
156	Bridgeport, CT	1.19	142	Fitchburg–Leominster, MA	4.41	–	Kansas City, MO–KS**	NA
–	Brockton, MA**	NA	186	Flint, MI	(8.98)	72	Kenosha, WI	28.71
24	Brownsville–Harlingen–San Benito, TX	59.46	207	Florence, AL	(18.21)	3	Killeen–Temple, TX	131.71
175	Bryan–College Station, TX	(4.43)	35	Florence, SC	49.13	124	Kokomo, IN	9.48
36	Buffalo–Niagara Falls, NY	48.88	130	Fort Collins–Loveland, CO	8.06	238	La Crosse, WI–MN	(32.98)
114	Canton–Massillon, OH	11.94	199	Fort Lauderdale, FL	(14.27)	12	Lafayette, IN	82.76
135	Charleston, WV	7.19	149	Fort Myers–Cape Coral, FL	3.06	184	Lafayette, LA	(7.74)
16	Charleston–North Charleston, SC	69.72	227	Fort Pierce–Port St. Lucie, FL	(25.71)	67	Lake Charles, LA	31.05
174	Charlottesville, VA	(4.09)	208	Fort Smith, AR–OK	(18.34)	214	Lakeland–Winter Haven, FL	(20.17)
79	Charlotte–Gastonia–Rock Hill, NC–SC	26.01	182	Fort Walton Beach, FL	(7.58)	27	Lancaster, PA	57.52
160	Chattanooga, TN–GA	0.05	223	Fort Wayne, IN	(23.59)	213	Lansing–East Lansing, MI	(19.93)

*Source: Morgan Quitno Corporation using data from U.S. Department of Justice, Federal Bureau of Investigation
"Crime in the United States 1993" (Uniform Crime Reports, December 4, 1994)
*Robbery is the taking or attempting to take anything of value by force or threat of force.
**Not available.*

20. Percent Change in Robbery Rate: 1989 to 1993 (continued)

National Percent Change = 9.8% Increase*

RANK	METRO AREA	% CHANGE	RANK	METRO AREA	% CHANGE	RANK	METRO AREA	CHANGE
187	Laredo, TX	(9.11)	102	Olympia, WA	17.18	129	Seattle-Bellevue-Everett, WA	8.33
71	Las Vegas, NV-AZ	28.94	–	Omaha, NE**	NA	8	Sheboygan, WI	94.83
19	Lawrence, MA-NH	65.79	81	Orange County, CA	25.74	46	Sherman-Denison, TX	40.83
64	Lawton, OK	32.20	212	Orlando, FL	(19.92)	155	Shreveport-Bossier City, LA	1.21
194	Lewiston-Auburn, ME	(12.59)	5	Owensboro, KY	107.17	65	Sioux City, IA-NE	31.87
42	Lexington, KY	41.74	119	Panama City, FL	11.38	101	Sioux Falls, SD	17.41
86	Lincoln, NE	23.31	107	Philadelphia, PA-NJ	16.36	–	South Bend, IN**	NA
138	Little Rock-North Little Rock, AR	6.36	99	Phoenix-Mesa, AZ	18.97	177	Spokane, WA	(6.00)
59	Longview-Marshall, TX	34.22	18	Pine Bluff, AR	67.16	193	Springfield, MA	(12.15)
103	Los Angeles-Long Beach, CA	17.07	110	Pittsburgh, PA	13.66	237	Springfield, MO	(32.95)
118	Louisville, KY-IN	11.39	–	Pittsfield, MA**	NA	148	Stamford-Norwalk, CT	3.15
150	Lubbock, TX	2.78	204	Portland, ME	(15.28)	–	Steubenville-Weirton, OH-WV**	NA
180	Lynchburg, VA	(6.38)	228	Portland-Vancouver, OR-WA	(27.37)	91	Stockton-Lodi, CA	22.47
205	Macon, GA	(15.99)	224	Providence-Fall River-Warwick, RI-MA	(24.05)	216	St. Cloud, MN	(20.61)
32	Madison, WI	51.88	–	Provo-Orem, UT**	NA	137	St. Joseph, MO	6.75
57	Manchester, NH	34.65	96	Pueblo, CO	20.21	–	St. Louis, MO-IL**	NA
233	Mansfield, OH	(30.78)	–	Punta Gorda, FL**	NA	–	Sumter, SC**	NA
6	McAllen-Edinburg-Mission, TX	104.12	128	Racine, WI	8.36	146	Syracuse, NY	3.98
104	Medford-Ashland, OR	16.88	11	Raleigh-Durham-Chapel Hill, NC	85.50	221	Tacoma, WA	(22.55)
73	Memphis, TN-AR-MS	28.49	183	Rapid City, SD	(7.65)	30	Tallahassee, FL	54.52
56	Merced, CA	35.15	–	Reading, PA**	NA	209	Tampa-St. Petersburg-Clearwater, FL	(18.65)
188	Miami, FL	(10.30)	13	Redding, CA	78.97	196	Texarkana, TX-AR	(13.55)
31	Middlesex-Sommerset-Hunterdon, NJ	54.43	190	Reno, NV	(10.51)	166	Toledo, OH	(1.22)
29	Milwaukee-Waukesha, WI	56.74	239	Richland-Kennewick-Pasco, WA	(34.29)	157	Trenton, NJ	0.91
112	Minneapolis-St. Paul, MN-WI	12.72	54	Richmond-Petersburg, VA	35.77	–	Tucson, AZ**	NA
37	Mobile, AL	48.35	–	Riverside-San Bernardino, CA**	NA	217	Tulsa, OK	(21.00)
94	Modesto, CA	20.61	181	Roanoke, VA	(7.52)	17	Tuscaloosa, AL	67.72
78	Monmouth-Ocean, NJ	26.06	211	Rochester, MN	(19.59)	105	Tyler, TX	16.63
144	Monroe, LA	4.12	90	Rochester, NY	22.49	55	Utica-Rome, NY	35.73
15	Montgomery, AL	73.67	–	Rocky Mount, NC**	NA	95	Vallejo-Fairfield-Napa, CA	20.28
–	Myrtle Beach, SC**	NA	68	Sacramento, CA	30.33	85	Ventura, CA	23.88
123	Naples, FL	9.54	45	Saginaw-Bay City-Midland, MI	40.84	39	Victoria, TX	44.08
178	Nashua, NH	(6.16)	220	Salem, OR	(22.45)	60	Vineland-Millville-Bridgeton, NJ	34.11
25	Nashville, TN	58.84	9	Salinas, CA	88.73	147	Visalia-Tulare-Porterville, CA	3.92
76	Nassau-Suffolk, NY	27.45	122	Salt Lake City-Ogden, UT	10.67	52	Waco, TX	38.10
203	New Bedford, MA	(14.59)	231	San Angelo, TX	(29.88)	173	Washington, DC-MD-VA-WV	(3.23)
201	New Haven-Meriden, CT	(14.41)	140	San Antonio, TX	4.96	165	Waterbury, CT	(0.85)
125	New London-Norwich, CT-RI	8.77	88	San Diego, CA	23.09	14	Waterloo-Cedar Falls, IA	73.91
153	New Orleans, LA	1.66	23	San Francisco, CA	61.40	144	Wausau, WI	4.12
176	New York, NY	(5.43)	108	San Jose, CA	14.64	–	West Palm Beach-Boca Raton, FL**	NA
152	Newark, NJ	2.37	–	San Luis Obispo-Atascadero, CA**	NA	232	Wichita Falls, TX	(30.27)
–	Newburgh, NY-PA**	NA	43	Santa Barbara-Santa Maria-Lompoc, CA	41.65	–	Williamsport, PA**	NA
26	Norfolk-Va Beach-Newport News, VA-NC	57.80	20	Santa Cruz-Watsonville, CA	65.62	185	Wilmington, NC	(8.63)
44	Oakland, CA	41.42	86	Santa Rosa, CA	23.31	–	Worcester, MA-CT**	NA
226	Ocala, FL	(25.13)	109	Sarasota-Bradenton, FL	14.44	215	Yakima, WA	(20.39)
172	Odessa-Midland, TX	(3.02)	49	Savannah, GA	39.20	–	Yolo, CA**	NA
162	Oklahoma City, OK	(0.24)	–	Scranton-Wilkes-Barre-Hazleton, PA**	NA	136	Yuba City, CA	7.18

Source: Morgan Quitno Corporation using data from U.S. Department of Justice, Federal Bureau of Investigation
  "Crime in the United States 1993" (Uniform Crime Reports, December 4, 1994)
*Robbery is the taking or attempting to take anything of value by force or threat of force.
**Not available.

20. Percent Change in Robbery Rate: 1989 to 1993 (continued)

National Percent Change = 9.8% Increase*

RANK	METRO AREA	% CHANGE	RANK	METRO AREA	% CHANGE	RANK	METRO AREA	% CHANGE
1	Danville, VA	184.39	48	Clarksville–Hopkinsville, TN–KY	39.70	95	Vallejo–Fairfield–Napa, CA	20.28
2	Baton Rouge, LA	133.89	49	Savannah, GA	39.20	96	Pueblo, CO	20.21
3	Killeen–Temple, TX	131.71	50	Denver, CO	38.46	97	Bellingham, WA	19.61
4	Jackson, MS	118.53	51	Cincinnati, OH–KY–IN	38.42	98	Atlantic City, NJ	19.07
5	Owensboro, KY	107.17	52	Waco, TX	38.10	99	Phoenix–Mesa, AZ	18.97
6	McAllen–Edinburg–Mission, TX	104.12	53	Decatur, AL	37.92	100	Columbia, MO	18.79
7	Gadsden, AL	100.49	54	Richmond–Petersburg, VA	35.77	101	Sioux Falls, SD	17.41
8	Sheboygan, WI	94.83	55	Utica–Rome, NY	35.73	102	Olympia, WA	17.18
9	Salinas, CA	88.73	56	Merced, CA	35.15	103	Los Angeles–Long Beach, CA	17.07
10	Anchorage, AK	85.96	57	Manchester, NH	34.65	104	Medford–Ashland, OR	16.88
11	Raleigh–Durham–Chapel Hill, NC	85.50	58	Jackson, TN	34.36	105	Tyler, TX	16.63
12	Lafayette, IN	82.76	59	Longview–Marshall, TX	34.22	106	Grand Rapids–Muskegon–Holland, MI	16.39
13	Redding, CA	78.97	60	Vineland–Millville–Bridgeton, NJ	34.11	107	Philadelphia, PA–NJ	16.36
14	Waterloo–Cedar Falls, IA	73.91	61	Erie, PA	33.25	108	San Jose, CA	14.64
15	Montgomery, AL	73.67	62	Fayetteville, NC	32.64	109	Sarasota–Bradenton, FL	14.44
16	Charleston–North Charleston, SC	69.72	63	Dothan, AL	32.51	110	Pittsburgh, PA	13.66
17	Tuscaloosa, AL	67.72	64	Lawton, OK	32.20	111	Columbus, OH	13.49
18	Pine Bluff, AR	67.16	65	Sioux City, IA–NE	31.87	112	Minneapolis–St. Paul, MN–WI	12.72
19	Lawrence, MA–NH	65.79	66	Columbia, SC	31.80	113	Detroit, MI	12.29
20	Santa Cruz–Watsonville, CA	65.62	67	Lake Charles, LA	31.05	114	Canton–Massillon, OH	11.94
21	Benton Harbor, MI	64.61	68	Sacramento, CA	30.33	115	Dubuque, IA	11.89
22	Gary–Hammond, IN	61.54	69	Danbury, CT	29.95	116	Gainesville, FL	11.74
23	San Francisco, CA	61.40	70	Honolulu, HI	29.06	117	Elkhart–Goshen, IN	11.60
24	Brownsville–Harlingen–San Benito, TX	59.46	71	Las Vegas, NV–AZ	28.94	118	Louisville, KY–IN	11.39
25	Nashville, TN	58.84	72	Kenosha, WI	28.71	119	Panama City, FL	11.38
26	Norfolk–Va Beach–Newport News, VA–NC	57.80	73	Memphis, TN–AR–MS	28.49	120	Glens Falls, NY	11.04
27	Lancaster, PA	57.52	74	El Paso, TX	28.25	121	Huntsville, AL	10.92
28	Chico–Paradise, CA	56.86	75	Greensboro–Winston Salem–High Point, NC	27.60	122	Salt Lake City–Ogden, UT	10.67
29	Milwaukee–Waukesha, WI	56.74	76	Nassau–Suffolk, NY	27.45	123	Naples, FL	9.54
30	Tallahassee, FL	54.52	77	Binghamton, NY	26.57	124	Kokomo, IN	9.48
31	Middlesex–Sommerset–Hunterdon, NJ	54.43	78	Monmouth–Ocean, NJ	26.06	125	New London–Norwich, CT–RI	8.77
32	Madison, WI	51.88	79	Charlotte–Gastonia–Rock Hill, NC–SC	26.01	126	Greenville–Spartanburg–Anderson, SC	8.63
33	Green Bay, WI	50.82	80	Brazoria, TX	25.83	127	Jersey City, NJ	8.56
34	Fresno, CA	49.86	81	Orange County, CA	25.74	128	Racine, WI	8.36
35	Florence, SC	49.13	82	Austin–San Marcos, TX	25.44	129	Seattle–Bellevue–Everett, WA	8.33
36	Buffalo–Niagara Falls, NY	48.88	83	Cumberland, MD–WV	25.12	130	Fort Collins–Loveland, CO	8.06
37	Mobile, AL	48.35	84	Hagerstown, MD	24.60	131	Beaumont–Port Arthur, TX	8.04
38	Janesville–Beloit, WI	47.35	85	Ventura, CA	23.88	132	Greeley, CO	7.91
39	Victoria, TX	44.08	86	Lincoln, NE	23.31	133	Altoona, PA	7.55
40	Jacksonville, NC	43.98	86	Santa Rosa, CA	23.31	134	Boise, ID	7.32
41	Baltimore, MD	42.97	88	San Diego, CA	23.09	135	Charleston, WV	7.19
42	Lexington, KY	41.74	89	Bangor, ME	22.84	136	Yuba City, CA	7.18
43	Santa Barbara–Santa Maria–Lompoc, CA	41.65	90	Rochester, NY	22.49	137	St. Joseph, MO	6.75
44	Oakland, CA	41.42	91	Stockton–Lodi, CA	22.47	138	Little Rock–North Little Rock, AR	6.36
45	Saginaw–Bay City–Midland, MI	40.84	92	Albuquerque, NM	22.17	139	Alexandria, LA	6.16
46	Sherman–Denison, TX	40.83	93	Joplin, MO	21.86	140	San Antonio, TX	4.96
47	Duluth–Superior, MN–WI	39.82	94	Modesto, CA	20.61	141	Fayetteville–Springdale–Rogers, AR	4.53

Source: Morgan Quitno Corporation using data from U.S. Department of Justice, Federal Bureau of Investigation
  "Crime in the United States 1993" (Uniform Crime Reports, December 4, 1994)
*Robbery is the taking or attempting to take anything of value by force or threat of force.
**Not available.

20. Percent Change in Robbery Rate: 1989 to 1993 (continued)

National Percent Change = 9.8% Increase*

RANK	METRO AREA	% CHANGE	RANK	METRO AREA	% CHANGE	RANK	METRO AREA	CHANGE
142	Fitchburg–Leominster, MA	4.41	189	Appleton–Oshkosh–Neenah, WI	(10.43)	236	Johnson City–Kingsport–Bristol, TN–VA	(31.98)
143	Colorado Springs, CO	4.26	190	Reno, NV	(10.51)	237	Springfield, MO	(32.95)
144	Monroe, LA	4.12	191	Asheville, NC	(11.65)	238	La Crosse, WI–MN	(32.98)
144	Wausau, WI	4.12	192	Jacksonville, FL	(11.85)	239	Richland–Kennewick–Pasco, WA	(34.29)
146	Syracuse, NY	3.98	193	Springfield, MA	(12.15)	240	Bloomington, IN	(36.79)
147	Visalia–Tulare–Porterville, CA	3.92	194	Lewiston–Auburn, ME	(12.59)	241	Daytona Beach, FL	(37.94)
148	Stamford–Norwalk, CT	3.15	195	Bergen–Passaic, NJ	(13.18)	242	Bismarck, ND	(38.30)
149	Fort Myers–Cape Coral, FL	3.06	196	Texarkana, TX–AR	(13.55)	243	Ann Arbor, MI	(45.32)
150	Lubbock, TX	2.78	197	Cheyenne, WY	(13.81)	244	Fargo–Moorhead, ND–MN	(49.62)
151	Galveston–Texas City, TX	2.38	198	Atlanta, GA	(13.90)	–	Akron, OH**	NA
152	Newark, NJ	2.37	199	Fort Lauderdale, FL	(14.27)	–	Albany, NY**	NA
153	New Orleans, LA	1.66	200	Corpus Christi, TX	(14.35)	–	Barnstable–Yarmouth, MA**	NA
154	Eugene–Springfield, OR	1.55	201	New Haven–Meriden, CT	(14.41)	–	Boston, MA–NH**	NA
155	Shreveport–Bossier City, LA	1.21	202	Huntington–Ashland, WV–KY–OH	(14.54)	–	Bremerton, WA**	NA
156	Bridgeport, CT	1.19	203	New Bedford, MA	(14.59)	–	Brockton, MA**	NA
157	Trenton, NJ	0.91	204	Portland, ME	(15.28)	–	Chicago, IL**	NA
158	Fort Worth–Arlington, TX	0.27	205	Macon, GA	(15.99)	–	Cleveland, OH**	NA
159	Evansville–Henderson, IN–KY	0.15	206	Jackson, MI	(17.02)	–	Dutchess County, NY**	NA
160	Chattanooga, TN–GA	0.05	207	Florence, AL	(18.21)	–	Goldsboro, NC**	NA
161	Albany, GA	(0.12)	208	Fort Smith, AR–OK	(18.34)	–	Greenville, NC**	NA
162	Oklahoma City, OK	(0.24)	209	Tampa–St. Petersburg–Clearwater, FL	(18.65)	–	Harrisburg–Lebanon–Carlisle, PA**	NA
163	Enid, OK	(0.61)	210	Anniston, AL	(18.70)	–	Hickory–Morganton, NC**	NA
164	Birmingham, AL	(0.73)	211	Rochester, MN	(19.59)	–	Houma, LA**	NA
165	Waterbury, CT	(0.85)	212	Orlando, FL	(19.92)	–	Houston, TX**	NA
166	Toledo, OH	(1.22)	213	Lansing–East Lansing, MI	(19.93)	–	Indianapolis, IN**	NA
167	Columbus, GA–AL	(1.25)	214	Lakeland–Winter Haven, FL	(20.17)	–	Johnstown, PA**	NA
168	Bakersfield, CA	(1.34)	215	Yakima, WA	(20.39)	–	Kansas City, MO–KS**	NA
169	Eau Claire, WI	(1.85)	216	St. Cloud, MN	(20.61)	–	Myrtle Beach, SC**	NA
170	Dayton–Springfield, OH	(2.26)	217	Tulsa, OK	(21.00)	–	Newburgh, NY–PA**	NA
171	Grand Forks, ND–MN	(2.53)	218	Amarillo, TX	(21.19)	–	Omaha, NE**	NA
172	Odessa–Midland, TX	(3.02)	219	Abilene, TX	(22.21)	–	Pittsfield, MA**	NA
173	Washington, DC–MD–VA–WV	(3.23)	220	Salem, OR	(22.45)	–	Provo–Orem, UT**	NA
174	Charlottesville, VA	(4.09)	221	Tacoma, WA	(22.55)	–	Punta Gorda, FL**	NA
175	Bryan–College Station, TX	(4.43)	222	Boulder–Longmont, CO	(22.60)	–	Reading, PA**	NA
176	New York, NY	(5.43)	223	Fort Wayne, IN	(23.59)	–	Riverside–San Bernardino, CA**	NA
177	Spokane, WA	(6.00)	224	Providence–Fall River–Warwick, RI–MA	(24.05)	–	Rocky Mount, NC**	NA
178	Nashua, NH	(6.16)	225	Augusta–Aiken, GA–SC	(24.15)	–	San Luis Obispo–Atascadero, CA**	NA
179	Athens, GA	(6.34)	226	Ocala, FL	(25.13)	–	Scranton–Wilkes-Barre–Hazleton, PA**	NA
180	Lynchburg, VA	(6.38)	227	Fort Pierce–Port St. Lucie, FL	(25.71)	–	South Bend, IN**	NA
181	Roanoke, VA	(7.52)	228	Portland–Vancouver, OR–WA	(27.37)	–	Steubenville–Weirton, OH–WV**	NA
182	Fort Walton Beach, FL	(7.58)	229	Dallas, TX	(27.93)	–	St. Louis, MO–IL**	NA
183	Rapid City, SD	(7.65)	230	Hartford, CT	(28.70)	–	Sumter, SC**	NA
184	Lafayette, LA	(7.74)	231	San Angelo, TX	(29.88)	–	Tucson, AZ**	NA
185	Wilmington, NC	(8.63)	232	Wichita Falls, TX	(30.27)	–	West Palm Beach–Boca Raton, FL**	NA
186	Flint, MI	(8.98)	233	Mansfield, OH	(30.78)	–	Williamsport, PA**	NA
187	Laredo, TX	(9.11)	234	Kalamazoo–Battle Creek, MI	(31.44)	–	Worcester, MA–CT**	NA
188	Miami, FL	(10.30)	235	Des Moines, IA	(31.51)	–	Yolo, CA**	NA

Source: Morgan Quitno Corporation using data from U.S. Department of Justice, Federal Bureau of Investigation
   "Crime in the United States 1993" (Uniform Crime Reports, December 4, 1994)
*Robbery is the taking or attempting to take anything of value by force or threat of force.
**Not available.

21. Aggravated Assaults in 1993

National Total = 1,135,099 Aggravated Assaults*

RANK	METRO AREA	ASSAULTS	RANK	METRO AREA	ASSAULTS	RANK	METRO AREA	ASSAULTS
177	Abilene, TX	690	265	Cheyenne, WY	98	24	Fort Worth-Arlington, TX	7,460
95	Akron, OH	1,716	–	Chicago, IL**	NA	40	Fresno, CA	4,778
185	Albany, GA	602	183	Chico-Paradise, CA	613	151	Gadsden, AL	914
–	Albany, NY**	NA	39	Cincinnati, OH–KY–IN	4,938	88	Gainesville, FL	1,791
33	Albuquerque, NM	5,955	121	Clarksville-Hopkinsville, TN–KY	1,260	124	Galveston-Texas City, TX	1,232
83	Alexandria, LA	2,186	–	Cleveland, OH**	NA	55	Gary-Hammond, IN	3,606
252	Altoona, PA	189	125	Colorado Springs, CO	1,226	209	Glens Falls, NY	456
160	Amarillo, TX	873	224	Columbia, MO	377	191	Goldsboro, NC	578
112	Anchorage, AK	1,410	56	Columbia, SC	3,581	259	Grand Forks, ND–MN	108
111	Ann Arbor, MI	1,460	148	Columbus, GA–AL	923	53	Grand Rapids-Muskegon-Holland, MI	3,741
130	Anniston, AL	1,146	49	Columbus, OH	4,099	233	Greeley, CO	318
241	Appleton-Oshkosh-Neenah, WI	264	92	Corpus Christi, TX	1,767	213	Green Bay, WI	441
217	Asheville, NC	416	223	Cumberland, MD–WV	383	45	Greensboro-Winston Salem-High Point, NC	4,622
193	Athens, GA	558	11	Dallas, TX	15,030	175	Greenville, NC	725
9	Atlanta, GA	16,132	254	Danbury, CT	133	27	Greenville-Spartanburg-Anderson, SC	7,237
106	Atlantic City, NJ	1,522	256	Danville, VA	127	241	Hagerstown, MD	264
87	Augusta-Aiken, GA–SC	1,876	74	Daytona Beach, FL	2,482	115	Harrisburg-Lebanon-Carlisle, PA	1,343
71	Austin-San Marcos, TX	2,548	72	Dayton-Springfield, OH	2,546	65	Hartford, CT	2,932
51	Bakersfield, CA	3,789	250	Decatur, AL	206	173	Hickory-Morganton, NC	746
10	Baltimore, MD	16,046	19	Denver, CO	8,652	136	Honolulu, HI	1,099
271	Bangor, ME	37	169	Des Moines, IA	799	166	Houma, LA	811
137	Barnstable-Yarmouth, MA	1,063	3	Detroit, MI	24,446	–	Houston, TX**	NA
34	Baton Rouge, LA	5,695	161	Dothan, AL	866	188	Huntington-Ashland, WV–KY–OH	592
93	Beaumont-Port Arthur, TX	1,752	253	Dubuque, IA	143	84	Huntsville, AL	2,139
251	Bellingham, WA	198	232	Duluth-Superior, MN–WI	337	–	Indianapolis, IN**	NA
123	Benton Harbor, MI	1,237	186	Dutchess County, NY	599	103	Jackson, MI	1,548
81	Bergen-Passaic, NJ	2,357	262	Eau Claire, WI	103	117	Jackson, MS	1,312
219	Binghamton, NY	410	46	El Paso, TX	4,583	174	Jackson, TN	728
29	Birmingham, AL	6,979	190	Elkhart-Goshen, IN	580	18	Jacksonville, FL	8,828
257	Bismarck, ND	116	229	Enid, OK	350	245	Jacksonville, NC	239
203	Bloomington, IN	500	200	Erie, PA	516	248	Janesville-Beloit, WI	231
155	Boise, ID	902	195	Eugene-Springfield, OR	552	66	Jersey City, NJ	2,859
6	Boston, MA–NH	18,289	134	Evansville-Henderson, IN–KY	1,117	167	Johnson City-Kingsport-Bristol, TN–VA	808
220	Boulder-Longmont, CO	394	261	Fargo-Moorhead, ND–MN	104	224	Johnstown, PA	377
210	Brazoria, TX	454	89	Fayetteville, NC	1,790	249	Joplin, MO	230
217	Bremerton, WA	416	236	Fayetteville-Springdale-Rogers, AR	309	80	Kalamazoo-Battle Creek, MI	2,360
138	Bridgeport, CT	1,058	152	Fitchburg-Leominster, MA	911	–	Kansas City, MO–KS**	NA
116	Brockton, MA	1,316	60	Flint, MI	3,315	230	Kenosha, WI	348
109	Brownsville-Harlingen-San Benito, TX	1,491	238	Florence, AL	296	133	Killeen-Temple, TX	1,121
208	Bryan-College Station, TX	467	156	Florence, SC	884	226	Kokomo, IN	372
38	Buffalo-Niagara Falls, NY	5,016	207	Fort Collins-Loveland, CO	470	266	La Crosse, WI–MN	90
162	Canton-Massillon, OH	854	22	Fort Lauderdale, FL	7,797	214	Lafayette, IN	438
186	Charleston, WV	599	100	Fort Myers-Cape Coral, FL	1,631	105	Lafayette, LA	1,526
57	Charleston-North Charleston, SC	3,536	110	Fort Pierce-Port St. Lucie, FL	1,476	120	Lake Charles, LA	1,269
244	Charlottesville, VA	249	182	Fort Smith, AR–OK	615	64	Lakeland-Winter Haven, FL	3,005
17	Charlotte-Gastonia-Rock Hill, NC–SC	9,825	215	Fort Walton Beach, FL	437	201	Lancaster, PA	506
69	Chattanooga, TN–GA	2,608	171	Fort Wayne, IN	780	99	Lansing-East Lansing, MI	1,640

Source: U.S. Department of Justice, Federal Bureau of Investigation
  "Crime in the United States 1993" (Uniform Crime Reports, December 4, 1994)
*Aggravated assault is an attack for the purpose of inflicting severe bodily injury.
**Not available.

21. Aggravated Assaults in 1993 (continued)

National Total = 1,135,099 Aggravated Assaults*

RANK	METRO AREA	ASSAULTS	RANK	METRO AREA	ASSAULTS	RANK	METRO AREA	ASSAULTS
153	Laredo, TX	907	245	Olympia, WA	239	31	Seattle-Bellevue-Everett, WA	6,583
41	Las Vegas, NV–AZ	4,764	–	Omaha, NE**	NA	269	Sheboygan, WI	69
127	Lawrence, MA–NH	1,205	28	Orange County, CA	7,147	236	Sherman-Denison, TX	309
184	Lawton, OK	604	16	Orlando, FL	10,743	77	Shreveport-Bossier City, LA	2,452
258	Lewiston-Auburn, ME	111	263	Owensboro, KY	102	132	Sioux City, IA–NE	1,132
86	Lexington, KY	1,940	170	Panama City, FL	787	227	Sioux Falls, SD	368
147	Lincoln, NE	929	12	Philadelphia, PA–NJ	14,512	168	South Bend, IN	806
36	Little Rock-North Little Rock, AR	5,589	15	Phoenix-Mesa, AZ	13,290	119	Spokane, WA	1,297
142	Longview-Marshall, TX	946	194	Pine Bluff, AR	556	–	Springfield, MA**	NA
1	Los Angeles-Long Beach, CA	82,250	43	Pittsburgh, PA	4,695	197	Springfield, MO	536
50	Louisville, KY–IN	3,920	228	Pittsfield, MA	351	221	Stamford-Norwalk, CT	391
139	Lubbock, TX	1,004	230	Portland, ME	348	205	Steubenville-Weirton, OH–WV	478
189	Lynchburg, VA	591	25	Portland-Vancouver, OR–WA	7,440	61	Stockton-Lodi, CA	3,296
165	Macon, GA	820	73	Providence-Fall River-Warwick, RI–MA	2,544	264	St. Cloud, MN	99
179	Madison, WI	626	243	Provo-Orem, UT	259	240	St. Joseph, MO	274
268	Manchester, NH	76	108	Pueblo, CO	1,515	–	St. Louis, MO–IL**	NA
122	Mansfield, OH	1,248	239	Punta Gorda, FL	280	145	Sumter, SC	941
68	McAllen-Edinburg-Mission, TX	2,634	222	Racine, WI	390	129	Syracuse, NY	1,173
202	Medford-Ashland, OR	504	62	Raleigh-Durham-Chapel Hill, NC	3,282	54	Tacoma, WA	3,671
42	Memphis, TN–AR–MS	4,746	245	Rapid City, SD	239	70	Tallahassee, FL	2,593
157	Merced, CA	879	181	Reading, PA	620	7	Tampa-St. Petersburg-Clearwater, FL	18,259
4	Miami, FL	23,468	196	Redding, CA	546	176	Texarkana, TX–AR	704
91	Middlesex-Sommerset-Hunterdon, NJ	1,768	163	Reno, NV	848	107	Toledo, OH	1,519
85	Milwaukee-Waukesha, WI	1,951	212	Richland-Kennewick-Pasco, WA	447	135	Trenton, NJ	1,104
32	Minneapolis-St. Paul, MN–WI	6,243	78	Richmond-Petersburg, VA	2,441	52	Tucson, AZ	3,771
79	Mobile, AL	2,378	5	Riverside-San Bernardino, CA	20,587	48	Tulsa, OK	4,171
63	Modesto, CA	3,133	211	Roanoke, VA	450	131	Tuscaloosa, AL	1,137
97	Monmouth-Ocean, NJ	1,679	259	Rochester, MN	108	164	Tyler, TX	828
128	Monroe, LA	1,204	102	Rochester, NY	1,562	206	Utica-Rome, NY	476
94	Montgomery, AL	1,744	178	Rocky Mount, NC	663	74	Vallejo-Fairfield-Napa, CA	2,482
150	Myrtle Beach, SC	918	30	Sacramento, CA	6,734	82	Ventura, CA	2,323
159	Naples, FL	875	76	Saginaw-Bay City-Midland, MI	2,480	204	Victoria, TX	491
267	Nashua, NH	79	216	Salem, OR	426	171	Vineland-Millville-Bridgeton, NJ	780
23	Nashville, TN	7,492	96	Salinas, CA	1,702	98	Visalia-Tulare-Porterville, CA	1,656
58	Nassau-Suffolk, NY	3,471	67	Salt Lake City-Ogden, UT	2,751	114	Waco, TX	1,347
126	New Bedford, MA	1,224	198	San Angelo, TX	524	8	Washington, DC-MD-VA-WV	17,519
101	New Haven-Meriden, CT	1,565	44	San Antonio, TX	4,629	235	Waterbury, CT	310
192	New London-Norwich, CT–RI	570	13	San Diego, CA	14,417	234	Waterloo-Cedar Falls, IA	316
20	New Orleans, LA	8,370	26	San Francisco, CA	7,395	270	Wausau, WI	68
2	New York, NY	65,497	35	San Jose, CA	5,649	–	West Palm Beach-Boca Raton, FL**	NA
21	Newark, NJ	8,156	143	San Luis Obispo-Atascadero, CA	945	180	Wichita Falls, TX	624
140	Newburgh, NY–PA	989	113	Santa Barbara-Santa Maria-Lompoc, CA	1,368	255	Williamsport, PA	129
47	Norfolk-Va Beach-Newport News, VA–NC	4,543	118	Santa Cruz-Watsonville, CA	1,304	146	Wilmington, NC	930
14	Oakland, CA	13,607	104	Santa Rosa, CA	1,542	–	Worcester, MA–CT**	NA
90	Ocala, FL	1,778	59	Sarasota-Bradenton, FL	3,366	158	Yakima, WA	876
149	Odessa-Midland, TX	920	154	Savannah, GA	906	199	Yolo, CA	522
37	Oklahoma City, OK	5,355	141	Scranton-Wilkes-Barre-Hazleton, PA	950	144	Yuba City, CA	944

Source: U.S. Department of Justice, Federal Bureau of Investigation
"Crime in the United States 1993" (Uniform Crime Reports, December 4, 1994)
*Aggravated assault is an attack for the purpose of inflicting severe bodily injury.
**Not available.

21. Aggravated Assaults in 1993 (continued)

National Total = 1,135,099 Aggravated Assaults*

RANK	METRO AREA	ASSAULTS	RANK	METRO AREA	ASSAULTS	RANK	METRO AREA	ASSAULTS
1	Los Angeles–Long Beach, CA	82,250	48	Tulsa, OK	4,171	95	Akron, OH	1,716
2	New York, NY	65,497	49	Columbus, OH	4,099	96	Salinas, CA	1,702
3	Detroit, MI	24,446	50	Louisville, KY–IN	3,920	97	Monmouth–Ocean, NJ	1,679
4	Miami, FL	23,468	51	Bakersfield, CA	3,789	98	Visalia–Tulare–Porterville, CA	1,656
5	Riverside–San Bernardino, CA	20,587	52	Tucson, AZ	3,771	99	Lansing–East Lansing, MI	1,640
6	Boston, MA–NH	18,289	53	Grand Rapids–Muskegon–Holland, MI	3,741	100	Fort Myers–Cape Coral, FL	1,631
7	Tampa–St. Petersburg–Clearwater, FL	18,259	54	Tacoma, WA	3,671	101	New Haven–Meriden, CT	1,565
8	Washington, DC–MD–VA–WV	17,519	55	Gary–Hammond, IN	3,606	102	Rochester, NY	1,562
9	Atlanta, GA	16,132	56	Columbia, SC	3,581	103	Jackson, MI	1,548
10	Baltimore, MD	16,046	57	Charleston–North Charleston, SC	3,536	104	Santa Rosa, CA	1,542
11	Dallas, TX	15,030	58	Nassau–Suffolk, NY	3,471	105	Lafayette, LA	1,526
12	Philadelphia, PA–NJ	14,512	59	Sarasota–Bradenton, FL	3,366	106	Atlantic City, NJ	1,522
13	San Diego, CA	14,417	60	Flint, MI	3,315	107	Toledo, OH	1,519
14	Oakland, CA	13,607	61	Stockton–Lodi, CA	3,296	108	Pueblo, CO	1,515
15	Phoenix–Mesa, AZ	13,290	62	Raleigh–Durham–Chapel Hill, NC	3,282	109	Brownsville–Harlingen–San Benito, TX	1,491
16	Orlando, FL	10,743	63	Modesto, CA	3,133	110	Fort Pierce–Port St. Lucie, FL	1,476
17	Charlotte–Gastonia–Rock Hill, NC–SC	9,825	64	Lakeland–Winter Haven, FL	3,005	111	Ann Arbor, MI	1,460
18	Jacksonville, FL	8,828	65	Hartford, CT	2,932	112	Anchorage, AK	1,410
19	Denver, CO	8,652	66	Jersey City, NJ	2,859	113	Santa Barbara–Santa Maria–Lompoc, CA	1,368
20	New Orleans, LA	8,370	67	Salt Lake City–Ogden, UT	2,751	114	Waco, TX	1,347
21	Newark, NJ	8,156	68	McAllen–Edinburg–Mission, TX	2,634	115	Harrisburg–Lebanon–Carlisle, PA	1,343
22	Fort Lauderdale, FL	7,797	69	Chattanooga, TN–GA	2,608	116	Brockton, MA	1,316
23	Nashville, TN	7,492	70	Tallahassee, FL	2,593	117	Jackson, MS	1,312
24	Fort Worth–Arlington, TX	7,460	71	Austin–San Marcos, TX	2,548	118	Santa Cruz–Watsonville, CA	1,304
25	Portland–Vancouver, OR–WA	7,440	72	Dayton–Springfield, OH	2,546	119	Spokane, WA	1,297
26	San Francisco, CA	7,395	73	Providence–Fall River–Warwick, RI–MA	2,544	120	Lake Charles, LA	1,269
27	Greenville–Spartanburg–Anderson, SC	7,237	74	Daytona Beach, FL	2,482	121	Clarksville–Hopkinsville, TN–KY	1,260
28	Orange County, CA	7,147	74	Vallejo–Fairfield–Napa, CA	2,482	122	Mansfield, OH	1,248
29	Birmingham, AL	6,979	76	Saginaw–Bay City–Midland, MI	2,480	123	Benton Harbor, MI	1,237
30	Sacramento, CA	6,734	77	Shreveport–Bossier City, LA	2,452	124	Galveston–Texas City, TX	1,232
31	Seattle–Bellevue–Everett, WA	6,583	78	Richmond–Petersburg, VA	2,441	125	Colorado Springs, CO	1,226
32	Minneapolis–St. Paul, MN–WI	6,243	79	Mobile, AL	2,378	126	New Bedford, MA	1,224
33	Albuquerque, NM	5,955	80	Kalamazoo–Battle Creek, MI	2,360	127	Lawrence, MA–NH	1,205
34	Baton Rouge, LA	5,695	81	Bergen–Passaic, NJ	2,357	128	Monroe, LA	1,204
35	San Jose, CA	5,649	82	Ventura, CA	2,323	129	Syracuse, NY	1,173
36	Little Rock–North Little Rock, AR	5,589	83	Alexandria, LA	2,186	130	Anniston, AL	1,146
37	Oklahoma City, OK	5,355	84	Huntsville, AL	2,139	131	Tuscaloosa, AL	1,137
38	Buffalo–Niagara Falls, NY	5,016	85	Milwaukee–Waukesha, WI	1,951	132	Sioux City, IA–NE	1,132
39	Cincinnati, OH–KY–IN	4,938	86	Lexington, KY	1,940	133	Killeen–Temple, TX	1,121
40	Fresno, CA	4,778	87	Augusta–Aiken, GA–SC	1,876	134	Evansville–Henderson, IN–KY	1,117
41	Las Vegas, NV–AZ	4,764	88	Gainesville, FL	1,791	135	Trenton, NJ	1,104
42	Memphis, TN–AR–MS	4,746	89	Fayetteville, NC	1,790	136	Honolulu, HI	1,099
43	Pittsburgh, PA	4,695	90	Ocala, FL	1,778	137	Barnstable–Yarmouth, MA	1,063
44	San Antonio, TX	4,629	91	Middlesex–Somerset–Hunterdon, NJ	1,768	138	Bridgeport, CT	1,058
45	Greensboro–Winston Salem–High Point, NC	4,622	92	Corpus Christi, TX	1,767	139	Lubbock, TX	1,004
46	El Paso, TX	4,583	93	Beaumont–Port Arthur, TX	1,752	140	Newburgh, NY–PA	989
47	Norfolk–Va Beach–Newport News, VA–NC	4,543	94	Montgomery, AL	1,744	141	Scranton–Wilkes-Barre–Hazleton, PA	950

Source: U.S. Department of Justice, Federal Bureau of Investigation
   "Crime in the United States 1993" (Uniform Crime Reports, December 4, 1994)
*Aggravated assault is an attack for the purpose of inflicting severe bodily injury.
**Not available.

21. Aggravated Assaults in 1993 (continued)

National Total = 1,135,099 Aggravated Assaults*

RANK	METRO AREA	ASSAULTS	RANK	METRO AREA	ASSAULTS	RANK	METRO AREA	ASSAULTS
142	Longview-Marshall, TX	946	189	Lynchburg, VA	591	236	Fayetteville-Springdale-Rogers, AR	309
143	San Luis Obispo-Atascadero, CA	945	190	Elkhart-Goshen, IN	580	236	Sherman-Denison, TX	309
144	Yuba City, CA	944	191	Goldsboro, NC	578	238	Florence, AL	296
145	Sumter, SC	941	192	New London-Norwich, CT-RI	570	239	Punta Gorda, FL	280
146	Wilmington, NC	930	193	Athens, GA	558	240	St. Joseph, MO	274
147	Lincoln, NE	929	194	Pine Bluff, AR	556	241	Appleton-Oshkosh-Neenah, WI	264
148	Columbus, GA-AL	923	195	Eugene-Springfield, OR	552	241	Hagerstown, MD	264
149	Odessa-Midland, TX	920	196	Redding, CA	546	243	Provo-Orem, UT	259
150	Myrtle Beach, SC	918	197	Springfield, MO	536	244	Charlottesville, VA	249
151	Gadsden, AL	914	198	San Angelo, TX	524	245	Jacksonville, NC	239
152	Fitchburg-Leominster, MA	911	199	Yolo, CA	522	245	Olympia, WA	239
153	Laredo, TX	907	200	Erie, PA	516	245	Rapid City, SD	239
154	Savannah, GA	906	201	Lancaster, PA	506	248	Janesville-Beloit, WI	231
155	Boise, ID	902	202	Medford-Ashland, OR	504	249	Joplin, MO	230
156	Florence, SC	884	203	Bloomington, IN	500	250	Decatur, AL	206
157	Merced, CA	879	204	Victoria, TX	491	251	Bellingham, WA	198
158	Yakima, WA	876	205	Steubenville-Weirton, OH-WV	478	252	Altoona, PA	189
159	Naples, FL	875	206	Utica-Rome, NY	476	253	Dubuque, IA	143
160	Amarillo, TX	873	207	Fort Collins-Loveland, CO	470	254	Danbury, CT	133
161	Dothan, AL	866	208	Bryan-College Station, TX	467	255	Williamsport, PA	129
162	Canton-Massillon, OH	854	209	Glens Falls, NY	456	256	Danville, VA	127
163	Reno, NV	848	210	Brazoria, TX	454	257	Bismarck, ND	116
164	Tyler, TX	828	211	Roanoke, VA	450	258	Lewiston-Auburn, ME	111
165	Macon, GA	820	212	Richland-Kennewick-Pasco, WA	447	259	Grand Forks, ND-MN	108
166	Houma, LA	811	213	Green Bay, WI	441	259	Rochester, MN	108
167	Johnson City-Kingsport-Bristol, TN-VA	808	214	Lafayette, IN	438	261	Fargo-Moorhead, ND-MN	104
168	South Bend, IN	806	215	Fort Walton Beach, FL	437	262	Eau Claire, WI	103
169	Des Moines, IA	799	216	Salem, OR	426	263	Owensboro, KY	102
170	Panama City, FL	787	217	Asheville, NC	416	264	St. Cloud, MN	99
171	Fort Wayne, IN	780	217	Bremerton, WA	416	265	Cheyenne, WY	98
171	Vineland-Millville-Bridgeton, NJ	780	219	Binghamton, NY	410	266	La Crosse, WI-MN	90
173	Hickory-Morganton, NC	746	220	Boulder-Longmont, CO	394	267	Nashua, NH	79
174	Jackson, TN	728	221	Stamford-Norwalk, CT	391	268	Manchester, NH	76
175	Greenville, NC	725	222	Racine, WI	390	269	Sheboygan, WI	69
176	Texarkana, TX-AR	704	223	Cumberland, MD-WV	383	270	Wausau, WI	68
177	Abilene, TX	690	224	Columbia, MO	377	271	Bangor, ME	37
178	Rocky Mount, NC	663	224	Johnstown, PA	377	–	Albany, NY**	NA
179	Madison, WI	626	226	Kokomo, IN	372	–	Chicago, IL**	NA
180	Wichita Falls, TX	624	227	Sioux Falls, SD	368	–	Cleveland, OH**	NA
181	Reading, PA	620	228	Pittsfield, MA	351	–	Houston, TX**	NA
182	Fort Smith, AR-OK	615	229	Enid, OK	350	–	Indianapolis, IN**	NA
183	Chico-Paradise, CA	613	230	Kenosha, WI	348	–	Kansas City, MO-KS**	NA
184	Lawton, OK	604	230	Portland, ME	348	–	Omaha, NE**	NA
185	Albany, GA	602	232	Duluth-Superior, MN-WI	337	–	Springfield, MA**	NA
186	Charleston, WV	599	233	Greeley, CO	318	–	St. Louis, MO-IL**	NA
186	Dutchess County, NY	599	234	Waterloo-Cedar Falls, IA	316	–	West Palm Beach-Boca Raton, FL**	NA
188	Huntington-Ashland, WV-KY-OH	592	235	Waterbury, CT	310	–	Worcester, MA-CT**	NA

Source: U.S. Department of Justice, Federal Bureau of Investigation
  "Crime in the United States 1993" (Uniform Crime Reports, December 4, 1994)
Aggravated assault is an attack for the purpose of inflicting severe bodily injury.
**Not available.*

Alpha Order – Metro

22. Aggravated Assault Rate in 1993

National Rate = 440.1 Aggravated Assaults per 100,000 Population*

RANK	METRO AREA	RATE	RANK	METRO AREA	RATE	RANK	METRO AREA	RATE
74	Abilene, TX	561.3	250	Cheyenne, WY	127.5	101	Fort Worth–Arlington, TX	484.8
189	Akron, OH	256.9	–	Chicago, IL**	NA	64	Fresno, CA	587.8
94	Albany, GA	511.6	158	Chico–Paradise, CA	322.1	13	Gadsden, AL	908.9
–	Albany, NY**	NA	165	Cincinnati, OH–KY–IN	314.3	11	Gainesville, FL	932.0
10	Albuquerque, NM	945.5	40	Clarksville–Hopkinsville, TN–KY	698.4	87	Galveston–Texas City, TX	529.7
1	Alexandria, LA	1,668.2	–	Cleveland, OH**	NA	67	Gary–Hammond, IN	579.0
241	Altoona, PA	143.3	173	Colorado Springs, CO	282.8	137	Glens Falls, NY	375.2
117	Amarillo, TX	446.8	161	Columbia, MO	319.9	88	Goldsboro, NC	528.2
73	Anchorage, AK	562.4	29	Columbia, SC	749.7	258	Grand Forks, ND–MN	104.2
171	Ann Arbor, MI	289.7	156	Columbus, GA–AL	331.6	134	Grand Rapids–Muskegon–Holland, MI	386.1
8	Anniston, AL	973.0	169	Columbus, OH	292.5	200	Greeley, CO	227.4
262	Appleton–Oshkosh–Neenah, WI	80.0	102	Corpus Christi, TX	478.2	205	Green Bay, WI	217.1
209	Asheville, NC	207.4	138	Cumberland, MD–WV	374.0	125	Greensboro–Winston Salem–High Point, NC	421.7
143	Athens, GA	361.2	80	Dallas, TX	546.3	50	Greenville, NC	646.5
97	Atlanta, GA	500.1	261	Danbury, CT	81.8	19	Greenville–Spartanburg–Anderson, SC	837.9
110	Atlantic City, NJ	463.0	254	Danville, VA	114.4	208	Hagerstown, MD	208.4
129	Augusta–Aiken, GA–SC	415.5	65	Daytona Beach, FL	580.1	202	Harrisburg–Lebanon–Carlisle, PA	222.0
179	Austin–San Marcos, TX	277.3	187	Dayton–Springfield, OH	263.0	177	Hartford, CT	278.2
53	Bakersfield, CA	638.2	236	Decatur, AL	150.6	192	Hickory–Morganton, NC	245.4
47	Baltimore, MD	653.0	100	Denver, CO	492.2	251	Honolulu, HI	125.5
268	Bangor, ME	54.7	211	Des Moines, IA	195.8	120	Houma, LA	433.2
25	Barnstable–Yarmouth, MA	775.2	71	Detroit, MI	564.5	–	Houston, TX**	NA
6	Baton Rouge, LA	1,038.5	52	Dothan, AL	642.1	216	Huntington–Ashland, WV–KY–OH	186.7
108	Beaumont–Port Arthur, TX	464.6	229	Dubuque, IA	163.2	42	Huntsville, AL	686.2
243	Bellingham, WA	140.5	244	Duluth–Superior, MN–WI	138.4	–	Indianapolis, IN**	NA
26	Benton Harbor, MI	762.6	201	Dutchess County, NY	226.8	7	Jackson, MI	1,015.5
220	Bergen–Passaic, NJ	181.2	264	Eau Claire, WI	73.0	159	Jackson, MS	320.6
235	Binghamton, NY	153.0	36	El Paso, TX	715.2	15	Jackson, TN	894.2
22	Birmingham, AL	802.8	144	Elkhart–Goshen, IN	360.6	12	Jacksonville, FL	913.5
246	Bismarck, ND	134.6	57	Enid, OK	616.0	230	Jacksonville, NC	162.8
118	Bloomington, IN	445.7	218	Erie, PA	183.7	232	Janesville–Beloit, WI	160.4
181	Boise, ID	273.6	217	Eugene–Springfield, OR	186.0	95	Jersey City, NJ	511.3
82	Boston, MA–NH	539.0	133	Evansville–Henderson, IN–KY	391.1	222	Johnson City–Kingsport–Bristol, TN–VA	179.2
231	Boulder–Longmont, CO	160.7	265	Fargo–Moorhead, ND–MN	65.7	233	Johnstown, PA	155.9
203	Brazoria, TX	218.4	54	Fayetteville, NC	635.3	228	Joplin, MO	165.9
213	Bremerton, WA	193.2	245	Fayetteville–Springdale–Rogers, AR	135.2	83	Kalamazoo–Battle Creek, MI	538.3
197	Bridgeport, CT	233.6	44	Fitchburg–Leominster, MA	665.0	–	Kansas City, MO–KS**	NA
84	Brockton, MA	534.4	27	Flint, MI	761.3	188	Kenosha, WI	257.4
90	Brownsville–Harlingen–San Benito, TX	524.7	204	Florence, AL	217.9	122	Killeen–Temple, TX	431.4
141	Bryan–College Station, TX	365.9	30	Florence, SC	737.2	140	Kokomo, IN	373.7
128	Buffalo–Niagara Falls, NY	417.4	199	Fort Collins–Loveland, CO	230.5	263	La Crosse, WI–MN	75.6
207	Canton–Massillon, OH	212.5	63	Fort Lauderdale, FL	590.6	186	Lafayette, IN	263.1
196	Charleston, WV	235.5	113	Fort Myers–Cape Coral, FL	456.6	123	Lafayette, LA	430.3
46	Charleston–North Charleston, SC	661.6	79	Fort Pierce–Port St. Lucie, FL	548.2	30	Lake Charles, LA	737.2
219	Charlottesville, VA	182.4	150	Fort Smith, AR–OK	336.7	37	Lakeland–Winter Haven, FL	707.0
23	Charlotte–Gastonia–Rock Hill, NC–SC	798.2	175	Fort Walton Beach, FL	280.8	253	Lancaster, PA	116.0
62	Chattanooga, TN–GA	595.2	225	Fort Wayne, IN	166.8	138	Lansing–East Lansing, MI	374.0

Source: U.S. Department of Justice, Federal Bureau of Investigation
"Crime in the United States 1993" (Uniform Crime Reports, December 4, 1994)
*Aggravated assault is an attack for the purpose of inflicting severe bodily injury.
**Not available.

22. Aggravated Assault Rate in 1993 (continued)

National Rate = 440.1 Aggravated Assaults per 100,000 Population*

RANK	METRO AREA	RATE	RANK	METRO AREA	RATE	RANK	METRO AREA	RATE
60	Laredo, TX	599.1	248	Olympia, WA	132.5	164	Seattle-Bellevue-Everett, WA	317.1
106	Las Vegas, NV-AZ	472.6	–	Omaha, NE**	NA	266	Sheboygan, WI	65.1
130	Lawrence, MA-NH	407.2	172	Orange County, CA	284.7	162	Sherman-Denison, TX	318.8
98	Lawton, OK	497.4	21	Orlando, FL	811.6	48	Shreveport-Bossier City, LA	652.8
256	Lewiston-Auburn, ME	106.6	255	Owensboro, KY	113.8	9	Sioux City, IA-NE	962.8
85	Lexington, KY	532.6	68	Panama City, FL	578.9	191	Sioux Falls, SD	248.0
126	Lincoln, NE	421.5	170	Philadelphia, PA-NJ	292.0	163	South Bend, IN	318.6
4	Little Rock-North Little Rock, AR	1,050.3	77	Phoenix-Mesa, AZ	555.3	154	Spokane, WA	333.0
109	Longview-Marshall, TX	464.1	51	Pine Bluff, AR	644.1	–	Springfield, MA**	NA
14	Los Angeles-Long Beach, CA	899.3	212	Pittsburgh, PA	193.7	214	Springfield, MO	192.9
131	Louisville, KY-IN	401.4	147	Pittsfield, MA	356.3	252	Stamford-Norwalk, CT	118.6
119	Lubbock, TX	439.9	238	Portland, ME	148.9	151	Steubenville-Weirton, OH-WV	335.7
168	Lynchburg, VA	293.4	114	Portland-Vancouver, OR-WA	453.4	49	Stockton-Lodi, CA	647.2
183	Macon, GA	268.9	185	Providence-Fall River-Warwick, RI-MA	265.9	267	St. Cloud, MN	64.1
226	Madison, WI	166.2	260	Provo-Orem, UT	91.7	179	St. Joseph, MO	277.3
271	Manchester, NH	45.5	2	Pueblo, CO	1,189.5	–	St. Louis, MO-IL**	NA
38	Mansfield, OH	706.8	198	Punta Gorda, FL	231.4	16	Sumter, SC	883.4
58	McAllen-Edinburg-Mission, TX	613.7	206	Racine, WI	215.3	234	Syracuse, NY	155.0
159	Medford-Ashland, OR	320.6	148	Raleigh-Durham-Chapel Hill, NC	355.5	66	Tacoma, WA	579.2
115	Memphis, TN-AR-MS	452.7	176	Rapid City, SD	278.4	5	Tallahassee, FL	1,042.0
111	Merced, CA	460.1	221	Reading, PA	179.9	17	Tampa-St. Petersburg-Clearwater, FL	854.1
3	Miami, FL	1,151.8	149	Redding, CA	342.9	69	Texarkana, TX-AR	572.2
223	Middlesex-Sommerset-Hunterdon, NJ	167.6	166	Reno, NV	303.7	193	Toledo, OH	245.3
247	Milwaukee-Waukesha, WI	134.2	182	Richland-Kennewick-Pasco, WA	271.9	153	Trenton, NJ	334.4
195	Minneapolis-St. Paul, MN-WI	235.7	184	Richmond-Petersburg, VA	268.3	86	Tucson, AZ	531.9
105	Mobile, AL	474.2	33	Riverside-San Bernardino, CA	725.5	70	Tulsa, OK	565.4
24	Modesto, CA	784.7	210	Roanoke, VA	195.9	32	Tuscaloosa, AL	731.4
226	Monmouth-Ocean, NJ	166.2	259	Rochester, MN	96.7	89	Tyler, TX	526.0
20	Monroe, LA	827.8	240	Rochester, NY	143.8	237	Utica-Rome, NY	149.9
72	Montgomery, AL	563.6	104	Rocky Mount, NC	475.6	93	Vallejo-Fairfield-Napa, CA	517.1
61	Myrtle Beach, SC	596.1	107	Sacramento, CA	469.9	152	Ventura, CA	334.9
91	Naples, FL	523.6	59	Saginaw-Bay City-Midland, MI	613.2	56	Victoria, TX	625.0
269	Nashua, NH	49.3	241	Salem, OR	143.3	75	Vineland-Millville-Bridgeton, NJ	559.0
34	Nashville, TN	721.4	112	Salinas, CA	457.4	99	Visalia-Tulare-Porterville, CA	495.1
249	Nassau-Suffolk, NY	132.1	194	Salt Lake City-Ogden, UT	237.5	41	Waco, TX	689.6
39	New Bedford, MA	701.0	92	San Angelo, TX	518.5	132	Washington, DC-MD-VA-WV	398.2
178	New Haven-Meriden, CT	278.1	157	San Antonio, TX	329.3	224	Waterbury, CT	167.2
215	New London-Norwich, CT-RI	189.2	78	San Diego, CA	548.7	190	Waterloo-Cedar Falls, IA	251.0
45	New Orleans, LA	663.8	116	San Francisco, CA	450.2	270	Wausau, WI	49.1
28	New York, NY	759.9	142	San Jose, CA	365.8	–	West Palm Beach-Boca Raton, FL**	NA
127	Newark, NJ	420.9	124	San Luis Obispo-Atascadero, CA	424.1	103	Wichita Falls, TX	477.8
174	Newburgh, NY-PA	282.6	144	Santa Barbara-Santa Maria-Lompoc, CA	360.6	256	Williamsport, PA	106.6
167	Norfolk-Va Beach-Newport News, VA-NC	299.0	76	Santa Cruz-Watsonville, CA	558.8	96	Wilmington, NC	502.3
55	Oakland, CA	627.0	136	Santa Rosa, CA	380.7	–	Worcester, MA-CT**	NA
18	Ocala, FL	842.6	43	Sarasota-Bradenton, FL	665.2	121	Yakima, WA	433.0
135	Odessa-Midland, TX	385.9	155	Savannah, GA	331.8	146	Yolo, CA	356.8
81	Oklahoma City, OK	540.1	239	Scranton-Wilkes-Barre-Hazleton, PA	148.1	35	Yuba City, CA	717.0

Source: U.S. Department of Justice, Federal Bureau of Investigation
    "Crime in the United States 1993" (Uniform Crime Reports, December 4, 1994)
*Aggravated assault is an attack for the purpose of inflicting severe bodily injury.
**Not available.

22. Aggravated Assault Rate in 1993 (continued)

National Rate = 440.1 Aggravated Assaults per 100,000 Population*

RANK	METRO AREA	RATE	RANK	METRO AREA	RATE	RANK	METRO AREA	RATE
1	Alexandria, LA	1,668.2	48	Shreveport-Bossier City, LA	652.8	95	Jersey City, NJ	511.3
2	Pueblo, CO	1,189.5	49	Stockton-Lodi, CA	647.2	96	Wilmington, NC	502.3
3	Miami, FL	1,151.8	50	Greenville, NC	646.5	97	Atlanta, GA	500.1
4	Little Rock-North Little Rock, AR	1,050.3	51	Pine Bluff, AR	644.1	98	Lawton, OK	497.4
5	Tallahassee, FL	1,042.0	52	Dothan, AL	642.1	99	Visalia-Tulare-Porterville, CA	495.1
6	Baton Rouge, LA	1,038.5	53	Bakersfield, CA	638.2	100	Denver, CO	492.2
7	Jackson, MI	1,015.5	54	Fayetteville, NC	635.3	101	Fort Worth-Arlington, TX	484.8
8	Anniston, AL	973.0	55	Oakland, CA	627.0	102	Corpus Christi, TX	478.2
9	Sioux City, IA-NE	962.8	56	Victoria, TX	625.0	103	Wichita Falls, TX	477.8
10	Albuquerque, NM	945.5	57	Enid, OK	616.0	104	Rocky Mount, NC	475.6
11	Gainesville, FL	932.0	58	McAllen-Edinburg-Mission, TX	613.7	105	Mobile, AL	474.2
12	Jacksonville, FL	913.5	59	Saginaw-Bay City-Midland, MI	613.2	106	Las Vegas, NV-AZ	472.6
13	Gadsden, AL	908.9	60	Laredo, TX	599.1	107	Sacramento, CA	469.9
14	Los Angeles-Long Beach, CA	899.3	61	Myrtle Beach, SC	596.1	108	Beaumont-Port Arthur, TX	464.6
15	Jackson, TN	894.2	62	Chattanooga, TN-GA	595.2	109	Longview-Marshall, TX	464.1
16	Sumter, SC	883.4	63	Fort Lauderdale, FL	590.6	110	Atlantic City, NJ	463.0
17	Tampa-St. Petersburg-Clearwater, FL	854.1	64	Fresno, CA	587.8	111	Merced, CA	460.1
18	Ocala, FL	842.6	65	Daytona Beach, FL	580.1	112	Salinas, CA	457.4
19	Greenville-Spartanburg-Anderson, SC	837.9	66	Tacoma, WA	579.2	113	Fort Myers-Cape Coral, FL	456.6
20	Monroe, LA	827.8	67	Gary-Hammond, IN	579.0	114	Portland-Vancouver, OR-WA	453.4
21	Orlando, FL	811.6	68	Panama City, FL	578.9	115	Memphis, TN-AR-MS	452.7
22	Birmingham, AL	802.8	69	Texarkana, TX-AR	572.2	116	San Francisco, CA	450.2
23	Charlotte-Gastonia-Rock Hill, NC-SC	798.2	70	Tulsa, OK	565.4	117	Amarillo, TX	446.8
24	Modesto, CA	784.7	71	Detroit, MI	564.5	118	Bloomington, IN	445.7
25	Barnstable-Yarmouth, MA	775.2	72	Montgomery, AL	563.6	119	Lubbock, TX	439.9
26	Benton Harbor, MI	762.6	73	Anchorage, AK	562.4	120	Houma, LA	433.2
27	Flint, MI	761.3	74	Abilene, TX	561.3	121	Yakima, WA	433.0
28	New York, NY	759.9	75	Vineland-Millville-Bridgeton, NJ	559.0	122	Killeen-Temple, TX	431.4
29	Columbia, SC	749.7	76	Santa Cruz-Watsonville, CA	558.8	123	Lafayette, LA	430.3
30	Florence, SC	737.2	77	Phoenix-Mesa, AZ	555.3	124	San Luis Obispo-Atascadero, CA	424.1
30	Lake Charles, LA	737.2	78	San Diego, CA	548.7	125	Greensboro-Winston Salem-High Point, NC	421.7
32	Tuscaloosa, AL	731.4	79	Fort Pierce-Port St. Lucie, FL	548.2	126	Lincoln, NE	421.5
33	Riverside-San Bernardino, CA	725.5	80	Dallas, TX	546.3	127	Newark, NJ	420.9
34	Nashville, TN	721.4	81	Oklahoma City, OK	540.1	128	Buffalo-Niagara Falls, NY	417.4
35	Yuba City, CA	717.0	82	Boston, MA-NH	539.0	129	Augusta-Aiken, GA-SC	415.5
36	El Paso, TX	715.2	83	Kalamazoo-Battle Creek, MI	538.3	130	Lawrence, MA-NH	407.2
37	Lakeland-Winter Haven, FL	707.0	84	Brockton, MA	534.4	131	Louisville, KY-IN	401.4
38	Mansfield, OH	706.8	85	Lexington, KY	532.6	132	Washington, DC-MD-VA-WV	398.2
39	New Bedford, MA	701.0	86	Tucson, AZ	531.9	133	Evansville-Henderson, IN-KY	391.1
40	Clarksville-Hopkinsville, TN-KY	698.4	87	Galveston-Texas City, TX	529.7	134	Grand Rapids-Muskegon-Holland, MI	386.1
41	Waco, TX	689.6	88	Goldsboro, NC	528.2	135	Odessa-Midland, TX	385.9
42	Huntsville, AL	686.2	89	Tyler, TX	526.0	136	Santa Rosa, CA	380.7
43	Sarasota-Bradenton, FL	665.2	90	Brownsville-Harlingen-San Benito, TX	524.7	137	Glens Falls, NY	375.2
44	Fitchburg-Leominster, MA	665.0	91	Naples, FL	523.6	138	Cumberland, MD-WV	374.0
45	New Orleans, LA	663.8	92	San Angelo, TX	518.5	138	Lansing-East Lansing, MI	374.0
46	Charleston-North Charleston, SC	661.6	93	Vallejo-Fairfield-Napa, CA	517.1	140	Kokomo, IN	373.7
47	Baltimore, MD	653.0	94	Albany, GA	511.6	141	Bryan-College Station, TX	365.9

Source: U.S. Department of Justice, Federal Bureau of Investigation
   "Crime in the United States 1993" (Uniform Crime Reports, December 4, 1994)
*Aggravated assault is an attack for the purpose of inflicting severe bodily injury.
**Not available.

22. Aggravated Assault Rate in 1993 (continued)

National Rate = 440.1 Aggravated Assaults per 100,000 Population*

RANK	METRO AREA	RATE	RANK	METRO AREA	RATE	RANK	METRO AREA	RATE
142	San Jose, CA	365.8	189	Akron, OH	256.9	236	Decatur, AL	150.6
143	Athens, GA	361.2	190	Waterloo–Cedar Falls, IA	251.0	237	Utica–Rome, NY	149.9
144	Elkhart–Goshen, IN	360.6	191	Sioux Falls, SD	248.0	238	Portland, ME	148.9
144	Santa Barbara–Santa Maria–Lompoc, CA	360.6	192	Hickory–Morganton, NC	245.4	239	Scranton–Wilkes-Barre–Hazleton, PA	148.1
146	Yolo, CA	356.8	193	Toledo, OH	245.3	240	Rochester, NY	143.8
147	Pittsfield, MA	356.3	194	Salt Lake City–Ogden, UT	237.5	241	Altoona, PA	143.3
148	Raleigh–Durham–Chapel Hill, NC	355.5	195	Minneapolis–St. Paul, MN–WI	235.7	241	Salem, OR	143.3
149	Redding, CA	342.9	196	Charleston, WV	235.5	243	Bellingham, WA	140.5
150	Fort Smith, AR–OK	336.7	197	Bridgeport, CT	233.6	244	Duluth–Superior, MN–WI	138.4
151	Steubenville–Weirton, OH–WV	335.7	198	Punta Gorda, FL	231.4	245	Fayetteville–Springdale–Rogers, AR	135.2
152	Ventura, CA	334.9	199	Fort Collins–Loveland, CO	230.5	246	Bismarck, ND	134.6
153	Trenton, NJ	334.4	200	Greeley, CO	227.4	247	Milwaukee–Waukesha, WI	134.2
154	Spokane, WA	333.0	201	Dutchess County, NY	226.8	248	Olympia, WA	132.5
155	Savannah, GA	331.8	202	Harrisburg–Lebanon–Carlisle, PA	222.0	249	Nassau–Suffolk, NY	132.1
156	Columbus, GA–AL	331.6	203	Brazoria, TX	218.4	250	Cheyenne, WY	127.5
157	San Antonio, TX	329.3	204	Florence, AL	217.9	251	Honolulu, HI	125.5
158	Chico–Paradise, CA	322.1	205	Green Bay, WI	217.1	252	Stamford–Norwalk, CT	118.6
159	Jackson, MS	320.6	206	Racine, WI	215.3	253	Lancaster, PA	116.0
159	Medford–Ashland, OR	320.6	207	Canton–Massillon, OH	212.5	254	Danville, VA	114.4
161	Columbia, MO	319.9	208	Hagerstown, MD	208.4	255	Owensboro, KY	113.8
162	Sherman–Denison, TX	318.8	209	Asheville, NC	207.4	256	Lewiston–Auburn, ME	106.6
163	South Bend, IN	318.6	210	Roanoke, VA	195.9	256	Williamsport, PA	106.6
164	Seattle–Bellevue–Everett, WA	317.1	211	Des Moines, IA	195.8	258	Grand Forks, ND–MN	104.2
165	Cincinnati, OH–KY–IN	314.3	212	Pittsburgh, PA	193.7	259	Rochester, MN	96.7
166	Reno, NV	303.7	213	Bremerton, WA	193.2	260	Provo–Orem, UT	91.7
167	Norfolk–Va Beach–Newport News, VA–NC	299.0	214	Springfield, MO	192.9	261	Danbury, CT	81.8
168	Lynchburg, VA	293.4	215	New London–Norwich, CT–RI	189.2	262	Appleton–Oshkosh–Neenah, WI	80.0
169	Columbus, OH	292.5	216	Huntington–Ashland, WV–KY–OH	186.7	263	La Crosse, WI–MN	75.6
170	Philadelphia, PA–NJ	292.0	217	Eugene–Springfield, OR	186.0	264	Eau Claire, WI	73.0
171	Ann Arbor, MI	289.7	218	Erie, PA	183.7	265	Fargo–Moorhead, ND–MN	65.7
172	Orange County, CA	284.7	219	Charlottesville, VA	182.4	266	Sheboygan, WI	65.1
173	Colorado Springs, CO	282.8	220	Bergen–Passaic, NJ	181.2	267	St. Cloud, MN	64.1
174	Newburgh, NY–PA	282.6	221	Reading, PA	179.9	268	Bangor, ME	54.7
175	Fort Walton Beach, FL	280.8	222	Johnson City–Kingsport–Bristol, TN–VA	179.2	269	Nashua, NH	49.3
176	Rapid City, SD	278.4	223	Middlesex–Somerset–Hunterdon, NJ	167.6	270	Wausau, WI	49.1
177	Hartford, CT	278.2	224	Waterbury, CT	167.2	271	Manchester, NH	45.5
178	New Haven–Meriden, CT	278.1	225	Fort Wayne, IN	166.8	–	Albany, NY**	NA
179	Austin–San Marcos, TX	277.3	226	Madison, WI	166.2	–	Chicago, IL**	NA
179	St. Joseph, MO	277.3	226	Monmouth–Ocean, NJ	166.2	–	Cleveland, OH**	NA
181	Boise, ID	273.6	228	Joplin, MO	165.9	–	Houston, TX**	NA
182	Richland–Kennewick–Pasco, WA	271.9	229	Dubuque, IA	163.2	–	Indianapolis, IN**	NA
183	Macon, GA	268.9	230	Jacksonville, NC	162.8	–	Kansas City, MO–KS**	NA
184	Richmond–Petersburg, VA	268.3	231	Boulder–Longmont, CO	160.7	–	Omaha, NE**	NA
185	Providence–Fall River–Warwick, RI–MA	265.9	232	Janesville–Beloit, WI	160.4	–	Springfield, MA**	NA
186	Lafayette, IN	263.1	233	Johnstown, PA	155.9	–	St. Louis, MO–IL**	NA
187	Dayton–Springfield, OH	263.0	234	Syracuse, NY	155.0	–	West Palm Beach–Boca Raton, FL**	NA
188	Kenosha, WI	257.4	235	Binghamton, NY	153.0	–	Worcester, MA–CT**	NA

Source: U.S. Department of Justice, Federal Bureau of Investigation
"Crime in the United States 1993" (Uniform Crime Reports, December 4, 1994)
Aggravated assault is an attack for the purpose of inflicting severe bodily injury.
**Not available.*

23. Percent Change in Aggravated Assault Rate: 1992 to 1993

National Percent Change = 0.4% Decrease*

RANK	METRO AREA	% CHANGE	RANK	METRO AREA	% CHANGE	RANK	METRO AREA	% CHANGE
62	Abilene, TX	7.74	244	Cheyenne, WY	(31.53)	228	Fort Worth–Arlington, TX	(18.25)
233	Akron, OH	(19.84)	–	Chicago, IL**	NA	42	Fresno, CA	11.47
137	Albany, GA	(0.49)	214	Chico–Paradise, CA	(13.83)	217	Gadsden, AL	(14.70)
–	Albany, NY**	NA	222	Cincinnati, OH–KY–IN	(17.09)	111	Gainesville, FL	1.98
65	Albuquerque, NM	7.46	247	Clarksville–Hopkinsville, TN–KY	(35.35)	37	Galveston–Texas City, TX	11.87
31	Alexandria, LA	14.03	–	Cleveland, OH**	NA	177	Gary–Hammond, IN	(6.67)
5	Altoona, PA	61.56	73	Colorado Springs, CO	5.96	211	Glens Falls, NY	(13.21)
60	Amarillo, TX	7.79	133	Columbia, MO	(0.31)	50	Goldsboro, NC	9.95
39	Anchorage, AK	11.63	25	Columbia, SC	16.07	235	Grand Forks, ND–MN	(22.87)
125	Ann Arbor, MI	0.28	44	Columbus, GA–AL	11.09	102	Grand Rapids–Muskegon–Holland, MI	2.80
23	Anniston, AL	16.26	156	Columbus, OH	(3.05)	52	Greeley, CO	9.27
83	Appleton–Oshkosh–Neenah, WI	5.12	236	Corpus Christi, TX	(23.29)	100	Green Bay, WI	3.43
225	Asheville, NC	(17.93)	74	Cumberland, MD–WV	5.89	126	Greensboro–Winston Salem–High Point, NC	0.21
196	Athens, GA	(9.38)	209	Dallas, TX	(11.92)	18	Greenville, NC	21.32
124	Atlanta, GA	0.46	183	Danbury, CT	(7.15)	21	Greenville–Spartanburg–Anderson, SC	17.88
167	Atlantic City, NJ	(5.10)	112	Danville, VA	1.69	200	Hagerstown, MD	(10.13)
107	Augusta–Aiken, GA–SC	2.31	121	Daytona Beach, FL	0.85	191	Harrisburg–Lebanon–Carlisle, PA	(8.75)
122	Austin–San Marcos, TX	0.84	223	Dayton–Springfield, OH	(17.19)	90	Hartford, CT	4.16
230	Bakersfield, CA	(18.98)	231	Decatur, AL	(19.38)	221	Hickory–Morganton, NC	(16.95)
127	Baltimore, MD	0.20	155	Denver, CO	(2.92)	55	Honolulu, HI	8.56
210	Bangor, ME	(12.76)	240	Des Moines, IA	(27.02)	40	Houma, LA	11.59
32	Barnstable–Yarmouth, MA	13.98	72	Detroit, MI	6.19	–	Houston, TX**	NA
179	Baton Rouge, LA	(6.88)	49	Dothan, AL	10.06	20	Huntington–Ashland, WV–KY–OH	19.14
245	Beaumont–Port Arthur, TX	(32.41)	8	Dubuque, IA	38.78	6	Huntsville, AL	50.91
216	Bellingham, WA	(14.64)	189	Duluth–Superior, MN–WI	(8.53)	–	Indianapolis, IN**	NA
170	Benton Harbor, MI	(5.50)	–	Dutchess County, NY**	NA	81	Jackson, MI	5.31
–	Bergen–Passaic, NJ**	NA	8	Eau Claire, WI	38.78	165	Jackson, MS	(4.78)
163	Binghamton, NY	(4.49)	88	El Paso, TX	4.39	213	Jackson, TN	(13.77)
26	Birmingham, AL	15.99	86	Elkhart–Goshen, IN	4.58	135	Jacksonville, FL	(0.35)
190	Bismarck, ND	(8.68)	11	Enid, OK	30.70	234	Jacksonville, NC	(20.82)
57	Bloomington, IN	8.31	108	Erie, PA	2.11	207	Janesville–Beloit, WI	(10.54)
34	Boise, ID	12.92	68	Eugene–Springfield, OR	7.02	–	Jersey City, NJ**	NA
–	Boston, MA–NH**	NA	219	Evansville–Henderson, IN–KY	(15.93)	202	Johnson City–Kingsport–Bristol, TN–VA	(10.22)
194	Boulder–Longmont, CO	(9.21)	101	Fargo–Moorhead, ND–MN	3.30	98	Johnstown, PA	3.59
70	Brazoria, TX	6.90	38	Fayetteville, NC	11.85	–	Joplin, MO**	NA
109	Bremerton, WA	2.06	89	Fayetteville–Springdale–Rogers, AR	4.32	193	Kalamazoo–Battle Creek, MI	(9.15)
172	Bridgeport, CT	(5.73)	–	Fitchburg–Leominster, MA**	NA	–	Kansas City, MO–KS**	NA
82	Brockton, MA	5.30	130	Flint, MI	(0.05)	7	Kenosha, WI	43.08
114	Brownsville–Harlingen–San Benito, TX	1.39	181	Florence, AL	(7.00)	29	Killeen–Temple, TX	14.25
164	Bryan–College Station, TX	(4.64)	77	Florence, SC	5.57	14	Kokomo, IN	25.82
–	Buffalo–Niagara Falls, NY**	NA	–	Fort Collins–Loveland, CO**	NA	3	La Crosse, WI–MN	66.89
215	Canton–Massillon, OH	(14.35)	115	Fort Lauderdale, FL	1.30	63	Lafayette, IN	7.48
203	Charleston, WV	(10.32)	76	Fort Myers–Cape Coral, FL	5.72	75	Lafayette, LA	5.88
94	Charleston–North Charleston, SC	3.78	54	Fort Pierce–Port St. Lucie, FL	9.20	–	Lake Charles, LA**	NA
119	Charlottesville, VA	1.00	17	Fort Smith, AR–OK	21.64	113	Lakeland–Winter Haven, FL	1.65
151	Charlotte–Gastonia–Rock Hill, NC–SC	(2.34)	184	Fort Walton Beach, FL	(7.51)	22	Lancaster, PA	16.58
161	Chattanooga, TN–GA	(4.39)	35	Fort Wayne, IN	12.78	206	Lansing–East Lansing, MI	(10.53)

Source: Morgan Quitno Corporation using data from U.S. Department of Justice, Federal Bureau of Investigation
"Crime in the United States 1993" (Uniform Crime Reports, December 4, 1994)
Aggravated assault is an attack for the purpose of inflicting severe bodily injury.
**Not available.*

23. Percent Change in Aggravated Assault Rate: 1992 to 1993 (continued)

National Percent Change = 0.4% Decrease*

RANK	METRO AREA	% CHANGE	RANK	METRO AREA	% CHANGE	RANK	METRO AREA	CHANGE
47	Laredo, TX	10.47	212	Olympia, WA	(13.62)	133	Seattle-Bellevue-Everett, WA	(0.31)
2	Las Vegas, NV-AZ	74.39	–	Omaha, NE**	NA	199	Sheboygan, WI	(10.08)
–	Lawrence, MA-NH**	NA	110	Orange County, CA	2.04	24	Sherman-Denison, TX	16.18
224	Lawton, OK	(17.70)	80	Orlando, FL	5.35	78	Shreveport-Bossier City, LA	5.53
1	Lewiston-Auburn, ME	105.00	248	Owensboro, KY	(36.03)	–	Sioux City, IA-NE**	NA
153	Lexington, KY	(2.54)	232	Panama City, FL	(19.42)	96	Sioux Falls, SD	3.68
203	Lincoln, NE	(10.32)	150	Philadelphia, PA-NJ	(2.31)	16	South Bend, IN	21.79
51	Little Rock-North Little Rock, AR	9.44	59	Phoenix-Mesa, AZ	7.97	143	Spokane, WA	(1.62)
154	Longview-Marshall, TX	(2.62)	43	Pine Bluff, AR	11.26	–	Springfield, MA**	NA
178	Los Angeles-Long Beach, CA	(6.87)	144	Pittsburgh, PA	(1.68)	129	Springfield, MO	0.10
195	Louisville, KY-IN	(9.25)	45	Pittsfield, MA	10.93	123	Stamford-Norwalk, CT	0.68
41	Lubbock, TX	11.48	220	Portland, ME	(16.77)	71	Steubenville-Weirton, OH-WV	6.77
174	Lynchburg, VA	(5.96)	96	Portland-Vancouver, OR-WA	3.68	48	Stockton-Lodi, CA	10.29
246	Macon, GA	(33.46)	131	Providence-Fall River-Warwick, RI-MA	(0.30)	238	St. Cloud, MN	(25.90)
227	Madison, WI	(18.13)	33	Provo-Orem, UT	13.07	229	St. Joseph, MO	(18.42)
–	Manchester, NH**	NA	28	Pueblo, CO	14.30	–	St. Louis, MO-IL**	NA
140	Mansfield, OH	(1.19)	–	Punta Gorda, FL**	NA	139	Sumter, SC	(0.64)
13	McAllen-Edinburg-Mission, TX	26.12	226	Racine, WI	(18.11)	192	Syracuse, NY	(8.93)
27	Medford-Ashland, OR	15.12	198	Raleigh-Durham-Chapel Hill, NC	(9.98)	93	Tacoma, WA	3.80
63	Memphis, TN-AR-MS	7.48	160	Rapid City, SD	(3.97)	208	Tallahassee, FL	(10.90)
4	Merced, CA	64.32	205	Reading, PA	(10.41)	158	Tampa-St. Petersburg-Clearwater, FL	(3.87)
56	Miami, FL	8.33	188	Redding, CA	(8.27)	65	Texarkana, TX-AR	7.46
–	Middlesex-Sommerset-Hunterdon, NJ**	NA	105	Reno, NV	2.39	147	Toledo, OH	(1.92)
141	Milwaukee-Waukesha, WI	(1.40)	159	Richland-Kennewick-Pasco, WA	(3.92)	165	Trenton, NJ	(4.78)
145	Minneapolis-St. Paul, MN-WI	(1.71)	106	Richmond-Petersburg, VA	2.33	84	Tucson, AZ	4.91
–	Mobile, AL**	NA	148	Riverside-San Bernardino, CA	(2.05)	92	Tulsa, OK	3.82
12	Modesto, CA	29.04	103	Roanoke, VA	2.78	171	Tuscaloosa, AL	(5.72)
–	Monmouth-Ocean, NJ**	NA	157	Rochester, MN	(3.30)	104	Tyler, TX	2.45
167	Monroe, LA	(5.10)	116	Rochester, NY	1.27	36	Utica-Rome, NY	12.20
53	Montgomery, AL	9.25	99	Rocky Mount, NC	3.55	201	Vallejo-Fairfield-Napa, CA	(10.15)
128	Myrtle Beach, SC	0.15	69	Sacramento, CA	6.97	173	Ventura, CA	(5.87)
182	Naples, FL	(7.03)	46	Saginaw-Bay City-Midland, MI	10.63	218	Victoria, TX	(15.25)
10	Nashua, NH	35.07	30	Salem, OR	14.09	175	Vineland-Millville-Bridgeton, NJ	(6.10)
61	Nashville, TN	7.75	176	Salinas, CA	(6.37)	119	Visalia-Tulare-Porterville, CA	1.00
–	Nassau-Suffolk, NY**	NA	136	Salt Lake City-Ogden, UT	(0.42)	19	Waco, TX	19.43
–	New Bedford, MA**	NA	197	San Angelo, TX	(9.61)	138	Washington, DC-MD-VA-WV	(0.55)
243	New Haven-Meriden, CT	(31.28)	67	San Antonio, TX	7.23	242	Waterbury, CT	(29.92)
180	New London-Norwich, CT-RI	(6.94)	186	San Diego, CA	(7.95)	–	Waterloo-Cedar Falls, IA**	NA
152	New Orleans, LA	(2.40)	146	San Francisco, CA	(1.81)	237	Wausau, WI	(24.11)
–	New York, NY**	NA	79	San Jose, CA	5.39	–	West Palm Beach-Boca Raton, FL**	NA
–	Newark, NJ**	NA	–	San Luis Obispo-Atascadero, CA**	NA	185	Wichita Falls, TX	(7.78)
–	Newburgh, NY-PA**	NA	162	Santa Barbara-Santa Maria-Lompoc, CA	(4.40)	169	Williamsport, PA	(5.24)
131	Norfolk-Va Beach-Newport News, VA-NC	(0.30)	58	Santa Cruz-Watsonville, CA	8.06	149	Wilmington, NC	(2.24)
85	Oakland, CA	4.62	95	Santa Rosa, CA	3.70	–	Worcester, MA-CT**	NA
118	Ocala, FL	1.03	87	Sarasota-Bradenton, FL	4.51	142	Yakima, WA	(1.61)
187	Odessa-Midland, TX	(8.25)	15	Savannah, GA	24.27	239	Yolo, CA	(26.46)
117	Oklahoma City, OK	1.24	241	Scranton-Wilkes-Barre-Hazleton, PA	(29.00)	91	Yuba City, CA	3.99

Source: Morgan Quitno Corporation using data from U.S. Department of Justice, Federal Bureau of Investigation
"Crime in the United States 1993" (Uniform Crime Reports, December 4, 1994)
Aggravated assault is an attack for the purpose of inflicting severe bodily injury.
**Not available.*

23. Percent Change in Aggravated Assault Rate: 1992 to 1993 (continued)

National Percent Change = 0.4% Decrease*

RANK	METRO AREA	% CHANGE	RANK	METRO AREA	% CHANGE	RANK	METRO AREA	% CHANGE
1	Lewiston–Auburn, ME	105.00	48	Stockton–Lodi, CA	10.29	95	Santa Rosa, CA	3.70
2	Las Vegas, NV–AZ	74.39	49	Dothan, AL	10.06	96	Portland–Vancouver, OR–WA	3.68
3	La Crosse, WI–MN	66.89	50	Goldsboro, NC	9.95	96	Sioux Falls, SD	3.68
4	Merced, CA	64.32	51	Little Rock–North Little Rock, AR	9.44	98	Johnstown, PA	3.59
5	Altoona, PA	61.56	52	Greeley, CO	9.27	99	Rocky Mount, NC	3.55
6	Huntsville, AL	50.91	53	Montgomery, AL	9.25	100	Green Bay, WI	3.43
7	Kenosha, WI	43.08	54	Fort Pierce–Port St. Lucie, FL	9.20	101	Fargo–Moorhead, ND–MN	3.30
8	Dubuque, IA	38.78	55	Honolulu, HI	8.56	102	Grand Rapids–Muskegon–Holland, MI	2.80
8	Eau Claire, WI	38.78	56	Miami, FL	8.33	103	Roanoke, VA	2.78
10	Nashua, NH	35.07	57	Bloomington, IN	8.31	104	Tyler, TX	2.45
11	Enid, OK	30.70	58	Santa Cruz–Watsonville, CA	8.06	105	Reno, NV	2.39
12	Modesto, CA	29.04	59	Phoenix–Mesa, AZ	7.97	106	Richmond–Petersburg, VA	2.33
13	McAllen–Edinburg–Mission, TX	26.12	60	Amarillo, TX	7.79	107	Augusta–Aiken, GA–SC	2.31
14	Kokomo, IN	25.82	61	Nashville, TN	7.75	108	Erie, PA	2.11
15	Savannah, GA	24.27	62	Abilene, TX	7.74	109	Bremerton, WA	2.06
16	South Bend, IN	21.79	63	Lafayette, IN	7.48	110	Orange County, CA	2.04
17	Fort Smith, AR–OK	21.64	63	Memphis, TN–AR–MS	7.48	111	Gainesville, FL	1.98
18	Greenville, NC	21.32	65	Albuquerque, NM	7.46	112	Danville, VA	1.69
19	Waco, TX	19.43	65	Texarkana, TX–AR	7.46	113	Lakeland–Winter Haven, FL	1.65
20	Huntington–Ashland, WV–KY–OH	19.14	67	San Antonio, TX	7.23	114	Brownsville–Harlingen–San Benito, TX	1.39
21	Greenville–Spartanburg–Anderson, SC	17.88	68	Eugene–Springfield, OR	7.02	115	Fort Lauderdale, FL	1.30
22	Lancaster, PA	16.58	69	Sacramento, CA	6.97	116	Rochester, NY	1.27
23	Anniston, AL	16.26	70	Brazoria, TX	6.90	117	Oklahoma City, OK	1.24
24	Sherman–Denison, TX	16.18	71	Steubenville–Weirton, OH–WV	6.77	118	Ocala, FL	1.03
25	Columbia, SC	16.07	72	Detroit, MI	6.19	119	Charlottesville, VA	1.00
26	Birmingham, AL	15.99	73	Colorado Springs, CO	5.96	119	Visalia–Tulare–Porterville, CA	1.00
27	Medford–Ashland, OR	15.12	74	Cumberland, MD–WV	5.89	121	Daytona Beach, FL	0.85
28	Pueblo, CO	14.30	75	Lafayette, LA	5.88	122	Austin–San Marcos, TX	0.84
29	Killeen–Temple, TX	14.25	76	Fort Myers–Cape Coral, FL	5.72	123	Stamford–Norwalk, CT	0.68
30	Salem, OR	14.09	77	Florence, SC	5.57	124	Atlanta, GA	0.46
31	Alexandria, LA	14.03	78	Shreveport–Bossier City, LA	5.53	125	Ann Arbor, MI	0.28
32	Barnstable–Yarmouth, MA	13.98	79	San Jose, CA	5.39	126	Greensboro–Winston Salem–High Point, NC	0.21
33	Provo–Orem, UT	13.07	80	Orlando, FL	5.35	127	Baltimore, MD	0.20
34	Boise, ID	12.92	81	Jackson, MI	5.31	128	Myrtle Beach, SC	0.15
35	Fort Wayne, IN	12.78	82	Brockton, MA	5.30	129	Springfield, MO	0.10
36	Utica–Rome, NY	12.20	83	Appleton–Oshkosh–Neenah, WI	5.12	130	Flint, MI	(0.05)
37	Galveston–Texas City, TX	11.87	84	Tucson, AZ	4.91	131	Norfolk–Va Beach–Newport News, VA–NC	(0.30)
38	Fayetteville, NC	11.85	85	Oakland, CA	4.62	131	Providence–Fall River–Warwick, RI–MA	(0.30)
39	Anchorage, AK	11.63	86	Elkhart–Goshen, IN	4.58	133	Columbia, MO	(0.31)
40	Houma, LA	11.59	87	Sarasota–Bradenton, FL	4.51	133	Seattle–Bellevue–Everett, WA	(0.31)
41	Lubbock, TX	11.48	88	El Paso, TX	4.39	135	Jacksonville, FL	(0.35)
42	Fresno, CA	11.47	89	Fayetteville–Springdale–Rogers, AR	4.32	136	Salt Lake City–Ogden, UT	(0.42)
43	Pine Bluff, AR	11.26	90	Hartford, CT	4.16	137	Albany, GA	(0.49)
44	Columbus, GA–AL	11.09	91	Yuba City, CA	3.99	138	Washington, DC–MD–VA–WV	(0.55)
45	Pittsfield, MA	10.93	92	Tulsa, OK	3.82	139	Sumter, SC	(0.64)
46	Saginaw–Bay City–Midland, MI	10.63	93	Tacoma, WA	3.80	140	Mansfield, OH	(1.19)
47	Laredo, TX	10.47	94	Charleston–North Charleston, SC	3.78	141	Milwaukee–Waukesha, WI	(1.40)

Source: Morgan Quitno Corporation using data from U.S. Department of Justice, Federal Bureau of Investigation
    "Crime in the United States 1993" (Uniform Crime Reports, December 4, 1994)
Aggravated assault is an attack for the purpose of inflicting severe bodily injury.
**Not available.*

23. Percent Change in Aggravated Assault Rate: 1992 to 1993 (continued)

National Percent Change = 0.4% Decrease*

RANK	METRO AREA	% CHANGE	RANK	METRO AREA	% CHANGE	RANK	METRO AREA	CHANGE
142	Yakima, WA	(1.61)	189	Duluth–Superior, MN–WI	(8.53)	236	Corpus Christi, TX	(23.29)
143	Spokane, WA	(1.62)	190	Bismarck, ND	(8.68)	237	Wausau, WI	(24.11)
144	Pittsburgh, PA	(1.68)	191	Harrisburg–Lebanon–Carlisle, PA	(8.75)	238	St. Cloud, MN	(25.90)
145	Minneapolis–St. Paul, MN–WI	(1.71)	192	Syracuse, NY	(8.93)	239	Yolo, CA	(26.46)
146	San Francisco, CA	(1.81)	193	Kalamazoo–Battle Creek, MI	(9.15)	240	Des Moines, IA	(27.02)
147	Toledo, OH	(1.92)	194	Boulder–Longmont, CO	(9.21)	241	Scranton–Wilkes-Barre–Hazleton, PA	(29.00)
148	Riverside–San Bernardino, CA	(2.05)	195	Louisville, KY–IN	(9.25)	242	Waterbury, CT	(29.92)
149	Wilmington, NC	(2.24)	196	Athens, GA	(9.38)	243	New Haven–Meriden, CT	(31.28)
150	Philadelphia, PA–NJ	(2.31)	197	San Angelo, TX	(9.61)	244	Cheyenne, WY	(31.53)
151	Charlotte–Gastonia–Rock Hill, NC–SC	(2.34)	198	Raleigh–Durham–Chapel Hill, NC	(9.98)	245	Beaumont–Port Arthur, TX	(32.41)
152	New Orleans, LA	(2.40)	199	Sheboygan, WI	(10.08)	246	Macon, GA	(33.46)
153	Lexington, KY	(2.54)	200	Hagerstown, MD	(10.13)	247	Clarksville–Hopkinsville, TN–KY	(35.35)
154	Longview–Marshall, TX	(2.62)	201	Vallejo–Fairfield–Napa, CA	(10.15)	248	Owensboro, KY	(36.03)
155	Denver, CO	(2.92)	202	Johnson City–Kingsport–Bristol, TN–VA	(10.22)	–	Albany, NY**	NA
156	Columbus, OH	(3.05)	203	Charleston, WV	(10.32)	–	Bergen–Passaic, NJ**	NA
157	Rochester, MN	(3.30)	203	Lincoln, NE	(10.32)	–	Boston, MA–NH**	NA
158	Tampa–St. Petersburg–Clearwater, FL	(3.87)	205	Reading, PA	(10.41)	–	Buffalo–Niagara Falls, NY**	NA
159	Richland–Kennewick–Pasco, WA	(3.92)	206	Lansing–East Lansing, MI	(10.53)	–	Chicago, IL**	NA
160	Rapid City, SD	(3.97)	207	Janesville–Beloit, WI	(10.54)	–	Cleveland, OH**	NA
161	Chattanooga, TN–GA	(4.39)	208	Tallahassee, FL	(10.90)	–	Dutchess County, NY**	NA
162	Santa Barbara–Santa Maria–Lompoc, CA	(4.40)	209	Dallas, TX	(11.92)	–	Fitchburg–Leominster, MA**	NA
163	Binghamton, NY	(4.49)	210	Bangor, ME	(12.76)	–	Fort Collins–Loveland, CO**	NA
164	Bryan–College Station, TX	(4.64)	211	Glens Falls, NY	(13.21)	–	Houston, TX**	NA
165	Jackson, MS	(4.78)	212	Olympia, WA	(13.62)	–	Indianapolis, IN**	NA
165	Trenton, NJ	(4.78)	213	Jackson, TN	(13.77)	–	Jersey City, NJ**	NA
167	Atlantic City, NJ	(5.10)	214	Chico–Paradise, CA	(13.83)	–	Joplin, MO**	NA
167	Monroe, LA	(5.10)	215	Canton–Massillon, OH	(14.35)	–	Kansas City, MO–KS**	NA
169	Williamsport, PA	(5.24)	216	Bellingham, WA	(14.64)	–	Lake Charles, LA**	NA
170	Benton Harbor, MI	(5.50)	217	Gadsden, AL	(14.70)	–	Lawrence, MA–NH**	NA
171	Tuscaloosa, AL	(5.72)	218	Victoria, TX	(15.25)	–	Manchester, NH**	NA
172	Bridgeport, CT	(5.73)	219	Evansville–Henderson, IN–KY	(15.93)	–	Middlesex–Sommerset–Hunterdon, NJ**	NA
173	Ventura, CA	(5.87)	220	Portland, ME	(16.77)	–	Mobile, AL**	NA
174	Lynchburg, VA	(5.96)	221	Hickory–Morganton, NC	(16.95)	–	Monmouth–Ocean, NJ**	NA
175	Vineland–Millville–Bridgeton, NJ	(6.10)	222	Cincinnati, OH–KY–IN	(17.09)	–	Nassau–Suffolk, NY**	NA
176	Salinas, CA	(6.37)	223	Dayton–Springfield, OH	(17.19)	–	New Bedford, MA**	NA
177	Gary–Hammond, IN	(6.67)	224	Lawton, OK	(17.70)	–	New York, NY**	NA
178	Los Angeles–Long Beach, CA	(6.87)	225	Asheville, NC	(17.93)	–	Newark, NJ**	NA
179	Baton Rouge, LA	(6.88)	226	Racine, WI	(18.11)	–	Newburgh, NY–PA**	NA
180	New London–Norwich, CT–RI	(6.94)	227	Madison, WI	(18.13)	–	Omaha, NE**	NA
181	Florence, AL	(7.00)	228	Fort Worth–Arlington, TX	(18.25)	–	Punta Gorda, FL**	NA
182	Naples, FL	(7.03)	229	St. Joseph, MO	(18.42)	–	San Luis Obispo–Atascadero, CA**	NA
183	Danbury, CT	(7.15)	230	Bakersfield, CA	(18.98)	–	Sioux City, IA–NE**	NA
184	Fort Walton Beach, FL	(7.51)	231	Decatur, AL	(19.38)	–	Springfield, MA**	NA
185	Wichita Falls, TX	(7.78)	232	Panama City, FL	(19.42)	–	St. Louis, MO–IL**	NA
186	San Diego, CA	(7.95)	233	Akron, OH	(19.84)	–	Waterloo–Cedar Falls, IA**	NA
187	Odessa–Midland, TX	(8.25)	234	Jacksonville, NC	(20.82)	–	West Palm Beach–Boca Raton, FL**	NA
188	Redding, CA	(8.27)	235	Grand Forks, ND–MN	(22.87)	–	Worcester, MA–CT**	NA

Source: Morgan Quitno Corporation using data from U.S. Department of Justice, Federal Bureau of Investigation
"Crime in the United States 1993" (Uniform Crime Reports, December 4, 1994)
Aggravated assault is an attack for the purpose of inflicting severe bodily injury.
**Not available.*

24. Percent Change in Aggravated Assault Rate: 1989 to 1993

National Percent Change = 14.8% Increase*

RANK	METRO AREA	% CHANGE	RANK	METRO AREA	% CHANGE	RANK	METRO AREA	% CHANGE
68	Abilene, TX	32.66	225	Cheyenne, WY	(22.11)	136	Fort Worth–Arlington, TX	10.76
–	Akron, OH**	NA	–	Chicago, IL**	NA	214	Fresno, CA	(14.56)
89	Albany, GA	26.07	170	Chico-Paradise, CA	2.64	22	Gadsden, AL	75.60
–	Albany, NY**	NA	94	Cincinnati, OH–KY–IN	23.64	117	Gainesville, FL	16.70
74	Albuquerque, NM	29.93	14	Clarksville-Hopkinsville, TN–KY	86.99	13	Galveston–Texas City, TX	90.88
10	Alexandria, LA	131.31	–	Cleveland, OH**	NA	104	Gary–Hammond, IN	20.20
134	Altoona, PA	11.34	137	Colorado Springs, CO	10.60	78	Glens Falls, NY	28.89
52	Amarillo, TX	42.34	171	Columbia, MO	2.60	–	Goldsboro, NC**	NA
20	Anchorage, AK	77.19	181	Columbia, SC	(1.17)	5	Grand Forks, ND–MN	202.91
236	Ann Arbor, MI	(36.59)	144	Columbus, GA–AL	8.61	145	Grand Rapids-Muskegon-Holland, MI	8.06
38	Anniston, AL	54.13	180	Columbus, OH	(1.15)	231	Greeley, CO	(28.78)
221	Appleton-Oshkosh-Neenah, WI	(20.56)	114	Corpus Christi, TX	16.98	45	Green Bay, WI	50.24
75	Asheville, NC	29.87	8	Cumberland, MD–WV	137.01	135	Greensboro-Winston Salem-High Point, NC	11.03
148	Athens, GA	6.86	188	Dallas, TX	(3.02)	–	Greenville, NC**	NA
193	Atlanta, GA	(5.61)	32	Danbury, CT	62.62	75	Greenville-Spartanburg-Anderson, SC	29.87
192	Atlantic City, NJ	(4.95)	169	Danville, VA	2.79	215	Hagerstown, MD	(14.63)
64	Augusta-Aiken, GA–SC	34.47	86	Daytona Beach, FL	26.91	–	Harrisburg-Lebanon-Carlisle, PA**	NA
165	Austin-San Marcos, TX	3.35	213	Dayton-Springfield, OH	(14.28)	227	Hartford, CT	(22.59)
143	Bakersfield, CA	9.79	233	Decatur, AL	(35.48)	–	Hickory-Morganton, NC**	NA
142	Baltimore, MD	9.84	90	Denver, CO	25.95	163	Honolulu, HI	3.72
55	Bangor, ME	38.48	237	Des Moines, IA	(41.53)	–	Houma, LA**	NA
–	Barnstable-Yarmouth, MA**	NA	92	Detroit, MI	24.45	–	Houston, TX**	NA
54	Baton Rouge, LA	39.41	116	Dothan, AL	16.81	62	Huntington-Ashland, WV–KY–OH	35.98
203	Beaumont–Port Arthur, TX	(8.78)	240	Dubuque, IA	(56.12)	7	Huntsville, AL	137.52
149	Bellingham, WA	6.76	69	Duluth–Superior, MN–WI	32.19	–	Indianapolis, IN**	NA
132	Benton Harbor, MI	11.95	–	Dutchess County, NY**	NA	36	Jackson, MI	56.59
207	Bergen-Passaic, NJ	(10.61)	60	Eau Claire, WI	36.96	39	Jackson, MS	52.96
25	Binghamton, NY	70.38	101	El Paso, TX	21.20	155	Jackson, TN	6.28
21	Birmingham, AL	76.91	26	Elkhart-Goshen, IN	68.74	47	Jacksonville, FL	47.60
6	Bismarck, ND	178.10	57	Enid, OK	37.90	234	Jacksonville, NC	(35.63)
83	Bloomington, IN	27.74	175	Erie, PA	0.66	195	Janesville-Beloit, WI	(5.92)
161	Boise, ID	3.79	127	Eugene-Springfield, OR	13.83	131	Jersey City, NJ	12.13
–	Boston, MA–NH**	NA	87	Evansville-Henderson, IN–KY	26.90	156	Johnson City-Kingsport-Bristol, TN–VA	5.79
232	Boulder-Longmont, CO	(30.88)	210	Fargo-Moorhead, ND–MN	(11.81)	–	Johnstown, PA**	NA
157	Brazoria, TX	5.66	190	Fayetteville, NC	(3.77)	173	Joplin, MO	0.97
–	Bremerton, WA**	NA	206	Fayetteville-Springdale-Rogers, AR	(10.58)	205	Kalamazoo-Battle Creek, MI	(10.22)
218	Bridgeport, CT	(16.84)	27	Fitchburg-Leominster, MA	66.58	–	Kansas City, MO–KS**	NA
–	Brockton, MA**	NA	133	Flint, MI	11.53	1	Kenosha, WI	345.33
65	Brownsville-Harlingen-San Benito, TX	33.65	164	Florence, AL	3.56	16	Killeen-Temple, TX	83.65
191	Bryan-College Station, TX	(3.91)	111	Florence, SC	17.58	37	Kokomo, IN	55.64
138	Buffalo-Niagara Falls, NY	10.13	194	Fort Collins-Loveland, CO	(5.69)	230	La Crosse, WI–MN	(26.89)
219	Canton-Massillon, OH	(16.89)	120	Fort Lauderdale, FL	16.12	2	Lafayette, IN	331.31
9	Charleston, WV	134.10	3	Fort Myers-Cape Coral, FL	233.28	121	Lafayette, LA	15.89
97	Charleston-North Charleston, SC	22.77	141	Fort Pierce-Port St. Lucie, FL	9.97	112	Lake Charles, LA	17.31
179	Charlottesville, VA	(0.05)	152	Fort Smith, AR–OK	6.45	146	Lakeland-Winter Haven, FL	7.50
113	Charlotte-Gastonia-Rock Hill, NC–SC	17.07	105	Fort Walton Beach, FL	20.00	93	Lancaster, PA	24.20
118	Chattanooga, TN–GA	16.61	150	Fort Wayne, IN	6.51	176	Lansing-East Lansing, MI	0.59

Source: Morgan Quitno Corporation using data from U.S. Department of Justice, Federal Bureau of Investigation
"Crime in the United States 1993" (Uniform Crime Reports, December 4, 1994)
Aggravated assault is an attack for the purpose of inflicting severe bodily injury.
**Not available.*

24. Percent Change in Aggravated Assault Rate: 1989 to 1993 (continued)

National Percent Change = 14.8% Increase*

RANK	METRO AREA	% CHANGE	RANK	METRO AREA	% CHANGE	RANK	METRO AREA	CHANGE
224	Laredo, TX	(21.60)	189	Olympia, WA	(3.43)	151	Seattle–Bellevue–Everett, WA	6.48
28	Las Vegas, NV–AZ	66.41	–	Omaha, NE**	NA	243	Sheboygan, WI	(65.17)
77	Lawrence, MA–NH	29.48	162	Orange County, CA	3.75	147	Sherman–Denison, TX	7.48
66	Lawton, OK	33.21	81	Orlando, FL	28.17	88	Shreveport–Bossier City, LA	26.32
98	Lewiston–Auburn, ME	22.67	153	Owensboro, KY	6.36	4	Sioux City, IA–NE	209.38
61	Lexington, KY	36.32	19	Panama City, FL	78.12	46	Sioux Falls, SD	49.31
96	Lincoln, NE	22.85	168	Philadelphia, PA–NJ	3.03	–	South Bend, IN**	NA
30	Little Rock–North Little Rock, AR	63.88	59	Phoenix–Mesa, AZ	37.38	42	Spokane, WA	51.36
50	Longview–Marshall, TX	43.60	186	Pine Bluff, AR	(2.39)	–	Springfield, MA**	NA
185	Los Angeles–Long Beach, CA	(2.38)	196	Pittsburgh, PA	(5.97)	182	Springfield, MO	(1.63)
31	Louisville, KY–IN	63.64	–	Pittsfield, MA**	NA	198	Stamford–Norwalk, CT	(6.69)
43	Lubbock, TX	51.12	217	Portland, ME	(16.40)	–	Steubenville–Weirton, OH–WV**	NA
177	Lynchburg, VA	0.17	199	Portland–Vancouver, OR–WA	(7.09)	33	Stockton–Lodi, CA	61.28
212	Macon, GA	(12.98)	166	Providence–Fall River–Warwick, RI–MA	3.34	167	St. Cloud, MN	3.05
126	Madison, WI	13.91	–	Provo–Orem, UT**	NA	238	St. Joseph, MO	(49.66)
242	Manchester, NH	(56.91)	48	Pueblo, CO	46.09	–	St. Louis, MO–IL**	NA
103	Mansfield, OH	20.86	–	Punta Gorda, FL**	NA	–	Sumter, SC**	NA
18	McAllen–Edinburg–Mission, TX	78.35	223	Racine, WI	(21.51)	204	Syracuse, NY	(10.14)
80	Medford–Ashland, OR	28.19	73	Raleigh–Durham–Chapel Hill, NC	30.27	70	Tacoma, WA	31.91
154	Memphis, TN–AR–MS	6.32	63	Rapid City, SD	35.41	125	Tallahassee, FL	14.44
24	Merced, CA	72.65	–	Reading, PA**	NA	91	Tampa–St. Petersburg–Clearwater, FL	25.40
158	Miami, FL	4.77	202	Redding, CA	(8.61)	12	Texarkana, TX–AR	91.37
100	Middlesex–Sommerset–Hunterdon, NJ	21.80	229	Reno, NV	(23.42)	209	Toledo, OH	(11.09)
197	Milwaukee–Waukesha, WI	(6.09)	99	Richland–Kennewick–Pasco, WA	22.42	184	Trenton, NJ	(2.02)
160	Minneapolis–St. Paul, MN–WI	4.57	211	Richmond–Petersburg, VA	(12.21)	–	Tucson, AZ**	NA
235	Mobile, AL	(35.84)	–	Riverside–San Bernardino, CA**	NA	106	Tulsa, OK	18.83
109	Modesto, CA	18.18	56	Roanoke, VA	37.96	110	Tuscaloosa, AL	17.74
201	Monmouth–Ocean, NJ	(7.82)	40	Rochester, MN	51.81	35	Tyler, TX	58.15
85	Monroe, LA	27.02	216	Rochester, NY	(16.15)	17	Utica–Rome, NY	82.80
11	Montgomery, AL	122.68	–	Rocky Mount, NC**	NA	222	Vallejo–Fairfield–Napa, CA	(20.96)
–	Myrtle Beach, SC**	NA	102	Sacramento, CA	20.89	82	Ventura, CA	27.87
122	Naples, FL	14.95	79	Saginaw–Bay City–Midland, MI	28.58	67	Victoria, TX	32.75
241	Nashua, NH	(56.60)	228	Salem, OR	(22.75)	124	Vineland–Millville–Bridgeton, NJ	14.50
29	Nashville, TN	64.37	174	Salinas, CA	0.90	186	Visalia–Tulare–Porterville, CA	(2.39)
172	Nassau–Suffolk, NY	1.54	115	Salt Lake City–Ogden, UT	16.82	34	Waco, TX	58.97
23	New Bedford, MA	74.51	107	San Angelo, TX	18.35	119	Washington, DC–MD–VA–WV	16.19
226	New Haven–Meriden, CT	(22.34)	53	San Antonio, TX	41.63	183	Waterbury, CT	(1.88)
220	New London–Norwich, CT–RI	(18.10)	128	San Diego, CA	13.77	130	Waterloo–Cedar Falls, IA	13.01
123	New Orleans, LA	14.78	178	San Francisco, CA	(0.02)	239	Wausau, WI	(54.03)
208	New York, NY	(10.72)	139	San Jose, CA	10.02	–	West Palm Beach–Boca Raton, FL**	NA
200	Newark, NJ	(7.70)	–	San Luis Obispo–Atascadero, CA**	NA	71	Wichita Falls, TX	31.73
–	Newburgh, NY–PA**	NA	159	Santa Barbara–Santa Maria–Lompoc, CA	4.61	–	Williamsport, PA**	NA
72	Norfolk–Va Beach–Newport News, VA–NC	30.62	15	Santa Cruz–Watsonville, CA	84.73	95	Wilmington, NC	23.29
51	Oakland, CA	43.05	58	Santa Rosa, CA	37.79	–	Worcester, MA–CT**	NA
49	Ocala, FL	45.50	84	Sarasota–Bradenton, FL	27.58	108	Yakima, WA	18.21
41	Odessa–Midland, TX	51.57	129	Savannah, GA	13.51	–	Yolo, CA**	NA
44	Oklahoma City, OK	51.03	–	Scranton–Wilkes-Barre–Hazleton, PA**	NA	140	Yuba City, CA	9.99

Source: Morgan Quitno Corporation using data from U.S. Department of Justice, Federal Bureau of Investigation
 "Crime in the United States 1993" (Uniform Crime Reports, December 4, 1994)
*Aggravated assault is an attack for the purpose of inflicting severe bodily injury.
**Not available.

24. Percent Change in Aggravated Assault Rate: 1989 to 1993 (continued)

National Percent Change = 14.8% Increase*

RANK	METRO AREA	% CHANGE	RANK	METRO AREA	% CHANGE	RANK	METRO AREA	% CHANGE
1	Kenosha, WI	345.33	48	Pueblo, CO	46.09	95	Wilmington, NC	23.29
2	Lafayette, IN	331.31	49	Ocala, FL	45.50	96	Lincoln, NE	22.85
3	Fort Myers-Cape Coral, FL	233.28	50	Longview-Marshall, TX	43.60	97	Charleston-North Charleston, SC	22.77
4	Sioux City, IA-NE	209.38	51	Oakland, CA	43.05	98	Lewiston-Auburn, ME	22.67
5	Grand Forks, ND-MN	202.91	52	Amarillo, TX	42.34	99	Richland-Kennewick-Pasco, WA	22.42
6	Bismarck, ND	178.10	53	San Antonio, TX	41.63	100	Middlesex-Sommerset-Hunterdon, NJ	21.80
7	Huntsville, AL	137.52	54	Baton Rouge, LA	39.41	101	El Paso, TX	21.20
8	Cumberland, MD-WV	137.01	55	Bangor, ME	38.48	102	Sacramento, CA	20.89
9	Charleston, WV	134.10	56	Roanoke, VA	37.96	103	Mansfield, OH	20.86
10	Alexandria, LA	131.31	57	Enid, OK	37.90	104	Gary-Hammond, IN	20.20
11	Montgomery, AL	122.68	58	Santa Rosa, CA	37.79	105	Fort Walton Beach, FL	20.00
12	Texarkana, TX-AR	91.37	59	Phoenix-Mesa, AZ	37.38	106	Tulsa, OK	18.83
13	Galveston-Texas City, TX	90.88	60	Eau Claire, WI	36.96	107	San Angelo, TX	18.35
14	Clarksville-Hopkinsville, TN-KY	86.99	61	Lexington, KY	36.32	108	Yakima, WA	18.21
15	Santa Cruz-Watsonville, CA	84.73	62	Huntington-Ashland, WV-KY-OH	35.98	109	Modesto, CA	18.18
16	Killeen-Temple, TX	83.65	63	Rapid City, SD	35.41	110	Tuscaloosa, AL	17.74
17	Utica-Rome, NY	82.80	64	Augusta-Aiken, GA-SC	34.47	111	Florence, SC	17.58
18	McAllen-Edinburg-Mission, TX	78.35	65	Brownsville-Harlingen-San Benito, TX	33.65	112	Lake Charles, LA	17.31
19	Panama City, FL	78.12	66	Lawton, OK	33.21	113	Charlotte-Gastonia-Rock Hill, NC-SC	17.07
20	Anchorage, AK	77.19	67	Victoria, TX	32.75	114	Corpus Christi, TX	16.98
21	Birmingham, AL	76.91	68	Abilene, TX	32.66	115	Salt Lake City-Ogden, UT	16.82
22	Gadsden, AL	75.60	69	Duluth-Superior, MN-WI	32.19	116	Dothan, AL	16.81
23	New Bedford, MA	74.51	70	Tacoma, WA	31.91	117	Gainesville, FL	16.70
24	Merced, CA	72.65	71	Wichita Falls, TX	31.73	118	Chattanooga, TN-GA	16.61
25	Binghamton, NY	70.38	72	Norfolk-Va Beach-Newport News, VA-NC	30.62	119	Washington, DC-MD-VA-WV	16.19
26	Elkhart-Goshen, IN	68.74	73	Raleigh-Durham-Chapel Hill, NC	30.27	120	Fort Lauderdale, FL	16.12
27	Fitchburg-Leominster, MA	66.58	74	Albuquerque, NM	29.93	121	Lafayette, LA	15.89
28	Las Vegas, NV-AZ	66.41	75	Asheville, NC	29.87	122	Naples, FL	14.95
29	Nashville, TN	64.37	75	Greenville-Spartanburg-Anderson, SC	29.87	123	New Orleans, LA	14.78
30	Little Rock-North Little Rock, AR	63.88	77	Lawrence, MA-NH	29.48	124	Vineland-Millville-Bridgeton, NJ	14.50
31	Louisville, KY-IN	63.64	78	Glens Falls, NY	28.89	125	Tallahassee, FL	14.44
32	Danbury, CT	62.62	79	Saginaw-Bay City-Midland, MI	28.58	126	Madison, WI	13.91
33	Stockton-Lodi, CA	61.28	80	Medford-Ashland, OR	28.19	127	Eugene-Springfield, OR	13.83
34	Waco, TX	58.97	81	Orlando, FL	28.17	128	San Diego, CA	13.77
35	Tyler, TX	58.15	82	Ventura, CA	27.87	129	Savannah, GA	13.51
36	Jackson, MI	56.59	83	Bloomington, IN	27.74	130	Waterloo-Cedar Falls, IA	13.01
37	Kokomo, IN	55.64	84	Sarasota-Bradenton, FL	27.58	131	Jersey City, NJ	12.13
38	Anniston, AL	54.13	85	Monroe, LA	27.02	132	Benton Harbor, MI	11.95
39	Jackson, MS	52.96	86	Daytona Beach, FL	26.91	133	Flint, MI	11.53
40	Rochester, MN	51.81	87	Evansville-Henderson, IN-KY	26.90	134	Altoona, PA	11.34
41	Odessa-Midland, TX	51.57	88	Shreveport-Bossier City, LA	26.32	135	Greensboro-Winston Salem-High Point, NC	11.03
42	Spokane, WA	51.36	89	Albany, GA	26.07	136	Fort Worth-Arlington, TX	10.76
43	Lubbock, TX	51.12	90	Denver, CO	25.95	137	Colorado Springs, CO	10.60
44	Oklahoma City, OK	51.03	91	Tampa-St. Petersburg-Clearwater, FL	25.40	138	Buffalo-Niagara Falls, NY	10.13
45	Green Bay, WI	50.24	92	Detroit, MI	24.45	139	San Jose, CA	10.02
46	Sioux Falls, SD	49.31	93	Lancaster, PA	24.20	140	Yuba City, CA	9.99
47	Jacksonville, FL	47.60	94	Cincinnati, OH-KY-IN	23.64	141	Fort Pierce-Port St. Lucie, FL	9.97

Source: Morgan Quitno Corporation using data from U.S. Department of Justice, Federal Bureau of Investigation
"Crime in the United States 1993" (Uniform Crime Reports, December 4, 1994)
*Aggravated assault is an attack for the purpose of inflicting severe bodily injury.
**Not available.

24. Percent Change in Aggravated Assault Rate: 1989 to 1993 (continued)

National Percent Change = 14.8% Increase*

RANK	METRO AREA	% CHANGE	RANK	METRO AREA	% CHANGE	RANK	METRO AREA	CHANGE
142	Baltimore, MD	9.84	189	Olympia, WA	(3.43)	236	Ann Arbor, MI	(36.59)
143	Bakersfield, CA	9.79	190	Fayetteville, NC	(3.77)	237	Des Moines, IA	(41.53)
144	Columbus, GA–AL	8.61	191	Bryan–College Station, TX	(3.91)	238	St. Joseph, MO	(49.66)
145	Grand Rapids–Muskegon–Holland, MI	8.06	192	Atlantic City, NJ	(4.95)	239	Wausau, WI	(54.03)
146	Lakeland–Winter Haven, FL	7.50	193	Atlanta, GA	(5.61)	240	Dubuque, IA	(56.12)
147	Sherman–Denison, TX	7.48	194	Fort Collins–Loveland, CO	(5.69)	241	Nashua, NH	(56.60)
148	Athens, GA	6.86	195	Janesville–Beloit, WI	(5.92)	242	Manchester, NH	(56.91)
149	Bellingham, WA	6.76	196	Pittsburgh, PA	(5.97)	243	Sheboygan, WI	(65.17)
150	Fort Wayne, IN	6.51	197	Milwaukee–Waukesha, WI	(6.09)	–	Akron, OH**	NA
151	Seattle–Bellevue–Everett, WA	6.48	198	Stamford–Norwalk, CT	(6.69)	–	Albany, NY**	NA
152	Fort Smith, AR–OK	6.45	199	Portland–Vancouver, OR–WA	(7.09)	–	Barnstable–Yarmouth, MA**	NA
153	Owensboro, KY	6.36	200	Newark, NJ	(7.70)	–	Boston, MA–NH**	NA
154	Memphis, TN–AR–MS	6.32	201	Monmouth–Ocean, NJ	(7.82)	–	Bremerton, WA**	NA
155	Jackson, TN	6.28	202	Redding, CA	(8.61)	–	Brockton, MA**	NA
156	Johnson City–Kingsport–Bristol, TN–VA	5.79	203	Beaumont–Port Arthur, TX	(8.78)	–	Chicago, IL**	NA
157	Brazoria, TX	5.66	204	Syracuse, NY	(10.14)	–	Cleveland, OH**	NA
158	Miami, FL	4.77	205	Kalamazoo–Battle Creek, MI	(10.22)	–	Dutchess County, NY**	NA
159	Santa Barbara–Santa Maria–Lompoc, CA	4.61	206	Fayetteville–Springdale–Rogers, AR	(10.58)	–	Goldsboro, NC**	NA
160	Minneapolis–St. Paul, MN–WI	4.57	207	Bergen–Passaic, NJ	(10.61)	–	Greenville, NC**	NA
161	Boise, ID	3.79	208	New York, NY	(10.72)	–	Harrisburg–Lebanon–Carlisle, PA**	NA
162	Orange County, CA	3.75	209	Toledo, OH	(11.09)	–	Hickory–Morganton, NC**	NA
163	Honolulu, HI	3.72	210	Fargo–Moorhead, ND–MN	(11.81)	–	Houma, LA**	NA
164	Florence, AL	3.56	211	Richmond–Petersburg, VA	(12.21)	–	Houston, TX**	NA
165	Austin–San Marcos, TX	3.35	212	Macon, GA	(12.98)	–	Indianapolis, IN**	NA
166	Providence–Fall River–Warwick, RI–MA	3.34	213	Dayton–Springfield, OH	(14.28)	–	Johnstown, PA**	NA
167	St. Cloud, MN	3.05	214	Fresno, CA	(14.56)	–	Kansas City, MO–KS**	NA
168	Philadelphia, PA–NJ	3.03	215	Hagerstown, MD	(14.63)	–	Myrtle Beach, SC**	NA
169	Danville, VA	2.79	216	Rochester, NY	(16.15)	–	Newburgh, NY–PA**	NA
170	Chico–Paradise, CA	2.64	217	Portland, ME	(16.40)	–	Omaha, NE**	NA
171	Columbia, MO	2.60	218	Bridgeport, CT	(16.84)	–	Pittsfield, MA**	NA
172	Nassau–Suffolk, NY	1.54	219	Canton–Massillon, OH	(16.89)	–	Provo–Orem, UT**	NA
173	Joplin, MO	0.97	220	New London–Norwich, CT–RI	(18.10)	–	Punta Gorda, FL**	NA
174	Salinas, CA	0.90	221	Appleton–Oshkosh–Neenah, WI	(20.56)	–	Reading, PA**	NA
175	Erie, PA	0.66	222	Vallejo–Fairfield–Napa, CA	(20.96)	–	Riverside–San Bernardino, CA**	NA
176	Lansing–East Lansing, MI	0.59	223	Racine, WI	(21.51)	–	Rocky Mount, NC**	NA
177	Lynchburg, VA	0.17	224	Laredo, TX	(21.60)	–	San Luis Obispo–Atascadero, CA**	NA
178	San Francisco, CA	(0.02)	225	Cheyenne, WY	(22.11)	–	Scranton–Wilkes-Barre–Hazleton, PA**	NA
179	Charlottesville, VA	(0.05)	226	New Haven–Meriden, CT	(22.34)	–	South Bend, IN**	NA
180	Columbus, OH	(1.15)	227	Hartford, CT	(22.59)	–	Springfield, MA**	NA
181	Columbia, SC	(1.17)	228	Salem, OR	(22.75)	–	Steubenville–Weirton, OH–WV**	NA
182	Springfield, MO	(1.63)	229	Reno, NV	(23.42)	–	St. Louis, MO–IL**	NA
183	Waterbury, CT	(1.88)	230	La Crosse, WI–MN	(26.89)	–	Sumter, SC**	NA
184	Trenton, NJ	(2.02)	231	Greeley, CO	(28.78)	–	Tucson, AZ**	NA
185	Los Angeles–Long Beach, CA	(2.38)	232	Boulder–Longmont, CO	(30.88)	–	West Palm Beach–Boca Raton, FL**	NA
186	Pine Bluff, AR	(2.39)	233	Decatur, AL	(35.48)	–	Williamsport, PA**	NA
186	Visalia–Tulare–Porterville, CA	(2.39)	234	Jacksonville, NC	(35.63)	–	Worcester, MA–CT**	NA
188	Dallas, TX	(3.02)	235	Mobile, AL	(35.84)	–	Yolo, CA**	NA

Source: Morgan Quitno Corporation using data from U.S. Department of Justice, Federal Bureau of Investigation
    "Crime in the United States 1993" (Uniform Crime Reports, December 4, 1994)
Aggravated assault is an attack for the purpose of inflicting severe bodily injury.
**Not available.*

25. Property Crimes in 1993

National Total = 12,216,764 Property Crimes*

RANK	METRO AREA	CRIMES	RANK	METRO AREA	CRIMES	RANK	METRO AREA	CRIMES
243	Abilene, TX	4,843	266	Cheyenne, WY	3,037	23	Fort Worth–Arlington, TX	93,196
82	Akron, OH	27,431	–	Chicago, IL**	NA	46	Fresno, CA	57,022
171	Albany, GA	9,077	176	Chico–Paradise, CA	8,713	229	Gadsden, AL	5,335
–	Albany, NY**	NA	37	Cincinnati, OH–KY–IN	66,935	117	Gainesville, FL	16,915
62	Albuquerque, NM	39,516	216	Clarksville–Hopkinsville, TN–KY	6,338	131	Galveston–Texas City, TX	14,560
211	Alexandria, LA	6,666	–	Cleveland, OH**	NA	74	Gary–Hammond, IN	29,614
269	Altoona, PA	2,907	98	Colorado Springs, CO	21,630	256	Glens Falls, NY	3,638
138	Amarillo, TX	13,596	225	Columbia, MO	5,462	234	Goldsboro, NC	5,229
136	Anchorage, AK	13,927	81	Columbia, SC	27,690	253	Grand Forks, ND–MN	3,890
102	Ann Arbor, MI	19,770	137	Columbus, GA–AL	13,707	59	Grand Rapids–Muskegon–Holland, MI	42,837
238	Anniston, AL	5,142	33	Columbus, OH	74,701	206	Greeley, CO	6,966
152	Appleton–Oshkosh–Neenah, WI	11,234	80	Corpus Christi, TX	28,395	198	Green Bay, WI	7,128
195	Asheville, NC	7,442	272	Cumberland, MD–WV	2,479	45	Greensboro–Winston Salem–High Point, NC	59,253
175	Athens, GA	8,831	9	Dallas, TX	174,542	191	Greenville, NC	7,841
5	Atlanta, GA	215,165	231	Danbury, CT	5,264	60	Greenville–Spartanburg–Anderson, SC	40,298
89	Atlantic City, NJ	25,186	268	Danville, VA	2,941	270	Hagerstown, MD	2,883
107	Augusta–Aiken, GA–SC	18,914	97	Daytona Beach, FL	21,884	111	Harrisburg–Lebanon–Carlisle, PA	17,888
41	Austin–San Marcos, TX	64,831	55	Dayton–Springfield, OH	45,462	53	Hartford, CT	45,815
69	Bakersfield, CA	33,583	246	Decatur, AL	4,628	147	Hickory–Morganton, NC	11,777
12	Baltimore, MD	145,454	22	Denver, CO	94,197	49	Honolulu, HI	53,904
273	Bangor, ME	2,314	99	Des Moines, IA	21,436	217	Houma, LA	6,321
244	Barnstable–Yarmouth, MA	4,776	3	Detroit, MI	234,223	7	Houston, TX	192,173
54	Baton Rouge, LA	45,763	227	Dothan, AL	5,423	179	Huntington–Ashland, WV–KY–OH	8,526
90	Beaumont–Port Arthur, TX	23,859	267	Dubuque, IA	2,992	121	Huntsville, AL	16,074
203	Bellingham, WA	7,084	170	Duluth–Superior, MN–WI	9,083	–	Indianapolis, IN**	NA
172	Benton Harbor, MI	9,032	202	Dutchess County, NY	7,089	233	Jackson, MI	5,237
57	Bergen–Passaic, NJ	44,223	241	Eau Claire, WI	4,892	78	Jackson, MS	28,784
183	Binghamton, NY	8,218	58	El Paso, TX	43,556	221	Jackson, TN	5,769
56	Birmingham, AL	44,694	205	Elkhart–Goshen, IN	6,988	35	Jacksonville, FL	69,370
265	Bismarck, ND	3,052	259	Enid, OK	3,508	218	Jacksonville, NC	6,310
255	Bloomington, IN	3,662	177	Erie, PA	8,587	201	Janesville–Beloit, WI	7,094
132	Boise, ID	14,280	124	Eugene–Springfield, OR	15,301	73	Jersey City, NJ	29,860
14	Boston, MA–NH	138,022	157	Evansville–Henderson, IN–KY	10,533	146	Johnson City–Kingsport–Bristol, TN–VA	12,113
148	Boulder–Longmont, CO	11,746	215	Fargo–Moorhead, ND–MN	6,345	264	Johnstown, PA	3,290
214	Brazoria, TX	6,378	101	Fayetteville, NC	20,288	235	Joplin, MO	5,222
188	Bremerton, WA	7,866	197	Fayetteville–Springdale–Rogers, AR	7,359	94	Kalamazoo–Battle Creek, MI	22,373
95	Bridgeport, CT	22,128	236	Fitchburg–Leominster, MA	5,193	–	Kansas City, MO–KS**	NA
162	Brockton, MA	10,205	85	Flint, MI	26,108	219	Kenosha, WI	6,200
104	Brownsville–Harlingen–San Benito, TX	19,406	261	Florence, AL	3,365	151	Killeen–Temple, TX	11,346
204	Bryan–College Station, TX	7,037	199	Florence, SC	7,101	260	Kokomo, IN	3,470
48	Buffalo–Niagara Falls, NY	54,425	196	Fort Collins–Loveland, CO	7,364	248	La Crosse, WI–MN	4,381
115	Canton–Massillon, OH	17,008	21	Fort Lauderdale, FL	104,277	213	Lafayette, IN	6,473
164	Charleston, WV	9,991	106	Fort Myers–Cape Coral, FL	19,093	130	Lafayette, LA	14,679
75	Charleston–North Charleston, SC	29,521	133	Fort Pierce–Port St. Lucie, FL	14,051	159	Lake Charles, LA	10,344
224	Charlottesville, VA	5,517	194	Fort Smith, AR–OK	7,617	71	Lakeland–Winter Haven, FL	33,310
32	Charlotte–Gastonia–Rock Hill, NC–SC	74,751	232	Fort Walton Beach, FL	5,258	149	Lancaster, PA	11,466
100	Chattanooga, TN–GA	20,301	103	Fort Wayne, IN	19,612	105	Lansing–East Lansing, MI	19,317

Source: U.S. Department of Justice, Federal Bureau of Investigation
"Crime in the United States 1993" (Uniform Crime Reports, December 4, 1994)
*Property crimes are offenses of burglary, larceny-theft and motor vehicle theft. They consist of taking money or property but there is no force or threat of force against victims.
**Not available.

25. Property Crimes in 1993 (continued)

National Total = 12,216,764 Property Crimes*

RANK	METRO AREA	CRIMES	RANK	METRO AREA	CRIMES	RANK	METRO AREA	CRIMES
169	Laredo, TX	9,361	184	Olympia, WA	8,180	17	Seattle–Bellevue–Everett, WA	130,616
47	Las Vegas, NV–AZ	56,738	–	Omaha, NE**	NA	251	Sheboygan, WI	4,032
145	Lawrence, MA–NH	12,237	19	Orange County, CA	121,756	239	Sherman–Denison, TX	4,985
223	Lawton, OK	5,536	29	Orlando, FL	84,647	84	Shreveport–Bossier City, LA	26,709
252	Lewiston–Auburn, ME	3,950	262	Owensboro, KY	3,361	209	Sioux City, IA–NE	6,877
108	Lexington, KY	18,414	168	Panama City, FL	9,682	237	Sioux Falls, SD	5,167
134	Lincoln, NE	13,995	8	Philadelphia, PA–NJ	183,521	129	South Bend, IN	14,763
61	Little Rock–North Little Rock, AR	39,548	11	Phoenix–Mesa, AZ	167,076	96	Spokane, WA	21,938
154	Longview–Marshall, TX	11,049	242	Pine Bluff, AR	4,844	86	Springfield, MA	25,817
1	Los Angeles–Long Beach, CA	490,882	40	Pittsburgh, PA	65,879	141	Springfield, MO	12,582
64	Louisville, KY–IN	38,654	271	Pittsfield, MA	2,483	142	Stamford–Norwalk, CT	12,455
140	Lubbock, TX	12,725	167	Portland, ME	9,691	274	Steubenville–Weirton, OH–WV	2,233
228	Lynchburg, VA	5,422	26	Portland–Vancouver, OR–WA	90,785	65	Stockton–Lodi, CA	37,871
113	Macon, GA	17,456	63	Providence–Fall River–Warwick, RI–MA	39,372	247	St. Cloud, MN	4,568
123	Madison, WI	15,983	153	Provo–Orem, UT	11,117	230	St. Joseph, MO	5,319
210	Manchester, NH	6,855	220	Pueblo, CO	5,988	–	St. Louis, MO–IL**	NA
186	Mansfield, OH	7,991	263	Punta Gorda, FL	3,332	226	Sumter, SC	5,424
77	McAllen–Edinburg–Mission, TX	29,445	180	Racine, WI	8,520	87	Syracuse, NY	25,459
182	Medford–Ashland, OR	8,290	50	Raleigh–Durham–Chapel Hill, NC	49,765	66	Tacoma, WA	37,254
38	Memphis, TN–AR–MS	66,038	249	Rapid City, SD	4,165	93	Tallahassee, FL	22,919
166	Merced, CA	9,775	158	Reading, PA	10,465	15	Tampa–St. Petersburg–Clearwater, FL	136,690
4	Miami, FL	231,554	200	Redding, CA	7,095	207	Texarkana, TX–AR	6,959
70	Middlesex–Sommerset–Hunterdon, NJ	33,367	119	Reno, NV	16,463	67	Toledo, OH	34,832
34	Milwaukee–Waukesha, WI	70,845	212	Richland–Kennewick–Pasco, WA	6,652	126	Trenton, NJ	14,882
18	Minneapolis–St. Paul, MN–WI	127,931	52	Richmond–Petersburg, VA	45,980	44	Tucson, AZ	60,016
83	Mobile, AL	26,724	10	Riverside–San Bernardino, CA	173,484	68	Tulsa, OK	34,544
88	Modesto, CA	25,397	173	Roanoke, VA	8,898	155	Tuscaloosa, AL	10,927
72	Monmouth–Ocean, NJ	33,243	254	Rochester, MN	3,836	160	Tyler, TX	10,307
178	Monroe, LA	8,584	51	Rochester, NY	48,937	174	Utica–Rome, NY	8,885
128	Montgomery, AL	14,788	189	Rocky Mount, NC	7,856	91	Vallejo–Fairfield–Napa, CA	23,506
144	Myrtle Beach, SC	12,264	28	Sacramento, CA	89,321	92	Ventura, CA	23,466
185	Naples, FL	8,083	116	Saginaw–Bay City–Midland, MI	16,936	240	Victoria, TX	4,937
250	Nashua, NH	4,094	114	Salem, OR	17,382	193	Vineland–Millville–Bridgeton, NJ	7,619
42	Nashville, TN	64,732	120	Salinas, CA	16,429	112	Visalia–Tulare–Porterville, CA	17,524
30	Nassau–Suffolk, NY	81,862	39	Salt Lake City–Ogden, UT	65,970	139	Waco, TX	12,838
187	New Bedford, MA	7,924	245	San Angelo, TX	4,706	6	Washington, DC–MD–VA–WV	206,360
79	New Haven–Meriden, CT	28,717	20	San Antonio, TX	109,947	161	Waterbury, CT	10,222
181	New London–Norwich, CT–RI	8,339	13	San Diego, CA	138,919	222	Waterloo–Cedar Falls, IA	5,692
27	New Orleans, LA	90,777	25	San Francisco, CA	92,147	257	Wausau, WI	3,588
2	New York, NY	488,505	43	San Jose, CA	63,552	–	West Palm Beach–Boca Raton, FL**	NA
24	Newark, NJ	92,482	192	San Luis Obispo–Atascadero, CA	7,632	190	Wichita Falls, TX	7,849
163	Newburgh, NY–PA	10,056	122	Santa Barbara–Santa Maria–Lompoc, CA	16,071	258	Williamsport, PA	3,566
31	Norfolk–Va Beach–Newport News, VA–NC	79,288	143	Santa Cruz–Watsonville, CA	12,344	150	Wilmington, NC	11,380
16	Oakland, CA	134,376	109	Santa Rosa, CA	18,085	118	Worcester, MA–CT	16,752
156	Ocala, FL	10,648	76	Sarasota–Bradenton, FL	29,504	127	Yakima, WA	14,807
125	Odessa–Midland, TX	14,953	110	Savannah, GA	17,927	165	Yolo, CA	9,877
36	Oklahoma City, OK	68,061	135	Scranton–Wilkes-Barre–Hazleton, PA	13,969	208	Yuba City, CA	6,881

Source: U.S. Department of Justice, Federal Bureau of Investigation
   "Crime in the United States 1993" (Uniform Crime Reports, December 4, 1994)
*Property crimes are offenses of burglary, larceny-theft and motor vehicle theft. They consist of taking money or property but there is no force or threat of force against victims.
**Not available.

25. Property Crimes in 1993 (continued)

National Total = 12,216,764 Property Crimes*

RANK	METRO AREA	CRIMES	RANK	METRO AREA	CRIMES	RANK	METRO AREA	CRIMES
1	Los Angeles–Long Beach, CA	490,882	48	Buffalo–Niagara Falls, NY	54,425	95	Bridgeport, CT	22,128
2	New York, NY	488,505	49	Honolulu, HI	53,904	96	Spokane, WA	21,938
3	Detroit, MI	234,223	50	Raleigh–Durham–Chapel Hill, NC	49,765	97	Daytona Beach, FL	21,884
4	Miami, FL	231,554	51	Rochester, NY	48,937	98	Colorado Springs, CO	21,630
5	Atlanta, GA	215,165	52	Richmond–Petersburg, VA	45,980	99	Des Moines, IA	21,436
6	Washington, DC–MD–VA–WV	206,360	53	Hartford, CT	45,815	100	Chattanooga, TN–GA	20,301
7	Houston, TX	192,173	54	Baton Rouge, LA	45,763	101	Fayetteville, NC	20,288
8	Philadelphia, PA–NJ	183,521	55	Dayton–Springfield, OH	45,462	102	Ann Arbor, MI	19,770
9	Dallas, TX	174,542	56	Birmingham, AL	44,694	103	Fort Wayne, IN	19,612
10	Riverside–San Bernardino, CA	173,484	57	Bergen–Passaic, NJ	44,223	104	Brownsville–Harlingen–San Benito, TX	19,406
11	Phoenix–Mesa, AZ	167,076	58	El Paso, TX	43,556	105	Lansing–East Lansing, MI	19,317
12	Baltimore, MD	145,454	59	Grand Rapids–Muskegon–Holland, MI	42,837	106	Fort Myers–Cape Coral, FL	19,093
13	San Diego, CA	138,919	60	Greenville–Spartanburg–Anderson, SC	40,298	107	Augusta–Aiken, GA–SC	18,914
14	Boston, MA–NH	138,022	61	Little Rock–North Little Rock, AR	39,548	108	Lexington, KY	18,414
15	Tampa–St. Petersburg–Clearwater, FL	136,690	62	Albuquerque, NM	39,516	109	Santa Rosa, CA	18,085
16	Oakland, CA	134,376	63	Providence–Fall River–Warwick, RI–MA	39,372	110	Savannah, GA	17,927
17	Seattle–Bellevue–Everett, WA	130,616	64	Louisville, KY–IN	38,654	111	Harrisburg–Lebanon–Carlisle, PA	17,888
18	Minneapolis–St. Paul, MN–WI	127,931	65	Stockton–Lodi, CA	37,871	112	Visalia–Tulare–Porterville, CA	17,524
19	Orange County, CA	121,756	66	Tacoma, WA	37,254	113	Macon, GA	17,456
20	San Antonio, TX	109,947	67	Toledo, OH	34,832	114	Salem, OR	17,382
21	Fort Lauderdale, FL	104,277	68	Tulsa, OK	34,544	115	Canton–Massillon, OH	17,008
22	Denver, CO	94,197	69	Bakersfield, CA	33,583	116	Saginaw–Bay City–Midland, MI	16,936
23	Fort Worth–Arlington, TX	93,196	70	Middlesex–Sommerset–Hunterdon, NJ	33,367	117	Gainesville, FL	16,915
24	Newark, NJ	92,482	71	Lakeland–Winter Haven, FL	33,310	118	Worcester, MA–CT	16,752
25	San Francisco, CA	92,147	72	Monmouth–Ocean, NJ	33,243	119	Reno, NV	16,463
26	Portland–Vancouver, OR–WA	90,785	73	Jersey City, NJ	29,860	120	Salinas, CA	16,429
27	New Orleans, LA	90,777	74	Gary–Hammond, IN	29,614	121	Huntsville, AL	16,074
28	Sacramento, CA	89,321	75	Charleston–North Charleston, SC	29,521	122	Santa Barbara–Santa Maria–Lompoc, CA	16,071
29	Orlando, FL	84,647	76	Sarasota–Bradenton, FL	29,504	123	Madison, WI	15,983
30	Nassau–Suffolk, NY	81,862	77	McAllen–Edinburg–Mission, TX	29,445	124	Eugene–Springfield, OR	15,301
31	Norfolk–Va Beach–Newport News, VA–NC	79,288	78	Jackson, MS	28,784	125	Odessa–Midland, TX	14,953
32	Charlotte–Gastonia–Rock Hill, NC–SC	74,751	79	New Haven–Meriden, CT	28,717	126	Trenton, NJ	14,882
33	Columbus, OH	74,701	80	Corpus Christi, TX	28,395	127	Yakima, WA	14,807
34	Milwaukee–Waukesha, WI	70,845	81	Columbia, SC	27,690	128	Montgomery, AL	14,788
35	Jacksonville, FL	69,370	82	Akron, OH	27,431	129	South Bend, IN	14,763
36	Oklahoma City, OK	68,061	83	Mobile, AL	26,724	130	Lafayette, LA	14,679
37	Cincinnati, OH–KY–IN	66,935	84	Shreveport–Bossier City, LA	26,709	131	Galveston–Texas City, TX	14,560
38	Memphis, TN–AR–MS	66,038	85	Flint, MI	26,108	132	Boise, ID	14,280
39	Salt Lake City–Ogden, UT	65,970	86	Springfield, MA	25,817	133	Fort Pierce–Port St. Lucie, FL	14,051
40	Pittsburgh, PA	65,879	87	Syracuse, NY	25,459	134	Lincoln, NE	13,995
41	Austin–San Marcos, TX	64,831	88	Modesto, CA	25,397	135	Scranton–Wilkes-Barre–Hazleton, PA	13,969
42	Nashville, TN	64,732	89	Atlantic City, NJ	25,186	136	Anchorage, AK	13,927
43	San Jose, CA	63,552	90	Beaumont–Port Arthur, TX	23,859	137	Columbus, GA–AL	13,707
44	Tucson, AZ	60,016	91	Vallejo–Fairfield–Napa, CA	23,506	138	Amarillo, TX	13,596
45	Greensboro–Winston Salem–High Point, NC	59,253	92	Ventura, CA	23,466	139	Waco, TX	12,838
46	Fresno, CA	57,022	93	Tallahassee, FL	22,919	140	Lubbock, TX	12,725
47	Las Vegas, NV–AZ	56,738	94	Kalamazoo–Battle Creek, MI	22,373	141	Springfield, MO	12,582

Source: U.S. Department of Justice, Federal Bureau of Investigation
"Crime in the United States 1993" (Uniform Crime Reports, December 4, 1994)
Property crimes are offenses of burglary, larceny-theft and motor vehicle theft. They consist of taking money or property but there is no force or threat of force against victims.
**Not available.*

25. Property Crimes in 1993 (continued)

National Total = 12,216,764 Property Crimes*

RANK	METRO AREA	CRIMES	RANK	METRO AREA	CRIMES	RANK	METRO AREA	CRIMES
142	Stamford–Norwalk, CT	12,455	189	Rocky Mount, NC	7,856	236	Fitchburg–Leominster, MA	5,193
143	Santa Cruz–Watsonville, CA	12,344	190	Wichita Falls, TX	7,849	237	Sioux Falls, SD	5,167
144	Myrtle Beach, SC	12,264	191	Greenville, NC	7,841	238	Anniston, AL	5,142
145	Lawrence, MA–NH	12,237	192	San Luis Obispo–Atascadero, CA	7,632	239	Sherman–Denison, TX	4,985
146	Johnson City–Kingsport–Bristol, TN–VA	12,113	193	Vineland–Millville–Bridgeton, NJ	7,619	240	Victoria, TX	4,937
147	Hickory–Morganton, NC	11,777	194	Fort Smith, AR–OK	7,617	241	Eau Claire, WI	4,892
148	Boulder–Longmont, CO	11,746	195	Asheville, NC	7,442	242	Pine Bluff, AR	4,844
149	Lancaster, PA	11,466	196	Fort Collins–Loveland, CO	7,364	243	Abilene, TX	4,843
150	Wilmington, NC	11,380	197	Fayetteville–Springdale–Rogers, AR	7,359	244	Barnstable–Yarmouth, MA	4,776
151	Killeen–Temple, TX	11,346	198	Green Bay, WI	7,128	245	San Angelo, TX	4,706
152	Appleton–Oshkosh–Neenah, WI	11,234	199	Florence, SC	7,101	246	Decatur, AL	4,628
153	Provo–Orem, UT	11,117	200	Redding, CA	7,095	247	St. Cloud, MN	4,568
154	Longview–Marshall, TX	11,049	201	Janesville–Beloit, WI	7,094	248	La Crosse, WI–MN	4,381
155	Tuscaloosa, AL	10,927	202	Dutchess County, NY	7,089	249	Rapid City, SD	4,165
156	Ocala, FL	10,648	203	Bellingham, WA	7,084	250	Nashua, NH	4,094
157	Evansville–Henderson, IN–KY	10,533	204	Bryan–College Station, TX	7,037	251	Sheboygan, WI	4,032
158	Reading, PA	10,465	205	Elkhart–Goshen, IN	6,988	252	Lewiston–Auburn, ME	3,950
159	Lake Charles, LA	10,344	206	Greeley, CO	6,966	253	Grand Forks, ND–MN	3,890
160	Tyler, TX	10,307	207	Texarkana, TX–AR	6,959	254	Rochester, MN	3,836
161	Waterbury, CT	10,222	208	Yuba City, CA	6,881	255	Bloomington, IN	3,662
162	Brockton, MA	10,205	209	Sioux City, IA–NE	6,877	256	Glens Falls, NY	3,638
163	Newburgh, NY–PA	10,056	210	Manchester, NH	6,855	257	Wausau, WI	3,588
164	Charleston, WV	9,991	211	Alexandria, LA	6,666	258	Williamsport, PA	3,566
165	Yolo, CA	9,877	212	Richland–Kennewick–Pasco, WA	6,652	259	Enid, OK	3,508
166	Merced, CA	9,775	213	Lafayette, IN	6,473	260	Kokomo, IN	3,470
167	Portland, ME	9,691	214	Brazoria, TX	6,378	261	Florence, AL	3,365
168	Panama City, FL	9,682	215	Fargo–Moorhead, ND–MN	6,345	262	Owensboro, KY	3,361
169	Laredo, TX	9,361	216	Clarksville–Hopkinsville, TN–KY	6,338	263	Punta Gorda, FL	3,332
170	Duluth–Superior, MN–WI	9,083	217	Houma, LA	6,321	264	Johnstown, PA	3,290
171	Albany, GA	9,077	218	Jacksonville, NC	6,310	265	Bismarck, ND	3,052
172	Benton Harbor, MI	9,032	219	Kenosha, WI	6,200	266	Cheyenne, WY	3,037
173	Roanoke, VA	8,898	220	Pueblo, CO	5,988	267	Dubuque, IA	2,992
174	Utica–Rome, NY	8,885	221	Jackson, TN	5,769	268	Danville, VA	2,941
175	Athens, GA	8,831	222	Waterloo–Cedar Falls, IA	5,692	269	Altoona, PA	2,907
176	Chico–Paradise, CA	8,713	223	Lawton, OK	5,536	270	Hagerstown, MD	2,883
177	Erie, PA	8,587	224	Charlottesville, VA	5,517	271	Pittsfield, MA	2,483
178	Monroe, LA	8,584	225	Columbia, MO	5,462	272	Cumberland, MD–WV	2,479
179	Huntington–Ashland, WV–KY–OH	8,526	226	Sumter, SC	5,424	273	Bangor, ME	2,314
180	Racine, WI	8,520	227	Dothan, AL	5,423	274	Steubenville–Weirton, OH–WV	2,233
181	New London–Norwich, CT–RI	8,339	228	Lynchburg, VA	5,422	–	Albany, NY**	NA
182	Medford–Ashland, OR	8,290	229	Gadsden, AL	5,335	–	Chicago, IL**	NA
183	Binghamton, NY	8,218	230	St. Joseph, MO	5,319	–	Cleveland, OH**	NA
184	Olympia, WA	8,180	231	Danbury, CT	5,264	–	Indianapolis, IN**	NA
185	Naples, FL	8,083	232	Fort Walton Beach, FL	5,258	–	Kansas City, MO–KS**	NA
186	Mansfield, OH	7,991	233	Jackson, MI	5,237	–	Omaha, NE**	NA
187	New Bedford, MA	7,924	234	Goldsboro, NC	5,229	–	St. Louis, MO–IL**	NA
188	Bremerton, WA	7,866	235	Joplin, MO	5,222	–	West Palm Beach–Boca Raton, FL**	NA

Source: U.S. Department of Justice, Federal Bureau of Investigation
    "Crime in the United States 1993" (Uniform Crime Reports, December 4, 1994)
Property crimes are offenses of burglary, larceny-theft and motor vehicle theft. They consist of taking money or property but there is no force or threat of force against victims.
**Not available.

26. Property Crime Rate in 1993

National Rate = 4,736.9 Property Crimes per 100,000 Population*

RANK	METRO AREA	RATE	RANK	METRO AREA	RATE	RANK	METRO AREA	RATE
199	Abilene, TX	3,939.7	198	Cheyenne, WY	3,950.3	59	Fort Worth-Arlington, TX	6,056.3
191	Akron, OH	4,106.5	–	Chicago, IL**	NA	25	Fresno, CA	7,015.0
10	Albany, GA	7,713.3	155	Chico-Paradise, CA	4,578.5	105	Gadsden, AL	5,305.5
–	Albany, NY**	NA	176	Cincinnati, OH-KY-IN	4,260.1	3	Gainesville, FL	8,802.7
47	Albuquerque, NM	6,274.2	222	Clarksville-Hopkinsville, TN-KY	3,513.2	49	Galveston-Texas City, TX	6,260.6
123	Alexandria, LA	5,087.0	–	Cleveland, OH**	NA	144	Gary-Hammond, IN	4,755.2
271	Altoona, PA	2,204.0	128	Colorado Springs, CO	4,990.1	250	Glens Falls, NY	2,993.7
28	Amarillo, TX	6,957.9	152	Columbia, MO	4,634.2	142	Goldsboro, NC	4,778.5
87	Anchorage, AK	5,554.8	72	Columbia, SC	5,797.4	211	Grand Forks, ND-MN	3,752.9
202	Ann Arbor, MI	3,923.4	130	Columbus, GA-AL	4,924.8	167	Grand Rapids-Muskegon-Holland, MI	4,421.5
171	Anniston, AL	4,365.7	103	Columbus, OH	5,330.5	129	Greeley, CO	4,981.9
233	Appleton-Oshkosh-Neenah, WI	3,404.5	11	Corpus Christi, TX	7,685.0	223	Green Bay, WI	3,508.4
214	Asheville, NC	3,709.8	269	Cumberland, MD-WV	2,420.7	95	Greensboro-Winston Salem-High Point, NC	5,405.6
74	Athens, GA	5,717.2	42	Dallas, TX	6,344.5	26	Greenville, NC	6,991.6
34	Atlanta, GA	6,670.6	242	Danbury, CT	3,237.6	150	Greenville-Spartanburg-Anderson, SC	4,665.9
12	Atlantic City, NJ	7,661.8	263	Danville, VA	2,650.1	270	Hagerstown, MD	2,275.4
181	Augusta-Aiken, GA-SC	4,189.1	119	Daytona Beach, FL	5,114.6	252	Harrisburg-Lebanon-Carlisle, PA	2,957.1
22	Austin-San Marcos, TX	7,056.3	147	Dayton-Springfield, OH	4,695.4	172	Hartford, CT	4,347.6
77	Bakersfield, CA	5,656.7	236	Decatur, AL	3,383.2	204	Hickory-Morganton, NC	3,874.3
64	Baltimore, MD	5,919.3	99	Denver, CO	5,359.0	55	Honolulu, HI	6,157.3
231	Bangor, ME	3,421.9	109	Des Moines, IA	5,251.7	238	Houma, LA	3,376.4
225	Barnstable-Yarmouth, MA	3,483.1	94	Detroit, MI	5,408.6	102	Houston, TX	5,337.0
5	Baton Rouge, LA	8,345.4	195	Dothan, AL	4,021.2	260	Huntington-Ashland, WV-KY-OH	2,688.2
43	Beaumont-Port Arthur, TX	6,327.1	232	Dubuque, IA	3,415.1	114	Huntsville, AL	5,157.0
127	Bellingham, WA	5,027.2	213	Duluth-Superior, MN-WI	3,729.8	–	Indianapolis, IN**	NA
86	Benton Harbor, MI	5,568.2	262	Dutchess County, NY	2,683.9	228	Jackson, MI	3,435.5
234	Bergen-Passaic, NJ	3,399.5	227	Eau Claire, WI	3,465.9	23	Jackson, MS	7,033.8
247	Binghamton, NY	3,066.6	32	El Paso, TX	6,796.7	21	Jackson, TN	7,086.4
117	Birmingham, AL	5,141.3	173	Elkhart-Goshen, IN	4,344.1	18	Jacksonville, FL	7,178.1
221	Bismarck, ND	3,541.3	54	Enid, OK	6,174.1	175	Jacksonville, NC	4,297.4
241	Bloomington, IN	3,264.3	248	Erie, PA	3,057.6	130	Janesville-Beloit, WI	4,924.8
174	Boise, ID	4,331.8	115	Eugene-Springfield, OR	5,155.0	101	Jersey City, NJ	5,340.4
192	Boston, MA-NH	4,067.6	216	Evansville-Henderson, IN-KY	3,688.4	261	Johnson City-Kingsport-Bristol, TN-VA	2,686.3
139	Boulder-Longmont, CO	4,792.0	196	Fargo-Moorhead, ND-MN	4,006.5	274	Johnstown, PA	1,360.4
246	Brazoria, TX	3,068.4	16	Fayetteville, NC	7,201.0	210	Joplin, MO	3,766.6
218	Bremerton, WA	3,652.6	243	Fayetteville-Springdale-Rogers, AR	3,219.8	120	Kalamazoo-Battle Creek, MI	5,103.6
133	Bridgeport, CT	4,886.2	208	Fitchburg-Leominster, MA	3,790.8	–	Kansas City, MO-KS**	NA
185	Brockton, MA	4,144.4	62	Flint, MI	5,995.8	154	Kenosha, WI	4,586.4
31	Brownsville-Harlingen-San Benito, TX	6,829.1	268	Florence, AL	2,477.7	170	Killeen-Temple, TX	4,366.0
91	Bryan-College Station, TX	5,514.0	63	Florence, SC	5,922.0	224	Kokomo, IN	3,486.2
159	Buffalo-Niagara Falls, NY	4,529.1	219	Fort Collins-Loveland, CO	3,611.6	217	La Crosse, WI-MN	3,678.5
179	Canton-Massillon, OH	4,232.4	7	Fort Lauderdale, FL	7,898.7	203	Lafayette, IN	3,888.9
201	Charleston, WV	3,928.8	100	Fort Myers-Cape Coral, FL	5,345.7	186	Lafayette, LA	4,139.5
89	Charleston-North Charleston, SC	5,523.7	112	Fort Pierce-Port St. Lucie, FL	5,218.5	61	Lake Charles, LA	6,008.9
194	Charlottesville, VA	4,042.2	183	Fort Smith, AR-OK	4,170.2	8	Lakeland-Winter Haven, FL	7,836.5
58	Charlotte-Gastonia-Rock Hill, NC-SC	6,072.6	237	Fort Walton Beach, FL	3,378.0	264	Lancaster, PA	2,627.9
153	Chattanooga, TN-GA	4,633.1	180	Fort Wayne, IN	4,192.8	169	Lansing-East Lansing, MI	4,405.5

Source: U.S. Department of Justice, Federal Bureau of Investigation
   "Crime in the United States 1993" (Uniform Crime Reports, December 4, 1994)
*Property crimes are offenses of burglary, larceny-theft and motor vehicle theft. They consist of taking money or property but there is no force or threat of force against victims.
**Not available.

26. Property Crime Rate in 1993 (continued)

National Rate = 4,736.9 Property Crimes per 100,000 Population*

RANK	METRO AREA	RATE	RANK	METRO AREA	RATE	RANK	METRO AREA	RATE
53	Laredo, TX	6,183.5	158	Olympia, WA	4,534.1	45	Seattle–Bellevue–Everett, WA	6,291.9
81	Las Vegas, NV–AZ	5,629.1	–	Omaha, NE**	NA	206	Sheboygan, WI	3,804.3
187	Lawrence, MA–NH	4,135.1	136	Orange County, CA	4,850.5	116	Sherman–Denison, TX	5,142.3
156	Lawton, OK	4,558.5	38	Orlando, FL	6,395.0	20	Shreveport–Bossier City, LA	7,110.5
207	Lewiston–Auburn, ME	3,794.7	212	Owensboro, KY	3,749.4	68	Sioux City, IA–NE	5,849.3
124	Lexington, KY	5,055.8	19	Panama City, FL	7,121.5	226	Sioux Falls, SD	3,482.8
41	Lincoln, NE	6,349.7	215	Philadelphia, PA–NJ	3,693.1	70	South Bend, IN	5,836.1
14	Little Rock–North Little Rock, AR	7,431.6	27	Phoenix–Mesa, AZ	6,981.1	80	Spokane, WA	5,632.6
93	Longview–Marshall, TX	5,420.0	83	Pine Bluff, AR	5,611.4	140	Springfield, MA	4,783.6
98	Los Angeles–Long Beach, CA	5,367.1	258	Pittsburgh, PA	2,717.8	160	Springfield, MO	4,527.5
197	Louisville, KY–IN	3,957.7	267	Pittsfield, MA	2,520.3	209	Stamford–Norwalk, CT	3,778.4
85	Lubbock, TX	5,575.0	184	Portland, ME	4,145.4	273	Steubenville–Weirton, OH–WV	1,568.1
259	Lynchburg, VA	2,692.2	88	Portland–Vancouver, OR–WA	5,532.8	13	Stockton–Lodi, CA	7,436.7
73	Macon, GA	5,723.9	189	Providence–Fall River–Warwick, RI–MA	4,115.0	251	St. Cloud, MN	2,959.2
177	Madison, WI	4,243.1	200	Provo–Orem, UT	3,935.2	97	St. Joseph, MO	5,383.8
190	Manchester, NH	4,107.8	146	Pueblo, CO	4,701.5	–	St. Louis, MO–IL**	NA
161	Mansfield, OH	4,525.6	257	Punta Gorda, FL	2,754.0	122	Sumter, SC	5,091.8
30	McAllen–Edinburg–Mission, TX	6,859.9	145	Racine, WI	4,704.0	239	Syracuse, NY	3,363.7
108	Medford–Ashland, OR	5,273.7	96	Raleigh–Durham–Chapel Hill, NC	5,391.0	67	Tacoma, WA	5,877.4
44	Memphis, TN–AR–MS	6,299.3	135	Rapid City, SD	4,851.3	2	Tallahassee, FL	9,210.3
118	Merced, CA	5,116.8	249	Reading, PA	3,036.5	39	Tampa–St. Petersburg–Clearwater, FL	6,393.7
1	Miami, FL	11,364.2	166	Redding, CA	4,456.4	78	Texarkana, TX–AR	5,656.5
244	Middlesex–Sommerset–Hunterdon, NJ	3,163.8	66	Reno, NV	5,896.7	82	Toledo, OH	5,625.3
134	Milwaukee–Waukesha, WI	4,873.6	193	Richland–Kennewick–Pasco, WA	4,046.1	163	Trenton, NJ	4,507.5
138	Minneapolis–St. Paul, MN–WI	4,830.6	125	Richmond–Petersburg, VA	5,054.7	4	Tucson, AZ	8,465.7
104	Mobile, AL	5,329.5	57	Riverside–San Bernardino, CA	6,113.8	149	Tulsa, OK	4,683.0
40	Modesto, CA	6,361.1	205	Roanoke, VA	3,873.5	24	Tuscaloosa, AL	7,029.2
240	Monmouth–Ocean, NJ	3,290.6	229	Rochester, MN	3,434.4	37	Tyler, TX	6,547.2
65	Monroe, LA	5,901.6	164	Rochester, NY	4,504.2	255	Utica–Rome, NY	2,797.7
141	Montgomery, AL	4,778.8	79	Rocky Mount, NC	5,635.7	132	Vallejo–Fairfield–Napa, CA	4,897.5
6	Myrtle Beach, SC	7,963.3	51	Sacramento, CA	6,232.9	235	Ventura, CA	3,383.3
137	Naples, FL	4,836.5	182	Saginaw–Bay City–Midland, MI	4,187.7	46	Victoria, TX	6,284.6
266	Nashua, NH	2,552.6	69	Salem, OR	5,849.0	92	Vineland–Millville–Bridgeton, NJ	5,460.2
50	Nashville, TN	6,233.1	168	Salinas, CA	4,415.5	110	Visalia–Tulare–Porterville, CA	5,239.5
245	Nassau–Suffolk, NY	3,114.9	75	Salt Lake City–Ogden, UT	5,694.6	35	Waco, TX	6,572.6
157	New Bedford, MA	4,538.1	151	San Angelo, TX	4,656.6	148	Washington, DC–MD–VA–WV	4,691.0
121	New Haven–Meriden, CT	5,102.2	9	San Antonio, TX	7,821.3	90	Waterbury, CT	5,514.6
256	New London–Norwich, CT–RI	2,767.6	107	San Diego, CA	5,286.8	162	Waterloo–Cedar Falls, IA	4,521.6
17	New Orleans, LA	7,199.1	84	San Francisco, CA	5,609.4	265	Wausau, WI	2,593.1
76	New York, NY	5,667.3	188	San Jose, CA	4,115.6	–	West Palm Beach–Boca Raton, FL**	NA
143	Newark, NJ	4,772.6	230	San Luis Obispo–Atascadero, CA	3,425.3	60	Wichita Falls, TX	6,009.8
254	Newburgh, NY–PA	2,873.4	178	Santa Barbara–Santa Maria–Lompoc, CA	4,236.4	253	Williamsport, PA	2,947.2
113	Norfolk–Va Beach–Newport News, VA–NC	5,218.4	106	Santa Cruz–Watsonville, CA	5,289.9	56	Wilmington, NC	6,146.6
52	Oakland, CA	6,192.1	165	Santa Rosa, CA	4,464.4	220	Worcester, MA–CT	3,558.4
126	Ocala, FL	5,046.3	71	Sarasota–Bradenton, FL	5,830.5	15	Yakima, WA	7,318.2
48	Odessa–Midland, TX	6,272.9	36	Savannah, GA	6,565.8	33	Yolo, CA	6,751.7
29	Oklahoma City, OK	6,864.4	272	Scranton–Wilkes-Barre–Hazleton, PA	2,177.7	111	Yuba City, CA	5,226.2

Source: U.S. Department of Justice, Federal Bureau of Investigation
    "Crime in the United States 1993" (Uniform Crime Reports, December 4, 1994)
*Property crimes are offenses of burglary, larceny-theft and motor vehicle theft. They consist of taking money or property but there is no force or threat of force against victims.
**Not available.

26. Property Crime Rate in 1993 (continued)

National Rate = 4,736.9 Property Crimes per 100,000 Population*

RANK	METRO AREA	RATE	RANK	METRO AREA	RATE	RANK	METRO AREA	RATE
1	Miami, FL	11,364.2	48	Odessa–Midland, TX	6,272.9	95	Greensboro–Winston Salem–High Point, NC	5,405.6
2	Tallahassee, FL	9,210.3	49	Galveston–Texas City, TX	6,260.6	96	Raleigh–Durham–Chapel Hill, NC	5,391.0
3	Gainesville, FL	8,802.7	50	Nashville, TN	6,233.1	97	St. Joseph, MO	5,383.8
4	Tucson, AZ	8,465.7	51	Sacramento, CA	6,232.9	98	Los Angeles–Long Beach, CA	5,367.1
5	Baton Rouge, LA	8,345.4	52	Oakland, CA	6,192.1	99	Denver, CO	5,359.0
6	Myrtle Beach, SC	7,963.3	53	Laredo, TX	6,183.5	100	Fort Myers–Cape Coral, FL	5,345.7
7	Fort Lauderdale, FL	7,898.7	54	Enid, OK	6,174.1	101	Jersey City, NJ	5,340.4
8	Lakeland–Winter Haven, FL	7,836.5	55	Honolulu, HI	6,157.3	102	Houston, TX	5,337.0
9	San Antonio, TX	7,821.3	56	Wilmington, NC	6,146.6	103	Columbus, OH	5,330.5
10	Albany, GA	7,713.3	57	Riverside–San Bernardino, CA	6,113.8	104	Mobile, AL	5,329.5
11	Corpus Christi, TX	7,685.0	58	Charlotte–Gastonia–Rock Hill, NC–SC	6,072.6	105	Gadsden, AL	5,305.5
12	Atlantic City, NJ	7,661.8	59	Fort Worth–Arlington, TX	6,056.3	106	Santa Cruz–Watsonville, CA	5,289.9
13	Stockton–Lodi, CA	7,436.7	60	Wichita Falls, TX	6,009.8	107	San Diego, CA	5,286.8
14	Little Rock–North Little Rock, AR	7,431.6	61	Lake Charles, LA	6,008.9	108	Medford–Ashland, OR	5,273.7
15	Yakima, WA	7,318.2	62	Flint, MI	5,995.8	109	Des Moines, IA	5,251.7
16	Fayetteville, NC	7,201.0	63	Florence, SC	5,922.0	110	Visalia–Tulare–Porterville, CA	5,239.5
17	New Orleans, LA	7,199.1	64	Baltimore, MD	5,919.3	111	Yuba City, CA	5,226.2
18	Jacksonville, FL	7,178.1	65	Monroe, LA	5,901.6	112	Fort Pierce–Port St. Lucie, FL	5,218.5
19	Panama City, FL	7,121.5	66	Reno, NV	5,896.7	113	Norfolk–Va Beach–Newport News, VA–NC	5,218.4
20	Shreveport–Bossier City, LA	7,110.5	67	Tacoma, WA	5,877.4	114	Huntsville, AL	5,157.0
21	Jackson, TN	7,086.4	68	Sioux City, IA–NE	5,849.3	115	Eugene–Springfield, OR	5,155.0
22	Austin–San Marcos, TX	7,056.3	69	Salem, OR	5,849.0	116	Sherman–Denison, TX	5,142.3
23	Jackson, MS	7,033.8	70	South Bend, IN	5,836.1	117	Birmingham, AL	5,141.3
24	Tuscaloosa, AL	7,029.2	71	Sarasota–Bradenton, FL	5,830.5	118	Merced, CA	5,116.8
25	Fresno, CA	7,015.0	72	Columbia, SC	5,797.4	119	Daytona Beach, FL	5,114.6
26	Greenville, NC	6,991.6	73	Macon, GA	5,723.9	120	Kalamazoo–Battle Creek, MI	5,103.6
27	Phoenix–Mesa, AZ	6,981.1	74	Athens, GA	5,717.2	121	New Haven–Meriden, CT	5,102.2
28	Amarillo, TX	6,957.9	75	Salt Lake City–Ogden, UT	5,694.6	122	Sumter, SC	5,091.8
29	Oklahoma City, OK	6,864.4	76	New York, NY	5,667.3	123	Alexandria, LA	5,087.0
30	McAllen–Edinburg–Mission, TX	6,859.9	77	Bakersfield, CA	5,656.7	124	Lexington, KY	5,055.8
31	Brownsville–Harlingen–San Benito, TX	6,829.1	78	Texarkana, TX–AR	5,656.5	125	Richmond–Petersburg, VA	5,054.7
32	El Paso, TX	6,796.7	79	Rocky Mount, NC	5,635.7	126	Ocala, FL	5,046.3
33	Yolo, CA	6,751.7	80	Spokane, WA	5,632.6	127	Bellingham, WA	5,027.2
34	Atlanta, GA	6,670.6	81	Las Vegas, NV–AZ	5,629.1	128	Colorado Springs, CO	4,990.1
35	Waco, TX	6,572.6	82	Toledo, OH	5,625.3	129	Greeley, CO	4,981.9
36	Savannah, GA	6,565.8	83	Pine Bluff, AR	5,611.4	130	Columbus, GA–AL	4,924.8
37	Tyler, TX	6,547.2	84	San Francisco, CA	5,609.4	130	Janesville–Beloit, WI	4,924.8
38	Orlando, FL	6,395.0	85	Lubbock, TX	5,575.0	132	Vallejo–Fairfield–Napa, CA	4,897.5
39	Tampa–St. Petersburg–Clearwater, FL	6,393.7	86	Benton Harbor, MI	5,568.2	133	Bridgeport, CT	4,886.2
40	Modesto, CA	6,361.1	87	Anchorage, AK	5,554.8	134	Milwaukee–Waukesha, WI	4,873.6
41	Lincoln, NE	6,349.7	88	Portland–Vancouver, OR–WA	5,532.8	135	Rapid City, SD	4,851.3
42	Dallas, TX	6,344.5	89	Charleston–North Charleston, SC	5,523.7	136	Orange County, CA	4,850.5
43	Beaumont–Port Arthur, TX	6,327.1	90	Waterbury, CT	5,514.6	137	Naples, FL	4,836.5
44	Memphis, TN–AR–MS	6,299.3	91	Bryan–College Station, TX	5,514.0	138	Minneapolis–St. Paul, MN–WI	4,830.6
45	Seattle–Bellevue–Everett, WA	6,291.9	92	Vineland–Millville–Bridgeton, NJ	5,460.2	139	Boulder–Longmont, CO	4,792.0
46	Victoria, TX	6,284.6	93	Longview–Marshall, TX	5,420.0	140	Springfield, MA	4,783.6
47	Albuquerque, NM	6,274.2	94	Detroit, MI	5,408.6	141	Montgomery, AL	4,778.8

Source: U.S. Department of Justice, Federal Bureau of Investigation
   "Crime in the United States 1993" (Uniform Crime Reports, December 4, 1994)
*Property crimes are offenses of burglary, larceny-theft and motor vehicle theft. They consist of taking money or property but there is no force or threat of force against victims.
**Not available.

26. Property Crime Rate in 1993 (continued)

National Rate = 4,736.9 Property Crimes per 100,000 Population*

RANK	METRO AREA	RATE	RANK	METRO AREA	RATE	RANK	METRO AREA	RATE
142	Goldsboro, NC	4,778.5	189	Providence–Fall River–Warwick, RI–MA	4,115.0	236	Decatur, AL	3,383.2
143	Newark, NJ	4,772.6	190	Manchester, NH	4,107.8	237	Fort Walton Beach, FL	3,378.0
144	Gary–Hammond, IN	4,755.2	191	Akron, OH	4,106.5	238	Houma, LA	3,376.4
145	Racine, WI	4,704.0	192	Boston, MA–NH	4,067.6	239	Syracuse, NY	3,363.7
146	Pueblo, CO	4,701.5	193	Richland–Kennewick–Pasco, WA	4,046.1	240	Monmouth–Ocean, NJ	3,290.6
147	Dayton–Springfield, OH	4,695.4	194	Charlottesville, VA	4,042.2	241	Bloomington, IN	3,264.3
148	Washington, DC–MD–VA–WV	4,691.0	195	Dothan, AL	4,021.2	242	Danbury, CT	3,237.6
149	Tulsa, OK	4,683.0	196	Fargo–Moorhead, ND–MN	4,006.5	243	Fayetteville–Springdale–Rogers, AR	3,219.8
150	Greenville–Spartanburg–Anderson, SC	4,665.9	197	Louisville, KY–IN	3,957.7	244	Middlesex–Sommerset–Hunterdon, NJ	3,163.8
151	San Angelo, TX	4,656.6	198	Cheyenne, WY	3,950.3	245	Nassau–Suffolk, NY	3,114.9
152	Columbia, MO	4,634.2	199	Abilene, TX	3,939.7	246	Brazoria, TX	3,068.4
153	Chattanooga, TN–GA	4,633.1	200	Provo–Orem, UT	3,935.2	247	Binghamton, NY	3,066.6
154	Kenosha, WI	4,586.4	201	Charleston, WV	3,928.8	248	Erie, PA	3,057.6
155	Chico–Paradise, CA	4,578.5	202	Ann Arbor, MI	3,923.4	249	Reading, PA	3,036.5
156	Lawton, OK	4,558.5	203	Lafayette, IN	3,888.9	250	Glens Falls, NY	2,993.7
157	New Bedford, MA	4,538.1	204	Hickory–Morganton, NC	3,874.3	251	St. Cloud, MN	2,959.2
158	Olympia, WA	4,534.1	205	Roanoke, VA	3,873.5	252	Harrisburg–Lebanon–Carlisle, PA	2,957.1
159	Buffalo–Niagara Falls, NY	4,529.1	206	Sheboygan, WI	3,804.3	253	Williamsport, PA	2,947.2
160	Springfield, MO	4,527.5	207	Lewiston–Auburn, ME	3,794.7	254	Newburgh, NY–PA	2,873.4
161	Mansfield, OH	4,525.6	208	Fitchburg–Leominster, MA	3,790.8	255	Utica–Rome, NY	2,797.7
162	Waterloo–Cedar Falls, IA	4,521.6	209	Stamford–Norwalk, CT	3,778.4	256	New London–Norwich, CT–RI	2,767.6
163	Trenton, NJ	4,507.5	210	Joplin, MO	3,766.6	257	Punta Gorda, FL	2,754.0
164	Rochester, NY	4,504.2	211	Grand Forks, ND–MN	3,752.9	258	Pittsburgh, PA	2,717.8
165	Santa Rosa, CA	4,464.4	212	Owensboro, KY	3,749.4	259	Lynchburg, VA	2,692.2
166	Redding, CA	4,456.4	213	Duluth–Superior, MN–WI	3,729.8	260	Huntington–Ashland, WV–KY–OH	2,688.2
167	Grand Rapids–Muskegon–Holland, MI	4,421.5	214	Asheville, NC	3,709.8	261	Johnson City–Kingsport–Bristol, TN–VA	2,686.3
168	Salinas, CA	4,415.5	215	Philadelphia, PA–NJ	3,693.1	262	Dutchess County, NY	2,683.9
169	Lansing–East Lansing, MI	4,405.5	216	Evansville–Henderson, IN–KY	3,688.4	263	Danville, VA	2,650.1
170	Killeen–Temple, TX	4,366.0	217	La Crosse, WI–MN	3,678.5	264	Lancaster, PA	2,627.9
171	Anniston, AL	4,365.7	218	Bremerton, WA	3,652.6	265	Wausau, WI	2,593.1
172	Hartford, CT	4,347.6	219	Fort Collins–Loveland, CO	3,611.6	266	Nashua, NH	2,552.6
173	Elkhart–Goshen, IN	4,344.1	220	Worcester, MA–CT	3,558.4	267	Pittsfield, MA	2,520.3
174	Boise, ID	4,331.8	221	Bismarck, ND	3,541.3	268	Florence, AL	2,477.7
175	Jacksonville, NC	4,297.4	222	Clarksville–Hopkinsville, TN–KY	3,513.2	269	Cumberland, MD–WV	2,420.7
176	Cincinnati, OH–KY–IN	4,260.1	223	Green Bay, WI	3,508.4	270	Hagerstown, MD	2,275.4
177	Madison, WI	4,243.1	224	Kokomo, IN	3,486.2	271	Altoona, PA	2,204.0
178	Santa Barbara–Santa Maria–Lompoc, CA	4,236.4	225	Barnstable–Yarmouth, MA	3,483.1	272	Scranton–Wilkes-Barre–Hazleton, PA	2,177.7
179	Canton–Massillon, OH	4,232.4	226	Sioux Falls, SD	3,482.8	273	Steubenville–Weirton, OH–WV	1,568.1
180	Fort Wayne, IN	4,192.8	227	Eau Claire, WI	3,465.9	274	Johnstown, PA	1,360.4
181	Augusta–Aiken, GA–SC	4,189.1	228	Jackson, MI	3,435.5	–	Albany, NY**	NA
182	Saginaw–Bay City–Midland, MI	4,187.7	229	Rochester, MN	3,434.4	–	Chicago, IL**	NA
183	Fort Smith, AR–OK	4,170.2	230	San Luis Obispo–Atascadero, CA	3,425.3	–	Cleveland, OH**	NA
184	Portland, ME	4,145.4	231	Bangor, ME	3,421.9	–	Indianapolis, IN**	NA
185	Brockton, MA	4,144.4	232	Dubuque, IA	3,415.1	–	Kansas City, MO–KS**	NA
186	Lafayette, LA	4,139.5	233	Appleton–Oshkosh–Neenah, WI	3,404.5	–	Omaha, NE**	NA
187	Lawrence, MA–NH	4,135.1	234	Bergen–Passaic, NJ	3,399.5	–	St. Louis, MO–IL**	NA
188	San Jose, CA	4,115.6	235	Ventura, CA	3,383.3	–	West Palm Beach–Boca Raton, FL**	NA

Source: U.S. Department of Justice, Federal Bureau of Investigation
   "Crime in the United States 1993" (Uniform Crime Reports, December 4, 1994)
*Property crimes are offenses of burglary, larceny-theft and motor vehicle theft. They consist of taking money or property but there is no force or threat of force against victims.
**Not available.

27. Percent Change in Property Crime Rate: 1992 to 1993

National Percent Change = 3.4% Decrease*

RANK	METRO AREA	% CHANGE	RANK	METRO AREA	% CHANGE	RANK	METRO AREA	% CHANGE
48	Abilene, TX	1.44	242	Cheyenne, WY	(14.10)	247	Fort Worth-Arlington, TX	(19.16)
164	Akron, OH	(5.87)	–	Chicago, IL**	NA	199	Fresno, CA	(8.43)
151	Albany, GA	(4.97)	142	Chico-Paradise, CA	(4.49)	100	Gadsden, AL	(2.46)
–	Albany, NY**	NA	162	Cincinnati, OH-KY-IN	(5.72)	182	Gainesville, FL	(6.96)
83	Albuquerque, NM	(1.35)	59	Clarksville-Hopkinsville, TN-KY	0.34	223	Galveston-Texas City, TX	(10.21)
105	Alexandria, LA	(2.67)	–	Cleveland, OH**	NA	175	Gary-Hammond, IN	(6.21)
6	Altoona, PA	11.19	132	Colorado Springs, CO	(3.88)	106	Glens Falls, NY	(2.70)
54	Amarillo, TX	0.79	178	Columbia, MO	(6.49)	66	Goldsboro, NC	(0.27)
228	Anchorage, AK	(10.98)	81	Columbia, SC	(1.16)	172	Grand Forks, ND-MN	(6.03)
194	Ann Arbor, MI	(7.99)	59	Columbus, GA-AL	0.34	181	Grand Rapids-Muskegon-Holland, MI	(6.84)
177	Anniston, AL	(6.29)	187	Columbus, OH	(7.18)	138	Greeley, CO	(4.30)
185	Appleton-Oshkosh-Neenah, WI	(7.16)	112	Corpus Christi, TX	(3.20)	85	Green Bay, WI	(1.48)
233	Asheville, NC	(11.88)	223	Cumberland, MD-WV	(10.21)	64	Greensboro-Winston Salem-High Point, NC	(0.14)
241	Athens, GA	(13.90)	237	Dallas, TX	(13.41)	165	Greenville, NC	(5.88)
143	Atlanta, GA	(4.59)	128	Danbury, CT	(3.82)	76	Greenville-Spartanburg-Anderson, SC	(0.99)
192	Atlantic City, NJ	(7.88)	96	Danville, VA	(2.33)	50	Hagerstown, MD	1.04
248	Augusta-Aiken, GA-SC	(19.26)	71	Daytona Beach, FL	(0.41)	201	Harrisburg-Lebanon-Carlisle, PA	(8.75)
188	Austin-San Marcos, TX	(7.25)	111	Dayton-Springfield, OH	(3.09)	219	Hartford, CT	(10.07)
56	Bakersfield, CA	0.68	137	Decatur, AL	(4.28)	20	Hickory-Morganton, NC	5.70
86	Baltimore, MD	(1.72)	203	Denver, CO	(8.86)	22	Honolulu, HI	5.31
69	Bangor, ME	(0.39)	225	Des Moines, IA	(10.23)	108	Houma, LA	(2.80)
209	Barnstable-Yarmouth, MA	(9.52)	87	Detroit, MI	(1.77)	221	Houston, TX	(10.09)
130	Baton Rouge, LA	(3.83)	211	Dothan, AL	(9.64)	214	Huntington-Ashland, WV-KY-OH	(9.78)
125	Beaumont-Port Arthur, TX	(3.76)	3	Dubuque, IA	14.43	222	Huntsville, AL	(10.20)
176	Bellingham, WA	(6.25)	113	Duluth-Superior, MN-WI	(3.23)	–	Indianapolis, IN**	NA
94	Benton Harbor, MI	(2.23)	–	Dutchess County, NY**	NA	183	Jackson, MI	(7.10)
–	Bergen-Passaic, NJ**	NA	126	Eau Claire, WI	(3.77)	152	Jackson, MS	(5.05)
13	Binghamton, NY	7.72	198	El Paso, TX	(8.36)	87	Jackson, TN	(1.77)
167	Birmingham, AL	(5.90)	6	Elkhart-Goshen, IN	11.19	184	Jacksonville, FL	(7.12)
208	Bismarck, ND	(9.37)	17	Enid, OK	6.26	43	Jacksonville, NC	2.01
38	Bloomington, IN	2.63	37	Erie, PA	2.81	218	Janesville-Beloit, WI	(10.04)
118	Boise, ID	(3.39)	53	Eugene-Springfield, OR	1.00	–	Jersey City, NJ**	NA
–	Boston, MA-NH**	NA	154	Evansville-Henderson, IN-KY	(5.10)	157	Johnson City-Kingsport-Bristol, TN-VA	(5.32)
226	Boulder-Longmont, CO	(10.36)	84	Fargo-Moorhead, ND-MN	(1.44)	229	Johnstown, PA	(11.26)
240	Brazoria, TX	(13.80)	79	Fayetteville, NC	(1.11)	–	Joplin, MO**	NA
235	Bremerton, WA	(12.79)	246	Fayetteville-Springdale-Rogers, AR	(18.82)	153	Kalamazoo-Battle Creek, MI	(5.06)
212	Bridgeport, CT	(9.74)	–	Fitchburg-Leominster, MA**	NA	–	Kansas City, MO-KS**	NA
243	Brockton, MA	(14.37)	140	Flint, MI	(4.42)	119	Kenosha, WI	(3.48)
31	Brownsville-Harlingen-San Benito, TX	3.76	212	Florence, AL	(9.74)	69	Killeen-Temple, TX	(0.39)
75	Bryan-College Station, TX	(0.98)	46	Florence, SC	1.65	19	Kokomo, IN	6.00
–	Buffalo-Niagara Falls, NY**	NA	–	Fort Collins-Loveland, CO**	NA	80	La Crosse, WI-MN	(1.13)
33	Canton-Massillon, OH	3.57	27	Fort Lauderdale, FL	4.65	196	Lafayette, IN	(8.19)
102	Charleston, WV	(2.52)	124	Fort Myers-Cape Coral, FL	(3.70)	114	Lafayette, LA	(3.24)
36	Charleston-North Charleston, SC	2.88	141	Fort Pierce-Port St. Lucie, FL	(4.48)	–	Lake Charles, LA**	NA
4	Charlottesville, VA	12.02	67	Fort Smith, AR-OK	(0.31)	61	Lakeland-Winter Haven, FL	0.30
180	Charlotte-Gastonia-Rock Hill, NC-SC	(6.81)	67	Fort Walton Beach, FL	(0.31)	236	Lancaster, PA	(12.87)
95	Chattanooga, TN-GA	(2.27)	179	Fort Wayne, IN	(6.56)	155	Lansing-East Lansing, MI	(5.28)

Source: Morgan Quitno Corporation using data from U.S. Department of Justice, Federal Bureau of Investigation
   "Crime in the United States 1993" (Uniform Crime Reports, December 4, 1994)
*Property crimes are offenses of burglary, larceny-theft and motor vehicle theft. They consist of taking money or property but there is no force or threat of force against victims.
**Not available.

27. Percent Change in Property Crime Rate: 1992 to 1993 (continued)

National Percent Change = 3.4% Decrease*

RANK	METRO AREA	% CHANGE	RANK	METRO AREA	% CHANGE	RANK	METRO AREA	CHANGE
205	Laredo, TX	(8.90)	16	Olympia, WA	6.31	49	Seattle-Bellevue-Everett, WA	1.24
173	Las Vegas, NV–AZ	(6.11)	–	Omaha, NE**	NA	126	Sheboygan, WI	(3.77)
–	Lawrence, MA–NH**	NA	146	Orange County, CA	(4.65)	170	Sherman-Denison, TX	(5.95)
41	Lawton, OK	2.37	122	Orlando, FL	(3.66)	24	Shreveport-Bossier City, LA	5.11
23	Lewiston-Auburn, ME	5.16	8	Owensboro, KY	10.36	–	Sioux City, IA–NE**	NA
42	Lexington, KY	2.10	18	Panama City, FL	6.11	25	Sioux Falls, SD	4.86
206	Lincoln, NE	(8.98)	91	Philadelphia, PA–NJ	(2.01)	65	South Bend, IN	(0.24)
45	Little Rock-North Little Rock, AR	1.69	30	Phoenix-Mesa, AZ	3.97	97	Spokane, WA	(2.34)
77	Longview-Marshall, TX	(1.04)	2	Pine Bluff, AR	17.43	204	Springfield, MA	(8.89)
146	Los Angeles-Long Beach, CA	(4.65)	158	Pittsburgh, PA	(5.37)	150	Springfield, MO	(4.90)
101	Louisville, KY–IN	(2.50)	135	Pittsfield, MA	(4.21)	144	Stamford-Norwalk, CT	(4.60)
194	Lubbock, TX	(7.99)	249	Portland, ME	(21.85)	117	Steubenville-Weirton, OH–WV	(3.28)
131	Lynchburg, VA	(3.85)	99	Portland-Vancouver, OR–WA	(2.45)	29	Stockton-Lodi, CA	4.29
63	Macon, GA	0.12	92	Providence-Fall River-Warwick, RI–MA	(2.07)	58	St. Cloud, MN	0.60
220	Madison, WI	(10.08)	136	Provo-Orem, UT	(4.23)	1	St. Joseph, MO	22.14
–	Manchester, NH**	NA	145	Pueblo, CO	(4.64)	–	St. Louis, MO–IL**	NA
107	Mansfield, OH	(2.73)	–	Punta Gorda, FL**	NA	234	Sumter, SC	(12.69)
149	McAllen-Edinburg-Mission, TX	(4.73)	171	Racine, WI	(6.02)	169	Syracuse, NY	(5.92)
5	Medford-Ashland, OR	11.41	197	Raleigh-Durham-Chapel Hill, NC	(8.35)	55	Tacoma, WA	0.78
34	Memphis, TN–AR–MS	3.56	190	Rapid City, SD	(7.42)	73	Tallahassee, FL	(0.79)
12	Merced, CA	7.94	148	Reading, PA	(4.69)	134	Tampa-St. Petersburg-Clearwater, FL	(4.17)
9	Miami, FL	10.34	32	Redding, CA	3.60	26	Texarkana, TX–AR	4.85
–	Middlesex-Sommerset-Hunterdon, NJ**	NA	44	Reno, NV	1.97	128	Toledo, OH	(3.82)
193	Milwaukee-Waukesha, WI	(7.93)	245	Richland-Kennewick-Pasco, WA	(18.62)	200	Trenton, NJ	(8.45)
159	Minneapolis-St. Paul, MN–WI	(5.44)	115	Richmond-Petersburg, VA	(3.26)	10	Tucson, AZ	10.26
–	Mobile, AL**	NA	116	Riverside-San Bernardino, CA	(3.27)	189	Tulsa, OK	(7.31)
11	Modesto, CA	8.27	238	Roanoke, VA	(13.55)	40	Tuscaloosa, AL	2.52
–	Monmouth-Ocean, NJ**	NA	185	Rochester, MN	(7.16)	217	Tyler, TX	(9.95)
202	Monroe, LA	(8.76)	163	Rochester, NY	(5.75)	227	Utica-Rome, NY	(10.37)
98	Montgomery, AL	(2.37)	168	Rocky Mount, NC	(5.91)	121	Vallejo-Fairfield-Napa, CA	(3.58)
21	Myrtle Beach, SC	5.66	52	Sacramento, CA	1.02	215	Ventura, CA	(9.86)
160	Naples, FL	(5.45)	138	Saginaw-Bay City-Midland, MI	(4.30)	156	Victoria, TX	(5.30)
123	Nashua, NH	(3.67)	82	Salem, OR	(1.31)	89	Vineland-Millville-Bridgeton, NJ	(1.95)
14	Nashville, TN	6.84	102	Salinas, CA	(2.52)	191	Visalia-Tulare-Porterville, CA	(7.55)
–	Nassau-Suffolk, NY**	NA	210	Salt Lake City-Ogden, UT	(9.56)	28	Waco, TX	4.57
–	New Bedford, MA**	NA	244	San Angelo, TX	(15.48)	93	Washington, DC-MD-VA-WV	(2.20)
207	New Haven-Meriden, CT	(9.30)	230	San Antonio, TX	(11.47)	72	Waterbury, CT	(0.63)
78	New London-Norwich, CT–RI	(1.10)	174	San Diego, CA	(6.14)	–	Waterloo-Cedar Falls, IA**	NA
62	New Orleans, LA	0.18	165	San Francisco, CA	(5.88)	231	Wausau, WI	(11.50)
–	New York, NY**	NA	109	San Jose, CA	(3.01)	–	West Palm Beach-Boca Raton, FL**	NA
–	Newark, NJ**	NA	–	San Luis Obispo-Atascadero, CA**	NA	133	Wichita Falls, TX	(4.16)
–	Newburgh, NY–PA**	NA	110	Santa Barbara-Santa Maria-Lompoc, CA	(3.03)	120	Williamsport, PA	(3.50)
161	Norfolk-Va Beach-Newport News, VA–NC	(5.66)	47	Santa Cruz-Watsonville, CA	1.57	250	Wilmington, NC	(23.66)
74	Oakland, CA	(0.96)	39	Santa Rosa, CA	2.59	–	Worcester, MA–CT**	NA
216	Ocala, FL	(9.89)	232	Sarasota-Bradenton, FL	(11.67)	51	Yakima, WA	1.03
239	Odessa-Midland, TX	(13.67)	57	Savannah, GA	0.67	15	Yolo, CA	6.61
90	Oklahoma City, OK	(1.96)	104	Scranton-Wilkes-Barre-Hazleton, PA	(2.65)	35	Yuba City, CA	3.51

Source: Morgan Quitno Corporation using data from U.S. Department of Justice, Federal Bureau of Investigation
"Crime in the United States 1993" (Uniform Crime Reports, December 4, 1994)
*Property crimes are offenses of burglary, larceny-theft and motor vehicle theft. They consist of taking money or property but there is no force or threat of force against victims.
**Not available.

27. Percent Change in Property Crime Rate: 1992 to 1993 (continued)

National Percent Change = 3.4% Decrease*

RANK	METRO AREA	% CHANGE	RANK	METRO AREA	% CHANGE	RANK	METRO AREA	% CHANGE
1	St. Joseph, MO	22.14	48	Abilene, TX	1.44	95	Chattanooga, TN–GA	(2.27)
2	Pine Bluff, AR	17.43	49	Seattle–Bellevue–Everett, WA	1.24	96	Danville, VA	(2.33)
3	Dubuque, IA	14.43	50	Hagerstown, MD	1.04	97	Spokane, WA	(2.34)
4	Charlottesville, VA	12.02	51	Yakima, WA	1.03	98	Montgomery, AL	(2.37)
5	Medford–Ashland, OR	11.41	52	Sacramento, CA	1.02	99	Portland–Vancouver, OR–WA	(2.45)
6	Altoona, PA	11.19	53	Eugene–Springfield, OR	1.00	100	Gadsden, AL	(2.46)
6	Elkhart–Goshen, IN	11.19	54	Amarillo, TX	0.79	101	Louisville, KY–IN	(2.50)
8	Owensboro, KY	10.36	55	Tacoma, WA	0.78	102	Charleston, WV	(2.52)
9	Miami, FL	10.34	56	Bakersfield, CA	0.68	102	Salinas, CA	(2.52)
10	Tucson, AZ	10.26	57	Savannah, GA	0.67	104	Scranton–Wilkes-Barre–Hazleton, PA	(2.65)
11	Modesto, CA	8.27	58	St. Cloud, MN	0.60	105	Alexandria, LA	(2.67)
12	Merced, CA	7.94	59	Clarksville–Hopkinsville, TN–KY	0.34	106	Glens Falls, NY	(2.70)
13	Binghamton, NY	7.72	59	Columbus, GA–AL	0.34	107	Mansfield, OH	(2.73)
14	Nashville, TN	6.84	61	Lakeland–Winter Haven, FL	0.30	108	Houma, LA	(2.80)
15	Yolo, CA	6.61	62	New Orleans, LA	0.18	109	San Jose, CA	(3.01)
16	Olympia, WA	6.31	63	Macon, GA	0.12	110	Santa Barbara–Santa Maria–Lompoc, CA	(3.03)
17	Enid, OK	6.26	64	Greensboro–Winston Salem–High Point, NC	(0.14)	111	Dayton–Springfield, OH	(3.09)
18	Panama City, FL	6.11	65	South Bend, IN	(0.24)	112	Corpus Christi, TX	(3.20)
19	Kokomo, IN	6.00	66	Goldsboro, NC	(0.27)	113	Duluth–Superior, MN–WI	(3.23)
20	Hickory–Morganton, NC	5.70	67	Fort Smith, AR–OK	(0.31)	114	Lafayette, LA	(3.24)
21	Myrtle Beach, SC	5.66	67	Fort Walton Beach, FL	(0.31)	115	Richmond–Petersburg, VA	(3.26)
22	Honolulu, HI	5.31	69	Bangor, ME	(0.39)	116	Riverside–San Bernardino, CA	(3.27)
23	Lewiston–Auburn, ME	5.16	69	Killeen–Temple, TX	(0.39)	117	Steubenville–Weirton, OH–WV	(3.28)
24	Shreveport–Bossier City, LA	5.11	71	Daytona Beach, FL	(0.41)	118	Boise, ID	(3.39)
25	Sioux Falls, SD	4.86	72	Waterbury, CT	(0.63)	119	Kenosha, WI	(3.48)
26	Texarkana, TX–AR	4.85	73	Tallahassee, FL	(0.79)	120	Williamsport, PA	(3.50)
27	Fort Lauderdale, FL	4.65	74	Oakland, CA	(0.96)	121	Vallejo–Fairfield–Napa, CA	(3.58)
28	Waco, TX	4.57	75	Bryan–College Station, TX	(0.98)	122	Orlando, FL	(3.66)
29	Stockton–Lodi, CA	4.29	76	Greenville–Spartanburg–Anderson, SC	(0.99)	123	Nashua, NH	(3.67)
30	Phoenix–Mesa, AZ	3.97	77	Longview–Marshall, TX	(1.04)	124	Fort Myers–Cape Coral, FL	(3.70)
31	Brownsville–Harlingen–San Benito, TX	3.76	78	New London–Norwich, CT–RI	(1.10)	125	Beaumont–Port Arthur, TX	(3.76)
32	Redding, CA	3.60	79	Fayetteville, NC	(1.11)	126	Eau Claire, WI	(3.77)
33	Canton–Massillon, OH	3.57	80	La Crosse, WI–MN	(1.13)	126	Sheboygan, WI	(3.77)
34	Memphis, TN–AR–MS	3.56	81	Columbia, SC	(1.16)	128	Danbury, CT	(3.82)
35	Yuba City, CA	3.51	82	Salem, OR	(1.31)	128	Toledo, OH	(3.82)
36	Charleston–North Charleston, SC	2.88	83	Albuquerque, NM	(1.35)	130	Baton Rouge, LA	(3.83)
37	Erie, PA	2.81	84	Fargo–Moorhead, ND–MN	(1.44)	131	Lynchburg, VA	(3.85)
38	Bloomington, IN	2.63	85	Green Bay, WI	(1.48)	132	Colorado Springs, CO	(3.88)
39	Santa Rosa, CA	2.59	86	Baltimore, MD	(1.72)	133	Wichita Falls, TX	(4.16)
40	Tuscaloosa, AL	2.52	87	Detroit, MI	(1.77)	134	Tampa–St. Petersburg–Clearwater, FL	(4.17)
41	Lawton, OK	2.37	87	Jackson, TN	(1.77)	135	Pittsfield, MA	(4.21)
42	Lexington, KY	2.10	89	Vineland–Millville–Bridgeton, NJ	(1.95)	136	Provo–Orem, UT	(4.23)
43	Jacksonville, NC	2.01	90	Oklahoma City, OK	(1.96)	137	Decatur, AL	(4.28)
44	Reno, NV	1.97	91	Philadelphia, PA–NJ	(2.01)	138	Greeley, CO	(4.30)
45	Little Rock–North Little Rock, AR	1.69	92	Providence–Fall River–Warwick, RI–MA	(2.07)	138	Saginaw–Bay City–Midland, MI	(4.30)
46	Florence, SC	1.65	93	Washington, DC–MD–VA–WV	(2.20)	140	Flint, MI	(4.42)
47	Santa Cruz–Watsonville, CA	1.57	94	Benton Harbor, MI	(2.23)	141	Fort Pierce–Port St. Lucie, FL	(4.48)

Source: Morgan Quitno Corporation using data from U.S. Department of Justice, Federal Bureau of Investigation
    "Crime in the United States 1993" (Uniform Crime Reports, December 4, 1994)
*Property crimes are offenses of burglary, larceny-theft and motor vehicle theft. They consist of taking money or property but there is no
force or threat of force against victims.
**Not available.

27. Percent Change in Property Crime Rate: 1992 to 1993 (continued)

National Percent Change = 3.4% Decrease*

RANK	METRO AREA	% CHANGE	RANK	METRO AREA	% CHANGE	RANK	METRO AREA	CHANGE
142	Chico-Paradise, CA	(4.49)	189	Tulsa, OK	(7.31)	236	Lancaster, PA	(12.87)
143	Atlanta, GA	(4.59)	190	Rapid City, SD	(7.42)	237	Dallas, TX	(13.41)
144	Stamford-Norwalk, CT	(4.60)	191	Visalia-Tulare-Porterville, CA	(7.55)	238	Roanoke, VA	(13.55)
145	Pueblo, CO	(4.64)	192	Atlantic City, NJ	(7.88)	239	Odessa-Midland, TX	(13.67)
146	Los Angeles-Long Beach, CA	(4.65)	193	Milwaukee-Waukesha, WI	(7.93)	240	Brazoria, TX	(13.80)
146	Orange County, CA	(4.65)	194	Ann Arbor, MI	(7.99)	241	Athens, GA	(13.90)
148	Reading, PA	(4.69)	194	Lubbock, TX	(7.99)	242	Cheyenne, WY	(14.10)
149	McAllen-Edinburg-Mission, TX	(4.73)	196	Lafayette, IN	(8.19)	243	Brockton, MA	(14.37)
150	Springfield, MO	(4.90)	197	Raleigh-Durham-Chapel Hill, NC	(8.35)	244	San Angelo, TX	(15.48)
151	Albany, GA	(4.97)	198	El Paso, TX	(8.36)	245	Richland-Kennewick-Pasco, WA	(18.62)
152	Jackson, MS	(5.05)	199	Fresno, CA	(8.43)	246	Fayetteville-Springdale-Rogers, AR	(18.82)
153	Kalamazoo-Battle Creek, MI	(5.06)	200	Trenton, NJ	(8.45)	247	Fort Worth-Arlington, TX	(19.16)
154	Evansville-Henderson, IN-KY	(5.10)	201	Harrisburg-Lebanon-Carlisle, PA	(8.75)	248	Augusta-Aiken, GA-SC	(19.26)
155	Lansing-East Lansing, MI	(5.28)	202	Monroe, LA	(8.76)	249	Portland, ME	(21.85)
156	Victoria, TX	(5.30)	203	Denver, CO	(8.86)	250	Wilmington, NC	(23.66)
157	Johnson City-Kingsport-Bristol, TN-VA	(5.32)	204	Springfield, MA	(8.89)	–	Albany, NY**	NA
158	Pittsburgh, PA	(5.37)	205	Laredo, TX	(8.90)	–	Bergen-Passaic, NJ**	NA
159	Minneapolis-St. Paul, MN-WI	(5.44)	206	Lincoln, NE	(8.98)	–	Boston, MA-NH**	NA
160	Naples, FL	(5.45)	207	New Haven-Meriden, CT	(9.30)	–	Buffalo-Niagara Falls, NY**	NA
161	Norfolk-Va Beach-Newport News, VA-NC	(5.66)	208	Bismarck, ND	(9.37)	–	Chicago, IL**	NA
162	Cincinnati, OH-KY-IN	(5.72)	209	Barnstable-Yarmouth, MA	(9.52)	–	Cleveland, OH**	NA
163	Rochester, NY	(5.75)	210	Salt Lake City-Ogden, UT	(9.56)	–	Dutchess County, NY**	NA
164	Akron, OH	(5.87)	211	Dothan, AL	(9.64)	–	Fitchburg-Leominster, MA**	NA
165	Greenville, NC	(5.88)	212	Bridgeport, CT	(9.74)	–	Fort Collins-Loveland, CO**	NA
165	San Francisco, CA	(5.88)	212	Florence, AL	(9.74)	–	Indianapolis, IN**	NA
167	Birmingham, AL	(5.90)	214	Huntington-Ashland, WV-KY-OH	(9.78)	–	Jersey City, NJ**	NA
168	Rocky Mount, NC	(5.91)	215	Ventura, CA	(9.86)	–	Joplin, MO**	NA
169	Syracuse, NY	(5.92)	216	Ocala, FL	(9.89)	–	Kansas City, MO-KS**	NA
170	Sherman-Denison, TX	(5.95)	217	Tyler, TX	(9.95)	–	Lake Charles, LA**	NA
171	Racine, WI	(6.02)	218	Janesville-Beloit, WI	(10.04)	–	Lawrence, MA-NH**	NA
172	Grand Forks, ND-MN	(6.03)	219	Hartford, CT	(10.07)	–	Manchester, NH**	NA
173	Las Vegas, NV-AZ	(6.11)	220	Madison, WI	(10.08)	–	Middlesex-Sommerset-Hunterdon, NJ**	NA
174	San Diego, CA	(6.14)	221	Houston, TX	(10.09)	–	Mobile, AL**	NA
175	Gary-Hammond, IN	(6.21)	222	Huntsville, AL	(10.20)	–	Monmouth-Ocean, NJ**	NA
176	Bellingham, WA	(6.25)	223	Cumberland, MD-WV	(10.21)	–	Nassau-Suffolk, NY**	NA
177	Anniston, AL	(6.29)	223	Galveston-Texas City, TX	(10.21)	–	New Bedford, MA**	NA
178	Columbia, MO	(6.49)	225	Des Moines, IA	(10.23)	–	New York, NY**	NA
179	Fort Wayne, IN	(6.56)	226	Boulder-Longmont, CO	(10.36)	–	Newark, NJ**	NA
180	Charlotte-Gastonia-Rock Hill, NC-SC	(6.81)	227	Utica-Rome, NY	(10.37)	–	Newburgh, NY-PA**	NA
181	Grand Rapids-Muskegon-Holland, MI	(6.84)	228	Anchorage, AK	(10.98)	–	Omaha, NE**	NA
182	Gainesville, FL	(6.96)	229	Johnstown, PA	(11.26)	–	Punta Gorda, FL**	NA
183	Jackson, MI	(7.10)	230	San Antonio, TX	(11.47)	–	San Luis Obispo-Atascadero, CA**	NA
184	Jacksonville, FL	(7.12)	231	Wausau, WI	(11.50)	–	Sioux City, IA-NE**	NA
185	Appleton-Oshkosh-Neenah, WI	(7.16)	232	Sarasota-Bradenton, FL	(11.67)	–	St. Louis, MO-IL**	NA
185	Rochester, MN	(7.16)	233	Asheville, NC	(11.88)	–	Waterloo-Cedar Falls, IA**	NA
187	Columbus, OH	(7.18)	234	Sumter, SC	(12.69)	–	West Palm Beach-Boca Raton, FL**	NA
188	Austin-San Marcos, TX	(7.25)	235	Bremerton, WA	(12.79)	–	Worcester, MA-CT**	NA

Source: Morgan Quitno Corporation using data from U.S. Department of Justice, Federal Bureau of Investigation
"Crime in the United States 1993" (Uniform Crime Reports, December 4, 1994)
*Property crimes are offenses of burglary, larceny-theft and motor vehicle theft. They consist of taking money or property but there is no force or threat of force against victims.
**Not available.

28. Percent Change in Property Crime Rate: 1989 to 1993

National Percent Change = 6.7% Decrease*

RANK	METRO AREA	% CHANGE	RANK	METRO AREA	% CHANGE	RANK	METRO AREA	% CHANGE
223	Abilene, TX	(22.43)	114	Cheyenne, WY	(6.19)	241	Fort Worth-Arlington, TX	(31.14)
–	Akron, OH**	NA	–	Chicago, IL**	NA	108	Fresno, CA	(5.91)
71	Albany, GA	(0.12)	141	Chico-Paradise, CA	(9.53)	3	Gadsden, AL	34.70
–	Albany, NY**	NA	101	Cincinnati, OH-KY-IN	(4.02)	19	Gainesville, FL	14.73
194	Albuquerque, NM	(15.76)	95	Clarksville-Hopkinsville, TN-KY	(3.46)	151	Galveston-Texas City, TX	(10.93)
70	Alexandria, LA	(0.07)	–	Cleveland, OH**	NA	49	Gary-Hammond, IN	3.62
100	Altoona, PA	(3.95)	197	Colorado Springs, CO	(16.03)	27	Glens Falls, NY	9.71
64	Amarillo, TX	0.35	150	Columbia, MO	(10.68)	–	Goldsboro, NC**	NA
25	Anchorage, AK	11.93	57	Columbia, SC	1.14	121	Grand Forks, ND-MN	(6.84)
245	Ann Arbor, MI	(35.91)	102	Columbus, GA-AL	(4.48)	112	Grand Rapids-Muskegon-Holland, MI	(6.09)
12	Anniston, AL	19.88	164	Columbus, OH	(12.14)	106	Greeley, CO	(5.58)
55	Appleton-Oshkosh-Neenah, WI	1.35	117	Corpus Christi, TX	(6.38)	111	Green Bay, WI	(6.08)
206	Asheville, NC	(18.00)	56	Cumberland, MD-WV	1.31	35	Greensboro-Winston Salem-High Point, NC	7.85
54	Athens, GA	1.40	244	Dallas, TX	(35.47)	–	Greenville, NC**	NA
220	Atlanta, GA	(21.09)	30	Danbury, CT	9.01	203	Greenville-Spartanburg-Anderson, SC	(17.76)
193	Atlantic City, NJ	(15.75)	10	Danville, VA	20.45	62	Hagerstown, MD	0.41
219	Augusta-Aiken, GA-SC	(21.02)	201	Daytona Beach, FL	(17.32)	–	Harrisburg-Lebanon-Carlisle, PA**	NA
179	Austin-San Marcos, TX	(13.87)	136	Dayton-Springfield, OH	(9.26)	162	Hartford, CT	(12.09)
89	Bakersfield, CA	(2.20)	28	Decatur, AL	9.67	–	Hickory-Morganton, NC**	NA
24	Baltimore, MD	12.32	154	Denver, CO	(11.01)	50	Honolulu, HI	3.28
207	Bangor, ME	(18.03)	163	Des Moines, IA	(12.12)	–	Houma, LA**	NA
–	Barnstable-Yarmouth, MA**	NA	155	Detroit, MI	(11.10)	238	Houston, TX	(30.41)
14	Baton Rouge, LA	17.41	210	Dothan, AL	(18.49)	126	Huntington-Ashland, WV-KY-OH	(7.41)
60	Beaumont-Port Arthur, TX	0.65	40	Dubuque, IA	5.34	184	Huntsville, AL	(14.25)
109	Bellingham, WA	(6.02)	66	Duluth-Superior, MN-WI	0.11	–	Indianapolis, IN**	NA
127	Benton Harbor, MI	(7.45)	–	Dutchess County, NY**	NA	190	Jackson, MI	(15.42)
183	Bergen-Passaic, NJ	(14.20)	140	Eau Claire, WI	(9.48)	4	Jackson, MS	28.09
84	Binghamton, NY	(1.57)	227	El Paso, TX	(23.16)	21	Jackson, TN	13.99
31	Birmingham, AL	8.91	146	Elkhart-Goshen, IN	(10.10)	118	Jacksonville, FL	(6.54)
51	Bismarck, ND	2.25	22	Enid, OK	13.57	34	Jacksonville, NC	7.89
161	Bloomington, IN	(11.93)	104	Erie, PA	(5.08)	52	Janesville-Beloit, WI	2.08
48	Boise, ID	3.65	158	Eugene-Springfield, OR	(11.28)	214	Jersey City, NJ	(19.09)
–	Boston, MA-NH**	NA	172	Evansville-Henderson, IN-KY	(13.29)	159	Johnson City-Kingsport-Bristol, TN-VA	(11.41)
195	Boulder-Longmont, CO	(15.81)	76	Fargo-Moorhead, ND-MN	(0.75)	–	Johnstown, PA**	NA
202	Brazoria, TX	(17.61)	142	Fayetteville, NC	(9.63)	177	Joplin, MO	(13.82)
–	Bremerton, WA**	NA	231	Fayetteville-Springdale-Rogers, AR	(24.50)	189	Kalamazoo-Battle Creek, MI	(15.33)
176	Bridgeport, CT	(13.68)	168	Fitchburg-Leominster, MA	(12.51)	–	Kansas City, MO-KS**	NA
–	Brockton, MA**	NA	171	Flint, MI	(13.00)	41	Kenosha, WI	5.24
38	Brownsville-Harlingen-San Benito, TX	5.85	149	Florence, AL	(10.30)	86	Killeen-Temple, TX	(1.94)
237	Bryan-College Station, TX	(28.01)	1	Florence, SC	41.54	33	Kokomo, IN	8.14
43	Buffalo-Niagara Falls, NY	4.79	204	Fort Collins-Loveland, CO	(17.85)	157	La Crosse, WI-MN	(11.24)
37	Canton-Massillon, OH	6.27	66	Fort Lauderdale, FL	0.11	26	Lafayette, IN	9.76
58	Charleston, WV	1.07	18	Fort Myers-Cape Coral, FL	14.91	133	Lafayette, LA	(8.34)
36	Charleston-North Charleston, SC	7.36	229	Fort Pierce-Port St. Lucie, FL	(23.24)	46	Lake Charles, LA	4.19
80	Charlottesville, VA	(0.94)	43	Fort Smith, AR-OK	4.79	170	Lakeland-Winter Haven, FL	(12.95)
165	Charlotte-Gastonia-Rock Hill, NC-SC	(12.34)	78	Fort Walton Beach, FL	(0.84)	47	Lancaster, PA	4.01
91	Chattanooga, TN-GA	(2.43)	226	Fort Wayne, IN	(22.88)	151	Lansing-East Lansing, MI	(10.93)

Source: Morgan Quitno Corporation using data from U.S. Department of Justice, Federal Bureau of Investigation
    "Crime in the United States 1993" (Uniform Crime Reports, December 4, 1994)
*Property crimes are offenses of burglary, larceny-theft and motor vehicle theft. They consist of taking money or property but there is no force or threat of force against victims.
**Not available.

28. Percent Change in Property Crime Rate: 1989 to 1993 (continued)

National Percent Change = 6.7% Decrease*

RANK	METRO AREA	% CHANGE	RANK	METRO AREA	% CHANGE	RANK	METRO AREA	CHANGE
217	Laredo, TX	(20.10)	45	Olympia, WA	4.55	145	Seattle–Bellevue–Everett, WA	(10.09)
122	Las Vegas, NV–AZ	(6.89)	–	Omaha, NE**	NA	20	Sheboygan, WI	14.60
137	Lawrence, MA–NH	(9.28)	155	Orange County, CA	(11.10)	232	Sherman–Denison, TX	(24.61)
8	Lawton, OK	22.72	198	Orlando, FL	(16.39)	185	Shreveport–Bossier City, LA	(14.54)
160	Lewiston–Auburn, ME	(11.86)	81	Owensboro, KY	(0.99)	185	Sioux City, IA–NE	(14.54)
90	Lexington, KY	(2.32)	6	Panama City, FL	23.32	85	Sioux Falls, SD	(1.65)
82	Lincoln, NE	(1.02)	139	Philadelphia, PA–NJ	(9.45)	–	South Bend, IN**	NA
62	Little Rock–North Little Rock, AR	0.41	166	Phoenix–Mesa, AZ	(12.42)	143	Spokane, WA	(9.72)
93	Longview–Marshall, TX	(3.09)	9	Pine Bluff, AR	22.20	17	Springfield, MA	14.93
129	Los Angeles–Long Beach, CA	(7.83)	116	Pittsburgh, PA	(6.34)	234	Springfield, MO	(25.11)
138	Louisville, KY–IN	(9.42)	–	Pittsfield, MA**	NA	215	Stamford–Norwalk, CT	(19.67)
208	Lubbock, TX	(18.38)	235	Portland, ME	(25.13)	–	Steubenville–Weirton, OH–WV**	NA
236	Lynchburg, VA	(25.91)	196	Portland–Vancouver, OR–WA	(15.99)	92	Stockton–Lodi, CA	(2.68)
188	Macon, GA	(14.95)	225	Providence–Fall River–Warwick, RI–MA	(22.67)	73	St. Cloud, MN	(0.26)
199	Madison, WI	(16.48)	–	Provo–Orem, UT**	NA	15	St. Joseph, MO	16.47
239	Manchester, NH	(30.77)	205	Pueblo, CO	(17.86)	–	St. Louis, MO–IL**	NA
115	Mansfield, OH	(6.26)	–	Punta Gorda, FL**	NA	–	Sumter, SC**	NA
16	McAllen–Edinburg–Mission, TX	16.20	173	Racine, WI	(13.32)	169	Syracuse, NY	(12.67)
23	Medford–Ashland, OR	13.06	83	Raleigh–Durham–Chapel Hill, NC	(1.45)	187	Tacoma, WA	(14.57)
61	Memphis, TN–AR–MS	0.43	72	Rapid City, SD	(0.23)	11	Tallahassee, FL	20.40
13	Merced, CA	17.75	–	Reading, PA**	NA	182	Tampa–St. Petersburg–Clearwater, FL	(14.17)
98	Miami, FL	(3.76)	153	Redding, CA	(10.94)	191	Texarkana, TX–AR	(15.56)
113	Middlesex–Sommerset–Hunterdon, NJ	(6.11)	128	Reno, NV	(7.78)	178	Toledo, OH	(13.85)
132	Milwaukee–Waukesha, WI	(8.28)	240	Richland–Kennewick–Pasco, WA	(31.09)	209	Trenton, NJ	(18.41)
123	Minneapolis–St. Paul, MN–WI	(6.91)	69	Richmond–Petersburg, VA	(0.05)	–	Tucson, AZ**	NA
103	Mobile, AL	(4.64)	–	Riverside–San Bernardino, CA**	NA	192	Tulsa, OK	(15.66)
53	Modesto, CA	1.81	212	Roanoke, VA	(18.99)	7	Tuscaloosa, AL	22.90
96	Monmouth–Ocean, NJ	(3.67)	135	Rochester, MN	(8.65)	130	Tyler, TX	(8.09)
29	Monroe, LA	9.39	131	Rochester, NY	(8.12)	39	Utica–Rome, NY	5.49
107	Montgomery, AL	(5.86)	–	Rocky Mount, NC**	NA	94	Vallejo–Fairfield–Napa, CA	(3.32)
–	Myrtle Beach, SC**	NA	87	Sacramento, CA	(1.99)	79	Ventura, CA	(0.93)
228	Naples, FL	(23.20)	148	Saginaw–Bay City–Midland, MI	(10.28)	5	Victoria, TX	23.77
222	Nashua, NH	(22.21)	74	Salem, OR	(0.60)	42	Vineland–Millville–Bridgeton, NJ	4.99
2	Nashville, TN	40.74	65	Salinas, CA	0.18	32	Visalia–Tulare–Porterville, CA	8.67
147	Nassau–Suffolk, NY	(10.25)	167	Salt Lake City–Ogden, UT	(12.49)	218	Waco, TX	(20.71)
211	New Bedford, MA	(18.65)	242	San Angelo, TX	(32.47)	88	Washington, DC–MD–VA–WV	(2.00)
175	New Haven–Meriden, CT	(13.47)	224	San Antonio, TX	(22.46)	124	Waterbury, CT	(7.26)
213	New London–Norwich, CT–RI	(19.08)	216	San Diego, CA	(19.97)	110	Waterloo–Cedar Falls, IA	(6.04)
97	New Orleans, LA	(3.75)	98	San Francisco, CA	(3.76)	180	Wausau, WI	(14.11)
200	New York, NY	(17.14)	105	San Jose, CA	(5.57)	–	West Palm Beach–Boca Raton, FL**	NA
181	Newark, NJ	(14.16)	–	San Luis Obispo–Atascadero, CA**	NA	243	Wichita Falls, TX	(32.68)
–	Newburgh, NY–PA**	NA	134	Santa Barbara–Santa Maria–Lompoc, CA	(8.51)	–	Williamsport, PA**	NA
125	Norfolk–Va Beach–Newport News, VA–NC	(7.36)	77	Santa Cruz–Watsonville, CA	(0.83)	221	Wilmington, NC	(21.36)
119	Oakland, CA	(6.77)	59	Santa Rosa, CA	0.73	–	Worcester, MA–CT**	NA
230	Ocala, FL	(23.76)	174	Sarasota–Bradenton, FL	(13.40)	144	Yakima, WA	(10.03)
233	Odessa–Midland, TX	(24.75)	75	Savannah, GA	(0.74)	–	Yolo, CA**	NA
120	Oklahoma City, OK	(6.80)	–	Scranton–Wilkes-Barre–Hazleton, PA**	NA	66	Yuba City, CA	0.11

Source: Morgan Quitno Corporation using data from U.S. Department of Justice, Federal Bureau of Investigation
   "Crime in the United States 1993" (Uniform Crime Reports, December 4, 1994)
*Property crimes are offenses of burglary, larceny-theft and motor vehicle theft. They consist of taking money or property but there is no force or threat of force against victims.
**Not available.

28. Percent Change in Property Crime Rate: 1989 to 1993 (continued)

National Percent Change = 6.7% Decrease*

RANK	METRO AREA	% CHANGE	RANK	METRO AREA	% CHANGE	RANK	METRO AREA	% CHANGE
1	Florence, SC	41.54	48	Boise, ID	3.65	95	Clarksville-Hopkinsville, TN-KY	(3.46)
2	Nashville, TN	40.74	49	Gary-Hammond, IN	3.62	96	Monmouth-Ocean, NJ	(3.67)
3	Gadsden, AL	34.70	50	Honolulu, HI	3.28	97	New Orleans, LA	(3.75)
4	Jackson, MS	28.09	51	Bismarck, ND	2.25	98	Miami, FL	(3.76)
5	Victoria, TX	23.77	52	Janesville-Beloit, WI	2.08	98	San Francisco, CA	(3.76)
6	Panama City, FL	23.32	53	Modesto, CA	1.81	100	Altoona, PA	(3.95)
7	Tuscaloosa, AL	22.90	54	Athens, GA	1.40	101	Cincinnati, OH-KY-IN	(4.02)
8	Lawton, OK	22.72	55	Appleton-Oshkosh-Neenah, WI	1.35	102	Columbus, GA-AL	(4.48)
9	Pine Bluff, AR	22.20	56	Cumberland, MD-WV	1.31	103	Mobile, AL	(4.64)
10	Danville, VA	20.45	57	Columbia, SC	1.14	104	Erie, PA	(5.08)
11	Tallahassee, FL	20.40	58	Charleston, WV	1.07	105	San Jose, CA	(5.57)
12	Anniston, AL	19.88	59	Santa Rosa, CA	0.73	106	Greeley, CO	(5.58)
13	Merced, CA	17.75	60	Beaumont-Port Arthur, TX	0.65	107	Montgomery, AL	(5.86)
14	Baton Rouge, LA	17.41	61	Memphis, TN-AR-MS	0.43	108	Fresno, CA	(5.91)
15	St. Joseph, MO	16.47	62	Hagerstown, MD	0.41	109	Bellingham, WA	(6.02)
16	McAllen-Edinburg-Mission, TX	16.20	62	Little Rock-North Little Rock, AR	0.41	110	Waterloo-Cedar Falls, IA	(6.04)
17	Springfield, MA	14.93	64	Amarillo, TX	0.35	111	Green Bay, WI	(6.08)
18	Fort Myers-Cape Coral, FL	14.91	65	Salinas, CA	0.18	112	Grand Rapids-Muskegon-Holland, MI	(6.09)
19	Gainesville, FL	14.73	66	Duluth-Superior, MN-WI	0.11	113	Middlesex-Sommerset-Hunterdon, NJ	(6.11)
20	Sheboygan, WI	14.60	66	Fort Lauderdale, FL	0.11	114	Cheyenne, WY	(6.19)
21	Jackson, TN	13.99	66	Yuba City, CA	0.11	115	Mansfield, OH	(6.26)
22	Enid, OK	13.57	69	Richmond-Petersburg, VA	(0.05)	116	Pittsburgh, PA	(6.34)
23	Medford-Ashland, OR	13.06	70	Alexandria, LA	(0.07)	117	Corpus Christi, TX	(6.38)
24	Baltimore, MD	12.32	71	Albany, GA	(0.12)	118	Jacksonville, FL	(6.54)
25	Anchorage, AK	11.93	72	Rapid City, SD	(0.23)	119	Oakland, CA	(6.77)
26	Lafayette, IN	9.76	73	St. Cloud, MN	(0.26)	120	Oklahoma City, OK	(6.80)
27	Glens Falls, NY	9.71	74	Salem, OR	(0.60)	121	Grand Forks, ND-MN	(6.84)
28	Decatur, AL	9.67	75	Savannah, GA	(0.74)	122	Las Vegas, NV-AZ	(6.89)
29	Monroe, LA	9.39	76	Fargo-Moorhead, ND-MN	(0.75)	123	Minneapolis-St. Paul, MN-WI	(6.91)
30	Danbury, CT	9.01	77	Santa Cruz-Watsonville, CA	(0.83)	124	Waterbury, CT	(7.26)
31	Birmingham, AL	8.91	78	Fort Walton Beach, FL	(0.84)	125	Norfolk-Va Beach-Newport News, VA-NC	(7.36)
32	Visalia-Tulare-Porterville, CA	8.67	79	Ventura, CA	(0.93)	126	Huntington-Ashland, WV-KY-OH	(7.41)
33	Kokomo, IN	8.14	80	Charlottesville, VA	(0.94)	127	Benton Harbor, MI	(7.45)
34	Jacksonville, NC	7.89	81	Owensboro, KY	(0.99)	128	Reno, NV	(7.78)
35	Greensboro-Winston Salem-High Point, NC	7.85	82	Lincoln, NE	(1.02)	129	Los Angeles-Long Beach, CA	(7.83)
36	Charleston-North Charleston, SC	7.36	83	Raleigh-Durham-Chapel Hill, NC	(1.45)	130	Tyler, TX	(8.09)
37	Canton-Massillon, OH	6.27	84	Binghamton, NY	(1.57)	131	Rochester, NY	(8.12)
38	Brownsville-Harlingen-San Benito, TX	5.85	85	Sioux Falls, SD	(1.65)	132	Milwaukee-Waukesha, WI	(8.28)
39	Utica-Rome, NY	5.49	86	Killeen-Temple, TX	(1.94)	133	Lafayette, LA	(8.34)
40	Dubuque, IA	5.34	87	Sacramento, CA	(1.99)	134	Santa Barbara-Santa Maria-Lompoc, CA	(8.51)
41	Kenosha, WI	5.24	88	Washington, DC-MD-VA-WV	(2.00)	135	Rochester, MN	(8.65)
42	Vineland-Millville-Bridgeton, NJ	4.99	89	Bakersfield, CA	(2.20)	136	Dayton-Springfield, OH	(9.26)
43	Buffalo-Niagara Falls, NY	4.79	90	Lexington, KY	(2.32)	137	Lawrence, MA-NH	(9.28)
43	Fort Smith, AR-OK	4.79	91	Chattanooga, TN-GA	(2.43)	138	Louisville, KY-IN	(9.42)
45	Olympia, WA	4.55	92	Stockton-Lodi, CA	(2.68)	139	Philadelphia, PA-NJ	(9.45)
46	Lake Charles, LA	4.19	93	Longview-Marshall, TX	(3.09)	140	Eau Claire, WI	(9.48)
47	Lancaster, PA	4.01	94	Vallejo-Fairfield-Napa, CA	(3.32)	141	Chico-Paradise, CA	(9.53)

Source: Morgan Quitno Corporation using data from U.S. Department of Justice, Federal Bureau of Investigation
  "Crime in the United States 1993" (Uniform Crime Reports, December 4, 1994)
Property crimes are offenses of burglary, larceny-theft and motor vehicle theft. They consist of taking money or property but there is no force or threat of force against victims.
**Not available.*

28. Percent Change in Property Crime Rate: 1989 to 1993 (continued)

National Percent Change = 6.7% Decrease*

RANK	METRO AREA	% CHANGE	RANK	METRO AREA	% CHANGE	RANK	METRO AREA	CHANGE
142	Fayetteville, NC	(9.63)	189	Kalamazoo–Battle Creek, MI	(15.33)	236	Lynchburg, VA	(25.91)
143	Spokane, WA	(9.72)	190	Jackson, MI	(15.42)	237	Bryan–College Station, TX	(28.01)
144	Yakima, WA	(10.03)	191	Texarkana, TX–AR	(15.56)	238	Houston, TX	(30.41)
145	Seattle–Bellevue–Everett, WA	(10.09)	192	Tulsa, OK	(15.66)	239	Manchester, NH	(30.77)
146	Elkhart–Goshen, IN	(10.10)	193	Atlantic City, NJ	(15.75)	240	Richland–Kennewick–Pasco, WA	(31.09)
147	Nassau–Suffolk, NY	(10.25)	194	Albuquerque, NM	(15.76)	241	Fort Worth–Arlington, TX	(31.14)
148	Saginaw–Bay City–Midland, MI	(10.28)	195	Boulder–Longmont, CO	(15.81)	242	San Angelo, TX	(32.47)
149	Florence, AL	(10.30)	196	Portland–Vancouver, OR–WA	(15.99)	243	Wichita Falls, TX	(32.68)
150	Columbia, MO	(10.68)	197	Colorado Springs, CO	(16.03)	244	Dallas, TX	(35.47)
151	Galveston–Texas City, TX	(10.93)	198	Orlando, FL	(16.39)	245	Ann Arbor, MI	(35.91)
151	Lansing–East Lansing, MI	(10.93)	199	Madison, WI	(16.48)	–	Akron, OH**	NA
153	Redding, CA	(10.94)	200	New York, NY	(17.14)	–	Albany, NY**	NA
154	Denver, CO	(11.01)	201	Daytona Beach, FL	(17.32)	–	Barnstable–Yarmouth, MA**	NA
155	Detroit, MI	(11.10)	202	Brazoria, TX	(17.61)	–	Boston, MA–NH**	NA
155	Orange County, CA	(11.10)	203	Greenville–Spartanburg–Anderson, SC	(17.76)	–	Bremerton, WA**	NA
157	La Crosse, WI–MN	(11.24)	204	Fort Collins–Loveland, CO	(17.85)	–	Brockton, MA**	NA
158	Eugene–Springfield, OR	(11.28)	205	Pueblo, CO	(17.86)	–	Chicago, IL**	NA
159	Johnson City–Kingsport–Bristol, TN–VA	(11.41)	206	Asheville, NC	(18.00)	–	Cleveland, OH**	NA
160	Lewiston–Auburn, ME	(11.86)	207	Bangor, ME	(18.03)	–	Dutchess County, NY**	NA
161	Bloomington, IN	(11.93)	208	Lubbock, TX	(18.38)	–	Goldsboro, NC**	NA
162	Hartford, CT	(12.09)	209	Trenton, NJ	(18.41)	–	Greenville, NC**	NA
163	Des Moines, IA	(12.12)	210	Dothan, AL	(18.49)	–	Harrisburg–Lebanon–Carlisle, PA**	NA
164	Columbus, OH	(12.14)	211	New Bedford, MA	(18.65)	–	Hickory–Morganton, NC**	NA
165	Charlotte–Gastonia–Rock Hill, NC–SC	(12.34)	212	Roanoke, VA	(18.99)	–	Houma, LA**	NA
166	Phoenix–Mesa, AZ	(12.42)	213	New London–Norwich, CT–RI	(19.08)	–	Indianapolis, IN**	NA
167	Salt Lake City–Ogden, UT	(12.49)	214	Jersey City, NJ	(19.09)	–	Johnstown, PA**	NA
168	Fitchburg–Leominster, MA	(12.51)	215	Stamford–Norwalk, CT	(19.67)	–	Kansas City, MO–KS**	NA
169	Syracuse, NY	(12.67)	216	San Diego, CA	(19.97)	–	Myrtle Beach, SC**	NA
170	Lakeland–Winter Haven, FL	(12.95)	217	Laredo, TX	(20.10)	–	Newburgh, NY–PA**	NA
171	Flint, MI	(13.00)	218	Waco, TX	(20.71)	–	Omaha, NE**	NA
172	Evansville–Henderson, IN–KY	(13.29)	219	Augusta–Aiken, GA–SC	(21.02)	–	Pittsfield, MA**	NA
173	Racine, WI	(13.32)	220	Atlanta, GA	(21.09)	–	Provo–Orem, UT**	NA
174	Sarasota–Bradenton, FL	(13.40)	221	Wilmington, NC	(21.36)	–	Punta Gorda, FL**	NA
175	New Haven–Meriden, CT	(13.47)	222	Nashua, NH	(22.21)	–	Reading, PA**	NA
176	Bridgeport, CT	(13.68)	223	Abilene, TX	(22.43)	–	Riverside–San Bernardino, CA**	NA
177	Joplin, MO	(13.82)	224	San Antonio, TX	(22.46)	–	Rocky Mount, NC**	NA
178	Toledo, OH	(13.85)	225	Providence–Fall River–Warwick, RI–MA	(22.67)	–	San Luis Obispo–Atascadero, CA**	NA
179	Austin–San Marcos, TX	(13.87)	226	Fort Wayne, IN	(22.88)	–	Scranton–Wilkes-Barre–Hazleton, PA**	NA
180	Wausau, WI	(14.11)	227	El Paso, TX	(23.16)	–	South Bend, IN**	NA
181	Newark, NJ	(14.16)	228	Naples, FL	(23.20)	–	Steubenville–Weirton, OH–WV**	NA
182	Tampa–St. Petersburg–Clearwater, FL	(14.17)	229	Fort Pierce–Port St. Lucie, FL	(23.24)	–	St. Louis, MO–IL**	NA
183	Bergen–Passaic, NJ	(14.20)	230	Ocala, FL	(23.76)	–	Sumter, SC**	NA
184	Huntsville, AL	(14.25)	231	Fayetteville–Springdale–Rogers, AR	(24.50)	–	Tucson, AZ**	NA
185	Shreveport–Bossier City, LA	(14.54)	232	Sherman–Denison, TX	(24.61)	–	West Palm Beach–Boca Raton, FL**	NA
185	Sioux City, IA–NE	(14.54)	233	Odessa–Midland, TX	(24.75)	–	Williamsport, PA**	NA
187	Tacoma, WA	(14.57)	234	Springfield, MO	(25.11)	–	Worcester, MA–CT**	NA
188	Macon, GA	(14.95)	235	Portland, ME	(25.13)	–	Yolo, CA**	NA

Source: Morgan Quitno Corporation using data from U.S. Department of Justice, Federal Bureau of Investigation
   "Crime in the United States 1993" (Uniform Crime Reports, December 4, 1994)
*Property crimes are offenses of burglary, larceny-theft and motor vehicle theft. They consist of taking money or property but there is no force or threat of force against victims.
**Not available.

29. Burglaries in 1993

National Total = 2,834,808 Burglaries*

RANK	METRO AREA	CRIMES	RANK	METRO AREA	CRIMES	RANK	METRO AREA	CRIMES
229	Abilene, TX	1,177	273	Cheyenne, WY	329	26	Fort Worth–Arlington, TX	21,369
94	Akron, OH	5,684	–	Chicago, IL**	NA	37	Fresno, CA	15,056
136	Albany, GA	3,029	151	Chico–Paradise, CA	2,660	227	Gadsden, AL	1,229
–	Albany, NY**	NA	41	Cincinnati, OH–KY–IN	13,669	107	Gainesville, FL	4,462
53	Albuquerque, NM	10,462	196	Clarksville–Hopkinsville, TN–KY	1,682	137	Galveston–Texas City, TX	3,024
218	Alexandria, LA	1,418	–	Cleveland, OH**	NA	86	Gary–Hammond, IN	6,230
256	Altoona, PA	730	105	Colorado Springs, CO	4,497	258	Glens Falls, NY	715
139	Amarillo, TX	2,974	252	Columbia, MO	781	201	Goldsboro, NC	1,620
187	Anchorage, AK	1,880	78	Columbia, SC	6,793	271	Grand Forks, ND–MN	467
114	Ann Arbor, MI	4,012	130	Columbus, GA–AL	3,142	64	Grand Rapids–Muskegon–Holland, MI	9,329
208	Anniston, AL	1,531	31	Columbus, OH	18,127	224	Greeley, CO	1,306
195	Appleton–Oshkosh–Neenah, WI	1,688	93	Corpus Christi, TX	5,750	234	Green Bay, WI	1,084
177	Asheville, NC	2,036	269	Cumberland, MD–WV	490	33	Greensboro–Winston Salem–High Point, NC	17,883
186	Athens, GA	1,892	9	Dallas, TX	38,948	156	Greenville, NC	2,463
5	Atlanta, GA	48,216	239	Danbury, CT	960	52	Greenville–Spartanburg–Anderson, SC	10,508
98	Atlantic City, NJ	5,185	262	Danville, VA	650	254	Hagerstown, MD	755
95	Augusta–Aiken, GA–SC	5,529	80	Daytona Beach, FL	6,659	122	Harrisburg–Lebanon–Carlisle, PA	3,399
45	Austin–San Marcos, TX	12,666	62	Dayton–Springfield, OH	9,478	54	Hartford, CT	10,395
60	Bakersfield, CA	9,892	240	Decatur, AL	956	121	Hickory–Morganton, NC	3,418
13	Baltimore, MD	34,072	28	Denver, CO	20,288	65	Honolulu, HI	9,296
274	Bangor, ME	289	126	Des Moines, IA	3,221	189	Houma, LA	1,856
198	Barnstable–Yarmouth, MA	1,645	6	Detroit, MI	45,741	7	Houston, TX	45,375
49	Baton Rouge, LA	10,934	232	Dothan, AL	1,152	175	Huntington–Ashland, WV–KY–OH	2,072
90	Beaumont–Port Arthur, TX	5,989	257	Dubuque, IA	727	125	Huntsville, AL	3,300
215	Bellingham, WA	1,470	171	Duluth–Superior, MN–WI	2,163	–	Indianapolis, IN**	NA
167	Benton Harbor, MI	2,211	204	Dutchess County, NY	1,581	241	Jackson, MI	949
66	Bergen–Passaic, NJ	9,295	243	Eau Claire, WI	942	68	Jackson, MS	8,977
211	Binghamton, NY	1,495	83	El Paso, TX	6,397	209	Jackson, TN	1,516
48	Birmingham, AL	11,444	219	Elkhart–Goshen, IN	1,388	30	Jacksonville, FL	18,333
270	Bismarck, ND	489	253	Enid, OK	775	192	Jacksonville, NC	1,794
266	Bloomington, IN	591	190	Erie, PA	1,836	228	Janesville–Beloit, WI	1,226
152	Boise, ID	2,583	138	Eugene–Springfield, OR	3,016	73	Jersey City, NJ	7,944
16	Boston, MA–NH	30,253	160	Evansville–Henderson, IN–KY	2,417	140	Johnson City–Kingsport–Bristol, TN–VA	2,972
164	Boulder–Longmont, CO	2,249	251	Fargo–Moorhead, ND–MN	797	244	Johnstown, PA	934
216	Brazoria, TX	1,436	92	Fayetteville, NC	5,767	223	Joplin, MO	1,309
199	Bremerton, WA	1,637	213	Fayetteville–Springdale–Rogers, AR	1,486	96	Kalamazoo–Battle Creek, MI	5,376
91	Bridgeport, CT	5,897	203	Fitchburg–Leominster, MA	1,610	–	Kansas City, MO–KS**	NA
145	Brockton, MA	2,889	85	Flint, MI	6,285	231	Kenosha, WI	1,155
104	Brownsville–Harlingen–San Benito, TX	4,591	264	Florence, AL	607	146	Killeen–Temple, TX	2,853
217	Bryan–College Station, TX	1,433	176	Florence, SC	2,044	260	Kokomo, IN	674
44	Buffalo–Niagara Falls, NY	13,251	226	Fort Collins–Loveland, CO	1,233	272	La Crosse, WI–MN	420
110	Canton–Massillon, OH	4,269	20	Fort Lauderdale, FL	23,520	236	Lafayette, IN	1,034
161	Charleston, WV	2,361	100	Fort Myers–Cape Coral, FL	5,099	123	Lafayette, LA	3,337
81	Charleston–North Charleston, SC	6,613	111	Fort Pierce–Port St. Lucie, FL	4,264	157	Lake Charles, LA	2,432
246	Charlottesville, VA	901	197	Fort Smith, AR–OK	1,670	67	Lakeland–Winter Haven, FL	9,184
25	Charlotte–Gastonia–Rock Hill, NC–SC	21,496	230	Fort Walton Beach, FL	1,160	169	Lancaster, PA	2,171
101	Chattanooga, TN–GA	4,931	127	Fort Wayne, IN	3,210	124	Lansing–East Lansing, MI	3,325

Source: U.S. Department of Justice, Federal Bureau of Investigation
    "Crime in the United States 1993" (Uniform Crime Reports, December 4, 1994)
*Burglary is the unlawful entry of a structure to commit a felony or theft. Attempts are included.
**Not available.

29. Burglaries in 1993 (continued)

National Total = 2,834,808 Burglaries*

RANK	METRO AREA	CRIMES	RANK	METRO AREA	CRIMES	RANK	METRO AREA	CRIMES
188	Laredo, TX	1,875	206	Olympia, WA	1,548	22	Seattle–Bellevue–Everett, WA	23,087
40	Las Vegas, NV–AZ	14,251	–	Omaha, NE**	NA	267	Sheboygan, WI	528
147	Lawrence, MA–NH	2,752	17	Orange County, CA	27,418	233	Sherman–Denison, TX	1,104
221	Lawton, OK	1,351	19	Orlando, FL	24,269	84	Shreveport–Bossier City, LA	6,316
247	Lewiston–Auburn, ME	874	249	Owensboro, KY	821	214	Sioux City, IA–NE	1,477
113	Lexington, KY	4,085	166	Panama City, FL	2,217	238	Sioux Falls, SD	977
170	Lincoln, NE	2,170	10	Philadelphia, PA–NJ	38,034	117	South Bend, IN	3,722
61	Little Rock–North Little Rock, AR	9,571	8	Phoenix–Mesa, AZ	38,976	112	Spokane, WA	4,263
143	Longview–Marshall, TX	2,892	179	Pine Bluff, AR	1,994	82	Springfield, MA	6,400
1	Los Angeles–Long Beach, CA	116,374	42	Pittsburgh, PA	13,530	148	Springfield, MO	2,705
63	Louisville, KY–IN	9,395	255	Pittsfield, MA	747	154	Stamford–Norwalk, CT	2,516
143	Lubbock, TX	2,892	165	Portland, ME	2,240	265	Steubenville–Weirton, OH–WV	606
235	Lynchburg, VA	1,051	35	Portland–Vancouver, OR–WA	17,379	59	Stockton–Lodi, CA	9,948
120	Macon, GA	3,479	56	Providence–Fall River–Warwick, RI–MA	10,100	263	St. Cloud, MN	621
159	Madison, WI	2,425	200	Provo–Orem, UT	1,624	237	St. Joseph, MO	999
205	Manchester, NH	1,566	207	Pueblo, CO	1,544	–	St. Louis, MO–IL**	NA
172	Mansfield, OH	2,144	242	Punta Gorda, FL	948	178	Sumter, SC	2,022
72	McAllen–Edinburg–Mission, TX	8,016	193	Racine, WI	1,754	89	Syracuse, NY	6,028
210	Medford–Ashland, OR	1,497	39	Raleigh–Durham–Chapel Hill, NC	14,265	71	Tacoma, WA	8,403
29	Memphis, TN–AR–MS	19,207	259	Rapid City, SD	679	88	Tallahassee, FL	6,037
131	Merced, CA	3,075	162	Reading, PA	2,357	12	Tampa–St. Petersburg–Clearwater, FL	34,349
4	Miami, FL	52,880	185	Redding, CA	1,915	212	Texarkana, TX–AR	1,492
75	Middlesex–Sommerset–Hunterdon, NJ	7,236	129	Reno, NV	3,158	76	Toledo, OH	7,050
46	Milwaukee–Waukesha, WI	12,090	222	Richland–Kennewick–Pasco, WA	1,334	135	Trenton, NJ	3,030
18	Minneapolis–St. Paul, MN–WI	26,205	55	Richmond–Petersburg, VA	10,244	58	Tucson, AZ	10,001
69	Mobile, AL	8,532	3	Riverside–San Bernardino, CA	54,730	57	Tulsa, OK	10,086
77	Modesto, CA	7,021	194	Roanoke, VA	1,753	191	Tuscaloosa, AL	1,798
74	Monmouth–Ocean, NJ	7,258	250	Rochester, MN	819	149	Tyler, TX	2,699
182	Monroe, LA	1,961	50	Rochester, NY	10,588	180	Utica–Rome, NY	1,990
102	Montgomery, AL	4,822	158	Rocky Mount, NC	2,431	97	Vallejo–Fairfield–Napa, CA	5,212
141	Myrtle Beach, SC	2,954	21	Sacramento, CA	23,360	87	Ventura, CA	6,110
155	Naples, FL	2,512	118	Saginaw–Bay City–Midland, MI	3,713	225	Victoria, TX	1,289
261	Nashua, NH	656	132	Salem, OR	3,066	173	Vineland–Millville–Bridgeton, NJ	2,139
43	Nashville, TN	13,367	115	Salinas, CA	3,876	106	Visalia–Tulare–Porterville, CA	4,495
32	Nassau–Suffolk, NY	17,926	51	Salt Lake City–Ogden, UT	10,559	128	Waco, TX	3,199
150	New Bedford, MA	2,672	245	San Angelo, TX	926	11	Washington, DC–MD–VA–WV	36,255
79	New Haven–Meriden, CT	6,742	23	San Antonio, TX	22,074	168	Waterbury, CT	2,191
181	New London–Norwich, CT–RI	1,969	14	San Diego, CA	32,027	220	Waterloo–Cedar Falls, IA	1,369
27	New Orleans, LA	20,686	34	San Francisco, CA	17,814	268	Wausau, WI	502
2	New York, NY	106,706	47	San Jose, CA	11,806	–	West Palm Beach–Boca Raton, FL**	NA
24	Newark, NJ	21,621	183	San Luis Obispo–Atascadero, CA	1,949	202	Wichita Falls, TX	1,618
163	Newburgh, NY–PA	2,348	109	Santa Barbara–Santa Maria–Lompoc, CA	4,311	248	Williamsport, PA	823
38	Norfolk–Va Beach–Newport News, VA–NC	14,890	153	Santa Cruz–Watsonville, CA	2,539	134	Wilmington, NC	3,040
15	Oakland, CA	30,798	103	Santa Rosa, CA	4,792	99	Worcester, MA–CT	5,116
133	Ocala, FL	3,052	70	Sarasota–Bradenton, FL	8,491	119	Yakima, WA	3,547
116	Odessa–Midland, TX	3,739	108	Savannah, GA	4,398	174	Yolo, CA	2,105
36	Oklahoma City, OK	15,599	142	Scranton–Wilkes-Barre–Hazleton, PA	2,946	184	Yuba City, CA	1,946

Source: U.S. Department of Justice, Federal Bureau of Investigation
   "Crime in the United States 1993" (Uniform Crime Reports, December 4, 1994)
*Burglary is the unlawful entry of a structure to commit a felony or theft. Attempts are included.
**Not available.

29. Burglaries in 1993 (continued)

National Total = 2,834,808 Burglaries*

RANK	METRO AREA	CRIMES	RANK	METRO AREA	CRIMES	RANK	METRO AREA	CRIMES
1	Los Angeles–Long Beach, CA	116,374	48	Birmingham, AL	11,444	95	Augusta–Aiken, GA–SC	5,529
2	New York, NY	106,706	49	Baton Rouge, LA	10,934	96	Kalamazoo–Battle Creek, MI	5,376
3	Riverside–San Bernardino, CA	54,730	50	Rochester, NY	10,588	97	Vallejo–Fairfield–Napa, CA	5,212
4	Miami, FL	52,880	51	Salt Lake City–Ogden, UT	10,559	98	Atlantic City, NJ	5,185
5	Atlanta, GA	48,216	52	Greenville–Spartanburg–Anderson, SC	10,508	99	Worcester, MA–CT	5,116
6	Detroit, MI	45,741	53	Albuquerque, NM	10,462	100	Fort Myers–Cape Coral, FL	5,099
7	Houston, TX	45,375	54	Hartford, CT	10,395	101	Chattanooga, TN–GA	4,931
8	Phoenix–Mesa, AZ	38,976	55	Richmond–Petersburg, VA	10,244	102	Montgomery, AL	4,822
9	Dallas, TX	38,948	56	Providence–Fall River–Warwick, RI–MA	10,100	103	Santa Rosa, CA	4,792
10	Philadelphia, PA–NJ	38,034	57	Tulsa, OK	10,086	104	Brownsville–Harlingen–San Benito, TX	4,591
11	Washington, DC–MD–VA–WV	36,255	58	Tucson, AZ	10,001	105	Colorado Springs, CO	4,497
12	Tampa–St. Petersburg–Clearwater, FL	34,349	59	Stockton–Lodi, CA	9,948	106	Visalia–Tulare–Porterville, CA	4,495
13	Baltimore, MD	34,072	60	Bakersfield, CA	9,892	107	Gainesville, FL	4,462
14	San Diego, CA	32,027	61	Little Rock–North Little Rock, AR	9,571	108	Savannah, GA	4,398
15	Oakland, CA	30,798	62	Dayton–Springfield, OH	9,478	109	Santa Barbara–Santa Maria–Lompoc, CA	4,311
16	Boston, MA–NH	30,253	63	Louisville, KY–IN	9,395	110	Canton–Massillon, OH	4,269
17	Orange County, CA	27,418	64	Grand Rapids–Muskegon–Holland, MI	9,329	111	Fort Pierce–Port St. Lucie, FL	4,264
18	Minneapolis–St. Paul, MN–WI	26,205	65	Honolulu, HI	9,296	112	Spokane, WA	4,263
19	Orlando, FL	24,269	66	Bergen–Passaic, NJ	9,295	113	Lexington, KY	4,085
20	Fort Lauderdale, FL	23,520	67	Lakeland–Winter Haven, FL	9,184	114	Ann Arbor, MI	4,012
21	Sacramento, CA	23,360	68	Jackson, MS	8,977	115	Salinas, CA	3,876
22	Seattle–Bellevue–Everett, WA	23,087	69	Mobile, AL	8,532	116	Odessa–Midland, TX	3,739
23	San Antonio, TX	22,074	70	Sarasota–Bradenton, FL	8,491	117	South Bend, IN	3,722
24	Newark, NJ	21,621	71	Tacoma, WA	8,403	118	Saginaw–Bay City–Midland, MI	3,713
25	Charlotte–Gastonia–Rock Hill, NC–SC	21,496	72	McAllen–Edinburg–Mission, TX	8,016	119	Yakima, WA	3,547
26	Fort Worth–Arlington, TX	21,369	73	Jersey City, NJ	7,944	120	Macon, GA	3,479
27	New Orleans, LA	20,686	74	Monmouth–Ocean, NJ	7,258	121	Hickory–Morganton, NC	3,418
28	Denver, CO	20,288	75	Middlesex–Somerset–Hunterdon, NJ	7,236	122	Harrisburg–Lebanon–Carlisle, PA	3,399
29	Memphis, TN–AR–MS	19,207	76	Toledo, OH	7,050	123	Lafayette, LA	3,337
30	Jacksonville, FL	18,333	77	Modesto, CA	7,021	124	Lansing–East Lansing, MI	3,325
31	Columbus, OH	18,127	78	Columbia, SC	6,793	125	Huntsville, AL	3,300
32	Nassau–Suffolk, NY	17,926	79	New Haven–Meriden, CT	6,742	126	Des Moines, IA	3,221
33	Greensboro–Winston Salem–High Point, NC	17,883	80	Daytona Beach, FL	6,659	127	Fort Wayne, IN	3,210
34	San Francisco, CA	17,814	81	Charleston–North Charleston, SC	6,613	128	Waco, TX	3,199
35	Portland–Vancouver, OR–WA	17,379	82	Springfield, MA	6,400	129	Reno, NV	3,158
36	Oklahoma City, OK	15,599	83	El Paso, TX	6,397	130	Columbus, GA–AL	3,142
37	Fresno, CA	15,056	84	Shreveport–Bossier City, LA	6,316	131	Merced, CA	3,075
38	Norfolk–Va Beach–Newport News, VA–NC	14,890	85	Flint, MI	6,285	132	Salem, OR	3,066
39	Raleigh–Durham–Chapel Hill, NC	14,265	86	Gary–Hammond, IN	6,230	133	Ocala, FL	3,052
40	Las Vegas, NV–AZ	14,251	87	Ventura, CA	6,110	134	Wilmington, NC	3,040
41	Cincinnati, OH–KY–IN	13,669	88	Tallahassee, FL	6,037	135	Trenton, NJ	3,030
42	Pittsburgh, PA	13,530	89	Syracuse, NY	6,028	136	Albany, GA	3,029
43	Nashville, TN	13,367	90	Beaumont–Port Arthur, TX	5,989	137	Galveston–Texas City, TX	3,024
44	Buffalo–Niagara Falls, NY	13,251	91	Bridgeport, CT	5,897	138	Eugene–Springfield, OR	3,016
45	Austin–San Marcos, TX	12,666	92	Fayetteville, NC	5,767	139	Amarillo, TX	2,974
46	Milwaukee–Waukesha, WI	12,090	93	Corpus Christi, TX	5,750	140	Johnson City–Kingsport–Bristol, TN–VA	2,972
47	San Jose, CA	11,806	94	Akron, OH	5,684	141	Myrtle Beach, SC	2,954

Source: U.S. Department of Justice, Federal Bureau of Investigation
   "Crime in the United States 1993" (Uniform Crime Reports, December 4, 1994)
*Burglary is the unlawful entry of a structure to commit a felony or theft. Attempts are included.
**Not available.

29. Burglaries in 1993 (continued)

National Total = 2,834,808 Burglaries*

RANK	METRO AREA	CRIMES	RANK	METRO AREA	CRIMES	RANK	METRO AREA	CRIMES
142	Scranton–Wilkes-Barre–Hazleton, PA	2,946	189	Houma, LA	1,856	236	Lafayette, IN	1,034
143	Longview–Marshall, TX	2,892	190	Erie, PA	1,836	237	St. Joseph, MO	999
143	Lubbock, TX	2,892	191	Tuscaloosa, AL	1,798	238	Sioux Falls, SD	977
145	Brockton, MA	2,889	192	Jacksonville, NC	1,794	239	Danbury, CT	960
146	Killeen–Temple, TX	2,853	193	Racine, WI	1,754	240	Decatur, AL	956
147	Lawrence, MA–NH	2,752	194	Roanoke, VA	1,753	241	Jackson, MI	949
148	Springfield, MO	2,705	195	Appleton–Oshkosh–Neenah, WI	1,688	242	Punta Gorda, FL	948
149	Tyler, TX	2,699	196	Clarksville–Hopkinsville, TN–KY	1,682	243	Eau Claire, WI	942
150	New Bedford, MA	2,672	197	Fort Smith, AR–OK	1,670	244	Johnstown, PA	934
151	Chico–Paradise, CA	2,660	198	Barnstable–Yarmouth, MA	1,645	245	San Angelo, TX	926
152	Boise, ID	2,583	199	Bremerton, WA	1,637	246	Charlottesville, VA	901
153	Santa Cruz–Watsonville, CA	2,539	200	Provo–Orem, UT	1,624	247	Lewiston–Auburn, ME	874
154	Stamford–Norwalk, CT	2,516	201	Goldsboro, NC	1,620	248	Williamsport, PA	823
155	Naples, FL	2,512	202	Wichita Falls, TX	1,618	249	Owensboro, KY	821
156	Greenville, NC	2,463	203	Fitchburg–Leominster, MA	1,610	250	Rochester, MN	819
157	Lake Charles, LA	2,432	204	Dutchess County, NY	1,581	251	Fargo–Moorhead, ND–MN	797
158	Rocky Mount, NC	2,431	205	Manchester, NH	1,566	252	Columbia, MO	781
159	Madison, WI	2,425	206	Olympia, WA	1,548	253	Enid, OK	775
160	Evansville–Henderson, IN–KY	2,417	207	Pueblo, CO	1,544	254	Hagerstown, MD	755
161	Charleston, WV	2,361	208	Anniston, AL	1,531	255	Pittsfield, MA	747
162	Reading, PA	2,357	209	Jackson, TN	1,516	256	Altoona, PA	730
163	Newburgh, NY–PA	2,348	210	Medford–Ashland, OR	1,497	257	Dubuque, IA	727
164	Boulder–Longmont, CO	2,249	211	Binghamton, NY	1,495	258	Glens Falls, NY	715
165	Portland, ME	2,240	212	Texarkana, TX–AR	1,492	259	Rapid City, SD	679
166	Panama City, FL	2,217	213	Fayetteville–Springdale–Rogers, AR	1,486	260	Kokomo, IN	674
167	Benton Harbor, MI	2,211	214	Sioux City, IA–NE	1,477	261	Nashua, NH	656
168	Waterbury, CT	2,191	215	Bellingham, WA	1,470	262	Danville, VA	650
169	Lancaster, PA	2,171	216	Brazoria, TX	1,436	263	St. Cloud, MN	621
170	Lincoln, NE	2,170	217	Bryan–College Station, TX	1,433	264	Florence, AL	607
171	Duluth–Superior, MN–WI	2,163	218	Alexandria, LA	1,418	265	Steubenville–Weirton, OH–WV	606
172	Mansfield, OH	2,144	219	Elkhart–Goshen, IN	1,388	266	Bloomington, IN	591
173	Vineland–Millville–Bridgeton, NJ	2,139	220	Waterloo–Cedar Falls, IA	1,369	267	Sheboygan, WI	528
174	Yolo, CA	2,105	221	Lawton, OK	1,351	268	Wausau, WI	502
175	Huntington–Ashland, WV–KY–OH	2,072	222	Richland–Kennewick–Pasco, WA	1,334	269	Cumberland, MD–WV	490
176	Florence, SC	2,044	223	Joplin, MO	1,309	270	Bismarck, ND	489
177	Asheville, NC	2,036	224	Greeley, CO	1,306	271	Grand Forks, ND–MN	467
178	Sumter, SC	2,022	225	Victoria, TX	1,289	272	La Crosse, WI–MN	420
179	Pine Bluff, AR	1,994	226	Fort Collins–Loveland, CO	1,233	273	Cheyenne, WY	329
180	Utica–Rome, NY	1,990	227	Gadsden, AL	1,229	274	Bangor, ME	289
181	New London–Norwich, CT–RI	1,969	228	Janesville–Beloit, WI	1,226	–	Albany, NY**	NA
182	Monroe, LA	1,961	229	Abilene, TX	1,177	–	Chicago, IL**	NA
183	San Luis Obispo–Atascadero, CA	1,949	230	Fort Walton Beach, FL	1,160	–	Cleveland, OH**	NA
184	Yuba City, CA	1,946	231	Kenosha, WI	1,155	–	Indianapolis, IN**	NA
185	Redding, CA	1,915	232	Dothan, AL	1,152	–	Kansas City, MO–KS**	NA
186	Athens, GA	1,892	233	Sherman–Denison, TX	1,104	–	Omaha, NE**	NA
187	Anchorage, AK	1,880	234	Green Bay, WI	1,084	–	St. Louis, MO–IL**	NA
188	Laredo, TX	1,875	235	Lynchburg, VA	1,051	–	West Palm Beach–Boca Raton, FL**	NA

Source: U.S. Department of Justice, Federal Bureau of Investigation
   "Crime in the United States 1993" (Uniform Crime Reports, December 4, 1994)
Burglary is the unlawful entry of a structure to commit a felony or theft. Attempts are included.
**Not available.

30. Burglary Rate in 1993

National Rate = 1,099.2 Burglaries per 100,000 Population*

RANK	METRO AREA	RATE	RANK	METRO AREA	RATE	RANK	METRO AREA	RATE
171	Abilene, TX	957.5	267	Cheyenne, WY	427.9	77	Fort Worth-Arlington, TX	1,388.7
197	Akron, OH	850.9	–	Chicago, IL**	NA	18	Fresno, CA	1,852.2
2	Albany, GA	2,573.9	76	Chico-Paradise, CA	1,397.8	103	Gadsden, AL	1,222.2
–	Albany, NY**	NA	191	Cincinnati, OH-KY-IN	870.0	4	Gainesville, FL	2,322.0
33	Albuquerque, NM	1,661.1	177	Clarksville-Hopkinsville, TN-KY	932.3	88	Galveston-Texas City, TX	1,300.3
143	Alexandria, LA	1,082.1	–	Cleveland, OH**	NA	157	Gary-Hammond, IN	1,000.4
255	Altoona, PA	553.5	152	Colorado Springs, CO	1,037.5	248	Glens Falls, NY	588.4
58	Amarillo, TX	1,522.0	232	Columbia, MO	662.6	61	Goldsboro, NC	1,480.4
217	Anchorage, AK	749.8	68	Columbia, SC	1,422.2	265	Grand Forks, ND-MN	450.5
205	Ann Arbor, MI	796.2	125	Columbus, GA-AL	1,128.9	168	Grand Rapids-Muskegon-Holland, MI	962.9
89	Anniston, AL	1,299.9	90	Columbus, OH	1,293.5	176	Greeley, CO	934.0
259	Appleton-Oshkosh-Neenah, WI	511.6	54	Corpus Christi, TX	1,556.2	256	Green Bay, WI	533.5
155	Asheville, NC	1,014.9	263	Cumberland, MD-WV	478.5	38	Greensboro-Winston Salem-High Point, NC	1,631.5
101	Athens, GA	1,224.9	72	Dallas, TX	1,415.7	6	Greenville, NC	2,196.2
60	Atlanta, GA	1,494.8	247	Danbury, CT	590.4	106	Greenville-Spartanburg-Anderson, SC	1,216.7
48	Atlantic City, NJ	1,577.3	249	Danville, VA	585.7	246	Hagerstown, MD	595.9
102	Augusta-Aiken, GA-SC	1,224.6	53	Daytona Beach, FL	1,556.3	252	Harrisburg-Lebanon-Carlisle, PA	561.9
79	Austin-San Marcos, TX	1,378.6	164	Dayton-Springfield, OH	978.9	161	Hartford, CT	986.4
32	Bakersfield, CA	1,666.2	222	Decatur, AL	698.9	128	Hickory-Morganton, NC	1,124.4
78	Baltimore, MD	1,386.6	119	Denver, CO	1,154.2	145	Honolulu, HI	1,061.8
268	Bangor, ME	427.4	207	Des Moines, IA	789.1	159	Houma, LA	991.4
111	Barnstable-Yarmouth, MA	1,199.7	148	Detroit, MI	1,056.2	94	Houston, TX	1,260.1
10	Baton Rouge, LA	1,993.9	195	Dothan, AL	854.2	238	Huntington-Ashland, WV-KY-OH	653.3
46	Beaumont-Port Arthur, TX	1,588.2	201	Dubuque, IA	829.8	147	Huntsville, AL	1,058.7
150	Bellingham, WA	1,043.2	188	Duluth-Superior, MN-WI	888.2	–	Indianapolis, IN**	NA
82	Benton Harbor, MI	1,363.1	245	Dutchess County, NY	598.6	242	Jackson, MI	622.5
221	Bergen-Passaic, NJ	714.5	231	Eau Claire, WI	667.4	7	Jackson, MS	2,193.7
254	Binghamton, NY	557.9	158	El Paso, TX	998.2	17	Jackson, TN	1,862.2
86	Birmingham, AL	1,316.4	192	Elkhart-Goshen, IN	862.8	15	Jacksonville, FL	1,897.0
251	Bismarck, ND	567.4	81	Enid, OK	1,364.0	104	Jacksonville, NC	1,221.8
257	Bloomington, IN	526.8	236	Erie, PA	653.7	196	Janesville-Beloit, WI	851.1
208	Boise, ID	783.6	154	Eugene-Springfield, OR	1,016.1	69	Jersey City, NJ	1,420.8
187	Boston, MA-NH	891.6	198	Evansville-Henderson, IN-KY	846.4	234	Johnson City-Kingsport-Bristol, TN-VA	659.1
182	Boulder-Longmont, CO	917.5	260	Fargo-Moorhead, ND-MN	503.3	272	Johnstown, PA	386.2
223	Brazoria, TX	690.8	9	Fayetteville, NC	2,046.9	173	Joplin, MO	944.2
214	Bremerton, WA	760.1	239	Fayetteville-Springdale-Rogers, AR	650.2	100	Kalamazoo-Battle Creek, MI	1,226.3
87	Bridgeport, CT	1,302.2	116	Fitchburg-Leominster, MA	1,175.3	–	Kansas City, MO-KS**	NA
117	Brockton, MA	1,173.3	65	Flint, MI	1,443.4	194	Kenosha, WI	854.4
42	Brownsville-Harlingen-San Benito, TX	1,615.6	266	Florence, AL	446.9	135	Killeen-Temple, TX	1,097.9
129	Bryan-College Station, TX	1,122.9	28	Florence, SC	1,704.6	229	Kokomo, IN	677.1
134	Buffalo-Niagara Falls, NY	1,102.7	244	Fort Collins-Loveland, CO	604.7	274	La Crosse, WI-MN	352.6
144	Canton-Massillon, OH	1,062.3	22	Fort Lauderdale, FL	1,781.6	243	Lafayette, IN	621.2
179	Charleston, WV	928.4	67	Fort Myers-Cape Coral, FL	1,427.6	174	Lafayette, LA	941.0
99	Charleston-North Charleston, SC	1,237.4	47	Fort Pierce-Port St. Lucie, FL	1,583.6	74	Lake Charles, LA	1,412.8
233	Charlottesville, VA	660.2	185	Fort Smith, AR-OK	914.3	8	Lakeland-Winter Haven, FL	2,160.6
25	Charlotte-Gastonia-Rock Hill, NC-SC	1,746.3	218	Fort Walton Beach, FL	745.2	262	Lancaster, PA	497.6
127	Chattanooga, TN-GA	1,125.3	224	Fort Wayne, IN	686.3	215	Lansing-East Lansing, MI	758.3

Source: U.S. Department of Justice, Federal Bureau of Investigation
   "Crime in the United States 1993" (Uniform Crime Reports, December 4, 1994)
*Burglary is the unlawful entry of a structure to commit a felony or theft. Attempts are included.
**Not available.

30. Burglary Rate in 1993 (continued)

National Rate = 1,099.2 Burglaries per 100,000 Population*

RANK	METRO AREA	RATE	RANK	METRO AREA	RATE	RANK	METRO AREA	RATE
97	Laredo, TX	1,238.6	193	Olympia, WA	858.0	133	Seattle–Bellevue–Everett, WA	1,112.1
73	Las Vegas, NV–AZ	1,413.9	–	Omaha, NE**	NA	261	Sheboygan, WI	498.2
178	Lawrence, MA–NH	929.9	137	Orange County, CA	1,092.3	121	Sherman–Denison, TX	1,138.8
132	Lawton, OK	1,112.5	19	Orlando, FL	1,833.5	30	Shreveport–Bossier City, LA	1,681.4
199	Lewiston–Auburn, ME	839.6	184	Owensboro, KY	915.9	95	Sioux City, IA–NE	1,256.3
130	Lexington, KY	1,121.6	39	Panama City, FL	1,630.7	235	Sioux Falls, SD	658.5
162	Lincoln, NE	984.6	210	Philadelphia, PA–NJ	765.4	63	South Bend, IN	1,471.4
21	Little Rock–North Little Rock, AR	1,798.5	41	Phoenix–Mesa, AZ	1,628.6	136	Spokane, WA	1,094.5
71	Longview–Marshall, TX	1,418.7	5	Pine Bluff, AR	2,309.9	113	Springfield, MA	1,185.8
92	Los Angeles–Long Beach, CA	1,272.4	253	Pittsburgh, PA	558.2	166	Springfield, MO	973.4
169	Louisville, KY–IN	961.9	216	Pittsfield, MA	758.2	212	Stamford–Norwalk, CT	763.3
93	Lubbock, TX	1,267.0	170	Portland, ME	958.2	269	Steubenville–Weirton, OH–WV	425.5
258	Lynchburg, VA	521.8	146	Portland–Vancouver, OR–WA	1,059.1	11	Stockton–Lodi, CA	1,953.5
120	Macon, GA	1,140.8	149	Providence–Fall River–Warwick, RI–MA	1,055.6	271	St. Cloud, MN	402.3
240	Madison, WI	643.8	250	Provo–Orem, UT	574.9	156	St. Joseph, MO	1,011.2
175	Manchester, NH	938.4	109	Pueblo, CO	1,212.3	–	St. Louis, MO–IL**	NA
107	Mansfield, OH	1,214.2	208	Punta Gorda, FL	783.6	14	Sumter, SC	1,898.2
16	McAllen–Edinburg–Mission, TX	1,867.5	167	Racine, WI	968.4	204	Syracuse, NY	796.4
172	Medford–Ashland, OR	952.3	55	Raleigh–Durham–Chapel Hill, NC	1,545.3	85	Tacoma, WA	1,325.7
20	Memphis, TN–AR–MS	1,832.1	206	Rapid City, SD	790.9	3	Tallahassee, FL	2,426.1
44	Merced, CA	1,609.6	226	Reading, PA	683.9	45	Tampa–St. Petersburg–Clearwater, FL	1,606.7
1	Miami, FL	2,595.3	110	Redding, CA	1,202.8	108	Texarkana, TX–AR	1,212.7
225	Middlesex–Sommerset–Hunterdon, NJ	686.1	124	Reno, NV	1,131.1	122	Toledo, OH	1,138.6
200	Milwaukee–Waukesha, WI	831.7	203	Richland–Kennewick–Pasco, WA	811.4	181	Trenton, NJ	917.7
160	Minneapolis–St. Paul, MN–WI	989.5	126	Richmond–Petersburg, VA	1,126.1	75	Tucson, AZ	1,410.7
29	Mobile, AL	1,701.5	12	Riverside–San Bernardino, CA	1,928.8	80	Tulsa, OK	1,367.3
23	Modesto, CA	1,758.5	213	Roanoke, VA	763.1	118	Tuscaloosa, AL	1,156.6
220	Monmouth–Ocean, NJ	718.4	219	Rochester, MN	733.3	27	Tyler, TX	1,714.5
83	Monroe, LA	1,348.2	165	Rochester, NY	974.5	241	Utica–Rome, NY	626.6
52	Montgomery, AL	1,558.2	26	Rocky Mount, NC	1,744.0	141	Vallejo–Fairfield–Napa, CA	1,085.9
13	Myrtle Beach, SC	1,918.1	40	Sacramento, CA	1,630.1	189	Ventura, CA	880.9
59	Naples, FL	1,503.1	180	Saginaw–Bay City–Midland, MI	918.1	35	Victoria, TX	1,640.8
270	Nashua, NH	409.0	153	Salem, OR	1,031.7	56	Vineland–Millville–Bridgeton, NJ	1,532.9
91	Nashville, TN	1,287.1	151	Salinas, CA	1,041.7	84	Visalia–Tulare–Porterville, CA	1,343.9
227	Nassau–Suffolk, NY	682.1	186	Salt Lake City–Ogden, UT	911.5	37	Waco, TX	1,637.8
57	New Bedford, MA	1,530.3	183	San Angelo, TX	916.3	202	Washington, DC–MD–VA–WV	824.2
112	New Haven–Meriden, CT	1,197.9	50	San Antonio, TX	1,570.3	115	Waterbury, CT	1,182.0
237	New London–Norwich, CT–RI	653.5	105	San Diego, CA	1,218.8	139	Waterloo–Cedar Falls, IA	1,087.5
36	New Orleans, LA	1,640.5	142	San Francisco, CA	1,084.4	273	Wausau, WI	362.8
98	New York, NY	1,237.9	211	San Jose, CA	764.6	–	West Palm Beach–Boca Raton, FL**	NA
131	Newark, NJ	1,115.8	190	San Luis Obispo–Atascadero, CA	874.7	96	Wichita Falls, TX	1,238.9
230	Newburgh, NY–PA	670.9	123	Santa Barbara–Santa Maria–Lompoc, CA	1,136.4	228	Williamsport, PA	680.2
163	Norfolk–Va Beach–Newport News, VA–NC	980.0	138	Santa Cruz–Watsonville, CA	1,088.1	34	Wilmington, NC	1,642.0
70	Oakland, CA	1,419.2	114	Santa Rosa, CA	1,182.9	140	Worcester, MA–CT	1,086.7
64	Ocala, FL	1,446.4	31	Sarasota–Bradenton, FL	1,678.0	24	Yakima, WA	1,753.1
51	Odessa–Midland, TX	1,568.5	43	Savannah, GA	1,610.8	66	Yolo, CA	1,438.9
49	Oklahoma City, OK	1,573.3	264	Scranton–Wilkes-Barre–Hazleton, PA	459.3	62	Yuba City, CA	1,478.0

Source: U.S. Department of Justice, Federal Bureau of Investigation
   "Crime in the United States 1993" (Uniform Crime Reports, December 4, 1994)
Burglary is the unlawful entry of a structure to commit a felony or theft. Attempts are included.
**Not available.*

30. Burglary Rate in 1993 (continued)

National Rate = 1,099.2 Burglaries per 100,000 Population*

RANK	METRO AREA	RATE	RANK	METRO AREA	RATE	RANK	METRO AREA	RATE
1	Miami, FL	2,595.3	48	Atlantic City, NJ	1,577.3	95	Sioux City, IA–NE	1,256.3
2	Albany, GA	2,573.9	49	Oklahoma City, OK	1,573.3	96	Wichita Falls, TX	1,238.9
3	Tallahassee, FL	2,426.1	50	San Antonio, TX	1,570.3	97	Laredo, TX	1,238.6
4	Gainesville, FL	2,322.0	51	Odessa–Midland, TX	1,568.5	98	New York, NY	1,237.9
5	Pine Bluff, AR	2,309.9	52	Montgomery, AL	1,558.2	99	Charleston–North Charleston, SC	1,237.4
6	Greenville, NC	2,196.2	53	Daytona Beach, FL	1,556.3	100	Kalamazoo–Battle Creek, MI	1,226.3
7	Jackson, MS	2,193.7	54	Corpus Christi, TX	1,556.2	101	Athens, GA	1,224.9
8	Lakeland–Winter Haven, FL	2,160.6	55	Raleigh–Durham–Chapel Hill, NC	1,545.3	102	Augusta–Aiken, GA–SC	1,224.6
9	Fayetteville, NC	2,046.9	56	Vineland–Millville–Bridgeton, NJ	1,532.9	103	Gadsden, AL	1,222.2
10	Baton Rouge, LA	1,993.9	57	New Bedford, MA	1,530.3	104	Jacksonville, NC	1,221.8
11	Stockton–Lodi, CA	1,953.5	58	Amarillo, TX	1,522.0	105	San Diego, CA	1,218.8
12	Riverside–San Bernardino, CA	1,928.8	59	Naples, FL	1,503.1	106	Greenville–Spartanburg–Anderson, SC	1,216.7
13	Myrtle Beach, SC	1,918.1	60	Atlanta, GA	1,494.8	107	Mansfield, OH	1,214.2
14	Sumter, SC	1,898.2	61	Goldsboro, NC	1,480.4	108	Texarkana, TX–AR	1,212.7
15	Jacksonville, FL	1,897.0	62	Yuba City, CA	1,478.0	109	Pueblo, CO	1,212.3
16	McAllen–Edinburg–Mission, TX	1,867.5	63	South Bend, IN	1,471.4	110	Redding, CA	1,202.8
17	Jackson, TN	1,862.2	64	Ocala, FL	1,446.4	111	Barnstable–Yarmouth, MA	1,199.7
18	Fresno, CA	1,852.2	65	Flint, MI	1,443.4	112	New Haven–Meriden, CT	1,197.9
19	Orlando, FL	1,833.5	66	Yolo, CA	1,438.9	113	Springfield, MA	1,185.8
20	Memphis, TN–AR–MS	1,832.1	67	Fort Myers–Cape Coral, FL	1,427.6	114	Santa Rosa, CA	1,182.9
21	Little Rock–North Little Rock, AR	1,798.5	68	Columbia, SC	1,422.2	115	Waterbury, CT	1,182.0
22	Fort Lauderdale, FL	1,781.6	69	Jersey City, NJ	1,420.8	116	Fitchburg–Leominster, MA	1,175.3
23	Modesto, CA	1,758.5	70	Oakland, CA	1,419.2	117	Brockton, MA	1,173.3
24	Yakima, WA	1,753.1	71	Longview–Marshall, TX	1,418.7	118	Tuscaloosa, AL	1,156.6
25	Charlotte–Gastonia–Rock Hill, NC–SC	1,746.3	72	Dallas, TX	1,415.7	119	Denver, CO	1,154.2
26	Rocky Mount, NC	1,744.0	73	Las Vegas, NV–AZ	1,413.9	120	Macon, GA	1,140.8
27	Tyler, TX	1,714.5	74	Lake Charles, LA	1,412.8	121	Sherman–Denison, TX	1,138.8
28	Florence, SC	1,704.6	75	Tucson, AZ	1,410.7	122	Toledo, OH	1,138.6
29	Mobile, AL	1,701.5	76	Chico–Paradise, CA	1,397.8	123	Santa Barbara–Santa Maria–Lompoc, CA	1,136.4
30	Shreveport–Bossier City, LA	1,681.4	77	Fort Worth–Arlington, TX	1,388.7	124	Reno, NV	1,131.1
31	Sarasota–Bradenton, FL	1,678.0	78	Baltimore, MD	1,386.6	125	Columbus, GA–AL	1,128.9
32	Bakersfield, CA	1,666.2	79	Austin–San Marcos, TX	1,378.6	126	Richmond–Petersburg, VA	1,126.1
33	Albuquerque, NM	1,661.1	80	Tulsa, OK	1,367.3	127	Chattanooga, TN–GA	1,125.3
34	Wilmington, NC	1,642.0	81	Enid, OK	1,364.0	128	Hickory–Morganton, NC	1,124.4
35	Victoria, TX	1,640.8	82	Benton Harbor, MI	1,363.1	129	Bryan–College Station, TX	1,122.9
36	New Orleans, LA	1,640.5	83	Monroe, LA	1,348.2	130	Lexington, KY	1,121.6
37	Waco, TX	1,637.8	84	Visalia–Tulare–Porterville, CA	1,343.9	131	Newark, NJ	1,115.8
38	Greensboro–Winston Salem–High Point, NC	1,631.5	85	Tacoma, WA	1,325.7	132	Lawton, OK	1,112.5
39	Panama City, FL	1,630.7	86	Birmingham, AL	1,316.4	133	Seattle–Bellevue–Everett, WA	1,112.1
40	Sacramento, CA	1,630.1	87	Bridgeport, CT	1,302.2	134	Buffalo–Niagara Falls, NY	1,102.7
41	Phoenix–Mesa, AZ	1,628.6	88	Galveston–Texas City, TX	1,300.3	135	Killeen–Temple, TX	1,097.9
42	Brownsville–Harlingen–San Benito, TX	1,615.6	89	Anniston, AL	1,299.9	136	Spokane, WA	1,094.5
43	Savannah, GA	1,610.8	90	Columbus, OH	1,293.5	137	Orange County, CA	1,092.3
44	Merced, CA	1,609.6	91	Nashville, TN	1,287.1	138	Santa Cruz–Watsonville, CA	1,088.1
45	Tampa–St. Petersburg–Clearwater, FL	1,606.7	92	Los Angeles–Long Beach, CA	1,272.4	139	Waterloo–Cedar Falls, IA	1,087.5
46	Beaumont–Port Arthur, TX	1,588.2	93	Lubbock, TX	1,267.0	140	Worcester, MA–CT	1,086.7
47	Fort Pierce–Port St. Lucie, FL	1,583.6	94	Houston, TX	1,260.1	141	Vallejo–Fairfield–Napa, CA	1,085.9

Source: U.S. Department of Justice, Federal Bureau of Investigation
"Crime in the United States 1993" (Uniform Crime Reports, December 4, 1994)
*Burglary is the unlawful entry of a structure to commit a felony or theft. Attempts are included.
**Not available.

30. Burglary Rate in 1993 (continued)

National Rate = 1,099.2 Burglaries per 100,000 Population*

RANK	METRO AREA	RATE	RANK	METRO AREA	RATE	RANK	METRO AREA	RATE
142	San Francisco, CA	1,084.4	189	Ventura, CA	880.9	236	Erie, PA	653.7
143	Alexandria, LA	1,082.1	190	San Luis Obispo-Atascadero, CA	874.7	237	New London-Norwich, CT-RI	653.5
144	Canton-Massillon, OH	1,062.3	191	Cincinnati, OH-KY-IN	870.0	238	Huntington-Ashland, WV-KY-OH	653.3
145	Honolulu, HI	1,061.8	192	Elkhart-Goshen, IN	862.8	239	Fayetteville-Springdale-Rogers, AR	650.2
146	Portland-Vancouver, OR-WA	1,059.1	193	Olympia, WA	858.0	240	Madison, WI	643.8
147	Huntsville, AL	1,058.7	194	Kenosha, WI	854.4	241	Utica-Rome, NY	626.6
148	Detroit, MI	1,056.2	195	Dothan, AL	854.2	242	Jackson, MI	622.5
149	Providence-Fall River-Warwick, RI-MA	1,055.6	196	Janesville-Beloit, WI	851.1	243	Lafayette, IN	621.2
150	Bellingham, WA	1,043.2	197	Akron, OH	850.9	244	Fort Collins-Loveland, CO	604.7
151	Salinas, CA	1,041.7	198	Evansville-Henderson, IN-KY	846.4	245	Dutchess County, NY	598.6
152	Colorado Springs, CO	1,037.5	199	Lewiston-Auburn, ME	839.6	246	Hagerstown, MD	595.9
153	Salem, OR	1,031.7	200	Milwaukee-Waukesha, WI	831.7	247	Danbury, CT	590.4
154	Eugene-Springfield, OR	1,016.1	201	Dubuque, IA	829.8	248	Glens Falls, NY	588.4
155	Asheville, NC	1,014.9	202	Washington, DC-MD-VA-WV	824.2	249	Danville, VA	585.7
156	St. Joseph, MO	1,011.2	203	Richland-Kennewick-Pasco, WA	811.4	250	Provo-Orem, UT	574.9
157	Gary-Hammond, IN	1,000.4	204	Syracuse, NY	796.4	251	Bismarck, ND	567.4
158	El Paso, TX	998.2	205	Ann Arbor, MI	796.2	252	Harrisburg-Lebanon-Carlisle, PA	561.9
159	Houma, LA	991.4	206	Rapid City, SD	790.9	253	Pittsburgh, PA	558.2
160	Minneapolis-St. Paul, MN-WI	989.5	207	Des Moines, IA	789.1	254	Binghamton, NY	557.9
161	Hartford, CT	986.4	208	Boise, ID	783.6	255	Altoona, PA	553.5
162	Lincoln, NE	984.6	208	Punta Gorda, FL	783.6	256	Green Bay, WI	533.5
163	Norfolk-Va Beach-Newport News, VA-NC	980.0	210	Philadelphia, PA-NJ	765.4	257	Bloomington, IN	526.8
164	Dayton-Springfield, OH	978.9	211	San Jose, CA	764.6	258	Lynchburg, VA	521.8
165	Rochester, NY	974.5	212	Stamford-Norwalk, CT	763.3	259	Appleton-Oshkosh-Neenah, WI	511.6
166	Springfield, MO	973.4	213	Roanoke, VA	763.1	260	Fargo-Moorhead, ND-MN	503.3
167	Racine, WI	968.4	214	Bremerton, WA	760.1	261	Sheboygan, WI	498.2
168	Grand Rapids-Muskegon-Holland, MI	962.9	215	Lansing-East Lansing, MI	758.3	262	Lancaster, PA	497.6
169	Louisville, KY-IN	961.9	216	Pittsfield, MA	758.2	263	Cumberland, MD-WV	478.5
170	Portland, ME	958.2	217	Anchorage, AK	749.8	264	Scranton-Wilkes-Barre-Hazleton, PA	459.3
171	Abilene, TX	957.5	218	Fort Walton Beach, FL	745.2	265	Grand Forks, ND-MN	450.5
172	Medford-Ashland, OR	952.3	219	Rochester, MN	733.3	266	Florence, AL	446.9
173	Joplin, MO	944.2	220	Monmouth-Ocean, NJ	718.4	267	Cheyenne, WY	427.9
174	Lafayette, LA	941.0	221	Bergen-Passaic, NJ	714.5	268	Bangor, ME	427.4
175	Manchester, NH	938.4	222	Decatur, AL	698.9	269	Steubenville-Weirton, OH-WV	425.5
176	Greeley, CO	934.0	223	Brazoria, TX	690.8	270	Nashua, NH	409.0
177	Clarksville-Hopkinsville, TN-KY	932.3	224	Fort Wayne, IN	686.3	271	St. Cloud, MN	402.3
178	Lawrence, MA-NH	929.9	225	Middlesex-Sommerset-Hunterdon, NJ	686.1	272	Johnstown, PA	386.2
179	Charleston, WV	928.4	226	Reading, PA	683.9	273	Wausau, WI	362.8
180	Saginaw-Bay City-Midland, MI	918.1	227	Nassau-Suffolk, NY	682.1	274	La Crosse, WI-MN	352.6
181	Trenton, NJ	917.7	228	Williamsport, PA	680.2	–	Albany, NY**	NA
182	Boulder-Longmont, CO	917.5	229	Kokomo, IN	677.1	–	Chicago, IL**	NA
183	San Angelo, TX	916.3	230	Newburgh, NY-PA	670.9	–	Cleveland, OH**	NA
184	Owensboro, KY	915.9	231	Eau Claire, WI	667.4	–	Indianapolis, IN**	NA
185	Fort Smith, AR-OK	914.3	232	Columbia, MO	662.6	–	Kansas City, MO-KS**	NA
186	Salt Lake City-Ogden, UT	911.5	233	Charlottesville, VA	660.2	–	Omaha, NE**	NA
187	Boston, MA-NH	891.6	234	Johnson City-Kingsport-Bristol, TN-VA	659.1	–	St. Louis, MO-IL**	NA
188	Duluth-Superior, MN-WI	888.2	235	Sioux Falls, SD	658.5	–	West Palm Beach-Boca Raton, FL**	NA

Source: U.S. Department of Justice, Federal Bureau of Investigation
    "Crime in the United States 1993" (Uniform Crime Reports, December 4, 1994)
*Burglary is the unlawful entry of a structure to commit a felony or theft. Attempts are included.
**Not available.

31. Percent Change in Burglary Rate: 1992 to 1993

National Percent Change = 5.9% Decrease*

RANK	METRO AREA	% CHANGE	RANK	METRO AREA	% CHANGE	RANK	METRO AREA	% CHANGE
237	Abilene, TX	(21.61)	196	Cheyenne, WY	(14.21)	236	Fort Worth-Arlington, TX	(21.27)
88	Akron, OH	(3.98)	–	Chicago, IL**	NA	141	Fresno, CA	(8.63)
210	Albany, GA	(16.02)	60	Chico-Paradise, CA	(0.85)	177	Gadsden, AL	(11.88)
–	Albany, NY**	NA	190	Cincinnati, OH-KY-IN	(13.84)	183	Gainesville, FL	(12.73)
125	Albuquerque, NM	(7.57)	154	Clarksville-Hopkinsville, TN-KY	(9.60)	228	Galveston-Texas City, TX	(20.07)
235	Alexandria, LA	(20.76)	–	Cleveland, OH**	NA	100	Gary-Hammond, IN	(5.20)
46	Altoona, PA	1.41	108	Colorado Springs, CO	(5.93)	122	Glens Falls, NY	(7.34)
58	Amarillo, TX	(0.64)	200	Columbia, MO	(14.61)	130	Goldsboro, NC	(7.86)
249	Anchorage, AK	(31.65)	19	Columbia, SC	7.73	244	Grand Forks, ND-MN	(24.58)
115	Ann Arbor, MI	(6.78)	182	Columbus, GA-AL	(12.66)	206	Grand Rapids-Muskegon-Holland, MI	(15.35)
170	Anniston, AL	(11.01)	187	Columbus, OH	(13.28)	220	Greeley, CO	(17.82)
37	Appleton-Oshkosh-Neenah, WI	3.08	185	Corpus Christi, TX	(12.87)	12	Green Bay, WI	10.23
230	Asheville, NC	(20.20)	198	Cumberland, MD-WV	(14.29)	77	Greensboro-Winston Salem-High Point, NC	(3.01)
250	Athens, GA	(34.38)	211	Dallas, TX	(16.03)	212	Greenville, NC	(16.13)
137	Atlanta, GA	(8.39)	243	Danbury, CT	(24.39)	114	Greenville-Spartanburg-Anderson, SC	(6.57)
80	Atlantic City, NJ	(3.48)	23	Danville, VA	6.36	18	Hagerstown, MD	8.23
234	Augusta-Aiken, GA-SC	(20.60)	50	Daytona Beach, FL	0.56	199	Harrisburg-Lebanon-Carlisle, PA	(14.40)
222	Austin-San Marcos, TX	(17.89)	68	Dayton-Springfield, OH	(2.00)	166	Hartford, CT	(10.72)
59	Bakersfield, CA	(0.80)	229	Decatur, AL	(20.19)	33	Hickory-Morganton, NC	4.11
41	Baltimore, MD	2.11	143	Denver, CO	(8.69)	42	Honolulu, HI	2.07
247	Bangor, ME	(29.17)	98	Des Moines, IA	(5.09)	49	Houma, LA	1.01
129	Barnstable-Yarmouth, MA	(7.77)	61	Detroit, MI	(0.87)	202	Houston, TX	(14.87)
93	Baton Rouge, LA	(4.42)	183	Dothan, AL	(12.73)	193	Huntington-Ashland, WV-KY-OH	(14.01)
218	Beaumont-Port Arthur, TX	(17.00)	1	Dubuque, IA	61.09	173	Huntsville, AL	(11.59)
5	Bellingham, WA	18.21	92	Duluth-Superior, MN-WI	(4.40)	–	Indianapolis, IN**	NA
102	Benton Harbor, MI	(5.74)	–	Dutchess County, NY**	NA	225	Jackson, MI	(19.67)
–	Bergen-Passaic, NJ**	NA	13	Eau Claire, WI	9.00	112	Jackson, MS	(6.41)
25	Binghamton, NY	5.60	245	El Paso, TX	(28.10)	118	Jackson, TN	(7.09)
146	Birmingham, AL	(8.91)	9	Elkhart-Goshen, IN	12.62	133	Jacksonville, FL	(8.17)
30	Bismarck, ND	4.76	111	Enid, OK	(6.38)	34	Jacksonville, NC	3.89
45	Bloomington, IN	1.44	165	Erie, PA	(10.62)	161	Janesville-Beloit, WI	(10.05)
167	Boise, ID	(10.75)	109	Eugene-Springfield, OR	(5.97)	–	Jersey City, NJ**	NA
–	Boston, MA-NH**	NA	119	Evansville-Henderson, IN-KY	(7.14)	205	Johnson City-Kingsport-Bristol, TN-VA	(15.22)
27	Boulder-Longmont, CO	5.19	22	Fargo-Moorhead, ND-MN	6.43	242	Johnstown, PA	(23.21)
221	Brazoria, TX	(17.88)	120	Fayetteville, NC	(7.16)	–	Joplin, MO**	NA
217	Bremerton, WA	(16.93)	225	Fayetteville-Springdale-Rogers, AR	(19.67)	142	Kalamazoo-Battle Creek, MI	(8.64)
126	Bridgeport, CT	(7.67)	–	Fitchburg-Leominster, MA**	NA	–	Kansas City, MO-KS**	NA
241	Brockton, MA	(23.13)	160	Flint, MI	(10.00)	79	Kenosha, WI	(3.20)
155	Brownsville-Harlingen-San Benito, TX	(9.62)	231	Florence, AL	(20.22)	156	Killeen-Temple, TX	(9.75)
136	Bryan-College Station, TX	(8.24)	152	Florence, SC	(9.52)	44	Kokomo, IN	1.73
–	Buffalo-Niagara Falls, NY**	NA	–	Fort Collins-Loveland, CO**	NA	2	La Crosse, WI-MN	30.06
76	Canton-Massillon, OH	(2.67)	66	Fort Lauderdale, FL	(1.70)	151	Lafayette, IN	(9.46)
40	Charleston, WV	2.56	178	Fort Myers-Cape Coral, FL	(12.02)	69	Lafayette, LA	(2.01)
124	Charleston-North Charleston, SC	(7.49)	157	Fort Pierce-Port St. Lucie, FL	(9.76)	–	Lake Charles, LA**	NA
3	Charlottesville, VA	22.37	72	Fort Smith, AR-OK	(2.30)	113	Lakeland-Winter Haven, FL	(6.54)
189	Charlotte-Gastonia-Rock Hill, NC-SC	(13.51)	57	Fort Walton Beach, FL	(0.45)	214	Lancaster, PA	(16.68)
158	Chattanooga, TN-GA	(9.84)	172	Fort Wayne, IN	(11.39)	107	Lansing-East Lansing, MI	(5.91)

Source: Morgan Quitno Corporation using data from U.S. Department of Justice, Federal Bureau of Investigation
   "Crime in the United States 1993" (Uniform Crime Reports, December 4, 1994)
*Burglary is the unlawful entry of a structure to commit a felony or theft. Attempts are included.
**Not available.

31. Percent Change in Burglary Rate: 1992 to 1993 (continued)

National Percent Change = 5.9% Decrease*

RANK	METRO AREA	% CHANGE	RANK	METRO AREA	% CHANGE	RANK	METRO AREA	CHANGE
195	Laredo, TX	(14.19)	56	Olympia, WA	(0.35)	48	Seattle-Bellevue-Everett, WA	1.25
81	Las Vegas, NV-AZ	(3.51)	–	Omaha, NE**	NA	121	Sheboygan, WI	(7.24)
–	Lawrence, MA-NH**	NA	153	Orange County, CA	(9.53)	150	Sherman-Denison, TX	(9.45)
39	Lawton, OK	2.71	78	Orlando, FL	(3.05)	14	Shreveport-Bossier City, LA	8.73
194	Lewiston-Auburn, ME	(14.12)	6	Owensboro, KY	14.92	–	Sioux City, IA-NE**	NA
14	Lexington, KY	8.73	17	Panama City, FL	8.32	8	Sioux Falls, SD	12.85
169	Lincoln, NE	(10.98)	74	Philadelphia, PA-NJ	(2.41)	181	South Bend, IN	(12.42)
36	Little Rock-North Little Rock, AR	3.63	38	Phoenix-Mesa, AZ	2.77	176	Spokane, WA	(11.81)
132	Longview-Marshall, TX	(7.95)	7	Pine Bluff, AR	13.85	203	Springfield, MA	(15.03)
148	Los Angeles-Long Beach, CA	(9.13)	145	Pittsburgh, PA	(8.90)	73	Springfield, MO	(2.31)
83	Louisville, KY-IN	(3.66)	201	Pittsfield, MA	(14.66)	248	Stamford-Norwalk, CT	(29.77)
175	Lubbock, TX	(11.74)	239	Portland, ME	(22.74)	95	Steubenville-Weirton, OH-WV	(4.60)
144	Lynchburg, VA	(8.86)	180	Portland-Vancouver, OR-WA	(12.33)	21	Stockton-Lodi, CA	6.72
204	Macon, GA	(15.13)	54	Providence-Fall River-Warwick, RI-MA	0.12	188	St. Cloud, MN	(13.45)
207	Madison, WI	(15.69)	71	Provo-Orem, UT	(2.11)	31	St. Joseph, MO	4.67
–	Manchester, NH**	NA	43	Pueblo, CO	1.99	–	St. Louis, MO-IL**	NA
101	Mansfield, OH	(5.32)	–	Punta Gorda, FL**	NA	28	Sumter, SC	5.18
147	McAllen-Edinburg-Mission, TX	(9.01)	162	Racine, WI	(10.20)	103	Syracuse, NY	(5.75)
20	Medford-Ashland, OR	7.28	223	Raleigh-Durham-Chapel Hill, NC	(18.85)	26	Tacoma, WA	5.52
89	Memphis, TN-AR-MS	(3.99)	55	Rapid City, SD	0.09	137	Tallahassee, FL	(8.39)
4	Merced, CA	21.21	130	Reading, PA	(7.86)	140	Tampa-St. Petersburg-Clearwater, FL	(8.55)
11	Miami, FL	10.50	67	Redding, CA	(1.80)	168	Texarkana, TX-AR	(10.77)
–	Middlesex-Sommerset-Hunterdon, NJ**	NA	53	Reno, NV	0.30	159	Toledo, OH	(9.87)
94	Milwaukee-Waukesha, WI	(4.53)	117	Richland-Kennewick-Pasco, WA	(7.05)	116	Trenton, NJ	(6.81)
106	Minneapolis-St. Paul, MN-WI	(5.90)	52	Richmond-Petersburg, VA	0.43	35	Tucson, AZ	3.82
–	Mobile, AL**	NA	62	Riverside-San Bernardino, CA	(1.47)	179	Tulsa, OK	(12.26)
10	Modesto, CA	11.46	96	Roanoke, VA	(4.67)	240	Tuscaloosa, AL	(23.11)
–	Monmouth-Ocean, NJ**	NA	231	Rochester, MN	(20.22)	50	Tyler, TX	0.56
233	Monroe, LA	(20.48)	128	Rochester, NY	(7.75)	164	Utica-Rome, NY	(10.58)
65	Montgomery, AL	(1.61)	110	Rocky Mount, NC	(6.16)	163	Vallejo-Fairfield-Napa, CA	(10.52)
135	Myrtle Beach, SC	(8.20)	24	Sacramento, CA	5.97	196	Ventura, CA	(14.21)
90	Naples, FL	(4.05)	149	Saginaw-Bay City-Midland, MI	(9.38)	224	Victoria, TX	(19.17)
213	Nashua, NH	(16.39)	97	Salem, OR	(4.85)	84	Vineland-Millville-Bridgeton, NJ	(3.78)
174	Nashville, TN	(11.70)	75	Salinas, CA	(2.43)	190	Visalia-Tulare-Porterville, CA	(13.84)
–	Nassau-Suffolk, NY**	NA	186	Salt Lake City-Ogden, UT	(13.08)	82	Waco, TX	(3.59)
–	New Bedford, MA**	NA	246	San Angelo, TX	(28.85)	64	Washington, DC-MD-VA-WV	(1.55)
139	New Haven-Meriden, CT	(8.45)	227	San Antonio, TX	(20.02)	216	Waterbury, CT	(16.88)
63	New London-Norwich, CT-RI	(1.54)	133	San Diego, CA	(8.17)	–	Waterloo-Cedar Falls, IA**	NA
105	New Orleans, LA	(5.77)	70	San Francisco, CA	(2.04)	86	Wausau, WI	(3.84)
–	New York, NY**	NA	98	San Jose, CA	(5.09)	–	West Palm Beach-Boca Raton, FL**	NA
–	Newark, NJ**	NA	–	San Luis Obispo-Atascadero, CA**	NA	215	Wichita Falls, TX	(16.70)
–	Newburgh, NY-PA**	NA	87	Santa Barbara-Santa Maria-Lompoc, CA	(3.94)	127	Williamsport, PA	(7.68)
104	Norfolk-Va Beach-Newport News, VA-NC	(5.76)	123	Santa Cruz-Watsonville, CA	(7.44)	238	Wilmington, NC	(22.45)
47	Oakland, CA	1.34	32	Santa Rosa, CA	4.31	–	Worcester, MA-CT**	NA
219	Ocala, FL	(17.78)	208	Sarasota-Bradenton, FL	(15.73)	192	Yakima, WA	(14.00)
209	Odessa-Midland, TX	(15.92)	91	Savannah, GA	(4.32)	16	Yolo, CA	8.48
171	Oklahoma City, OK	(11.07)	85	Scranton-Wilkes-Barre-Hazleton, PA	(3.81)	29	Yuba City, CA	5.14

Source: Morgan Quitno Corporation using data from U.S. Department of Justice, Federal Bureau of Investigation
"Crime in the United States 1993" (Uniform Crime Reports, December 4, 1994)
*Burglary is the unlawful entry of a structure to commit a felony or theft. Attempts are included.
**Not available.

31. Percent Change in Burglary Rate: 1992 to 1993 (continued)

National Percent Change = 5.9% Decrease*

RANK	METRO AREA	% CHANGE	RANK	METRO AREA	% CHANGE	RANK	METRO AREA	% CHANGE
1	Dubuque, IA	61.09	48	Seattle–Bellevue–Everett, WA	1.25	95	Steubenville–Weirton, OH–WV	(4.60)
2	La Crosse, WI–MN	30.06	49	Houma, LA	1.01	96	Roanoke, VA	(4.67)
3	Charlottesville, VA	22.37	50	Daytona Beach, FL	0.56	97	Salem, OR	(4.85)
4	Merced, CA	21.21	50	Tyler, TX	0.56	98	Des Moines, IA	(5.09)
5	Bellingham, WA	18.21	52	Richmond–Petersburg, VA	0.43	98	San Jose, CA	(5.09)
6	Owensboro, KY	14.92	53	Reno, NV	0.30	100	Gary–Hammond, IN	(5.20)
7	Pine Bluff, AR	13.85	54	Providence–Fall River–Warwick, RI–MA	0.12	101	Mansfield, OH	(5.32)
8	Sioux Falls, SD	12.85	55	Rapid City, SD	0.09	102	Benton Harbor, MI	(5.74)
9	Elkhart–Goshen, IN	12.62	56	Olympia, WA	(0.35)	103	Syracuse, NY	(5.75)
10	Modesto, CA	11.46	57	Fort Walton Beach, FL	(0.45)	104	Norfolk–Va Beach–Newport News, VA–NC	(5.76)
11	Miami, FL	10.50	58	Amarillo, TX	(0.64)	105	New Orleans, LA	(5.77)
12	Green Bay, WI	10.23	59	Bakersfield, CA	(0.80)	106	Minneapolis–St. Paul, MN–WI	(5.90)
13	Eau Claire, WI	9.00	60	Chico–Paradise, CA	(0.85)	107	Lansing–East Lansing, MI	(5.91)
14	Lexington, KY	8.73	61	Detroit, MI	(0.87)	108	Colorado Springs, CO	(5.93)
14	Shreveport–Bossier City, LA	8.73	62	Riverside–San Bernardino, CA	(1.47)	109	Eugene–Springfield, OR	(5.97)
16	Yolo, CA	8.48	63	New London–Norwich, CT–RI	(1.54)	110	Rocky Mount, NC	(6.16)
17	Panama City, FL	8.32	64	Washington, DC–MD–VA–WV	(1.55)	111	Enid, OK	(6.38)
18	Hagerstown, MD	8.23	65	Montgomery, AL	(1.61)	112	Jackson, MS	(6.41)
19	Columbia, SC	7.73	66	Fort Lauderdale, FL	(1.70)	113	Lakeland–Winter Haven, FL	(6.54)
20	Medford–Ashland, OR	7.28	67	Redding, CA	(1.80)	114	Greenville–Spartanburg–Anderson, SC	(6.57)
21	Stockton–Lodi, CA	6.72	68	Dayton–Springfield, OH	(2.00)	115	Ann Arbor, MI	(6.78)
22	Fargo–Moorhead, ND–MN	6.43	69	Lafayette, LA	(2.01)	116	Trenton, NJ	(6.81)
23	Danville, VA	6.36	70	San Francisco, CA	(2.04)	117	Richland–Kennewick–Pasco, WA	(7.05)
24	Sacramento, CA	5.97	71	Provo–Orem, UT	(2.11)	118	Jackson, TN	(7.09)
25	Binghamton, NY	5.60	72	Fort Smith, AR–OK	(2.30)	119	Evansville–Henderson, IN–KY	(7.14)
26	Tacoma, WA	5.52	73	Springfield, MO	(2.31)	120	Fayetteville, NC	(7.16)
27	Boulder–Longmont, CO	5.19	74	Philadelphia, PA–NJ	(2.41)	121	Sheboygan, WI	(7.24)
28	Sumter, SC	5.18	75	Salinas, CA	(2.43)	122	Glens Falls, NY	(7.34)
29	Yuba City, CA	5.14	76	Canton–Massillon, OH	(2.67)	123	Santa Cruz–Watsonville, CA	(7.44)
30	Bismarck, ND	4.76	77	Greensboro–Winston Salem–High Point, NC	(3.01)	124	Charleston–North Charleston, SC	(7.49)
31	St. Joseph, MO	4.67	78	Orlando, FL	(3.05)	125	Albuquerque, NM	(7.57)
32	Santa Rosa, CA	4.31	79	Kenosha, WI	(3.20)	126	Bridgeport, CT	(7.67)
33	Hickory–Morganton, NC	4.11	80	Atlantic City, NJ	(3.48)	127	Williamsport, PA	(7.68)
34	Jacksonville, NC	3.89	81	Las Vegas, NV–AZ	(3.51)	128	Rochester, NY	(7.75)
35	Tucson, AZ	3.82	82	Waco, TX	(3.59)	129	Barnstable–Yarmouth, MA	(7.77)
36	Little Rock–North Little Rock, AR	3.63	83	Louisville, KY–IN	(3.66)	130	Goldsboro, NC	(7.86)
37	Appleton–Oshkosh–Neenah, WI	3.08	84	Vineland–Millville–Bridgeton, NJ	(3.78)	130	Reading, PA	(7.86)
38	Phoenix–Mesa, AZ	2.77	85	Scranton–Wilkes-Barre–Hazleton, PA	(3.81)	132	Longview–Marshall, TX	(7.95)
39	Lawton, OK	2.71	86	Wausau, WI	(3.84)	133	Jacksonville, FL	(8.17)
40	Charleston, WV	2.56	87	Santa Barbara–Santa Maria–Lompoc, CA	(3.94)	133	San Diego, CA	(8.17)
41	Baltimore, MD	2.11	88	Akron, OH	(3.98)	135	Myrtle Beach, SC	(8.20)
42	Honolulu, HI	2.07	89	Memphis, TN–AR–MS	(3.99)	136	Bryan–College Station, TX	(8.24)
43	Pueblo, CO	1.99	90	Naples, FL	(4.05)	137	Atlanta, GA	(8.39)
44	Kokomo, IN	1.73	91	Savannah, GA	(4.32)	137	Tallahassee, FL	(8.39)
45	Bloomington, IN	1.44	92	Duluth–Superior, MN–WI	(4.40)	139	New Haven–Meriden, CT	(8.45)
46	Altoona, PA	1.41	93	Baton Rouge, LA	(4.42)	140	Tampa–St. Petersburg–Clearwater, FL	(8.55)
47	Oakland, CA	1.34	94	Milwaukee–Waukesha, WI	(4.53)	141	Fresno, CA	(8.63)

Source: Morgan Quitno Corporation using data from U.S. Department of Justice, Federal Bureau of Investigation
"Crime in the United States 1993" (Uniform Crime Reports, December 4, 1994)
*Burglary is the unlawful entry of a structure to commit a felony or theft. Attempts are included.
**Not available.

31. Percent Change in Burglary Rate: 1992 to 1993 (continued)

National Percent Change = 5.9% Decrease*

RANK	METRO AREA	% CHANGE	RANK	METRO AREA	% CHANGE	RANK	METRO AREA	CHANGE
142	Kalamazoo–Battle Creek, MI	(8.64)	189	Charlotte–Gastonia–Rock Hill, NC–SC	(13.51)	236	Fort Worth–Arlington, TX	(21.27)
143	Denver, CO	(8.69)	190	Cincinnati, OH–KY–IN	(13.84)	237	Abilene, TX	(21.61)
144	Lynchburg, VA	(8.86)	190	Visalia–Tulare–Porterville, CA	(13.84)	238	Wilmington, NC	(22.45)
145	Pittsburgh, PA	(8.90)	192	Yakima, WA	(14.00)	239	Portland, ME	(22.74)
146	Birmingham, AL	(8.91)	193	Huntington–Ashland, WV–KY–OH	(14.01)	240	Tuscaloosa, AL	(23.11)
147	McAllen–Edinburg–Mission, TX	(9.01)	194	Lewiston–Auburn, ME	(14.12)	241	Brockton, MA	(23.13)
148	Los Angeles–Long Beach, CA	(9.13)	195	Laredo, TX	(14.19)	242	Johnstown, PA	(23.21)
149	Saginaw–Bay City–Midland, MI	(9.38)	196	Cheyenne, WY	(14.21)	243	Danbury, CT	(24.39)
150	Sherman–Denison, TX	(9.45)	196	Ventura, CA	(14.21)	244	Grand Forks, ND–MN	(24.58)
151	Lafayette, IN	(9.46)	198	Cumberland, MD–WV	(14.29)	245	El Paso, TX	(28.10)
152	Florence, SC	(9.52)	199	Harrisburg–Lebanon–Carlisle, PA	(14.40)	246	San Angelo, TX	(28.85)
153	Orange County, CA	(9.53)	200	Columbia, MO	(14.61)	247	Bangor, ME	(29.17)
154	Clarksville–Hopkinsville, TN–KY	(9.60)	201	Pittsfield, MA	(14.66)	248	Stamford–Norwalk, CT	(29.77)
155	Brownsville–Harlingen–San Benito, TX	(9.62)	202	Houston, TX	(14.87)	249	Anchorage, AK	(31.65)
156	Killeen–Temple, TX	(9.75)	203	Springfield, MA	(15.03)	250	Athens, GA	(34.38)
157	Fort Pierce–Port St. Lucie, FL	(9.76)	204	Macon, GA	(15.13)	–	Albany, NY**	NA
158	Chattanooga, TN–GA	(9.84)	205	Johnson City–Kingsport–Bristol, TN–VA	(15.22)	–	Bergen–Passaic, NJ**	NA
159	Toledo, OH	(9.87)	206	Grand Rapids–Muskegon–Holland, MI	(15.35)	–	Boston, MA–NH**	NA
160	Flint, MI	(10.00)	207	Madison, WI	(15.69)	–	Buffalo–Niagara Falls, NY**	NA
161	Janesville–Beloit, WI	(10.05)	208	Sarasota–Bradenton, FL	(15.73)	–	Chicago, IL**	NA
162	Racine, WI	(10.20)	209	Odessa–Midland, TX	(15.92)	–	Cleveland, OH**	NA
163	Vallejo–Fairfield–Napa, CA	(10.52)	210	Albany, GA	(16.02)	–	Dutchess County, NY**	NA
164	Utica–Rome, NY	(10.58)	211	Dallas, TX	(16.03)	–	Fitchburg–Leominster, MA**	NA
165	Erie, PA	(10.62)	212	Greenville, NC	(16.13)	–	Fort Collins–Loveland, CO**	NA
166	Hartford, CT	(10.72)	213	Nashua, NH	(16.39)	–	Indianapolis, IN**	NA
167	Boise, ID	(10.75)	214	Lancaster, PA	(16.68)	–	Jersey City, NJ**	NA
168	Texarkana, TX–AR	(10.77)	215	Wichita Falls, TX	(16.70)	–	Joplin, MO**	NA
169	Lincoln, NE	(10.98)	216	Waterbury, CT	(16.88)	–	Kansas City, MO–KS**	NA
170	Anniston, AL	(11.01)	217	Bremerton, WA	(16.93)	–	Lake Charles, LA**	NA
171	Oklahoma City, OK	(11.07)	218	Beaumont–Port Arthur, TX	(17.00)	–	Lawrence, MA–NH**	NA
172	Fort Wayne, IN	(11.39)	219	Ocala, FL	(17.78)	–	Manchester, NH**	NA
173	Huntsville, AL	(11.59)	220	Greeley, CO	(17.82)	–	Middlesex–Sommerset–Hunterdon, NJ**	NA
174	Nashville, TN	(11.70)	221	Brazoria, TX	(17.88)	–	Mobile, AL**	NA
175	Lubbock, TX	(11.74)	222	Austin–San Marcos, TX	(17.89)	–	Monmouth–Ocean, NJ**	NA
176	Spokane, WA	(11.81)	223	Raleigh–Durham–Chapel Hill, NC	(18.85)	–	Nassau–Suffolk, NY**	NA
177	Gadsden, AL	(11.88)	224	Victoria, TX	(19.17)	–	New Bedford, MA**	NA
178	Fort Myers–Cape Coral, FL	(12.02)	225	Fayetteville–Springdale–Rogers, AR	(19.67)	–	New York, NY**	NA
179	Tulsa, OK	(12.26)	225	Jackson, MI	(19.67)	–	Newark, NJ**	NA
180	Portland–Vancouver, OR–WA	(12.33)	227	San Antonio, TX	(20.02)	–	Newburgh, NY–PA**	NA
181	South Bend, IN	(12.42)	228	Galveston–Texas City, TX	(20.07)	–	Omaha, NE**	NA
182	Columbus, GA–AL	(12.66)	229	Decatur, AL	(20.19)	–	Punta Gorda, FL**	NA
183	Dothan, AL	(12.73)	230	Asheville, NC	(20.20)	–	San Luis Obispo–Atascadero, CA**	NA
183	Gainesville, FL	(12.73)	231	Florence, AL	(20.22)	–	Sioux City, IA–NE**	NA
185	Corpus Christi, TX	(12.87)	231	Rochester, MN	(20.22)	–	St. Louis, MO–IL**	NA
186	Salt Lake City–Ogden, UT	(13.08)	233	Monroe, LA	(20.48)	–	Waterloo–Cedar Falls, IA**	NA
187	Columbus, OH	(13.28)	234	Augusta–Aiken, GA–SC	(20.60)	–	West Palm Beach–Boca Raton, FL**	NA
188	St. Cloud, MN	(13.45)	235	Alexandria, LA	(20.76)	–	Worcester, MA–CT**	NA

Source: Morgan Quitno Corporation using data from U.S. Department of Justice, Federal Bureau of Investigation
   "Crime in the United States 1993" (Uniform Crime Reports, December 4, 1994)
Burglary is the unlawful entry of a structure to commit a felony or theft. Attempts are included.
**Not available.*

32. Percent Change in Burglary Rate: 1989 to 1993

National Percent Change = 13.9% Decrease*

RANK	METRO AREA	% CHANGE	RANK	METRO AREA	% CHANGE	RANK	METRO AREA	% CHANGE
245	Abilene, TX	(55.53)	197	Cheyenne, WY	(27.52)	237	Fort Worth-Arlington, TX	(41.20)
–	Akron, OH**	NA	–	Chicago, IL**	NA	72	Fresno, CA	(6.17)
87	Albany, GA	(9.15)	61	Chico-Paradise, CA	(4.40)	1	Gadsden, AL	44.38
–	Albany, NY**	NA	79	Cincinnati, OH-KY-IN	(8.03)	106	Gainesville, FL	(11.83)
186	Albuquerque, NM	(25.73)	47	Clarksville-Hopkinsville, TN-KY	(2.47)	205	Galveston-Texas City, TX	(29.31)
158	Alexandria, LA	(20.00)	–	Cleveland, OH**	NA	35	Gary-Hammond, IN	0.59
177	Altoona, PA	(23.84)	167	Colorado Springs, CO	(22.02)	119	Glens Falls, NY	(14.23)
136	Amarillo, TX	(16.93)	179	Columbia, MO	(24.52)	–	Goldsboro, NC**	NA
45	Anchorage, AK	(1.95)	42	Columbia, SC	(1.24)	83	Grand Forks, ND-MN	(9.01)
212	Ann Arbor, MI	(31.19)	153	Columbus, GA-AL	(19.77)	63	Grand Rapids-Muskegon-Holland, MI	(4.73)
9	Anniston, AL	15.61	139	Columbus, OH	(17.69)	204	Greeley, CO	(28.94)
94	Appleton-Oshkosh-Neenah, WI	(10.20)	214	Corpus Christi, TX	(31.41)	14	Green Bay, WI	11.05
195	Asheville, NC	(27.31)	159	Cumberland, MD-WV	(20.02)	18	Greensboro-Winston Salem-High Point, NC	7.93
225	Athens, GA	(35.94)	240	Dallas, TX	(45.80)	–	Greenville, NC**	NA
188	Atlanta, GA	(25.99)	171	Danbury, CT	(22.84)	157	Greenville-Spartanburg-Anderson, SC	(19.95)
43	Atlantic City, NJ	(1.42)	3	Danville, VA	35.42	90	Hagerstown, MD	(9.30)
218	Augusta-Aiken, GA-SC	(32.95)	187	Daytona Beach, FL	(25.94)	–	Harrisburg-Lebanon-Carlisle, PA**	NA
217	Austin-San Marcos, TX	(32.43)	108	Dayton-Springfield, OH	(12.02)	165	Hartford, CT	(21.79)
31	Bakersfield, CA	2.67	138	Decatur, AL	(17.55)	–	Hickory-Morganton, NC**	NA
23	Baltimore, MD	6.52	162	Denver, CO	(20.84)	133	Honolulu, HI	(15.64)
227	Bangor, ME	(36.75)	172	Des Moines, IA	(23.22)	–	Houma, LA**	NA
–	Barnstable-Yarmouth, MA**	NA	168	Detroit, MI	(22.33)	239	Houston, TX	(42.83)
20	Baton Rouge, LA	6.84	173	Dothan, AL	(23.36)	137	Huntington-Ashland, WV-KY-OH	(17.25)
182	Beaumont-Port Arthur, TX	(25.13)	2	Dubuque, IA	40.84	36	Huntsville, AL	0.25
62	Bellingham, WA	(4.42)	21	Duluth-Superior, MN-WI	6.77	–	Indianapolis, IN**	NA
130	Benton Harbor, MI	(15.46)	–	Dutchess County, NY**	NA	221	Jackson, MI	(34.09)
54	Bergen-Passaic, NJ	(3.24)	76	Eau Claire, WI	(6.83)	13	Jackson, MS	11.67
53	Binghamton, NY	(3.21)	242	El Paso, TX	(51.38)	51	Jackson, TN	(3.07)
65	Birmingham, AL	(5.05)	65	Elkhart-Goshen, IN	(5.05)	178	Jacksonville, FL	(24.23)
5	Bismarck, ND	32.17	141	Enid, OK	(18.39)	17	Jacksonville, NC	8.57
213	Bloomington, IN	(31.33)	166	Erie, PA	(21.91)	107	Janesville-Beloit, WI	(11.96)
210	Boise, ID	(30.28)	150	Eugene-Springfield, OR	(19.24)	64	Jersey City, NJ	(4.85)
–	Boston, MA-NH**	NA	111	Evansville-Henderson, IN-KY	(12.43)	143	Johnson City-Kingsport-Bristol, TN-VA	(18.57)
121	Boulder-Longmont, CO	(14.48)	74	Fargo-Moorhead, ND-MN	(6.59)	–	Johnstown, PA**	NA
169	Brazoria, TX	(22.34)	146	Fayetteville, NC	(18.75)	49	Joplin, MO	(2.54)
–	Bremerton, WA**	NA	228	Fayetteville-Springdale-Rogers, AR	(37.01)	98	Kalamazoo-Battle Creek, MI	(10.80)
104	Bridgeport, CT	(11.69)	7	Fitchburg-Leominster, MA	19.51	–	Kansas City, MO-KS**	NA
–	Brockton, MA**	NA	199	Flint, MI	(27.96)	52	Kenosha, WI	(3.12)
149	Brownsville-Harlingen-San Benito, TX	(19.15)	219	Florence, AL	(33.67)	84	Killeen-Temple, TX	(9.03)
231	Bryan-College Station, TX	(39.12)	8	Florence, SC	19.22	69	Kokomo, IN	(5.87)
58	Buffalo-Niagara Falls, NY	(3.72)	163	Fort Collins-Loveland, CO	(21.62)	12	La Crosse, WI-MN	11.79
16	Canton-Massillon, OH	9.20	127	Fort Lauderdale, FL	(14.74)	115	Lafayette, IN	(13.65)
46	Charleston, WV	(2.29)	77	Fort Myers-Cape Coral, FL	(6.85)	161	Lafayette, LA	(20.51)
102	Charleston-North Charleston, SC	(11.51)	198	Fort Pierce-Port St. Lucie, FL	(27.55)	88	Lake Charles, LA	(9.24)
216	Charlottesville, VA	(32.42)	154	Fort Smith, AR-OK	(19.78)	110	Lakeland-Winter Haven, FL	(12.41)
151	Charlotte-Gastonia-Rock Hill, NC-SC	(19.42)	117	Fort Walton Beach, FL	(14.03)	99	Lancaster, PA	(10.87)
174	Chattanooga, TN-GA	(23.57)	238	Fort Wayne, IN	(42.14)	188	Lansing-East Lansing, MI	(25.99)

Source: Morgan Quitno Corporation using data from U.S. Department of Justice, Federal Bureau of Investigation
    "Crime in the United States 1993" (Uniform Crime Reports, December 4, 1994)
*Burglary is the unlawful entry of a structure to commit a felony or theft. Attempts are included.
**Not available.

32. Percent Change in Burglary Rate: 1989 to 1993 (continued)

National Percent Change = 13.9% Decrease*

RANK	METRO AREA	% CHANGE	RANK	METRO AREA	% CHANGE	RANK	METRO AREA	CHANGE
202	Laredo, TX	(28.52)	118	Olympia, WA	(14.04)	215	Seattle–Bellevue–Everett, WA	(31.98)
80	Las Vegas, NV–AZ	(8.07)	–	Omaha, NE**	NA	60	Sheboygan, WI	(4.38)
123	Lawrence, MA–NH	(14.60)	126	Orange County, CA	(14.70)	224	Sherman–Denison, TX	(35.82)
93	Lawton, OK	(9.97)	203	Orlando, FL	(28.72)	194	Shreveport–Bossier City, LA	(27.09)
175	Lewiston–Auburn, ME	(23.64)	22	Owensboro, KY	6.76	222	Sioux City, IA–NE	(34.18)
70	Lexington, KY	(5.90)	10	Panama City, FL	12.78	19	Sioux Falls, SD	7.48
86	Lincoln, NE	(9.12)	132	Philadelphia, PA–NJ	(15.53)	–	South Bend, IN**	NA
109	Little Rock–North Little Rock, AR	(12.12)	114	Phoenix–Mesa, AZ	(13.30)	229	Spokane, WA	(38.03)
152	Longview–Marshall, TX	(19.55)	4	Pine Bluff, AR	32.20	50	Springfield, MA	(2.97)
82	Los Angeles–Long Beach, CA	(8.37)	196	Pittsburgh, PA	(27.43)	201	Springfield, MO	(28.15)
112	Louisville, KY–IN	(12.55)	–	Pittsfield, MA**	NA	207	Stamford–Norwalk, CT	(30.00)
208	Lubbock, TX	(30.08)	181	Portland, ME	(24.99)	–	Steubenville–Weirton, OH–WV**	NA
144	Lynchburg, VA	(18.65)	232	Portland–Vancouver, OR–WA	(39.68)	71	Stockton–Lodi, CA	(5.93)
236	Macon, GA	(40.75)	122	Providence–Fall River–Warwick, RI–MA	(14.50)	142	St. Cloud, MN	(18.50)
223	Madison, WI	(34.96)	–	Provo–Orem, UT**	NA	75	St. Joseph, MO	(6.63)
233	Manchester, NH	(39.83)	92	Pueblo, CO	(9.73)	–	St. Louis, MO–IL**	NA
125	Mansfield, OH	(14.69)	–	Punta Gorda, FL**	NA	–	Sumter, SC**	NA
11	McAllen–Edinburg–Mission, TX	12.25	211	Racine, WI	(30.65)	148	Syracuse, NY	(18.92)
55	Medford–Ashland, OR	(3.65)	39	Raleigh–Durham–Chapel Hill, NC	(0.71)	209	Tacoma, WA	(30.12)
65	Memphis, TN–AR–MS	(5.05)	56	Rapid City, SD	(3.67)	27	Tallahassee, FL	5.97
6	Merced, CA	20.91	–	Reading, PA**	NA	164	Tampa–St. Petersburg–Clearwater, FL	(21.69)
144	Miami, FL	(18.65)	119	Redding, CA	(14.23)	226	Texarkana, TX–AR	(36.15)
47	Middlesex–Sommerset–Hunterdon, NJ	(2.47)	155	Reno, NV	(19.82)	180	Toledo, OH	(24.90)
101	Milwaukee–Waukesha, WI	(11.42)	241	Richland–Kennewick–Pasco, WA	(49.64)	191	Trenton, NJ	(26.43)
124	Minneapolis–St. Paul, MN–WI	(14.64)	34	Richmond–Petersburg, VA	1.73	–	Tucson, AZ**	NA
105	Mobile, AL	(11.77)	–	Riverside–San Bernardino, CA**	NA	156	Tulsa, OK	(19.84)
25	Modesto, CA	6.40	131	Roanoke, VA	(15.47)	129	Tuscaloosa, AL	(15.45)
37	Monmouth–Ocean, NJ	0.22	91	Rochester, MN	(9.48)	147	Tyler, TX	(18.87)
78	Monroe, LA	(7.78)	57	Rochester, NY	(3.68)	100	Utica–Rome, NY	(11.03)
25	Montgomery, AL	6.40	–	Rocky Mount, NC**	NA	96	Vallejo–Fairfield–Napa, CA	(10.54)
–	Myrtle Beach, SC**	NA	29	Sacramento, CA	4.05	81	Ventura, CA	(8.34)
193	Naples, FL	(26.86)	170	Saginaw–Bay City–Midland, MI	(22.50)	32	Victoria, TX	2.60
184	Nashua, NH	(25.31)	176	Salem, OR	(23.76)	15	Vineland–Millville–Bridgeton, NJ	9.96
24	Nashville, TN	6.48	33	Salinas, CA	2.10	41	Visalia–Tulare–Porterville, CA	(1.10)
95	Nassau–Suffolk, NY	(10.38)	135	Salt Lake City–Ogden, UT	(16.79)	235	Waco, TX	(40.41)
85	New Bedford, MA	(9.11)	243	San Angelo, TX	(52.25)	113	Washington, DC–MD–VA–WV	(13.07)
185	New Haven–Meriden, CT	(25.32)	230	San Antonio, TX	(38.05)	190	Waterbury, CT	(26.29)
191	New London–Norwich, CT–RI	(26.43)	115	San Diego, CA	(13.65)	134	Waterloo–Cedar Falls, IA	(15.81)
128	New Orleans, LA	(14.90)	44	San Francisco, CA	(1.57)	40	Wausau, WI	(1.09)
140	New York, NY	(18.36)	73	San Jose, CA	(6.30)	–	West Palm Beach–Boca Raton, FL**	NA
37	Newark, NJ	0.22	–	San Luis Obispo–Atascadero, CA**	NA	244	Wichita Falls, TX	(55.32)
–	Newburgh, NY–PA**	NA	59	Santa Barbara–Santa Maria–Lompoc, CA	(4.12)	–	Williamsport, PA**	NA
97	Norfolk–Va Beach–Newport News, VA–NC	(10.68)	103	Santa Cruz–Watsonville, CA	(11.62)	200	Wilmington, NC	(28.11)
89	Oakland, CA	(9.26)	68	Santa Rosa, CA	(5.25)	–	Worcester, MA–CT**	NA
234	Ocala, FL	(40.28)	160	Sarasota–Bradenton, FL	(20.08)	183	Yakima, WA	(25.23)
220	Odessa–Midland, TX	(33.97)	30	Savannah, GA	3.01	–	Yolo, CA**	NA
206	Oklahoma City, OK	(29.60)	–	Scranton–Wilkes-Barre–Hazleton, PA**	NA	28	Yuba City, CA	4.52

Source: Morgan Quitno Corporation using data from U.S. Department of Justice, Federal Bureau of Investigation
   "Crime in the United States 1993" (Uniform Crime Reports, December 4, 1994)
*Burglary is the unlawful entry of a structure to commit a felony or theft. Attempts are included.
**Not available.

32. Percent Change in Burglary Rate: 1989 to 1993 (continued)

National Percent Change = 13.9% Decrease*

RANK	METRO AREA	% CHANGE	RANK	METRO AREA	% CHANGE	RANK	METRO AREA	% CHANGE
1	Gadsden, AL	44.38	47	Middlesex–Sommerset–Hunterdon, NJ	(2.47)	95	Nassau–Suffolk, NY	(10.38)
2	Dubuque, IA	40.84	49	Joplin, MO	(2.54)	96	Vallejo–Fairfield–Napa, CA	(10.54)
3	Danville, VA	35.42	50	Springfield, MA	(2.97)	97	Norfolk–Va Beach–Newport News, VA–NC	(10.68)
4	Pine Bluff, AR	32.20	51	Jackson, TN	(3.07)	98	Kalamazoo–Battle Creek, MI	(10.80)
5	Bismarck, ND	32.17	52	Kenosha, WI	(3.12)	99	Lancaster, PA	(10.87)
6	Merced, CA	20.91	53	Binghamton, NY	(3.21)	100	Utica–Rome, NY	(11.03)
7	Fitchburg–Leominster, MA	19.51	54	Bergen–Passaic, NJ	(3.24)	101	Milwaukee–Waukesha, WI	(11.42)
8	Florence, SC	19.22	55	Medford–Ashland, OR	(3.65)	102	Charleston–North Charleston, SC	(11.51)
9	Anniston, AL	15.61	56	Rapid City, SD	(3.67)	103	Santa Cruz–Watsonville, CA	(11.62)
10	Panama City, FL	12.78	57	Rochester, NY	(3.68)	104	Bridgeport, CT	(11.69)
11	McAllen–Edinburg–Mission, TX	12.25	58	Buffalo–Niagara Falls, NY	(3.72)	105	Mobile, AL	(11.77)
12	La Crosse, WI–MN	11.79	59	Santa Barbara–Santa Maria–Lompoc, CA	(4.12)	106	Gainesville, FL	(11.83)
13	Jackson, MS	11.67	60	Sheboygan, WI	(4.38)	107	Janesville–Beloit, WI	(11.96)
14	Green Bay, WI	11.05	61	Chico–Paradise, CA	(4.40)	108	Dayton–Springfield, OH	(12.02)
15	Vineland–Millville–Bridgeton, NJ	9.96	62	Bellingham, WA	(4.42)	109	Little Rock–North Little Rock, AR	(12.12)
16	Canton–Massillon, OH	9.20	63	Grand Rapids–Muskegon–Holland, MI	(4.73)	110	Lakeland–Winter Haven, FL	(12.41)
17	Jacksonville, NC	8.57	64	Jersey City, NJ	(4.85)	111	Evansville–Henderson, IN–KY	(12.43)
18	Greensboro–Winston Salem–High Point, NC	7.93	65	Birmingham, AL	(5.05)	112	Louisville, KY–IN	(12.55)
19	Sioux Falls, SD	7.48	65	Elkhart–Goshen, IN	(5.05)	113	Washington, DC–MD–VA–WV	(13.07)
20	Baton Rouge, LA	6.84	65	Memphis, TN–AR–MS	(5.05)	114	Phoenix–Mesa, AZ	(13.30)
21	Duluth–Superior, MN–WI	6.77	68	Santa Rosa, CA	(5.25)	115	Lafayette, IN	(13.65)
22	Owensboro, KY	6.76	69	Kokomo, IN	(5.87)	115	San Diego, CA	(13.65)
23	Baltimore, MD	6.52	70	Lexington, KY	(5.90)	117	Fort Walton Beach, FL	(14.03)
24	Nashville, TN	6.48	71	Stockton–Lodi, CA	(5.93)	118	Olympia, WA	(14.04)
25	Modesto, CA	6.40	72	Fresno, CA	(6.17)	119	Glens Falls, NY	(14.23)
25	Montgomery, AL	6.40	73	San Jose, CA	(6.30)	119	Redding, CA	(14.23)
27	Tallahassee, FL	5.97	74	Fargo–Moorhead, ND–MN	(6.59)	121	Boulder–Longmont, CO	(14.48)
28	Yuba City, CA	4.52	75	St. Joseph, MO	(6.63)	122	Providence–Fall River–Warwick, RI–MA	(14.50)
29	Sacramento, CA	4.05	76	Eau Claire, WI	(6.83)	123	Lawrence, MA–NH	(14.60)
30	Savannah, GA	3.01	77	Fort Myers–Cape Coral, FL	(6.85)	124	Minneapolis–St. Paul, MN–WI	(14.64)
31	Bakersfield, CA	2.67	78	Monroe, LA	(7.78)	125	Mansfield, OH	(14.69)
32	Victoria, TX	2.60	79	Cincinnati, OH–KY–IN	(8.03)	126	Orange County, CA	(14.70)
33	Salinas, CA	2.10	80	Las Vegas, NV–AZ	(8.07)	127	Fort Lauderdale, FL	(14.74)
34	Richmond–Petersburg, VA	1.73	81	Ventura, CA	(8.34)	128	New Orleans, LA	(14.90)
35	Gary–Hammond, IN	0.59	82	Los Angeles–Long Beach, CA	(8.37)	129	Tuscaloosa, AL	(15.45)
36	Huntsville, AL	0.25	83	Grand Forks, ND–MN	(9.01)	130	Benton Harbor, MI	(15.46)
37	Monmouth–Ocean, NJ	0.22	84	Killeen–Temple, TX	(9.03)	131	Roanoke, VA	(15.47)
37	Newark, NJ	0.22	85	New Bedford, MA	(9.11)	132	Philadelphia, PA–NJ	(15.53)
39	Raleigh–Durham–Chapel Hill, NC	(0.71)	86	Lincoln, NE	(9.12)	133	Honolulu, HI	(15.64)
40	Wausau, WI	(1.09)	87	Albany, GA	(9.15)	134	Waterloo–Cedar Falls, IA	(15.81)
41	Visalia–Tulare–Porterville, CA	(1.10)	88	Lake Charles, LA	(9.24)	135	Salt Lake City–Ogden, UT	(16.79)
42	Columbia, SC	(1.24)	89	Oakland, CA	(9.26)	136	Amarillo, TX	(16.93)
43	Atlantic City, NJ	(1.42)	90	Hagerstown, MD	(9.30)	137	Huntington–Ashland, WV–KY–OH	(17.25)
44	San Francisco, CA	(1.57)	91	Rochester, MN	(9.48)	138	Decatur, AL	(17.55)
45	Anchorage, AK	(1.95)	92	Pueblo, CO	(9.73)	139	Columbus, OH	(17.69)
46	Charleston, WV	(2.29)	93	Lawton, OK	(9.97)	140	New York, NY	(18.36)
47	Clarksville–Hopkinsville, TN–KY	(2.47)	94	Appleton–Oshkosh–Neenah, WI	(10.20)	141	Enid, OK	(18.39)

*Source: Morgan Quitno Corporation using data from U.S. Department of Justice, Federal Bureau of Investigation
"Crime in the United States 1993" (Uniform Crime Reports, December 4, 1994)*
Burglary is the unlawful entry of a structure to commit a felony or theft. Attempts are included.
**Not available.*

32. Percent Change in Burglary Rate: 1989 to 1993 (continued)

National Percent Change = 13.9% Decrease*

RANK	METRO AREA	% CHANGE	RANK	METRO AREA	% CHANGE	RANK	METRO AREA	CHANGE
142	St. Cloud, MN	(18.50)	188	Lansing–East Lansing, MI	(25.99)	236	Macon, GA	(40.75)
143	Johnson City–Kingsport–Bristol, TN–VA	(18.57)	190	Waterbury, CT	(26.29)	237	Fort Worth–Arlington, TX	(41.20)
144	Lynchburg, VA	(18.65)	191	New London–Norwich, CT–RI	(26.43)	238	Fort Wayne, IN	(42.14)
144	Miami, FL	(18.65)	191	Trenton, NJ	(26.43)	239	Houston, TX	(42.83)
146	Fayetteville, NC	(18.75)	193	Naples, FL	(26.86)	240	Dallas, TX	(45.80)
147	Tyler, TX	(18.87)	194	Shreveport–Bossier City, LA	(27.09)	241	Richland–Kennewick–Pasco, WA	(49.64)
148	Syracuse, NY	(18.92)	195	Asheville, NC	(27.31)	242	El Paso, TX	(51.38)
149	Brownsville–Harlingen–San Benito, TX	(19.15)	196	Pittsburgh, PA	(27.43)	243	San Angelo, TX	(52.25)
150	Eugene–Springfield, OR	(19.24)	197	Cheyenne, WY	(27.52)	244	Wichita Falls, TX	(55.32)
151	Charlotte–Gastonia–Rock Hill, NC–SC	(19.42)	198	Fort Pierce–Port St. Lucie, FL	(27.55)	245	Abilene, TX	(55.53)
152	Longview–Marshall, TX	(19.55)	199	Flint, MI	(27.96)	–	Akron, OH**	NA
153	Columbus, GA–AL	(19.77)	200	Wilmington, NC	(28.11)	–	Albany, NY**	NA
154	Fort Smith, AR–OK	(19.78)	201	Springfield, MO	(28.15)	–	Barnstable–Yarmouth, MA**	NA
155	Reno, NV	(19.82)	202	Laredo, TX	(28.52)	–	Boston, MA–NH**	NA
156	Tulsa, OK	(19.84)	203	Orlando, FL	(28.72)	–	Bremerton, WA**	NA
157	Greenville–Spartanburg–Anderson, SC	(19.95)	204	Greeley, CO	(28.94)	–	Brockton, MA**	NA
158	Alexandria, LA	(20.00)	205	Galveston–Texas City, TX	(29.31)	–	Chicago, IL**	NA
159	Cumberland, MD–WV	(20.02)	206	Oklahoma City, OK	(29.60)	–	Cleveland, OH**	NA
160	Sarasota–Bradenton, FL	(20.08)	207	Stamford–Norwalk, CT	(30.00)	–	Dutchess County, NY**	NA
161	Lafayette, LA	(20.51)	208	Lubbock, TX	(30.08)	–	Goldsboro, NC**	NA
162	Denver, CO	(20.84)	209	Tacoma, WA	(30.12)	–	Greenville, NC**	NA
163	Fort Collins–Loveland, CO	(21.62)	210	Boise, ID	(30.28)	–	Harrisburg–Lebanon–Carlisle, PA**	NA
164	Tampa–St. Petersburg–Clearwater, FL	(21.69)	211	Racine, WI	(30.65)	–	Hickory–Morganton, NC**	NA
165	Hartford, CT	(21.79)	212	Ann Arbor, MI	(31.19)	–	Houma, LA**	NA
166	Erie, PA	(21.91)	213	Bloomington, IN	(31.33)	–	Indianapolis, IN**	NA
167	Colorado Springs, CO	(22.02)	214	Corpus Christi, TX	(31.41)	–	Johnstown, PA**	NA
168	Detroit, MI	(22.33)	215	Seattle–Bellevue–Everett, WA	(31.98)	–	Kansas City, MO–KS**	NA
169	Brazoria, TX	(22.34)	216	Charlottesville, VA	(32.42)	–	Myrtle Beach, SC**	NA
170	Saginaw–Bay City–Midland, MI	(22.50)	217	Austin–San Marcos, TX	(32.43)	–	Newburgh, NY–PA**	NA
171	Danbury, CT	(22.84)	218	Augusta–Aiken, GA–SC	(32.95)	–	Omaha, NE**	NA
172	Des Moines, IA	(23.22)	219	Florence, AL	(33.67)	–	Pittsfield, MA**	NA
173	Dothan, AL	(23.36)	220	Odessa–Midland, TX	(33.97)	–	Provo–Orem, UT**	NA
174	Chattanooga, TN–GA	(23.57)	221	Jackson, MI	(34.09)	–	Punta Gorda, FL**	NA
175	Lewiston–Auburn, ME	(23.64)	222	Sioux City, IA–NE	(34.18)	–	Reading, PA**	NA
176	Salem, OR	(23.76)	223	Madison, WI	(34.96)	–	Riverside–San Bernardino, CA**	NA
177	Altoona, PA	(23.84)	224	Sherman–Denison, TX	(35.82)	–	Rocky Mount, NC**	NA
178	Jacksonville, FL	(24.23)	225	Athens, GA	(35.94)	–	San Luis Obispo–Atascadero, CA**	NA
179	Columbia, MO	(24.52)	226	Texarkana, TX–AR	(36.15)	–	Scranton–Wilkes-Barre–Hazleton, PA**	NA
180	Toledo, OH	(24.90)	227	Bangor, ME	(36.75)	–	South Bend, IN**	NA
181	Portland, ME	(24.99)	228	Fayetteville–Springdale–Rogers, AR	(37.01)	–	Steubenville–Weirton, OH–WV**	NA
182	Beaumont–Port Arthur, TX	(25.13)	229	Spokane, WA	(38.03)	–	St. Louis, MO–IL**	NA
183	Yakima, WA	(25.23)	230	San Antonio, TX	(38.05)	–	Sumter, SC**	NA
184	Nashua, NH	(25.31)	231	Bryan–College Station, TX	(39.12)	–	Tucson, AZ**	NA
185	New Haven–Meriden, CT	(25.32)	232	Portland–Vancouver, OR–WA	(39.68)	–	West Palm Beach–Boca Raton, FL**	NA
186	Albuquerque, NM	(25.73)	233	Manchester, NH	(39.83)	–	Williamsport, PA**	NA
187	Daytona Beach, FL	(25.94)	234	Ocala, FL	(40.28)	–	Worcester, MA–CT**	NA
188	Atlanta, GA	(25.99)	235	Waco, TX	(40.41)	–	Yolo, CA**	NA

Source: Morgan Quitno Corporation using data from U.S. Department of Justice, Federal Bureau of Investigation
    "Crime in the United States 1993" (Uniform Crime Reports, December 4, 1994)
Burglary is the unlawful entry of a structure to commit a felony or theft. Attempts are included.
**Not available.*

33. Larceny and Theft in 1993

National Total = 7,820,909 Larcenies and Thefts*

RANK	METRO AREA	THEFTS	RANK	METRO AREA	THEFTS	RANK	METRO AREA	THEFTS
240	Abilene, TX	3,479	259	Cheyenne, WY	2,612	23	Fort Worth-Arlington, TX	60,530
77	Akron, OH	18,934	–	Chicago, IL**	NA	61	Fresno, CA	25,341
187	Albany, GA	5,493	188	Chico-Paradise, CA	5,482	237	Gadsden, AL	3,608
–	Albany, NY**	NA	30	Cincinnati, OH-KY-IN	49,219	120	Gainesville, FL	11,069
64	Albuquerque, NM	24,977	216	Clarksville-Hopkinsville, TN-KY	4,376	130	Galveston-Texas City, TX	9,960
208	Alexandria, LA	4,780	–	Cleveland, OH**	NA	83	Gary-Hammond, IN	17,141
269	Altoona, PA	1,968	87	Colorado Springs, CO	15,946	254	Glens Falls, NY	2,830
133	Amarillo, TX	9,911	214	Columbia, MO	4,478	246	Goldsboro, NC	3,299
126	Anchorage, AK	10,660	78	Columbia, SC	18,611	247	Grand Forks, ND-MN	3,142
97	Ann Arbor, MI	14,557	134	Columbus, GA-AL	9,299	53	Grand Rapids-Muskegon-Holland, MI	30,868
244	Anniston, AL	3,346	34	Columbus, OH	47,996	192	Greeley, CO	5,354
138	Appleton-Oshkosh-Neenah, WI	9,168	70	Corpus Christi, TX	20,800	184	Green Bay, WI	5,696
206	Asheville, NC	4,899	272	Cumberland, MD-WV	1,867	45	Greensboro-Winston Salem-High Point, NC	37,954
173	Athens, GA	6,247	7	Dallas, TX	111,455	203	Greenville, NC	4,944
5	Atlanta, GA	138,057	232	Danbury, CT	3,807	59	Greenville-Spartanburg-Anderson, SC	27,060
76	Atlantic City, NJ	18,954	266	Danville, VA	2,146	270	Hagerstown, MD	1,948
120	Augusta-Aiken, GA-SC	11,069	103	Daytona Beach, FL	13,422	102	Harrisburg-Lebanon-Carlisle, PA	13,458
35	Austin-San Marcos, TX	46,890	54	Dayton-Springfield, OH	30,755	56	Hartford, CT	29,429
73	Bakersfield, CA	19,984	243	Decatur, AL	3,374	151	Hickory-Morganton, NC	7,808
12	Baltimore, MD	91,733	22	Denver, CO	61,612	43	Honolulu, HI	40,148
271	Bangor, ME	1,933	84	Des Moines, IA	17,077	225	Houma, LA	4,023
255	Barnstable-Yarmouth, MA	2,820	4	Detroit, MI	143,361	9	Houston, TX	106,262
55	Baton Rouge, LA	29,722	228	Dothan, AL	3,936	179	Huntington-Ashland, WV-KY-OH	5,931
93	Beaumont-Port Arthur, TX	15,025	267	Dubuque, IA	2,107	114	Huntsville, AL	11,684
195	Bellingham, WA	5,251	170	Duluth-Superior, MN-WI	6,397	–	Indianapolis, IN**	NA
172	Benton Harbor, MI	6,310	198	Dutchess County, NY	5,153	226	Jackson, MI	3,987
57	Bergen-Passaic, NJ	27,882	234	Eau Claire, WI	3,753	91	Jackson, MS	15,362
166	Binghamton, NY	6,607	52	El Paso, TX	31,373	229	Jackson, TN	3,906
58	Birmingham, AL	27,736	193	Elkhart-Goshen, IN	5,298	42	Jacksonville, FL	41,282
263	Bismarck, ND	2,432	260	Enid, OK	2,584	219	Jacksonville, NC	4,217
253	Bloomington, IN	2,873	176	Erie, PA	6,160	186	Janesville-Beloit, WI	5,528
124	Boise, ID	10,957	115	Eugene-Springfield, OR	11,538	94	Jersey City, NJ	14,881
17	Boston, MA-NH	78,525	154	Evansville-Henderson, IN-KY	7,486	148	Johnson City-Kingsport-Bristol, TN-VA	8,290
141	Boulder-Longmont, CO	8,965	196	Fargo-Moorhead, ND-MN	5,206	268	Johnstown, PA	2,077
215	Brazoria, TX	4,393	105	Fayetteville, NC	12,922	238	Joplin, MO	3,601
183	Bremerton, WA	5,805	189	Fayetteville-Springdale-Rogers, AR	5,471	90	Kalamazoo-Battle Creek, MI	15,635
125	Bridgeport, CT	10,837	249	Fitchburg-Leominster, MA	3,038	–	Kansas City, MO-KS**	NA
210	Brockton, MA	4,720	86	Flint, MI	16,498	211	Kenosha, WI	4,629
104	Brownsville-Harlingen-San Benito, TX	13,349	258	Florence, AL	2,614	152	Killeen-Temple, TX	7,740
197	Bryan-College Station, TX	5,164	213	Florence, SC	4,562	257	Kokomo, IN	2,635
48	Buffalo-Niagara Falls, NY	32,656	181	Fort Collins-Loveland, CO	5,835	230	La Crosse, WI-MN	3,849
116	Canton-Massillon, OH	11,355	21	Fort Lauderdale, FL	67,436	199	Lafayette, IN	5,151
163	Charleston, WV	6,813	118	Fort Myers-Cape Coral, FL	11,258	127	Lafayette, LA	10,540
71	Charleston-North Charleston, SC	20,449	149	Fort Pierce-Port St. Lucie, FL	8,231	156	Lake Charles, LA	7,264
218	Charlottesville, VA	4,314	190	Fort Smith, AR-OK	5,426	72	Lakeland-Winter Haven, FL	20,188
31	Charlotte-Gastonia-Rock Hill, NC-SC	48,574	233	Fort Walton Beach, FL	3,778	144	Lancaster, PA	8,562
108	Chattanooga, TN-GA	12,501	98	Fort Wayne, IN	14,098	95	Lansing-East Lansing, MI	14,658

Source: U.S. Department of Justice, Federal Bureau of Investigation

   "Crime in the United States 1993" (Uniform Crime Reports, December 4, 1994)

Larceny and theft is the unlawful taking of property without use of force, violence or fraud. Attempts are included. Motor vehicle thefts are excluded.

**Not available.*

33. Larceny and Theft in 1993 (continued)

National Total = 7,820,909 Larcenies and Thefts*

RANK	METRO AREA	THEFTS	RANK	METRO AREA	THEFTS	RANK	METRO AREA	THEFTS
168	Laredo, TX	6,419	175	Olympia, WA	6,202	11	Seattle–Bellevue–Everett, WA	93,866
47	Las Vegas, NV–AZ	33,186	–	Omaha, NE**	NA	242	Sheboygan, WI	3,379
178	Lawrence, MA–NH	5,948	20	Orange County, CA	73,050	236	Sherman–Denison, TX	3,635
231	Lawton, OK	3,826	28	Orlando, FL	52,549	80	Shreveport–Bossier City, LA	18,450
252	Lewiston–Auburn, ME	2,939	262	Owensboro, KY	2,441	201	Sioux City, IA–NE	5,101
101	Lexington, KY	13,505	161	Panama City, FL	6,909	227	Sioux Falls, SD	3,967
117	Lincoln, NE	11,349	8	Philadelphia, PA–NJ	107,820	132	South Bend, IN	9,936
60	Little Rock–North Little Rock, AR	26,340	10	Phoenix–Mesa, AZ	103,077	85	Spokane, WA	16,542
155	Longview–Marshall, TX	7,267	264	Pine Bluff, AR	2,294	100	Springfield, MA	13,698
2	Los Angeles–Long Beach, CA	248,455	44	Pittsburgh, PA	39,756	135	Springfield, MO	9,274
62	Louisville, KY–IN	25,072	273	Pittsfield, MA	1,521	147	Stamford–Norwalk, CT	8,368
137	Lubbock, TX	9,175	160	Portland, ME	6,938	274	Steubenville–Weirton, OH–WV	1,470
221	Lynchburg, VA	4,085	24	Portland–Vancouver, OR–WA	59,729	69	Stockton–Lodi, CA	22,256
107	Macon, GA	12,750	67	Providence–Fall River–Warwick, RI–MA	22,675	235	St. Cloud, MN	3,675
110	Madison, WI	12,404	140	Provo–Orem, UT	9,025	224	St. Joseph, MO	4,054
209	Manchester, NH	4,731	220	Pueblo, CO	4,111	–	St. Louis, MO–IL**	NA
191	Mansfield, OH	5,420	265	Punta Gorda, FL	2,179	250	Sumter, SC	2,996
82	McAllen–Edinburg–Mission, TX	18,410	177	Racine, WI	6,141	81	Syracuse, NY	18,422
171	Medford–Ashland, OR	6,344	49	Raleigh–Durham–Chapel Hill, NC	32,588	63	Tacoma, WA	25,031
51	Memphis, TN–AR–MS	31,902	245	Rapid City, SD	3,306	99	Tallahassee, FL	14,096
185	Merced, CA	5,645	158	Reading, PA	7,167	15	Tampa–St. Petersburg–Clearwater, FL	85,051
6	Miami, FL	135,607	212	Redding, CA	4,572	200	Texarkana, TX–AR	5,120
68	Middlesex–Sommerset–Hunterdon, NJ	22,624	111	Reno, NV	12,212	66	Toledo, OH	22,697
36	Milwaukee–Waukesha, WI	46,314	204	Richland–Kennewick–Pasco, WA	4,918	150	Trenton, NJ	8,039
13	Minneapolis–St. Paul, MN–WI	89,491	50	Richmond–Petersburg, VA	32,077	41	Tucson, AZ	43,545
88	Mobile, AL	15,909	14	Riverside–San Bernardino, CA	87,878	75	Tulsa, OK	19,057
92	Modesto, CA	15,094	165	Roanoke, VA	6,736	142	Tuscaloosa, AL	8,627
65	Monmouth–Ocean, NJ	24,257	256	Rochester, MN	2,790	162	Tyler, TX	6,908
174	Monroe, LA	6,203	46	Rochester, NY	33,943	167	Utica–Rome, NY	6,470
143	Montgomery, AL	8,566	202	Rocky Mount, NC	5,038	89	Vallejo–Fairfield–Napa, CA	15,810
144	Myrtle Beach, SC	8,562	32	Sacramento, CA	48,184	96	Ventura, CA	14,580
207	Naples, FL	4,805	109	Saginaw–Bay City–Midland, MI	12,481	241	Victoria, TX	3,383
248	Nashua, NH	3,107	106	Salem, OR	12,835	204	Vineland–Millville–Bridgeton, NJ	4,918
38	Nashville, TN	45,419	119	Salinas, CA	11,200	122	Visalia–Tulare–Porterville, CA	11,053
33	Nassau–Suffolk, NY	48,059	29	Salt Lake City–Ogden, UT	52,005	146	Waco, TX	8,409
222	New Bedford, MA	4,075	239	San Angelo, TX	3,596	3	Washington, DC–MD–VA–WV	143,386
79	New Haven–Meriden, CT	18,469	18	San Antonio, TX	74,474	169	Waterbury, CT	6,403
180	New London–Norwich, CT–RI	5,847	19	San Diego, CA	73,694	223	Waterloo–Cedar Falls, IA	4,071
27	New Orleans, LA	55,034	25	San Francisco, CA	58,733	251	Wausau, WI	2,961
1	New York, NY	263,810	40	San Jose, CA	45,063	–	West Palm Beach–Boca Raton, FL**	NA
37	Newark, NJ	45,620	194	San Luis Obispo–Atascadero, CA	5,289	182	Wichita Falls, TX	5,812
157	Newburgh, NY–PA	7,262	123	Santa Barbara–Santa Maria–Lompoc, CA	10,974	261	Williamsport, PA	2,562
26	Norfolk–Va Beach–Newport News, VA–NC	57,496	139	Santa Cruz–Watsonville, CA	9,068	153	Wilmington, NC	7,733
16	Oakland, CA	84,235	112	Santa Rosa, CA	11,967	136	Worcester, MA–CT	9,204
159	Ocala, FL	7,023	74	Sarasota–Bradenton, FL	19,073	129	Yakima, WA	10,339
128	Odessa–Midland, TX	10,362	113	Savannah, GA	11,827	164	Yolo, CA	6,757
39	Oklahoma City, OK	45,196	131	Scranton–Wilkes-Barre–Hazleton, PA	9,951	217	Yuba City, CA	4,332

Source: U.S. Department of Justice, Federal Bureau of Investigation
   "Crime in the United States 1993" (Uniform Crime Reports, December 4, 1994)
Larceny and theft is the unlawful taking of property without use of force, violence or fraud. Attempts are included. Motor vehicle thefts are excluded.
**Not available.*

33. Larceny and Theft in 1993 (continued)

National Total = 7,820,909 Larcenies and Thefts*

RANK	METRO AREA	THEFTS	RANK	METRO AREA	THEFTS	RANK	METRO AREA	THEFTS
1	New York, NY	263,810	48	Buffalo–Niagara Falls, NY	32,656	95	Lansing–East Lansing, MI	14,658
2	Los Angeles–Long Beach, CA	248,455	49	Raleigh–Durham–Chapel Hill, NC	32,588	96	Ventura, CA	14,580
3	Washington, DC–MD–VA–WV	143,386	50	Richmond–Petersburg, VA	32,077	97	Ann Arbor, MI	14,557
4	Detroit, MI	143,361	51	Memphis, TN–AR–MS	31,902	98	Fort Wayne, IN	14,098
5	Atlanta, GA	138,057	52	El Paso, TX	31,373	99	Tallahassee, FL	14,096
6	Miami, FL	135,607	53	Grand Rapids–Muskegon–Holland, MI	30,868	100	Springfield, MA	13,698
7	Dallas, TX	111,455	54	Dayton–Springfield, OH	30,755	101	Lexington, KY	13,505
8	Philadelphia, PA–NJ	107,820	55	Baton Rouge, LA	29,722	102	Harrisburg–Lebanon–Carlisle, PA	13,458
9	Houston, TX	106,262	56	Hartford, CT	29,429	103	Daytona Beach, FL	13,422
10	Phoenix–Mesa, AZ	103,077	57	Bergen–Passaic, NJ	27,882	104	Brownsville–Harlingen–San Benito, TX	13,349
11	Seattle–Bellevue–Everett, WA	93,866	58	Birmingham, AL	27,736	105	Fayetteville, NC	12,922
12	Baltimore, MD	91,733	59	Greenville–Spartanburg–Anderson, SC	27,060	106	Salem, OR	12,835
13	Minneapolis–St. Paul, MN–WI	89,491	60	Little Rock–North Little Rock, AR	26,340	107	Macon, GA	12,750
14	Riverside–San Bernardino, CA	87,878	61	Fresno, CA	25,341	108	Chattanooga, TN–GA	12,501
15	Tampa–St. Petersburg–Clearwater, FL	85,051	62	Louisville, KY–IN	25,072	109	Saginaw–Bay City–Midland, MI	12,481
16	Oakland, CA	84,235	63	Tacoma, WA	25,031	110	Madison, WI	12,404
17	Boston, MA–NH	78,525	64	Albuquerque, NM	24,977	111	Reno, NV	12,212
18	San Antonio, TX	74,474	65	Monmouth–Ocean, NJ	24,257	112	Santa Rosa, CA	11,967
19	San Diego, CA	73,694	66	Toledo, OH	22,697	113	Savannah, GA	11,827
20	Orange County, CA	73,050	67	Providence–Fall River–Warwick, RI–MA	22,675	114	Huntsville, AL	11,684
21	Fort Lauderdale, FL	67,436	68	Middlesex–Somerset–Hunterdon, NJ	22,624	115	Eugene–Springfield, OR	11,538
22	Denver, CO	61,612	69	Stockton–Lodi, CA	22,256	116	Canton–Massillon, OH	11,355
23	Fort Worth–Arlington, TX	60,530	70	Corpus Christi, TX	20,800	117	Lincoln, NE	11,349
24	Portland–Vancouver, OR–WA	59,729	71	Charleston–North Charleston, SC	20,449	118	Fort Myers–Cape Coral, FL	11,258
25	San Francisco, CA	58,733	72	Lakeland–Winter Haven, FL	20,188	119	Salinas, CA	11,200
26	Norfolk–Va Beach–Newport News, VA–NC	57,496	73	Bakersfield, CA	19,984	120	Augusta–Aiken, GA–SC	11,069
27	New Orleans, LA	55,034	74	Sarasota–Bradenton, FL	19,073	120	Gainesville, FL	11,069
28	Orlando, FL	52,549	75	Tulsa, OK	19,057	122	Visalia–Tulare–Porterville, CA	11,053
29	Salt Lake City–Ogden, UT	52,005	76	Atlantic City, NJ	18,954	123	Santa Barbara–Santa Maria–Lompoc, CA	10,974
30	Cincinnati, OH–KY–IN	49,219	77	Akron, OH	18,934	124	Boise, ID	10,957
31	Charlotte–Gastonia–Rock Hill, NC–SC	48,574	78	Columbia, SC	18,611	125	Bridgeport, CT	10,837
32	Sacramento, CA	48,184	79	New Haven–Meriden, CT	18,469	126	Anchorage, AK	10,660
33	Nassau–Suffolk, NY	48,059	80	Shreveport–Bossier City, LA	18,450	127	Lafayette, LA	10,540
34	Columbus, OH	47,996	81	Syracuse, NY	18,422	128	Odessa–Midland, TX	10,362
35	Austin–San Marcos, TX	46,890	82	McAllen–Edinburg–Mission, TX	18,410	129	Yakima, WA	10,339
36	Milwaukee–Waukesha, WI	46,314	83	Gary–Hammond, IN	17,141	130	Galveston–Texas City, TX	9,960
37	Newark, NJ	45,620	84	Des Moines, IA	17,077	131	Scranton–Wilkes-Barre–Hazleton, PA	9,951
38	Nashville, TN	45,419	85	Spokane, WA	16,542	132	South Bend, IN	9,936
39	Oklahoma City, OK	45,196	86	Flint, MI	16,498	133	Amarillo, TX	9,911
40	San Jose, CA	45,063	87	Colorado Springs, CO	15,946	134	Columbus, GA–AL	9,299
41	Tucson, AZ	43,545	88	Mobile, AL	15,909	135	Springfield, MO	9,274
42	Jacksonville, FL	41,282	89	Vallejo–Fairfield–Napa, CA	15,810	136	Worcester, MA–CT	9,204
43	Honolulu, HI	40,148	90	Kalamazoo–Battle Creek, MI	15,635	137	Lubbock, TX	9,175
44	Pittsburgh, PA	39,756	91	Jackson, MS	15,362	138	Appleton–Oshkosh–Neenah, WI	9,168
45	Greensboro–Winston Salem–High Point, NC	37,954	92	Modesto, CA	15,094	139	Santa Cruz–Watsonville, CA	9,068
46	Rochester, NY	33,943	93	Beaumont–Port Arthur, TX	15,025	140	Provo–Orem, UT	9,025
47	Las Vegas, NV–AZ	33,186	94	Jersey City, NJ	14,881	141	Boulder–Longmont, CO	8,965

Source: U.S. Department of Justice, Federal Bureau of Investigation
    "Crime in the United States 1993" (Uniform Crime Reports, December 4, 1994)
*Larceny and theft is the unlawful taking of property without use of force, violence or fraud. Attempts are included. Motor vehicle thefts are excluded.
**Not available.

33. Larceny and Theft in 1993 (continued)

National Total = 7,820,909 Larcenies and Thefts*

RANK	METRO AREA	THEFTS	RANK	METRO AREA	THEFTS	RANK	METRO AREA	THEFTS
142	Tuscaloosa, AL	8,627	189	Fayetteville–Springdale–Rogers, AR	5,471	236	Sherman–Denison, TX	3,635
143	Montgomery, AL	8,566	190	Fort Smith, AR–OK	5,426	237	Gadsden, AL	3,608
144	Lancaster, PA	8,562	191	Mansfield, OH	5,420	238	Joplin, MO	3,601
144	Myrtle Beach, SC	8,562	192	Greeley, CO	5,354	239	San Angelo, TX	3,596
146	Waco, TX	8,409	193	Elkhart–Goshen, IN	5,298	240	Abilene, TX	3,479
147	Stamford–Norwalk, CT	8,368	194	San Luis Obispo–Atascadero, CA	5,289	241	Victoria, TX	3,383
148	Johnson City–Kingsport–Bristol, TN–VA	8,290	195	Bellingham, WA	5,251	242	Sheboygan, WI	3,379
149	Fort Pierce–Port St. Lucie, FL	8,231	196	Fargo–Moorhead, ND–MN	5,206	243	Decatur, AL	3,374
150	Trenton, NJ	8,039	197	Bryan–College Station, TX	5,164	244	Anniston, AL	3,346
151	Hickory–Morganton, NC	7,808	198	Dutchess County, NY	5,153	245	Rapid City, SD	3,306
152	Killeen–Temple, TX	7,740	199	Lafayette, IN	5,151	246	Goldsboro, NC	3,299
153	Wilmington, NC	7,733	200	Texarkana, TX–AR	5,120	247	Grand Forks, ND–MN	3,142
154	Evansville–Henderson, IN–KY	7,486	201	Sioux City, IA–NE	5,101	248	Nashua, NH	3,107
155	Longview–Marshall, TX	7,267	202	Rocky Mount, NC	5,038	249	Fitchburg–Leominster, MA	3,038
156	Lake Charles, LA	7,264	203	Greenville, NC	4,944	250	Sumter, SC	2,996
157	Newburgh, NY–PA	7,262	204	Richland–Kennewick–Pasco, WA	4,918	251	Wausau, WI	2,961
158	Reading, PA	7,167	204	Vineland–Millville–Bridgeton, NJ	4,918	252	Lewiston–Auburn, ME	2,939
159	Ocala, FL	7,023	206	Asheville, NC	4,899	253	Bloomington, IN	2,873
160	Portland, ME	6,938	207	Naples, FL	4,805	254	Glens Falls, NY	2,830
161	Panama City, FL	6,909	208	Alexandria, LA	4,780	255	Barnstable–Yarmouth, MA	2,820
162	Tyler, TX	6,908	209	Manchester, NH	4,731	256	Rochester, MN	2,790
163	Charleston, WV	6,813	210	Brockton, MA	4,720	257	Kokomo, IN	2,635
164	Yolo, CA	6,757	211	Kenosha, WI	4,629	258	Florence, AL	2,614
165	Roanoke, VA	6,736	212	Redding, CA	4,572	259	Cheyenne, WY	2,612
166	Binghamton, NY	6,607	213	Florence, SC	4,562	260	Enid, OK	2,584
167	Utica–Rome, NY	6,470	214	Columbia, MO	4,478	261	Williamsport, PA	2,562
168	Laredo, TX	6,419	215	Brazoria, TX	4,393	262	Owensboro, KY	2,441
169	Waterbury, CT	6,403	216	Clarksville–Hopkinsville, TN–KY	4,376	263	Bismarck, ND	2,432
170	Duluth–Superior, MN–WI	6,397	217	Yuba City, CA	4,332	264	Pine Bluff, AR	2,294
171	Medford–Ashland, OR	6,344	218	Charlottesville, VA	4,314	265	Punta Gorda, FL	2,179
172	Benton Harbor, MI	6,310	219	Jacksonville, NC	4,217	266	Danville, VA	2,146
173	Athens, GA	6,247	220	Pueblo, CO	4,111	267	Dubuque, IA	2,107
174	Monroe, LA	6,203	221	Lynchburg, VA	4,085	268	Johnstown, PA	2,077
175	Olympia, WA	6,202	222	New Bedford, MA	4,075	269	Altoona, PA	1,968
176	Erie, PA	6,160	223	Waterloo–Cedar Falls, IA	4,071	270	Hagerstown, MD	1,948
177	Racine, WI	6,141	224	St. Joseph, MO	4,054	271	Bangor, ME	1,933
178	Lawrence, MA–NH	5,948	225	Houma, LA	4,023	272	Cumberland, MD–WV	1,867
179	Huntington–Ashland, WV–KY–OH	5,931	226	Jackson, MI	3,987	273	Pittsfield, MA	1,521
180	New London–Norwich, CT–RI	5,847	227	Sioux Falls, SD	3,967	274	Steubenville–Weirton, OH–WV	1,470
181	Fort Collins–Loveland, CO	5,835	228	Dothan, AL	3,936	–	Albany, NY**	NA
182	Wichita Falls, TX	5,812	229	Jackson, TN	3,906	–	Chicago, IL**	NA
183	Bremerton, WA	5,805	230	La Crosse, WI–MN	3,849	–	Cleveland, OH**	NA
184	Green Bay, WI	5,696	231	Lawton, OK	3,826	–	Indianapolis, IN**	NA
185	Merced, CA	5,645	232	Danbury, CT	3,807	–	Kansas City, MO–KS**	NA
186	Janesville–Beloit, WI	5,528	233	Fort Walton Beach, FL	3,778	–	Omaha, NE**	NA
187	Albany, GA	5,493	234	Eau Claire, WI	3,753	–	St. Louis, MO–IL**	NA
188	Chico–Paradise, CA	5,482	235	St. Cloud, MN	3,675	–	West Palm Beach–Boca Raton, FL**	NA

Source: U.S. Department of Justice, Federal Bureau of Investigation
    "Crime in the United States 1993" (Uniform Crime Reports, December 4, 1994)
*Larceny and theft is the unlawful taking of property without use of force, violence or fraud. Attempts are included. Motor vehicle thefts are excluded.
**Not available.

34. Larceny and Theft Rate in 1993

National Rate = 3,032.4 Larcenies and Thefts Per 100,000 Population*

RANK	METRO AREA	RATE	RANK	METRO AREA	RATE	RANK	METRO AREA	RATE
186	Abilene, TX	2,830.1	113	Cheyenne, WY	3,397.5	70	Fort Worth–Arlington, TX	3,933.5
185	Akron, OH	2,834.5	–	Chicago, IL**	NA	150	Fresno, CA	3,117.5
23	Albany, GA	4,667.7	176	Chico–Paradise, CA	2,880.7	99	Gadsden, AL	3,588.1
–	Albany, NY**	NA	148	Cincinnati, OH–KY–IN	3,132.5	4	Gainesville, FL	5,760.4
67	Albuquerque, NM	3,965.8	225	Clarksville–Hopkinsville, TN–KY	2,425.6	46	Galveston–Texas City, TX	4,282.6
96	Alexandria, LA	3,647.7	–	Cleveland, OH**	NA	196	Gary–Hammond, IN	2,752.4
272	Altoona, PA	1,492.1	93	Colorado Springs, CO	3,678.8	236	Glens Falls, NY	2,328.8
16	Amarillo, TX	5,072.0	82	Columbia, MO	3,799.4	159	Goldsboro, NC	3,014.8
50	Anchorage, AK	4,251.8	72	Columbia, SC	3,896.6	158	Grand Forks, ND–MN	3,031.3
175	Ann Arbor, MI	2,888.9	119	Columbus, GA–AL	3,341.1	139	Grand Rapids–Muskegon–Holland, MI	3,186.1
183	Anniston, AL	2,840.9	111	Columbus, OH	3,424.9	79	Greeley, CO	3,829.0
194	Appleton–Oshkosh–Neenah, WI	2,778.4	6	Corpus Christi, TX	5,629.5	192	Green Bay, WI	2,803.6
221	Asheville, NC	2,442.1	266	Cumberland, MD–WV	1,823.1	108	Greensboro–Winston Salem–High Point, NC	3,462.5
61	Athens, GA	4,044.3	59	Dallas, TX	4,051.3	32	Greenville, NC	4,408.4
47	Atlanta, GA	4,280.1	234	Danbury, CT	2,341.5	147	Greenville–Spartanburg–Anderson, SC	3,133.2
3	Atlantic City, NJ	5,766.0	260	Danville, VA	1,933.7	271	Hagerstown, MD	1,537.5
220	Augusta–Aiken, GA–SC	2,451.6	146	Daytona Beach, FL	3,136.9	238	Harrisburg–Lebanon–Carlisle, PA	2,224.8
14	Austin–San Marcos, TX	5,103.6	141	Dayton–Springfield, OH	3,176.4	193	Hartford, CT	2,792.6
116	Bakersfield, CA	3,366.1	218	Decatur, AL	2,466.5	212	Hickory–Morganton, NC	2,568.6
90	Baltimore, MD	3,733.1	107	Denver, CO	3,505.2	26	Honolulu, HI	4,586.0
181	Bangor, ME	2,858.5	54	Des Moines, IA	4,183.8	242	Houma, LA	2,148.9
251	Barnstable–Yarmouth, MA	2,056.6	123	Detroit, MI	3,310.4	169	Houston, TX	2,951.1
9	Baton Rouge, LA	5,420.2	171	Dothan, AL	2,918.6	263	Huntington–Ashland, WV–KY–OH	1,870.0
64	Beaumont–Port Arthur, TX	3,984.4	226	Dubuque, IA	2,404.9	89	Huntsville, AL	3,748.5
91	Bellingham, WA	3,726.4	207	Duluth–Superior, MN–WI	2,626.8	–	Indianapolis, IN**	NA
73	Benton Harbor, MI	3,890.1	257	Dutchess County, NY	1,950.9	209	Jackson, MI	2,615.5
244	Bergen–Passaic, NJ	2,143.4	204	Eau Claire, WI	2,659.0	87	Jackson, MS	3,753.9
219	Binghamton, NY	2,465.5	19	El Paso, TX	4,895.6	20	Jackson, TN	4,797.9
137	Birmingham, AL	3,190.5	126	Elkhart–Goshen, IN	3,293.5	48	Jacksonville, FL	4,271.7
189	Bismarck, ND	2,821.9	28	Enid, OK	4,547.9	178	Jacksonville, NC	2,872.0
214	Bloomington, IN	2,561.0	240	Erie, PA	2,193.4	78	Janesville–Beloit, WI	3,837.6
122	Boise, ID	3,323.8	74	Eugene–Springfield, OR	3,887.2	203	Jersey City, NJ	2,661.5
237	Boston, MA–NH	2,314.2	208	Evansville–Henderson, IN–KY	2,621.4	264	Johnson City–Kingsport–Bristol, TN–VA	1,838.5
95	Boulder–Longmont, CO	3,657.4	130	Fargo–Moorhead, ND–MN	3,287.3	274	Johnstown, PA	858.8
247	Brazoria, TX	2,113.4	25	Fayetteville, NC	4,586.5	210	Joplin, MO	2,597.4
200	Bremerton, WA	2,695.5	228	Fayetteville–Springdale–Rogers, AR	2,393.7	101	Kalamazoo–Battle Creek, MI	3,566.5
229	Bridgeport, CT	2,393.0	239	Fitchburg–Leominster, MA	2,217.7	–	Kansas City, MO–KS**	NA
262	Brockton, MA	1,916.9	83	Flint, MI	3,788.8	112	Kenosha, WI	3,424.3
22	Brownsville–Harlingen–San Benito, TX	4,697.6	261	Florence, AL	1,924.7	163	Killeen–Temple, TX	2,978.4
60	Bryan–College Station, TX	4,046.4	81	Florence, SC	3,804.6	206	Kokomo, IN	2,647.3
198	Buffalo–Niagara Falls, NY	2,717.5	180	Fort Collins–Loveland, CO	2,861.7	134	La Crosse, WI–MN	3,231.8
187	Canton–Massillon, OH	2,825.6	13	Fort Lauderdale, FL	5,108.1	152	Lafayette, IN	3,094.6
201	Charleston, WV	2,679.1	144	Fort Myers–Cape Coral, FL	3,152.0	164	Lafayette, LA	2,972.3
80	Charleston–North Charleston, SC	3,826.2	156	Fort Pierce–Port St. Lucie, FL	3,057.0	53	Lake Charles, LA	4,219.7
143	Charlottesville, VA	3,160.8	165	Fort Smith, AR–OK	2,970.7	21	Lakeland–Winter Haven, FL	4,749.4
69	Charlotte–Gastonia–Rock Hill, NC–SC	3,946.0	224	Fort Walton Beach, FL	2,427.2	255	Lancaster, PA	1,962.3
182	Chattanooga, TN–GA	2,853.0	160	Fort Wayne, IN	3,014.0	118	Lansing–East Lansing, MI	3,343.0

Source: U.S. Department of Justice, Federal Bureau of Investigation
  "Crime in the United States 1993" (Uniform Crime Reports, December 4, 1994)
*Larceny and theft is the unlawful taking of property without use of force, violence or fraud. Attempts are included. Motor vehicle thefts are excluded.
**Not available.

34. Larceny and Theft Rate in 1993 (continued)

National Rate = 3,032.4 Larcenies and Thefts Per 100,000 Population*

RANK	METRO AREA	RATE	RANK	METRO AREA	RATE	RANK	METRO AREA	RATE
52	Laredo, TX	4,240.2	110	Olympia, WA	3,437.7	29	Seattle–Bellevue–Everett, WA	4,521.6
128	Las Vegas, NV–AZ	3,292.4	–	Omaha, NE**	NA	138	Sheboygan, WI	3,188.2
254	Lawrence, MA–NH	2,009.9	173	Orange County, CA	2,910.1	88	Sherman–Denison, TX	3,749.7
145	Lawton, OK	3,150.4	66	Orlando, FL	3,970.0	18	Shreveport–Bossier City, LA	4,911.7
188	Lewiston–Auburn, ME	2,823.5	197	Owensboro, KY	2,723.1	39	Sioux City, IA–NE	4,338.7
92	Lexington, KY	3,707.9	15	Panama City, FL	5,081.9	202	Sioux Falls, SD	2,673.9
11	Lincoln, NE	5,149.2	241	Philadelphia, PA–NJ	2,169.7	71	South Bend, IN	3,927.9
17	Little Rock–North Little Rock, AR	4,949.7	42	Phoenix–Mesa, AZ	4,307.0	51	Spokane, WA	4,247.1
102	Longview–Marshall, TX	3,564.8	205	Pine Bluff, AR	2,657.4	216	Springfield, MA	2,538.1
199	Los Angeles–Long Beach, CA	2,716.5	268	Pittsburgh, PA	1,640.1	120	Springfield, MO	3,337.2
213	Louisville, KY–IN	2,567.1	270	Pittsfield, MA	1,543.9	215	Stamford–Norwalk, CT	2,538.6
63	Lubbock, TX	4,019.7	166	Portland, ME	2,967.8	273	Steubenville–Weirton, OH–WV	1,032.3
253	Lynchburg, VA	2,028.3	97	Portland–Vancouver, OR–WA	3,640.1	36	Stockton–Lodi, CA	4,370.4
55	Macon, GA	4,180.8	232	Providence–Fall River–Warwick, RI–MA	2,369.9	230	St. Cloud, MN	2,380.7
127	Madison, WI	3,293.0	136	Provo–Orem, UT	3,194.7	58	St. Joseph, MO	4,103.4
184	Manchester, NH	2,835.0	135	Pueblo, CO	3,227.8	–	St. Louis, MO–IL**	NA
154	Mansfield, OH	3,069.6	267	Punta Gorda, FL	1,801.0	190	Sumter, SC	2,812.5
45	McAllen–Edinburg–Mission, TX	4,289.0	114	Racine, WI	3,390.6	223	Syracuse, NY	2,434.0
62	Medford–Ashland, OR	4,035.7	104	Raleigh–Durham–Chapel Hill, NC	3,530.2	68	Tacoma, WA	3,949.1
157	Memphis, TN–AR–MS	3,043.1	77	Rapid City, SD	3,850.8	5	Tallahassee, FL	5,664.7
167	Merced, CA	2,954.9	249	Reading, PA	2,079.6	65	Tampa–St. Petersburg–Clearwater, FL	3,978.3
1	Miami, FL	6,655.3	179	Redding, CA	2,871.7	57	Texarkana, TX–AR	4,161.7
243	Middlesex–Sommerset–Hunterdon, NJ	2,145.2	34	Reno, NV	4,374.1	94	Toledo, OH	3,665.5
139	Milwaukee–Waukesha, WI	3,186.1	162	Richland–Kennewick–Pasco, WA	2,991.4	222	Trenton, NJ	2,434.9
115	Minneapolis–St. Paul, MN–WI	3,379.2	105	Richmond–Petersburg, VA	3,526.3	2	Tucson, AZ	6,142.3
142	Mobile, AL	3,172.7	151	Riverside–San Bernardino, CA	3,096.9	211	Tulsa, OK	2,583.5
85	Modesto, CA	3,780.6	170	Roanoke, VA	2,932.4	8	Tuscaloosa, AL	5,549.6
227	Monmouth–Ocean, NJ	2,401.1	217	Rochester, MN	2,497.9	33	Tyler, TX	4,388.1
49	Monroe, LA	4,264.7	149	Rochester, NY	3,124.1	252	Utica–Rome, NY	2,037.3
195	Montgomery, AL	2,768.1	98	Rocky Mount, NC	3,614.2	125	Vallejo–Fairfield–Napa, CA	3,294.0
7	Myrtle Beach, SC	5,559.5	117	Sacramento, CA	3,362.3	248	Ventura, CA	2,102.1
177	Naples, FL	2,875.1	153	Saginaw–Bay City–Midland, MI	3,086.2	43	Victoria, TX	4,306.4
259	Nashua, NH	1,937.2	41	Salem, OR	4,319.0	106	Vineland–Millville–Bridgeton, NJ	3,524.5
35	Nashville, TN	4,373.5	161	Salinas, CA	3,010.1	124	Visalia–Tulare–Porterville, CA	3,304.7
265	Nassau–Suffolk, NY	1,828.7	30	Salt Lake City–Ogden, UT	4,489.1	44	Waco, TX	4,305.1
235	New Bedford, MA	2,333.8	103	San Angelo, TX	3,558.3	132	Washington, DC–MD–VA–WV	3,259.5
131	New Haven–Meriden, CT	3,281.4	10	San Antonio, TX	5,297.9	109	Waterbury, CT	3,454.3
258	New London–Norwich, CT–RI	1,940.6	191	San Diego, CA	2,804.5	133	Waterloo–Cedar Falls, IA	3,233.9
37	New Orleans, LA	4,364.5	100	San Francisco, CA	3,575.3	245	Wausau, WI	2,139.9
155	New York, NY	3,060.6	172	San Jose, CA	2,918.3	–	West Palm Beach–Boca Raton, FL**	NA
233	Newark, NJ	2,354.2	231	San Luis Obispo–Atascadero, CA	2,373.8	31	Wichita Falls, TX	4,450.1
250	Newburgh, NY–PA	2,075.0	174	Santa Barbara–Santa Maria–Lompoc, CA	2,892.8	246	Williamsport, PA	2,117.4
84	Norfolk–Va Beach–Newport News, VA–NC	3,784.2	75	Santa Cruz–Watsonville, CA	3,886.0	56	Wilmington, NC	4,176.8
76	Oakland, CA	3,881.6	168	Santa Rosa, CA	2,954.2	256	Worcester, MA–CT	1,955.1
121	Ocala, FL	3,328.3	86	Sarasota–Bradenton, FL	3,769.2	12	Yakima, WA	5,109.9
38	Odessa–Midland, TX	4,346.9	40	Savannah, GA	4,331.6	24	Yolo, CA	4,618.9
27	Oklahoma City, OK	4,558.3	269	Scranton–Wilkes-Barre–Hazleton, PA	1,551.3	129	Yuba City, CA	3,290.2

Source: U.S. Department of Justice, Federal Bureau of Investigation
     "Crime in the United States 1993" (Uniform Crime Reports, December 4, 1994)
*Larceny and theft is the unlawful taking of property without use of force, violence or fraud. Attempts are included. Motor vehicle thefts are excluded.
**Not available.

34. Larceny and Theft Rate in 1993 (continued)

National Rate = 3,032.4 Larcenies and Thefts Per 100,000 Population*

RANK	METRO AREA	RATE	RANK	METRO AREA	RATE	RANK	METRO AREA	RATE
1	Miami, FL	6,655.3	48	Jacksonville, FL	4,271.7	95	Boulder–Longmont, CO	3,657.4
2	Tucson, AZ	6,142.3	49	Monroe, LA	4,264.7	96	Alexandria, LA	3,647.7
3	Atlantic City, NJ	5,766.0	50	Anchorage, AK	4,251.8	97	Portland–Vancouver, OR–WA	3,640.1
4	Gainesville, FL	5,760.4	51	Spokane, WA	4,247.1	98	Rocky Mount, NC	3,614.2
5	Tallahassee, FL	5,664.7	52	Laredo, TX	4,240.2	99	Gadsden, AL	3,588.1
6	Corpus Christi, TX	5,629.5	53	Lake Charles, LA	4,219.7	100	San Francisco, CA	3,575.3
7	Myrtle Beach, SC	5,559.5	54	Des Moines, IA	4,183.8	101	Kalamazoo–Battle Creek, MI	3,566.5
8	Tuscaloosa, AL	5,549.6	55	Macon, GA	4,180.8	102	Longview–Marshall, TX	3,564.8
9	Baton Rouge, LA	5,420.2	56	Wilmington, NC	4,176.8	103	San Angelo, TX	3,558.3
10	San Antonio, TX	5,297.9	57	Texarkana, TX–AR	4,161.7	104	Raleigh–Durham–Chapel Hill, NC	3,530.2
11	Lincoln, NE	5,149.2	58	St. Joseph, MO	4,103.4	105	Richmond–Petersburg, VA	3,526.3
12	Yakima, WA	5,109.9	59	Dallas, TX	4,051.3	106	Vineland–Millville–Bridgeton, NJ	3,524.5
13	Fort Lauderdale, FL	5,108.1	60	Bryan–College Station, TX	4,046.4	107	Denver, CO	3,505.2
14	Austin–San Marcos, TX	5,103.6	61	Athens, GA	4,044.3	108	Greensboro–Winston Salem–High Point, NC	3,462.5
15	Panama City, FL	5,081.9	62	Medford–Ashland, OR	4,035.7	109	Waterbury, CT	3,454.3
16	Amarillo, TX	5,072.0	63	Lubbock, TX	4,019.7	110	Olympia, WA	3,437.7
17	Little Rock–North Little Rock, AR	4,949.7	64	Beaumont–Port Arthur, TX	3,984.4	111	Columbus, OH	3,424.9
18	Shreveport–Bossier City, LA	4,911.7	65	Tampa–St. Petersburg–Clearwater, FL	3,978.3	112	Kenosha, WI	3,424.3
19	El Paso, TX	4,895.6	66	Orlando, FL	3,970.0	113	Cheyenne, WY	3,397.5
20	Jackson, TN	4,797.9	67	Albuquerque, NM	3,965.8	114	Racine, WI	3,390.6
21	Lakeland–Winter Haven, FL	4,749.4	68	Tacoma, WA	3,949.1	115	Minneapolis–St. Paul, MN–WI	3,379.2
22	Brownsville–Harlingen–San Benito, TX	4,697.6	69	Charlotte–Gastonia–Rock Hill, NC–SC	3,946.0	116	Bakersfield, CA	3,366.1
23	Albany, GA	4,667.7	70	Fort Worth–Arlington, TX	3,933.5	117	Sacramento, CA	3,362.3
24	Yolo, CA	4,618.9	71	South Bend, IN	3,927.9	118	Lansing–East Lansing, MI	3,343.0
25	Fayetteville, NC	4,586.5	72	Columbia, SC	3,896.6	119	Columbus, GA–AL	3,341.1
26	Honolulu, HI	4,586.0	73	Benton Harbor, MI	3,890.1	120	Springfield, MO	3,337.2
27	Oklahoma City, OK	4,558.3	74	Eugene–Springfield, OR	3,887.2	121	Ocala, FL	3,328.3
28	Enid, OK	4,547.9	75	Santa Cruz–Watsonville, CA	3,886.0	122	Boise, ID	3,323.8
29	Seattle–Bellevue–Everett, WA	4,521.6	76	Oakland, CA	3,881.6	123	Detroit, MI	3,310.4
30	Salt Lake City–Ogden, UT	4,489.1	77	Rapid City, SD	3,850.8	124	Visalia–Tulare–Porterville, CA	3,304.7
31	Wichita Falls, TX	4,450.1	78	Janesville–Beloit, WI	3,837.6	125	Vallejo–Fairfield–Napa, CA	3,294.0
32	Greenville, NC	4,408.4	79	Greeley, CO	3,829.0	126	Elkhart–Goshen, IN	3,293.5
33	Tyler, TX	4,388.1	80	Charleston–North Charleston, SC	3,826.2	127	Madison, WI	3,293.0
34	Reno, NV	4,374.1	81	Florence, SC	3,804.6	128	Las Vegas, NV–AZ	3,292.4
35	Nashville, TN	4,373.5	82	Columbia, MO	3,799.4	129	Yuba City, CA	3,290.2
36	Stockton–Lodi, CA	4,370.4	83	Flint, MI	3,788.8	130	Fargo–Moorhead, ND–MN	3,287.3
37	New Orleans, LA	4,364.5	84	Norfolk–Va Beach–Newport News, VA–NC	3,784.2	131	New Haven–Meriden, CT	3,281.4
38	Odessa–Midland, TX	4,346.9	85	Modesto, CA	3,780.6	132	Washington, DC–MD–VA–WV	3,259.5
39	Sioux City, IA–NE	4,338.7	86	Sarasota–Bradenton, FL	3,769.2	133	Waterloo–Cedar Falls, IA	3,233.9
40	Savannah, GA	4,331.6	87	Jackson, MS	3,753.9	134	La Crosse, WI–MN	3,231.8
41	Salem, OR	4,319.0	88	Sherman–Denison, TX	3,749.7	135	Pueblo, CO	3,227.8
42	Phoenix–Mesa, AZ	4,307.0	89	Huntsville, AL	3,748.5	136	Provo–Orem, UT	3,194.7
43	Victoria, TX	4,306.4	90	Baltimore, MD	3,733.1	137	Birmingham, AL	3,190.5
44	Waco, TX	4,305.1	91	Bellingham, WA	3,726.4	138	Sheboygan, WI	3,188.2
45	McAllen–Edinburg–Mission, TX	4,289.0	92	Lexington, KY	3,707.9	139	Grand Rapids–Muskegon–Holland, MI	3,186.1
46	Galveston–Texas City, TX	4,282.6	93	Colorado Springs, CO	3,678.8	139	Milwaukee–Waukesha, WI	3,186.1
47	Atlanta, GA	4,280.1	94	Toledo, OH	3,665.5	141	Dayton–Springfield, OH	3,176.4

Source: U.S. Department of Justice, Federal Bureau of Investigation
   "Crime in the United States 1993" (Uniform Crime Reports, December 4, 1994)
Larceny and theft is the unlawful taking of property without use of force, violence or fraud. Attempts are included. Motor vehicle thefts are excluded.

***Not available.*

34. Larceny and Theft Rate in 1993 (continued)

National Rate = 3,032.4 Larcenies and Thefts Per 100,000 Population*

RANK	METRO AREA	RATE	RANK	METRO AREA	RATE	RANK	METRO AREA	RATE
142	Mobile, AL	3,172.7	189	Bismarck, ND	2,821.9	236	Glens Falls, NY	2,328.8
143	Charlottesville, VA	3,160.8	190	Sumter, SC	2,812.5	237	Boston, MA–NH	2,314.2
144	Fort Myers–Cape Coral, FL	3,152.0	191	San Diego, CA	2,804.5	238	Harrisburg–Lebanon–Carlisle, PA	2,224.8
145	Lawton, OK	3,150.4	192	Green Bay, WI	2,803.6	239	Fitchburg–Leominster, MA	2,217.7
146	Daytona Beach, FL	3,136.9	193	Hartford, CT	2,792.6	240	Erie, PA	2,193.4
147	Greenville–Spartanburg–Anderson, SC	3,133.2	194	Appleton–Oshkosh–Neenah, WI	2,778.4	241	Philadelphia, PA–NJ	2,169.7
148	Cincinnati, OH–KY–IN	3,132.5	195	Montgomery, AL	2,768.1	242	Houma, LA	2,148.9
149	Rochester, NY	3,124.1	196	Gary–Hammond, IN	2,752.4	243	Middlesex–Sommerset–Hunterdon, NJ	2,145.2
150	Fresno, CA	3,117.5	197	Owensboro, KY	2,723.1	244	Bergen–Passaic, NJ	2,143.4
151	Riverside–San Bernardino, CA	3,096.9	198	Buffalo–Niagara Falls, NY	2,717.5	245	Wausau, WI	2,139.9
152	Lafayette, IN	3,094.6	199	Los Angeles–Long Beach, CA	2,716.5	246	Williamsport, PA	2,117.4
153	Saginaw–Bay City–Midland, MI	3,086.2	200	Bremerton, WA	2,695.5	247	Brazoria, TX	2,113.4
154	Mansfield, OH	3,069.6	201	Charleston, WV	2,679.1	248	Ventura, CA	2,102.1
155	New York, NY	3,060.6	202	Sioux Falls, SD	2,673.9	249	Reading, PA	2,079.6
156	Fort Pierce–Port St. Lucie, FL	3,057.0	203	Jersey City, NJ	2,661.5	250	Newburgh, NY–PA	2,075.0
157	Memphis, TN–AR–MS	3,043.1	204	Eau Claire, WI	2,659.0	251	Barnstable–Yarmouth, MA	2,056.6
158	Grand Forks, ND–MN	3,031.3	205	Pine Bluff, AR	2,657.4	252	Utica–Rome, NY	2,037.3
159	Goldsboro, NC	3,014.8	206	Kokomo, IN	2,647.3	253	Lynchburg, VA	2,028.3
160	Fort Wayne, IN	3,014.0	207	Duluth–Superior, MN–WI	2,626.8	254	Lawrence, MA–NH	2,009.9
161	Salinas, CA	3,010.1	208	Evansville–Henderson, IN–KY	2,621.4	255	Lancaster, PA	1,962.3
162	Richland–Kennewick–Pasco, WA	2,991.4	209	Jackson, MI	2,615.5	256	Worcester, MA–CT	1,955.1
163	Killeen–Temple, TX	2,978.4	210	Joplin, MO	2,597.4	257	Dutchess County, NY	1,950.9
164	Lafayette, LA	2,972.3	211	Tulsa, OK	2,583.5	258	New London–Norwich, CT–RI	1,940.6
165	Fort Smith, AR–OK	2,970.7	212	Hickory–Morganton, NC	2,568.6	259	Nashua, NH	1,937.2
166	Portland, ME	2,967.8	213	Louisville, KY–IN	2,567.1	260	Danville, VA	1,933.7
167	Merced, CA	2,954.9	214	Bloomington, IN	2,561.0	261	Florence, AL	1,924.7
168	Santa Rosa, CA	2,954.2	215	Stamford–Norwalk, CT	2,538.6	262	Brockton, MA	1,916.9
169	Houston, TX	2,951.1	216	Springfield, MA	2,538.1	263	Huntington–Ashland, WV–KY–OH	1,870.0
170	Roanoke, VA	2,932.4	217	Rochester, MN	2,497.9	264	Johnson City–Kingsport–Bristol, TN–VA	1,838.5
171	Dothan, AL	2,918.6	218	Decatur, AL	2,466.5	265	Nassau–Suffolk, NY	1,828.7
172	San Jose, CA	2,918.3	219	Binghamton, NY	2,465.5	266	Cumberland, MD–WV	1,823.1
173	Orange County, CA	2,910.1	220	Augusta–Aiken, GA–SC	2,451.6	267	Punta Gorda, FL	1,801.0
174	Santa Barbara–Santa Maria–Lompoc, CA	2,892.8	221	Asheville, NC	2,442.1	268	Pittsburgh, PA	1,640.1
175	Ann Arbor, MI	2,888.9	222	Trenton, NJ	2,434.9	269	Scranton–Wilkes-Barre–Hazleton, PA	1,551.3
176	Chico–Paradise, CA	2,880.7	223	Syracuse, NY	2,434.0	270	Pittsfield, MA	1,543.9
177	Naples, FL	2,875.1	224	Fort Walton Beach, FL	2,427.2	271	Hagerstown, MD	1,537.5
178	Jacksonville, NC	2,872.0	225	Clarksville–Hopkinsville, TN–KY	2,425.6	272	Altoona, PA	1,492.1
179	Redding, CA	2,871.7	226	Dubuque, IA	2,404.9	273	Steubenville–Weirton, OH–WV	1,032.3
180	Fort Collins–Loveland, CO	2,861.7	227	Monmouth–Ocean, NJ	2,401.1	274	Johnstown, PA	858.8
181	Bangor, ME	2,858.5	228	Fayetteville–Springdale–Rogers, AR	2,393.7	–	Albany, NY**	NA
182	Chattanooga, TN–GA	2,853.0	229	Bridgeport, CT	2,393.0	–	Chicago, IL**	NA
183	Anniston, AL	2,840.9	230	St. Cloud, MN	2,380.7	–	Cleveland, OH**	NA
184	Manchester, NH	2,835.0	231	San Luis Obispo–Atascadero, CA	2,373.8	–	Indianapolis, IN**	NA
185	Akron, OH	2,834.5	232	Providence–Fall River–Warwick, RI–MA	2,369.9	–	Kansas City, MO–KS**	NA
186	Abilene, TX	2,830.1	233	Newark, NJ	2,354.2	–	Omaha, NE**	NA
187	Canton–Massillon, OH	2,825.6	234	Danbury, CT	2,341.5	–	St. Louis, MO–IL**	NA
188	Lewiston–Auburn, ME	2,823.5	235	New Bedford, MA	2,333.8	–	West Palm Beach–Boca Raton, FL**	NA

Source: U.S. Department of Justice, Federal Bureau of Investigation
"Crime in the United States 1993" (Uniform Crime Reports, December 4, 1994)
*Larceny and theft is the unlawful taking of property without use of force, violence or fraud. Attempts are included. Motor vehicle thefts are excluded.
**Not available.

35. Percent Change in Larceny and Theft Rate: 1992 to 1993

National Percent Change = 2.3% Decrease*

RANK	METRO AREA	% CHANGE	RANK	METRO AREA	% CHANGE	RANK	METRO AREA	% CHANGE
6	Abilene, TX	12.42	242	Cheyenne, WY	(14.61)	243	Fort Worth-Arlington, TX	(15.30)
189	Akron, OH	(6.05)	–	Chicago, IL**	NA	232	Fresno, CA	(11.50)
84	Albany, GA	0.02	172	Chico-Paradise, CA	(5.02)	54	Gadsden, AL	2.74
–	Albany, NY**	NA	128	Cincinnati, OH-KY-IN	(2.87)	187	Gainesville, FL	(5.91)
103	Albuquerque, NM	(1.39)	34	Clarksville-Hopkinsville, TN-KY	5.24	204	Galveston-Texas City, TX	(7.41)
67	Alexandria, LA	1.16	–	Cleveland, OH**	NA	83	Gary-Hammond, IN	0.09
5	Altoona, PA	13.19	132	Colorado Springs, CO	(3.16)	108	Glens Falls, NY	(1.63)
75	Amarillo, TX	0.56	167	Columbia, MO	(4.92)	39	Goldsboro, NC	4.67
171	Anchorage, AK	(5.01)	120	Columbia, SC	(2.48)	162	Grand Forks, ND-MN	(4.42)
211	Ann Arbor, MI	(8.86)	66	Columbus, GA-AL	1.20	157	Grand Rapids-Muskegon-Holland, MI	(4.25)
160	Anniston, AL	(4.31)	173	Columbus, OH	(5.19)	93	Greeley, CO	(0.65)
219	Appleton-Oshkosh-Neenah, WI	(9.62)	79	Corpus Christi, TX	0.30	155	Green Bay, WI	(4.15)
208	Asheville, NC	(7.94)	224	Cumberland, MD-WV	(9.97)	77	Greensboro-Winston Salem-High Point, NC	0.38
161	Athens, GA	(4.39)	234	Dallas, TX	(11.62)	85	Greenville, NC	(0.10)
164	Atlanta, GA	(4.65)	86	Danbury, CT	(0.12)	71	Greenville-Spartanburg-Anderson, SC	0.88
207	Atlantic City, NJ	(7.92)	148	Danville, VA	(3.88)	111	Hagerstown, MD	(2.06)
246	Augusta-Aiken, GA-SC	(19.04)	109	Daytona Beach, FL	(1.67)	156	Harrisburg-Lebanon-Carlisle, PA	(4.21)
142	Austin-San Marcos, TX	(3.63)	144	Dayton-Springfield, OH	(3.68)	196	Hartford, CT	(6.45)
100	Bakersfield, CA	(1.13)	69	Decatur, AL	1.01	24	Hickory-Morganton, NC	7.28
117	Baltimore, MD	(2.38)	209	Denver, CO	(8.24)	43	Honolulu, HI	4.09
29	Bangor, ME	6.32	236	Des Moines, IA	(12.43)	176	Houma, LA	(5.33)
229	Barnstable-Yarmouth, MA	(11.07)	124	Detroit, MI	(2.55)	182	Houston, TX	(5.56)
105	Baton Rouge, LA	(1.60)	226	Dothan, AL	(10.46)	223	Huntington-Ashland, WV-KY-OH	(9.84)
51	Beaumont-Port Arthur, TX	3.08	44	Dubuque, IA	3.72	237	Huntsville, AL	(12.50)
233	Bellingham, WA	(11.53)	118	Duluth-Superior, MN-WI	(2.45)	–	Indianapolis, IN**	NA
98	Benton Harbor, MI	(0.96)	–	Dutchess County, NY**	NA	146	Jackson, MI	(3.79)
–	Bergen-Passaic, NJ**	NA	200	Eau Claire, WI	(6.98)	173	Jackson, MS	(5.19)
15	Binghamton, NY	10.27	159	El Paso, TX	(4.29)	96	Jackson, TN	(0.87)
175	Birmingham, AL	(5.27)	16	Elkhart-Goshen, IN	9.96	205	Jacksonville, FL	(7.76)
231	Bismarck, ND	(11.49)	9	Enid, OK	11.35	65	Jacksonville, NC	1.40
33	Bloomington, IN	5.33	25	Erie, PA	7.27	228	Janesville-Beloit, WI	(10.71)
124	Boise, ID	(2.55)	45	Eugene-Springfield, OR	3.50	–	Jersey City, NJ**	NA
–	Boston, MA-NH**	NA	163	Evansville-Henderson, IN-KY	(4.58)	123	Johnson City-Kingsport-Bristol, TN-VA	(2.53)
239	Boulder-Longmont, CO	(13.10)	113	Fargo-Moorhead, ND-MN	(2.18)	168	Johnstown, PA	(4.97)
221	Brazoria, TX	(9.81)	53	Fayetteville, NC	2.79	–	Joplin, MO**	NA
221	Bremerton, WA	(9.81)	245	Fayetteville-Springdale-Rogers, AR	(18.56)	170	Kalamazoo-Battle Creek, MI	(4.98)
199	Bridgeport, CT	(6.91)	–	Fitchburg-Leominster, MA**	NA	–	Kansas City, MO-KS**	NA
145	Brockton, MA	(3.70)	102	Flint, MI	(1.29)	165	Kenosha, WI	(4.74)
12	Brownsville-Harlingen-San Benito, TX	10.75	198	Florence, AL	(6.84)	60	Killeen-Temple, TX	2.32
81	Bryan-College Station, TX	0.24	36	Florence, SC	5.10	22	Kokomo, IN	7.86
–	Buffalo-Niagara Falls, NY**	NA	–	Fort Collins-Loveland, CO**	NA	135	La Crosse, WI-MN	(3.33)
28	Canton-Massillon, OH	6.37	35	Fort Lauderdale, FL	5.22	206	Lafayette, IN	(7.78)
152	Charleston, WV	(3.96)	88	Fort Myers-Cape Coral, FL	(0.28)	94	Lafayette, LA	(0.76)
26	Charleston-North Charleston, SC	7.24	201	Fort Pierce-Port St. Lucie, FL	(7.04)	–	Lake Charles, LA**	NA
19	Charlottesville, VA	8.81	91	Fort Smith, AR-OK	(0.56)	73	Lakeland-Winter Haven, FL	0.74
166	Charlotte-Gastonia-Rock Hill, NC-SC	(4.90)	115	Fort Walton Beach, FL	(2.26)	230	Lancaster, PA	(11.38)
105	Chattanooga, TN-GA	(1.60)	202	Fort Wayne, IN	(7.13)	168	Lansing-East Lansing, MI	(4.97)

Source: Morgan Quitno Corporation using data from U.S. Department of Justice, Federal Bureau of Investigation
   "Crime in the United States 1993" (Uniform Crime Reports, December 4, 1994)
Larceny and theft is the unlawful taking of property without use of force, violence or fraud. Attempts are included. Motor vehicle thefts are excluded.
**Not available.*

35. Percent Change in Larceny and Theft Rate: 1992 to 1993 (continued)

National Percent Change = 2.3% Decrease*

RANK	METRO AREA	% CHANGE	RANK	METRO AREA	% CHANGE	RANK	METRO AREA	CHANGE
191	Laredo, TX	(6.15)	20	Olympia, WA	8.46	61	Seattle-Bellevue-Everett, WA	1.70
217	Las Vegas, NV-AZ	(9.36)	–	Omaha, NE**	NA	133	Sheboygan, WI	(3.26)
–	Lawrence, MA-NH**	NA	154	Orange County, CA	(4.11)	134	Sherman-Denison, TX	(3.28)
46	Lawton, OK	3.44	138	Orlando, FL	(3.46)	30	Shreveport-Bossier City, LA	6.21
4	Lewiston-Auburn, ME	13.86	7	Owensboro, KY	12.31	–	Sioux City, IA-NE**	NA
74	Lexington, KY	0.61	37	Panama City, FL	5.09	63	Sioux Falls, SD	1.48
215	Lincoln, NE	(9.24)	121	Philadelphia, PA-NJ	(2.49)	59	South Bend, IN	2.41
57	Little Rock-North Little Rock, AR	2.67	42	Phoenix-Mesa, AZ	4.34	82	Spokane, WA	0.11
62	Longview-Marshall, TX	1.69	2	Pine Bluff, AR	22.40	210	Springfield, MA	(8.65)
115	Los Angeles-Long Beach, CA	(2.26)	68	Pittsburgh, PA	1.05	186	Springfield, MO	(5.80)
110	Louisville, KY-IN	(1.74)	80	Pittsfield, MA	0.26	18	Stamford-Norwalk, CT	8.87
192	Lubbock, TX	(6.18)	247	Portland, ME	(21.93)	118	Steubenville-Weirton, OH-WV	(2.45)
130	Lynchburg, VA	(3.04)	101	Portland-Vancouver, OR-WA	(1.23)	48	Stockton-Lodi, CA	3.37
31	Macon, GA	5.92	76	Providence-Fall River-Warwick, RI-MA	0.49	41	St. Cloud, MN	4.44
235	Madison, WI	(11.80)	187	Provo-Orem, UT	(5.91)	1	St. Joseph, MO	27.59
–	Manchester, NH**	NA	203	Pueblo, CO	(7.24)	–	St. Louis, MO-IL**	NA
114	Mansfield, OH	(2.25)	–	Punta Gorda, FL**	NA	249	Sumter, SC	(23.38)
55	McAllen-Edinburg-Mission, TX	2.72	99	Racine, WI	(1.10)	183	Syracuse, NY	(5.64)
11	Medford-Ashland, OR	11.26	131	Raleigh-Durham-Chapel Hill, NC	(3.05)	122	Tacoma, WA	(2.52)
21	Memphis, TN-AR-MS	8.34	214	Rapid City, SD	(9.14)	70	Tallahassee, FL	0.97
107	Merced, CA	(1.61)	179	Reading, PA	(5.45)	139	Tampa-St. Petersburg-Clearwater, FL	(3.52)
23	Miami, FL	7.82	49	Redding, CA	3.34	14	Texarkana, TX-AR	10.50
–	Middlesex-Sommerset-Hunterdon, NJ**	NA	72	Reno, NV	0.75	157	Toledo, OH	(4.25)
150	Milwaukee-Waukesha, WI	(3.94)	248	Richland-Kennewick-Pasco, WA	(22.25)	241	Trenton, NJ	(13.86)
181	Minneapolis-St. Paul, MN-WI	(5.50)	150	Richmond-Petersburg, VA	(3.94)	8	Tucson, AZ	11.73
–	Mobile, AL**	NA	184	Riverside-San Bernardino, CA	(5.67)	146	Tulsa, OK	(3.79)
58	Modesto, CA	2.54	244	Roanoke, VA	(15.83)	10	Tuscaloosa, AL	11.29
–	Monmouth-Ocean, NJ**	NA	148	Rochester, MN	(3.88)	213	Tyler, TX	(9.09)
137	Monroe, LA	(3.43)	194	Rochester, NY	(6.36)	227	Utica-Rome, NY	(10.70)
129	Montgomery, AL	(3.01)	180	Rocky Mount, NC	(5.49)	126	Vallejo-Fairfield-Napa, CA	(2.56)
13	Myrtle Beach, SC	10.72	112	Sacramento, CA	(2.16)	219	Ventura, CA	(9.62)
212	Naples, FL	(9.00)	92	Saginaw-Bay City-Midland, MI	(0.62)	50	Victoria, TX	3.17
87	Nashua, NH	(0.14)	141	Salem, OR	(3.55)	97	Vineland-Millville-Bridgeton, NJ	(0.92)
3	Nashville, TN	15.87	142	Salinas, CA	(3.63)	185	Visalia-Tulare-Porterville, CA	(5.73)
–	Nassau-Suffolk, NY**	NA	216	Salt Lake City-Ogden, UT	(9.35)	17	Waco, TX	9.93
–	New Bedford, MA**	NA	225	San Angelo, TX	(10.31)	95	Washington, DC-MD-VA-WV	(0.82)
190	New Haven-Meriden, CT	(6.06)	197	San Antonio, TX	(6.65)	38	Waterbury, CT	4.76
89	New London-Norwich, CT-RI	(0.30)	193	San Diego, CA	(6.30)	–	Waterloo-Cedar Falls, IA**	NA
56	New Orleans, LA	2.71	195	San Francisco, CA	(6.44)	240	Wausau, WI	(13.39)
–	New York, NY**	NA	153	San Jose, CA	(4.04)	–	West Palm Beach-Boca Raton, FL**	NA
–	Newark, NJ**	NA	–	San Luis Obispo-Atascadero, CA**	NA	63	Wichita Falls, TX	1.48
–	Newburgh, NY-PA**	NA	136	Santa Barbara-Santa Maria-Lompoc, CA	(3.39)	139	Williamsport, PA	(3.52)
177	Norfolk-Va Beach-Newport News, VA-NC	(5.37)	47	Santa Cruz-Watsonville, CA	3.38	250	Wilmington, NC	(24.28)
127	Oakland, CA	(2.69)	90	Santa Rosa, CA	(0.31)	–	Worcester, MA-CT**	NA
178	Ocala, FL	(5.39)	218	Sarasota-Bradenton, FL	(9.42)	27	Yakima, WA	6.76
238	Odessa-Midland, TX	(12.73)	40	Savannah, GA	4.49	32	Yolo, CA	5.78
52	Oklahoma City, OK	3.04	104	Scranton-Wilkes-Barre-Hazleton, PA	(1.40)	78	Yuba City, CA	0.34

Source: Morgan Quitno Corporation using data from U.S. Department of Justice, Federal Bureau of Investigation
"Crime in the United States 1993" (Uniform Crime Reports, December 4, 1994)
*Larceny and theft is the unlawful taking of property without use of force, violence or fraud. Attempts are included. Motor vehicle thefts are excluded.
**Not available.

35. Percent Change in Larceny and Theft Rate: 1992 to 1993 (continued)

National Percent Change = 2.3% Decrease*

RANK	METRO AREA	% CHANGE	RANK	METRO AREA	% CHANGE	RANK	METRO AREA	% CHANGE
1	St. Joseph, MO	27.59	48	Stockton–Lodi, CA	3.37	95	Washington, DC–MD–VA–WV	(0.82)
2	Pine Bluff, AR	22.40	49	Redding, CA	3.34	96	Jackson, TN	(0.87)
3	Nashville, TN	15.87	50	Victoria, TX	3.17	97	Vineland–Millville–Bridgeton, NJ	(0.92)
4	Lewiston–Auburn, ME	13.86	51	Beaumont–Port Arthur, TX	3.08	98	Benton Harbor, MI	(0.96)
5	Altoona, PA	13.19	52	Oklahoma City, OK	3.04	99	Racine, WI	(1.10)
6	Abilene, TX	12.42	53	Fayetteville, NC	2.79	100	Bakersfield, CA	(1.13)
7	Owensboro, KY	12.31	54	Gadsden, AL	2.74	101	Portland–Vancouver, OR–WA	(1.23)
8	Tucson, AZ	11.73	55	McAllen–Edinburg–Mission, TX	2.72	102	Flint, MI	(1.29)
9	Enid, OK	11.35	56	New Orleans, LA	2.71	103	Albuquerque, NM	(1.39)
10	Tuscaloosa, AL	11.29	57	Little Rock–North Little Rock, AR	2.67	104	Scranton–Wilkes-Barre–Hazleton, PA	(1.40)
11	Medford–Ashland, OR	11.26	58	Modesto, CA	2.54	105	Baton Rouge, LA	(1.60)
12	Brownsville–Harlingen–San Benito, TX	10.75	59	South Bend, IN	2.41	105	Chattanooga, TN–GA	(1.60)
13	Myrtle Beach, SC	10.72	60	Killeen–Temple, TX	2.32	107	Merced, CA	(1.61)
14	Texarkana, TX–AR	10.50	61	Seattle–Bellevue–Everett, WA	1.70	108	Glens Falls, NY	(1.63)
15	Binghamton, NY	10.27	62	Longview–Marshall, TX	1.69	109	Daytona Beach, FL	(1.67)
16	Elkhart–Goshen, IN	9.96	63	Sioux Falls, SD	1.48	110	Louisville, KY–IN	(1.74)
17	Waco, TX	9.93	63	Wichita Falls, TX	1.48	111	Hagerstown, MD	(2.06)
18	Stamford–Norwalk, CT	8.87	65	Jacksonville, NC	1.40	112	Sacramento, CA	(2.16)
19	Charlottesville, VA	8.81	66	Columbus, GA–AL	1.20	113	Fargo–Moorhead, ND–MN	(2.18)
20	Olympia, WA	8.46	67	Alexandria, LA	1.16	114	Mansfield, OH	(2.25)
21	Memphis, TN–AR–MS	8.34	68	Pittsburgh, PA	1.05	115	Fort Walton Beach, FL	(2.26)
22	Kokomo, IN	7.86	69	Decatur, AL	1.01	115	Los Angeles–Long Beach, CA	(2.26)
23	Miami, FL	7.82	70	Tallahassee, FL	0.97	117	Baltimore, MD	(2.38)
24	Hickory–Morganton, NC	7.28	71	Greenville–Spartanburg–Anderson, SC	0.88	118	Duluth–Superior, MN–WI	(2.45)
25	Erie, PA	7.27	72	Reno, NV	0.75	118	Steubenville–Weirton, OH–WV	(2.45)
26	Charleston–North Charleston, SC	7.24	73	Lakeland–Winter Haven, FL	0.74	120	Columbia, SC	(2.48)
27	Yakima, WA	6.76	74	Lexington, KY	0.61	121	Philadelphia, PA–NJ	(2.49)
28	Canton–Massillon, OH	6.37	75	Amarillo, TX	0.56	122	Tacoma, WA	(2.52)
29	Bangor, ME	6.32	76	Providence–Fall River–Warwick, RI–MA	0.49	123	Johnson City–Kingsport–Bristol, TN–VA	(2.53)
30	Shreveport–Bossier City, LA	6.21	77	Greensboro–Winston Salem–High Point, NC	0.38	124	Boise, ID	(2.55)
31	Macon, GA	5.92	78	Yuba City, CA	0.34	124	Detroit, MI	(2.55)
32	Yolo, CA	5.78	79	Corpus Christi, TX	0.30	126	Vallejo–Fairfield–Napa, CA	(2.56)
33	Bloomington, IN	5.33	80	Pittsfield, MA	0.26	127	Oakland, CA	(2.69)
34	Clarksville–Hopkinsville, TN–KY	5.24	81	Bryan–College Station, TX	0.24	128	Cincinnati, OH–KY–IN	(2.87)
35	Fort Lauderdale, FL	5.22	82	Spokane, WA	0.11	129	Montgomery, AL	(3.01)
36	Florence, SC	5.10	83	Gary–Hammond, IN	0.09	130	Lynchburg, VA	(3.04)
37	Panama City, FL	5.09	84	Albany, GA	0.02	131	Raleigh–Durham–Chapel Hill, NC	(3.05)
38	Waterbury, CT	4.76	85	Greenville, NC	(0.10)	132	Colorado Springs, CO	(3.16)
39	Goldsboro, NC	4.67	86	Danbury, CT	(0.12)	133	Sheboygan, WI	(3.26)
40	Savannah, GA	4.49	87	Nashua, NH	(0.14)	134	Sherman–Denison, TX	(3.28)
41	St. Cloud, MN	4.44	88	Fort Myers–Cape Coral, FL	(0.28)	135	La Crosse, WI–MN	(3.33)
42	Phoenix–Mesa, AZ	4.34	89	New London–Norwich, CT–RI	(0.30)	136	Santa Barbara–Santa Maria–Lompoc, CA	(3.39)
43	Honolulu, HI	4.09	90	Santa Rosa, CA	(0.31)	137	Monroe, LA	(3.43)
44	Dubuque, IA	3.72	91	Fort Smith, AR–OK	(0.56)	138	Orlando, FL	(3.46)
45	Eugene–Springfield, OR	3.50	92	Saginaw–Bay City–Midland, MI	(0.62)	139	Tampa–St. Petersburg–Clearwater, FL	(3.52)
46	Lawton, OK	3.44	93	Greeley, CO	(0.65)	139	Williamsport, PA	(3.52)
47	Santa Cruz–Watsonville, CA	3.38	94	Lafayette, LA	(0.76)	141	Salem, OR	(3.55)

Source: Morgan Quitno Corporation using data from U.S. Department of Justice, Federal Bureau of Investigation
    "Crime in the United States 1993" (Uniform Crime Reports, December 4, 1994)
*Larceny and theft is the unlawful taking of property without use of force, violence or fraud. Attempts are included. Motor vehicle thefts are excluded.

**Not available.

35. Percent Change in Larceny and Theft Rate: 1992 to 1993 (continued)

National Percent Change = 2.3% Decrease*

RANK	METRO AREA	% CHANGE	RANK	METRO AREA	% CHANGE	RANK	METRO AREA	CHANGE
142	Austin–San Marcos, TX	(3.63)	189	Akron, OH	(6.05)	236	Des Moines, IA	(12.43)
142	Salinas, CA	(3.63)	190	New Haven–Meriden, CT	(6.06)	237	Huntsville, AL	(12.50)
144	Dayton–Springfield, OH	(3.68)	191	Laredo, TX	(6.15)	238	Odessa–Midland, TX	(12.73)
145	Brockton, MA	(3.70)	192	Lubbock, TX	(6.18)	239	Boulder–Longmont, CO	(13.10)
146	Jackson, MI	(3.79)	193	San Diego, CA	(6.30)	240	Wausau, WI	(13.39)
146	Tulsa, OK	(3.79)	194	Rochester, NY	(6.36)	241	Trenton, NJ	(13.86)
148	Danville, VA	(3.88)	195	San Francisco, CA	(6.44)	242	Cheyenne, WY	(14.61)
148	Rochester, MN	(3.88)	196	Hartford, CT	(6.45)	243	Fort Worth–Arlington, TX	(15.30)
150	Milwaukee–Waukesha, WI	(3.94)	197	San Antonio, TX	(6.65)	244	Roanoke, VA	(15.83)
150	Richmond–Petersburg, VA	(3.94)	198	Florence, AL	(6.84)	245	Fayetteville–Springdale–Rogers, AR	(18.56)
152	Charleston, WV	(3.96)	199	Bridgeport, CT	(6.91)	246	Augusta–Aiken, GA–SC	(19.04)
153	San Jose, CA	(4.04)	200	Eau Claire, WI	(6.98)	247	Portland, ME	(21.93)
154	Orange County, CA	(4.11)	201	Fort Pierce–Port St. Lucie, FL	(7.04)	248	Richland–Kennewick–Pasco, WA	(22.25)
155	Green Bay, WI	(4.15)	202	Fort Wayne, IN	(7.13)	249	Sumter, SC	(23.38)
156	Harrisburg–Lebanon–Carlisle, PA	(4.21)	203	Pueblo, CO	(7.24)	250	Wilmington, NC	(24.28)
157	Grand Rapids–Muskegon–Holland, MI	(4.25)	204	Galveston–Texas City, TX	(7.41)	–	Albany, NY**	NA
157	Toledo, OH	(4.25)	205	Jacksonville, FL	(7.76)	–	Bergen–Passaic, NJ**	NA
159	El Paso, TX	(4.29)	206	Lafayette, IN	(7.78)	–	Boston, MA–NH**	NA
160	Anniston, AL	(4.31)	207	Atlantic City, NJ	(7.92)	–	Buffalo–Niagara Falls, NY**	NA
161	Athens, GA	(4.39)	208	Asheville, NC	(7.94)	–	Chicago, IL**	NA
162	Grand Forks, ND–MN	(4.42)	209	Denver, CO	(8.24)	–	Cleveland, OH**	NA
163	Evansville–Henderson, IN–KY	(4.58)	210	Springfield, MA	(8.65)	–	Dutchess County, NY**	NA
164	Atlanta, GA	(4.65)	211	Ann Arbor, MI	(8.86)	–	Fitchburg–Leominster, MA**	NA
165	Kenosha, WI	(4.74)	212	Naples, FL	(9.00)	–	Fort Collins–Loveland, CO**	NA
166	Charlotte–Gastonia–Rock Hill, NC–SC	(4.90)	213	Tyler, TX	(9.09)	–	Indianapolis, IN**	NA
167	Columbia, MO	(4.92)	214	Rapid City, SD	(9.14)	–	Jersey City, NJ**	NA
168	Johnstown, PA	(4.97)	215	Lincoln, NE	(9.24)	–	Joplin, MO**	NA
168	Lansing–East Lansing, MI	(4.97)	216	Salt Lake City–Ogden, UT	(9.35)	–	Kansas City, MO–KS**	NA
170	Kalamazoo–Battle Creek, MI	(4.98)	217	Las Vegas, NV–AZ	(9.36)	–	Lake Charles, LA**	NA
171	Anchorage, AK	(5.01)	218	Sarasota–Bradenton, FL	(9.42)	–	Lawrence, MA–NH**	NA
172	Chico–Paradise, CA	(5.02)	219	Appleton–Oshkosh–Neenah, WI	(9.62)	–	Manchester, NH**	NA
173	Columbus, OH	(5.19)	219	Ventura, CA	(9.62)	–	Middlesex–Sommerset–Hunterdon, NJ**	NA
173	Jackson, MS	(5.19)	221	Brazoria, TX	(9.81)	–	Mobile, AL**	NA
175	Birmingham, AL	(5.27)	221	Bremerton, WA	(9.81)	–	Monmouth–Ocean, NJ**	NA
176	Houma, LA	(5.33)	223	Huntington–Ashland, WV–KY–OH	(9.84)	–	Nassau–Suffolk, NY**	NA
177	Norfolk–Va Beach–Newport News, VA–NC	(5.37)	224	Cumberland, MD–WV	(9.97)	–	New Bedford, MA**	NA
178	Ocala, FL	(5.39)	225	San Angelo, TX	(10.31)	–	New York, NY**	NA
179	Reading, PA	(5.45)	226	Dothan, AL	(10.46)	–	Newark, NJ**	NA
180	Rocky Mount, NC	(5.49)	227	Utica–Rome, NY	(10.70)	–	Newburgh, NY–PA**	NA
181	Minneapolis–St. Paul, MN–WI	(5.50)	228	Janesville–Beloit, WI	(10.71)	–	Omaha, NE**	NA
182	Houston, TX	(5.56)	229	Barnstable–Yarmouth, MA	(11.07)	–	Punta Gorda, FL**	NA
183	Syracuse, NY	(5.64)	230	Lancaster, PA	(11.38)	–	San Luis Obispo–Atascadero, CA**	NA
184	Riverside–San Bernardino, CA	(5.67)	231	Bismarck, ND	(11.49)	–	Sioux City, IA–NE**	NA
185	Visalia–Tulare–Porterville, CA	(5.73)	232	Fresno, CA	(11.50)	–	St. Louis, MO–IL**	NA
186	Springfield, MO	(5.80)	233	Bellingham, WA	(11.53)	–	Waterloo–Cedar Falls, IA**	NA
187	Gainesville, FL	(5.91)	234	Dallas, TX	(11.62)	–	West Palm Beach–Boca Raton, FL**	NA
187	Provo–Orem, UT	(5.91)	235	Madison, WI	(11.80)	–	Worcester, MA–CT**	NA

Source: Morgan Quitno Corporation using data from U.S. Department of Justice, Federal Bureau of Investigation
"Crime in the United States 1993" (Uniform Crime Reports, December 4, 1994)
*Larceny and theft is the unlawful taking of property without use of force, violence or fraud. Attempts are included. Motor vehicle thefts are excluded.
**Not available.

36. Percent Change in Larceny and Theft Rate: 1989 to 1993

National Percent Change = 4.4% Decrease*

RANK	METRO AREA	% CHANGE	RANK	METRO AREA	% CHANGE	RANK	METRO AREA	% CHANGE
57	Abilene, TX	5.57	102	Cheyenne, WY	(2.99)	239	Fort Worth–Arlington, TX	(25.80)
–	Akron, OH**	NA	–	Chicago, IL**	NA	242	Fresno, CA	(27.81)
68	Albany, GA	3.50	149	Chico–Paradise, CA	(8.14)	7	Gadsden, AL	27.47
–	Albany, NY**	NA	104	Cincinnati, OH–KY–IN	(3.49)	12	Gainesville, FL	23.41
199	Albuquerque, NM	(15.78)	103	Clarksville–Hopkinsville, TN–KY	(3.43)	133	Galveston–Texas City, TX	(6.53)
70	Alexandria, LA	3.27	–	Cleveland, OH**	NA	56	Gary–Hammond, IN	5.75
52	Altoona, PA	6.57	171	Colorado Springs, CO	(11.34)	15	Glens Falls, NY	21.30
53	Amarillo, TX	5.93	150	Columbia, MO	(8.23)	–	Goldsboro, NC**	NA
26	Anchorage, AK	15.55	58	Columbia, SC	5.53	164	Grand Forks, ND–MN	(10.65)
245	Ann Arbor, MI	(36.06)	100	Columbus, GA–AL	(2.85)	117	Grand Rapids–Muskegon–Holland, MI	(4.94)
11	Anniston, AL	23.96	168	Columbus, OH	(11.04)	77	Greeley, CO	1.99
74	Appleton–Oshkosh–Neenah, WI	2.73	78	Corpus Christi, TX	1.22	163	Green Bay, WI	(10.53)
181	Asheville, NC	(12.33)	50	Cumberland, MD–WV	6.93	41	Greensboro–Winston Salem–High Point, NC	8.39
16	Athens, GA	18.82	244	Dallas, TX	(29.35)	–	Greenville, NC**	NA
217	Atlanta, GA	(19.75)	17	Danbury, CT	18.31	210	Greenville–Spartanburg–Anderson, SC	(17.66)
212	Atlantic City, NJ	(18.23)	23	Danville, VA	17.07	54	Hagerstown, MD	5.90
213	Augusta–Aiken, GA–SC	(18.37)	197	Daytona Beach, FL	(15.50)	–	Harrisburg–Lebanon–Carlisle, PA**	NA
161	Austin–San Marcos, TX	(10.42)	172	Dayton–Springfield, OH	(11.38)	153	Hartford, CT	(8.53)
139	Bakersfield, CA	(7.26)	20	Decatur, AL	18.03	–	Hickory–Morganton, NC**	NA
33	Baltimore, MD	13.10	166	Denver, CO	(10.87)	47	Honolulu, HI	7.18
191	Bangor, ME	(14.28)	167	Des Moines, IA	(11.02)	–	Houma, LA**	NA
–	Barnstable–Yarmouth, MA**	NA	131	Detroit, MI	(6.35)	236	Houston, TX	(24.74)
27	Baton Rouge, LA	15.27	218	Dothan, AL	(19.76)	109	Huntington–Ashland, WV–KY–OH	(4.10)
48	Beaumont–Port Arthur, TX	7.01	121	Dubuque, IA	(5.15)	214	Huntsville, AL	(19.10)
129	Bellingham, WA	(6.20)	92	Duluth–Superior, MN–WI	(1.23)	–	Indianapolis, IN**	NA
126	Benton Harbor, MI	(5.74)	–	Dutchess County, NY**	NA	146	Jackson, MI	(7.88)
201	Bergen–Passaic, NJ	(16.55)	158	Eau Claire, WI	(10.03)	19	Jackson, MS	18.17
76	Binghamton, NY	2.21	200	El Paso, TX	(16.32)	13	Jackson, TN	22.14
21	Birmingham, AL	17.66	165	Elkhart–Goshen, IN	(10.81)	125	Jacksonville, FL	(5.70)
97	Bismarck, ND	(2.49)	8	Enid, OK	25.56	45	Jacksonville, NC	7.32
130	Bloomington, IN	(6.29)	81	Erie, PA	0.98	61	Janesville–Beloit, WI	5.03
25	Boise, ID	15.72	152	Eugene–Springfield, OR	(8.44)	222	Jersey City, NJ	(20.30)
–	Boston, MA–NH**	NA	190	Evansville–Henderson, IN–KY	(14.15)	154	Johnson City–Kingsport–Bristol, TN–VA	(9.02)
202	Boulder–Longmont, CO	(16.56)	89	Fargo–Moorhead, ND–MN	(0.54)	–	Johnstown, PA**	NA
205	Brazoria, TX	(16.65)	118	Fayetteville, NC	(5.00)	211	Joplin, MO	(18.13)
–	Bremerton, WA**	NA	208	Fayetteville–Springdale–Rogers, AR	(17.34)	209	Kalamazoo–Battle Creek, MI	(17.43)
185	Bridgeport, CT	(12.69)	232	Fitchburg–Leominster, MA	(24.00)	–	Kansas City, MO–KS**	NA
–	Brockton, MA**	NA	111	Flint, MI	(4.14)	44	Kenosha, WI	7.76
6	Brownsville–Harlingen–San Benito, TX	30.68	94	Florence, AL	(1.89)	93	Killeen–Temple, TX	(1.77)
233	Bryan–College Station, TX	(24.42)	1	Florence, SC	54.75	34	Kokomo, IN	12.76
86	Buffalo–Niagara Falls, NY	0.14	206	Fort Collins–Loveland, CO	(16.86)	178	La Crosse, WI–MN	(12.29)
60	Canton–Massillon, OH	5.32	62	Fort Lauderdale, FL	4.61	24	Lafayette, IN	16.28
79	Charleston, WV	1.21	14	Fort Myers–Cape Coral, FL	22.12	122	Lafayette, LA	(5.22)
32	Charleston–North Charleston, SC	13.47	234	Fort Pierce–Port St. Lucie, FL	(24.62)	46	Lake Charles, LA	7.27
39	Charlottesville, VA	8.98	28	Fort Smith, AR–OK	15.10	216	Lakeland–Winter Haven, FL	(19.55)
155	Charlotte–Gastonia–Rock Hill, NC–SC	(9.15)	72	Fort Walton Beach, FL	2.85	42	Lancaster, PA	8.26
55	Chattanooga, TN–GA	5.87	227	Fort Wayne, IN	(21.23)	132	Lansing–East Lansing, MI	(6.44)

Source: Morgan Quitno Corporation using data from U.S. Department of Justice, Federal Bureau of Investigation
   "Crime in the United States 1993" (Uniform Crime Reports, December 4, 1994)
*Larceny and theft is the unlawful taking of property without use of force, violence or fraud. Attempts are included. Motor vehicle thefts are excluded.
**Not available.

36. Percent Change in Larceny and Theft Rate: 1989 to 1993 (continued)

National Percent Change = 4.4% Decrease*

RANK	METRO AREA	% CHANGE	RANK	METRO AREA	% CHANGE	RANK	METRO AREA	CHANGE
229	Laredo, TX	(21.59)	38	Olympia, WA	9.91	113	Seattle–Bellevue–Everett, WA	(4.49)
184	Las Vegas, NV–AZ	(12.58)	–	Omaha, NE**	NA	22	Sheboygan, WI	17.50
134	Lawrence, MA–NH	(6.79)	182	Orange County, CA	(12.36)	224	Sherman–Denison, TX	(20.56)
3	Lawton, OK	38.89	156	Orlando, FL	(9.22)	186	Shreveport–Bossier City, LA	(12.85)
128	Lewiston–Auburn, ME	(5.96)	95	Owensboro, KY	(2.08)	127	Sioux City, IA–NE	(5.90)
85	Lexington, KY	0.29	9	Panama City, FL	25.05	106	Sioux Falls, SD	(3.78)
84	Lincoln, NE	0.43	147	Philadelphia, PA–NJ	(7.90)	–	South Bend, IN**	NA
75	Little Rock–North Little Rock, AR	2.71	204	Phoenix–Mesa, AZ	(16.64)	69	Spokane, WA	3.44
73	Longview–Marshall, TX	2.80	49	Pine Bluff, AR	6.98	37	Springfield, MA	9.96
157	Los Angeles–Long Beach, CA	(9.35)	40	Pittsburgh, PA	8.89	235	Springfield, MO	(24.69)
173	Louisville, KY–IN	(11.41)	–	Pittsfield, MA**	NA	194	Stamford–Norwalk, CT	(15.00)
189	Lubbock, TX	(13.98)	231	Portland, ME	(23.44)	–	Steubenville–Weirton, OH–WV**	NA
243	Lynchburg, VA	(27.95)	151	Portland–Vancouver, OR–WA	(8.33)	141	Stockton–Lodi, CA	(7.39)
108	Macon, GA	(4.03)	221	Providence–Fall River–Warwick, RI–MA	(20.24)	67	St. Cloud, MN	3.62
188	Madison, WI	(13.71)	–	Provo–Orem, UT**	NA	10	St. Joseph, MO	24.55
240	Manchester, NH	(26.90)	226	Pueblo, CO	(20.88)	–	St. Louis, MO–IL**	NA
105	Mansfield, OH	(3.61)	–	Punta Gorda, FL**	NA	–	Sumter, SC**	NA
29	McAllen–Edinburg–Mission, TX	14.86	138	Racine, WI	(7.21)	160	Syracuse, NY	(10.32)
17	Medford–Ashland, OR	18.31	91	Raleigh–Durham–Chapel Hill, NC	(1.14)	159	Tacoma, WA	(10.22)
66	Memphis, TN–AR–MS	3.96	82	Rapid City, SD	0.70	30	Tallahassee, FL	14.82
36	Merced, CA	10.46	–	Reading, PA**	NA	193	Tampa–St. Petersburg–Clearwater, FL	(14.86)
80	Miami, FL	1.10	148	Redding, CA	(7.94)	140	Texarkana, TX–AR	(7.27)
116	Middlesex–Sommerset–Hunterdon, NJ	(4.91)	107	Reno, NV	(3.87)	168	Toledo, OH	(11.04)
175	Milwaukee–Waukesha, WI	(11.80)	237	Richland–Kennewick–Pasco, WA	(24.92)	228	Trenton, NJ	(21.54)
99	Minneapolis–St. Paul, MN–WI	(2.79)	90	Richmond–Petersburg, VA	(0.58)	–	Tucson, AZ**	NA
115	Mobile, AL	(4.83)	–	Riverside–San Bernardino, CA**	NA	162	Tulsa, OK	(10.46)
137	Modesto, CA	(7.03)	219	Roanoke, VA	(20.17)	4	Tuscaloosa, AL	36.12
101	Monmouth–Ocean, NJ	(2.89)	170	Rochester, MN	(11.21)	123	Tyler, TX	(5.43)
31	Monroe, LA	13.88	183	Rochester, NY	(12.57)	35	Utica–Rome, NY	12.53
203	Montgomery, AL	(16.61)	–	Rocky Mount, NC**	NA	87	Vallejo–Fairfield–Napa, CA	(0.41)
–	Myrtle Beach, SC**	NA	174	Sacramento, CA	(11.79)	88	Ventura, CA	(0.51)
241	Naples, FL	(27.01)	119	Saginaw–Bay City–Midland, MI	(5.13)	5	Victoria, TX	32.87
225	Nashua, NH	(20.71)	63	Salem, OR	4.57	64	Vineland–Millville–Bridgeton, NJ	4.54
2	Nashville, TN	52.90	96	Salinas, CA	(2.38)	51	Visalia–Tulare–Porterville, CA	6.78
187	Nassau–Suffolk, NY	(13.50)	177	Salt Lake City–Ogden, UT	(12.17)	192	Waco, TX	(14.65)
143	New Bedford, MA	(7.57)	238	San Angelo, TX	(25.16)	59	Washington, DC–MD–VA–WV	5.44
98	New Haven–Meriden, CT	(2.55)	196	San Antonio, TX	(15.26)	110	Waterbury, CT	(4.13)
195	New London–Norwich, CT–RI	(15.09)	220	San Diego, CA	(20.18)	112	Waterloo–Cedar Falls, IA	(4.23)
83	New Orleans, LA	0.59	142	San Francisco, CA	(7.43)	198	Wausau, WI	(15.59)
207	New York, NY	(17.03)	119	San Jose, CA	(5.13)	–	West Palm Beach–Boca Raton, FL**	NA
178	Newark, NJ	(12.29)	–	San Luis Obispo–Atascadero, CA**	NA	223	Wichita Falls, TX	(20.49)
–	Newburgh, NY–PA**	NA	144	Santa Barbara–Santa Maria–Lompoc, CA	(7.58)	–	Williamsport, PA**	NA
136	Norfolk–Va Beach–Newport News, VA–NC	(6.99)	71	Santa Cruz–Watsonville, CA	3.13	215	Wilmington, NC	(19.34)
145	Oakland, CA	(7.69)	65	Santa Rosa, CA	4.21	–	Worcester, MA–CT**	NA
175	Ocala, FL	(11.80)	180	Sarasota–Bradenton, FL	(12.32)	124	Yakima, WA	(5.54)
230	Odessa–Midland, TX	(22.34)	135	Savannah, GA	(6.80)	–	Yolo, CA**	NA
43	Oklahoma City, OK	8.07	–	Scranton–Wilkes-Barre–Hazleton, PA**	NA	114	Yuba City, CA	(4.58)

Source: Morgan Quitno Corporation using data from U.S. Department of Justice, Federal Bureau of Investigation
    "Crime in the United States 1993" (Uniform Crime Reports, December 4, 1994)
*Larceny and theft is the unlawful taking of property without use of force, violence or fraud. Attempts are included. Motor vehicle thefts are excluded.
**Not available.

36. Percent Change in Larceny and Theft Rate: 1989 to 1993 (continued)

National Percent Change = 4.4% Decrease*

RANK	METRO AREA	% CHANGE	RANK	METRO AREA	% CHANGE	RANK	METRO AREA	% CHANGE
1	Florence, SC	54.75	48	Beaumont–Port Arthur, TX	7.01	95	Owensboro, KY	(2.08)
2	Nashville, TN	52.90	49	Pine Bluff, AR	6.98	96	Salinas, CA	(2.38)
3	Lawton, OK	38.89	50	Cumberland, MD–WV	6.93	97	Bismarck, ND	(2.49)
4	Tuscaloosa, AL	36.12	51	Visalia–Tulare–Porterville, CA	6.78	98	New Haven–Meriden, CT	(2.55)
5	Victoria, TX	32.87	52	Altoona, PA	6.57	99	Minneapolis–St. Paul, MN–WI	(2.79)
6	Brownsville–Harlingen–San Benito, TX	30.68	53	Amarillo, TX	5.93	100	Columbus, GA–AL	(2.85)
7	Gadsden, AL	27.47	54	Hagerstown, MD	5.90	101	Monmouth–Ocean, NJ	(2.89)
8	Enid, OK	25.56	55	Chattanooga, TN–GA	5.87	102	Cheyenne, WY	(2.99)
9	Panama City, FL	25.05	56	Gary–Hammond, IN	5.75	103	Clarksville–Hopkinsville, TN–KY	(3.43)
10	St. Joseph, MO	24.55	57	Abilene, TX	5.57	104	Cincinnati, OH–KY–IN	(3.49)
11	Anniston, AL	23.96	58	Columbia, SC	5.53	105	Mansfield, OH	(3.61)
12	Gainesville, FL	23.41	59	Washington, DC–MD–VA–WV	5.44	106	Sioux Falls, SD	(3.78)
13	Jackson, TN	22.14	60	Canton–Massillon, OH	5.32	107	Reno, NV	(3.87)
14	Fort Myers–Cape Coral, FL	22.12	61	Janesville–Beloit, WI	5.03	108	Macon, GA	(4.03)
15	Glens Falls, NY	21.30	62	Fort Lauderdale, FL	4.61	109	Huntington–Ashland, WV–KY–OH	(4.10)
16	Athens, GA	18.82	63	Salem, OR	4.57	110	Waterbury, CT	(4.13)
17	Danbury, CT	18.31	64	Vineland–Millville–Bridgeton, NJ	4.54	111	Flint, MI	(4.14)
17	Medford–Ashland, OR	18.31	65	Santa Rosa, CA	4.21	112	Waterloo–Cedar Falls, IA	(4.23)
19	Jackson, MS	18.17	66	Memphis, TN–AR–MS	3.96	113	Seattle–Bellevue–Everett, WA	(4.49)
20	Decatur, AL	18.03	67	St. Cloud, MN	3.62	114	Yuba City, CA	(4.58)
21	Birmingham, AL	17.66	68	Albany, GA	3.50	115	Mobile, AL	(4.83)
22	Sheboygan, WI	17.50	69	Spokane, WA	3.44	116	Middlesex–Sommerset–Hunterdon, NJ	(4.91)
23	Danville, VA	17.07	70	Alexandria, LA	3.27	117	Grand Rapids–Muskegon–Holland, MI	(4.94)
24	Lafayette, IN	16.28	71	Santa Cruz–Watsonville, CA	3.13	118	Fayetteville, NC	(5.00)
25	Boise, ID	15.72	72	Fort Walton Beach, FL	2.85	119	Saginaw–Bay City–Midland, MI	(5.13)
26	Anchorage, AK	15.55	73	Longview–Marshall, TX	2.80	119	San Jose, CA	(5.13)
27	Baton Rouge, LA	15.27	74	Appleton–Oshkosh–Neenah, WI	2.73	121	Dubuque, IA	(5.15)
28	Fort Smith, AR–OK	15.10	75	Little Rock–North Little Rock, AR	2.71	122	Lafayette, LA	(5.22)
29	McAllen–Edinburg–Mission, TX	14.86	76	Binghamton, NY	2.21	123	Tyler, TX	(5.43)
30	Tallahassee, FL	14.82	77	Greeley, CO	1.99	124	Yakima, WA	(5.54)
31	Monroe, LA	13.88	78	Corpus Christi, TX	1.22	125	Jacksonville, FL	(5.70)
32	Charleston–North Charleston, SC	13.47	79	Charleston, WV	1.21	126	Benton Harbor, MI	(5.74)
33	Baltimore, MD	13.10	80	Miami, FL	1.10	127	Sioux City, IA–NE	(5.90)
34	Kokomo, IN	12.76	81	Erie, PA	0.98	128	Lewiston–Auburn, ME	(5.96)
35	Utica–Rome, NY	12.53	82	Rapid City, SD	0.70	129	Bellingham, WA	(6.20)
36	Merced, CA	10.46	83	New Orleans, LA	0.59	130	Bloomington, IN	(6.29)
37	Springfield, MA	9.96	84	Lincoln, NE	0.43	131	Detroit, MI	(6.35)
38	Olympia, WA	9.91	85	Lexington, KY	0.29	132	Lansing–East Lansing, MI	(6.44)
39	Charlottesville, VA	8.98	86	Buffalo–Niagara Falls, NY	0.14	133	Galveston–Texas City, TX	(6.53)
40	Pittsburgh, PA	8.89	87	Vallejo–Fairfield–Napa, CA	(0.41)	134	Lawrence, MA–NH	(6.79)
41	Greensboro–Winston Salem–High Point, NC	8.39	88	Ventura, CA	(0.51)	135	Savannah, GA	(6.80)
42	Lancaster, PA	8.26	89	Fargo–Moorhead, ND–MN	(0.54)	136	Norfolk–Va Beach–Newport News, VA–NC	(6.99)
43	Oklahoma City, OK	8.07	90	Richmond–Petersburg, VA	(0.58)	137	Modesto, CA	(7.03)
44	Kenosha, WI	7.76	91	Raleigh–Durham–Chapel Hill, NC	(1.14)	138	Racine, WI	(7.21)
45	Jacksonville, NC	7.32	92	Duluth–Superior, MN–WI	(1.23)	139	Bakersfield, CA	(7.26)
46	Lake Charles, LA	7.27	93	Killeen–Temple, TX	(1.77)	140	Texarkana, TX–AR	(7.27)
47	Honolulu, HI	7.18	94	Florence, AL	(1.89)	141	Stockton–Lodi, CA	(7.39)

Source: Morgan Quitno Corporation using data from U.S. Department of Justice, Federal Bureau of Investigation "Crime in the United States 1993" (Uniform Crime Reports, December 4, 1994)
*Larceny and theft is the unlawful taking of property without use of force, violence or fraud. Attempts are included. Motor vehicle thefts are excluded.
**Not available.

36. Percent Change in Larceny and Theft Rate: 1989 to 1993 (continued)

National Percent Change = 4.4% Decrease*

RANK	METRO AREA	% CHANGE	RANK	METRO AREA	% CHANGE	RANK	METRO AREA	CHANGE
142	San Francisco, CA	(7.43)	189	Lubbock, TX	(13.98)	236	Houston, TX	(24.74)
143	New Bedford, MA	(7.57)	190	Evansville-Henderson, IN-KY	(14.15)	237	Richland-Kennewick-Pasco, WA	(24.92)
144	Santa Barbara-Santa Maria-Lompoc, CA	(7.58)	191	Bangor, ME	(14.28)	238	San Angelo, TX	(25.16)
145	Oakland, CA	(7.69)	192	Waco, TX	(14.65)	239	Fort Worth-Arlington, TX	(25.80)
146	Jackson, MI	(7.88)	193	Tampa-St. Petersburg-Clearwater, FL	(14.86)	240	Manchester, NH	(26.90)
147	Philadelphia, PA-NJ	(7.90)	194	Stamford-Norwalk, CT	(15.00)	241	Naples, FL	(27.01)
148	Redding, CA	(7.94)	195	New London-Norwich, CT-RI	(15.09)	242	Fresno, CA	(27.81)
149	Chico-Paradise, CA	(8.14)	196	San Antonio, TX	(15.26)	243	Lynchburg, VA	(27.95)
150	Columbia, MO	(8.23)	197	Daytona Beach, FL	(15.50)	244	Dallas, TX	(29.35)
151	Portland-Vancouver, OR-WA	(8.33)	198	Wausau, WI	(15.59)	245	Ann Arbor, MI	(36.06)
152	Eugene-Springfield, OR	(8.44)	199	Albuquerque, NM	(15.78)	–	Akron, OH**	NA
153	Hartford, CT	(8.53)	200	El Paso, TX	(16.32)	–	Albany, NY**	NA
154	Johnson City-Kingsport-Bristol, TN-VA	(9.02)	201	Bergen-Passaic, NJ	(16.55)	–	Barnstable-Yarmouth, MA**	NA
155	Charlotte-Gastonia-Rock Hill, NC-SC	(9.15)	202	Boulder-Longmont, CO	(16.56)	–	Boston, MA-NH**	NA
156	Orlando, FL	(9.22)	203	Montgomery, AL	(16.61)	–	Bremerton, WA**	NA
157	Los Angeles-Long Beach, CA	(9.35)	204	Phoenix-Mesa, AZ	(16.64)	–	Brockton, MA**	NA
158	Eau Claire, WI	(10.03)	205	Brazoria, TX	(16.65)	–	Chicago, IL**	NA
159	Tacoma, WA	(10.22)	206	Fort Collins-Loveland, CO	(16.86)	–	Cleveland, OH**	NA
160	Syracuse, NY	(10.32)	207	New York, NY	(17.03)	–	Dutchess County, NY**	NA
161	Austin-San Marcos, TX	(10.42)	208	Fayetteville-Springdale-Rogers, AR	(17.34)	–	Goldsboro, NC**	NA
162	Tulsa, OK	(10.46)	209	Kalamazoo-Battle Creek, MI	(17.43)	–	Greenville, NC**	NA
163	Green Bay, WI	(10.53)	210	Greenville-Spartanburg-Anderson, SC	(17.66)	–	Harrisburg-Lebanon-Carlisle, PA**	NA
164	Grand Forks, ND-MN	(10.65)	211	Joplin, MO	(18.13)	–	Hickory-Morganton, NC**	NA
165	Elkhart-Goshen, IN	(10.81)	212	Atlantic City, NJ	(18.23)	–	Houma, LA**	NA
166	Denver, CO	(10.87)	213	Augusta-Aiken, GA-SC	(18.37)	–	Indianapolis, IN**	NA
167	Des Moines, IA	(11.02)	214	Huntsville, AL	(19.10)	–	Johnstown, PA**	NA
168	Columbus, OH	(11.04)	215	Wilmington, NC	(19.34)	–	Kansas City, MO-KS**	NA
168	Toledo, OH	(11.04)	216	Lakeland-Winter Haven, FL	(19.55)	–	Myrtle Beach, SC**	NA
170	Rochester, MN	(11.21)	217	Atlanta, GA	(19.75)	–	Newburgh, NY-PA**	NA
171	Colorado Springs, CO	(11.34)	218	Dothan, AL	(19.76)	–	Omaha, NE**	NA
172	Dayton-Springfield, OH	(11.38)	219	Roanoke, VA	(20.17)	–	Pittsfield, MA**	NA
173	Louisville, KY-IN	(11.41)	220	San Diego, CA	(20.18)	–	Provo-Orem, UT**	NA
174	Sacramento, CA	(11.79)	221	Providence-Fall River-Warwick, RI-MA	(20.24)	–	Punta Gorda, FL**	NA
175	Milwaukee-Waukesha, WI	(11.80)	222	Jersey City, NJ	(20.30)	–	Reading, PA**	NA
175	Ocala, FL	(11.80)	223	Wichita Falls, TX	(20.49)	–	Riverside-San Bernardino, CA**	NA
177	Salt Lake City-Ogden, UT	(12.17)	224	Sherman-Denison, TX	(20.56)	–	Rocky Mount, NC**	NA
178	La Crosse, WI-MN	(12.29)	225	Nashua, NH	(20.71)	–	San Luis Obispo-Atascadero, CA**	NA
178	Newark, NJ	(12.29)	226	Pueblo, CO	(20.88)	–	Scranton-Wilkes-Barre-Hazleton, PA**	NA
180	Sarasota-Bradenton, FL	(12.32)	227	Fort Wayne, IN	(21.23)	–	South Bend, IN**	NA
181	Asheville, NC	(12.33)	228	Trenton, NJ	(21.54)	–	Steubenville-Weirton, OH-WV**	NA
182	Orange County, CA	(12.36)	229	Laredo, TX	(21.59)	–	St. Louis, MO-IL**	NA
183	Rochester, NY	(12.57)	230	Odessa-Midland, TX	(22.34)	–	Sumter, SC**	NA
184	Las Vegas, NV-AZ	(12.58)	231	Portland, ME	(23.44)	–	Tucson, AZ**	NA
185	Bridgeport, CT	(12.69)	232	Fitchburg-Leominster, MA	(24.00)	–	West Palm Beach-Boca Raton, FL**	NA
186	Shreveport-Bossier City, LA	(12.85)	233	Bryan-College Station, TX	(24.42)	–	Williamsport, PA**	NA
187	Nassau-Suffolk, NY	(13.50)	234	Fort Pierce-Port St. Lucie, FL	(24.62)	–	Worcester, MA-CT**	NA
188	Madison, WI	(13.71)	235	Springfield, MO	(24.69)	–	Yolo, CA**	NA

Source: Morgan Quitno Corporation using data from U.S. Department of Justice, Federal Bureau of Investigation "Crime in the United States 1993" (Uniform Crime Reports, December 4, 1994)

*Larceny and theft is the unlawful taking of property without use of force, violence or fraud. Attempts are included. Motor vehicle thefts are excluded.

**Not available.

37. Motor Vehicle Thefts in 1993

National Total = 1,561,047 Motor Vehicle Thefts*

RANK	METRO AREA	THEFTS	RANK	METRO AREA	THEFTS	RANK	METRO AREA	THEFTS
253	Abilene, TX	187	272	Cheyenne, WY	96	33	Fort Worth–Arlington, TX	11,297
83	Akron, OH	2,813	–	Chicago, IL**	NA	20	Fresno, CA	16,625
173	Albany, GA	555	168	Chico–Paradise, CA	571	186	Gadsden, AL	498
–	Albany, NY**	NA	65	Cincinnati, OH–KY–IN	4,047	113	Gainesville, FL	1,384
64	Albuquerque, NM	4,077	237	Clarksville–Hopkinsville, TN–KY	280	106	Galveston–Texas City, TX	1,576
190	Alexandria, LA	468	–	Cleveland, OH**	NA	46	Gary–Hammond, IN	6,243
248	Altoona, PA	209	123	Colorado Springs, CO	1,187	273	Glens Falls, NY	93
155	Amarillo, TX	711	250	Columbia, MO	203	225	Goldsboro, NC	310
112	Anchorage, AK	1,387	95	Columbia, SC	2,286	236	Grand Forks, ND–MN	281
122	Ann Arbor, MI	1,201	119	Columbus, GA–AL	1,266	88	Grand Rapids–Muskegon–Holland, MI	2,640
241	Anniston, AL	265	36	Columbus, OH	8,578	226	Greeley, CO	306
210	Appleton–Oshkosh–Neenah, WI	378	100	Corpus Christi, TX	1,845	214	Green Bay, WI	348
184	Asheville, NC	507	268	Cumberland, MD–WV	122	75	Greensboro–Winston Salem–High Point, NC	3,416
157	Athens, GA	692	14	Dallas, TX	24,139	196	Greenville, NC	434
10	Atlanta, GA	28,892	187	Danbury, CT	497	87	Greenville–Spartanburg–Anderson, SC	2,730
134	Atlantic City, NJ	1,047	262	Danville, VA	145	256	Hagerstown, MD	180
93	Augusta–Aiken, GA–SC	2,316	101	Daytona Beach, FL	1,803	135	Harrisburg–Lebanon–Carlisle, PA	1,031
55	Austin–San Marcos, TX	5,275	56	Dayton–Springfield, OH	5,229	47	Hartford, CT	5,991
69	Bakersfield, CA	3,707	232	Decatur, AL	298	174	Hickory–Morganton, NC	551
16	Baltimore, MD	19,649	31	Denver, CO	12,297	60	Honolulu, HI	4,460
274	Bangor, ME	92	126	Des Moines, IA	1,138	194	Houma, LA	442
224	Barnstable–Yarmouth, MA	311	3	Detroit, MI	45,121	5	Houston, TX	40,536
57	Baton Rouge, LA	5,107	219	Dothan, AL	335	178	Huntington–Ashland, WV–KY–OH	523
82	Beaumont–Port Arthur, TX	2,845	259	Dubuque, IA	158	130	Huntsville, AL	1,090
211	Bellingham, WA	363	178	Duluth–Superior, MN–WI	523	–	Indianapolis, IN**	NA
183	Benton Harbor, MI	511	213	Dutchess County, NY	355	229	Jackson, MI	301
40	Bergen–Passaic, NJ	7,046	252	Eau Claire, WI	197	61	Jackson, MS	4,445
269	Binghamton, NY	116	49	El Paso, TX	5,786	215	Jackson, TN	347
52	Birmingham, AL	5,514	227	Elkhart–Goshen, IN	302	34	Jacksonville, FL	9,755
265	Bismarck, ND	131	261	Enid, OK	149	230	Jacksonville, NC	299
251	Bloomington, IN	198	166	Erie, PA	591	218	Janesville–Beloit, WI	340
152	Boise, ID	740	150	Eugene–Springfield, OR	747	41	Jersey City, NJ	7,035
9	Boston, MA–NH	29,244	160	Evansville–Henderson, IN–KY	630	142	Johnson City–Kingsport–Bristol, TN–VA	851
177	Boulder–Longmont, CO	532	217	Fargo–Moorhead, ND–MN	342	238	Johnstown, PA	279
175	Brazoria, TX	549	105	Fayetteville, NC	1,599	223	Joplin, MO	312
200	Bremerton, WA	424	206	Fayetteville–Springdale–Rogers, AR	402	115	Kalamazoo–Battle Creek, MI	1,362
54	Bridgeport, CT	5,394	176	Fitchburg–Leominster, MA	545	–	Kansas City, MO–KS**	NA
89	Brockton, MA	2,596	77	Flint, MI	3,325	203	Kenosha, WI	416
110	Brownsville–Harlingen–San Benito, TX	1,466	263	Florence, AL	144	148	Killeen–Temple, TX	753
195	Bryan–College Station, TX	440	188	Florence, SC	495	258	Kokomo, IN	161
37	Buffalo–Niagara Falls, NY	8,518	233	Fort Collins–Loveland, CO	296	270	La Crosse, WI–MN	112
113	Canton–Massillon, OH	1,384	28	Fort Lauderdale, FL	13,321	234	Lafayette, IN	288
144	Charleston, WV	817	86	Fort Myers–Cape Coral, FL	2,736	145	Lafayette, LA	802
91	Charleston–North Charleston, SC	2,459	108	Fort Pierce–Port St. Lucie, FL	1,556	159	Lake Charles, LA	648
227	Charlottesville, VA	302	181	Fort Smith, AR–OK	521	66	Lakeland–Winter Haven, FL	3,938
59	Charlotte–Gastonia–Rock Hill, NC–SC	4,681	222	Fort Walton Beach, FL	320	154	Lancaster, PA	733
81	Chattanooga, TN–GA	2,869	94	Fort Wayne, IN	2,304	117	Lansing–East Lansing, MI	1,334

Source: U.S. Department of Justice, Federal Bureau of Investigation
  "Crime in the United States 1993" (Uniform Crime Reports, December 4, 1994)
Includes the theft or attempted theft of a self-propelled vehicle. Excludes motorboats, construction equipment, airplanes and farming equipment.
***Not available.*

37. Motor Vehicle Thefts in 1993 (continued)

National Total = 1,561,047 Motor Vehicle Thefts*

RANK	METRO AREA	THEFTS	RANK	METRO AREA	THEFTS	RANK	METRO AREA	THEFTS
132	Laredo, TX	1,067	197	Olympia, WA	430	26	Seattle-Bellevue-Everett, WA	13,663
35	Las Vegas, NV-AZ	9,301	–	Omaha, NE**	NA	266	Sheboygan, WI	125
72	Lawrence, MA-NH	3,537	15	Orange County, CA	21,288	244	Sherman-Denison, TX	246
212	Lawton, OK	359	38	Orlando, FL	7,829	98	Shreveport-Bossier City, LA	1,943
264	Lewiston-Auburn, ME	137	271	Owensboro, KY	99	230	Sioux City, IA-NE	299
143	Lexington, KY	824	171	Panama City, FL	556	246	Sioux Falls, SD	223
189	Lincoln, NE	476	6	Philadelphia, PA-NJ	37,667	128	South Bend, IN	1,105
71	Little Rock-North Little Rock, AR	3,637	13	Phoenix-Mesa, AZ	25,023	127	Spokane, WA	1,133
140	Longview-Marshall, TX	890	171	Pine Bluff, AR	556	50	Springfield, MA	5,719
1	Los Angeles-Long Beach, CA	126,053	29	Pittsburgh, PA	12,593	164	Springfield, MO	603
63	Louisville, KY-IN	4,187	247	Pittsfield, MA	215	107	Stamford-Norwalk, CT	1,571
158	Lubbock, TX	658	182	Portland, ME	513	260	Steubenville-Weirton, OH-WV	157
235	Lynchburg, VA	286	25	Portland-Vancouver, OR-WA	13,677	51	Stockton-Lodi, CA	5,667
121	Macon, GA	1,227	44	Providence-Fall River-Warwick, RI-MA	6,597	239	St. Cloud, MN	272
125	Madison, WI	1,154	190	Provo-Orem, UT	468	240	St. Joseph, MO	266
170	Manchester, NH	558	220	Pueblo, CO	333	–	St. Louis, MO-IL**	NA
198	Mansfield, OH	427	249	Punta Gorda, FL	205	205	Sumter, SC	406
79	McAllen-Edinburg-Mission, TX	3,019	161	Racine, WI	625	137	Syracuse, NY	1,009
192	Medford-Ashland, OR	449	80	Raleigh-Durham-Chapel Hill, NC	2,912	67	Tacoma, WA	3,820
24	Memphis, TN-AR-MS	14,929	256	Rapid City, SD	180	84	Tallahassee, FL	2,786
133	Merced, CA	1,055	138	Reading, PA	941	19	Tampa-St. Petersburg-Clearwater, FL	17,290
4	Miami, FL	43,067	162	Redding, CA	608	215	Texarkana, TX-AR	347
73	Middlesex-Sommerset-Hunterdon, NJ	3,507	129	Reno, NV	1,093	58	Toledo, OH	5,085
30	Milwaukee-Waukesha, WI	12,441	207	Richland-Kennewick-Pasco, WA	400	68	Trenton, NJ	3,813
32	Minneapolis-St. Paul, MN-WI	12,235	70	Richmond-Petersburg, VA	3,659	45	Tucson, AZ	6,470
96	Mobile, AL	2,283	8	Riverside-San Bernardino, CA	30,876	53	Tulsa, OK	5,401
78	Modesto, CA	3,282	204	Roanoke, VA	409	185	Tuscaloosa, AL	502
102	Monmouth-Ocean, NJ	1,728	245	Rochester, MN	227	156	Tyler, TX	700
201	Monroe, LA	420	62	Rochester, NY	4,406	199	Utica-Rome, NY	425
111	Montgomery, AL	1,400	209	Rocky Mount, NC	387	90	Vallejo-Fairfield-Napa, CA	2,484
149	Myrtle Beach, SC	748	18	Sacramento, CA	17,777	85	Ventura, CA	2,776
147	Naples, FL	766	151	Saginaw-Bay City-Midland, MI	742	241	Victoria, TX	265
221	Nashua, NH	331	109	Salem, OR	1,481	169	Vineland-Millville-Bridgeton, NJ	562
48	Nashville, TN	5,946	116	Salinas, CA	1,353	97	Visalia-Tulare-Porterville, CA	1,976
21	Nassau-Suffolk, NY	15,877	76	Salt Lake City-Ogden, UT	3,406	120	Waco, TX	1,230
124	New Bedford, MA	1,177	254	San Angelo, TX	184	11	Washington, DC-MD-VA-WV	26,719
74	New Haven-Meriden, CT	3,506	27	San Antonio, TX	13,399	104	Waterbury, CT	1,628
178	New London-Norwich, CT-RI	523	7	San Diego, CA	33,198	243	Waterloo-Cedar Falls, IA	252
23	New Orleans, LA	15,057	22	San Francisco, CA	15,600	266	Wausau, WI	125
2	New York, NY	117,989	43	San Jose, CA	6,683	–	West Palm Beach-Boca Raton, FL**	NA
12	Newark, NJ	25,241	208	San Luis Obispo-Atascadero, CA	394	202	Wichita Falls, TX	419
193	Newburgh, NY-PA	446	146	Santa Barbara-Santa Maria-Lompoc, CA	786	255	Williamsport, PA	181
42	Norfolk-Va Beach-Newport News, VA-NC	6,902	153	Santa Cruz-Watsonville, CA	737	163	Wilmington, NC	607
17	Oakland, CA	19,343	118	Santa Rosa, CA	1,326	92	Worcester, MA-CT	2,432
167	Ocala, FL	573	99	Sarasota-Bradenton, FL	1,940	139	Yakima, WA	921
141	Odessa-Midland, TX	852	103	Savannah, GA	1,702	136	Yolo, CA	1,015
39	Oklahoma City, OK	7,266	131	Scranton-Wilkes-Barre-Hazleton, PA	1,072	164	Yuba City, CA	603

Source: U.S. Department of Justice, Federal Bureau of Investigation
    "Crime in the United States 1993" (Uniform Crime Reports, December 4, 1994)
*Includes the theft or attempted theft of a self-propelled vehicle. Excludes motorboats, construction equipment, airplanes and farming equipment.
**Not available.

37. Motor Vehicle Thefts in 1993 (continued)

National Total = 1,561,047 Motor Vehicle Thefts*

RANK	METRO AREA	THEFTS	RANK	METRO AREA	THEFTS	RANK	METRO AREA	THEFTS
1	Los Angeles–Long Beach, CA	126,053	48	Nashville, TN	5,946	95	Columbia, SC	2,286
2	New York, NY	117,989	49	El Paso, TX	5,786	96	Mobile, AL	2,283
3	Detroit, MI	45,121	50	Springfield, MA	5,719	97	Visalia–Tulare–Porterville, CA	1,976
4	Miami, FL	43,067	51	Stockton–Lodi, CA	5,667	98	Shreveport–Bossier City, LA	1,943
5	Houston, TX	40,536	52	Birmingham, AL	5,514	99	Sarasota–Bradenton, FL	1,940
6	Philadelphia, PA–NJ	37,667	53	Tulsa, OK	5,401	100	Corpus Christi, TX	1,845
7	San Diego, CA	33,198	54	Bridgeport, CT	5,394	101	Daytona Beach, FL	1,803
8	Riverside–San Bernardino, CA	30,876	55	Austin–San Marcos, TX	5,275	102	Monmouth–Ocean, NJ	1,728
9	Boston, MA–NH	29,244	56	Dayton–Springfield, OH	5,229	103	Savannah, GA	1,702
10	Atlanta, GA	28,892	57	Baton Rouge, LA	5,107	104	Waterbury, CT	1,628
11	Washington, DC–MD–VA–WV	26,719	58	Toledo, OH	5,085	105	Fayetteville, NC	1,599
12	Newark, NJ	25,241	59	Charlotte–Gastonia–Rock Hill, NC–SC	4,681	106	Galveston–Texas City, TX	1,576
13	Phoenix–Mesa, AZ	25,023	60	Honolulu, HI	4,460	107	Stamford–Norwalk, CT	1,571
14	Dallas, TX	24,139	61	Jackson, MS	4,445	108	Fort Pierce–Port St. Lucie, FL	1,556
15	Orange County, CA	21,288	62	Rochester, NY	4,406	109	Salem, OR	1,481
16	Baltimore, MD	19,649	63	Louisville, KY–IN	4,187	110	Brownsville–Harlingen–San Benito, TX	1,466
17	Oakland, CA	19,343	64	Albuquerque, NM	4,077	111	Montgomery, AL	1,400
18	Sacramento, CA	17,777	65	Cincinnati, OH–KY–IN	4,047	112	Anchorage, AK	1,387
19	Tampa–St. Petersburg–Clearwater, FL	17,290	66	Lakeland–Winter Haven, FL	3,938	113	Canton–Massillon, OH	1,384
20	Fresno, CA	16,625	67	Tacoma, WA	3,820	113	Gainesville, FL	1,384
21	Nassau–Suffolk, NY	15,877	68	Trenton, NJ	3,813	115	Kalamazoo–Battle Creek, MI	1,362
22	San Francisco, CA	15,600	69	Bakersfield, CA	3,707	116	Salinas, CA	1,353
23	New Orleans, LA	15,057	70	Richmond–Petersburg, VA	3,659	117	Lansing–East Lansing, MI	1,334
24	Memphis, TN–AR–MS	14,929	71	Little Rock–North Little Rock, AR	3,637	118	Santa Rosa, CA	1,326
25	Portland–Vancouver, OR–WA	13,677	72	Lawrence, MA–NH	3,537	119	Columbus, GA–AL	1,266
26	Seattle–Bellevue–Everett, WA	13,663	73	Middlesex–Sommerset–Hunterdon, NJ	3,507	120	Waco, TX	1,230
27	San Antonio, TX	13,399	74	New Haven–Meriden, CT	3,506	121	Macon, GA	1,227
28	Fort Lauderdale, FL	13,321	75	Greensboro–Winston Salem–High Point, NC	3,416	122	Ann Arbor, MI	1,201
29	Pittsburgh, PA	12,593	76	Salt Lake City–Ogden, UT	3,406	123	Colorado Springs, CO	1,187
30	Milwaukee–Waukesha, WI	12,441	77	Flint, MI	3,325	124	New Bedford, MA	1,177
31	Denver, CO	12,297	78	Modesto, CA	3,282	125	Madison, WI	1,154
32	Minneapolis–St. Paul, MN–WI	12,235	79	McAllen–Edinburg–Mission, TX	3,019	126	Des Moines, IA	1,138
33	Fort Worth–Arlington, TX	11,297	80	Raleigh–Durham–Chapel Hill, NC	2,912	127	Spokane, WA	1,133
34	Jacksonville, FL	9,755	81	Chattanooga, TN–GA	2,869	128	South Bend, IN	1,105
35	Las Vegas, NV–AZ	9,301	82	Beaumont–Port Arthur, TX	2,845	129	Reno, NV	1,093
36	Columbus, OH	8,578	83	Akron, OH	2,813	130	Huntsville, AL	1,090
37	Buffalo–Niagara Falls, NY	8,518	84	Tallahassee, FL	2,786	131	Scranton–Wilkes-Barre–Hazleton, PA	1,072
38	Orlando, FL	7,829	85	Ventura, CA	2,776	132	Laredo, TX	1,067
39	Oklahoma City, OK	7,266	86	Fort Myers–Cape Coral, FL	2,736	133	Merced, CA	1,055
40	Bergen–Passaic, NJ	7,046	87	Greenville–Spartanburg–Anderson, SC	2,730	134	Atlantic City, NJ	1,047
41	Jersey City, NJ	7,035	88	Grand Rapids–Muskegon–Holland, MI	2,640	135	Harrisburg–Lebanon–Carlisle, PA	1,031
42	Norfolk–Va Beach–Newport News, VA–NC	6,902	89	Brockton, MA	2,596	136	Yolo, CA	1,015
43	San Jose, CA	6,683	90	Vallejo–Fairfield–Napa, CA	2,484	137	Syracuse, NY	1,009
44	Providence–Fall River–Warwick, RI–MA	6,597	91	Charleston–North Charleston, SC	2,459	138	Reading, PA	941
45	Tucson, AZ	6,470	92	Worcester, MA–CT	2,432	139	Yakima, WA	921
46	Gary–Hammond, IN	6,243	93	Augusta–Aiken, GA–SC	2,316	140	Longview–Marshall, TX	890
47	Hartford, CT	5,991	94	Fort Wayne, IN	2,304	141	Odessa–Midland, TX	852

Source: U.S. Department of Justice, Federal Bureau of Investigation
"Crime in the United States 1993" (Uniform Crime Reports, December 4, 1994)
*Includes the theft or attempted theft of a self-propelled vehicle. Excludes motorboats, construction equipment, airplanes and farming equipment.
**Not available.

37. Motor Vehicle Thefts in 1993 (continued)

National Total = 1,561,047 Motor Vehicle Thefts*

RANK	METRO AREA	THEFTS	RANK	METRO AREA	THEFTS	RANK	METRO AREA	THEFTS
142	Johnson City–Kingsport–Bristol, TN–VA	851	189	Lincoln, NE	476	236	Grand Forks, ND–MN	281
143	Lexington, KY	824	190	Alexandria, LA	468	237	Clarksville–Hopkinsville, TN–KY	280
144	Charleston, WV	817	190	Provo–Orem, UT	468	238	Johnstown, PA	279
145	Lafayette, LA	802	192	Medford–Ashland, OR	449	239	St. Cloud, MN	272
146	Santa Barbara–Santa Maria–Lompoc, CA	786	193	Newburgh, NY–PA	446	240	St. Joseph, MO	266
147	Naples, FL	766	194	Houma, LA	442	241	Anniston, AL	265
148	Killeen–Temple, TX	753	195	Bryan–College Station, TX	440	241	Victoria, TX	265
149	Myrtle Beach, SC	748	196	Greenville, NC	434	243	Waterloo–Cedar Falls, IA	252
150	Eugene–Springfield, OR	747	197	Olympia, WA	430	244	Sherman–Denison, TX	246
151	Saginaw–Bay City–Midland, MI	742	198	Mansfield, OH	427	245	Rochester, MN	227
152	Boise, ID	740	199	Utica–Rome, NY	425	246	Sioux Falls, SD	223
153	Santa Cruz–Watsonville, CA	737	200	Bremerton, WA	424	247	Pittsfield, MA	215
154	Lancaster, PA	733	201	Monroe, LA	420	248	Altoona, PA	209
155	Amarillo, TX	711	202	Wichita Falls, TX	419	249	Punta Gorda, FL	205
156	Tyler, TX	700	203	Kenosha, WI	416	250	Columbia, MO	203
157	Athens, GA	692	204	Roanoke, VA	409	251	Bloomington, IN	198
158	Lubbock, TX	658	205	Sumter, SC	406	252	Eau Claire, WI	197
159	Lake Charles, LA	648	206	Fayetteville–Springdale–Rogers, AR	402	253	Abilene, TX	187
160	Evansville–Henderson, IN–KY	630	207	Richland–Kennewick–Pasco, WA	400	254	San Angelo, TX	184
161	Racine, WI	625	208	San Luis Obispo–Atascadero, CA	394	255	Williamsport, PA	181
162	Redding, CA	608	209	Rocky Mount, NC	387	256	Hagerstown, MD	180
163	Wilmington, NC	607	210	Appleton–Oshkosh–Neenah, WI	378	256	Rapid City, SD	180
164	Springfield, MO	603	211	Bellingham, WA	363	258	Kokomo, IN	161
164	Yuba City, CA	603	212	Lawton, OK	359	259	Dubuque, IA	158
166	Erie, PA	591	213	Dutchess County, NY	355	260	Steubenville–Weirton, OH–WV	157
167	Ocala, FL	573	214	Green Bay, WI	348	261	Enid, OK	149
168	Chico–Paradise, CA	571	215	Jackson, TN	347	262	Danville, VA	145
169	Vineland–Millville–Bridgeton, NJ	562	215	Texarkana, TX–AR	347	263	Florence, AL	144
170	Manchester, NH	558	217	Fargo–Moorhead, ND–MN	342	264	Lewiston–Auburn, ME	137
171	Panama City, FL	556	218	Janesville–Beloit, WI	340	265	Bismarck, ND	131
171	Pine Bluff, AR	556	219	Dothan, AL	335	266	Sheboygan, WI	125
173	Albany, GA	555	220	Pueblo, CO	333	266	Wausau, WI	125
174	Hickory–Morganton, NC	551	221	Nashua, NH	331	268	Cumberland, MD–WV	122
175	Brazoria, TX	549	222	Fort Walton Beach, FL	320	269	Binghamton, NY	116
176	Fitchburg–Leominster, MA	545	223	Joplin, MO	312	270	La Crosse, WI–MN	112
177	Boulder–Longmont, CO	532	224	Barnstable–Yarmouth, MA	311	271	Owensboro, KY	99
178	Duluth–Superior, MN–WI	523	225	Goldsboro, NC	310	272	Cheyenne, WY	96
178	Huntington–Ashland, WV–KY–OH	523	226	Greeley, CO	306	273	Glens Falls, NY	93
178	New London–Norwich, CT–RI	523	227	Charlottesville, VA	302	274	Bangor, ME	92
181	Fort Smith, AR–OK	521	227	Elkhart–Goshen, IN	302	–	Albany, NY**	NA
182	Portland, ME	513	229	Jackson, MI	301	–	Chicago, IL**	NA
183	Benton Harbor, MI	511	230	Jacksonville, NC	299	–	Cleveland, OH**	NA
184	Asheville, NC	507	230	Sioux City, IA–NE	299	–	Indianapolis, IN**	NA
185	Tuscaloosa, AL	502	232	Decatur, AL	298	–	Kansas City, MO–KS**	NA
186	Gadsden, AL	498	233	Fort Collins–Loveland, CO	296	–	Omaha, NE**	NA
187	Danbury, CT	497	234	Lafayette, IN	288	–	St. Louis, MO–IL**	NA
188	Florence, SC	495	235	Lynchburg, VA	286	–	West Palm Beach–Boca Raton, FL**	NA

Source: U.S. Department of Justice, Federal Bureau of Investigation
   "Crime in the United States 1993" (Uniform Crime Reports, December 4, 1994)
*Includes the theft or attempted theft of a self-propelled vehicle. Excludes motorboats, construction equipment, airplanes and farming equipment.
**Not available.

149

38. Motor Vehicle Theft Rate in 1993

National Rate = 605.3 Motor Vehicle Thefts per 100,000 Population*

RANK	METRO AREA	RATE	RANK	METRO AREA	RATE	RANK	METRO AREA	RATE
248	Abilene, TX	152.1	263	Cheyenne, WY	124.9	49	Fort Worth–Arlington, TX	734.1
118	Akron, OH	421.1	–	Chicago, IL**	NA	2	Fresno, CA	2,045.3
100	Albany, GA	471.6	161	Chico–Paradise, CA	300.0	95	Gadsden, AL	495.2
–	Albany, NY**	NA	183	Cincinnati, OH–KY–IN	257.6	52	Gainesville, FL	720.2
64	Albuquerque, NM	647.3	247	Clarksville–Hopkinsville, TN–KY	155.2	60	Galveston–Texas City, TX	677.7
137	Alexandria, LA	357.1	–	Cleveland, OH**	NA	25	Gary–Hammond, IN	1,002.5
246	Altoona, PA	158.5	174	Colorado Springs, CO	273.8	273	Glens Falls, NY	76.5
134	Amarillo, TX	363.9	236	Columbia, MO	172.2	170	Goldsboro, NC	283.3
82	Anchorage, AK	553.2	98	Columbia, SC	478.6	178	Grand Forks, ND–MN	271.1
192	Ann Arbor, MI	238.3	107	Columbus, GA–AL	454.9	176	Grand Rapids–Muskegon–Holland, MI	272.5
199	Anniston, AL	225.0	71	Columbus, OH	612.1	205	Greeley, CO	218.8
267	Appleton–Oshkosh–Neenah, WI	114.6	93	Corpus Christi, TX	499.3	237	Green Bay, WI	171.3
187	Asheville, NC	252.7	264	Cumberland, MD–WV	119.1	155	Greensboro–Winston Salem–High Point, NC	311.6
110	Athens, GA	448.0	36	Dallas, TX	877.4	128	Greenville, NC	387.0
33	Atlanta, GA	895.7	159	Danbury, CT	305.7	151	Greenville–Spartanburg–Anderson, SC	316.1
150	Atlantic City, NJ	318.5	261	Danville, VA	130.7	253	Hagerstown, MD	142.1
91	Augusta–Aiken, GA–SC	513.0	117	Daytona Beach, FL	421.4	239	Harrisburg–Lebanon–Carlisle, PA	170.4
78	Austin–San Marcos, TX	574.1	85	Dayton–Springfield, OH	540.1	80	Hartford, CT	568.5
68	Bakersfield, CA	624.4	207	Decatur, AL	217.8	227	Hickory–Morganton, NC	181.3
44	Baltimore, MD	799.6	56	Denver, CO	699.6	92	Honolulu, HI	509.4
256	Bangor, ME	136.0	172	Des Moines, IA	278.8	194	Houma, LA	236.1
196	Barnstable–Yarmouth, MA	226.8	22	Detroit, MI	1,041.9	14	Houston, TX	1,125.8
28	Baton Rouge, LA	931.3	189	Dothan, AL	248.4	244	Huntington–Ashland, WV–KY–OH	164.9
48	Beaumont–Port Arthur, TX	754.5	228	Dubuque, IA	180.3	138	Huntsville, AL	349.7
183	Bellingham, WA	257.6	212	Duluth–Superior, MN–WI	214.8	–	Indianapolis, IN**	NA
154	Benton Harbor, MI	315.0	257	Dutchess County, NY	134.4	221	Jackson, MI	197.5
84	Bergen–Passaic, NJ	541.6	255	Eau Claire, WI	139.6	18	Jackson, MS	1,086.2
274	Binghamton, NY	43.3	32	El Paso, TX	902.9	116	Jackson, TN	426.2
66	Birmingham, AL	634.3	224	Elkhart–Goshen, IN	187.7	23	Jacksonville, FL	1,009.4
249	Bismarck, ND	152.0	181	Enid, OK	262.2	218	Jacksonville, NC	203.6
231	Bloomington, IN	176.5	213	Erie, PA	210.4	195	Janesville–Beloit, WI	236.0
201	Boise, ID	224.5	188	Eugene–Springfield, OR	251.7	8	Jersey City, NJ	1,258.2
37	Boston, MA–NH	861.8	203	Evansville–Henderson, IN–KY	220.6	223	Johnson City–Kingsport–Bristol, TN–VA	188.7
208	Boulder–Longmont, CO	217.0	210	Fargo–Moorhead, ND–MN	216.0	266	Johnstown, PA	115.4
180	Brazoria, TX	264.1	81	Fayetteville, NC	567.5	199	Joplin, MO	225.0
222	Bremerton, WA	196.9	233	Fayetteville–Springdale–Rogers, AR	175.9	156	Kalamazoo–Battle Creek, MI	310.7
12	Bridgeport, CT	1,191.1	126	Fitchburg–Leominster, MA	397.8	–	Kansas City, MO–KS**	NA
20	Brockton, MA	1,054.3	46	Flint, MI	763.6	157	Kenosha, WI	307.7
90	Brownsville–Harlingen–San Benito, TX	515.9	270	Florence, AL	106.0	165	Killeen–Temple, TX	289.8
140	Bryan–College Station, TX	344.8	119	Florence, SC	412.8	245	Kokomo, IN	161.8
53	Buffalo–Niagara Falls, NY	708.8	252	Fort Collins–Loveland, CO	145.2	271	La Crosse, WI–MN	94.0
141	Canton–Massillon, OH	344.4	24	Fort Lauderdale, FL	1,009.0	235	Lafayette, IN	173.0
148	Charleston, WV	321.3	45	Fort Myers–Cape Coral, FL	766.0	197	Lafayette, LA	226.2
102	Charleston–North Charleston, SC	460.1	77	Fort Pierce–Port St. Lucie, FL	577.9	133	Lake Charles, LA	376.4
202	Charlottesville, VA	221.3	169	Fort Smith, AR–OK	285.2	29	Lakeland–Winter Haven, FL	926.5
132	Charlotte–Gastonia–Rock Hill, NC–SC	380.3	217	Fort Walton Beach, FL	205.6	241	Lancaster, PA	168.0
63	Chattanooga, TN–GA	654.8	96	Fort Wayne, IN	492.6	160	Lansing–East Lansing, MI	304.2

Source: U.S. Department of Justice, Federal Bureau of Investigation
    "Crime in the United States 1993" (Uniform Crime Reports, December 4, 1994)
*Includes the theft or attempted theft of a self-propelled vehicle. Excludes motorboats, construction equipment, airplanes and farming equipment.
**Not available.

38. Motor Vehicle Theft Rate in 1993 (continued)

National Rate = 605.3 Motor Vehicle Thefts per 100,000 Population*

RANK	METRO AREA	RATE	RANK	METRO AREA	RATE	RANK	METRO AREA	RATE
54	Laredo, TX	704.8	192	Olympia, WA	238.3	62	Seattle–Bellevue–Everett, WA	658.2
30	Las Vegas, NV–AZ	922.8	–	Omaha, NE**	NA	265	Sheboygan, WI	117.9
10	Lawrence, MA–NH	1,195.2	39	Orange County, CA	848.1	186	Sherman–Denison, TX	253.8
162	Lawton, OK	295.6	75	Orlando, FL	591.5	88	Shreveport–Bossier City, LA	517.3
260	Lewiston–Auburn, ME	131.6	268	Owensboro, KY	110.4	185	Sioux City, IA–NE	254.3
197	Lexington, KY	226.2	120	Panama City, FL	409.0	250	Sioux Falls, SD	150.3
210	Lincoln, NE	216.0	47	Philadelphia, PA–NJ	758.0	112	South Bend, IN	436.8
59	Little Rock–North Little Rock, AR	683.4	21	Phoenix–Mesa, AZ	1,045.6	164	Spokane, WA	290.9
113	Longview–Marshall, TX	436.6	65	Pine Bluff, AR	644.1	19	Springfield, MA	1,059.7
4	Los Angeles–Long Beach, CA	1,378.2	86	Pittsburgh, PA	519.5	208	Springfield, MO	217.0
115	Louisville, KY–IN	428.7	206	Pittsfield, MA	218.2	99	Stamford–Norwalk, CT	476.6
167	Lubbock, TX	288.3	204	Portland, ME	219.4	269	Steubenville–Weirton, OH–WV	110.2
254	Lynchburg, VA	142.0	40	Portland–Vancouver, OR–WA	833.5	16	Stockton–Lodi, CA	1,112.8
123	Macon, GA	402.3	58	Providence–Fall River–Warwick, RI–MA	689.5	232	St. Cloud, MN	176.2
158	Madison, WI	306.4	243	Provo–Orem, UT	165.7	179	St. Joseph, MO	269.2
143	Manchester, NH	334.4	182	Pueblo, CO	261.5	–	St. Louis, MO–IL**	NA
191	Mansfield, OH	241.8	240	Punta Gorda, FL	169.4	131	Sumter, SC	381.1
55	McAllen–Edinburg–Mission, TX	703.3	139	Racine, WI	345.1	259	Syracuse, NY	133.3
168	Medford–Ashland, OR	285.6	153	Raleigh–Durham–Chapel Hill, NC	315.5	74	Tacoma, WA	602.7
3	Memphis, TN–AR–MS	1,424.1	214	Rapid City, SD	209.7	15	Tallahassee, FL	1,119.6
83	Merced, CA	552.2	175	Reading, PA	273.0	43	Tampa–St. Petersburg–Clearwater, FL	808.7
1	Miami, FL	2,113.6	130	Redding, CA	381.9	171	Texarkana, TX–AR	282.1
144	Middlesex–Sommerset–Hunterdon, NJ	332.5	127	Reno, NV	391.5	42	Toledo, OH	821.2
38	Milwaukee–Waukesha, WI	855.8	190	Richland–Kennewick–Pasco, WA	243.3	13	Trenton, NJ	1,154.9
101	Minneapolis–St. Paul, MN–WI	462.0	124	Richmond–Petersburg, VA	402.2	31	Tucson, AZ	912.6
105	Mobile, AL	455.3	17	Riverside–San Bernardino, CA	1,088.1	51	Tulsa, OK	732.2
41	Modesto, CA	822.0	229	Roanoke, VA	178.0	147	Tuscaloosa, AL	322.9
238	Monmouth–Ocean, NJ	171.0	219	Rochester, MN	203.2	111	Tyler, TX	444.7
166	Monroe, LA	288.8	121	Rochester, NY	405.5	258	Utica–Rome, NY	133.1
109	Montgomery, AL	452.4	173	Rocky Mount, NC	277.6	87	Vallejo–Fairfield–Napa, CA	517.5
97	Myrtle Beach, SC	485.7	9	Sacramento, CA	1,240.5	125	Ventura, CA	400.2
103	Naples, FL	458.3	225	Saginaw–Bay City–Midland, MI	183.5	142	Victoria, TX	337.3
216	Nashua, NH	206.4	94	Salem, OR	498.4	122	Vineland–Millville–Bridgeton, NJ	402.8
79	Nashville, TN	572.5	135	Salinas, CA	363.6	76	Visalia–Tulare–Porterville, CA	590.8
73	Nassau–Suffolk, NY	604.1	163	Salt Lake City–Ogden, UT	294.0	67	Waco, TX	629.7
61	New Bedford, MA	674.1	226	San Angelo, TX	182.1	72	Washington, DC–MD–VA–WV	607.4
70	New Haven–Meriden, CT	622.9	26	San Antonio, TX	953.2	35	Waterbury, CT	878.3
234	New London–Norwich, CT–RI	173.6	7	San Diego, CA	1,263.4	220	Waterloo–Cedar Falls, IA	200.2
11	New Orleans, LA	1,194.1	27	San Francisco, CA	949.6	272	Wausau, WI	90.3
5	New York, NY	1,368.8	114	San Jose, CA	432.8	–	West Palm Beach–Boca Raton, FL**	NA
6	Newark, NJ	1,302.6	230	San Luis Obispo–Atascadero, CA	176.8	149	Wichita Falls, TX	320.8
262	Newburgh, NY–PA	127.4	215	Santa Barbara–Santa Maria–Lompoc, CA	207.2	251	Williamsport, PA	149.6
108	Norfolk–Va Beach–Newport News, VA–NC	454.3	152	Santa Cruz–Watsonville, CA	315.8	145	Wilmington, NC	327.9
34	Oakland, CA	891.3	146	Santa Rosa, CA	327.3	89	Worcester, MA–CT	516.6
177	Ocala, FL	271.6	129	Sarasota–Bradenton, FL	383.4	106	Yakima, WA	455.2
136	Odessa–Midland, TX	357.4	69	Savannah, GA	623.4	89	Yolo, CA	693.8
50	Oklahoma City, OK	732.8	242	Scranton–Wilkes-Barre–Hazleton, PA	167.1	104	Yuba City, CA	458.0

Source: U.S. Department of Justice, Federal Bureau of Investigation
    "Crime in the United States 1993" (Uniform Crime Reports, December 4, 1994)
*Includes the theft or attempted theft of a self-propelled vehicle. Excludes motorboats, construction equipment, airplanes and farming equipment.
**Not available.

38. Motor Vehicle Theft Rate in 1993 (continued)

National Rate = 605.3 Motor Vehicle Thefts per 100,000 Population*

RANK	METRO AREA	RATE	RANK	METRO AREA	RATE	RANK	METRO AREA	RATE
1	Miami, FL	2,113.6	48	Beaumont-Port Arthur, TX	754.5	95	Gadsden, AL	495.2
2	Fresno, CA	2,045.3	49	Fort Worth-Arlington, TX	734.1	96	Fort Wayne, IN	492.6
3	Memphis, TN-AR-MS	1,424.1	50	Oklahoma City, OK	732.8	97	Myrtle Beach, SC	485.7
4	Los Angeles-Long Beach, CA	1,378.2	51	Tulsa, OK	732.2	98	Columbia, SC	478.6
5	New York, NY	1,368.8	52	Gainesville, FL	720.2	99	Stamford-Norwalk, CT	476.6
6	Newark, NJ	1,302.6	53	Buffalo-Niagara Falls, NY	708.8	100	Albany, GA	471.6
7	San Diego, CA	1,263.4	54	Laredo, TX	704.8	101	Minneapolis-St. Paul, MN-WI	462.0
8	Jersey City, NJ	1,258.2	55	McAllen-Edinburg-Mission, TX	703.3	102	Charleston-North Charleston, SC	460.1
9	Sacramento, CA	1,240.5	56	Denver, CO	699.6	103	Naples, FL	458.3
10	Lawrence, MA-NH	1,195.2	57	Yolo, CA	693.8	104	Yuba City, CA	458.0
11	New Orleans, LA	1,194.1	58	Providence-Fall River-Warwick, RI-MA	689.5	105	Mobile, AL	455.3
12	Bridgeport, CT	1,191.1	59	Little Rock-North Little Rock, AR	683.4	106	Yakima, WA	455.2
13	Trenton, NJ	1,154.9	60	Galveston-Texas City, TX	677.7	107	Columbus, GA-AL	454.9
14	Houston, TX	1,125.8	61	New Bedford, MA	674.1	108	Norfolk-Va Beach-Newport News, VA-NC	454.3
15	Tallahassee, FL	1,119.6	62	Seattle-Bellevue-Everett, WA	658.2	109	Montgomery, AL	452.4
16	Stockton-Lodi, CA	1,112.8	63	Chattanooga, TN-GA	654.8	110	Athens, GA	448.0
17	Riverside-San Bernardino, CA	1,088.1	64	Albuquerque, NM	647.3	111	Tyler, TX	444.7
18	Jackson, MS	1,086.2	65	Pine Bluff, AR	644.1	112	South Bend, IN	436.8
19	Springfield, MA	1,059.7	66	Birmingham, AL	634.3	113	Longview-Marshall, TX	436.6
20	Brockton, MA	1,054.3	67	Waco, TX	629.7	114	San Jose, CA	432.8
21	Phoenix-Mesa, AZ	1,045.6	68	Bakersfield, CA	624.4	115	Louisville, KY-IN	428.7
22	Detroit, MI	1,041.9	69	Savannah, GA	623.4	116	Jackson, TN	426.2
23	Jacksonville, FL	1,009.4	70	New Haven-Meriden, CT	622.9	117	Daytona Beach, FL	421.4
24	Fort Lauderdale, FL	1,009.0	71	Columbus, OH	612.1	118	Akron, OH	421.1
25	Gary-Hammond, IN	1,002.5	72	Washington, DC-MD-VA-WV	607.4	119	Florence, SC	412.8
26	San Antonio, TX	953.2	73	Nassau-Suffolk, NY	604.1	120	Panama City, FL	409.0
27	San Francisco, CA	949.6	74	Tacoma, WA	602.7	121	Rochester, NY	405.5
28	Baton Rouge, LA	931.3	75	Orlando, FL	591.5	122	Vineland-Millville-Bridgeton, NJ	402.8
29	Lakeland-Winter Haven, FL	926.5	76	Visalia-Tulare-Porterville, CA	590.8	123	Macon, GA	402.3
30	Las Vegas, NV-AZ	922.8	77	Fort Pierce-Port St. Lucie, FL	577.9	124	Richmond-Petersburg, VA	402.2
31	Tucson, AZ	912.6	78	Austin-San Marcos, TX	574.1	125	Ventura, CA	400.2
32	El Paso, TX	902.9	79	Nashville, TN	572.5	126	Fitchburg-Leominster, MA	397.8
33	Atlanta, GA	895.7	80	Hartford, CT	568.5	127	Reno, NV	391.5
34	Oakland, CA	891.3	81	Fayetteville, NC	567.5	128	Greenville, NC	387.0
35	Waterbury, CT	878.3	82	Anchorage, AK	553.2	129	Sarasota-Bradenton, FL	383.4
36	Dallas, TX	877.4	83	Merced, CA	552.2	130	Redding, CA	381.9
37	Boston, MA-NH	861.8	84	Bergen-Passaic, NJ	541.6	131	Sumter, SC	381.1
38	Milwaukee-Waukesha, WI	855.8	85	Dayton-Springfield, OH	540.1	132	Charlotte-Gastonia-Rock Hill, NC-SC	380.3
39	Orange County, CA	848.1	86	Pittsburgh, PA	519.5	133	Lake Charles, LA	376.4
40	Portland-Vancouver, OR-WA	833.5	87	Vallejo-Fairfield-Napa, CA	517.5	134	Amarillo, TX	363.9
41	Modesto, CA	822.0	88	Shreveport-Bossier City, LA	517.3	135	Salinas, CA	363.6
42	Toledo, OH	821.2	89	Worcester, MA-CT	516.6	136	Odessa-Midland, TX	357.4
43	Tampa-St. Petersburg-Clearwater, FL	808.7	90	Brownsville-Harlingen-San Benito, TX	515.9	137	Alexandria, LA	357.1
44	Baltimore, MD	799.6	91	Augusta-Aiken, GA-SC	513.0	138	Huntsville, AL	349.7
45	Fort Myers-Cape Coral, FL	766.0	92	Honolulu, HI	509.4	139	Racine, WI	345.1
46	Flint, MI	763.6	93	Corpus Christi, TX	499.3	140	Bryan-College Station, TX	344.8
47	Philadelphia, PA-NJ	758.0	94	Salem, OR	498.4	141	Canton-Massillon, OH	344.4

Source: U.S. Department of Justice, Federal Bureau of Investigation
  "Crime in the United States 1993" (Uniform Crime Reports, December 4, 1994)
*Includes the theft or attempted theft of a self-propelled vehicle. Excludes motorboats, construction equipment, airplanes and farming equipment.
**Not available.

38. Motor Vehicle Theft Rate in 1993 (continued)

National Rate = 605.3 Motor Vehicle Thefts per 100,000 Population*

RANK	METRO AREA	RATE	RANK	METRO AREA	RATE	RANK	METRO AREA	RATE
142	Victoria, TX	337.3	189	Dothan, AL	248.4	236	Columbia, MO	172.2
143	Manchester, NH	334.4	190	Richland–Kennewick–Pasco, WA	243.3	237	Green Bay, WI	171.3
144	Middlesex–Sommerset–Hunterdon, NJ	332.5	191	Mansfield, OH	241.8	238	Monmouth–Ocean, NJ	171.0
145	Wilmington, NC	327.9	192	Ann Arbor, MI	238.3	239	Harrisburg–Lebanon–Carlisle, PA	170.4
146	Santa Rosa, CA	327.3	192	Olympia, WA	238.3	240	Punta Gorda, FL	169.4
147	Tuscaloosa, AL	322.9	194	Houma, LA	236.1	241	Lancaster, PA	168.0
148	Charleston, WV	321.3	195	Janesville–Beloit, WI	236.0	242	Scranton–Wilkes-Barre–Hazleton, PA	167.1
149	Wichita Falls, TX	320.8	196	Barnstable–Yarmouth, MA	226.8	243	Provo–Orem, UT	165.7
150	Atlantic City, NJ	318.5	197	Lafayette, LA	226.2	244	Huntington–Ashland, WV–KY–OH	164.9
151	Greenville–Spartanburg–Anderson, SC	316.1	197	Lexington, KY	226.2	245	Kokomo, IN	161.8
152	Santa Cruz–Watsonville, CA	315.8	199	Anniston, AL	225.0	246	Altoona, PA	158.5
153	Raleigh–Durham–Chapel Hill, NC	315.5	199	Joplin, MO	225.0	247	Clarksville–Hopkinsville, TN–KY	155.2
154	Benton Harbor, MI	315.0	201	Boise, ID	224.5	248	Abilene, TX	152.1
155	Greensboro–Winston Salem–High Point, NC	311.6	202	Charlottesville, VA	221.3	249	Bismarck, ND	152.0
156	Kalamazoo–Battle Creek, MI	310.7	203	Evansville–Henderson, IN–KY	220.6	250	Sioux Falls, SD	150.3
157	Kenosha, WI	307.7	204	Portland, ME	219.4	251	Williamsport, PA	149.6
158	Madison, WI	306.4	205	Greeley, CO	218.8	252	Fort Collins–Loveland, CO	145.2
159	Danbury, CT	305.7	206	Pittsfield, MA	218.2	253	Hagerstown, MD	142.1
160	Lansing–East Lansing, MI	304.2	207	Decatur, AL	217.8	254	Lynchburg, VA	142.0
161	Chico–Paradise, CA	300.0	208	Boulder–Longmont, CO	217.0	255	Eau Claire, WI	139.6
162	Lawton, OK	295.6	208	Springfield, MO	217.0	256	Bangor, ME	136.0
163	Salt Lake City–Ogden, UT	294.0	210	Fargo–Moorhead, ND–MN	216.0	257	Dutchess County, NY	134.4
164	Spokane, WA	290.9	210	Lincoln, NE	216.0	258	Utica–Rome, NY	133.8
165	Killeen–Temple, TX	289.8	212	Duluth–Superior, MN–WI	214.8	259	Syracuse, NY	133.3
166	Monroe, LA	288.8	213	Erie, PA	210.4	260	Lewiston–Auburn, ME	131.6
167	Lubbock, TX	288.3	214	Rapid City, SD	209.7	261	Danville, VA	130.7
168	Medford–Ashland, OR	285.6	215	Santa Barbara–Santa Maria–Lompoc, CA	207.2	262	Newburgh, NY–PA	127.4
169	Fort Smith, AR–OK	285.2	216	Nashua, NH	206.4	263	Cheyenne, WY	124.9
170	Goldsboro, NC	283.3	217	Fort Walton Beach, FL	205.6	264	Cumberland, MD–WV	119.1
171	Texarkana, TX–AR	282.1	218	Jacksonville, NC	203.6	265	Sheboygan, WI	117.9
172	Des Moines, IA	278.8	219	Rochester, MN	203.2	266	Johnstown, PA	115.4
173	Rocky Mount, NC	277.6	220	Waterloo–Cedar Falls, IA	200.2	267	Appleton–Oshkosh–Neenah, WI	114.6
174	Colorado Springs, CO	273.8	221	Jackson, MI	197.5	268	Owensboro, KY	110.4
175	Reading, PA	273.0	222	Bremerton, WA	196.9	269	Steubenville–Weirton, OH–WV	110.2
176	Grand Rapids–Muskegon–Holland, MI	272.5	223	Johnson City–Kingsport–Bristol, TN–VA	188.7	270	Florence, AL	106.0
177	Ocala, FL	271.6	224	Elkhart–Goshen, IN	187.7	271	La Crosse, WI–MN	94.0
178	Grand Forks, ND–MN	271.1	225	Saginaw–Bay City–Midland, MI	183.5	272	Wausau, WI	90.3
179	St. Joseph, MO	269.2	226	San Angelo, TX	182.1	273	Glens Falls, NY	76.5
180	Brazoria, TX	264.1	227	Hickory–Morganton, NC	181.3	274	Binghamton, NY	43.3
181	Enid, OK	262.2	228	Dubuque, IA	180.3	–	Albany, NY**	NA
182	Pueblo, CO	261.5	229	Roanoke, VA	178.0	–	Chicago, IL**	NA
183	Bellingham, WA	257.6	230	San Luis Obispo–Atascadero, CA	176.8	–	Cleveland, OH**	NA
183	Cincinnati, OH–KY–IN	257.6	231	Bloomington, IN	176.5	–	Indianapolis, IN**	NA
185	Sioux City, IA–NE	254.3	232	St. Cloud, MN	176.2	–	Kansas City, MO–KS**	NA
186	Sherman–Denison, TX	253.8	233	Fayetteville–Springdale–Rogers, AR	175.9	–	Omaha, NE**	NA
187	Asheville, NC	252.7	234	New London–Norwich, CT–RI	173.6	–	St. Louis, MO–IL**	NA
188	Eugene–Springfield, OR	251.7	235	Lafayette, IN	173.0	–	West Palm Beach–Boca Raton, FL**	NA

Source: U.S. Department of Justice, Federal Bureau of Investigation

"Crime in the United States 1993" (Uniform Crime Reports, December 4, 1994)

Includes the theft or attempted theft of a self-propelled vehicle. Excludes motorboats, construction equipment, airplanes and farming equipment.

**Not available.*

39. Percent Change in Motor Vehicle Theft Rate: 1992 to 1993

National Percent Change = 4.1% Decrease*

RANK	METRO AREA	% CHANGE	RANK	METRO AREA	% CHANGE	RANK	METRO AREA	% CHANGE
83	Abilene, TX	5.11	94	Cheyenne, WY	3.14	246	Fort Worth-Arlington, TX	(32.25)
179	Akron, OH	(8.26)	–	Chicago, IL**	NA	135	Fresno, CA	(3.11)
24	Albany, GA	22.37	210	Chico-Paradise, CA	(14.53)	197	Gadsden, AL	(11.62)
–	Albany, NY**	NA	183	Cincinnati, OH-KY-IN	(9.20)	76	Gainesville, FL	6.27
27	Albuquerque, NM	19.63	161	Clarksville-Hopkinsville, TN-KY	(6.05)	159	Galveston-Texas City, TX	(5.94)
3	Alexandria, LA	39.93	–	Cleveland, OH**	NA	230	Gary-Hammond, IN	(20.73)
10	Altoona, PA	34.09	157	Colorado Springs, CO	(5.62)	97	Glens Falls, NY	2.55
53	Amarillo, TX	11.01	164	Columbia, MO	(6.46)	169	Goldsboro, NC	(6.96)
220	Anchorage, AK	(17.05)	205	Columbia, SC	(12.93)	26	Grand Forks, ND-MN	20.60
117	Ann Arbor, MI	(0.83)	2	Columbus, GA-AL	44.96	134	Grand Rapids-Muskegon-Holland, MI	(2.99)
124	Anniston, AL	(1.75)	147	Columbus, OH	(4.19)	102	Greeley, CO	1.63
30	Appleton-Oshkosh-Neenah, WI	18.88	173	Corpus Christi, TX	(7.54)	45	Green Bay, WI	12.62
195	Asheville, NC	(11.49)	80	Cumberland, MD-WV	5.77	54	Greensboro-Winston Salem-High Point, NC	10.61
221	Athens, GA	(17.62)	219	Dallas, TX	(17.00)	131	Greenville, NC	(2.45)
95	Atlanta, GA	2.82	21	Danbury, CT	26.85	90	Greenville-Spartanburg-Anderson, SC	3.84
237	Atlantic City, NJ	(24.35)	206	Danville, VA	(13.33)	68	Hagerstown, MD	7.98
218	Augusta-Aiken, GA-SC	(16.96)	78	Daytona Beach, FL	5.88	247	Harrisburg-Lebanon-Carlisle, PA	(34.91)
185	Austin-San Marcos, TX	(9.33)	121	Dayton-Springfield, OH	(1.53)	235	Hartford, CT	(23.66)
35	Bakersfield, CA	16.86	106	Decatur, AL	0.51	155	Hickory-Morganton, NC	(5.18)
150	Baltimore, MD	(4.88)	201	Denver, CO	(12.11)	20	Honolulu, HI	27.13
154	Bangor, ME	(5.16)	36	Des Moines, IA	15.64	77	Houma, LA	6.16
145	Barnstable-Yarmouth, MA	(4.06)	110	Detroit, MI	(0.17)	214	Houston, TX	(15.40)
207	Baton Rouge, LA	(14.03)	34	Dothan, AL	17.23	44	Huntington-Ashland, WV-KY-OH	13.10
153	Beaumont-Port Arthur, TX	(5.13)	28	Dubuque, IA	19.56	11	Huntsville, AL	33.98
142	Bellingham, WA	(3.77)	172	Duluth-Superior, MN-WI	(7.53)	–	Indianapolis, IN**	NA
127	Benton Harbor, MI	(1.90)	–	Dutchess County, NY**	NA	138	Jackson, MI	(3.47)
–	Bergen-Passaic, NJ**	NA	73	Eau Claire, WI	6.81	123	Jackson, MS	(1.69)
250	Binghamton, NY	(47.64)	120	El Paso, TX	(1.12)	38	Jackson, TN	15.28
132	Birmingham, AL	(2.49)	16	Elkhart-Goshen, IN	29.09	129	Jacksonville, FL	(2.15)
208	Bismarck, ND	(14.27)	133	Enid, OK	(2.64)	114	Jacksonville, NC	(0.34)
234	Bloomington, IN	(23.26)	75	Erie, PA	6.37	98	Janesville-Beloit, WI	2.43
39	Boise, ID	15.25	159	Eugene-Springfield, OR	(5.94)	–	Jersey City, NJ**	NA
–	Boston, MA-NH**	NA	136	Evansville-Henderson, IN-KY	(3.20)	63	Johnson City-Kingsport-Bristol, TN-VA	8.76
223	Boulder-Longmont, CO	(18.11)	167	Fargo-Moorhead, ND-MN	(6.74)	180	Johnstown, PA	(8.63)
242	Brazoria, TX	(29.65)	174	Fayetteville, NC	(7.71)	–	Joplin, MO**	NA
245	Bremerton, WA	(30.84)	226	Fayetteville-Springdale-Rogers, AR	(19.09)	52	Kalamazoo-Battle Creek, MI	11.04
217	Bridgeport, CT	(16.83)	–	Fitchburg-Leominster, MA**	NA	–	Kansas City, MO-KS**	NA
228	Brockton, MA	(20.29)	178	Flint, MI	(8.10)	46	Kenosha, WI	12.14
166	Brownsville-Harlingen-San Benito, TX	(6.57)	194	Florence, AL	(10.92)	43	Killeen-Temple, TX	13.25
47	Bryan-College Station, TX	11.98	18	Florence, SC	28.36	146	Kokomo, IN	(4.09)
–	Buffalo-Niagara Falls, NY**	NA	–	Fort Collins-Loveland, CO**	NA	199	La Crosse, WI-MN	(11.82)
101	Canton-Massillon, OH	1.65	41	Fort Lauderdale, FL	14.65	193	Lafayette, IN	(10.78)
148	Charleston, WV	(4.23)	111	Fort Myers-Cape Coral, FL	(0.18)	243	Lafayette, LA	(29.97)
116	Charleston-North Charleston, SC	(0.75)	5	Fort Pierce-Port St. Lucie, FL	37.63	–	Lake Charles, LA**	NA
8	Charlottesville, VA	34.69	58	Fort Smith, AR-OK	9.65	33	Lakeland-Winter Haven, FL	17.76
60	Charlotte-Gastonia-Rock Hill, NC-SC	9.25	13	Fort Walton Beach, FL	31.12	222	Lancaster, PA	(17.85)
56	Chattanooga, TN-GA	10.35	81	Fort Wayne, IN	5.44	171	Lansing-East Lansing, MI	(7.09)

Source: Morgan Quitno Corporation using data from U.S. Department of Justice, Federal Bureau of Investigation
   "Crime in the United States 1993" (Uniform Crime Reports, December 4, 1994)
*Includes the theft or attempted theft of a self-propelled vehicle. Excludes motorboats, construction equipment, airplanes and farming equipment.
**Not available.

39. Percent Change in Motor Vehicle Theft Rate: 1992 to 1993 (continued)

National Percent Change = 4.1% Decrease*

RANK	METRO AREA	% CHANGE	RANK	METRO AREA	% CHANGE	RANK	METRO AREA	CHANGE
211	Laredo, TX	(14.68)	103	Olympia, WA	1.62	125	Seattle-Bellevue-Everett, WA	(1.78)
96	Las Vegas, NV–AZ	2.77	–	Omaha, NE**	NA	128	Sheboygan, WI	(2.08)
–	Lawrence, MA–NH**	NA	107	Orange County, CA	0.38	236	Sherman-Denison, TX	(23.81)
181	Lawton, OK	(8.79)	168	Orlando, FL	(6.81)	203	Shreveport-Bossier City, LA	(12.88)
204	Lewiston-Auburn, ME	(12.91)	248	Owensboro, KY	(37.13)	–	Sioux City, IA–NE**	NA
139	Lexington, KY	(3.70)	55	Panama City, FL	10.51	1	Sioux Falls, SD	46.06
59	Lincoln, NE	9.48	112	Philadelphia, PA–NJ	(0.20)	15	South Bend, IN	30.58
182	Little Rock-North Little Rock, AR	(9.07)	87	Phoenix-Mesa, AZ	4.34	98	Spokane, WA	2.43
104	Longview-Marshall, TX	1.53	50	Pine Bluff, AR	11.26	122	Springfield, MA	(1.57)
151	Los Angeles-Long Beach, CA	(4.92)	224	Pittsburgh, PA	(18.38)	130	Springfield, MO	(2.16)
149	Louisville, KY–IN	(4.31)	69	Pittsfield, MA	7.59	200	Stamford-Norwalk, CT	(12.02)
213	Lubbock, TX	(15.11)	216	Portland, ME	(16.51)	158	Steubenville-Weirton, OH–WV	(5.81)
85	Lynchburg, VA	4.80	71	Portland-Vancouver, OR–WA	7.06	92	Stockton-Lodi, CA	3.79
156	Macon, GA	(5.45)	202	Providence-Fall River-Warwick, RI–MA	(12.64)	192	St. Cloud, MN	(10.69)
4	Madison, WI	38.20	12	Provo-Orem, UT	31.30	29	St. Joseph, MO	19.17
–	Manchester, NH**	NA	113	Pueblo, CO	(0.23)	–	St. Louis, MO–IL**	NA
82	Mansfield, OH	5.22	–	Punta Gorda, FL**	NA	72	Sumter, SC	6.93
239	McAllen-Edinburg-Mission, TX	(27.68)	244	Racine, WI	(30.77)	196	Syracuse, NY	(11.60)
14	Medford-Ashland, OR	30.71	163	Raleigh-Durham-Chapel Hill, NC	(6.38)	40	Tacoma, WA	14.87
88	Memphis, TN–AR–MS	4.27	118	Rapid City, SD	(0.94)	61	Tallahassee, FL	9.19
7	Merced, CA	34.98	49	Reading, PA	11.75	100	Tampa-St. Petersburg-Clearwater, FL	2.20
31	Miami, FL	18.85	19	Redding, CA	28.28	86	Texarkana, TX–AR	4.52
–	Middlesex-Sommerset-Hunterdon, NJ**	NA	23	Reno, NV	24.80	65	Toledo, OH	8.47
233	Milwaukee-Waukesha, WI	(22.58)	137	Richland-Kennewick-Pasco, WA	(3.22)	89	Trenton, NJ	3.85
143	Minneapolis-St. Paul, MN–WI	(3.91)	170	Richmond-Petersburg, VA	(7.07)	51	Tucson, AZ	11.05
–	Mobile, AL**	NA	105	Riverside-San Bernardino, CA	0.72	187	Tulsa, OK	(9.46)
9	Modesto, CA	34.64	184	Roanoke, VA	(9.28)	198	Tuscaloosa, AL	(11.66)
–	Monmouth-Ocean, NJ**	NA	48	Rochester, MN	11.89	249	Tyler, TX	(39.79)
225	Monroe, LA	(18.99)	84	Rochester, NY	4.97	144	Utica-Rome, NY	(3.95)
119	Montgomery, AL	(1.05)	188	Rocky Mount, NC	(9.64)	74	Vallejo-Fairfield-Napa, CA	6.64
42	Myrtle Beach, SC	14.04	91	Sacramento, CA	3.80	108	Ventura, CA	(0.15)
32	Naples, FL	17.78	241	Saginaw-Bay City-Midland, MI	(28.68)	232	Victoria, TX	(21.94)
165	Nashua, NH	(6.48)	6	Salem, OR	36.77	140	Vineland-Millville-Bridgeton, NJ	(3.73)
151	Nashville, TN	(4.92)	70	Salinas, CA	7.38	126	Visalia-Tulare-Porterville, CA	(1.88)
–	Nassau-Suffolk, NY**	NA	115	Salt Lake City-Ogden, UT	(0.51)	162	Waco, TX	(6.09)
–	New Bedford, MA**	NA	240	San Angelo, TX	(28.34)	189	Washington, DC-MD-VA-WV	(9.76)
238	New Haven-Meriden, CT	(24.39)	229	San Antonio, TX	(20.31)	79	Waterbury, CT	5.81
175	New London-Norwich, CT–RI	(7.81)	141	San Diego, CA	(3.74)	–	Waterloo-Cedar Falls, IA**	NA
108	New Orleans, LA	(0.15)	177	San Francisco, CA	(7.95)	57	Wausau, WI	9.85
–	New York, NY**	NA	62	San Jose, CA	9.16	–	West Palm Beach-Boca Raton, FL**	NA
–	Newark, NJ**	NA	–	San Luis Obispo-Atascadero, CA**	NA	227	Wichita Falls, TX	(19.52)
–	Newburgh, NY–PA**	NA	67	Santa Barbara-Santa Maria-Lompoc, CA	8.37	25	Williamsport, PA	22.12
175	Norfolk-Va Beach-Newport News, VA–NC	(7.81)	37	Santa Cruz-Watsonville, CA	15.59	231	Wilmington, NC	(21.70)
93	Oakland, CA	3.27	17	Santa Rosa, CA	28.71	–	Worcester, MA–CT**	NA
215	Ocala, FL	(15.91)	209	Sarasota-Bradenton, FL	(14.42)	64	Yakima, WA	8.61
212	Odessa-Midland, TX	(14.84)	190	Savannah, GA	(10.07)	65	Yolo, CA	8.47
186	Oklahoma City, OK	(9.41)	191	Scranton-Wilkes-Barre-Hazleton, PA	(10.21)	22	Yuba City, CA	25.82

Source: Morgan Quitno Corporation using data from U.S. Department of Justice, Federal Bureau of Investigation
    "Crime in the United States 1993" (Uniform Crime Reports, December 4, 1994)
*Includes the theft or attempted theft of a self-propelled vehicle. Excludes motorboats, construction equipment, airplanes and farming equipment.
**Not available.

39. Percent Change in Motor Vehicle Theft Rate: 1992 to 1993 (continued)

National Percent Change = 4.1% Decrease*

RANK	METRO AREA	% CHANGE	RANK	METRO AREA	% CHANGE	RANK	METRO AREA	% CHANGE
1	Sioux Falls, SD	46.06	48	Rochester, MN	11.89	95	Atlanta, GA	2.82
2	Columbus, GA–AL	44.96	49	Reading, PA	11.75	96	Las Vegas, NV–AZ	2.77
3	Alexandria, LA	39.93	50	Pine Bluff, AR	11.26	97	Glens Falls, NY	2.55
4	Madison, WI	38.20	51	Tucson, AZ	11.05	98	Janesville–Beloit, WI	2.43
5	Fort Pierce–Port St. Lucie, FL	37.63	52	Kalamazoo–Battle Creek, MI	11.04	98	Spokane, WA	2.43
6	Salem, OR	36.77	53	Amarillo, TX	11.01	100	Tampa–St. Petersburg–Clearwater, FL	2.20
7	Merced, CA	34.98	54	Greensboro–Winston Salem–High Point, NC	10.61	101	Canton–Massillon, OH	1.65
8	Charlottesville, VA	34.69	55	Panama City, FL	10.51	102	Greeley, CO	1.63
9	Modesto, CA	34.64	56	Chattanooga, TN–GA	10.35	103	Olympia, WA	1.62
10	Altoona, PA	34.09	57	Wausau, WI	9.85	104	Longview–Marshall, TX	1.53
11	Huntsville, AL	33.98	58	Fort Smith, AR–OK	9.65	105	Riverside–San Bernardino, CA	0.72
12	Provo–Orem, UT	31.30	59	Lincoln, NE	9.48	106	Decatur, AL	0.51
13	Fort Walton Beach, FL	31.12	60	Charlotte–Gastonia–Rock Hill, NC–SC	9.25	107	Orange County, CA	0.38
14	Medford–Ashland, OR	30.71	61	Tallahassee, FL	9.19	108	New Orleans, LA	(0.15)
15	South Bend, IN	30.58	62	San Jose, CA	9.16	108	Ventura, CA	(0.15)
16	Elkhart–Goshen, IN	29.09	63	Johnson City–Kingsport–Bristol, TN–VA	8.76	110	Detroit, MI	(0.17)
17	Santa Rosa, CA	28.71	64	Yakima, WA	8.61	111	Fort Myers–Cape Coral, FL	(0.18)
18	Florence, SC	28.36	65	Toledo, OH	8.47	112	Philadelphia, PA–NJ	(0.20)
19	Redding, CA	28.28	65	Yolo, CA	8.47	113	Pueblo, CO	(0.23)
20	Honolulu, HI	27.13	67	Santa Barbara–Santa Maria–Lompoc, CA	8.37	114	Jacksonville, NC	(0.34)
21	Danbury, CT	26.85	68	Hagerstown, MD	7.98	115	Salt Lake City–Ogden, UT	(0.51)
22	Yuba City, CA	25.82	69	Pittsfield, MA	7.59	116	Charleston–North Charleston, SC	(0.75)
23	Reno, NV	24.80	70	Salinas, CA	7.38	117	Ann Arbor, MI	(0.83)
24	Albany, GA	22.37	71	Portland–Vancouver, OR–WA	7.06	118	Rapid City, SD	(0.94)
25	Williamsport, PA	22.12	72	Sumter, SC	6.93	119	Montgomery, AL	(1.05)
26	Grand Forks, ND–MN	20.60	73	Eau Claire, WI	6.81	120	El Paso, TX	(1.12)
27	Albuquerque, NM	19.63	74	Vallejo–Fairfield–Napa, CA	6.64	121	Dayton–Springfield, OH	(1.53)
28	Dubuque, IA	19.56	75	Erie, PA	6.37	122	Springfield, MA	(1.57)
29	St. Joseph, MO	19.17	76	Gainesville, FL	6.27	123	Jackson, MS	(1.69)
30	Appleton–Oshkosh–Neenah, WI	18.88	77	Houma, LA	6.16	124	Anniston, AL	(1.75)
31	Miami, FL	18.85	78	Daytona Beach, FL	5.88	125	Seattle–Bellevue–Everett, WA	(1.78)
32	Naples, FL	17.78	79	Waterbury, CT	5.81	126	Visalia–Tulare–Porterville, CA	(1.88)
33	Lakeland–Winter Haven, FL	17.76	80	Cumberland, MD–WV	5.77	127	Benton Harbor, MI	(1.90)
34	Dothan, AL	17.23	81	Fort Wayne, IN	5.44	128	Sheboygan, WI	(2.08)
35	Bakersfield, CA	16.86	82	Mansfield, OH	5.22	129	Jacksonville, FL	(2.15)
36	Des Moines, IA	15.64	83	Abilene, TX	5.11	130	Springfield, MO	(2.16)
37	Santa Cruz–Watsonville, CA	15.59	84	Rochester, NY	4.97	131	Greenville, NC	(2.45)
38	Jackson, TN	15.28	85	Lynchburg, VA	4.80	132	Birmingham, AL	(2.49)
39	Boise, ID	15.25	86	Texarkana, TX–AR	4.52	133	Enid, OK	(2.64)
40	Tacoma, WA	14.87	87	Phoenix–Mesa, AZ	4.34	134	Grand Rapids–Muskegon–Holland, MI	(2.99)
41	Fort Lauderdale, FL	14.65	88	Memphis, TN–AR–MS	4.27	135	Fresno, CA	(3.11)
42	Myrtle Beach, SC	14.04	89	Trenton, NJ	3.85	136	Evansville–Henderson, IN–KY	(3.20)
43	Killeen–Temple, TX	13.25	90	Greenville–Spartanburg–Anderson, SC	3.84	137	Richland–Kennewick–Pasco, WA	(3.22)
44	Huntington–Ashland, WV–KY–OH	13.10	91	Sacramento, CA	3.80	138	Jackson, MI	(3.47)
45	Green Bay, WI	12.62	92	Stockton–Lodi, CA	3.79	139	Lexington, KY	(3.70)
46	Kenosha, WI	12.14	93	Oakland, CA	3.27	140	Vineland–Millville–Bridgeton, NJ	(3.73)
47	Bryan–College Station, TX	11.98	94	Cheyenne, WY	3.14	141	San Diego, CA	(3.74)

Source: Morgan Quitno Corporation using data from U.S. Department of Justice, Federal Bureau of Investigation
    "Crime in the United States 1993" (Uniform Crime Reports, December 4, 1994)
Includes the theft or attempted theft of a self-propelled vehicle. Excludes motorboats, construction equipment, airplanes and farming equipment.
**Not available.*

39. Percent Change in Motor Vehicle Theft Rate: 1992 to 1993 (continued)

National Percent Change = 4.1% Decrease*

RANK	METRO AREA	% CHANGE	RANK	METRO AREA	% CHANGE	RANK	METRO AREA	CHANGE
142	Bellingham, WA	(3.77)	189	Washington, DC–MD–VA–WV	(9.76)	236	Sherman–Denison, TX	(23.81)
143	Minneapolis–St. Paul, MN–WI	(3.91)	190	Savannah, GA	(10.07)	237	Atlantic City, NJ	(24.35)
144	Utica–Rome, NY	(3.95)	191	Scranton–Wilkes-Barre–Hazleton, PA	(10.21)	238	New Haven–Meriden, CT	(24.39)
145	Barnstable–Yarmouth, MA	(4.06)	192	St. Cloud, MN	(10.69)	239	McAllen–Edinburg–Mission, TX	(27.68)
146	Kokomo, IN	(4.09)	193	Lafayette, IN	(10.78)	240	San Angelo, TX	(28.34)
147	Columbus, OH	(4.19)	194	Florence, AL	(10.92)	241	Saginaw–Bay City–Midland, MI	(28.68)
148	Charleston, WV	(4.23)	195	Asheville, NC	(11.49)	242	Brazoria, TX	(29.65)
149	Louisville, KY–IN	(4.31)	196	Syracuse, NY	(11.60)	243	Lafayette, LA	(29.97)
150	Baltimore, MD	(4.88)	197	Gadsden, AL	(11.62)	244	Racine, WI	(30.77)
151	Los Angeles–Long Beach, CA	(4.92)	198	Tuscaloosa, AL	(11.66)	245	Bremerton, WA	(30.84)
151	Nashville, TN	(4.92)	199	La Crosse, WI–MN	(11.82)	246	Fort Worth–Arlington, TX	(32.25)
153	Beaumont–Port Arthur, TX	(5.13)	200	Stamford–Norwalk, CT	(12.02)	247	Harrisburg–Lebanon–Carlisle, PA	(34.91)
154	Bangor, ME	(5.16)	201	Denver, CO	(12.11)	248	Owensboro, KY	(37.13)
155	Hickory–Morganton, NC	(5.18)	202	Providence–Fall River–Warwick, RI–MA	(12.64)	249	Tyler, TX	(39.79)
156	Macon, GA	(5.45)	203	Shreveport–Bossier City, LA	(12.88)	250	Binghamton, NY	(47.64)
157	Colorado Springs, CO	(5.62)	204	Lewiston–Auburn, ME	(12.91)	–	Albany, NY**	NA
158	Steubenville–Weirton, OH–WV	(5.81)	205	Columbia, SC	(12.93)	–	Bergen–Passaic, NJ**	NA
159	Eugene–Springfield, OR	(5.94)	206	Danville, VA	(13.33)	–	Boston, MA–NH**	NA
159	Galveston–Texas City, TX	(5.94)	207	Baton Rouge, LA	(14.03)	–	Buffalo–Niagara Falls, NY**	NA
161	Clarksville–Hopkinsville, TN–KY	(6.05)	208	Bismarck, ND	(14.27)	–	Chicago, IL**	NA
162	Waco, TX	(6.09)	209	Sarasota–Bradenton, FL	(14.42)	–	Cleveland, OH**	NA
163	Raleigh–Durham–Chapel Hill, NC	(6.38)	210	Chico–Paradise, CA	(14.53)	–	Dutchess County, NY**	NA
164	Columbia, MO	(6.46)	211	Laredo, TX	(14.68)	–	Fitchburg–Leominster, MA**	NA
165	Nashua, NH	(6.48)	212	Odessa–Midland, TX	(14.84)	–	Fort Collins–Loveland, CO**	NA
166	Brownsville–Harlingen–San Benito, TX	(6.57)	213	Lubbock, TX	(15.11)	–	Indianapolis, IN**	NA
167	Fargo–Moorhead, ND–MN	(6.74)	214	Houston, TX	(15.40)	–	Jersey City, NJ**	NA
168	Orlando, FL	(6.81)	215	Ocala, FL	(15.91)	–	Joplin, MO**	NA
169	Goldsboro, NC	(6.96)	216	Portland, ME	(16.51)	–	Kansas City, MO–KS**	NA
170	Richmond–Petersburg, VA	(7.07)	217	Bridgeport, CT	(16.83)	–	Lake Charles, LA**	NA
171	Lansing–East Lansing, MI	(7.09)	218	Augusta–Aiken, GA–SC	(16.96)	–	Lawrence, MA–NH**	NA
172	Duluth–Superior, MN–WI	(7.53)	219	Dallas, TX	(17.00)	–	Manchester, NH**	NA
173	Corpus Christi, TX	(7.54)	220	Anchorage, AK	(17.05)	–	Middlesex–Sommerset–Hunterdon, NJ**	NA
174	Fayetteville, NC	(7.71)	221	Athens, GA	(17.62)	–	Mobile, AL**	NA
175	New London–Norwich, CT–RI	(7.81)	222	Lancaster, PA	(17.85)	–	Monmouth–Ocean, NJ**	NA
175	Norfolk–Va Beach–Newport News, VA–NC	(7.81)	223	Boulder–Longmont, CO	(18.11)	–	Nassau–Suffolk, NY**	NA
177	San Francisco, CA	(7.95)	224	Pittsburgh, PA	(18.38)	–	New Bedford, MA**	NA
178	Flint, MI	(8.10)	225	Monroe, LA	(18.99)	–	New York, NY**	NA
179	Akron, OH	(8.26)	226	Fayetteville–Springdale–Rogers, AR	(19.09)	–	Newark, NJ**	NA
180	Johnstown, PA	(8.63)	227	Wichita Falls, TX	(19.52)	–	Newburgh, NY–PA**	NA
181	Lawton, OK	(8.79)	228	Brockton, MA	(20.29)	–	Omaha, NE**	NA
182	Little Rock–North Little Rock, AR	(9.07)	229	San Antonio, TX	(20.31)	–	Punta Gorda, FL**	NA
183	Cincinnati, OH–KY–IN	(9.20)	230	Gary–Hammond, IN	(20.73)	–	San Luis Obispo–Atascadero, CA**	NA
184	Roanoke, VA	(9.28)	231	Wilmington, NC	(21.70)	–	Sioux City, IA–NE**	NA
185	Austin–San Marcos, TX	(9.33)	232	Victoria, TX	(21.94)	–	St. Louis, MO–IL**	NA
186	Oklahoma City, OK	(9.41)	233	Milwaukee–Waukesha, WI	(22.58)	–	Waterloo–Cedar Falls, IA**	NA
187	Tulsa, OK	(9.46)	234	Bloomington, IN	(23.26)	–	West Palm Beach–Boca Raton, FL**	NA
188	Rocky Mount, NC	(9.64)	235	Hartford, CT	(23.66)	–	Worcester, MA–CT**	NA

Source: Morgan Quitno Corporation using data from U.S. Department of Justice, Federal Bureau of Investigation
"Crime in the United States 1993" (Uniform Crime Reports, December 4, 1994)
Includes the theft or attempted theft of a self-propelled vehicle. Excludes motorboats, construction equipment, airplanes and farming equipment.
**Not available.*

Alpha Order – Metro

40. Percent Change in Motor Vehicle Theft Rate: 1989 to 1993

National Percent Change = 4.0% Decrease*

RANK	METRO AREA	% CHANGE	RANK	METRO AREA	% CHANGE	RANK	METRO AREA	% CHANGE
235	Abilene, TX	(37.89)	108	Cheyenne, WY	5.76	230	Fort Worth-Arlington, TX	(35.17)
–	Akron, OH**	NA	–	Chicago, IL**	NA	8	Fresno, CA	75.92
57	Albany, GA	24.24	231	Chico-Paradise, CA	(35.18)	7	Gadsden, AL	78.58
–	Albany, NY**	NA	113	Cincinnati, OH-KY-IN	4.50	3	Gainesville, FL	93.91
48	Albuquerque, NM	28.87	167	Clarksville-Hopkinsville, TN-KY	(9.45)	91	Galveston-Texas City, TX	11.59
9	Alexandria, LA	73.52	–	Cleveland, OH**	NA	123	Gary-Hammond, IN	1.10
146	Altoona, PA	(5.54)	238	Colorado Springs, CO	(40.81)	234	Glens Falls, NY	(37.70)
71	Amarillo, TX	16.15	124	Columbia, MO	1.00	–	Goldsboro, NC**	NA
106	Anchorage, AK	6.71	202	Columbia, SC	(20.17)	4	Grand Forks, ND-MN	92.82
242	Ann Arbor, MI	(46.61)	27	Columbus, GA-AL	46.88	206	Grand Rapids-Muskegon-Holland, MI	(21.13)
129	Anniston, AL	(0.22)	145	Columbus, OH	(5.17)	110	Greeley, CO	5.45
45	Appleton-Oshkosh-Neenah, WI	35.30	46	Corpus Christi, TX	32.02	31	Green Bay, WI	40.99
218	Asheville, NC	(26.15)	39	Cumberland, MD-WV	38.17	121	Greensboro-Winston Salem-High Point, NC	1.80
37	Athens, GA	39.00	239	Dallas, TX	(40.90)	–	Greenville, NC**	NA
195	Atlanta, GA	(18.61)	44	Danbury, CT	35.51	165	Greenville-Spartanburg-Anderson, SC	(9.30)
221	Atlantic City, NJ	(28.09)	85	Danville, VA	12.77	168	Hagerstown, MD	(9.55)
102	Augusta-Aiken, GA-SC	8.11	82	Daytona Beach, FL	13.07	–	Harrisburg-Lebanon-Carlisle, PA**	NA
54	Austin-San Marcos, TX	26.01	81	Dayton-Springfield, OH	13.09	171	Hartford, CT	(9.96)
69	Bakersfield, CA	17.52	26	Decatur, AL	47.76	–	Hickory-Morganton, NC**	NA
64	Baltimore, MD	19.81	94	Denver, CO	10.78	62	Honolulu, HI	20.06
188	Bangor, ME	(17.07)	83	Des Moines, IA	13.06	–	Houma, LA**	NA
–	Barnstable-Yarmouth, MA**	NA	176	Detroit, MI	(12.38)	220	Houston, TX	(27.06)
10	Baton Rouge, LA	72.59	40	Dothan, AL	36.71	125	Huntington-Ashland, WV-KY-OH	0.67
11	Beaumont-Port Arthur, TX	70.70	22	Dubuque, IA	53.58	103	Huntsville, AL	7.87
170	Bellingham, WA	(9.74)	160	Duluth-Superior, MN-WI	(8.32)	–	Indianapolis, IN**	NA
79	Benton Harbor, MI	13.76	–	Dutchess County, NY**	NA	223	Jackson, MI	(28.93)
190	Bergen-Passaic, NJ	(17.38)	173	Eau Claire, WI	(11.14)	1	Jackson, MS	210.17
245	Binghamton, NY	(65.88)	142	El Paso, TX	(4.09)	73	Jackson, TN	15.97
120	Birmingham, AL	1.83	196	Elkhart-Goshen, IN	(18.67)	16	Jacksonville, FL	55.89
101	Bismarck, ND	8.34	5	Enid, OK	83.10	88	Jacksonville, NC	11.99
181	Bloomington, IN	(14.40)	131	Erie, PA	(0.75)	74	Janesville-Beloit, WI	15.57
58	Boise, ID	22.81	192	Eugene-Springfield, OR	(17.99)	222	Jersey City, NJ	(28.84)
–	Boston, MA-NH**	NA	147	Evansville-Henderson, IN-KY	(5.61)	150	Johnson City-Kingsport-Bristol, TN-VA	(6.63)
156	Boulder-Longmont, CO	(7.74)	89	Fargo-Moorhead, ND-MN	11.98	–	Johnstown, PA**	NA
174	Brazoria, TX	(11.67)	162	Fayetteville, NC	(8.59)	136	Joplin, MO	(1.96)
–	Bremerton, WA**	NA	243	Fayetteville-Springdale-Rogers, AR	(47.74)	151	Kalamazoo-Battle Creek, MI	(6.81)
191	Bridgeport, CT	(17.59)	157	Fitchburg-Leominster, MA	(7.83)	–	Kansas City, MO-KS**	NA
–	Brockton, MA**	NA	194	Flint, MI	(18.38)	118	Kenosha, WI	3.05
237	Brownsville-Harlingen-San Benito, TX	(39.93)	183	Florence, AL	(16.21)	43	Killeen-Temple, TX	35.80
215	Bryan-College Station, TX	(25.29)	33	Florence, SC	39.70	117	Kokomo, IN	3.25
23	Buffalo-Niagara Falls, NY	53.12	203	Fort Collins-Loveland, CO	(20.48)	229	La Crosse, WI-MN	(34.77)
111	Canton-Massillon, OH	5.39	97	Fort Lauderdale, FL	9.95	107	Lafayette, IN	6.53
93	Charleston, WV	10.87	29	Fort Myers-Cape Coral, FL	42.22	76	Lafayette, LA	15.29
59	Charleston-North Charleston, SC	22.76	115	Fort Pierce-Port St. Lucie, FL	3.77	42	Lake Charles, LA	35.84
100	Charlottesville, VA	8.91	95	Fort Smith, AR-OK	10.16	28	Lakeland-Winter Haven, FL	46.57
163	Charlotte-Gastonia-Rock Hill, NC-SC	(8.82)	78	Fort Walton Beach, FL	14.41	104	Lancaster, PA	7.83
86	Chattanooga, TN-GA	12.64	72	Fort Wayne, IN	16.07	177	Lansing-East Lansing, MI	(12.76)

Source: Morgan Quitno Corporation using data from U.S. Department of Justice, Federal Bureau of Investigation
"Crime in the United States 1993" (Uniform Crime Reports, December 4, 1994)
*Includes the theft or attempted theft of a self-propelled vehicle. Excludes motorboats, construction equipment, airplanes and farming equipment.
**Not available.

158

40. Percent Change in Motor Vehicle Theft Rate: 1989 to 1993 (continued)

National Percent Change = 4.0% Decrease*

RANK	METRO AREA	% CHANGE	RANK	METRO AREA	% CHANGE	RANK	METRO AREA	CHANGE
67	Laredo, TX	17.84	80	Olympia, WA	13.10	112	Seattle–Bellevue–Everett, WA	4.63
55	Las Vegas, NV–AZ	24.55	–	Omaha, NE**	NA	38	Sheboygan, WI	38.38
164	Lawrence, MA–NH	(8.95)	132	Orange County, CA	(0.83)	209	Sherman–Denison, TX	(22.15)
32	Lawton, OK	40.29	182	Orlando, FL	(15.87)	41	Shreveport–Bossier City, LA	36.60
232	Lewiston–Auburn, ME	(35.33)	216	Owensboro, KY	(25.35)	208	Sioux City, IA–NE	(21.75)
207	Lexington, KY	(21.21)	20	Panama City, FL	54.17	126	Sioux Falls, SD	0.60
109	Lincoln, NE	5.62	152	Philadelphia, PA–NJ	(7.16)	–	South Bend, IN**	NA
51	Little Rock–North Little Rock, AR	27.60	84	Phoenix–Mesa, AZ	12.88	205	Spokane, WA	(20.80)
60	Longview–Marshall, TX	20.67	6	Pine Bluff, AR	78.62	12	Springfield, MA	67.65
143	Los Angeles–Long Beach, CA	(4.15)	189	Pittsburgh, PA	(17.08)	186	Springfield, MO	(16.51)
75	Louisville, KY–IN	15.40	–	Pittsfield, MA**	NA	212	Stamford–Norwalk, CT	(23.90)
185	Lubbock, TX	(16.43)	241	Portland, ME	(42.73)	–	Steubenville–Weirton, OH–WV**	NA
200	Lynchburg, VA	(20.05)	140	Portland–Vancouver, OR–WA	(3.01)	47	Stockton–Lodi, CA	31.58
172	Macon, GA	(10.30)	236	Providence–Fall River–Warwick, RI–MA	(38.18)	128	St. Cloud, MN	0.23
90	Madison, WI	11.66	–	Provo–Orem, UT**	NA	98	St. Joseph, MO	9.83
226	Manchester, NH	(32.55)	178	Pueblo, CO	(13.12)	–	St. Louis, MO–IL**	NA
96	Mansfield, OH	9.96	–	Punta Gorda, FL**	NA	–	Sumter, SC**	NA
36	McAllen–Edinburg–Mission, TX	39.02	161	Racine, WI	(8.34)	180	Syracuse, NY	(14.28)
105	Medford–Ashland, OR	7.81	158	Raleigh–Durham–Chapel Hill, NC	(8.04)	116	Tacoma, WA	3.26
127	Memphis, TN–AR–MS	0.57	141	Rapid City, SD	(3.67)	2	Tallahassee, FL	162.14
13	Merced, CA	62.75	–	Reading, PA**	NA	92	Tampa–St. Petersburg–Clearwater, FL	11.54
114	Miami, FL	3.86	204	Redding, CA	(20.75)	166	Texarkana, TX–AR	(9.41)
198	Middlesex–Sommerset–Hunterdon, NJ	(18.96)	169	Reno, NV	(9.67)	159	Toledo, OH	(8.05)
87	Milwaukee–Waukesha, WI	12.25	175	Richland–Kennewick–Pasco, WA	(11.88)	134	Trenton, NJ	(1.62)
187	Minneapolis–St. Paul, MN–WI	(16.56)	130	Richmond–Petersburg, VA	(0.30)	–	Tucson, AZ**	NA
34	Mobile, AL	39.41	–	Riverside–San Bernardino, CA**	NA	211	Tulsa, OK	(23.83)
17	Modesto, CA	55.36	179	Roanoke, VA	(13.26)	68	Tuscaloosa, AL	17.72
213	Monmouth–Ocean, NJ	(24.50)	25	Rochester, MN	49.19	61	Tyler, TX	20.09
21	Monroe, LA	53.70	49	Rochester, NY	27.80	138	Utica–Rome, NY	(2.62)
18	Montgomery, AL	54.83	–	Rocky Mount, NC**	NA	144	Vallejo–Fairfield–Napa, CA	(4.91)
–	Myrtle Beach, SC**	NA	53	Sacramento, CA	26.41	70	Ventura, CA	17.29
24	Naples, FL	50.96	201	Saginaw–Bay City–Midland, MI	(20.08)	30	Victoria, TX	42.08
224	Nashua, NH	(29.00)	56	Salem, OR	24.32	155	Vineland–Millville–Bridgeton, NJ	(7.53)
15	Nashville, TN	59.20	65	Salinas, CA	19.76	14	Visalia–Tulare–Porterville, CA	60.72
122	Nassau–Suffolk, NY	1.51	137	Salt Lake City–Ogden, UT	(2.13)	52	Waco, TX	26.80
244	New Bedford, MA	(50.79)	193	San Angelo, TX	(18.19)	197	Washington, DC–MD–VA–WV	(18.72)
227	New Haven–Meriden, CT	(32.67)	219	San Antonio, TX	(26.69)	66	Waterbury, CT	18.75
225	New London–Norwich, CT–RI	(29.52)	214	San Diego, CA	(24.84)	35	Waterloo–Cedar Falls, IA	39.22
133	New Orleans, LA	(1.60)	99	San Francisco, CA	9.81	210	Wausau, WI	(23.02)
184	New York, NY	(16.29)	153	San Jose, CA	(7.20)	–	West Palm Beach–Boca Raton, FL**	NA
217	Newark, NJ	(26.08)	–	San Luis Obispo–Atascadero, CA**	NA	240	Wichita Falls, TX	(42.46)
–	Newburgh, NY–PA**	NA	228	Santa Barbara–Santa Maria–Lompoc, CA	(34.20)	–	Williamsport, PA**	NA
139	Norfolk–Va Beach–Newport News, VA–NC	(2.82)	148	Santa Cruz–Watsonville, CA	(5.79)	154	Wilmington, NC	(7.24)
119	Oakland, CA	2.17	149	Santa Rosa, CA	(6.14)	–	Worcester, MA–CT**	NA
233	Ocala, FL	(35.90)	77	Sarasota–Bradenton, FL	14.89	63	Yakima, WA	19.95
135	Odessa–Midland, TX	(1.68)	19	Savannah, GA	54.46	–	Yolo, CA**	NA
199	Oklahoma City, OK	(19.68)	–	Scranton–Wilkes-Barre–Hazleton, PA**	NA	50	Yuba City, CA	27.79

Source: Morgan Quitno Corporation using data from U.S. Department of Justice, Federal Bureau of Investigation
   "Crime in the United States 1993" (Uniform Crime Reports, December 4, 1994)
*Includes the theft or attempted theft of a self-propelled vehicle. Excludes motorboats, construction equipment, airplanes and farming equipment.
**Not available.

40. Percent Change in Motor Vehicle Theft Rate: 1989 to 1993 (continued)

National Percent Change = 4.0% Decrease*

RANK	METRO AREA	% CHANGE	RANK	METRO AREA	% CHANGE	RANK	METRO AREA	% CHANGE
1	Jackson, MS	210.17	48	Albuquerque, NM	28.87	95	Fort Smith, AR–OK	10.16
2	Tallahassee, FL	162.14	49	Rochester, NY	27.80	96	Mansfield, OH	9.96
3	Gainesville, FL	93.91	50	Yuba City, CA	27.79	97	Fort Lauderdale, FL	9.95
4	Grand Forks, ND–MN	92.82	51	Little Rock–North Little Rock, AR	27.60	98	St. Joseph, MO	9.83
5	Enid, OK	83.10	52	Waco, TX	26.80	99	San Francisco, CA	9.81
6	Pine Bluff, AR	78.62	53	Sacramento, CA	26.41	100	Charlottesville, VA	8.91
7	Gadsden, AL	78.58	54	Austin–San Marcos, TX	26.01	101	Bismarck, ND	8.34
8	Fresno, CA	75.92	55	Las Vegas, NV–AZ	24.55	102	Augusta–Aiken, GA–SC	8.11
9	Alexandria, LA	73.52	56	Salem, OR	24.32	103	Huntsville, AL	7.87
10	Baton Rouge, LA	72.59	57	Albany, GA	24.24	104	Lancaster, PA	7.83
11	Beaumont–Port Arthur, TX	70.70	58	Boise, ID	22.81	105	Medford–Ashland, OR	7.81
12	Springfield, MA	67.65	59	Charleston–North Charleston, SC	22.76	106	Anchorage, AK	6.71
13	Merced, CA	62.75	60	Longview–Marshall, TX	20.67	107	Lafayette, IN	6.53
14	Visalia–Tulare–Porterville, CA	60.72	61	Tyler, TX	20.09	108	Cheyenne, WY	5.76
15	Nashville, TN	59.20	62	Honolulu, HI	20.06	109	Lincoln, NE	5.62
16	Jacksonville, FL	55.89	63	Yakima, WA	19.95	110	Greeley, CO	5.45
17	Modesto, CA	55.36	64	Baltimore, MD	19.81	111	Canton–Massillon, OH	5.39
18	Montgomery, AL	54.83	65	Salinas, CA	19.76	112	Seattle–Bellevue–Everett, WA	4.63
19	Savannah, GA	54.46	66	Waterbury, CT	18.75	113	Cincinnati, OH–KY–IN	4.50
20	Panama City, FL	54.17	67	Laredo, TX	17.84	114	Miami, FL	3.86
21	Monroe, LA	53.70	68	Tuscaloosa, AL	17.72	115	Fort Pierce–Port St. Lucie, FL	3.77
22	Dubuque, IA	53.58	69	Bakersfield, CA	17.52	116	Tacoma, WA	3.26
23	Buffalo–Niagara Falls, NY	53.12	70	Ventura, CA	17.29	117	Kokomo, IN	3.25
24	Naples, FL	50.96	71	Amarillo, TX	16.15	118	Kenosha, WI	3.05
25	Rochester, MN	49.19	72	Fort Wayne, IN	16.07	119	Oakland, CA	2.17
26	Decatur, AL	47.76	73	Jackson, TN	15.97	120	Birmingham, AL	1.83
27	Columbus, GA–AL	46.88	74	Janesville–Beloit, WI	15.57	121	Greensboro–Winston Salem–High Point, NC	1.80
28	Lakeland–Winter Haven, FL	46.57	75	Louisville, KY–IN	15.40	122	Nassau–Suffolk, NY	1.51
29	Fort Myers–Cape Coral, FL	42.22	76	Lafayette, LA	15.29	123	Gary–Hammond, IN	1.10
30	Victoria, TX	42.08	77	Sarasota–Bradenton, FL	14.89	124	Columbia, MO	1.00
31	Green Bay, WI	40.99	78	Fort Walton Beach, FL	14.41	125	Huntington–Ashland, WV–KY–OH	0.67
32	Lawton, OK	40.29	79	Benton Harbor, MI	13.76	126	Sioux Falls, SD	0.60
33	Florence, SC	39.70	80	Olympia, WA	13.10	127	Memphis, TN–AR–MS	0.57
34	Mobile, AL	39.41	81	Dayton–Springfield, OH	13.09	128	St. Cloud, MN	0.23
35	Waterloo–Cedar Falls, IA	39.22	82	Daytona Beach, FL	13.07	129	Anniston, AL	(0.22)
36	McAllen–Edinburg–Mission, TX	39.02	83	Des Moines, IA	13.06	130	Richmond–Petersburg, VA	(0.30)
37	Athens, GA	39.00	84	Phoenix–Mesa, AZ	12.88	131	Erie, PA	(0.75)
38	Sheboygan, WI	38.38	85	Danville, VA	12.77	132	Orange County, CA	(0.83)
39	Cumberland, MD–WV	38.17	86	Chattanooga, TN–GA	12.64	133	New Orleans, LA	(1.60)
40	Dothan, AL	36.71	87	Milwaukee–Waukesha, WI	12.25	134	Trenton, NJ	(1.62)
41	Shreveport–Bossier City, LA	36.60	88	Jacksonville, NC	11.99	135	Odessa–Midland, TX	(1.68)
42	Lake Charles, LA	35.84	89	Fargo–Moorhead, ND–MN	11.98	136	Joplin, MO	(1.96)
43	Killeen–Temple, TX	35.80	90	Madison, WI	11.66	137	Salt Lake City–Ogden, UT	(2.13)
44	Danbury, CT	35.51	91	Galveston–Texas City, TX	11.59	138	Utica–Rome, NY	(2.62)
45	Appleton–Oshkosh–Neenah, WI	35.30	92	Tampa–St. Petersburg–Clearwater, FL	11.54	139	Norfolk–Va Beach–Newport News, VA–NC	(2.82)
46	Corpus Christi, TX	32.02	93	Charleston, WV	10.87	140	Portland–Vancouver, OR–WA	(3.01)
47	Stockton–Lodi, CA	31.58	94	Denver, CO	10.78	141	Rapid City, SD	(3.67)

Source: Morgan Quitno Corporation using data from U.S. Department of Justice, Federal Bureau of Investigation
"Crime in the United States 1993" (Uniform Crime Reports, December 4, 1994)
*Includes the theft or attempted theft of a self-propelled vehicle. Excludes motorboats, construction equipment, airplanes and farming equipment.
**Not available.

40. Percent Change in Motor Vehicle Theft Rate: 1989 to 1993 (continued)

National Percent Change = 4.0% Decrease*

RANK	METRO AREA	% CHANGE	RANK	METRO AREA	% CHANGE	RANK	METRO AREA	CHANGE
142	El Paso, TX	(4.09)	189	Pittsburgh, PA	(17.08)	236	Providence–Fall River–Warwick, RI-MA	(38.18)
143	Los Angeles–Long Beach, CA	(4.15)	190	Bergen–Passaic, NJ	(17.38)	237	Brownsville–Harlingen–San Benito, TX	(39.93)
144	Vallejo–Fairfield–Napa, CA	(4.91)	191	Bridgeport, CT	(17.59)	238	Colorado Springs, CO	(40.81)
145	Columbus, OH	(5.17)	192	Eugene–Springfield, OR	(17.99)	239	Dallas, TX	(40.90)
146	Altoona, PA	(5.54)	193	San Angelo, TX	(18.19)	240	Wichita Falls, TX	(42.46)
147	Evansville–Henderson, IN-KY	(5.61)	194	Flint, MI	(18.38)	241	Portland, ME	(42.73)
148	Santa Cruz–Watsonville, CA	(5.79)	195	Atlanta, GA	(18.61)	242	Ann Arbor, MI	(46.61)
149	Santa Rosa, CA	(6.14)	196	Elkhart–Goshen, IN	(18.67)	243	Fayetteville–Springdale–Rogers, AR	(47.74)
150	Johnson City–Kingsport–Bristol, TN-VA	(6.63)	197	Washington, DC-MD-VA-WV	(18.72)	244	New Bedford, MA	(50.79)
151	Kalamazoo–Battle Creek, MI	(6.81)	198	Middlesex–Somerset–Hunterdon, NJ	(18.96)	245	Binghamton, NY	(65.88)
152	Philadelphia, PA-NJ	(7.16)	199	Oklahoma City, OK	(19.68)	–	Akron, OH**	NA
153	San Jose, CA	(7.20)	200	Lynchburg, VA	(20.05)	–	Albany, NY**	NA
154	Wilmington, NC	(7.24)	201	Saginaw–Bay City–Midland, MI	(20.08)	–	Barnstable–Yarmouth, MA**	NA
155	Vineland–Millville–Bridgeton, NJ	(7.53)	202	Columbia, SC	(20.17)	–	Boston, MA-NH**	NA
156	Boulder–Longmont, CO	(7.74)	203	Fort Collins–Loveland, CO	(20.48)	–	Bremerton, WA**	NA
157	Fitchburg–Leominster, MA	(7.83)	204	Redding, CA	(20.75)	–	Brockton, MA**	NA
158	Raleigh–Durham–Chapel Hill, NC	(8.04)	205	Spokane, WA	(20.80)	–	Chicago, IL**	NA
159	Toledo, OH	(8.05)	206	Grand Rapids–Muskegon–Holland, MI	(21.13)	–	Cleveland, OH**	NA
160	Duluth–Superior, MN-WI	(8.32)	207	Lexington, KY	(21.21)	–	Dutchess County, NY**	NA
161	Racine, WI	(8.34)	208	Sioux City, IA-NE	(21.75)	–	Goldsboro, NC**	NA
162	Fayetteville, NC	(8.59)	209	Sherman–Denison, TX	(22.15)	–	Greenville, NC**	NA
163	Charlotte–Gastonia–Rock Hill, NC-SC	(8.82)	210	Wausau, WI	(23.02)	–	Harrisburg–Lebanon–Carlisle, PA**	NA
164	Lawrence, MA-NH	(8.95)	211	Tulsa, OK	(23.83)	–	Hickory–Morganton, NC**	NA
165	Greenville–Spartanburg–Anderson, SC	(9.30)	212	Stamford–Norwalk, CT	(23.90)	–	Houma, LA**	NA
166	Texarkana, TX-AR	(9.41)	213	Monmouth–Ocean, NJ	(24.50)	–	Indianapolis, IN**	NA
167	Clarksville–Hopkinsville, TN-KY	(9.45)	214	San Diego, CA	(24.84)	–	Johnstown, PA**	NA
168	Hagerstown, MD	(9.55)	215	Bryan–College Station, TX	(25.29)	–	Kansas City, MO-KS**	NA
169	Reno, NV	(9.67)	216	Owensboro, KY	(25.35)	–	Myrtle Beach, SC**	NA
170	Bellingham, WA	(9.74)	217	Newark, NJ	(26.08)	–	Newburgh, NY-PA**	NA
171	Hartford, CT	(9.96)	218	Asheville, NC	(26.15)	–	Omaha, NE**	NA
172	Macon, GA	(10.30)	219	San Antonio, TX	(26.69)	–	Pittsfield, MA**	NA
173	Eau Claire, WI	(11.14)	220	Houston, TX	(27.06)	–	Provo–Orem, UT**	NA
174	Brazoria, TX	(11.67)	221	Atlantic City, NJ	(28.09)	–	Punta Gorda, FL**	NA
175	Richland–Kennewick–Pasco, WA	(11.88)	222	Jersey City, NJ	(28.84)	–	Reading, PA**	NA
176	Detroit, MI	(12.38)	223	Jackson, MI	(28.93)	–	Riverside–San Bernardino, CA**	NA
177	Lansing–East Lansing, MI	(12.76)	224	Nashua, NH	(29.00)	–	Rocky Mount, NC**	NA
178	Pueblo, CO	(13.12)	225	New London–Norwich, CT-RI	(29.52)	–	San Luis Obispo–Atascadero, CA**	NA
179	Roanoke, VA	(13.26)	226	Manchester, NH	(32.55)	–	Scranton–Wilkes-Barre–Hazleton, PA**	NA
180	Syracuse, NY	(14.28)	227	New Haven–Meriden, CT	(32.67)	–	South Bend, IN**	NA
181	Bloomington, IN	(14.40)	228	Santa Barbara–Santa Maria–Lompoc, CA	(34.20)	–	Steubenville–Weirton, OH-WV**	NA
182	Orlando, FL	(15.87)	229	La Crosse, WI-MN	(34.77)	–	St. Louis, MO-IL**	NA
183	Florence, AL	(16.21)	230	Fort Worth–Arlington, TX	(35.17)	–	Sumter, SC**	NA
184	New York, NY	(16.29)	231	Chico–Paradise, CA	(35.18)	–	Tucson, AZ**	NA
185	Lubbock, TX	(16.43)	232	Lewiston–Auburn, ME	(35.33)	–	West Palm Beach–Boca Raton, FL**	NA
186	Springfield, MO	(16.51)	233	Ocala, FL	(35.90)	–	Williamsport, PA**	NA
187	Minneapolis–St. Paul, MN-WI	(16.56)	234	Glens Falls, NY	(37.70)	–	Worcester, MA-CT**	NA
188	Bangor, ME	(17.07)	235	Abilene, TX	(37.89)	–	Yolo, CA**	NA

Source: Morgan Quitno Corporation using data from U.S. Department of Justice, Federal Bureau of Investigation "Crime in the United States 1993" (Uniform Crime Reports, December 4, 1994)
Includes the theft or attempted theft of a self-propelled vehicle. Excludes motorboats, construction equipment, airplanes and farming equipment.
**Not available.*

161

II. 100 LARGEST CITIES CRIME STATISTICS

41. Crimes in 1993

National Total = 14,140,952 Crimes*

RANK	CITY	CRIMES	RANK	CITY	CRIMES
–	Akron, OH**	NA	75	Louisville, KY	17,329
39	Albuquerque, NM	39,025	85	Lubbock, TX	12,353
–	Anaheim, CA**	NA	89	Madison, WI	10,616
76	Anchorage, AK	16,140	16	Memphis, TN	62,150
69	Arlington, TX	20,202	57	Mesa, AZ	24,146
10	Atlanta, GA	69,914	11	Miami, FL	69,828
68	Aurora, CO	20,367	26	Milwaukee, WI	50,432
24	Austin, TX	51,468	35	Minneapolis, MN	40,463
79	Bakersfield, CA	15,614	74	Mobile, AL	18,567
7	Baltimore, MD	91,920	86	Montgomery, AL	12,310
42	Baton Rouge, LA	36,527	20	Nashville, TN	55,500
46	Birmingham, AL	31,776	22	New Orleans, LA	52,773
19	Boston, MA	55,555	1	New York, NY	600,346
45	Buffalo, NY	31,871	40	Newark, NJ	38,514
28	Charlotte, NC	49,758	88	Newport News, VA	12,230
–	Chicago, IL**	NA	61	Norfolk, VA	22,209
47	Cincinnati, OH	30,923	33	Oakland, CA	44,927
36	Cleveland, OH	40,005	25	Oklahoma City, OK	51,335
71	Colorado Springs, CO	19,608	64	Orlando, FL	21,953
87	Columbus, GA	12,266	5	Philadelphia, PA	97,659
18	Columbus, OH	56,322	6	Phoenix, AZ	96,476
53	Corpus Christi, TX	27,416	49	Pittsburgh, PA	28,613
3	Dallas, TX	110,799	23	Portland, OR	51,765
70	Dayton, OH	19,637	82	Raleigh, NC	15,255
37	Denver, CO	39,796	63	Richmond, VA	22,142
80	Des Moines, IA	15,505	62	Riverside, CA	22,147
–	Detroit, MI**	NA	54	Rochester, NY	25,520
31	El Paso, TX	46,738	38	Sacramento, CA	39,485
83	Fort Wayne, IN	14,857	4	San Antonio, TX	97,671
27	Fort Worth, TX	49,801	60	San Bernardino, CA	22,312
93	Fremont, CA	7,245	8	San Diego, CA	85,227
34	Fresno, CA	41,584	9	San Francisco, CA	70,132
–	Garland, TX**	NA	41	San Jose, CA	36,743
92	Glendale, CA	8,215	72	Santa Ana, CA	19,071
–	Grand Rapids, MI**	NA	15	Seattle, WA	62,679
81	Greensboro, NC	15,303	59	Shreveport, LA	22,631
17	Honolulu, HI	56,405	77	Spokane, WA	15,952
–	Houston, TX**	NA	56	Stockton, CA	24,849
91	Huntington Beach, CA	9,122	14	St. Louis, MO	64,438
44	Indianapolis, IN	33,530	67	St. Paul, MN	20,382
55	Jackson, MS	25,508	58	St. Petersburg, FL	23,022
13	Jacksonville, FL	67,513	65	Tacoma, WA	21,046
73	Jersey City, NJ	18,760	32	Tampa, FL	45,373
21	Kansas City, MO	55,165	50	Toledo, OH	28,461
30	Las Vegas, NV	48,365	29	Tucson, AZ	48,945
78	Lexington, KY	15,641	48	Tulsa, OK	29,354
84	Lincoln, NE	13,561	66	Virginia Beach, VA	20,516
51	Little Rock, AR	28,070	12	Washington, DC	67,946
43	Long Beach, CA	35,630	52	Wichita, KS	27,737
2	Los Angeles, CA	312,789	90	Yonkers, NY	9,494

Source: U.S. Department of Justice, Federal Bureau of Investigation
"Crime in the United States 1993" (Uniform Crime Reports, December 4, 1994)
Includes murder, rape, robbery, aggravated assault, burglary, larceny-theft and motor vehicle theft.
**Not available.*

41. Crimes in 1993 (continued)

National Total = 14,140,952 Crimes*

RANK	CITY	CRIMES	RANK	CITY	CRIMES
1	New York, NY	600,346	51	Little Rock, AR	28,070
2	Los Angeles, CA	312,789	52	Wichita, KS	27,737
3	Dallas, TX	110,799	53	Corpus Christi, TX	27,416
4	San Antonio, TX	97,671	54	Rochester, NY	25,520
5	Philadelphia, PA	97,659	55	Jackson, MS	25,508
6	Phoenix, AZ	96,476	56	Stockton, CA	24,849
7	Baltimore, MD	91,920	57	Mesa, AZ	24,146
8	San Diego, CA	85,227	58	St. Petersburg, FL	23,022
9	San Francisco, CA	70,132	59	Shreveport, LA	22,631
10	Atlanta, GA	69,914	60	San Bernardino, CA	22,312
11	Miami, FL	69,828	61	Norfolk, VA	22,209
12	Washington, DC	67,946	62	Riverside, CA	22,147
13	Jacksonville, FL	67,513	63	Richmond, VA	22,142
14	St. Louis, MO	64,438	64	Orlando, FL	21,953
15	Seattle, WA	62,679	65	Tacoma, WA	21,046
16	Memphis, TN	62,150	66	Virginia Beach, VA	20,516
17	Honolulu, HI	56,405	67	St. Paul, MN	20,382
18	Columbus, OH	56,322	68	Aurora, CO	20,367
19	Boston, MA	55,555	69	Arlington, TX	20,202
20	Nashville, TN	55,500	70	Dayton, OH	19,637
21	Kansas City, MO	55,165	71	Colorado Springs, CO	19,608
22	New Orleans, LA	52,773	72	Santa Ana, CA	19,071
23	Portland, OR	51,765	73	Jersey City, NJ	18,760
24	Austin, TX	51,468	74	Mobile, AL	18,567
25	Oklahoma City, OK	51,335	75	Louisville, KY	17,329
26	Milwaukee, WI	50,432	76	Anchorage, AK	16,140
27	Fort Worth, TX	49,801	77	Spokane, WA	15,952
28	Charlotte, NC	49,758	78	Lexington, KY	15,641
29	Tucson, AZ	48,945	79	Bakersfield, CA	15,614
30	Las Vegas, NV	48,365	80	Des Moines, IA	15,505
31	El Paso, TX	46,738	81	Greensboro, NC	15,303
32	Tampa, FL	45,373	82	Raleigh, NC	15,255
33	Oakland, CA	44,927	83	Fort Wayne, IN	14,857
34	Fresno, CA	41,584	84	Lincoln, NE	13,561
35	Minneapolis, MN	40,463	85	Lubbock, TX	12,353
36	Cleveland, OH	40,005	86	Montgomery, AL	12,310
37	Denver, CO	39,796	87	Columbus, GA	12,266
38	Sacramento, CA	39,485	88	Newport News, VA	12,230
39	Albuquerque, NM	39,025	89	Madison, WI	10,616
40	Newark, NJ	38,514	90	Yonkers, NY	9,494
41	San Jose, CA	36,743	91	Huntington Beach, CA	9,122
42	Baton Rouge, LA	36,527	92	Glendale, CA	8,215
43	Long Beach, CA	35,630	93	Fremont, CA	7,245
44	Indianapolis,IN	33,530	-	Akron, OH**	NA
45	Buffalo, NY	31,871	-	Anaheim, CA**	NA
46	Birmingham, AL	31,776	-	Chicago, IL**	NA
47	Cincinnati, OH	30,923	-	Detroit, MI**	NA
48	Tulsa, OK	29,354	-	Garland, TX**	NA
49	Pittsburgh, PA	28,613	-	Grand Rapids, MI**	NA
50	Toledo, OH	28,461	-	Houston, TX**	NA

Source: U.S. Department of Justice, Federal Bureau of Investigation
 "Crime in the United States 1993" (Uniform Crime Reports, December 4, 1994)
Includes murder, rape, robbery, aggravated assault, burglary, larceny-theft and motor vehicle theft.
**Not available.*

42. Crime Rate in 1993

National Rate = 5,842.9 Crimes per 100,000 Population*

RANK	CITY	RATE	RANK	CITY	RATE
–	Akron, OH**	NA	84	Louisville, KY	6,334.5
42	Albuquerque, NM	9,581.7	79	Lubbock, TX	6,446.0
–	Anaheim, CA**	NA	87	Madison, WI	5,391.0
83	Anchorage, AK	6,437.5	37	Memphis, TN	10,040.7
72	Arlington, TX	7,180.7	66	Mesa, AZ	7,924.6
2	Atlanta, GA	17,353.7	1	Miami, FL	18,744.8
57	Aurora, CO	8,258.8	61	Milwaukee, WI	8,093.5
33	Austin, TX	10,252.2	24	Minneapolis, MN	11,036.1
58	Bakersfield, CA	8,221.9	46	Mobile, AL	9,088.7
11	Baltimore, MD	12,540.8	85	Montgomery, AL	6,332.3
4	Baton Rouge, LA	16,195.1	27	Nashville, TN	10,805.1
14	Birmingham, AL	11,822.8	30	New Orleans, LA	10,734.5
38	Boston, MA	10,030.3	59	New York, NY	8,171.0
40	Buffalo, NY	9,810.8	7	Newark, NJ	14,270.2
16	Charlotte, NC	11,767.0	75	Newport News, VA	6,795.4
–	Chicago, IL**	NA	51	Norfolk, VA	8,620.9
54	Cincinnati, OH	8,435.3	13	Oakland, CA	11,915.8
67	Cleveland, OH	7,910.3	21	Oklahoma City, OK	11,222.0
82	Colorado Springs, CO	6,440.7	12	Orlando, FL	12,420.5
80	Columbus, GA	6,444.6	86	Philadelphia, PA	6,262.1
50	Columbus, OH	8,706.0	44	Phoenix, AZ	9,282.2
35	Corpus Christi, TX	10,095.6	68	Pittsburgh, PA	7,765.3
32	Dallas, TX	10,627.0	20	Portland, OR	11,379.7
31	Dayton, OH	10,651.9	74	Raleigh, NC	6,808.5
63	Denver, CO	7,984.7	28	Richmond, VA	10,783.6
64	Des Moines, IA	7,931.6	45	Riverside, CA	9,188.1
–	Detroit, MI**	NA	26	Rochester, NY	10,845.7
55	El Paso, TX	8,428.6	34	Sacramento, CA	10,209.9
53	Fort Wayne, IN	8,470.1	39	San Antonio, TX	9,911.2
29	Fort Worth, TX	10,747.5	9	San Bernardino, CA	12,807.2
93	Fremont, CA	3,999.8	71	San Diego, CA	7,343.3
25	Fresno, CA	10,943.8	43	San Francisco, CA	9,523.9
–	Garland, TX**	NA	92	San Jose, CA	4,538.8
91	Glendale, CA	4,576.9	78	Santa Ana, CA	6,574.6
–	Grand Rapids, MI**	NA	15	Seattle, WA	11,797.9
65	Greensboro, NC	7,931.0	19	Shreveport, LA	11,465.8
81	Honolulu, HI	6,442.9	56	Spokane, WA	8,329.5
–	Houston, TX**	NA	23	Stockton, CA	11,200.0
89	Huntington Beach, CA	4,879.4	3	St. Louis, MO	16,648.4
47	Indianapolis, IN	8,876.9	70	St. Paul, MN	7,515.3
8	Jackson, MS	12,868.1	41	St. Petersburg, FL	9,643.7
36	Jacksonville, FL	10,041.9	22	Tacoma, WA	11,200.9
60	Jersey City, NJ	8,146.0	5	Tampa, FL	15,706.7
10	Kansas City, MO	12,669.1	52	Toledo, OH	8,587.7
76	Las Vegas, NV	6,741.3	18	Tucson, AZ	11,480.2
77	Lexington, KY	6,653.1	69	Tulsa, OK	7,758.4
73	Lincoln, NE	6,841.1	90	Virginia Beach, VA	4,845.7
6	Little Rock, AR	15,688.2	17	Washington, DC	11,755.4
62	Long Beach, CA	8,038.2	49	Wichita, KS	8,844.8
48	Los Angeles, CA	8,872.6	88	Yonkers, NY	5,077.9

Source: U.S. Department of Justice, Federal Bureau of Investigation
"Crime in the United States 1993" (Uniform Crime Reports, December 4, 1994)
*Includes murder, rape, robbery, aggravated assault, burglary, larceny-theft and motor vehicle theft.
**Not available.

42. Crime Rate in 1993 (continued)

National Rate = 5,842.9 Crimes per 100,000 Population*

RANK	CITY	RATE	RANK	CITY	RATE
1	Miami, FL	18,744.8	51	Norfolk, VA	8,620.9
2	Atlanta, GA	17,353.7	52	Toledo, OH	8,587.7
3	St. Louis, MO	16,648.4	53	Fort Wayne, IN	8,470.1
4	Baton Rouge, LA	16,195.1	54	Cincinnati, OH	8,435.3
5	Tampa, FL	15,706.7	55	El Paso, TX	8,428.6
6	Little Rock, AR	15,688.2	56	Spokane, WA	8,329.5
7	Newark, NJ	14,270.2	57	Aurora, CO	8,258.8
8	Jackson, MS	12,868.1	58	Bakersfield, CA	8,221.9
9	San Bernardino, CA	12,807.2	59	New York, NY	8,171.0
10	Kansas City, MO	12,669.1	60	Jersey City, NJ	8,146.0
11	Baltimore, MD	12,540.8	61	Milwaukee, WI	8,093.5
12	Orlando, FL	12,420.5	62	Long Beach, CA	8,038.2
13	Oakland, CA	11,915.8	63	Denver, CO	7,984.7
14	Birmingham, AL	11,822.8	64	Des Moines, IA	7,931.6
15	Seattle, WA	11,797.9	65	Greensboro, NC	7,931.0
16	Charlotte, NC	11,767.0	66	Mesa, AZ	7,924.6
17	Washington, DC	11,755.4	67	Cleveland, OH	7,910.3
18	Tucson, AZ	11,480.2	68	Pittsburgh, PA	7,765.3
19	Shreveport, LA	11,465.8	69	Tulsa, OK	7,758.4
20	Portland, OR	11,379.7	70	St. Paul, MN	7,515.3
21	Oklahoma City, OK	11,222.0	71	San Diego, CA	7,343.3
22	Tacoma, WA	11,200.9	72	Arlington, TX	7,180.7
23	Stockton, CA	11,200.0	73	Lincoln, NE	6,841.1
24	Minneapolis, MN	11,036.1	74	Raleigh, NC	6,808.5
25	Fresno, CA	10,943.8	75	Newport News, VA	6,795.4
26	Rochester, NY	10,845.7	76	Las Vegas, NV	6,741.3
27	Nashville, TN	10,805.1	77	Lexington, KY	6,653.1
28	Richmond, VA	10,783.6	78	Santa Ana, CA	6,574.6
29	Fort Worth, TX	10,747.5	79	Lubbock, TX	6,446.0
30	New Orleans, LA	10,734.5	80	Columbus, GA	6,444.6
31	Dayton, OH	10,651.9	81	Honolulu, HI	6,442.9
32	Dallas, TX	10,627.0	82	Colorado Springs, CO	6,440.7
33	Austin, TX	10,252.2	83	Anchorage, AK	6,437.5
34	Sacramento, CA	10,209.9	84	Louisville, KY	6,334.5
35	Corpus Christi, TX	10,095.6	85	Montgomery, AL	6,332.3
36	Jacksonville, FL	10,041.9	86	Philadelphia, PA	6,262.1
37	Memphis, TN	10,040.7	87	Madison, WI	5,391.0
38	Boston, MA	10,030.3	88	Yonkers, NY	5,077.9
39	San Antonio, TX	9,911.2	89	Huntington Beach, CA	4,879.4
40	Buffalo, NY	9,810.8	90	Virginia Beach, VA	4,845.7
41	St. Petersburg, FL	9,643.7	91	Glendale, CA	4,576.9
42	Albuquerque, NM	9,581.7	92	San Jose, CA	4,538.8
43	San Francisco, CA	9,523.9	93	Fremont, CA	3,999.8
44	Phoenix, AZ	9,282.2	–	Akron, OH**	NA
45	Riverside, CA	9,188.1	–	Anaheim, CA**	NA
46	Mobile, AL	9,088.7	–	Chicago, IL**	NA
47	Indianapolis,IN	8,876.9	–	Detroit, MI**	NA
48	Los Angeles, CA	8,872.6	–	Garland, TX**	NA
49	Wichita, KS	8,844.8	–	Grand Rapids, MI**	NA
50	Columbus, OH	8,706.0	–	Houston, TX**	NA

Source: U.S. Department of Justice, Federal Bureau of Investigation
  "Crime in the United States 1993" (Uniform Crime Reports, December 4, 1994)
*Includes murder, rape, robbery, aggravated assault, burglary, larceny-theft and motor vehicle theft.
**Not available.

43. Percent Change in Crime Rate: 1992 to 1993

National Percent Change = 3.1% Decrease*

RANK	CITY	% CHANGE	RANK	CITY	% CHANGE
–	Akron, OH**	NA	75	Louisville, KY	(6.79)
33	Albuquerque, NM	1.14	74	Lubbock, TX	(6.66)
–	Anaheim, CA**	NA	81	Madison, WI	(8.29)
85	Anchorage, AK	(8.77)	27	Memphis, TN	1.95
91	Arlington, TX	(15.41)	3	Mesa, AZ	12.79
37	Atlanta, GA	0.04	11	Miami, FL	7.19
52	Aurora, CO	(3.47)	73	Milwaukee, WI	(6.64)
70	Austin, TX	(6.32)	38	Minneapolis, MN	(0.61)
25	Bakersfield, CA	2.74	93	Mobile, AL	(30.46)
15	Baltimore, MD	5.14	50	Montgomery, AL	(2.60)
2	Baton Rouge, LA	13.57	5	Nashville, TN	11.55
40	Birmingham, AL	(1.07)	9	New Orleans, LA	7.47
29	Boston, MA	1.87	54	New York, NY	(3.76)
48	Buffalo, NY	(2.19)	49	Newark, NJ	(2.42)
71	Charlotte, NC	(6.54)	62	Newport News, VA	(4.85)
–	Chicago, IL**	NA	26	Norfolk, VA	2.55
61	Cincinnati, OH	(4.58)	58	Oakland, CA	(4.33)
60	Cleveland, OH	(4.51)	36	Oklahoma City, OK	0.40
68	Colorado Springs, CO	(5.55)	18	Orlando, FL	4.37
13	Columbus, GA	5.67	24	Philadelphia, PA	3.11
55	Columbus, OH	(3.85)	35	Phoenix, AZ	0.65
47	Corpus Christi, TX	(2.15)	65	Pittsburgh, PA	(5.42)
90	Dallas, TX	(14.50)	34	Portland, OR	1.01
56	Dayton, OH	(3.95)	88	Raleigh, NC	(9.98)
45	Denver, CO	(2.08)	31	Richmond, VA	1.45
69	Des Moines, IA	(5.91)	10	Riverside, CA	7.42
–	Detroit, MI**	NA	80	Rochester, NY	(7.95)
76	El Paso, TX	(6.81)	28	Sacramento, CA	1.93
67	Fort Wayne, IN	(5.49)	89	San Antonio, TX	(11.65)
92	Fort Worth, TX	(23.96)	57	San Bernardino, CA	(4.29)
16	Fremont, CA	4.75	82	San Diego, CA	(8.32)
86	Fresno, CA	(9.65)	72	San Francisco, CA	(6.58)
–	Garland, TX**	NA	79	San Jose, CA	(7.48)
21	Glendale, CA	3.19	63	Santa Ana, CA	(4.96)
–	Grand Rapids, MI**	NA	44	Seattle, WA	(1.69)
53	Greensboro, NC	(3.64)	7	Shreveport, LA	8.43
14	Honolulu, HI	5.30	41	Spokane, WA	(1.18)
–	Houston, TX**	NA	23	Stockton, CA	3.13
8	Huntington Beach, CA	7.85	4	St. Louis, MO	12.49
1	Indianapolis, IN	22.12	46	St. Paul, MN	(2.09)
43	Jackson, MS	(1.59)	77	St. Petersburg, FL	(6.94)
59	Jacksonville, FL	(4.46)	17	Tacoma, WA	4.46
84	Jersey City, NJ	(8.54)	38	Tampa, FL	(0.61)
30	Kansas City, MO	1.56	42	Toledo, OH	(1.44)
82	Las Vegas, NV	(8.32)	6	Tucson, AZ	10.25
20	Lexington, KY	3.35	66	Tulsa, OK	(5.47)
87	Lincoln, NE	(9.82)	78	Virginia Beach, VA	(7.10)
19	Little Rock, AR	3.76	22	Washington, DC	3.14
32	Long Beach, CA	1.32	51	Wichita, KS	(3.05)
64	Los Angeles, CA	(5.24)	12	Yonkers, NY	5.86

Source: Morgan Quitno Corporation using data from U.S. Department of Justice, Federal Bureau of Investigation
"Crime in the United States 1993" (Uniform Crime Reports, December 4, 1994)
*Includes murder, rape, robbery, aggravated assault, burglary, larceny-theft and motor vehicle theft.
**Not available.

43. Percent Change in Crime Rate: 1992 to 1993 (continued)

National Percent Change = 3.1% Decrease*

RANK	CITY	% CHANGE	RANK	CITY	% CHANGE
1	Indianapolis, IN	22.12	51	Wichita, KS	(3.05)
2	Baton Rouge, LA	13.57	52	Aurora, CO	(3.47)
3	Mesa, AZ	12.79	53	Greensboro, NC	(3.64)
4	St. Louis, MO	12.49	54	New York, NY	(3.76)
5	Nashville, TN	11.55	55	Columbus, OH	(3.85)
6	Tucson, AZ	10.25	56	Dayton, OH	(3.95)
7	Shreveport, LA	8.43	57	San Bernardino, CA	(4.29)
8	Huntington Beach, CA	7.85	58	Oakland, CA	(4.33)
9	New Orleans, LA	7.47	59	Jacksonville, FL	(4.46)
10	Riverside, CA	7.42	60	Cleveland, OH	(4.51)
11	Miami, FL	7.19	61	Cincinnati, OH	(4.58)
12	Yonkers, NY	5.86	62	Newport News, VA	(4.85)
13	Columbus, GA	5.67	63	Santa Ana, CA	(4.96)
14	Honolulu, HI	5.30	64	Los Angeles, CA	(5.24)
15	Baltimore, MD	5.14	65	Pittsburgh, PA	(5.42)
16	Fremont, CA	4.75	66	Tulsa, OK	(5.47)
17	Tacoma, WA	4.46	67	Fort Wayne, IN	(5.49)
18	Orlando, FL	4.37	68	Colorado Springs, CO	(5.55)
19	Little Rock, AR	3.76	69	Des Moines, IA	(5.91)
20	Lexington, KY	3.35	70	Austin, TX	(6.32)
21	Glendale, CA	3.19	71	Charlotte, NC	(6.54)
22	Washington, DC	3.14	72	San Francisco, CA	(6.58)
23	Stockton, CA	3.13	73	Milwaukee, WI	(6.64)
24	Philadelphia, PA	3.11	74	Lubbock, TX	(6.66)
25	Bakersfield, CA	2.74	75	Louisville, KY	(6.79)
26	Norfolk, VA	2.55	76	El Paso, TX	(6.81)
27	Memphis, TN	1.95	77	St. Petersburg, FL	(6.94)
28	Sacramento, CA	1.93	78	Virginia Beach, VA	(7.10)
29	Boston, MA	1.87	79	San Jose, CA	(7.48)
30	Kansas City, MO	1.56	80	Rochester, NY	(7.95)
31	Richmond, VA	1.45	81	Madison, WI	(8.29)
32	Long Beach, CA	1.32	82	Las Vegas, NV	(8.32)
33	Albuquerque, NM	1.14	82	San Diego, CA	(8.32)
34	Portland, OR	1.01	84	Jersey City, NJ	(8.54)
35	Phoenix, AZ	0.65	85	Anchorage, AK	(8.77)
36	Oklahoma City, OK	0.40	86	Fresno, CA	(9.65)
37	Atlanta, GA	0.04	87	Lincoln, NE	(9.82)
38	Minneapolis, MN	(0.61)	88	Raleigh, NC	(9.98)
38	Tampa, FL	(0.61)	89	San Antonio, TX	(11.65)
40	Birmingham, AL	(1.07)	90	Dallas, TX	(14.50)
41	Spokane, WA	(1.18)	91	Arlington, TX	(15.41)
42	Toledo, OH	(1.44)	92	Fort Worth, TX	(23.96)
43	Jackson, MS	(1.59)	93	Mobile, AL	(30.46)
44	Seattle, WA	(1.69)	-	Akron, OH**	NA
45	Denver, CO	(2.08)	-	Anaheim, CA**	NA
46	St. Paul, MN	(2.09)	-	Chicago, IL**	NA
47	Corpus Christi, TX	(2.15)	-	Detroit, MI**	NA
48	Buffalo, NY	(2.19)	-	Garland, TX**	NA
49	Newark, NJ	(2.42)	-	Grand Rapids, MI**	NA
50	Montgomery, AL	(2.60)	-	Houston, TX**	NA

Source: Morgan Quitno Corporation using data from U.S. Department of Justice, Federal Bureau of Investigation "Crime in the United States 1993" (Uniform Crime Reports, December 4, 1994)
*Includes murder, rape, robbery, aggravated assault, burglary, larceny-theft and motor vehicle theft.
**Not available.

44. Percent Change in Crime Rate: 1989 to 1993

National Percent Change = 4.5% Decrease*

RANK	CITY	% CHANGE	RANK	CITY	% CHANGE
-	Akron, OH**	NA	38	Louisville, KY	(2.63)
40	Albuquerque, NM	(3.84)	73	Lubbock, TX	(15.10)
-	Anaheim, CA**	NA	87	Madison, WI	(23.17)
9	Anchorage, AK	17.71	13	Memphis, TN	13.05
79	Arlington, TX	(16.63)	8	Mesa, AZ	18.77
77	Atlanta, GA	(16.13)	25	Miami, FL	2.00
20	Aurora, CO	5.02	53	Milwaukee, WI	(7.62)
41	Austin, TX	(3.91)	56	Minneapolis, MN	(8.77)
64	Bakersfield, CA	(10.88)	67	Mobile, AL	(12.19)
5	Baltimore, MD	34.09	35	Montgomery, AL	(1.29)
3	Baton Rouge, LA	37.84	1	Nashville, TN	55.01
6	Birmingham, AL	24.75	43	New Orleans, LA	(4.69)
80	Boston, MA	(16.88)	76	New York, NY	(15.48)
10	Buffalo, NY	15.03	31	Newark, NJ	(0.52)
65	Charlotte, NC	(11.14)	7	Newport News, VA	18.96
-	Chicago, IL**	NA	22	Norfolk, VA	4.33
14	Cincinnati, OH	12.88	44	Oakland, CA	(4.94)
45	Cleveland, OH	(5.27)	27	Oklahoma City, OK	0.32
72	Colorado Springs, CO	(14.99)	49	Orlando, FL	(6.14)
24	Columbus, GA	2.05	62	Philadelphia, PA	(10.50)
78	Columbus, OH	(16.24)	71	Phoenix, AZ	(14.58)
47	Corpus Christi, TX	(5.93)	68	Pittsburgh, PA	(12.50)
91	Dallas, TX	(36.39)	63	Portland, OR	(10.77)
60	Dayton, OH	(9.88)	58	Raleigh, NC	(9.62)
21	Denver, CO	4.89	15	Richmond, VA	9.13
69	Des Moines, IA	(13.07)	18	Riverside, CA	6.59
-	Detroit, MI**	NA	52	Rochester, NY	(7.06)
84	El Paso, TX	(20.66)	34	Sacramento, CA	(1.06)
51	Fort Wayne, IN	(6.62)	86	San Antonio, TX	(22.06)
90	Fort Worth, TX	(31.44)	-	San Bernardino, CA**	NA
17	Fremont, CA	8.58	85	San Diego, CA	(21.67)
50	Fresno, CA	(6.41)	19	San Francisco, CA	5.57
-	Garland, TX**	NA	66	San Jose, CA	(11.64)
81	Glendale, CA	(17.92)	89	Santa Ana, CA	(25.00)
-	Grand Rapids, MI**	NA	54	Seattle, WA	(8.60)
32	Greensboro, NC	(0.99)	32	Shreveport, LA	(0.99)
23	Honolulu, HI	3.38	55	Spokane, WA	(8.62)
-	Houston, TX**	NA	46	Stockton, CA	(5.87)
36	Huntington Beach, CA	(1.94)	16	St. Louis, MO	8.63
4	Indianapolis, IN	36.42	59	St. Paul, MN	(9.70)
2	Jackson, MS	45.05	88	St. Petersburg, FL	(24.00)
39	Jacksonville, FL	(2.81)	83	Tacoma, WA	(19.00)
82	Jersey City, NJ	(17.93)	29	Tampa, FL	0.30
30	Kansas City, MO	(0.41)	61	Toledo, OH	(10.02)
57	Las Vegas, NV	(8.78)	-	Tucson, AZ**	NA
27	Lexington, KY	0.32	75	Tulsa, OK	(15.46)
37	Lincoln, NE	(2.07)	70	Virginia Beach, VA	(13.83)
12	Little Rock, AR	14.12	11	Washington, DC	14.30
74	Long Beach, CA	(15.30)	26	Wichita, KS	1.22
42	Los Angeles, CA	(4.31)	48	Yonkers, NY	(6.02)

Source: Morgan Quitno Corporation using data from U.S. Department of Justice, Federal Bureau of Investigation
"Crime in the United States 1993" (Uniform Crime Reports, December 4, 1994)
*Includes murder, rape, robbery, aggravated assault, burglary, larceny-theft and motor vehicle theft.
**Not available.

44. Percent Change in Crime Rate: 1989 to 1993 (continued)

National Percent Change = 4.5% Decrease*

RANK	CITY	% CHANGE	RANK	CITY	% CHANGE
1	Nashville, TN	55.01	51	Fort Wayne, IN	(6.62)
2	Jackson, MS	45.05	52	Rochester, NY	(7.06)
3	Baton Rouge, LA	37.84	53	Milwaukee, WI	(7.62)
4	Indianapolis,IN	36.42	54	Seattle, WA	(8.60)
5	Baltimore, MD	34.09	55	Spokane, WA	(8.62)
6	Birmingham, AL	24.75	56	Minneapolis, MN	(8.77)
7	Newport News, VA	18.96	57	Las Vegas, NV	(8.78)
8	Mesa, AZ	18.77	58	Raleigh, NC	(9.62)
9	Anchorage, AK	17.71	59	St. Paul, MN	(9.70)
10	Buffalo, NY	15.03	60	Dayton, OH	(9.88)
11	Washington, DC	14.30	61	Toledo, OH	(10.02)
12	Little Rock, AR	14.12	62	Philadelphia, PA	(10.50)
13	Memphis, TN	13.05	63	Portland, OR	(10.77)
14	Cincinnati, OH	12.88	64	Bakersfield, CA	(10.88)
15	Richmond, VA	9.13	65	Charlotte, NC	(11.14)
16	St. Louis, MO	8.63	66	San Jose, CA	(11.64)
17	Fremont, CA	8.58	67	Mobile, AL	(12.19)
18	Riverside, CA	6.59	68	Pittsburgh, PA	(12.50)
19	San Francisco, CA	5.57	69	Des Moines, IA	(13.07)
20	Aurora, CO	5.02	70	Virginia Beach, VA	(13.83)
21	Denver, CO	4.89	71	Phoenix, AZ	(14.58)
22	Norfolk, VA	4.33	72	Colorado Springs, CO	(14.99)
23	Honolulu, HI	3.38	73	Lubbock, TX	(15.10)
24	Columbus, GA	2.05	74	Long Beach, CA	(15.30)
25	Miami, FL	2.00	75	Tulsa, OK	(15.46)
26	Wichita, KS	1.22	76	New York, NY	(15.48)
27	Lexington, KY	0.32	77	Atlanta, GA	(16.13)
27	Oklahoma City, OK	0.32	78	Columbus, OH	(16.24)
29	Tampa, FL	0.30	79	Arlington, TX	(16.63)
30	Kansas City, MO	(0.41)	80	Boston, MA	(16.88)
31	Newark, NJ	(0.52)	81	Glendale, CA	(17.92)
32	Greensboro, NC	(0.99)	82	Jersey City, NJ	(17.93)
32	Shreveport, LA	(0.99)	83	Tacoma, WA	(19.00)
34	Sacramento, CA	(1.06)	84	El Paso, TX	(20.66)
35	Montgomery, AL	(1.29)	85	San Diego, CA	(21.67)
36	Huntington Beach, CA	(1.94)	86	San Antonio, TX	(22.06)
37	Lincoln, NE	(2.07)	87	Madison, WI	(23.17)
38	Louisville, KY	(2.63)	88	St. Petersburg, FL	(24.00)
39	Jacksonville, FL	(2.81)	89	Santa Ana, CA	(25.00)
40	Albuquerque, NM	(3.84)	90	Fort Worth, TX	(31.44)
41	Austin, TX	(3.91)	91	Dallas, TX	(36.39)
42	Los Angeles, CA	(4.31)	–	Akron, OH**	NA
43	New Orleans, LA	(4.69)	–	Anaheim, CA**	NA
44	Oakland, CA	(4.94)	–	Chicago, IL**	NA
45	Cleveland, OH	(5.27)	–	Detroit, MI**	NA
46	Stockton, CA	(5.87)	–	Garland, TX**	NA
47	Corpus Christi, TX	(5.93)	–	Grand Rapids, MI**	NA
48	Yonkers, NY	(6.02)	–	Houston, TX**	NA
49	Orlando, FL	(6.14)	–	San Bernardino, CA**	NA
50	Fresno, CA	(6.41)	–	Tucson, AZ**	NA

Source: Morgan Quitno Corporation using data from U.S. Department of Justice, Federal Bureau of Investigation "Crime in the United States 1993" (Uniform Crime Reports, December 4, 1994)
*Includes murder, rape, robbery, aggravated assault, burglary, larceny-theft and motor vehicle theft.
**Not available.

45. Violent Crimes in 1993

National Total = 1,924,188 Violent Crimes*

RANK	CITY	CRIMES	RANK	CITY	CRIMES
-	Akron, OH**	NA	65	Louisville, KY	2,724
32	Albuquerque, NM	6,696	84	Lubbock, TX	1,275
-	Anaheim, CA**	NA	93	Madison, WI	631
74	Anchorage, AK	2,213	17	Memphis, TN	10,113
71	Arlington, TX	2,259	70	Mesa, AZ	2,335
7	Atlanta, GA	16,281	9	Miami, FL	14,502
51	Aurora, CO	4,457	39	Milwaukee, WI	6,014
60	Austin, TX	3,011	34	Minneapolis, MN	6,481
78	Bakersfield, CA	1,871	73	Mobile, AL	2,220
3	Baltimore, MD	21,945	80	Montgomery, AL	1,695
30	Baton Rouge, LA	6,822	22	Nashville, TN	9,164
33	Birmingham, AL	6,678	18	New Orleans, LA	10,024
15	Boston, MA	10,843	1	New York, NY	153,543
38	Buffalo, NY	6,041	16	Newark, NJ	10,222
20	Charlotte, NC	9,725	75	Newport News, VA	2,178
-	Chicago, IL**	NA	63	Norfolk, VA	2,769
41	Cincinnati, OH	5,621	19	Oakland, CA	9,809
24	Cleveland, OH	8,310	35	Oklahoma City, OK	6,480
82	Colorado Springs, CO	1,555	53	Orlando, FL	4,140
86	Columbus, GA	1,163	4	Philadelphia, PA	19,576
27	Columbus, OH	7,146	12	Phoenix, AZ	11,911
72	Corpus Christi, TX	2,225	50	Pittsburgh, PA	4,479
5	Dallas, TX	18,176	23	Portland, OR	8,445
61	Dayton, OH	2,922	77	Raleigh, NC	2,030
45	Denver, CO	5,252	57	Richmond, VA	3,275
89	Des Moines, IA	902	54	Riverside, CA	3,975
-	Detroit, MI**	NA	66	Rochester, NY	2,704
37	El Paso, TX	6,109	48	Sacramento, CA	4,850
88	Fort Wayne, IN	1,027	31	San Antonio, TX	6,725
29	Fort Worth, TX	6,979	42	San Bernardino, CA	5,566
90	Fremont, CA	892	10	San Diego, CA	13,463
43	Fresno, CA	5,511	11	San Francisco, CA	13,365
-	Garland, TX**	NA	44	San Jose, CA	5,317
92	Glendale, CA	671	59	Santa Ana, CA	3,190
-	Grand Rapids, MI**	NA	25	Seattle, WA	7,437
79	Greensboro, NC	1,720	68	Shreveport, LA	2,570
69	Honolulu, HI	2,501	81	Spokane, WA	1,558
-	Houston, TX**	NA	55	Stockton, CA	3,500
91	Huntington Beach, CA	877	8	St. Louis, MO	14,998
36	Indianapolis,IN	6,292	66	St. Paul, MN	2,704
62	Jackson, MS	2,780	46	St. Petersburg, FL	5,173
13	Jacksonville, FL	11,417	56	Tacoma, WA	3,441
49	Jersey City, NJ	4,584	21	Tampa, FL	9,379
14	Kansas City, MO	10,961	58	Toledo, OH	3,191
26	Las Vegas, NV	7,281	52	Tucson, AZ	4,363
76	Lexington, KY	2,160	47	Tulsa, OK	4,921
87	Lincoln, NE	1,125	85	Virginia Beach, VA	1,248
40	Little Rock, AR	5,887	6	Washington, DC	16,888
28	Long Beach, CA	7,116	64	Wichita, KS	2,743
2	Los Angeles, CA	83,701	83	Yonkers, NY	1,351

Source: U.S. Department of Justice, Federal Bureau of Investigation
   "Crime in the United States 1993" (Uniform Crime Reports, December 4, 1994)
*Violent crimes are offenses of murder, forcible rape, robbery and aggravated assault.
**Not available.

45. Violent Crimes in 1993 (continued)

National Total = 1,924,188 Violent Crimes*

RANK	CITY	CRIMES	RANK	CITY	CRIMES
1	New York, NY	153,543	51	Aurora, CO	4,457
2	Los Angeles, CA	83,701	52	Tucson, AZ	4,363
3	Baltimore, MD	21,945	53	Orlando, FL	4,140
4	Philadelphia, PA	19,576	54	Riverside, CA	3,975
5	Dallas, TX	18,176	55	Stockton, CA	3,500
6	Washington, DC	16,888	56	Tacoma, WA	3,441
7	Atlanta, GA	16,281	57	Richmond, VA	3,275
8	St. Louis, MO	14,998	58	Toledo, OH	3,191
9	Miami, FL	14,502	59	Santa Ana, CA	3,190
10	San Diego, CA	13,463	60	Austin, TX	3,011
11	San Francisco, CA	13,365	61	Dayton, OH	2,922
12	Phoenix, AZ	11,911	62	Jackson, MS	2,780
13	Jacksonville, FL	11,417	63	Norfolk, VA	2,769
14	Kansas City, MO	10,961	64	Wichita, KS	2,743
15	Boston, MA	10,843	65	Louisville, KY	2,724
16	Newark, NJ	10,222	66	Rochester, NY	2,704
17	Memphis, TN	10,113	66	St. Paul, MN	2,704
18	New Orleans, LA	10,024	68	Shreveport, LA	2,570
19	Oakland, CA	9,809	69	Honolulu, HI	2,501
20	Charlotte, NC	9,725	70	Mesa, AZ	2,335
21	Tampa, FL	9,379	71	Arlington, TX	2,259
22	Nashville, TN	9,164	72	Corpus Christi, TX	2,225
23	Portland, OR	8,445	73	Mobile, AL	2,220
24	Cleveland, OH	8,310	74	Anchorage, AK	2,213
25	Seattle, WA	7,437	75	Newport News, VA	2,178
26	Las Vegas, NV	7,281	76	Lexington, KY	2,160
27	Columbus, OH	7,146	77	Raleigh, NC	2,030
28	Long Beach, CA	7,116	78	Bakersfield, CA	1,871
29	Fort Worth, TX	6,979	79	Greensboro, NC	1,720
30	Baton Rouge, LA	6,822	80	Montgomery, AL	1,695
31	San Antonio, TX	6,725	81	Spokane, WA	1,558
32	Albuquerque, NM	6,696	82	Colorado Springs, CO	1,555
33	Birmingham, AL	6,678	83	Yonkers, NY	1,351
34	Minneapolis, MN	6,481	84	Lubbock, TX	1,275
35	Oklahoma City, OK	6,480	85	Virginia Beach, VA	1,248
36	Indianapolis,IN	6,292	86	Columbus, GA	1,163
37	El Paso, TX	6,109	87	Lincoln, NE	1,125
38	Buffalo, NY	6,041	88	Fort Wayne, IN	1,027
39	Milwaukee, WI	6,014	89	Des Moines, IA	902
40	Little Rock, AR	5,887	90	Fremont, CA	892
41	Cincinnati, OH	5,621	91	Huntington Beach, CA	877
42	San Bernardino, CA	5,566	92	Glendale, CA	671
43	Fresno, CA	5,511	93	Madison, WI	631
44	San Jose, CA	5,317	–	Akron, OH**	NA
45	Denver, CO	5,252	–	Anaheim, CA**	NA
46	St. Petersburg, FL	5,173	–	Chicago, IL**	NA
47	Tulsa, OK	4,921	–	Detroit, MI**	NA
48	Sacramento, CA	4,850	–	Garland, TX**	NA
49	Jersey City, NJ	4,584	–	Grand Rapids, MI**	NA
50	Pittsburgh, PA	4,479	–	Houston, TX**	NA

Source: U.S. Department of Justice, Federal Bureau of Investigation
  "Crime in the United States 1993" (Uniform Crime Reports, December 4, 1994)
*Violent crimes are offenses of murder, forcible rape, robbery and aggravated assault.
**Not available.

46. Violent Crime Rate in 1993

National Rate = 746.1 Violent Crimes per 100,000 Population*

RANK	CITY	RATE	RANK	CITY	RATE
-	Akron, OH**	NA	64	Louisville, KY	995.7
33	Albuquerque, NM	1,644.1	80	Lubbock, TX	665.3
-	Anaheim, CA**	NA	91	Madison, WI	320.4
71	Anchorage, AK	882.7	35	Memphis, TN	1,633.8
76	Arlington, TX	803.0	77	Mesa, AZ	766.3
1	Atlanta, GA	4,041.2	2	Miami, FL	3,893.0
26	Aurora, CO	1,807.3	66	Milwaukee, WI	965.2
83	Austin, TX	599.8	28	Minneapolis, MN	1,767.7
65	Bakersfield, CA	985.2	58	Mobile, AL	1,086.7
9	Baltimore, MD	2,994.0	73	Montgomery, AL	871.9
8	Baton Rouge, LA	3,024.7	27	Nashville, TN	1,784.1
13	Birmingham, AL	2,484.7	19	New Orleans, LA	2,039.0
21	Boston, MA	1,957.7	18	New York, NY	2,089.8
22	Buffalo, NY	1,859.6	4	Newark, NJ	3,787.4
16	Charlotte, NC	2,299.8	51	Newport News, VA	1,210.2
-	Chicago, IL**	NA	59	Norfolk, VA	1,074.9
40	Cincinnati, OH	1,533.3	11	Oakland, CA	2,601.6
34	Cleveland, OH	1,643.2	43	Oklahoma City, OK	1,416.6
86	Colorado Springs, CO	510.8	15	Orlando, FL	2,342.3
82	Columbus, GA	611.0	48	Philadelphia, PA	1,255.2
55	Columbus, OH	1,104.6	54	Phoenix, AZ	1,146.0
74	Corpus Christi, TX	819.3	50	Pittsburgh, PA	1,215.6
29	Dallas, TX	1,743.3	23	Portland, OR	1,856.5
38	Dayton, OH	1,585.0	69	Raleigh, NC	906.0
60	Denver, CO	1,053.8	37	Richmond, VA	1,595.0
89	Des Moines, IA	461.4	32	Riverside, CA	1,649.1
-	Detroit, MI**	NA	53	Rochester, NY	1,149.2
56	El Paso, TX	1,101.7	49	Sacramento, CA	1,254.1
84	Fort Wayne, IN	585.5	79	San Antonio, TX	682.4
41	Fort Worth, TX	1,506.1	7	San Bernardino, CA	3,194.9
87	Fremont, CA	492.5	52	San Diego, CA	1,160.0
42	Fresno, CA	1,450.4	25	San Francisco, CA	1,815.0
-	Garland, TX**	NA	81	San Jose, CA	656.8
90	Glendale, CA	373.8	57	Santa Ana, CA	1,099.7
-	Grand Rapids, MI**	NA	45	Seattle, WA	1,399.8
70	Greensboro, NC	891.4	46	Shreveport, LA	1,302.1
93	Honolulu, HI	285.7	75	Spokane, WA	813.5
-	Houston, TX**	NA	39	Stockton, CA	1,577.5
88	Huntington Beach, CA	469.1	3	St. Louis, MO	3,874.9
31	Indianapolis, IN	1,665.8	63	St. Paul, MN	997.0
44	Jackson, MS	1,402.4	17	St. Petersburg, FL	2,166.9
30	Jacksonville, FL	1,698.2	24	Tacoma, WA	1,831.3
20	Jersey City, NJ	1,990.5	6	Tampa, FL	3,246.7
12	Kansas City, MO	2,517.3	67	Toledo, OH	962.8
62	Las Vegas, NV	1,014.9	61	Tucson, AZ	1,023.4
68	Lexington, KY	918.8	47	Tulsa, OK	1,300.6
85	Lincoln, NE	567.5	92	Virginia Beach, VA	294.8
5	Little Rock, AR	3,290.2	10	Washington, DC	2,921.8
36	Long Beach, CA	1,605.4	72	Wichita, KS	874.7
14	Los Angeles, CA	2,374.3	78	Yonkers, NY	722.6

Source: U.S. Department of Justice, Federal Bureau of Investigation
  "Crime in the United States 1993" (Uniform Crime Reports, December 4, 1994)
*Violent crimes are offenses of murder, forcible rape, robbery and aggravated assault.
**Not available.

46. Violent Crime Rate in 1993 (continued)

National Rate = 746.1 Violent Crimes per 100,000 Population*

RANK	CITY	RATE	RANK	CITY	RATE
1	Atlanta, GA	4,041.2	51	Newport News, VA	1,210.2
2	Miami, FL	3,893.0	52	San Diego, CA	1,160.0
3	St. Louis, MO	3,874.9	53	Rochester, NY	1,149.2
4	Newark, NJ	3,787.4	54	Phoenix, AZ	1,146.0
5	Little Rock, AR	3,290.2	55	Columbus, OH	1,104.6
6	Tampa, FL	3,246.7	56	El Paso, TX	1,101.7
7	San Bernardino, CA	3,194.9	57	Santa Ana, CA	1,099.7
8	Baton Rouge, LA	3,024.7	58	Mobile, AL	1,086.7
9	Baltimore, MD	2,994.0	59	Norfolk, VA	1,074.9
10	Washington, DC	2,921.8	60	Denver, CO	1,053.8
11	Oakland, CA	2,601.6	61	Tucson, AZ	1,023.4
12	Kansas City, MO	2,517.3	62	Las Vegas, NV	1,014.9
13	Birmingham, AL	2,484.7	63	St. Paul, MN	997.0
14	Los Angeles, CA	2,374.3	64	Louisville, KY	995.7
15	Orlando, FL	2,342.3	65	Bakersfield, CA	985.2
16	Charlotte, NC	2,299.8	66	Milwaukee, WI	965.2
17	St. Petersburg, FL	2,166.9	67	Toledo, OH	962.8
18	New York, NY	2,089.8	68	Lexington, KY	918.8
19	New Orleans, LA	2,039.0	69	Raleigh, NC	906.0
20	Jersey City, NJ	1,990.5	70	Greensboro, NC	891.4
21	Boston, MA	1,957.7	71	Anchorage, AK	882.7
22	Buffalo, NY	1,859.6	72	Wichita, KS	874.7
23	Portland, OR	1,856.5	73	Montgomery, AL	871.9
24	Tacoma, WA	1,831.3	74	Corpus Christi, TX	819.3
25	San Francisco, CA	1,815.0	75	Spokane, WA	813.5
26	Aurora, CO	1,807.3	76	Arlington, TX	803.0
27	Nashville, TN	1,784.1	77	Mesa, AZ	766.3
28	Minneapolis, MN	1,767.7	78	Yonkers, NY	722.6
29	Dallas, TX	1,743.3	79	San Antonio, TX	682.4
30	Jacksonville, FL	1,698.2	80	Lubbock, TX	665.3
31	Indianapolis, IN	1,665.8	81	San Jose, CA	656.8
32	Riverside, CA	1,649.1	82	Columbus, GA	611.0
33	Albuquerque, NM	1,644.1	83	Austin, TX	599.8
34	Cleveland, OH	1,643.2	84	Fort Wayne, IN	585.5
35	Memphis, TN	1,633.8	85	Lincoln, NE	567.5
36	Long Beach, CA	1,605.4	86	Colorado Springs, CO	510.8
37	Richmond, VA	1,595.0	87	Fremont, CA	492.5
38	Dayton, OH	1,585.0	88	Huntington Beach, CA	469.1
39	Stockton, CA	1,577.5	89	Des Moines, IA	461.4
40	Cincinnati, OH	1,533.3	90	Glendale, CA	373.8
41	Fort Worth, TX	1,506.1	91	Madison, WI	320.4
42	Fresno, CA	1,450.4	92	Virginia Beach, VA	294.8
43	Oklahoma City, OK	1,416.6	93	Honolulu, HI	285.7
44	Jackson, MS	1,402.4	–	Akron, OH**	NA
45	Seattle, WA	1,399.8	–	Anaheim, CA**	NA
46	Shreveport, LA	1,302.1	–	Chicago, IL**	NA
47	Tulsa, OK	1,300.6	–	Detroit, MI**	NA
48	Philadelphia, PA	1,255.2	–	Garland, TX**	NA
49	Sacramento, CA	1,254.1	–	Grand Rapids, MI**	NA
50	Pittsburgh, PA	1,215.6	–	Houston, TX**	NA

Source: U.S. Department of Justice, Federal Bureau of Investigation
"Crime in the United States 1993" (Uniform Crime Reports, December 4, 1994)
*Violent crimes are offenses of murder, forcible rape, robbery and aggravated assault.
**Not available.

47. Percent Change in Violent Crime Rate: 1992 to 1993

National Percent Change = 1.5% Decrease*

RANK	CITY	% CHANGE	RANK	CITY	% CHANGE
-	Akron, OH**	NA	83	Louisville, KY	(7.94)
22	Albuquerque, NM	6.95	30	Lubbock, TX	5.29
-	Anaheim, CA**	NA	88	Madison, WI	(12.03)
18	Anchorage, AK	8.19	31	Memphis, TN	5.23
25	Arlington, TX	6.25	10	Mesa, AZ	12.38
34	Atlanta, GA	4.72	36	Miami, FL	4.35
38	Aurora, CO	4.04	66	Milwaukee, WI	(1.83)
50	Austin, TX	1.85	19	Minneapolis, MN	7.60
26	Bakersfield, CA	6.21	93	Mobile, AL	(69.52)
40	Baltimore, MD	3.77	9	Montgomery, AL	12.45
7	Baton Rouge, LA	16.45	14	Nashville, TN	9.57
13	Birmingham, AL	10.17	47	New Orleans, LA	2.90
77	Boston, MA	(3.92)	74	New York, NY	(3.42)
76	Buffalo, NY	(3.48)	17	Newark, NJ	8.20
60	Charlotte, NC	(0.54)	15	Newport News, VA	9.15
-	Chicago, IL**	NA	21	Norfolk, VA	6.96
69	Cincinnati, OH	(2.14)	62	Oakland, CA	(0.94)
63	Cleveland, OH	(1.11)	53	Oklahoma City, OK	1.21
67	Colorado Springs, CO	(1.90)	3	Orlando, FL	24.43
2	Columbus, GA	32.74	29	Philadelphia, PA	5.37
55	Columbus, OH	1.05	32	Phoenix, AZ	5.06
90	Corpus Christi, TX	(14.39)	54	Pittsburgh, PA	1.10
91	Dallas, TX	(15.85)	51	Portland, OR	1.39
89	Dayton, OH	(12.71)	86	Raleigh, NC	(10.41)
68	Denver, CO	(2.10)	20	Richmond, VA	7.33
82	Des Moines, IA	(7.37)	12	Riverside, CA	10.92
-	Detroit, MI**	NA	24	Rochester, NY	6.30
52	El Paso, TX	1.30	48	Sacramento, CA	2.80
28	Fort Wayne, IN	5.92	81	San Antonio, TX	(6.90)
92	Fort Worth, TX	(25.39)	79	San Bernardino, CA	(6.14)
1	Fremont, CA	42.80	84	San Diego, CA	(9.67)
61	Fresno, CA	(0.64)	59	San Francisco, CA	(0.35)
-	Garland, TX**	NA	65	San Jose, CA	(1.81)
71	Glendale, CA	(2.50)	41	Santa Ana, CA	3.73
-	Grand Rapids, MI**	NA	37	Seattle, WA	4.11
39	Greensboro, NC	3.86	35	Shreveport, LA	4.42
33	Honolulu, HI	5.00	73	Spokane, WA	(3.11)
-	Houston, TX**	NA	46	Stockton, CA	3.02
49	Huntington Beach, CA	2.58	5	St. Louis, MO	17.76
4	Indianapolis, IN	20.60	27	St. Paul, MN	6.12
16	Jackson, MS	8.95	80	St. Petersburg, FL	(6.45)
70	Jacksonville, FL	(2.37)	58	Tacoma, WA	(0.32)
56	Jersey City, NJ	0.28	77	Tampa, FL	(3.92)
87	Kansas City, MO	(11.82)	45	Toledo, OH	3.08
8	Las Vegas, NV	14.24	57	Tucson, AZ	0.24
23	Lexington, KY	6.71	72	Tulsa, OK	(2.60)
85	Lincoln, NE	(10.09)	42	Virginia Beach, VA	3.40
11	Little Rock, AR	11.45	44	Washington, DC	3.17
43	Long Beach, CA	3.25	64	Wichita, KS	(1.59)
75	Los Angeles, CA	(3.46)	6	Yonkers, NY	16.98

Source: Morgan Quitno Corporation using data from U.S. Department of Justice, Federal Bureau of Investigation
"Crime in the United States 1993" (Uniform Crime Reports, December 4, 1994)
*Violent crimes are offenses of murder, forcible rape, robbery and aggravated assault.
**Not available.

47. Percent Change in Violent Crime Rate: 1992 to 1993 (continued)

National Percent Change = 1.5% Decrease*

RANK	CITY	% CHANGE	RANK	CITY	% CHANGE
1	Fremont, CA	42.80	51	Portland, OR	1.39
2	Columbus, GA	32.74	52	El Paso, TX	1.30
3	Orlando, FL	24.43	53	Oklahoma City, OK	1.21
4	Indianapolis, IN	20.60	54	Pittsburgh, PA	1.10
5	St. Louis, MO	17.76	55	Columbus, OH	1.05
6	Yonkers, NY	16.98	56	Jersey City, NJ	0.28
7	Baton Rouge, LA	16.45	57	Tucson, AZ	0.24
8	Las Vegas, NV	14.24	58	Tacoma, WA	(0.32)
9	Montgomery, AL	12.45	59	San Francisco, CA	(0.35)
10	Mesa, AZ	12.38	60	Charlotte, NC	(0.54)
11	Little Rock, AR	11.45	61	Fresno, CA	(0.64)
12	Riverside, CA	10.92	62	Oakland, CA	(0.94)
13	Birmingham, AL	10.17	63	Cleveland, OH	(1.11)
14	Nashville, TN	9.57	64	Wichita, KS	(1.59)
15	Newport News, VA	9.15	65	San Jose, CA	(1.81)
16	Jackson, MS	8.95	66	Milwaukee, WI	(1.83)
17	Newark, NJ	8.20	67	Colorado Springs, CO	(1.90)
18	Anchorage, AK	8.19	68	Denver, CO	(2.10)
19	Minneapolis, MN	7.60	69	Cincinnati, OH	(2.14)
20	Richmond, VA	7.33	70	Jacksonville, FL	(2.37)
21	Norfolk, VA	6.96	71	Glendale, CA	(2.50)
22	Albuquerque, NM	6.95	72	Tulsa, OK	(2.60)
23	Lexington, KY	6.71	73	Spokane, WA	(3.11)
24	Rochester, NY	6.30	74	New York, NY	(3.42)
25	Arlington, TX	6.25	75	Los Angeles, CA	(3.46)
26	Bakersfield, CA	6.21	76	Buffalo, NY	(3.48)
27	St. Paul, MN	6.12	77	Boston, MA	(3.92)
28	Fort Wayne, IN	5.92	77	Tampa, FL	(3.92)
29	Philadelphia, PA	5.37	79	San Bernardino, CA	(6.14)
30	Lubbock, TX	5.29	80	St. Petersburg, FL	(6.45)
31	Memphis, TN	5.23	81	San Antonio, TX	(6.90)
32	Phoenix, AZ	5.06	82	Des Moines, IA	(7.37)
33	Honolulu, HI	5.00	83	Louisville, KY	(7.94)
34	Atlanta, GA	4.72	84	San Diego, CA	(9.67)
35	Shreveport, LA	4.42	85	Lincoln, NE	(10.09)
36	Miami, FL	4.35	86	Raleigh, NC	(10.41)
37	Seattle, WA	4.11	87	Kansas City, MO	(11.82)
38	Aurora, CO	4.04	88	Madison, WI	(12.03)
39	Greensboro, NC	3.86	89	Dayton, OH	(12.71)
40	Baltimore, MD	3.77	90	Corpus Christi, TX	(14.39)
41	Santa Ana, CA	3.73	91	Dallas, TX	(15.85)
42	Virginia Beach, VA	3.40	92	Fort Worth, TX	(25.39)
43	Long Beach, CA	3.25	93	Mobile, AL	(69.52)
44	Washington, DC	3.17	–	Akron, OH**	NA
45	Toledo, OH	3.08	–	Anaheim, CA**	NA
46	Stockton, CA	3.02	–	Chicago, IL**	NA
47	New Orleans, LA	2.90	–	Detroit, MI**	NA
48	Sacramento, CA	2.80	–	Garland, TX**	NA
49	Huntington Beach, CA	2.58	–	Grand Rapids, MI**	NA
50	Austin, TX	1.85	–	Houston, TX**	NA

Source: Morgan Quitno Corporation using data from U.S. Department of Justice, Federal Bureau of Investigation "Crime in the United States 1993" (Uniform Crime Reports, December 4, 1994)
*Violent crimes are offenses of murder, forcible rape, robbery and aggravated assault.
**Not available.

48. Percent Change in Violent Crime Rate: 1989 to 1993

National Percent Change = 12.5% Increase*

RANK	CITY	% CHANGE	RANK	CITY	% CHANGE
-	Akron, OH**	NA	58	Louisville, KY	9.83
26	Albuquerque, NM	34.72	32	Lubbock, TX	29.11
-	Anaheim, CA**	NA	54	Madison, WI	13.74
5	Anchorage, AK	74.31	29	Memphis, TN	32.47
27	Arlington, TX	34.60	11	Mesa, AZ	56.48
76	Atlanta, GA	2.27	72	Miami, FL	5.30
20	Aurora, CO	38.94	24	Milwaukee, WI	35.87
64	Austin, TX	7.97	53	Minneapolis, MN	14.75
87	Bakersfield, CA	(10.93)	91	Mobile, AL	(35.92)
14	Baltimore, MD	46.30	1	Montgomery, AL	144.30
4	Baton Rouge, LA	80.75	8	Nashville, TN	71.04
6	Birmingham, AL	71.83	69	New Orleans, LA	5.64
88	Boston, MA	(12.09)	86	New York, NY	(9.14)
30	Buffalo, NY	30.49	51	Newark, NJ	14.95
56	Charlotte, NC	12.16	2	Newport News, VA	114.19
-	Chicago, IL**	NA	18	Norfolk, VA	43.21
12	Cincinnati, OH	54.69	7	Oakland, CA	71.55
62	Cleveland, OH	8.08	19	Oklahoma City, OK	42.09
63	Colorado Springs, CO	8.04	55	Orlando, FL	12.24
36	Columbus, GA	24.92	52	Philadelphia, PA	14.87
70	Columbus, OH	5.61	33	Phoenix, AZ	27.28
61	Corpus Christi, TX	8.19	78	Pittsburgh, PA	(0.07)
89	Dallas, TX	(18.18)	82	Portland, OR	(1.83)
81	Dayton, OH	(1.77)	22	Raleigh, NC	37.29
15	Denver, CO	45.92	48	Richmond, VA	17.79
90	Des Moines, IA	(30.48)	41	Riverside, CA	21.03
-	Detroit, MI**	NA	65	Rochester, NY	6.67
43	El Paso, TX	20.30	46	Sacramento, CA	19.02
80	Fort Wayne, IN	(0.41)	38	San Antonio, TX	23.38
83	Fort Worth, TX	(2.69)	-	San Bernardino, CA**	NA
45	Fremont, CA	19.45	34	San Diego, CA	25.88
66	Fresno, CA	6.60	25	San Francisco, CA	35.44
-	Garland, TX**	NA	59	San Jose, CA	9.78
74	Glendale, CA	2.58	50	Santa Ana, CA	16.65
-	Grand Rapids, MI**	NA	73	Seattle, WA	4.69
84	Greensboro, NC	(4.25)	43	Shreveport, LA	20.30
71	Honolulu, HI	5.58	35	Spokane, WA	25.70
-	Houston, TX**	NA	31	Stockton, CA	30.39
16	Huntington Beach, CA	45.14	37	St. Louis, MO	24.14
21	Indianapolis, IN	37.62	67	St. Paul, MN	6.02
3	Jackson, MS	96.36	75	St. Petersburg, FL	2.36
49	Jacksonville, FL	17.67	79	Tacoma, WA	(0.08)
57	Jersey City, NJ	11.19	47	Tampa, FL	18.81
39	Kansas City, MO	23.25	77	Toledo, OH	0.24
28	Las Vegas, NV	32.91	-	Tucson, AZ**	NA
13	Lexington, KY	49.76	60	Tulsa, OK	9.51
40	Lincoln, NE	21.55	17	Virginia Beach, VA	43.25
9	Little Rock, AR	60.29	23	Washington, DC	36.42
85	Long Beach, CA	(4.60)	42	Wichita, KS	20.60
68	Los Angeles, CA	5.71	10	Yonkers, NY	58.15

Source: Morgan Quitno Corporation using data from U.S. Department of Justice, Federal Bureau of Investigation
"Crime in the United States 1993" (Uniform Crime Reports, December 4, 1994)
*Violent crimes are offenses of murder, forcible rape, robbery and aggravated assault.
**Not available.

48. Percent Change in Violent Crime Rate: 1989 to 1993 (continued)

National Percent Change = 12.5% Increase*

RANK	CITY	% CHANGE		RANK	CITY	% CHANGE
1	Montgomery, AL	144.30		51	Newark, NJ	14.95
2	Newport News, VA	114.19		52	Philadelphia, PA	14.87
3	Jackson, MS	96.36		53	Minneapolis, MN	14.75
4	Baton Rouge, LA	80.75		54	Madison, WI	13.74
5	Anchorage, AK	74.31		55	Orlando, FL	12.24
6	Birmingham, AL	71.83		56	Charlotte, NC	12.16
7	Oakland, CA	71.55		57	Jersey City, NJ	11.19
8	Nashville, TN	71.04		58	Louisville, KY	9.83
9	Little Rock, AR	60.29		59	San Jose, CA	9.78
10	Yonkers, NY	58.15		60	Tulsa, OK	9.51
11	Mesa, AZ	56.48		61	Corpus Christi, TX	8.19
12	Cincinnati, OH	54.69		62	Cleveland, OH	8.08
13	Lexington, KY	49.76		63	Colorado Springs, CO	8.04
14	Baltimore, MD	46.30		64	Austin, TX	7.97
15	Denver, CO	45.92		65	Rochester, NY	6.67
16	Huntington Beach, CA	45.14		66	Fresno, CA	6.60
17	Virginia Beach, VA	43.25		67	St. Paul, MN	6.02
18	Norfolk, VA	43.21		68	Los Angeles, CA	5.71
19	Oklahoma City, OK	42.09		69	New Orleans, LA	5.64
20	Aurora, CO	38.94		70	Columbus, OH	5.61
21	Indianapolis, IN	37.62		71	Honolulu, HI	5.58
22	Raleigh, NC	37.29		72	Miami, FL	5.30
23	Washington, DC	36.42		73	Seattle, WA	4.69
24	Milwaukee, WI	35.87		74	Glendale, CA	2.58
25	San Francisco, CA	35.44		75	St. Petersburg, FL	2.36
26	Albuquerque, NM	34.72		76	Atlanta, GA	2.27
27	Arlington, TX	34.60		77	Toledo, OH	0.24
28	Las Vegas, NV	32.91		78	Pittsburgh, PA	(0.07)
29	Memphis, TN	32.47		79	Tacoma, WA	(0.08)
30	Buffalo, NY	30.49		80	Fort Wayne, IN	(0.41)
31	Stockton, CA	30.39		81	Dayton, OH	(1.77)
32	Lubbock, TX	29.11		82	Portland, OR	(1.83)
33	Phoenix, AZ	27.28		83	Fort Worth, TX	(2.69)
34	San Diego, CA	25.88		84	Greensboro, NC	(4.25)
35	Spokane, WA	25.70		85	Long Beach, CA	(4.60)
36	Columbus, GA	24.92		86	New York, NY	(9.14)
37	St. Louis, MO	24.14		87	Bakersfield, CA	(10.93)
38	San Antonio, TX	23.38		88	Boston, MA	(12.09)
39	Kansas City, MO	23.25		89	Dallas, TX	(18.18)
40	Lincoln, NE	21.55		90	Des Moines, IA	(30.48)
41	Riverside, CA	21.03		91	Mobile, AL	(35.92)
42	Wichita, KS	20.60		-	Akron, OH**	NA
43	El Paso, TX	20.30		-	Anaheim, CA**	NA
43	Shreveport, LA	20.30		-	Chicago, IL**	NA
45	Fremont, CA	19.45		-	Detroit, MI**	NA
46	Sacramento, CA	19.02		-	Garland, TX**	NA
47	Tampa, FL	18.81		-	Grand Rapids, MI**	NA
48	Richmond, VA	17.79		-	Houston, TX**	NA
49	Jacksonville, FL	17.67		-	San Bernardino, CA**	NA
50	Santa Ana, CA	16.65		-	Tucson, AZ**	NA

Source: Morgan Quitno Corporation using data from U.S. Department of Justice, Federal Bureau of Investigation "Crime in the United States 1993" (Uniform Crime Reports, December 4, 1994)
*Violent crimes are offenses of murder, forcible rape, robbery and aggravated assault.
**Not available.

49. Murders in 1993

National Total = 24,526 Murders*

RANK	CITY	MURDERS
83	Akron, OH	19
53	Albuquerque, NM	50
68	Anaheim, CA	33
78	Anchorage, AK	23
95	Arlington, TX	7
13	Atlanta, GA	203
83	Aurora, CO	19
65	Austin, TX	37
75	Bakersfield, CA	27
9	Baltimore, MD	353
43	Baton Rouge, LA	74
27	Birmingham, AL	121
30	Boston, MA	98
41	Buffalo, NY	76
26	Charlotte, NC	122
3	Chicago, IL	845
63	Cincinnati, OH	39
15	Cleveland, OH	167
83	Colorado Springs, CO	19
71	Columbus, GA	32
29	Columbus, OH	105
67	Corpus Christi, TX	34
10	Dallas, TX	317
54	Dayton, OH	49
43	Denver, CO	74
92	Des Moines, IA	9
4	Detroit, MI	579
56	El Paso, TX	47
74	Fort Wayne, IN	28
20	Fort Worth, TX	133
97	Fremont, CA	4
33	Fresno, CA	87
91	Garland, TX	12
92	Glendale, CA	9
68	Grand Rapids, MI	33
75	Greensboro, NC	27
72	Honolulu, HI	31
6	Houston, TX	446
99	Huntington Beach, CA	3
45	Indianapolis, IN	68
36	Jackson, MS	83
25	Jacksonville, FL	125
82	Jersey City, NJ	20
19	Kansas City, MO	153
32	Las Vegas, NV	91
94	Lexington, KY	8
97	Lincoln, NE	4
45	Little Rock, AR	68
24	Long Beach, CA	126
2	Los Angeles, CA	1,076
65	Louisville, KY	37
88	Lubbock, TX	17
100	Madison, WI	2
14	Memphis, TN	198
96	Mesa, AZ	6
23	Miami, FL	127
17	Milwaukee, WI	157
50	Minneapolis, MN	58
61	Mobile, AL	42
63	Montgomery, AL	39
33	Nashville, TN	87
8	New Orleans, LA	395
1	New York, NY	1,946
31	Newark, NJ	96
79	Newport News, VA	22
49	Norfolk, VA	62
18	Oakland, CA	154
38	Oklahoma City, OK	80
89	Orlando, FL	15
7	Philadelphia, PA	439
16	Phoenix, AZ	158
38	Pittsburgh, PA	80
50	Portland, OR	58
75	Raleigh, NC	27
28	Richmond, VA	112
68	Riverside, CA	33
48	Rochester, NY	64
35	Sacramento, CA	85
12	San Antonio, TX	220
37	San Bernardino, CA	82
20	San Diego, CA	133
22	San Francisco, CA	129
62	San Jose, CA	41
40	Santa Ana, CA	78
47	Seattle, WA	67
41	Shreveport, LA	76
90	Spokane, WA	13
57	Stockton, CA	45
11	St. Louis, MO	267
79	St. Paul, MN	22
83	St. Petersburg, FL	19
72	Tacoma, WA	31
60	Tampa, FL	43
57	Toledo, OH	45
59	Tucson, AZ	44
52	Tulsa, OK	54
79	Virginia Beach, VA	22
5	Washington, DC	454
55	Wichita, KS	48
83	Yonkers, NY	19

Source: U.S. Department of Justice, Federal Bureau of Investigation
   "Crime in the United States 1993" (Uniform Crime Reports, December 4, 1994)
*Includes nonnegligent manslaughter.

49. Murders in 1993 (continued)

National Total = 24,526 Murders*

RANK	CITY	MURDERS
1	New York, NY	1,946
2	Los Angeles, CA	1,076
3	Chicago, IL	845
4	Detroit, MI	579
5	Washington, DC	454
6	Houston, TX	446
7	Philadelphia, PA	439
8	New Orleans, LA	395
9	Baltimore, MD	353
10	Dallas, TX	317
11	St. Louis, MO	267
12	San Antonio, TX	220
13	Atlanta, GA	203
14	Memphis, TN	198
15	Cleveland, OH	167
16	Phoenix, AZ	158
17	Milwaukee, WI	157
18	Oakland, CA	154
19	Kansas City, MO	153
20	Fort Worth, TX	133
20	San Diego, CA	133
22	San Francisco, CA	129
23	Miami, FL	127
24	Long Beach, CA	126
25	Jacksonville, FL	125
26	Charlotte, NC	122
27	Birmingham, AL	121
28	Richmond, VA	112
29	Columbus, OH	105
30	Boston, MA	98
31	Newark, NJ	96
32	Las Vegas, NV	91
33	Fresno, CA	87
33	Nashville, TN	87
35	Sacramento, CA	85
36	Jackson, MS	83
37	San Bernardino, CA	82
38	Oklahoma City, OK	80
38	Pittsburgh, PA	80
40	Santa Ana, CA	78
41	Buffalo, NY	76
41	Shreveport, LA	76
43	Baton Rouge, LA	74
43	Denver, CO	74
45	Indianapolis,IN	68
45	Little Rock, AR	68
47	Seattle, WA	67
48	Rochester, NY	64
49	Norfolk, VA	62
50	Minneapolis, MN	58
50	Portland, OR	58
52	Tulsa, OK	54
53	Albuquerque, NM	50
54	Dayton, OH	49
55	Wichita, KS	48
56	El Paso, TX	47
57	Stockton, CA	45
57	Toledo, OH	45
59	Tucson, AZ	44
60	Tampa, FL	43
61	Mobile, AL	42
62	San Jose, CA	41
63	Cincinnati, OH	39
63	Montgomery, AL	39
65	Austin, TX	37
65	Louisville, KY	37
67	Corpus Christi, TX	34
68	Anaheim, CA	33
68	Grand Rapids, MI	33
68	Riverside, CA	33
71	Columbus, GA	32
72	Honolulu, HI	31
72	Tacoma, WA	31
74	Fort Wayne, IN	28
75	Bakersfield, CA	27
75	Greensboro, NC	27
75	Raleigh, NC	27
78	Anchorage, AK	23
79	Newport News, VA	22
79	St. Paul, MN	22
79	Virginia Beach, VA	22
82	Jersey City, NJ	20
83	Akron, OH	19
83	Aurora, CO	19
83	Colorado Springs, CO	19
83	St. Petersburg, FL	19
83	Yonkers, NY	19
88	Lubbock, TX	17
89	Orlando, FL	15
90	Spokane, WA	13
91	Garland, TX	12
92	Des Moines, IA	9
92	Glendale, CA	9
94	Lexington, KY	8
95	Arlington, TX	7
96	Mesa, AZ	6
97	Fremont, CA	4
97	Lincoln, NE	4
99	Huntington Beach, CA	3
100	Madison, WI	2

Source: U.S. Department of Justice, Federal Bureau of Investigation
"Crime in the United States 1993" (Uniform Crime Reports, December 4, 1994)
*Includes nonnegligent manslaughter.

Alpha Order – City

50. Murder Rate in 1993

National Rate = 9.5 Murders per 100,000 Population*

RANK	CITY	RATE		RANK	CITY	RATE
81	Akron, OH	8.4		63	Louisville, KY	13.5
68	Albuquerque, NM	12.3		77	Lubbock, TX	8.9
71	Anaheim, CA	11.9		100	Madison, WI	1.0
76	Anchorage, AK	9.2		19	Memphis, TN	32.0
95	Arlington, TX	2.5		97	Mesa, AZ	2.0
6	Atlanta, GA	50.4		16	Miami, FL	34.1
84	Aurora, CO	7.7		32	Milwaukee, WI	25.2
85	Austin, TX	7.4		53	Minneapolis, MN	15.8
59	Bakersfield, CA	14.2		39	Mobile, AL	20.6
7	Baltimore, MD	48.2		41	Montgomery, AL	20.1
18	Baton Rouge, LA	32.8		48	Nashville, TN	16.9
9	Birmingham, AL	45.0		1	New Orleans, LA	80.3
44	Boston, MA	17.7		30	New York, NY	26.5
34	Buffalo, NY	23.4		14	Newark, NJ	35.6
23	Charlotte, NC	28.9		69	Newport News, VA	12.2
22	Chicago, IL	30.3		33	Norfolk, VA	24.1
73	Cincinnati, OH	10.6		11	Oakland, CA	40.8
17	Cleveland, OH	33.0		45	Oklahoma City, OK	17.5
87	Colorado Springs, CO	6.2		79	Orlando, FL	8.5
49	Columbus, GA	16.8		26	Philadelphia, PA	28.1
51	Columbus, OH	16.2		55	Phoenix, AZ	15.2
67	Corpus Christi, TX	12.5		38	Pittsburgh, PA	21.7
21	Dallas, TX	30.4		64	Portland, OR	12.8
29	Dayton, OH	26.6		70	Raleigh, NC	12.1
57	Denver, CO	14.8		5	Richmond, VA	54.5
92	Des Moines, IA	4.6		61	Riverside, CA	13.7
4	Detroit, MI	56.8		27	Rochester, NY	27.2
79	El Paso, TX	8.5		37	Sacramento, CA	22.0
52	Fort Wayne, IN	16.0		36	San Antonio, TX	22.3
24	Fort Worth, TX	28.7		8	San Bernardino, CA	47.1
96	Fremont, CA	2.2		72	San Diego, CA	11.5
35	Fresno, CA	22.9		45	San Francisco, CA	17.5
87	Garland, TX	6.2		90	San Jose, CA	5.1
91	Glendale, CA	5.0		28	Santa Ana, CA	26.9
47	Grand Rapids, MI	17.2		66	Seattle, WA	12.6
60	Greensboro, NC	14.0		12	Shreveport, LA	38.5
93	Honolulu, HI	3.5		86	Spokane, WA	6.8
31	Houston, TX	25.9		40	Stockton, CA	20.3
99	Huntington Beach, CA	1.6		3	St. Louis, MO	69.0
43	Indianapolis,IN	18.0		82	St. Paul, MN	8.1
10	Jackson, MS	41.9		83	St. Petersburg, FL	8.0
42	Jacksonville, FL	18.6		50	Tacoma, WA	16.5
78	Jersey City, NJ	8.7		56	Tampa, FL	14.9
15	Kansas City, MO	35.1		62	Toledo, OH	13.6
65	Las Vegas, NV	12.7		74	Tucson, AZ	10.3
94	Lexington, KY	3.4		58	Tulsa, OK	14.3
97	Lincoln, NE	2.0		89	Virginia Beach, VA	5.2
13	Little Rock, AR	38.0		2	Washington, DC	78.5
25	Long Beach, CA	28.4		54	Wichita, KS	15.3
20	Los Angeles, CA	30.5		75	Yonkers, NY	10.2

Source: U.S. Department of Justice, Federal Bureau of Investigation
"Crime in the United States 1993" (Uniform Crime Reports, December 4, 1994)
*Includes nonnegligent manslaughter.

50. Murder Rate in 1993 (continued)

National Rate = 9.5 Murders per 100,000 Population*

RANK	CITY	RATE		RANK	CITY	RATE
1	New Orleans, LA	80.3		51	Columbus, OH	16.2
2	Washington, DC	78.5		52	Fort Wayne, IN	16.0
3	St. Louis, MO	69.0		53	Minneapolis, MN	15.8
4	Detroit, MI	56.8		54	Wichita, KS	15.3
5	Richmond, VA	54.5		55	Phoenix, AZ	15.2
6	Atlanta, GA	50.4		56	Tampa, FL	14.9
7	Baltimore, MD	48.2		57	Denver, CO	14.8
8	San Bernardino, CA	47.1		58	Tulsa, OK	14.3
9	Birmingham, AL	45.0		59	Bakersfield, CA	14.2
10	Jackson, MS	41.9		60	Greensboro, NC	14.0
11	Oakland, CA	40.8		61	Riverside, CA	13.7
12	Shreveport, LA	38.5		62	Toledo, OH	13.6
13	Little Rock, AR	38.0		63	Louisville, KY	13.5
14	Newark, NJ	35.6		64	Portland, OR	12.8
15	Kansas City, MO	35.1		65	Las Vegas, NV	12.7
16	Miami, FL	34.1		66	Seattle, WA	12.6
17	Cleveland, OH	33.0		67	Corpus Christi, TX	12.5
18	Baton Rouge, LA	32.8		68	Albuquerque, NM	12.3
19	Memphis, TN	32.0		69	Newport News, VA	12.2
20	Los Angeles, CA	30.5		70	Raleigh, NC	12.1
21	Dallas, TX	30.4		71	Anaheim, CA	11.9
22	Chicago, IL	30.3		72	San Diego, CA	11.5
23	Charlotte, NC	28.9		73	Cincinnati, OH	10.6
24	Fort Worth, TX	28.7		74	Tucson, AZ	10.3
25	Long Beach, CA	28.4		75	Yonkers, NY	10.2
26	Philadelphia, PA	28.1		76	Anchorage, AK	9.2
27	Rochester, NY	27.2		77	Lubbock, TX	8.9
28	Santa Ana, CA	26.9		78	Jersey City, NJ	8.7
29	Dayton, OH	26.6		79	El Paso, TX	8.5
30	New York, NY	26.5		79	Orlando, FL	8.5
31	Houston, TX	25.9		81	Akron, OH	8.4
32	Milwaukee, WI	25.2		82	St. Paul, MN	8.1
33	Norfolk, VA	24.1		83	St. Petersburg, FL	8.0
34	Buffalo, NY	23.4		84	Aurora, CO	7.7
35	Fresno, CA	22.9		85	Austin, TX	7.4
36	San Antonio, TX	22.3		86	Spokane, WA	6.8
37	Sacramento, CA	22.0		87	Colorado Springs, CO	6.2
38	Pittsburgh, PA	21.7		87	Garland, TX	6.2
39	Mobile, AL	20.6		89	Virginia Beach, VA	5.2
40	Stockton, CA	20.3		90	San Jose, CA	5.1
41	Montgomery, AL	20.1		91	Glendale, CA	5.0
42	Jacksonville, FL	18.6		92	Des Moines, IA	4.6
43	Indianapolis, IN	18.0		93	Honolulu, HI	3.5
44	Boston, MA	17.7		94	Lexington, KY	3.4
45	Oklahoma City, OK	17.5		95	Arlington, TX	2.5
45	San Francisco, CA	17.5		96	Fremont, CA	2.2
47	Grand Rapids, MI	17.2		97	Lincoln, NE	2.0
48	Nashville, TN	16.9		97	Mesa, AZ	2.0
49	Columbus, GA	16.8		99	Huntington Beach, CA	1.6
50	Tacoma, WA	16.5		100	Madison, WI	1.0

Source: U.S. Department of Justice, Federal Bureau of Investigation
"Crime in the United States 1993" (Uniform Crime Reports, December 4, 1994)
*Includes nonnegligent manslaughter.

51. Percent Change in Murder Rate: 1992 to 1993

National Percent Change = 2.2% Increase*

RANK	CITY	% CHANGE	RANK	CITY	% CHANGE
88	Akron, OH	(20.75)	71	Louisville, KY	(4.93)
31	Albuquerque, NM	17.14	24	Lubbock, TX	23.61
73	Anaheim, CA	(6.30)	92	Madison, WI	(33.33)
19	Anchorage, AK	31.43	34	Memphis, TN	14.29
99	Arlington, TX	(57.63)	92	Mesa, AZ	(33.33)
49	Atlanta, GA	4.56	60	Miami, FL	(0.29)
36	Aurora, CO	13.24	41	Milwaukee, WI	11.01
67	Austin, TX	(2.63)	63	Minneapolis, MN	(0.63)
7	Bakersfield, CA	61.36	30	Mobile, AL	18.39
42	Baltimore, MD	8.80	27	Montgomery, AL	20.36
17	Baton Rouge, LA	34.43	68	Nashville, TN	(3.43)
74	Birmingham, AL	(7.79)	11	New Orleans, LA	45.47
14	Boston, MA	39.37	65	New York, NY	(2.21)
55	Buffalo, NY	1.74	35	Newark, NJ	13.74
29	Charlotte, NC	19.42	95	Newport News, VA	(35.11)
76	Chicago, IL	(8.46)	84	Norfolk, VA	(17.75)
87	Cincinnati, OH	(20.30)	70	Oakland, CA	(4.45)
44	Cleveland, OH	7.84	20	Oklahoma City, OK	30.60
43	Colorado Springs, CO	8.77	38	Orlando, FL	11.84
2	Columbus, GA	110.00	48	Philadelphia, PA	6.04
75	Columbus, OH	(7.95)	39	Phoenix, AZ	11.76
40	Corpus Christi, TX	11.61	4	Pittsburgh, PA	83.90
85	Dallas, TX	(17.84)	22	Portland, OR	28.00
82	Dayton, OH	(13.64)	15	Raleigh, NC	35.96
90	Denver, CO	(23.32)	66	Richmond, VA	(2.50)
23	Des Moines, IA	27.78	13	Riverside, CA	39.80
61	Detroit, MI	(0.35)	21	Rochester, NY	29.52
53	El Paso, TX	3.66	3	Sacramento, CA	88.03
9	Fort Wayne, IN	56.86	64	San Antonio, TX	(0.89)
80	Fort Worth, TX	(12.77)	46	San Bernardino, CA	7.05
92	Fremont, CA	(33.33)	78	San Diego, CA	(9.45)
51	Fresno, CA	4.09	37	San Francisco, CA	12.18
89	Garland, TX	(22.50)	69	San Jose, CA	(3.77)
16	Glendale, CA	35.14	12	Santa Ana, CA	41.58
1	Grand Rapids, MI	152.94	33	Seattle, WA	14.55
32	Greensboro, NC	15.70	5	Shreveport, LA	65.24
59	Honolulu, HI	0.00	47	Spokane, WA	6.25
72	Houston, TX	(5.47)	83	Stockton, CA	(16.12)
100	Huntington Beach, CA	(61.90)	28	St. Louis, MO	20.21
56	Indianapolis, IN	1.12	91	St. Paul, MN	(31.36)
18	Jackson, MS	33.02	96	St. Petersburg, FL	(36.00)
58	Jacksonville, FL	0.54	62	Tacoma, WA	(0.60)
86	Jersey City, NJ	(20.18)	79	Tampa, FL	(11.31)
54	Kansas City, MO	3.24	45	Toledo, OH	7.09
81	Las Vegas, NV	(13.01)	52	Tucson, AZ	4.04
98	Lexington, KY	(56.41)	6	Tulsa, OK	62.50
97	Lincoln, NE	(44.44)	77	Virginia Beach, VA	(8.77)
26	Little Rock, AR	21.79	50	Washington, DC	4.39
25	Long Beach, CA	21.89	8	Wichita, KS	57.73
57	Los Angeles, CA	0.66	10	Yonkers, NY	47.83

*Source: Morgan Quitno Corporation using data from U.S. Department of Justice, Federal Bureau of Investigation
"Crime in the United States 1993" (Uniform Crime Reports, December 4, 1994)*
Includes nonnegligent manslaughter.

51. Percent Change in Murder Rate: 1992 to 1993 (continued)

National Percent Change = 2.2% Increase*

RANK	CITY	% CHANGE	RANK	CITY	% CHANGE
1	Grand Rapids, MI	152.94	51	Fresno, CA	4.09
2	Columbus, GA	110.00	52	Tucson, AZ	4.04
3	Sacramento, CA	88.03	53	El Paso, TX	3.66
4	Pittsburgh, PA	83.90	54	Kansas City, MO	3.24
5	Shreveport, LA	65.24	55	Buffalo, NY	1.74
6	Tulsa, OK	62.50	56	Indianapolis, IN	1.12
7	Bakersfield, CA	61.36	57	Los Angeles, CA	0.66
8	Wichita, KS	57.73	58	Jacksonville, FL	0.54
9	Fort Wayne, IN	56.86	59	Honolulu, HI	0.00
10	Yonkers, NY	47.83	60	Miami, FL	(0.29)
11	New Orleans, LA	45.47	61	Detroit, MI	(0.35)
12	Santa Ana, CA	41.58	62	Tacoma, WA	(0.60)
13	Riverside, CA	39.80	63	Minneapolis, MN	(0.63)
14	Boston, MA	39.37	64	San Antonio, TX	(0.89)
15	Raleigh, NC	35.96	65	New York, NY	(2.21)
16	Glendale, CA	35.14	66	Richmond, VA	(2.50)
17	Baton Rouge, LA	34.43	67	Austin, TX	(2.63)
18	Jackson, MS	33.02	68	Nashville, TN	(3.43)
19	Anchorage, AK	31.43	69	San Jose, CA	(3.77)
20	Oklahoma City, OK	30.60	70	Oakland, CA	(4.45)
21	Rochester, NY	29.52	71	Louisville, KY	(4.93)
22	Portland, OR	28.00	72	Houston, TX	(5.47)
23	Des Moines, IA	27.78	73	Anaheim, CA	(6.30)
24	Lubbock, TX	23.61	74	Birmingham, AL	(7.79)
25	Long Beach, CA	21.89	75	Columbus, OH	(7.95)
26	Little Rock, AR	21.79	76	Chicago, IL	(8.46)
27	Montgomery, AL	20.36	77	Virginia Beach, VA	(8.77)
28	St. Louis, MO	20.21	78	San Diego, CA	(9.45)
29	Charlotte, NC	19.42	79	Tampa, FL	(11.31)
30	Mobile, AL	18.39	80	Fort Worth, TX	(12.77)
31	Albuquerque, NM	17.14	81	Las Vegas, NV	(13.01)
32	Greensboro, NC	15.70	82	Dayton, OH	(13.64)
33	Seattle, WA	14.55	83	Stockton, CA	(16.12)
34	Memphis, TN	14.29	84	Norfolk, VA	(17.75)
35	Newark, NJ	13.74	85	Dallas, TX	(17.84)
36	Aurora, CO	13.24	86	Jersey City, NJ	(20.18)
37	San Francisco, CA	12.18	87	Cincinnati, OH	(20.30)
38	Orlando, FL	11.84	88	Akron, OH	(20.75)
39	Phoenix, AZ	11.76	89	Garland, TX	(22.50)
40	Corpus Christi, TX	11.61	90	Denver, CO	(23.32)
41	Milwaukee, WI	11.01	91	St. Paul, MN	(31.36)
42	Baltimore, MD	8.80	92	Fremont, CA	(33.33)
43	Colorado Springs, CO	8.77	92	Madison, WI	(33.33)
44	Cleveland, OH	7.84	92	Mesa, AZ	(33.33)
45	Toledo, OH	7.09	95	Newport News, VA	(35.11)
46	San Bernardino, CA	7.05	96	St. Petersburg, FL	(36.00)
47	Spokane, WA	6.25	97	Lincoln, NE	(44.44)
48	Philadelphia, PA	6.04	98	Lexington, KY	(56.41)
49	Atlanta, GA	4.56	99	Arlington, TX	(57.63)
50	Washington, DC	4.39	100	Huntington Beach, CA	(61.90)

Source: Morgan Quitno Corporation using data from U.S. Department of Justice, Federal Bureau of Investigation "Crime in the United States 1993" (Uniform Crime Reports, December 4, 1994)
Includes nonnegligent manslaughter.

52. Percent Change in Murder Rate: 1989 to 1993

National Percent Change = 9.2% Increase*

RANK	CITY	% CHANGE	RANK	CITY	% CHANGE
82	Akron, OH	(6.67)	50	Louisville, KY	19.47
56	Albuquerque, NM	14.95	60	Lubbock, TX	12.66
63	Anaheim, CA	10.19	98	Madison, WI	(74.36)
8	Anchorage, AK	87.76	26	Memphis, TN	47.47
94	Arlington, TX	(40.48)	95	Mesa, AZ	(42.86)
85	Atlanta, GA	(12.65)	76	Miami, FL	(1.45)
3	Aurora, CO	140.63	33	Milwaukee, WI	35.48
61	Austin, TX	12.12	48	Minneapolis, MN	19.70
23	Bakersfield, CA	63.22	66	Mobile, AL	7.85
32	Baltimore, MD	40.52	52	Montgomery, AL	18.24
9	Baton Rouge, LA	87.43	44	Nashville, TN	22.46
41	Birmingham, AL	25.00	20	New Orleans, LA	69.05
71	Boston, MA	3.51	73	New York, NY	2.71
6	Buffalo, NY	98.31	70	Newark, NJ	4.40
27	Charlotte, NC	47.45	54	Newport News, VA	16.19
45	Chicago, IL	22.18	37	Norfolk, VA	27.51
84	Cincinnati, OH	(12.40)	55	Oakland, CA	15.91
47	Cleveland, OH	20.00	43	Oklahoma City, OK	24.11
7	Colorado Springs, CO	93.75	90	Orlando, FL	(28.57)
39	Columbus, GA	26.32	77	Philadelphia, PA	(2.09)
72	Columbus, OH	3.18	57	Phoenix, AZ	13.43
15	Corpus Christi, TX	73.61	1	Pittsburgh, PA	164.63
86	Dallas, TX	(13.64)	28	Portland, OR	43.82
83	Dayton, OH	(10.14)	25	Raleigh, NC	53.16
34	Denver, CO	33.33	46	Richmond, VA	20.31
88	Des Moines, IA	(25.81)	53	Riverside, CA	18.10
80	Detroit, MI	(5.33)	14	Rochester, NY	74.36
68	El Paso, TX	6.25	16	Sacramento, CA	73.23
5	Fort Wayne, IN	107.79	40	San Antonio, TX	25.99
64	Fort Worth, TX	9.54	–	San Bernardino, CA**	NA
10	Fremont, CA	83.33	69	San Diego, CA	4.55
17	Fresno, CA	72.18	11	San Francisco, CA	80.41
38	Garland, TX	26.53	74	San Jose, CA	2.00
51	Glendale, CA	19.05	42	Santa Ana, CA	24.54
2	Grand Rapids, MI	145.71	18	Seattle, WA	70.27
67	Greensboro, NC	7.69	22	Shreveport, LA	63.83
92	Honolulu, HI	(31.37)	34	Spokane, WA	33.33
78	Houston, TX	(3.36)	81	Stockton, CA	(5.58)
93	Huntington Beach, CA	(38.46)	12	St. Louis, MO	76.92
4	Indianapolis, IN	111.76	30	St. Paul, MN	42.11
13	Jackson, MS	76.05	97	St. Petersburg, FL	(56.04)
89	Jacksonville, FL	(26.19)	36	Tacoma, WA	32.00
96	Jersey City, NJ	(47.27)	87	Tampa, FL	(24.37)
62	Kansas City, MO	10.38	58	Toledo, OH	13.33
75	Las Vegas, NV	1.60	–	Tucson, AZ**	NA
91	Lexington, KY	(30.61)	21	Tulsa, OK	64.37
79	Lincoln, NE	(4.76)	59	Virginia Beach, VA	13.04
29	Little Rock, AR	43.40	65	Washington, DC	9.18
31	Long Beach, CA	42.00	24	Wichita, KS	56.12
49	Los Angeles, CA	19.61	19	Yonkers, NY	70.00

Source: Morgan Quitno Corporation using data from U.S. Department of Justice, Federal Bureau of Investigation "Crime in the United States 1993" (Uniform Crime Reports, December 4, 1994)
*Includes nonnegligent manslaughter.
**Not available.

52. Percent Change in Murder Rate: 1989 to 1993 (continued)

National Percent Change = 9.2% Increase*

RANK	CITY	% CHANGE	RANK	CITY	% CHANGE
1	Pittsburgh, PA	164.63	51	Glendale, CA	19.05
2	Grand Rapids, MI	145.71	52	Montgomery, AL	18.24
3	Aurora, CO	140.63	53	Riverside, CA	18.10
4	Indianapolis,IN	111.76	54	Newport News, VA	16.19
5	Fort Wayne, IN	107.79	55	Oakland, CA	15.91
6	Buffalo, NY	98.31	56	Albuquerque, NM	14.95
7	Colorado Springs, CO	93.75	57	Phoenix, AZ	13.43
8	Anchorage, AK	87.76	58	Toledo, OH	13.33
9	Baton Rouge, LA	87.43	59	Virginia Beach, VA	13.04
10	Fremont, CA	83.33	60	Lubbock, TX	12.66
11	San Francisco, CA	80.41	61	Austin, TX	12.12
12	St. Louis, MO	76.92	62	Kansas City, MO	10.38
13	Jackson, MS	76.05	63	Anaheim, CA	10.19
14	Rochester, NY	74.36	64	Fort Worth, TX	9.54
15	Corpus Christi, TX	73.61	65	Washington, DC	9.18
16	Sacramento, CA	73.23	66	Mobile, AL	7.85
17	Fresno, CA	72.18	67	Greensboro, NC	7.69
18	Seattle, WA	70.27	68	El Paso, TX	6.25
19	Yonkers, NY	70.00	69	San Diego, CA	4.55
20	New Orleans, LA	69.05	70	Newark, NJ	4.40
21	Tulsa, OK	64.37	71	Boston, MA	3.51
22	Shreveport, LA	63.83	72	Columbus, OH	3.18
23	Bakersfield, CA	63.22	73	New York, NY	2.71
24	Wichita, KS	56.12	74	San Jose, CA	2.00
25	Raleigh, NC	53.16	75	Las Vegas, NV	1.60
26	Memphis, TN	47.47	76	Miami, FL	(1.45)
27	Charlotte, NC	47.45	77	Philadelphia, PA	(2.09)
28	Portland, OR	43.82	78	Houston, TX	(3.36)
29	Little Rock, AR	43.40	79	Lincoln, NE	(4.76)
30	St. Paul, MN	42.11	80	Detroit, MI	(5.33)
31	Long Beach, CA	42.00	81	Stockton, CA	(5.58)
32	Baltimore, MD	40.52	82	Akron, OH	(6.67)
33	Milwaukee, WI	35.48	83	Dayton, OH	(10.14)
34	Denver, CO	33.33	84	Cincinnati, OH	(12.40)
34	Spokane, WA	33.33	85	Atlanta, GA	(12.65)
36	Tacoma, WA	32.00	86	Dallas, TX	(13.64)
37	Norfolk, VA	27.51	87	Tampa, FL	(24.37)
38	Garland, TX	26.53	88	Des Moines, IA	(25.81)
39	Columbus, GA	26.32	89	Jacksonville, FL	(26.19)
40	San Antonio, TX	25.99	90	Orlando, FL	(28.57)
41	Birmingham, AL	25.00	91	Lexington, KY	(30.61)
42	Santa Ana, CA	24.54	92	Honolulu, HI	(31.37)
43	Oklahoma City, OK	24.11	93	Huntington Beach, CA	(38.46)
44	Nashville, TN	22.46	94	Arlington, TX	(40.48)
45	Chicago, IL	22.18	95	Mesa, AZ	(42.86)
46	Richmond, VA	20.31	96	Jersey City, NJ	(47.27)
47	Cleveland, OH	20.00	97	St. Petersburg, FL	(56.04)
48	Minneapolis, MN	19.70	98	Madison, WI	(74.36)
49	Los Angeles, CA	19.61	-	San Bernardino, CA**	NA
50	Louisville, KY	19.47	-	Tucson, AZ**	NA

Source: Morgan Quitno Corporation using data from U.S. Department of Justice, Federal Bureau of Investigation
"Crime in the United States 1993" (Uniform Crime Reports, December 4, 1994)
*Includes nonnegligent manslaughter.
**Not available.

53. Rapes in 1993

National Total = 104,806 Rapes*

RANK	CITY	RAPES	RANK	CITY	RAPES
55	Akron, OH	204	73	Louisville, KY	135
46	Albuquerque, NM	259	72	Lubbock, TX	136
91	Anaheim, CA	70	85	Madison, WI	99
53	Anchorage, AK	212	7	Memphis, TN	725
70	Arlington, TX	146	80	Mesa, AZ	111
18	Atlanta, GA	492	55	Miami, FL	204
67	Aurora, CO	166	24	Milwaukee, WI	424
42	Austin, TX	271	13	Minneapolis, MN	518
93	Bakersfield, CA	39	77	Mobile, AL	122
9	Baltimore, MD	668	87	Montgomery, AL	87
62	Baton Rouge, LA	177	11	Nashville, TN	577
38	Birmingham, AL	297	37	New Orleans, LA	298
19	Boston, MA	480	1	New York, NY	2,818
39	Buffalo, NY	295	47	Newark, NJ	257
30	Charlotte, NC	356	82	Newport News, VA	103
-	Chicago, IL**	NA	55	Norfolk, VA	204
21	Cincinnati, OH	449	32	Oakland, CA	353
5	Cleveland, OH	834	15	Oklahoma City, OK	515
44	Colorado Springs, CO	265	54	Orlando, FL	209
92	Columbus, GA	49	6	Philadelphia, PA	785
10	Columbus, OH	658	22	Phoenix, AZ	444
59	Corpus Christi, TX	194	50	Pittsburgh, PA	226
4	Dallas, TX	1,000	20	Portland, OR	479
43	Dayton, OH	269	86	Raleigh, NC	94
26	Denver, CO	393	64	Richmond, VA	174
88	Des Moines, IA	84	74	Riverside, CA	131
-	Detroit, MI**	NA	68	Rochester, NY	159
41	El Paso, TX	281	66	Sacramento, CA	167
75	Fort Wayne, IN	130	12	San Antonio, TX	553
17	Fort Worth, TX	507	76	San Bernardino, CA	129
93	Fremont, CA	39	25	San Diego, CA	396
51	Fresno, CA	216	28	San Francisco, CA	361
78	Garland, TX	114	27	San Jose, CA	391
97	Glendale, CA	30	90	Santa Ana, CA	77
-	Grand Rapids, MI**	NA	30	Seattle, WA	356
81	Greensboro, NC	105	83	Shreveport, LA	100
40	Honolulu, HI	286	79	Spokane, WA	112
3	Houston, TX	1,109	69	Stockton, CA	157
95	Huntington Beach, CA	38	35	St. Louis, MO	319
14	Indianapolis,IN	517	49	St. Paul, MN	242
65	Jackson, MS	173	63	St. Petersburg, FL	176
8	Jacksonville, FL	699	60	Tacoma, WA	191
83	Jersey City, NJ	100	48	Tampa, FL	247
15	Kansas City, MO	515	29	Toledo, OH	357
23	Las Vegas, NV	435	36	Tucson, AZ	314
71	Lexington, KY	139	33	Tulsa, OK	339
89	Lincoln, NE	83	61	Virginia Beach, VA	181
52	Little Rock, AR	215	34	Washington, DC	324
58	Long Beach, CA	200	44	Wichita, KS	265
2	Los Angeles, CA	1,773	96	Yonkers, NY	34

Source: U.S. Department of Justice, Federal Bureau of Investigation
    "Crime in the United States 1993" (Uniform Crime Reports, December 4, 1994)
*Forcible rape is the carnal knowledge of a female forcibly and against her will. Assaults or attempts to commit rape by force or threat of force are included. However, statutory rape without force and other sex offenses are excluded.
**Not available.   188

53. Rapes in 1993 (continued)

National Total = 104,806 Rapes*

RANK	CITY	RAPES	RANK	CITY	RAPES
1	New York, NY	2,818	51	Fresno, CA	216
2	Los Angeles, CA	1,773	52	Little Rock, AR	215
3	Houston, TX	1,109	53	Anchorage, AK	212
4	Dallas, TX	1,000	54	Orlando, FL	209
5	Cleveland, OH	834	55	Akron, OH	204
6	Philadelphia, PA	785	55	Miami, FL	204
7	Memphis, TN	725	55	Norfolk, VA	204
8	Jacksonville, FL	699	58	Long Beach, CA	200
9	Baltimore, MD	668	59	Corpus Christi, TX	194
10	Columbus, OH	658	60	Tacoma, WA	191
11	Nashville, TN	577	61	Virginia Beach, VA	181
12	San Antonio, TX	553	62	Baton Rouge, LA	177
13	Minneapolis, MN	518	63	St. Petersburg, FL	176
14	Indianapolis,IN	517	64	Richmond, VA	174
15	Kansas City, MO	515	65	Jackson, MS	173
15	Oklahoma City, OK	515	66	Sacramento, CA	167
17	Fort Worth, TX	507	67	Aurora, CO	166
18	Atlanta, GA	492	68	Rochester, NY	159
19	Boston, MA	480	69	Stockton, CA	157
20	Portland, OR	479	70	Arlington, TX	146
21	Cincinnati, OH	449	71	Lexington, KY	139
22	Phoenix, AZ	444	72	Lubbock, TX	136
23	Las Vegas, NV	435	73	Louisville, KY	135
24	Milwaukee, WI	424	74	Riverside, CA	131
25	San Diego, CA	396	75	Fort Wayne, IN	130
26	Denver, CO	393	76	San Bernardino, CA	129
27	San Jose, CA	391	77	Mobile, AL	122
28	San Francisco, CA	361	78	Garland, TX	114
29	Toledo, OH	357	79	Spokane, WA	112
30	Charlotte, NC	356	80	Mesa, AZ	111
30	Seattle, WA	356	81	Greensboro, NC	105
32	Oakland, CA	353	82	Newport News, VA	103
33	Tulsa, OK	339	83	Jersey City, NJ	100
34	Washington, DC	324	83	Shreveport, LA	100
35	St. Louis, MO	319	85	Madison, WI	99
36	Tucson, AZ	314	86	Raleigh, NC	94
37	New Orleans, LA	298	87	Montgomery, AL	87
38	Birmingham, AL	297	88	Des Moines, IA	84
39	Buffalo, NY	295	89	Lincoln, NE	83
40	Honolulu, HI	286	90	Santa Ana, CA	77
41	El Paso, TX	281	91	Anaheim, CA	70
42	Austin, TX	271	92	Columbus, GA	49
43	Dayton, OH	269	93	Bakersfield, CA	39
44	Colorado Springs, CO	265	93	Fremont, CA	39
44	Wichita, KS	265	95	Huntington Beach, CA	38
46	Albuquerque, NM	259	96	Yonkers, NY	34
47	Newark, NJ	257	97	Glendale, CA	30
48	Tampa, FL	247	-	Chicago, IL**	NA
49	St. Paul, MN	242	-	Detroit, MI**	NA
50	Pittsburgh, PA	226	-	Grand Rapids, MI**	NA

Source: U.S. Department of Justice, Federal Bureau of Investigation
"Crime in the United States 1993" (Uniform Crime Reports, December 4, 1994)
*Forcible rape is the carnal knowledge of a female forcibly and against her will. Assaults or attempts to commit rape by force or threat of force are included. However, statutory rape without force and other sex offenses are excluded.
**Not available.

54. Rape Rate in 1993

National Rate = 40.6 Rapes per 100,000 Population*

RANK	CITY	RATE		RANK	CITY	RATE
25	Akron, OH	90.7		74	Louisville, KY	49.3
52	Albuquerque, NM	63.6		45	Lubbock, TX	71.0
92	Anaheim, CA	25.3		71	Madison, WI	50.3
33	Anchorage, AK	84.6		10	Memphis, TN	117.1
68	Arlington, TX	51.9		87	Mesa, AZ	36.4
6	Atlanta, GA	122.1		64	Miami, FL	54.8
49	Aurora, CO	67.3		47	Milwaukee, WI	68.0
67	Austin, TX	54.0		3	Minneapolis, MN	141.3
94	Bakersfield, CA	20.5		56	Mobile, AL	59.7
23	Baltimore, MD	91.1		78	Montgomery, AL	44.8
39	Baton Rouge, LA	78.5		12	Nashville, TN	112.3
13	Birmingham, AL	110.5		54	New Orleans, LA	60.6
30	Boston, MA	86.7		86	New York, NY	38.4
24	Buffalo, NY	90.8		21	Newark, NJ	95.2
35	Charlotte, NC	84.2		60	Newport News, VA	57.2
-	Chicago, IL**	NA		37	Norfolk, VA	79.2
5	Cincinnati, OH	122.5		22	Oakland, CA	93.6
1	Cleveland, OH	164.9		11	Oklahoma City, OK	112.6
29	Colorado Springs, CO	87.0		9	Orlando, FL	118.2
91	Columbus, GA	25.7		71	Philadelphia, PA	50.3
18	Columbus, OH	101.7		83	Phoenix, AZ	42.7
44	Corpus Christi, TX	71.4		53	Pittsburgh, PA	61.3
20	Dallas, TX	95.9		16	Portland, OR	105.3
2	Dayton, OH	145.9		84	Raleigh, NC	42.0
38	Denver, CO	78.9		32	Richmond, VA	84.7
81	Des Moines, IA	43.0		66	Riverside, CA	54.3
-	Detroit, MI**	NA		48	Rochester, NY	67.6
69	El Paso, TX	50.7		80	Sacramento, CA	43.2
40	Fort Wayne, IN	74.1		62	San Antonio, TX	56.1
14	Fort Worth, TX	109.4		41	San Bernardino, CA	74.0
93	Fremont, CA	21.5		88	San Diego, CA	34.1
61	Fresno, CA	56.8		75	San Francisco, CA	49.0
58	Garland, TX	58.5		76	San Jose, CA	48.3
97	Glendale, CA	16.7		90	Santa Ana, CA	26.5
-	Grand Rapids, MI**	NA		50	Seattle, WA	67.0
65	Greensboro, NC	54.4		69	Shreveport, LA	50.7
89	Honolulu, HI	32.7		58	Spokane, WA	58.5
51	Houston, TX	64.3		46	Stockton, CA	70.8
95	Huntington Beach, CA	20.3		36	St. Louis, MO	82.4
4	Indianapolis, IN	136.9		27	St. Paul, MN	89.2
28	Jackson, MS	87.3		42	St. Petersburg, FL	73.7
17	Jacksonville, FL	104.0		18	Tacoma, WA	101.7
79	Jersey City, NJ	43.4		31	Tampa, FL	85.5
8	Kansas City, MO	118.3		15	Toledo, OH	107.7
54	Las Vegas, NV	60.6		43	Tucson, AZ	73.6
57	Lexington, KY	59.1		26	Tulsa, OK	89.6
85	Lincoln, NE	41.9		82	Virginia Beach, VA	42.8
7	Little Rock, AR	120.2		62	Washington, DC	56.1
77	Long Beach, CA	45.1		34	Wichita, KS	84.5
71	Los Angeles, CA	50.3		96	Yonkers, NY	18.2

Source: U.S. Department of Justice, Federal Bureau of Investigation
    "Crime in the United States 1993" (Uniform Crime Reports, December 4, 1994)
*Forcible rape is the carnal knowledge of a female forcibly and against her will. Assaults or attempts to commit rape by force or threat of force are included. However, statutory rape without force and other sex offenses are excluded.
**Not available.

54. Rape Rate in 1993 (continued)

National Rate = 40.6 Rapes per 100,000 Population*

RANK	CITY	RATE	RANK	CITY	RATE
1	Cleveland, OH	164.9	51	Houston, TX	64.3
2	Dayton, OH	145.9	52	Albuquerque, NM	63.6
3	Minneapolis, MN	141.3	53	Pittsburgh, PA	61.3
4	Indianapolis, IN	136.9	54	Las Vegas, NV	60.6
5	Cincinnati, OH	122.5	54	New Orleans, LA	60.6
6	Atlanta, GA	122.1	56	Mobile, AL	59.7
7	Little Rock, AR	120.2	57	Lexington, KY	59.1
8	Kansas City, MO	118.3	58	Garland, TX	58.5
9	Orlando, FL	118.2	58	Spokane, WA	58.5
10	Memphis, TN	117.1	60	Newport News, VA	57.2
11	Oklahoma City, OK	112.6	61	Fresno, CA	56.8
12	Nashville, TN	112.3	62	San Antonio, TX	56.1
13	Birmingham, AL	110.5	62	Washington, DC	56.1
14	Fort Worth, TX	109.4	64	Miami, FL	54.8
15	Toledo, OH	107.7	65	Greensboro, NC	54.4
16	Portland, OR	105.3	66	Riverside, CA	54.3
17	Jacksonville, FL	104.0	67	Austin, TX	54.0
18	Columbus, OH	101.7	68	Arlington, TX	51.9
18	Tacoma, WA	101.7	69	El Paso, TX	50.7
20	Dallas, TX	95.9	69	Shreveport, LA	50.7
21	Newark, NJ	95.2	71	Los Angeles, CA	50.3
22	Oakland, CA	93.6	71	Madison, WI	50.3
23	Baltimore, MD	91.1	71	Philadelphia, PA	50.3
24	Buffalo, NY	90.8	74	Louisville, KY	49.3
25	Akron, OH	90.7	75	San Francisco, CA	49.0
26	Tulsa, OK	89.6	76	San Jose, CA	48.3
27	St. Paul, MN	89.2	77	Long Beach, CA	45.1
28	Jackson, MS	87.3	78	Montgomery, AL	44.8
29	Colorado Springs, CO	87.0	79	Jersey City, NJ	43.4
30	Boston, MA	86.7	80	Sacramento, CA	43.2
31	Tampa, FL	85.5	81	Des Moines, IA	43.0
32	Richmond, VA	84.7	82	Virginia Beach, VA	42.8
33	Anchorage, AK	84.6	83	Phoenix, AZ	42.7
34	Wichita, KS	84.5	84	Raleigh, NC	42.0
35	Charlotte, NC	84.2	85	Lincoln, NE	41.9
36	St. Louis, MO	82.4	86	New York, NY	38.4
37	Norfolk, VA	79.2	87	Mesa, AZ	36.4
38	Denver, CO	78.9	88	San Diego, CA	34.1
39	Baton Rouge, LA	78.5	89	Honolulu, HI	32.7
40	Fort Wayne, IN	74.1	90	Santa Ana, CA	26.5
41	San Bernardino, CA	74.0	91	Columbus, GA	25.7
42	St. Petersburg, FL	73.7	92	Anaheim, CA	25.3
43	Tucson, AZ	73.6	93	Fremont, CA	21.5
44	Corpus Christi, TX	71.4	94	Bakersfield, CA	20.5
45	Lubbock, TX	71.0	95	Huntington Beach, CA	20.3
46	Stockton, CA	70.8	96	Yonkers, NY	18.2
47	Milwaukee, WI	68.0	97	Glendale, CA	16.7
48	Rochester, NY	67.6	-	Chicago, IL**	NA
49	Aurora, CO	67.3	-	Detroit, MI**	NA
50	Seattle, WA	67.0	-	Grand Rapids, MI**	NA

Source: U.S. Department of Justice, Federal Bureau of Investigation
"Crime in the United States 1993" (Uniform Crime Reports, December 4, 1994)
Forcible rape is the carnal knowledge of a female forcibly and against her will. Assaults or attempts to commit rape by force or threat of force are included. However, statutory rape without force and other sex offenses are excluded.
**Not available.

191

Alpha Order – City

55. Percent Change in Rape Rate: 1992 to 1993

National Percent Change = 5.1% Decrease*

RANK	CITY	% CHANGE	RANK	CITY	% CHANGE
25	Akron, OH	0.67	11	Louisville, KY	12.81
71	Albuquerque, NM	(13.23)	70	Lubbock, TX	(12.99)
87	Anaheim, CA	(22.39)	5	Madison, WI	21.50
84	Anchorage, AK	(19.20)	16	Memphis, TN	7.04
39	Arlington, TX	(3.35)	51	Mesa, AZ	(7.85)
86	Atlanta, GA	(19.99)	88	Miami, FL	(24.73)
73	Aurora, CO	(13.50)	76	Milwaukee, WI	(14.89)
62	Austin, TX	(11.04)	64	Minneapolis, MN	(11.13)
92	Bakersfield, CA	(27.05)	95	Mobile, AL	(30.26)
52	Baltimore, MD	(8.07)	93	Montgomery, AL	(28.55)
13	Baton Rouge, LA	10.25	7	Nashville, TN	16.13
78	Birmingham, AL	(16.85)	17	New Orleans, LA	6.69
49	Boston, MA	(7.47)	26	New York, NY	0.52
72	Buffalo, NY	(13.28)	77	Newark, NJ	(15.60)
41	Charlotte, NC	(4.64)	69	Newport News, VA	(12.80)
-	Chicago, IL**	NA	82	Norfolk, VA	(17.93)
45	Cincinnati, OH	(6.84)	74	Oakland, CA	(13.57)
29	Cleveland, OH	(0.84)	14	Oklahoma City, OK	8.37
8	Colorado Springs, CO	14.02	2	Orlando, FL	45.03
75	Columbus, GA	(14.33)	31	Philadelphia, PA	(1.18)
40	Columbus, OH	(4.42)	61	Phoenix, AZ	(10.29)
3	Corpus Christi, TX	32.71	21	Pittsburgh, PA	3.72
53	Dallas, TX	(8.40)	32	Portland, OR	(1.59)
59	Dayton, OH	(9.49)	90	Raleigh, NC	(24.87)
63	Denver, CO	(11.05)	28	Richmond, VA	(0.47)
58	Des Moines, IA	(9.47)	33	Riverside, CA	(1.81)
-	Detroit, MI**	NA	47	Rochester, NY	(7.27)
27	El Paso, TX	(0.20)	94	Sacramento, CA	(30.21)
20	Fort Wayne, IN	3.93	65	San Antonio, TX	(11.37)
37	Fort Worth, TX	(3.01)	54	San Bernardino, CA	(8.64)
9	Fremont, CA	13.76	83	San Diego, CA	(19.00)
23	Fresno, CA	2.71	45	San Francisco, CA	(6.84)
67	Garland, TX	(12.16)	68	San Jose, CA	(12.50)
81	Glendale, CA	(17.73)	12	Santa Ana, CA	12.29
-	Grand Rapids, MI**	NA	22	Seattle, WA	3.40
35	Greensboro, NC	(2.86)	89	Shreveport, LA	(24.78)
66	Honolulu, HI	(12.10)	6	Spokane, WA	18.90
44	Houston, TX	(6.81)	56	Stockton, CA	(8.88)
97	Huntington Beach, CA	(40.29)	42	St. Louis, MO	(4.96)
4	Indianapolis, IN	24.79	18	St. Paul, MN	4.94
79	Jackson, MS	(16.86)	43	St. Petersburg, FL	(5.99)
38	Jacksonville, FL	(3.17)	96	Tacoma, WA	(38.62)
15	Jersey City, NJ	7.43	80	Tampa, FL	(17.63)
48	Kansas City, MO	(7.43)	30	Toledo, OH	(1.01)
19	Las Vegas, NV	4.66	85	Tucson, AZ	(19.21)
60	Lexington, KY	(10.18)	55	Tulsa, OK	(8.66)
91	Lincoln, NE	(24.91)	10	Virginia Beach, VA	13.23
34	Little Rock, AR	(2.83)	1	Washington, DC	53.70
50	Long Beach, CA	(7.77)	24	Wichita, KS	2.67
36	Los Angeles, CA	(2.90)	57	Yonkers, NY	(9.45)

Source: Morgan Quitno Corporation using data from U.S. Department of Justice, Federal Bureau of Investigation
"Crime in the United States 1993" (Uniform Crime Reports, December 4, 1994)
*Forcible rape is the carnal knowledge of a female forcibly and against her will. Assaults or attempts to commit rape by force or threat of force are included. However, statutory rape without force and other sex offenses are excluded.
**Not available.   192

55. Percent Change in Rape Rate: 1992 to 1993 (continued)

National Percent Change = 5.1% Decrease*

RANK	CITY	% CHANGE	RANK	CITY	% CHANGE
1	Washington, DC	53.70	51	Mesa, AZ	(7.85)
2	Orlando, FL	45.03	52	Baltimore, MD	(8.07)
3	Corpus Christi, TX	32.71	53	Dallas, TX	(8.40)
4	Indianapolis, IN	24.79	54	San Bernardino, CA	(8.64)
5	Madison, WI	21.50	55	Tulsa, OK	(8.66)
6	Spokane, WA	18.90	56	Stockton, CA	(8.88)
7	Nashville, TN	16.13	57	Yonkers, NY	(9.45)
8	Colorado Springs, CO	14.02	58	Des Moines, IA	(9.47)
9	Fremont, CA	13.76	59	Dayton, OH	(9.49)
10	Virginia Beach, VA	13.23	60	Lexington, KY	(10.18)
11	Louisville, KY	12.81	61	Phoenix, AZ	(10.29)
12	Santa Ana, CA	12.29	62	Austin, TX	(11.04)
13	Baton Rouge, LA	10.25	63	Denver, CO	(11.05)
14	Oklahoma City, OK	8.37	64	Minneapolis, MN	(11.13)
15	Jersey City, NJ	7.43	65	San Antonio, TX	(11.37)
16	Memphis, TN	7.04	66	Honolulu, HI	(12.10)
17	New Orleans, LA	6.69	67	Garland, TX	(12.16)
18	St. Paul, MN	4.94	68	San Jose, CA	(12.50)
19	Las Vegas, NV	4.66	69	Newport News, VA	(12.80)
20	Fort Wayne, IN	3.93	70	Lubbock, TX	(12.99)
21	Pittsburgh, PA	3.72	71	Albuquerque, NM	(13.23)
22	Seattle, WA	3.40	72	Buffalo, NY	(13.28)
23	Fresno, CA	2.71	73	Aurora, CO	(13.50)
24	Wichita, KS	2.67	74	Oakland, CA	(13.57)
25	Akron, OH	0.67	75	Columbus, GA	(14.33)
26	New York, NY	0.52	76	Milwaukee, WI	(14.89)
27	El Paso, TX	(0.20)	77	Newark, NJ	(15.60)
28	Richmond, VA	(0.47)	78	Birmingham, AL	(16.85)
29	Cleveland, OH	(0.84)	79	Jackson, MS	(16.86)
30	Toledo, OH	(1.01)	80	Tampa, FL	(17.63)
31	Philadelphia, PA	(1.18)	81	Glendale, CA	(17.73)
32	Portland, OR	(1.59)	82	Norfolk, VA	(17.93)
33	Riverside, CA	(1.81)	83	San Diego, CA	(19.00)
34	Little Rock, AR	(2.83)	84	Anchorage, AK	(19.20)
35	Greensboro, NC	(2.86)	85	Tucson, AZ	(19.21)
36	Los Angeles, CA	(2.90)	86	Atlanta, GA	(19.99)
37	Fort Worth, TX	(3.01)	87	Anaheim, CA	(22.39)
38	Jacksonville, FL	(3.17)	88	Miami, FL	(24.73)
39	Arlington, TX	(3.35)	89	Shreveport, LA	(24.78)
40	Columbus, OH	(4.42)	90	Raleigh, NC	(24.87)
41	Charlotte, NC	(4.64)	91	Lincoln, NE	(24.91)
42	St. Louis, MO	(4.96)	92	Bakersfield, CA	(27.05)
43	St. Petersburg, FL	(5.99)	93	Montgomery, AL	(28.55)
44	Houston, TX	(6.81)	94	Sacramento, CA	(30.21)
45	Cincinnati, OH	(6.84)	95	Mobile, AL	(30.26)
45	San Francisco, CA	(6.84)	96	Tacoma, WA	(38.62)
47	Rochester, NY	(7.27)	97	Huntington Beach, CA	(40.29)
48	Kansas City, MO	(7.43)	-	Chicago, IL**	NA
49	Boston, MA	(7.47)	-	Detroit, MI**	NA
50	Long Beach, CA	(7.77)	-	Grand Rapids, MI**	NA

Source: Morgan Quitno Corporation using data from U.S. Department of Justice, Federal Bureau of Investigation "Crime in the United States 1993" (Uniform Crime Reports, December 4, 1994)
*Forcible rape is the carnal knowledge of a female forcibly and against her will. Assaults or attempts to commit rape by force or threat of force are included. However, statutory rape without force and other sex offenses are excluded.
**Not available.   193

56. Percent Change in Rape Rate: 1989 to 1993

National Percent Change = 6.6% Increase*

RANK	CITY	% CHANGE	RANK	CITY	% CHANGE
28	Akron, OH	12.81	25	Louisville, KY	14.12
9	Albuquerque, NM	37.37	27	Lubbock, TX	13.24
94	Anaheim, CA	(43.78)	3	Madison, WI	69.93
11	Anchorage, AK	36.01	58	Memphis, TN	(2.42)
5	Arlington, TX	53.10	18	Mesa, AZ	22.56
87	Atlanta, GA	(24.63)	88	Miami, FL	(26.74)
17	Aurora, CO	23.26	72	Milwaukee, WI	(11.34)
34	Austin, TX	7.78	38	Minneapolis, MN	6.56
92	Bakersfield, CA	(36.14)	64	Mobile, AL	(5.98)
14	Baltimore, MD	28.49	41	Montgomery, AL	6.16
4	Baton Rouge, LA	62.53	23	Nashville, TN	17.84
22	Birmingham, AL	19.07	78	New Orleans, LA	(17.44)
46	Boston, MA	4.08	74	New York, NY	(13.12)
40	Buffalo, NY	6.45	81	Newark, NJ	(20.53)
61	Charlotte, NC	(3.44)	26	Newport News, VA	13.27
-	Chicago, IL**	NA	19	Norfolk, VA	21.66
13	Cincinnati, OH	29.90	85	Oakland, CA	(22.45)
48	Cleveland, OH	3.19	8	Oklahoma City, OK	38.16
12	Colorado Springs, CO	30.24	35	Orlando, FL	7.55
93	Columbus, GA	(42.76)	43	Philadelphia, PA	5.89
36	Columbus, OH	7.17	54	Phoenix, AZ	0.71
59	Corpus Christi, TX	(2.59)	44	Pittsburgh, PA	5.33
79	Dallas, TX	(19.34)	33	Portland, OR	8.00
76	Dayton, OH	(14.73)	83	Raleigh, NC	(22.08)
20	Denver, CO	20.09	51	Richmond, VA	1.80
31	Des Moines, IA	9.41	52	Riverside, CA	1.12
-	Detroit, MI**	NA	70	Rochester, NY	(9.99)
32	El Paso, TX	8.57	80	Sacramento, CA	(19.85)
7	Fort Wayne, IN	38.25	30	San Antonio, TX	11.75
47	Fort Worth, TX	3.80	-	San Bernardino, CA**	NA
50	Fremont, CA	1.90	68	San Diego, CA	(8.58)
86	Fresno, CA	(23.45)	60	San Francisco, CA	(3.16)
69	Garland, TX	(9.72)	66	San Jose, CA	(8.17)
95	Glendale, CA	(48.77)	73	Santa Ana, CA	(11.96)
-	Grand Rapids, MI**	NA	89	Seattle, WA	(27.88)
45	Greensboro, NC	4.41	65	Shreveport, LA	(7.65)
91	Honolulu, HI	(32.58)	71	Spokane, WA	(10.96)
62	Houston, TX	(4.32)	82	Stockton, CA	(21.68)
77	Huntington Beach, CA	(17.14)	53	St. Louis, MO	1.10
10	Indianapolis, IN	37.17	16	St. Paul, MN	23.55
57	Jackson, MS	(2.35)	24	St. Petersburg, FL	17.36
29	Jacksonville, FL	11.83	90	Tacoma, WA	(32.25)
55	Jersey City, NJ	(0.46)	6	Tampa, FL	41.32
49	Kansas City, MO	2.78	63	Toledo, OH	(5.94)
39	Las Vegas, NV	6.50	-	Tucson, AZ**	NA
15	Lexington, KY	28.48	37	Tulsa, OK	6.92
56	Lincoln, NE	(2.33)	21	Virginia Beach, VA	19.22
67	Little Rock, AR	(8.24)	1	Washington, DC	82.14
84	Long Beach, CA	(22.24)	42	Wichita, KS	6.02
75	Los Angeles, CA	(13.28)	2	Yonkers, NY	75.00

Source: Morgan Quitno Corporation using data from U.S. Department of Justice, Federal Bureau of Investigation "Crime in the United States 1993" (Uniform Crime Reports, December 4, 1994)
Forcible rape is the carnal knowledge of a female forcibly and against her will. Assaults or attempts to commit rape by force or threat of force are included. However, statutory rape without force and other sex offenses are excluded.
Not available.

56. Percent Change in Rape Rate: 1989 to 1993 (continued)

National Percent Change = 6.6% Increase*

RANK	CITY	% CHANGE	RANK	CITY	% CHANGE
1	Washington, DC	82.14	51	Richmond, VA	1.80
2	Yonkers, NY	75.00	52	Riverside, CA	1.12
3	Madison, WI	69.93	53	St. Louis, MO	1.10
4	Baton Rouge, LA	62.53	54	Phoenix, AZ	0.71
5	Arlington, TX	53.10	55	Jersey City, NJ	(0.46)
6	Tampa, FL	41.32	56	Lincoln, NE	(2.33)
7	Fort Wayne, IN	38.25	57	Jackson, MS	(2.35)
8	Oklahoma City, OK	38.16	58	Memphis, TN	(2.42)
9	Albuquerque, NM	37.37	59	Corpus Christi, TX	(2.59)
10	Indianapolis, IN	37.17	60	San Francisco, CA	(3.16)
11	Anchorage, AK	36.01	61	Charlotte, NC	(3.44)
12	Colorado Springs, CO	30.24	62	Houston, TX	(4.32)
13	Cincinnati, OH	29.90	63	Toledo, OH	(5.94)
14	Baltimore, MD	28.49	64	Mobile, AL	(5.98)
15	Lexington, KY	28.48	65	Shreveport, LA	(7.65)
16	St. Paul, MN	23.55	66	San Jose, CA	(8.17)
17	Aurora, CO	23.26	67	Little Rock, AR	(8.24)
18	Mesa, AZ	22.56	68	San Diego, CA	(8.58)
19	Norfolk, VA	21.66	69	Garland, TX	(9.72)
20	Denver, CO	20.09	70	Rochester, NY	(9.99)
21	Virginia Beach, VA	19.22	71	Spokane, WA	(10.96)
22	Birmingham, AL	19.07	72	Milwaukee, WI	(11.34)
23	Nashville, TN	17.84	73	Santa Ana, CA	(11.96)
24	St. Petersburg, FL	17.36	74	New York, NY	(13.12)
25	Louisville, KY	14.12	75	Los Angeles, CA	(13.28)
26	Newport News, VA	13.27	76	Dayton, OH	(14.73)
27	Lubbock, TX	13.24	77	Huntington Beach, CA	(17.14)
28	Akron, OH	12.81	78	New Orleans, LA	(17.44)
29	Jacksonville, FL	11.83	79	Dallas, TX	(19.34)
30	San Antonio, TX	11.75	80	Sacramento, CA	(19.85)
31	Des Moines, IA	9.41	81	Newark, NJ	(20.53)
32	El Paso, TX	8.57	82	Stockton, CA	(21.68)
33	Portland, OR	8.00	83	Raleigh, NC	(22.08)
34	Austin, TX	7.78	84	Long Beach, CA	(22.24)
35	Orlando, FL	7.55	85	Oakland, CA	(22.45)
36	Columbus, OH	7.17	86	Fresno, CA	(23.45)
37	Tulsa, OK	6.92	87	Atlanta, GA	(24.63)
38	Minneapolis, MN	6.56	88	Miami, FL	(26.74)
39	Las Vegas, NV	6.50	89	Seattle, WA	(27.88)
40	Buffalo, NY	6.45	90	Tacoma, WA	(32.25)
41	Montgomery, AL	6.16	91	Honolulu, HI	(32.58)
42	Wichita, KS	6.02	92	Bakersfield, CA	(36.14)
43	Philadelphia, PA	5.89	93	Columbus, GA	(42.76)
44	Pittsburgh, PA	5.33	94	Anaheim, CA	(43.78)
45	Greensboro, NC	4.41	95	Glendale, CA	(48.77)
46	Boston, MA	4.08	-	Chicago, IL**	NA
47	Fort Worth, TX	3.80	-	Detroit, MI**	NA
48	Cleveland, OH	3.19	-	Grand Rapids, MI**	NA
49	Kansas City, MO	2.78	-	San Bernardino, CA**	NA
50	Fremont, CA	1.90	-	Tucson, AZ**	NA

Source: Morgan Quitno Corporation using data from U.S. Department of Justice, Federal Bureau of Investigation "Crime in the United States 1993" (Uniform Crime Reports, December 4, 1994)
Forcible rape is the carnal knowledge of a female forcibly and against her will. Assaults or attempts to commit rape by force or threat of force are included. However, statutory rape without force and other sex offenses are excluded.

57. Robberies in 1993

National Total = 659,757 Robberies*

RANK	CITY	ROBBERIES	RANK	CITY	ROBBERIES
74	Akron, OH	840	59	Louisville, KY	1,393
54	Albuquerque, NM	1,552	95	Lubbock, TX	282
70	Anaheim, CA	909	93	Madison, WI	316
82	Anchorage, AK	568	14	Memphis, TN	5,366
80	Arlington, TX	710	89	Mesa, AZ	410
12	Atlanta, GA	6,045	10	Miami, FL	7,082
78	Aurora, CO	740	20	Milwaukee, WI	4,022
52	Austin, TX	1,555	28	Minneapolis, MN	3,178
82	Bakersfield, CA	568	62	Mobile, AL	1,186
5	Baltimore, MD	12,376	84	Montgomery, AL	562
43	Baton Rouge, LA	1,866	35	Nashville, TN	2,709
46	Birmingham, AL	1,706	15	New Orleans, LA	5,179
19	Boston, MA	4,081	1	New York, NY	86,001
31	Buffalo, NY	2,898	13	Newark, NJ	5,892
27	Charlotte, NC	3,227	79	Newport News, VA	719
3	Chicago, IL	35,189	58	Norfolk, VA	1,428
38	Cincinnati, OH	2,327	17	Oakland, CA	4,559
18	Cleveland, OH	4,297	45	Oklahoma City, OK	1,724
90	Colorado Springs, CO	389	66	Orlando, FL	1,107
88	Columbus, GA	451	6	Philadelphia, PA	11,531
22	Columbus, OH	3,887	26	Phoenix, AZ	3,437
87	Corpus Christi, TX	509	33	Pittsburgh, PA	2,784
8	Dallas, TX	7,420	40	Portland, OR	2,305
57	Dayton, OH	1,475	76	Raleigh, NC	795
44	Denver, CO	1,863	50	Richmond, VA	1,578
96	Des Moines, IA	271	61	Riverside, CA	1,287
4	Detroit, MI	13,591	47	Rochester, NY	1,638
51	El Paso, TX	1,561	39	Sacramento, CA	2,310
86	Fort Wayne, IN	552	29	San Antonio, TX	2,979
34	Fort Worth, TX	2,750	55	San Bernardino, CA	1,550
98	Fremont, CA	135	16	San Diego, CA	4,651
32	Fresno, CA	2,879	7	San Francisco, CA	8,454
94	Garland, TX	293	62	San Jose, CA	1,186
91	Glendale, CA	355	42	Santa Ana, CA	1,886
75	Grand Rapids, MI	829	36	Seattle, WA	2,670
77	Greensboro, NC	791	73	Shreveport, LA	842
67	Honolulu, HI	1,085	92	Spokane, WA	354
–	Houston, TX**	NA	53	Stockton, CA	1,554
97	Huntington Beach, CA	174	11	St. Louis, MO	6,223
41	Indianapolis,IN	2,050	69	St. Paul, MN	954
56	Jackson, MS	1,505	48	St. Petersburg, FL	1,599
24	Jacksonville, FL	3,604	68	Tacoma, WA	1,015
37	Jersey City, NJ	2,500	30	Tampa, FL	2,965
21	Kansas City, MO	3,891	49	Toledo, OH	1,594
25	Las Vegas, NV	3,572	71	Tucson, AZ	894
85	Lexington, KY	558	64	Tulsa, OK	1,143
99	Lincoln, NE	127	81	Virginia Beach, VA	631
65	Little Rock, AR	1,136	9	Washington, DC	7,107
23	Long Beach, CA	3,717	60	Wichita, KS	1,327
2	Los Angeles, CA	38,415	72	Yonkers, NY	852

Source: U.S. Department of Justice, Federal Bureau of Investigation
  "Crime in the United States 1993" (Uniform Crime Reports, December 4, 1994)
Robbery is the taking or attempting to take anything of value by force or threat of force.
**Not available.*

57. Robberies in 1993 (continued)

National Total = 659,757 Robberies*

RANK	CITY	ROBBERIES	RANK	CITY	ROBBERIES
1	New York, NY	86,001	51	El Paso, TX	1,561
2	Los Angeles, CA	38,415	52	Austin, TX	1,555
3	Chicago, IL	35,189	53	Stockton, CA	1,554
4	Detroit, MI	13,591	54	Albuquerque, NM	1,552
5	Baltimore, MD	12,376	55	San Bernardino, CA	1,550
6	Philadelphia, PA	11,531	56	Jackson, MS	1,505
7	San Francisco, CA	8,454	57	Dayton, OH	1,475
8	Dallas, TX	7,420	58	Norfolk, VA	1,428
9	Washington, DC	7,107	59	Louisville, KY	1,393
10	Miami, FL	7,082	60	Wichita, KS	1,327
11	St. Louis, MO	6,223	61	Riverside, CA	1,287
12	Atlanta, GA	6,045	62	Mobile, AL	1,186
13	Newark, NJ	5,892	62	San Jose, CA	1,186
14	Memphis, TN	5,366	64	Tulsa, OK	1,143
15	New Orleans, LA	5,179	65	Little Rock, AR	1,136
16	San Diego, CA	4,651	66	Orlando, FL	1,107
17	Oakland, CA	4,559	67	Honolulu, HI	1,085
18	Cleveland, OH	4,297	68	Tacoma, WA	1,015
19	Boston, MA	4,081	69	St. Paul, MN	954
20	Milwaukee, WI	4,022	70	Anaheim, CA	909
21	Kansas City, MO	3,891	71	Tucson, AZ	894
22	Columbus, OH	3,887	72	Yonkers, NY	852
23	Long Beach, CA	3,717	73	Shreveport, LA	842
24	Jacksonville, FL	3,604	74	Akron, OH	840
25	Las Vegas, NV	3,572	75	Grand Rapids, MI	829
26	Phoenix, AZ	3,437	76	Raleigh, NC	795
27	Charlotte, NC	3,227	77	Greensboro, NC	791
28	Minneapolis, MN	3,178	78	Aurora, CO	740
29	San Antonio, TX	2,979	79	Newport News, VA	719
30	Tampa, FL	2,965	80	Arlington, TX	710
31	Buffalo, NY	2,898	81	Virginia Beach, VA	631
32	Fresno, CA	2,879	82	Anchorage, AK	568
33	Pittsburgh, PA	2,784	82	Bakersfield, CA	568
34	Fort Worth, TX	2,750	84	Montgomery, AL	562
35	Nashville, TN	2,709	85	Lexington, KY	558
36	Seattle, WA	2,670	86	Fort Wayne, IN	552
37	Jersey City, NJ	2,500	87	Corpus Christi, TX	509
38	Cincinnati, OH	2,327	88	Columbus, GA	451
39	Sacramento, CA	2,310	89	Mesa, AZ	410
40	Portland, OR	2,305	90	Colorado Springs, CO	389
41	Indianapolis, IN	2,050	91	Glendale, CA	355
42	Santa Ana, CA	1,886	92	Spokane, WA	354
43	Baton Rouge, LA	1,866	93	Madison, WI	316
44	Denver, CO	1,863	94	Garland, TX	293
45	Oklahoma City, OK	1,724	95	Lubbock, TX	282
46	Birmingham, AL	1,706	96	Des Moines, IA	271
47	Rochester, NY	1,638	97	Huntington Beach, CA	174
48	St. Petersburg, FL	1,599	98	Fremont, CA	135
49	Toledo, OH	1,594	99	Lincoln, NE	127
50	Richmond, VA	1,578	–	Houston, TX**	NA

Source: U.S. Department of Justice, Federal Bureau of Investigation
 "Crime in the United States 1993" (Uniform Crime Reports, December 4, 1994)
*Robbery is the taking or attempting to take anything of value by force or threat of force.
**Not available.

58. Robbery Rate in 1993

National Rate = 255.8 Robberies per 100,000 Population*

RANK	CITY	RATE	RANK	CITY	RATE
67	Akron, OH	373.3	52	Louisville, KY	509.2
64	Albuquerque, NM	381.1	91	Lubbock, TX	147.2
71	Anaheim, CA	328.5	88	Madison, WI	160.5
83	Anchorage, AK	226.5	19	Memphis, TN	866.9
80	Arlington, TX	252.4	94	Mesa, AZ	134.6
5	Atlanta, GA	1,500.5	2	Miami, FL	1,901.1
76	Aurora, CO	300.1	37	Milwaukee, WI	645.5
73	Austin, TX	309.7	20	Minneapolis, MN	866.8
77	Bakersfield, CA	299.1	45	Mobile, AL	580.6
3	Baltimore, MD	1,688.5	78	Montgomery, AL	289.1
23	Baton Rouge, LA	827.3	51	Nashville, TN	527.4
40	Birmingham, AL	634.7	14	New Orleans, LA	1,053.5
31	Boston, MA	736.8	10	New York, NY	1,170.5
17	Buffalo, NY	892.1	1	Newark, NJ	2,183.1
26	Charlotte, NC	763.1	63	Newport News, VA	399.5
7	Chicago, IL	1,261.7	46	Norfolk, VA	554.3
39	Cincinnati, OH	634.8	9	Oakland, CA	1,209.2
21	Cleveland, OH	849.7	65	Oklahoma City, OK	376.9
95	Colorado Springs, CO	127.8	41	Orlando, FL	626.3
82	Columbus, GA	237.0	30	Philadelphia, PA	739.4
42	Columbus, OH	600.8	70	Phoenix, AZ	330.7
86	Corpus Christi, TX	187.4	29	Pittsburgh, PA	755.6
32	Dallas, TX	711.7	53	Portland, OR	506.7
24	Dayton, OH	800.1	68	Raleigh, NC	354.8
66	Denver, CO	373.8	25	Richmond, VA	768.5
93	Des Moines, IA	138.6	50	Riverside, CA	533.9
6	Detroit, MI	1,332.4	34	Rochester, NY	696.1
79	El Paso, TX	281.5	43	Sacramento, CA	597.3
72	Fort Wayne, IN	314.7	74	San Antonio, TX	302.3
44	Fort Worth, TX	593.5	18	San Bernardino, CA	889.7
98	Fremont, CA	74.5	62	San Diego, CA	400.7
28	Fresno, CA	757.7	11	San Francisco, CA	1,148.1
89	Garland, TX	150.3	92	San Jose, CA	146.5
85	Glendale, CA	197.8	36	Santa Ana, CA	650.2
58	Grand Rapids, MI	431.5	54	Seattle, WA	502.6
61	Greensboro, NC	409.9	59	Shreveport, LA	426.6
96	Honolulu, HI	123.9	87	Spokane, WA	184.8
-	Houston, TX**	NA	33	Stockton, CA	700.4
97	Huntington Beach, CA	93.1	4	St. Louis, MO	1,607.8
47	Indianapolis, IN	542.7	69	St. Paul, MN	351.8
27	Jackson, MS	759.2	35	St. Petersburg, FL	669.8
49	Jacksonville, FL	536.1	48	Tacoma, WA	540.2
13	Jersey City, NJ	1,085.6	15	Tampa, FL	1,026.4
16	Kansas City, MO	893.6	56	Toledo, OH	481.0
55	Las Vegas, NV	497.9	84	Tucson, AZ	209.7
81	Lexington, KY	237.4	75	Tulsa, OK	302.1
99	Lincoln, NE	64.1	90	Virginia Beach, VA	149.0
38	Little Rock, AR	634.9	8	Washington, DC	1,229.6
22	Long Beach, CA	838.6	60	Wichita, KS	423.2
12	Los Angeles, CA	1,089.7	57	Yonkers, NY	455.7

Source: U.S. Department of Justice, Federal Bureau of Investigation
 "Crime in the United States 1993" (Uniform Crime Reports, December 4, 1994)
*Robbery is the taking or attempting to take anything of value by force or threat of force.
**Not available.

58. Robbery Rate in 1993 (continued)

National Rate = 255.8 Robberies per 100,000 Population*

RANK	CITY	RATE	RANK	CITY	RATE
1	Newark, NJ	2,183.1	51	Nashville, TN	527.4
2	Miami, FL	1,901.1	52	Louisville, KY	509.2
3	Baltimore, MD	1,688.5	53	Portland, OR	506.7
4	St. Louis, MO	1,607.8	54	Seattle, WA	502.6
5	Atlanta, GA	1,500.5	55	Las Vegas, NV	497.9
6	Detroit, MI	1,332.4	56	Toledo, OH	481.0
7	Chicago, IL	1,261.7	57	Yonkers, NY	455.7
8	Washington, DC	1,229.6	58	Grand Rapids, MI	431.5
9	Oakland, CA	1,209.2	59	Shreveport, LA	426.6
10	New York, NY	1,170.5	60	Wichita, KS	423.2
11	San Francisco, CA	1,148.1	61	Greensboro, NC	409.9
12	Los Angeles, CA	1,089.7	62	San Diego, CA	400.7
13	Jersey City, NJ	1,085.6	63	Newport News, VA	399.5
14	New Orleans, LA	1,053.5	64	Albuquerque, NM	381.1
15	Tampa, FL	1,026.4	65	Oklahoma City, OK	376.9
16	Kansas City, MO	893.6	66	Denver, CO	373.8
17	Buffalo, NY	892.1	67	Akron, OH	373.3
18	San Bernardino, CA	889.7	68	Raleigh, NC	354.8
19	Memphis, TN	866.9	69	St. Paul, MN	351.8
20	Minneapolis, MN	866.8	70	Phoenix, AZ	330.7
21	Cleveland, OH	849.7	71	Anaheim, CA	328.5
22	Long Beach, CA	838.6	72	Fort Wayne, IN	314.7
23	Baton Rouge, LA	827.3	73	Austin, TX	309.7
24	Dayton, OH	800.1	74	San Antonio, TX	302.3
25	Richmond, VA	768.5	75	Tulsa, OK	302.1
26	Charlotte, NC	763.1	76	Aurora, CO	300.1
27	Jackson, MS	759.2	77	Bakersfield, CA	299.1
28	Fresno, CA	757.7	78	Montgomery, AL	289.1
29	Pittsburgh, PA	755.6	79	El Paso, TX	281.5
30	Philadelphia, PA	739.4	80	Arlington, TX	252.4
31	Boston, MA	736.8	81	Lexington, KY	237.4
32	Dallas, TX	711.7	82	Columbus, GA	237.0
33	Stockton, CA	700.4	83	Anchorage, AK	226.5
34	Rochester, NY	696.1	84	Tucson, AZ	209.7
35	St. Petersburg, FL	669.8	85	Glendale, CA	197.8
36	Santa Ana, CA	650.2	86	Corpus Christi, TX	187.4
37	Milwaukee, WI	645.5	87	Spokane, WA	184.8
38	Little Rock, AR	634.9	88	Madison, WI	160.5
39	Cincinnati, OH	634.8	89	Garland, TX	150.3
40	Birmingham, AL	634.7	90	Virginia Beach, VA	149.0
41	Orlando, FL	626.3	91	Lubbock, TX	147.2
42	Columbus, OH	600.8	92	San Jose, CA	146.5
43	Sacramento, CA	597.3	93	Des Moines, IA	138.6
44	Fort Worth, TX	593.5	94	Mesa, AZ	134.6
45	Mobile, AL	580.6	95	Colorado Springs, CO	127.8
46	Norfolk, VA	554.3	96	Honolulu, HI	123.9
47	Indianapolis,IN	542.7	97	Huntington Beach, CA	93.1
48	Tacoma, WA	540.2	98	Fremont, CA	74.5
49	Jacksonville, FL	536.1	99	Lincoln, NE	64.1
50	Riverside, CA	533.9	-	Houston, TX**	NA

Source: U.S. Department of Justice, Federal Bureau of Investigation
 "Crime in the United States 1993" (Uniform Crime Reports, December 4, 1994)
*Robbery is the taking or attempting to take anything of value by force or threat of force.
**Not available.

59. Percent Change in Robbery Rate: 1992 to 1993

National Percent Change = 3.0% Decrease*

RANK	CITY	% CHANGE	RANK	CITY	% CHANGE
87	Akron, OH	(12.47)	15	Louisville, KY	12.56
31	Albuquerque, NM	4.73	97	Lubbock, TX	(19.08)
45	Anaheim, CA	1.86	17	Madison, WI	11.85
14	Anchorage, AK	13.02	43	Memphis, TN	2.07
70	Arlington, TX	(5.29)	2	Mesa, AZ	37.49
29	Atlanta, GA	5.86	49	Miami, FL	0.58
32	Aurora, CO	4.46	69	Milwaukee, WI	(4.23)
39	Austin, TX	3.37	26	Minneapolis, MN	6.37
27	Bakersfield, CA	6.33	64	Mobile, AL	(1.81)
36	Baltimore, MD	4.03	40	Montgomery, AL	3.10
8	Baton Rouge, LA	18.59	46	Nashville, TN	1.76
75	Birmingham, AL	(6.74)	54	New Orleans, LA	(0.39)
85	Boston, MA	(11.42)	71	New York, NY	(5.38)
63	Buffalo, NY	(1.66)	16	Newark, NJ	12.43
44	Charlotte, NC	2.05	20	Newport News, VA	8.06
78	Chicago, IL	(7.04)	6	Norfolk, VA	22.88
41	Cincinnati, OH	2.30	48	Oakland, CA	1.27
58	Cleveland, OH	(1.36)	76	Oklahoma City, OK	(6.75)
93	Colorado Springs, CO	(15.53)	3	Orlando, FL	33.09
1	Columbus, GA	41.92	47	Philadelphia, PA	1.51
21	Columbus, OH	7.77	30	Phoenix, AZ	5.32
61	Corpus Christi, TX	(1.47)	72	Pittsburgh, PA	(5.49)
99	Dallas, TX	(21.86)	90	Portland, OR	(13.58)
92	Dayton, OH	(14.84)	91	Raleigh, NC	(14.13)
42	Denver, CO	2.08	18	Richmond, VA	10.23
37	Des Moines, IA	3.98	22	Riverside, CA	7.49
11	Detroit, MI	14.09	25	Rochester, NY	6.55
73	El Paso, TX	(6.35)	60	Sacramento, CA	(1.45)
33	Fort Wayne, IN	4.34	94	San Antonio, TX	(15.61)
98	Fort Worth, TX	(20.84)	96	San Bernardino, CA	(17.44)
56	Fremont, CA	(0.80)	89	San Diego, CA	(13.27)
84	Fresno, CA	(10.03)	35	San Francisco, CA	4.15
88	Garland, TX	(12.62)	68	San Jose, CA	(3.43)
57	Glendale, CA	(0.95)	52	Santa Ana, CA	(0.26)
19	Grand Rapids, MI	9.60	28	Seattle, WA	6.28
13	Greensboro, NC	13.04	12	Shreveport, LA	13.79
24	Honolulu, HI	7.09	80	Spokane, WA	(7.60)
–	Houston, TX**	NA	50	Stockton, CA	0.09
81	Huntington Beach, CA	(7.73)	4	St. Louis, MO	31.13
5	Indianapolis, IN	24.10	9	St. Paul, MN	17.46
7	Jackson, MS	21.55	77	St. Petersburg, FL	(7.01)
62	Jacksonville, FL	(1.52)	54	Tacoma, WA	(0.39)
67	Jersey City, NJ	(3.22)	51	Tampa, FL	(0.09)
86	Kansas City, MO	(12.28)	23	Toledo, OH	7.34
74	Las Vegas, NV	(6.41)	83	Tucson, AZ	(8.39)
38	Lexington, KY	3.85	95	Tulsa, OK	(15.69)
82	Lincoln, NE	(7.90)	59	Virginia Beach, VA	(1.39)
78	Little Rock, AR	(7.04)	66	Washington, DC	(2.87)
34	Long Beach, CA	4.25	65	Wichita, KS	(2.11)
53	Los Angeles, CA	(0.28)	10	Yonkers, NY	14.93

Source: Morgan Quitno Corporation using data from U.S. Department of Justice, Federal Bureau of Investigation "Crime in the United States 1993" (Uniform Crime Reports, December 4, 1994)
Robbery is the taking or attempting to take anything of value by force or threat of force.
**Not available.*

59. Percent Change in Robbery Rate: 1992 to 1993 (continued)

National Percent Change = 3.0% Decrease*

RANK	CITY	% CHANGE		RANK	CITY	% CHANGE
1	Columbus, GA	41.92		51	Tampa, FL	(0.09)
2	Mesa, AZ	37.49		52	Santa Ana, CA	(0.26)
3	Orlando, FL	33.09		53	Los Angeles, CA	(0.28)
4	St. Louis, MO	31.13		54	New Orleans, LA	(0.39)
5	Indianapolis,IN	24.10		54	Tacoma, WA	(0.39)
6	Norfolk, VA	22.88		56	Fremont, CA	(0.80)
7	Jackson, MS	21.55		57	Glendale, CA	(0.95)
8	Baton Rouge, LA	18.59		58	Cleveland, OH	(1.36)
9	St. Paul, MN	17.46		59	Virginia Beach, VA	(1.39)
10	Yonkers, NY	14.93		60	Sacramento, CA	(1.45)
11	Detroit, MI	14.09		61	Corpus Christi, TX	(1.47)
12	Shreveport, LA	13.79		62	Jacksonville, FL	(1.52)
13	Greensboro, NC	13.04		63	Buffalo, NY	(1.66)
14	Anchorage, AK	13.02		64	Mobile, AL	(1.81)
15	Louisville, KY	12.56		65	Wichita, KS	(2.11)
16	Newark, NJ	12.43		66	Washington, DC	(2.87)
17	Madison, WI	11.85		67	Jersey City, NJ	(3.22)
18	Richmond, VA	10.23		68	San Jose, CA	(3.43)
19	Grand Rapids, MI	9.60		69	Milwaukee, WI	(4.23)
20	Newport News, VA	8.06		70	Arlington, TX	(5.29)
21	Columbus, OH	7.77		71	New York, NY	(5.38)
22	Riverside, CA	7.49		72	Pittsburgh, PA	(5.49)
23	Toledo, OH	7.34		73	El Paso, TX	(6.35)
24	Honolulu, HI	7.09		74	Las Vegas, NV	(6.41)
25	Rochester, NY	6.55		75	Birmingham, AL	(6.74)
26	Minneapolis, MN	6.37		76	Oklahoma City, OK	(6.75)
27	Bakersfield, CA	6.33		77	St. Petersburg, FL	(7.01)
28	Seattle, WA	6.28		78	Chicago, IL	(7.04)
29	Atlanta, GA	5.86		78	Little Rock, AR	(7.04)
30	Phoenix, AZ	5.32		80	Spokane, WA	(7.60)
31	Albuquerque, NM	4.73		81	Huntington Beach, CA	(7.73)
32	Aurora, CO	4.46		82	Lincoln, NE	(7.90)
33	Fort Wayne, IN	4.34		83	Tucson, AZ	(8.39)
34	Long Beach, CA	4.25		84	Fresno, CA	(10.03)
35	San Francisco, CA	4.15		85	Boston, MA	(11.42)
36	Baltimore, MD	4.03		86	Kansas City, MO	(12.28)
37	Des Moines, IA	3.98		87	Akron, OH	(12.47)
38	Lexington, KY	3.85		88	Garland, TX	(12.62)
39	Austin, TX	3.37		89	San Diego, CA	(13.27)
40	Montgomery, AL	3.10		90	Portland, OR	(13.58)
41	Cincinnati, OH	2.30		91	Raleigh, NC	(14.13)
42	Denver, CO	2.08		92	Dayton, OH	(14.84)
43	Memphis, TN	2.07		93	Colorado Springs, CO	(15.53)
44	Charlotte, NC	2.05		94	San Antonio, TX	(15.61)
45	Anaheim, CA	1.86		95	Tulsa, OK	(15.69)
46	Nashville, TN	1.76		96	San Bernardino, CA	(17.44)
47	Philadelphia, PA	1.51		97	Lubbock, TX	(19.08)
48	Oakland, CA	1.27		98	Fort Worth, TX	(20.84)
49	Miami, FL	0.58		99	Dallas, TX	(21.86)
50	Stockton, CA	0.09		-	Houston, TX**	NA

Source: Morgan Quitno Corporation using data from U.S. Department of Justice, Federal Bureau of Investigation "Crime in the United States 1993" (Uniform Crime Reports, December 4, 1994)
*Robbery is the taking or attempting to take anything of value by force or threat of force.
**Not available.

60. Percent Change in Robbery Rate: 1989 to 1993

National Percent Change = 9.8% Increase*

RANK	CITY	% CHANGE	RANK	CITY	% CHANGE
60	Akron, OH	11.53	46	Louisville, KY	20.24
30	Albuquerque, NM	42.10	71	Lubbock, TX	4.25
64	Anaheim, CA	9.28	26	Madison, WI	44.99
5	Anchorage, AK	85.96	22	Memphis, TN	49.29
54	Arlington, TX	18.78	6	Mesa, AZ	80.67
84	Atlanta, GA	(5.84)	79	Miami, FL	(0.58)
8	Aurora, CO	74.48	15	Milwaukee, WI	60.61
28	Austin, TX	42.52	48	Minneapolis, MN	19.64
91	Bakersfield, CA	(20.39)	27	Mobile, AL	43.61
14	Baltimore, MD	61.76	4	Montgomery, AL	89.08
1	Baton Rouge, LA	165.08	13	Nashville, TN	64.45
78	Birmingham, AL	(0.08)	75	New Orleans, LA	2.19
95	Boston, MA	(27.14)	85	New York, NY	(7.62)
19	Buffalo, NY	53.28	39	Newark, NJ	29.02
47	Charlotte, NC	20.02	3	Newport News, VA	128.29
51	Chicago, IL	19.35	11	Norfolk, VA	69.46
12	Cincinnati, OH	65.48	31	Oakland, CA	37.39
62	Cleveland, OH	10.05	77	Oklahoma City, OK	0.69
70	Colorado Springs, CO	4.50	89	Orlando, FL	(15.62)
65	Columbus, GA	8.22	49	Philadelphia, PA	19.37
63	Columbus, OH	9.96	52	Phoenix, AZ	19.13
88	Corpus Christi, TX	(13.44)	56	Pittsburgh, PA	15.10
94	Dallas, TX	(24.90)	90	Portland, OR	(19.11)
80	Dayton, OH	(1.91)	7	Raleigh, NC	76.61
24	Denver, CO	45.90	20	Richmond, VA	53.15
93	Des Moines, IA	(24.51)	34	Riverside, CA	35.16
55	Detroit, MI	16.38	32	Rochester, NY	36.79
40	El Paso, TX	27.43	41	Sacramento, CA	25.38
69	Fort Wayne, IN	4.52	67	San Antonio, TX	5.92
76	Fort Worth, TX	1.26	-	San Bernardino, CA**	NA
37	Fremont, CA	30.02	42	San Diego, CA	22.80
16	Fresno, CA	56.61	10	San Francisco, CA	72.26
18	Garland, TX	53.68	59	San Jose, CA	11.58
44	Glendale, CA	20.76	29	Santa Ana, CA	42.12
33	Grand Rapids, MI	36.08	68	Seattle, WA	5.61
49	Greensboro, NC	19.37	61	Shreveport, LA	10.46
38	Honolulu, HI	29.06	87	Spokane, WA	(12.08)
-	Houston, TX**	NA	57	Stockton, CA	14.43
53	Huntington Beach, CA	19.05	17	St. Louis, MO	54.33
25	Indianapolis,IN	45.46	66	St. Paul, MN	7.65
2	Jackson, MS	136.29	96	St. Petersburg, FL	(28.06)
86	Jacksonville, FL	(10.92)	97	Tacoma, WA	(28.11)
74	Jersey City, NJ	2.59	83	Tampa, FL	(5.29)
73	Kansas City, MO	2.93	72	Toledo, OH	4.04
36	Las Vegas, NV	30.48	-	Tucson, AZ**	NA
23	Lexington, KY	47.36	92	Tulsa, OK	(21.86)
43	Lincoln, NE	22.33	9	Virginia Beach, VA	73.46
81	Little Rock, AR	(1.99)	58	Washington, DC	13.55
82	Long Beach, CA	(5.06)	34	Wichita, KS	35.16
45	Los Angeles, CA	20.73	21	Yonkers, NY	50.59

Source: Morgan Quitno Corporation using data from U.S. Department of Justice, Federal Bureau of Investigation
"Crime in the United States 1993" (Uniform Crime Reports, December 4, 1994)
*Robbery is the taking or attempting to take anything of value by force or threat of force.
**Not available.

60. Percent Change in Robbery Rate: 1989 to 1993 (continued)

National Percent Change = 9.8% Increase*

RANK	CITY	% CHANGE	RANK	CITY	% CHANGE
1	Baton Rouge, LA	165.08	51	Chicago, IL	19.35
2	Jackson, MS	136.29	52	Phoenix, AZ	19.13
3	Newport News, VA	128.29	53	Huntington Beach, CA	19.05
4	Montgomery, AL	89.08	54	Arlington, TX	18.78
5	Anchorage, AK	85.96	55	Detroit, MI	16.38
6	Mesa, AZ	80.67	56	Pittsburgh, PA	15.10
7	Raleigh, NC	76.61	57	Stockton, CA	14.43
8	Aurora, CO	74.48	58	Washington, DC	13.55
9	Virginia Beach, VA	73.46	59	San Jose, CA	11.58
10	San Francisco, CA	72.26	60	Akron, OH	11.53
11	Norfolk, VA	69.46	61	Shreveport, LA	10.46
12	Cincinnati, OH	65.48	62	Cleveland, OH	10.05
13	Nashville, TN	64.45	63	Columbus, OH	9.96
14	Baltimore, MD	61.76	64	Anaheim, CA	9.28
15	Milwaukee, WI	60.61	65	Columbus, GA	8.22
16	Fresno, CA	56.61	66	St. Paul, MN	7.65
17	St. Louis, MO	54.33	67	San Antonio, TX	5.92
18	Garland, TX	53.68	68	Seattle, WA	5.61
19	Buffalo, NY	53.28	69	Fort Wayne, IN	4.52
20	Richmond, VA	53.15	70	Colorado Springs, CO	4.50
21	Yonkers, NY	50.59	71	Lubbock, TX	4.25
22	Memphis, TN	49.29	72	Toledo, OH	4.04
23	Lexington, KY	47.36	73	Kansas City, MO	2.93
24	Denver, CO	45.90	74	Jersey City, NJ	2.59
25	Indianapolis, IN	45.46	75	New Orleans, LA	2.19
26	Madison, WI	44.99	76	Fort Worth, TX	1.26
27	Mobile, AL	43.61	77	Oklahoma City, OK	0.69
28	Austin, TX	42.52	78	Birmingham, AL	(0.08)
29	Santa Ana, CA	42.12	79	Miami, FL	(0.58)
30	Albuquerque, NM	42.10	80	Dayton, OH	(1.91)
31	Oakland, CA	37.39	81	Little Rock, AR	(1.99)
32	Rochester, NY	36.79	82	Long Beach, CA	(5.06)
33	Grand Rapids, MI	36.08	83	Tampa, FL	(5.29)
34	Riverside, CA	35.16	84	Atlanta, GA	(5.84)
34	Wichita, KS	35.16	85	New York, NY	(7.62)
36	Las Vegas, NV	30.48	86	Jacksonville, FL	(10.92)
37	Fremont, CA	30.02	87	Spokane, WA	(12.08)
38	Honolulu, HI	29.06	88	Corpus Christi, TX	(13.44)
39	Newark, NJ	29.02	89	Orlando, FL	(15.62)
40	El Paso, TX	27.43	90	Portland, OR	(19.11)
41	Sacramento, CA	25.38	91	Bakersfield, CA	(20.39)
42	San Diego, CA	22.80	92	Tulsa, OK	(21.86)
43	Lincoln, NE	22.33	93	Des Moines, IA	(24.51)
44	Glendale, CA	20.76	94	Dallas, TX	(24.90)
45	Los Angeles, CA	20.73	95	Boston, MA	(27.14)
46	Louisville, KY	20.24	96	St. Petersburg, FL	(28.06)
47	Charlotte, NC	20.02	97	Tacoma, WA	(28.11)
48	Minneapolis, MN	19.64	-	Houston, TX**	NA
49	Greensboro, NC	19.37	-	San Bernardino, CA**	NA
49	Philadelphia, PA	19.37	-	Tucson, AZ**	NA

Source: Morgan Quitno Corporation using data from U.S. Department of Justice, Federal Bureau of Investigation
"Crime in the United States 1993" (Uniform Crime Reports, December 4, 1994)
*Robbery is the taking or attempting to take anything of value by force or threat of force.
**Not available.

Alpha Order – City

61. Aggravated Assaults in 1993

National Total = 1,135,099 Aggravated Assaults*

RANK	CITY	ASSAULTS	RANK	CITY	ASSAULTS
–	Akron, OH**	NA	71	Louisville, KY	1,159
21	Albuquerque, NM	4,835	86	Lubbock, TX	840
–	Anaheim, CA**	NA	96	Madison, WI	214
65	Anchorage, AK	1,410	32	Memphis, TN	3,824
66	Arlington, TX	1,396	56	Mesa, AZ	1,808
5	Atlanta, GA	9,541	12	Miami, FL	7,089
37	Aurora, CO	3,532	63	Milwaukee, WI	1,411
73	Austin, TX	1,148	49	Minneapolis, MN	2,727
69	Bakersfield, CA	1,237	84	Mobile, AL	870
8	Baltimore, MD	8,548	81	Montgomery, AL	1,007
23	Baton Rouge, LA	4,705	19	Nashville, TN	5,791
24	Birmingham, AL	4,554	30	New Orleans, LA	4,152
16	Boston, MA	6,184	1	New York, NY	62,778
48	Buffalo, NY	2,772	31	Newark, NJ	3,977
18	Charlotte, NC	6,020	68	Newport News, VA	1,334
3	Chicago, IL	39,753	79	Norfolk, VA	1,075
47	Cincinnati, OH	2,806	22	Oakland, CA	4,743
43	Cleveland, OH	3,012	29	Oklahoma City, OK	4,161
83	Colorado Springs, CO	882	46	Orlando, FL	2,809
90	Columbus, GA	631	14	Philadelphia, PA	6,821
51	Columbus, OH	2,496	11	Phoenix, AZ	7,872
60	Corpus Christi, TX	1,488	67	Pittsburgh, PA	1,389
6	Dallas, TX	9,439	20	Portland, OR	5,603
74	Dayton, OH	1,129	75	Raleigh, NC	1,114
45	Denver, CO	2,922	63	Richmond, VA	1,411
91	Des Moines, IA	538	50	Riverside, CA	2,524
4	Detroit, MI	12,999	85	Rochester, NY	843
28	El Paso, TX	4,220	53	Sacramento, CA	2,288
94	Fort Wayne, IN	317	44	San Antonio, TX	2,973
36	Fort Worth, TX	3,589	33	San Bernardino, CA	3,805
88	Fremont, CA	714	9	San Diego, CA	8,283
52	Fresno, CA	2,329	26	San Francisco, CA	4,421
–	Garland, TX**	NA	34	San Jose, CA	3,699
95	Glendale, CA	277	72	Santa Ana, CA	1,149
57	Grand Rapids, MI	1,793	27	Seattle, WA	4,344
87	Greensboro, NC	797	59	Shreveport, LA	1,552
77	Honolulu, HI	1,099	78	Spokane, WA	1,079
–	Houston, TX**	NA	58	Stockton, CA	1,744
89	Huntington Beach, CA	662	10	St. Louis, MO	8,189
35	Indianapolis, IN	3,657	61	St. Paul, MN	1,486
80	Jackson, MS	1,019	39	St. Petersburg, FL	3,379
13	Jacksonville, FL	6,989	54	Tacoma, WA	2,204
55	Jersey City, NJ	1,964	17	Tampa, FL	6,124
15	Kansas City, MO	6,402	70	Toledo, OH	1,195
40	Las Vegas, NV	3,183	41	Tucson, AZ	3,111
62	Lexington, KY	1,455	38	Tulsa, OK	3,385
82	Lincoln, NE	911	93	Virginia Beach, VA	414
25	Little Rock, AR	4,468	7	Washington, DC	9,003
42	Long Beach, CA	3,073	76	Wichita, KS	1,103
2	Los Angeles, CA	42,437	92	Yonkers, NY	446

Source: U.S. Department of Justice, Federal Bureau of Investigation
"Crime in the United States 1993" (Uniform Crime Reports, December 4, 1994)
*Aggravated assault is an attack for the purpose of inflicting severe bodily injury.
**Not available.

61. Aggravated Assaults in 1993 (continued)

National Total = 1,135,099 Aggravated Assaults*

RANK	CITY	ASSAULTS	RANK	CITY	ASSAULTS
1	New York, NY	62,778	51	Columbus, OH	2,496
2	Los Angeles, CA	42,437	52	Fresno, CA	2,329
3	Chicago, IL	39,753	53	Sacramento, CA	2,288
4	Detroit, MI	12,999	54	Tacoma, WA	2,204
5	Atlanta, GA	9,541	55	Jersey City, NJ	1,964
6	Dallas, TX	9,439	56	Mesa, AZ	1,808
7	Washington, DC	9,003	57	Grand Rapids, MI	1,793
8	Baltimore, MD	8,548	58	Stockton, CA	1,744
9	San Diego, CA	8,283	59	Shreveport, LA	1,552
10	St. Louis, MO	8,189	60	Corpus Christi, TX	1,488
11	Phoenix, AZ	7,872	61	St. Paul, MN	1,486
12	Miami, FL	7,089	62	Lexington, KY	1,455
13	Jacksonville, FL	6,989	63	Milwaukee, WI	1,411
14	Philadelphia, PA	6,821	63	Richmond, VA	1,411
15	Kansas City, MO	6,402	65	Anchorage, AK	1,410
16	Boston, MA	6,184	66	Arlington, TX	1,396
17	Tampa, FL	6,124	67	Pittsburgh, PA	1,389
18	Charlotte, NC	6,020	68	Newport News, VA	1,334
19	Nashville, TN	5,791	69	Bakersfield, CA	1,237
20	Portland, OR	5,603	70	Toledo, OH	1,195
21	Albuquerque, NM	4,835	71	Louisville, KY	1,159
22	Oakland, CA	4,743	72	Santa Ana, CA	1,149
23	Baton Rouge, LA	4,705	73	Austin, TX	1,148
24	Birmingham, AL	4,554	74	Dayton, OH	1,129
25	Little Rock, AR	4,468	75	Raleigh, NC	1,114
26	San Francisco, CA	4,421	76	Wichita, KS	1,103
27	Seattle, WA	4,344	77	Honolulu, HI	1,099
28	El Paso, TX	4,220	78	Spokane, WA	1,079
29	Oklahoma City, OK	4,161	79	Norfolk, VA	1,075
30	New Orleans, LA	4,152	80	Jackson, MS	1,019
31	Newark, NJ	3,977	81	Montgomery, AL	1,007
32	Memphis, TN	3,824	82	Lincoln, NE	911
33	San Bernardino, CA	3,805	83	Colorado Springs, CO	882
34	San Jose, CA	3,699	84	Mobile, AL	870
35	Indianapolis,IN	3,657	85	Rochester, NY	843
36	Fort Worth, TX	3,589	86	Lubbock, TX	840
37	Aurora, CO	3,532	87	Greensboro, NC	797
38	Tulsa, OK	3,385	88	Fremont, CA	714
39	St. Petersburg, FL	3,379	89	Huntington Beach, CA	662
40	Las Vegas, NV	3,183	90	Columbus, GA	631
41	Tucson, AZ	3,111	91	Des Moines, IA	538
42	Long Beach, CA	3,073	92	Yonkers, NY	446
43	Cleveland, OH	3,012	93	Virginia Beach, VA	414
44	San Antonio, TX	2,973	94	Fort Wayne, IN	317
45	Denver, CO	2,922	95	Glendale, CA	277
46	Orlando, FL	2,809	96	Madison, WI	214
47	Cincinnati, OH	2,806	-	Akron, OH**	NA
48	Buffalo, NY	2,772	-	Anaheim, CA**	NA
49	Minneapolis, MN	2,727	-	Garland, TX**	NA
50	Riverside, CA	2,524	-	Houston, TX**	NA

Source: U.S. Department of Justice, Federal Bureau of Investigation
"Crime in the United States 1993" (Uniform Crime Reports, December 4, 1994)
*Aggravated assault is an attack for the purpose of inflicting severe bodily injury.
**Not available.

62. Aggravated Assault Rate in 1993

National Rate = 440.1 Aggravated Assaults per 100,000 Population*

RANK	CITY	RATE	RANK	CITY	RATE
-	Akron, OH**	NA	74	Louisville, KY	423.7
21	Albuquerque, NM	1,187.1	71	Lubbock, TX	438.3
-	Anaheim, CA**	NA	95	Madison, WI	108.7
61	Anchorage, AK	562.4	52	Memphis, TN	617.8
67	Arlington, TX	496.2	57	Mesa, AZ	593.4
2	Atlanta, GA	2,368.2	7	Miami, FL	1,903.0
13	Aurora, CO	1,432.2	91	Milwaukee, WI	226.4
90	Austin, TX	228.7	44	Minneapolis, MN	743.8
50	Bakersfield, CA	651.4	73	Mobile, AL	425.9
23	Baltimore, MD	1,166.2	64	Montgomery, AL	518.0
6	Baton Rouge, LA	2,086.1	24	Nashville, TN	1,127.4
8	Birmingham, AL	1,694.4	36	New Orleans, LA	844.6
25	Boston, MA	1,116.5	33	New York, NY	854.4
34	Buffalo, NY	853.3	11	Newark, NJ	1,473.6
15	Charlotte, NC	1,423.6	45	Newport News, VA	741.2
14	Chicago, IL	1,425.4	75	Norfolk, VA	417.3
41	Cincinnati, OH	765.4	18	Oakland, CA	1,258.0
56	Cleveland, OH	595.6	30	Oklahoma City, OK	909.6
87	Colorado Springs, CO	289.7	9	Orlando, FL	1,589.3
85	Columbus, GA	331.5	72	Philadelphia, PA	437.4
79	Columbus, OH	385.8	43	Phoenix, AZ	757.4
62	Corpus Christi, TX	547.9	80	Pittsburgh, PA	377.0
31	Dallas, TX	905.3	19	Portland, OR	1,231.7
54	Dayton, OH	612.4	66	Raleigh, NC	497.2
59	Denver, CO	586.3	49	Richmond, VA	687.2
88	Des Moines, IA	275.2	26	Riverside, CA	1,047.1
17	Detroit, MI	1,274.3	82	Rochester, NY	358.3
42	El Paso, TX	761.0	58	Sacramento, CA	591.6
92	Fort Wayne, IN	180.7	86	San Antonio, TX	301.7
40	Fort Worth, TX	774.5	3	San Bernardino, CA	2,184.1
78	Fremont, CA	394.2	47	San Diego, CA	713.7
53	Fresno, CA	612.9	55	San Francisco, CA	600.4
-	Garland, TX**	NA	69	San Jose, CA	456.9
93	Glendale, CA	154.3	77	Santa Ana, CA	396.1
29	Grand Rapids, MI	933.3	37	Seattle, WA	817.7
76	Greensboro, NC	413.1	38	Shreveport, LA	786.3
94	Honolulu, HI	125.5	60	Spokane, WA	563.4
-	Houston, TX**	NA	39	Stockton, CA	786.1
83	Huntington Beach, CA	354.1	5	St. Louis, MO	2,115.7
28	Indianapolis, IN	968.2	62	St. Paul, MN	547.9
65	Jackson, MS	514.1	16	St. Petersburg, FL	1,415.4
27	Jacksonville, FL	1,039.6	22	Tacoma, WA	1,173.0
35	Jersey City, NJ	852.8	4	Tampa, FL	2,119.9
12	Kansas City, MO	1,470.3	81	Toledo, OH	360.6
70	Las Vegas, NV	443.7	46	Tucson, AZ	729.7
51	Lexington, KY	618.9	32	Tulsa, OK	894.7
68	Lincoln, NE	459.6	96	Virginia Beach, VA	97.8
1	Little Rock, AR	2,497.1	10	Washington, DC	1,557.6
48	Long Beach, CA	693.3	84	Wichita, KS	351.7
20	Los Angeles, CA	1,203.8	89	Yonkers, NY	238.5

Source: U.S. Department of Justice, Federal Bureau of Investigation
   "Crime in the United States 1993" (Uniform Crime Reports, December 4, 1994)
*Aggravated assault is an attack for the purpose of inflicting severe bodily injury.
**Not available.

62. Aggravated Assault Rate in 1993 (continued)

National Rate = 440.1 Aggravated Assaults per 100,000 Population*

RANK	CITY	RATE	RANK	CITY	RATE
1	Little Rock, AR	2,497.1	51	Lexington, KY	618.9
2	Atlanta, GA	2,368.2	52	Memphis, TN	617.8
3	San Bernardino, CA	2,184.1	53	Fresno, CA	612.9
4	Tampa, FL	2,119.9	54	Dayton, OH	612.4
5	St. Louis, MO	2,115.7	55	San Francisco, CA	600.4
6	Baton Rouge, LA	2,086.1	56	Cleveland, OH	595.6
7	Miami, FL	1,903.0	57	Mesa, AZ	593.4
8	Birmingham, AL	1,694.4	58	Sacramento, CA	591.6
9	Orlando, FL	1,589.3	59	Denver, CO	586.3
10	Washington, DC	1,557.6	60	Spokane, WA	563.4
11	Newark, NJ	1,473.6	61	Anchorage, AK	562.4
12	Kansas City, MO	1,470.3	62	Corpus Christi, TX	547.9
13	Aurora, CO	1,432.2	62	St. Paul, MN	547.9
14	Chicago, IL	1,425.4	64	Montgomery, AL	518.0
15	Charlotte, NC	1,423.6	65	Jackson, MS	514.1
16	St. Petersburg, FL	1,415.4	66	Raleigh, NC	497.2
17	Detroit, MI	1,274.3	67	Arlington, TX	496.2
18	Oakland, CA	1,258.0	68	Lincoln, NE	459.6
19	Portland, OR	1,231.7	69	San Jose, CA	456.9
20	Los Angeles, CA	1,203.8	70	Las Vegas, NV	443.7
21	Albuquerque, NM	1,187.1	71	Lubbock, TX	438.3
22	Tacoma, WA	1,173.0	72	Philadelphia, PA	437.4
23	Baltimore, MD	1,166.2	73	Mobile, AL	425.9
24	Nashville, TN	1,127.4	74	Louisville, KY	423.7
25	Boston, MA	1,116.5	75	Norfolk, VA	417.3
26	Riverside, CA	1,047.1	76	Greensboro, NC	413.1
27	Jacksonville, FL	1,039.6	77	Santa Ana, CA	396.1
28	Indianapolis, IN	968.2	78	Fremont, CA	394.2
29	Grand Rapids, MI	933.3	79	Columbus, OH	385.8
30	Oklahoma City, OK	909.6	80	Pittsburgh, PA	377.0
31	Dallas, TX	905.3	81	Toledo, OH	360.6
32	Tulsa, OK	894.7	82	Rochester, NY	358.3
33	New York, NY	854.4	83	Huntington Beach, CA	354.1
34	Buffalo, NY	853.3	84	Wichita, KS	351.7
35	Jersey City, NJ	852.8	85	Columbus, GA	331.5
36	New Orleans, LA	844.6	86	San Antonio, TX	301.7
37	Seattle, WA	817.7	87	Colorado Springs, CO	289.7
38	Shreveport, LA	786.3	88	Des Moines, IA	275.2
39	Stockton, CA	786.1	89	Yonkers, NY	238.5
40	Fort Worth, TX	774.5	90	Austin, TX	228.7
41	Cincinnati, OH	765.4	91	Milwaukee, WI	226.4
42	El Paso, TX	761.0	92	Fort Wayne, IN	180.7
43	Phoenix, AZ	757.4	93	Glendale, CA	154.3
44	Minneapolis, MN	743.8	94	Honolulu, HI	125.5
45	Newport News, VA	741.2	95	Madison, WI	108.7
46	Tucson, AZ	729.7	96	Virginia Beach, VA	97.8
47	San Diego, CA	713.7	–	Akron, OH**	NA
48	Long Beach, CA	693.3	–	Anaheim, CA**	NA
49	Richmond, VA	687.2	–	Garland, TX**	NA
50	Bakersfield, CA	651.4	–	Houston, TX**	NA

Source: U.S. Department of Justice, Federal Bureau of Investigation
    "Crime in the United States 1993" (Uniform Crime Reports, December 4, 1994)
Aggravated assault is an attack for the purpose of inflicting severe bodily injury.
**Not available.*

63. Percent Change in Aggravated Assault Rate: 1992 to 1993

National Percent Change = 0.4% Decrease*

RANK	CITY	% CHANGE	RANK	CITY	% CHANGE
-	Akron, OH**	NA	93	Louisville, KY	(25.82)
30	Albuquerque, NM	8.95	7	Lubbock, TX	21.35
-	Anaheim, CA**	NA	95	Madison, WI	(38.86)
20	Anchorage, AK	11.63	29	Memphis, TN	9.17
12	Arlington, TX	15.48	26	Mesa, AZ	9.58
42	Atlanta, GA	5.69	24	Miami, FL	9.77
46	Aurora, CO	4.90	25	Milwaukee, WI	9.64
53	Austin, TX	3.53	13	Minneapolis, MN	13.91
38	Bakersfield, CA	6.89	96	Mobile, AL	(85.16)
49	Baltimore, MD	4.25	4	Montgomery, AL	24.64
11	Baton Rouge, LA	15.62	18	Nashville, TN	13.22
6	Birmingham, AL	21.63	51	New Orleans, LA	4.03
57	Boston, MA	1.56	63	New York, NY	(0.81)
78	Buffalo, NY	(4.32)	50	Newark, NJ	4.17
68	Charlotte, NC	(1.96)	17	Newport News, VA	13.25
66	Chicago, IL	(1.70)	70	Norfolk, VA	(2.52)
79	Cincinnati, OH	(4.53)	67	Oakland, CA	(1.82)
65	Cleveland, OH	(1.28)	52	Oklahoma City, OK	3.59
59	Colorado Springs, CO	0.80	8	Orlando, FL	20.16
3	Columbus, GA	29.85	15	Philadelphia, PA	13.49
82	Columbus, OH	(6.27)	41	Phoenix, AZ	5.84
92	Corpus Christi, TX	(21.93)	14	Pittsburgh, PA	13.55
89	Dallas, TX	(11.18)	28	Portland, OR	9.21
88	Dayton, OH	(10.49)	84	Raleigh, NC	(6.79)
71	Denver, CO	(2.64)	40	Richmond, VA	6.07
91	Des Moines, IA	(12.27)	19	Riverside, CA	13.20
37	Detroit, MI	7.01	35	Rochester, NY	7.31
47	El Paso, TX	4.52	27	Sacramento, CA	9.49
39	Fort Wayne, IN	6.48	48	San Antonio, TX	4.39
94	Fort Worth, TX	(31.05)	62	San Bernardino, CA	(0.78)
1	Fremont, CA	59.27	85	San Diego, CA	(7.01)
16	Fresno, CA	13.44	86	San Francisco, CA	(7.73)
-	Garland, TX**	NA	61	San Jose, CA	0.04
73	Glendale, CA	(3.32)	32	Santa Ana, CA	8.34
77	Grand Rapids, MI	(3.55)	55	Seattle, WA	2.74
74	Greensboro, NC	(3.37)	60	Shreveport, LA	0.61
31	Honolulu, HI	8.56	75	Spokane, WA	(3.53)
-	Houston, TX**	NA	34	Stockton, CA	7.76
21	Huntington Beach, CA	11.28	23	St. Louis, MO	10.17
9	Indianapolis, IN	18.58	58	St. Paul, MN	0.88
69	Jackson, MS	(2.28)	81	St. Petersburg, FL	(5.95)
72	Jacksonville, FL	(2.76)	44	Tacoma, WA	5.45
45	Jersey City, NJ	5.01	80	Tampa, FL	(4.98)
90	Kansas City, MO	(12.18)	64	Toledo, OH	(1.04)
2	Las Vegas, NV	56.29	43	Tucson, AZ	5.59
22	Lexington, KY	10.78	54	Tulsa, OK	2.84
87	Lincoln, NE	(8.48)	33	Virginia Beach, VA	7.95
10	Little Rock, AR	18.11	36	Washington, DC	7.10
56	Long Beach, CA	2.26	76	Wichita, KS	(3.54)
83	Los Angeles, CA	(6.30)	5	Yonkers, NY	22.75

Source: Morgan Quitno Corporation using data from U.S. Department of Justice, Federal Bureau of Investigation
"Crime in the United States 1993" (Uniform Crime Reports, December 4, 1994)
*Aggravated assault is an attack for the purpose of inflicting severe bodily injury.
**Not available.

63. Percent Change in Aggravated Assault Rate: 1992 to 1993 (continued)

National Percent Change = 0.4% Decrease*

RANK	CITY	% CHANGE	RANK	CITY	% CHANGE
1	Fremont, CA	59.27	51	New Orleans, LA	4.03
2	Las Vegas, NV	56.29	52	Oklahoma City, OK	3.59
3	Columbus, GA	29.85	53	Austin, TX	3.53
4	Montgomery, AL	24.64	54	Tulsa, OK	2.84
5	Yonkers, NY	22.75	55	Seattle, WA	2.74
6	Birmingham, AL	21.63	56	Long Beach, CA	2.26
7	Lubbock, TX	21.35	57	Boston, MA	1.56
8	Orlando, FL	20.16	58	St. Paul, MN	0.88
9	Indianapolis,IN	18.58	59	Colorado Springs, CO	0.80
10	Little Rock, AR	18.11	60	Shreveport, LA	0.61
11	Baton Rouge, LA	15.62	61	San Jose, CA	0.04
12	Arlington, TX	15.48	62	San Bernardino, CA	(0.78)
13	Minneapolis, MN	13.91	63	New York, NY	(0.81)
14	Pittsburgh, PA	13.55	64	Toledo, OH	(1.04)
15	Philadelphia, PA	13.49	65	Cleveland, OH	(1.28)
16	Fresno, CA	13.44	66	Chicago, IL	(1.70)
17	Newport News, VA	13.25	67	Oakland, CA	(1.82)
18	Nashville, TN	13.22	68	Charlotte, NC	(1.96)
19	Riverside, CA	13.20	69	Jackson, MS	(2.28)
20	Anchorage, AK	11.63	70	Norfolk, VA	(2.52)
21	Huntington Beach, CA	11.28	71	Denver, CO	(2.64)
22	Lexington, KY	10.78	72	Jacksonville, FL	(2.76)
23	St. Louis, MO	10.17	73	Glendale, CA	(3.32)
24	Miami, FL	9.77	74	Greensboro, NC	(3.37)
25	Milwaukee, WI	9.64	75	Spokane, WA	(3.53)
26	Mesa, AZ	9.58	76	Wichita, KS	(3.54)
27	Sacramento, CA	9.49	77	Grand Rapids, MI	(3.55)
28	Portland, OR	9.21	78	Buffalo, NY	(4.32)
29	Memphis, TN	9.17	79	Cincinnati, OH	(4.53)
30	Albuquerque, NM	8.95	80	Tampa, FL	(4.98)
31	Honolulu, HI	8.56	81	St. Petersburg, FL	(5.95)
32	Santa Ana, CA	8.34	82	Columbus, OH	(6.27)
33	Virginia Beach, VA	7.95	83	Los Angeles, CA	(6.30)
34	Stockton, CA	7.76	84	Raleigh, NC	(6.79)
35	Rochester, NY	7.31	85	San Diego, CA	(7.01)
36	Washington, DC	7.10	86	San Francisco, CA	(7.73)
37	Detroit, MI	7.01	87	Lincoln, NE	(8.48)
38	Bakersfield, CA	6.89	88	Dayton, OH	(10.49)
39	Fort Wayne, IN	6.48	89	Dallas, TX	(11.18)
40	Richmond, VA	6.07	90	Kansas City, MO	(12.18)
41	Phoenix, AZ	5.84	91	Des Moines, IA	(12.27)
42	Atlanta, GA	5.69	92	Corpus Christi, TX	(21.93)
43	Tucson, AZ	5.59	93	Louisville, KY	(25.82)
44	Tacoma, WA	5.45	94	Fort Worth, TX	(31.05)
45	Jersey City, NJ	5.01	95	Madison, WI	(38.86)
46	Aurora, CO	4.90	96	Mobile, AL	(85.16)
47	El Paso, TX	4.52	–	Akron, OH**	NA
48	San Antonio, TX	4.39	–	Anaheim, CA**	NA
49	Baltimore, MD	4.25	–	Garland, TX**	NA
50	Newark, NJ	4.17	–	Houston, TX**	NA

Source: Morgan Quitno Corporation using data from U.S. Department of Justice, Federal Bureau of Investigation "Crime in the United States 1993" (Uniform Crime Reports, December 4, 1994)
*Aggravated assault is an attack for the purpose of inflicting severe bodily injury.
**Not available.

64. Percent Change in Aggravated Assault Rate: 1989 to 1993

National Percent Change = 14.8% Increase*

RANK	CITY	% CHANGE	RANK	CITY	% CHANGE
-	Akron, OH**	NA	74	Louisville, KY	(1.12)
31	Albuquerque, NM	32.59	22	Lubbock, TX	44.42
-	Anaheim, CA**	NA	89	Madison, WI	(20.95)
8	Anchorage, AK	77.19	45	Memphis, TN	20.90
24	Arlington, TX	43.41	16	Mesa, AZ	55.34
57	Atlanta, GA	10.76	53	Miami, FL	13.58
28	Aurora, CO	33.71	65	Milwaukee, WI	6.19
86	Austin, TX	(18.76)	56	Minneapolis, MN	10.98
80	Bakersfield, CA	(5.54)	94	Mobile, AL	(64.77)
34	Baltimore, MD	29.94	1	Montgomery, AL	257.98
14	Baton Rouge, LA	61.03	7	Nashville, TN	83.83
3	Birmingham, AL	148.45	61	New Orleans, LA	8.49
72	Boston, MA	0.09	84	New York, NY	(11.26)
52	Buffalo, NY	14.37	71	Newark, NJ	1.71
60	Charlotte, NC	8.85	4	Newport News, VA	125.29
54	Chicago, IL	13.23	44	Norfolk, VA	22.92
19	Cincinnati, OH	52.71	2	Oakland, CA	161.81
66	Cleveland, OH	6.17	10	Oklahoma City, OK	72.57
68	Colorado Springs, CO	3.28	33	Orlando, FL	29.96
15	Columbus, GA	56.52	58	Philadelphia, PA	10.12
73	Columbus, OH	(0.80)	29	Phoenix, AZ	33.58
47	Corpus Christi, TX	19.03	91	Pittsburgh, PA	(23.62)
85	Dallas, TX	(12.00)	64	Portland, OR	6.34
69	Dayton, OH	2.56	40	Raleigh, NC	25.21
21	Denver, CO	50.64	79	Richmond, VA	(5.06)
93	Des Moines, IA	(36.66)	50	Riverside, CA	16.04
46	Detroit, MI	20.36	92	Rochester, NY	(24.98)
48	El Paso, TX	18.87	51	Sacramento, CA	15.84
87	Fort Wayne, IN	(19.83)	20	San Antonio, TX	50.93
82	Fort Worth, TX	(6.69)	-	San Bernardino, CA**	NA
49	Fremont, CA	18.45	32	San Diego, CA	30.50
90	Fresno, CA	(22.35)	75	San Francisco, CA	(2.10)
-	Garland, TX**	NA	55	San Jose, CA	11.60
81	Glendale, CA	(5.80)	83	Santa Ana, CA	(8.63)
42	Grand Rapids, MI	23.22	63	Seattle, WA	7.46
88	Greensboro, NC	(20.94)	37	Shreveport, LA	27.27
67	Honolulu, HI	3.72	18	Spokane, WA	53.85
-	Houston, TX**	NA	13	Stockton, CA	61.78
12	Huntington Beach, CA	62.51	62	St. Louis, MO	7.99
30	Indianapolis, IN	32.81	70	St. Paul, MN	2.28
6	Jackson, MS	83.87	35	St. Petersburg, FL	28.11
23	Jacksonville, FL	43.75	36	Tacoma, WA	27.67
38	Jersey City, NJ	26.90	27	Tampa, FL	35.13
25	Kansas City, MO	43.11	76	Toledo, OH	(3.01)
26	Las Vegas, NV	41.94	-	Tucson, AZ**	NA
17	Lexington, KY	54.15	39	Tulsa, OK	26.30
41	Lincoln, NE	24.38	43	Virginia Beach, VA	23.17
5	Little Rock, AR	100.18	11	Washington, DC	62.91
77	Long Beach, CA	(3.92)	59	Wichita, KS	8.95
78	Los Angeles, CA	(4.46)	9	Yonkers, NY	72.95

Source: Morgan Quitno Corporation using data from U.S. Department of Justice, Federal Bureau of Investigation
   "Crime in the United States 1993" (Uniform Crime Reports, December 4, 1994)
*Aggravated assault is an attack for the purpose of inflicting severe bodily injury.
**Not available.

64. Percent Change in Aggravated Assault Rate: 1989 to 1993 (continued)

National Percent Change = 14.8% Increase*

RANK	CITY	% CHANGE	RANK	CITY	% CHANGE
1	Montgomery, AL	257.98	51	Sacramento, CA	15.84
2	Oakland, CA	161.81	52	Buffalo, NY	14.37
3	Birmingham, AL	148.45	53	Miami, FL	13.58
4	Newport News, VA	125.29	54	Chicago, IL	13.23
5	Little Rock, AR	100.18	55	San Jose, CA	11.60
6	Jackson, MS	83.87	56	Minneapolis, MN	10.98
7	Nashville, TN	83.83	57	Atlanta, GA	10.76
8	Anchorage, AK	77.19	58	Philadelphia, PA	10.12
9	Yonkers, NY	72.95	59	Wichita, KS	8.95
10	Oklahoma City, OK	72.57	60	Charlotte, NC	8.85
11	Washington, DC	62.91	61	New Orleans, LA	8.49
12	Huntington Beach, CA	62.51	62	St. Louis, MO	7.99
13	Stockton, CA	61.78	63	Seattle, WA	7.46
14	Baton Rouge, LA	61.03	64	Portland, OR	6.34
15	Columbus, GA	56.52	65	Milwaukee, WI	6.19
16	Mesa, AZ	55.34	66	Cleveland, OH	6.17
17	Lexington, KY	54.15	67	Honolulu, HI	3.72
18	Spokane, WA	53.85	68	Colorado Springs, CO	3.28
19	Cincinnati, OH	52.71	69	Dayton, OH	2.56
20	San Antonio, TX	50.93	70	St. Paul, MN	2.28
21	Denver, CO	50.64	71	Newark, NJ	1.71
22	Lubbock, TX	44.42	72	Boston, MA	0.09
23	Jacksonville, FL	43.75	73	Columbus, OH	(0.80)
24	Arlington, TX	43.41	74	Louisville, KY	(1.12)
25	Kansas City, MO	43.11	75	San Francisco, CA	(2.10)
26	Las Vegas, NV	41.94	76	Toledo, OH	(3.01)
27	Tampa, FL	35.13	77	Long Beach, CA	(3.92)
28	Aurora, CO	33.71	78	Los Angeles, CA	(4.46)
29	Phoenix, AZ	33.58	79	Richmond, VA	(5.06)
30	Indianapolis, IN	32.81	80	Bakersfield, CA	(5.54)
31	Albuquerque, NM	32.59	81	Glendale, CA	(5.80)
32	San Diego, CA	30.50	82	Fort Worth, TX	(6.69)
33	Orlando, FL	29.96	83	Santa Ana, CA	(8.63)
34	Baltimore, MD	29.94	84	New York, NY	(11.26)
35	St. Petersburg, FL	28.11	85	Dallas, TX	(12.00)
36	Tacoma, WA	27.67	86	Austin, TX	(18.76)
37	Shreveport, LA	27.27	87	Fort Wayne, IN	(19.83)
38	Jersey City, NJ	26.90	88	Greensboro, NC	(20.94)
39	Tulsa, OK	26.30	89	Madison, WI	(20.95)
40	Raleigh, NC	25.21	90	Fresno, CA	(22.35)
41	Lincoln, NE	24.38	91	Pittsburgh, PA	(23.62)
42	Grand Rapids, MI	23.22	92	Rochester, NY	(24.98)
43	Virginia Beach, VA	23.17	93	Des Moines, IA	(36.66)
44	Norfolk, VA	22.92	94	Mobile, AL	(64.77)
45	Memphis, TN	20.90	-	Akron, OH**	NA
46	Detroit, MI	20.36	-	Anaheim, CA**	NA
47	Corpus Christi, TX	19.03	-	Garland, TX**	NA
48	El Paso, TX	18.87	-	Houston, TX**	NA
49	Fremont, CA	18.45	-	San Bernardino, CA**	NA
50	Riverside, CA	16.04	-	Tucson, AZ**	NA

Source: Morgan Quitno Corporation using data from U.S. Department of Justice, Federal Bureau of Investigation "Crime in the United States 1993" (Uniform Crime Reports, December 4, 1994)
*Aggravated assault is an attack for the purpose of inflicting severe bodily injury.
**Not available.

65. Property Crimes in 1993

National Total = 12,216,764 Property Crimes*

RANK	CITY	CRIMES	RANK	CITY	CRIMES
82	Akron, OH	14,085	78	Louisville, KY	14,605
41	Albuquerque, NM	32,329	93	Lubbock, TX	11,078
74	Anaheim, CA	16,694	96	Madison, WI	9,985
83	Anchorage, AK	13,927	18	Memphis, TN	52,037
67	Arlington, TX	17,943	59	Mesa, AZ	21,811
17	Atlanta, GA	53,633	14	Miami, FL	55,326
76	Aurora, CO	15,910	27	Milwaukee, WI	44,418
22	Austin, TX	48,457	40	Minneapolis, MN	33,982
85	Bakersfield, CA	13,743	75	Mobile, AL	16,347
11	Baltimore, MD	69,975	94	Montgomery, AL	10,615
44	Baton Rouge, LA	29,705	23	Nashville, TN	46,336
52	Birmingham, AL	25,098	31	New Orleans, LA	42,749
25	Boston, MA	44,712	1	New York, NY	446,803
48	Buffalo, NY	25,830	46	Newark, NJ	28,292
34	Charlotte, NC	40,033	95	Newport News, VA	10,052
3	Chicago, IL	207,422	62	Norfolk, VA	19,440
49	Cincinnati, OH	25,302	37	Oakland, CA	35,118
42	Cleveland, OH	31,695	24	Oklahoma City, OK	44,855
66	Colorado Springs, CO	18,053	69	Orlando, FL	17,813
92	Columbus, GA	11,103	9	Philadelphia, PA	78,083
21	Columbus, OH	49,176	8	Phoenix, AZ	84,565
51	Corpus Christi, TX	25,191	55	Pittsburgh, PA	24,134
6	Dallas, TX	92,623	29	Portland, OR	43,320
73	Dayton, OH	16,715	88	Raleigh, NC	13,225
39	Denver, CO	34,544	64	Richmond, VA	18,867
79	Des Moines, IA	14,603	65	Riverside, CA	18,172
5	Detroit, MI	93,971	56	Rochester, NY	22,816
33	El Paso, TX	40,629	38	Sacramento, CA	34,635
84	Fort Wayne, IN	13,830	7	San Antonio, TX	90,946
30	Fort Worth, TX	42,822	72	San Bernardino, CA	16,746
100	Fremont, CA	6,353	10	San Diego, CA	71,764
35	Fresno, CA	36,073	12	San Francisco, CA	56,767
91	Garland, TX	11,212	43	San Jose, CA	31,426
99	Glendale, CA	7,544	77	Santa Ana, CA	15,881
89	Grand Rapids, MI	13,063	15	Seattle, WA	55,242
86	Greensboro, NC	13,583	61	Shreveport, LA	20,061
16	Honolulu, HI	53,904	80	Spokane, WA	14,394
4	Houston, TX	116,110	60	Stockton, CA	21,349
97	Huntington Beach, CA	8,245	20	St. Louis, MO	49,440
47	Indianapolis, IN	27,238	70	St. Paul, MN	17,678
57	Jackson, MS	22,728	68	St. Petersburg, FL	17,849
13	Jacksonville, FL	56,096	71	Tacoma, WA	17,605
81	Jersey City, NJ	14,176	36	Tampa, FL	35,994
28	Kansas City, MO	44,204	50	Toledo, OH	25,270
32	Las Vegas, NV	41,084	26	Tucson, AZ	44,582
87	Lexington, KY	13,481	54	Tulsa, OK	24,433
90	Lincoln, NE	12,436	63	Virginia Beach, VA	19,268
58	Little Rock, AR	22,183	19	Washington, DC	51,058
45	Long Beach, CA	28,514	53	Wichita, KS	24,994
2	Los Angeles, CA	229,088	98	Yonkers, NY	8,143

Source: U.S. Department of Justice, Federal Bureau of Investigation
"Crime in the United States 1993" (Uniform Crime Reports, December 4, 1994)
*Property crimes are offenses of burglary, larceny-theft and motor vehicle theft. They consist of taking money or property but there is no force or threat of force against victims.
**Not available.

65. Property Crimes in 1993 (continued)

National Total = 12,216,764 Property Crimes*

RANK	CITY	CRIMES	RANK	CITY	CRIMES
1	New York, NY	446,803	51	Corpus Christi, TX	25,191
2	Los Angeles, CA	229,088	52	Birmingham, AL	25,098
3	Chicago, IL	207,422	53	Wichita, KS	24,994
4	Houston, TX	116,110	54	Tulsa, OK	24,433
5	Detroit, MI	93,971	55	Pittsburgh, PA	24,134
6	Dallas, TX	92,623	56	Rochester, NY	22,816
7	San Antonio, TX	90,946	57	Jackson, MS	22,728
8	Phoenix, AZ	84,565	58	Little Rock, AR	22,183
9	Philadelphia, PA	78,083	59	Mesa, AZ	21,811
10	San Diego, CA	71,764	60	Stockton, CA	21,349
11	Baltimore, MD	69,975	61	Shreveport, LA	20,061
12	San Francisco, CA	56,767	62	Norfolk, VA	19,440
13	Jacksonville, FL	56,096	63	Virginia Beach, VA	19,268
14	Miami, FL	55,326	64	Richmond, VA	18,867
15	Seattle, WA	55,242	65	Riverside, CA	18,172
16	Honolulu, HI	53,904	66	Colorado Springs, CO	18,053
17	Atlanta, GA	53,633	67	Arlington, TX	17,943
18	Memphis, TN	52,037	68	St. Petersburg, FL	17,849
19	Washington, DC	51,058	69	Orlando, FL	17,813
20	St. Louis, MO	49,440	70	St. Paul, MN	17,678
21	Columbus, OH	49,176	71	Tacoma, WA	17,605
22	Austin, TX	48,457	72	San Bernardino, CA	16,746
23	Nashville, TN	46,336	73	Dayton, OH	16,715
24	Oklahoma City, OK	44,855	74	Anaheim, CA	16,694
25	Boston, MA	44,712	75	Mobile, AL	16,347
26	Tucson, AZ	44,582	76	Aurora, CO	15,910
27	Milwaukee, WI	44,418	77	Santa Ana, CA	15,881
28	Kansas City, MO	44,204	78	Louisville, KY	14,605
29	Portland, OR	43,320	79	Des Moines, IA	14,603
30	Fort Worth, TX	42,822	80	Spokane, WA	14,394
31	New Orleans, LA	42,749	81	Jersey City, NJ	14,176
32	Las Vegas, NV	41,084	82	Akron, OH	14,085
33	El Paso, TX	40,629	83	Anchorage, AK	13,927
34	Charlotte, NC	40,033	84	Fort Wayne, IN	13,830
35	Fresno, CA	36,073	85	Bakersfield, CA	13,743
36	Tampa, FL	35,994	86	Greensboro, NC	13,583
37	Oakland, CA	35,118	87	Lexington, KY	13,481
38	Sacramento, CA	34,635	88	Raleigh, NC	13,225
39	Denver, CO	34,544	89	Grand Rapids, MI	13,063
40	Minneapolis, MN	33,982	90	Lincoln, NE	12,436
41	Albuquerque, NM	32,329	91	Garland, TX	11,212
42	Cleveland, OH	31,695	92	Columbus, GA	11,103
43	San Jose, CA	31,426	93	Lubbock, TX	11,078
44	Baton Rouge, LA	29,705	94	Montgomery, AL	10,615
45	Long Beach, CA	28,514	95	Newport News, VA	10,052
46	Newark, NJ	28,292	96	Madison, WI	9,985
47	Indianapolis, IN	27,238	97	Huntington Beach, CA	8,245
48	Buffalo, NY	25,830	98	Yonkers, NY	8,143
49	Cincinnati, OH	25,302	99	Glendale, CA	7,544
50	Toledo, OH	25,270	100	Fremont, CA	6,353

Source: U.S. Department of Justice, Federal Bureau of Investigation
  "Crime in the United States 1993" (Uniform Crime Reports, December 4, 1994)
Property crimes are offenses of burglary, larceny-theft and motor vehicle theft. They consist of taking money
or property but there is no force or threat of force against victims.
**Not available.*

66. Property Crime Rate in 1993

National Rate = 4,736.9 Property Crimes per 100,000 Population*

RANK	CITY	RATE	RANK	CITY	RATE
75	Akron, OH	6,258.9	92	Louisville, KY	5,338.8
45	Albuquerque, NM	7,937.7	84	Lubbock, TX	5,780.7
80	Anaheim, CA	6,033.3	93	Madison, WI	5,070.6
89	Anchorage, AK	5,554.8	38	Memphis, TN	8,406.9
72	Arlington, TX	6,377.8	59	Mesa, AZ	7,158.3
2	Atlanta, GA	13,312.5	1	Miami, FL	14,851.9
70	Aurora, CO	6,451.5	60	Milwaukee, WI	7,128.4
16	Austin, TX	9,652.4	27	Minneapolis, MN	9,268.4
57	Bakersfield, CA	7,236.7	42	Mobile, AL	8,002.0
19	Baltimore, MD	9,546.8	91	Montgomery, AL	5,460.4
3	Baton Rouge, LA	13,170.4	33	Nashville, TN	9,021.0
24	Birmingham, AL	9,338.2	37	New Orleans, LA	8,695.6
41	Boston, MA	8,072.7	79	New York, NY	6,081.2
44	Buffalo, NY	7,951.2	8	Newark, NJ	10,482.7
22	Charlotte, NC	9,467.2	88	Newport News, VA	5,585.2
55	Chicago, IL	7,437.2	50	Norfolk, VA	7,546.1
63	Cincinnati, OH	6,902.0	25	Oakland, CA	9,314.2
74	Cleveland, OH	6,267.2	14	Oklahoma City, OK	9,805.5
81	Colorado Springs, CO	5,929.9	13	Orlando, FL	10,078.2
83	Columbus, GA	5,833.5	94	Philadelphia, PA	5,006.8
49	Columbus, OH	7,601.4	40	Phoenix, AZ	8,136.2
26	Corpus Christi, TX	9,276.3	66	Pittsburgh, PA	6,549.7
35	Dallas, TX	8,883.7	20	Portland, OR	9,523.2
32	Dayton, OH	9,066.9	82	Raleigh, NC	5,902.5
62	Denver, CO	6,931.0	31	Richmond, VA	9,188.6
54	Des Moines, IA	7,470.1	51	Riverside, CA	7,539.0
30	Detroit, MI	9,212.3	15	Rochester, NY	9,696.5
56	El Paso, TX	7,326.9	34	Sacramento, CA	8,955.8
46	Fort Wayne, IN	7,884.6	29	San Antonio, TX	9,228.8
28	Fort Worth, TX	9,241.4	18	San Bernardino, CA	9,612.3
100	Fremont, CA	3,507.3	76	San Diego, CA	6,183.3
21	Fresno, CA	9,493.5	47	San Francisco, CA	7,709.0
85	Garland, TX	5,751.8	99	San Jose, CA	3,882.0
98	Glendale, CA	4,203.1	90	Santa Ana, CA	5,474.9
64	Grand Rapids, MI	6,799.4	10	Seattle, WA	10,398.0
61	Greensboro, NC	7,039.6	11	Shreveport, LA	10,163.7
77	Honolulu, HI	6,157.3	52	Spokane, WA	7,516.0
65	Houston, TX	6,733.6	17	Stockton, CA	9,622.4
96	Huntington Beach, CA	4,410.3	4	St. Louis, MO	12,773.4
58	Indianapolis, IN	7,211.1	67	St. Paul, MN	6,518.2
7	Jackson, MS	11,465.6	53	St. Petersburg, FL	7,476.7
39	Jacksonville, FL	8,343.8	23	Tacoma, WA	9,369.6
78	Jersey City, NJ	6,155.5	5	Tampa, FL	12,460.0
12	Kansas City, MO	10,151.9	48	Toledo, OH	7,624.9
87	Las Vegas, NV	5,726.5	9	Tucson, AZ	10,456.8
86	Lexington, KY	5,734.3	69	Tulsa, OK	6,457.8
73	Lincoln, NE	6,273.6	95	Virginia Beach, VA	4,550.9
6	Little Rock, AR	12,398.0	36	Washington, DC	8,833.6
71	Long Beach, CA	6,432.8	43	Wichita, KS	7,970.1
68	Los Angeles, CA	6,498.4	97	Yonkers, NY	4,355.3

Source: U.S. Department of Justice, Federal Bureau of Investigation
"Crime in the United States 1993" (Uniform Crime Reports, December 4, 1994)
Property crimes are offenses of burglary, larceny-theft and motor vehicle theft. They consist of taking money or property but there is no force or threat of force against victims.
**Not available.*

66. Property Crime Rate in 1993 (continued)

National Rate = 4,736.9 Property Crimes per 100,000 Population*

RANK	CITY	RATE	RANK	CITY	RATE
1	Miami, FL	14,851.9	51	Riverside, CA	7,539.0
2	Atlanta, GA	13,312.5	52	Spokane, WA	7,516.0
3	Baton Rouge, LA	13,170.4	53	St. Petersburg, FL	7,476.7
4	St. Louis, MO	12,773.4	54	Des Moines, IA	7,470.1
5	Tampa, FL	12,460.0	55	Chicago, IL	7,437.2
6	Little Rock, AR	12,398.0	56	El Paso, TX	7,326.9
7	Jackson, MS	11,465.6	57	Bakersfield, CA	7,236.7
8	Newark, NJ	10,482.7	58	Indianapolis, IN	7,211.1
9	Tucson, AZ	10,456.8	59	Mesa, AZ	7,158.3
10	Seattle, WA	10,398.0	60	Milwaukee, WI	7,128.4
11	Shreveport, LA	10,163.7	61	Greensboro, NC	7,039.6
12	Kansas City, MO	10,151.9	62	Denver, CO	6,931.0
13	Orlando, FL	10,078.2	63	Cincinnati, OH	6,902.0
14	Oklahoma City, OK	9,805.5	64	Grand Rapids, MI	6,799.4
15	Rochester, NY	9,696.5	65	Houston, TX	6,733.6
16	Austin, TX	9,652.4	66	Pittsburgh, PA	6,549.7
17	Stockton, CA	9,622.4	67	St. Paul, MN	6,518.2
18	San Bernardino, CA	9,612.3	68	Los Angeles, CA	6,498.4
19	Baltimore, MD	9,546.8	69	Tulsa, OK	6,457.8
20	Portland, OR	9,523.2	70	Aurora, CO	6,451.5
21	Fresno, CA	9,493.5	71	Long Beach, CA	6,432.8
22	Charlotte, NC	9,467.2	72	Arlington, TX	6,377.8
23	Tacoma, WA	9,369.6	73	Lincoln, NE	6,273.6
24	Birmingham, AL	9,338.2	74	Cleveland, OH	6,267.2
25	Oakland, CA	9,314.2	75	Akron, OH	6,258.9
26	Corpus Christi, TX	9,276.3	76	San Diego, CA	6,183.3
27	Minneapolis, MN	9,268.4	77	Honolulu, HI	6,157.3
28	Fort Worth, TX	9,241.4	78	Jersey City, NJ	6,155.5
29	San Antonio, TX	9,228.8	79	New York, NY	6,081.2
30	Detroit, MI	9,212.3	80	Anaheim, CA	6,033.3
31	Richmond, VA	9,188.6	81	Colorado Springs, CO	5,929.9
32	Dayton, OH	9,066.9	82	Raleigh, NC	5,902.5
33	Nashville, TN	9,021.0	83	Columbus, GA	5,833.5
34	Sacramento, CA	8,955.8	84	Lubbock, TX	5,780.7
35	Dallas, TX	8,883.7	85	Garland, TX	5,751.8
36	Washington, DC	8,833.6	86	Lexington, KY	5,734.3
37	New Orleans, LA	8,695.6	87	Las Vegas, NV	5,726.5
38	Memphis, TN	8,406.9	88	Newport News, VA	5,585.2
39	Jacksonville, FL	8,343.8	89	Anchorage, AK	5,554.8
40	Phoenix, AZ	8,136.2	90	Santa Ana, CA	5,474.9
41	Boston, MA	8,072.7	91	Montgomery, AL	5,460.4
42	Mobile, AL	8,002.0	92	Louisville, KY	5,338.8
43	Wichita, KS	7,970.1	93	Madison, WI	5,070.6
44	Buffalo, NY	7,951.2	94	Philadelphia, PA	5,006.8
45	Albuquerque, NM	7,937.7	95	Virginia Beach, VA	4,550.9
46	Fort Wayne, IN	7,884.6	96	Huntington Beach, CA	4,410.3
47	San Francisco, CA	7,709.0	97	Yonkers, NY	4,355.3
48	Toledo, OH	7,624.9	98	Glendale, CA	4,203.1
49	Columbus, OH	7,601.4	99	San Jose, CA	3,882.0
50	Norfolk, VA	7,546.1	100	Fremont, CA	3,507.3

Source: U.S. Department of Justice, Federal Bureau of Investigation
"Crime in the United States 1993" (Uniform Crime Reports, December 4, 1994)
Property crimes are offenses of burglary, larceny-theft and motor vehicle theft. They consist of taking money or property but there is no force or threat of force against victims.
**Not available.*

67. Percent Change in Property Crime Rate: 1992 to 1993

National Percent Change = 3.4% Decrease*

RANK	CITY	% CHANGE	RANK	CITY	% CHANGE
51	Akron, OH	(2.85)	73	Louisville, KY	(6.57)
38	Albuquerque, NM	0.02	82	Lubbock, TX	(7.86)
43	Anaheim, CA	(1.84)	86	Madison, WI	(8.04)
93	Anchorage, AK	(10.98)	29	Memphis, TN	1.34
99	Arlington, TX	(17.53)	3	Mesa, AZ	12.83
41	Atlanta, GA	(1.30)	10	Miami, FL	7.96
64	Aurora, CO	(5.39)	77	Milwaukee, WI	(7.25)
75	Austin, TX	(6.78)	46	Minneapolis, MN	(2.03)
25	Bakersfield, CA	2.28	98	Mobile, AL	(15.80)
13	Baltimore, MD	5.58	59	Montgomery, AL	(4.63)
2	Baton Rouge, LA	12.92	4	Nashville, TN	11.95
55	Birmingham, AL	(3.68)	8	New Orleans, LA	8.61
20	Boston, MA	3.39	56	New York, NY	(3.88)
44	Buffalo, NY	(1.88)	65	Newark, NJ	(5.76)
83	Charlotte, NC	(7.89)	79	Newport News, VA	(7.42)
42	Chicago, IL	(1.42)	26	Norfolk, VA	1.95
61	Cincinnati, OH	(5.10)	62	Oakland, CA	(5.23)
63	Cleveland, OH	(5.36)	35	Oklahoma City, OK	0.29
67	Colorado Springs, CO	(5.86)	33	Orlando, FL	0.60
19	Columbus, GA	3.46	24	Philadelphia, PA	2.55
58	Columbus, OH	(4.52)	37	Phoenix, AZ	0.06
39	Corpus Christi, TX	(0.89)	72	Pittsburgh, PA	(6.54)
97	Dallas, TX	(14.23)	31	Portland, OR	0.94
48	Dayton, OH	(2.23)	91	Raleigh, NC	(9.92)
47	Denver, CO	(2.08)	34	Richmond, VA	0.49
66	Des Moines, IA	(5.82)	11	Riverside, CA	6.69
12	Detroit, MI	5.93	89	Rochester, NY	(9.39)
84	El Paso, TX	(7.91)	28	Sacramento, CA	1.81
70	Fort Wayne, IN	(6.24)	96	San Antonio, TX	(11.98)
100	Fort Worth, TX	(23.73)	54	San Bernardino, CA	(3.65)
30	Fremont, CA	0.97	87	San Diego, CA	(8.06)
92	Fresno, CA	(10.88)	85	San Francisco, CA	(7.94)
78	Garland, TX	(7.29)	88	San Jose, CA	(8.37)
18	Glendale, CA	3.73	71	Santa Ana, CA	(6.53)
74	Grand Rapids, MI	(6.58)	49	Seattle, WA	(2.43)
57	Greensboro, NC	(4.51)	7	Shreveport, LA	8.97
16	Honolulu, HI	5.31	40	Spokane, WA	(0.96)
80	Houston, TX	(7.53)	21	Stockton, CA	3.14
9	Huntington Beach, CA	8.44	6	St. Louis, MO	10.99
1	Indianapolis, IN	22.48	53	St. Paul, MN	(3.24)
50	Jackson, MS	(2.74)	76	St. Petersburg, FL	(7.09)
60	Jacksonville, FL	(4.87)	15	Tacoma, WA	5.45
94	Jersey City, NJ	(11.06)	35	Tampa, FL	0.29
14	Kansas City, MO	5.53	45	Toledo, OH	(1.99)
95	Las Vegas, NV	(11.41)	5	Tucson, AZ	11.34
23	Lexington, KY	2.83	69	Tulsa, OK	(6.03)
90	Lincoln, NE	(9.80)	81	Virginia Beach, VA	(7.71)
27	Little Rock, AR	1.89	22	Washington, DC	3.12
32	Long Beach, CA	0.84	52	Wichita, KS	(3.21)
68	Los Angeles, CA	(5.88)	17	Yonkers, NY	4.22

Source: Morgan Quitno Corporation using data from U.S. Department of Justice, Federal Bureau of Investigation "Crime in the United States 1993" (Uniform Crime Reports, December 4, 1994)
Property crimes are offenses of burglary, larceny-theft and motor vehicle theft. They consist of taking money or property but there is no force or threat of force against victims.
**Not available.*

67. Percent Change in Property Crime Rate: 1992 to 1993 (continued)

National Percent Change = 3.4% Decrease*

RANK	CITY	% CHANGE	RANK	CITY	% CHANGE
1	Indianapolis,IN	22.48	51	Akron, OH	(2.85)
2	Baton Rouge, LA	12.92	52	Wichita, KS	(3.21)
3	Mesa, AZ	12.83	53	St. Paul, MN	(3.24)
4	Nashville, TN	11.95	54	San Bernardino, CA	(3.65)
5	Tucson, AZ	11.34	55	Birmingham, AL	(3.68)
6	St. Louis, MO	10.99	56	New York, NY	(3.88)
7	Shreveport, LA	8.97	57	Greensboro, NC	(4.51)
8	New Orleans, LA	8.61	58	Columbus, OH	(4.52)
9	Huntington Beach, CA	8.44	59	Montgomery, AL	(4.63)
10	Miami, FL	7.96	60	Jacksonville, FL	(4.87)
11	Riverside, CA	6.69	61	Cincinnati, OH	(5.10)
12	Detroit, MI	5.93	62	Oakland, CA	(5.23)
13	Baltimore, MD	5.58	63	Cleveland, OH	(5.36)
14	Kansas City, MO	5.53	64	Aurora, CO	(5.39)
15	Tacoma, WA	5.45	65	Newark, NJ	(5.76)
16	Honolulu, HI	5.31	66	Des Moines, IA	(5.82)
17	Yonkers, NY	4.22	67	Colorado Springs, CO	(5.86)
18	Glendale, CA	3.73	68	Los Angeles, CA	(5.88)
19	Columbus, GA	3.46	69	Tulsa, OK	(6.03)
20	Boston, MA	3.39	70	Fort Wayne, IN	(6.24)
21	Stockton, CA	3.14	71	Santa Ana, CA	(6.53)
22	Washington, DC	3.12	72	Pittsburgh, PA	(6.54)
23	Lexington, KY	2.83	73	Louisville, KY	(6.57)
24	Philadelphia, PA	2.55	74	Grand Rapids, MI	(6.58)
25	Bakersfield, CA	2.28	75	Austin, TX	(6.78)
26	Norfolk, VA	1.95	76	St. Petersburg, FL	(7.09)
27	Little Rock, AR	1.89	77	Milwaukee, WI	(7.25)
28	Sacramento, CA	1.81	78	Garland, TX	(7.29)
29	Memphis, TN	1.34	79	Newport News, VA	(7.42)
30	Fremont, CA	0.97	80	Houston, TX	(7.53)
31	Portland, OR	0.94	81	Virginia Beach, VA	(7.71)
32	Long Beach, CA	0.84	82	Lubbock, TX	(7.86)
33	Orlando, FL	0.60	83	Charlotte, NC	(7.89)
34	Richmond, VA	0.49	84	El Paso, TX	(7.91)
35	Oklahoma City, OK	0.29	85	San Francisco, CA	(7.94)
35	Tampa, FL	0.29	86	Madison, WI	(8.04)
37	Phoenix, AZ	0.06	87	San Diego, CA	(8.06)
38	Albuquerque, NM	0.02	88	San Jose, CA	(8.37)
39	Corpus Christi, TX	(0.89)	89	Rochester, NY	(9.39)
40	Spokane, WA	(0.96)	90	Lincoln, NE	(9.80)
41	Atlanta, GA	(1.30)	91	Raleigh, NC	(9.92)
42	Chicago, IL	(1.42)	92	Fresno, CA	(10.88)
43	Anaheim, CA	(1.84)	93	Anchorage, AK	(10.98)
44	Buffalo, NY	(1.88)	94	Jersey City, NJ	(11.06)
45	Toledo, OH	(1.99)	95	Las Vegas, NV	(11.41)
46	Minneapolis, MN	(2.03)	96	San Antonio, TX	(11.98)
47	Denver, CO	(2.08)	97	Dallas, TX	(14.23)
48	Dayton, OH	(2.23)	98	Mobile, AL	(15.80)
49	Seattle, WA	(2.43)	99	Arlington, TX	(17.53)
50	Jackson, MS	(2.74)	100	Fort Worth, TX	(23.73)

Source: Morgan Quitno Corporation using data from U.S. Department of Justice, Federal Bureau of Investigation "Crime in the United States 1993" (Uniform Crime Reports, December 4, 1994)
Property crimes are offenses of burglary, larceny-theft and motor vehicle theft. They consist of taking money or property but there is no force or threat of force against victims.
**Not available.*

68. Percent Change in Property Crime Rate: 1989 to 1993

National Percent Change = 6.7% Decrease*

RANK	CITY	% CHANGE
33	Akron, OH	(3.76)
54	Albuquerque, NM	(9.22)
53	Anaheim, CA	(8.79)
8	Anchorage, AK	11.93
86	Arlington, TX	(20.44)
87	Atlanta, GA	(20.47)
28	Aurora, CO	(1.70)
36	Austin, TX	(4.56)
59	Bakersfield, CA	(10.87)
5	Baltimore, MD	30.67
4	Baton Rouge, LA	30.72
6	Birmingham, AL	16.27
80	Boston, MA	(17.96)
8	Buffalo, NY	11.93
74	Charlotte, NC	(15.41)
29	Chicago, IL	(2.37)
15	Cincinnati, OH	6.49
51	Cleveland, OH	(8.24)
77	Colorado Springs, CO	(16.52)
24	Columbus, GA	0.13
83	Columbus, OH	(18.69)
46	Corpus Christi, TX	(7.00)
98	Dallas, TX	(39.05)
60	Dayton, OH	(11.17)
21	Denver, CO	0.59
64	Des Moines, IA	(11.70)
39	Detroit, MI	(4.92)
91	El Paso, TX	(24.52)
47	Fort Wayne, IN	(7.05)
97	Fort Worth, TX	(34.59)
14	Fremont, CA	7.21
50	Fresno, CA	(8.12)
27	Garland, TX	(1.18)
85	Glendale, CA	(19.35)
43	Grand Rapids, MI	(5.79)
26	Greensboro, NC	(0.56)
19	Honolulu, HI	3.28
96	Houston, TX	(30.41)
42	Huntington Beach, CA	(5.21)
3	Indianapolis,IN	36.14
2	Jackson, MS	40.55
44	Jacksonville, FL	(6.14)
90	Jersey City, NJ	(24.34)
40	Kansas City, MO	(4.93)
69	Las Vegas, NV	(13.59)
38	Lexington, KY	(4.72)
33	Lincoln, NE	(3.76)
16	Little Rock, AR	6.02
79	Long Beach, CA	(17.61)
48	Los Angeles, CA	(7.51)

RANK	CITY	% CHANGE
37	Louisville, KY	(4.65)
81	Lubbock, TX	(18.32)
92	Madison, WI	(24.71)
10	Memphis, TN	9.91
7	Mesa, AZ	15.79
20	Miami, FL	1.17
63	Milwaukee, WI	(11.45)
67	Minneapolis, MN	(12.20)
49	Mobile, AL	(7.55)
56	Montgomery, AL	(9.87)
1	Nashville, TN	52.19
45	New Orleans, LA	(6.83)
78	New York, NY	(17.46)
41	Newark, NJ	(5.13)
11	Newport News, VA	8.51
22	Norfolk, VA	0.44
75	Oakland, CA	(15.46)
33	Oklahoma City, OK	(3.76)
55	Orlando, FL	(9.59)
73	Philadelphia, PA	(15.20)
82	Phoenix, AZ	(18.36)
72	Pittsburgh, PA	(14.48)
68	Portland, OR	(12.33)
70	Raleigh, NC	(14.13)
13	Richmond, VA	7.75
18	Riverside, CA	3.88
52	Rochester, NY	(8.46)
31	Sacramento, CA	(3.34)
89	San Antonio, TX	(24.13)
-	San Bernardino, CA**	NA
93	San Diego, CA	(26.85)
23	San Francisco, CA	0.36
71	San Jose, CA	(14.47)
95	Santa Ana, CA	(30.01)
58	Seattle, WA	(10.13)
30	Shreveport, LA	(3.19)
62	Spokane, WA	(11.25)
57	Stockton, CA	(9.97)
17	St. Louis, MO	4.66
64	St. Paul, MN	(11.70)
94	St. Petersburg, FL	(29.28)
88	Tacoma, WA	(21.90)
32	Tampa, FL	(3.61)
60	Toledo, OH	(11.17)
-	Tucson, AZ**	NA
84	Tulsa, OK	(19.18)
76	Virginia Beach, VA	(16.00)
12	Washington, DC	8.48
25	Wichita, KS	(0.53)
66	Yonkers, NY	(11.94)

Source: Morgan Quitno Corporation using data from U.S. Department of Justice, Federal Bureau of Investigation
"Crime in the United States 1993" (Uniform Crime Reports, December 4, 1994)
*Property crimes are offenses of burglary, larceny-theft and motor vehicle theft. They consist of taking money
or property but there is no force or threat of force against victims.
**Not available.

68. Percent Change in Property Crime Rate: 1989 to 1993 (continued)

National Percent Change = 6.7% Decrease*

RANK	CITY	% CHANGE		RANK	CITY	% CHANGE
1	Nashville, TN	52.19		51	Cleveland, OH	(8.24)
2	Jackson, MS	40.55		52	Rochester, NY	(8.46)
3	Indianapolis, IN	36.14		53	Anaheim, CA	(8.79)
4	Baton Rouge, LA	30.72		54	Albuquerque, NM	(9.22)
5	Baltimore, MD	30.67		55	Orlando, FL	(9.59)
6	Birmingham, AL	16.27		56	Montgomery, AL	(9.87)
7	Mesa, AZ	15.79		57	Stockton, CA	(9.97)
8	Anchorage, AK	11.93		58	Seattle, WA	(10.13)
8	Buffalo, NY	11.93		59	Bakersfield, CA	(10.87)
10	Memphis, TN	9.91		60	Dayton, OH	(11.17)
11	Newport News, VA	8.51		60	Toledo, OH	(11.17)
12	Washington, DC	8.48		62	Spokane, WA	(11.25)
13	Richmond, VA	7.75		63	Milwaukee, WI	(11.45)
14	Fremont, CA	7.21		64	Des Moines, IA	(11.70)
15	Cincinnati, OH	6.49		64	St. Paul, MN	(11.70)
16	Little Rock, AR	6.02		66	Yonkers, NY	(11.94)
17	St. Louis, MO	4.66		67	Minneapolis, MN	(12.20)
18	Riverside, CA	3.88		68	Portland, OR	(12.33)
19	Honolulu, HI	3.28		69	Las Vegas, NV	(13.59)
20	Miami, FL	1.17		70	Raleigh, NC	(14.13)
21	Denver, CO	0.59		71	San Jose, CA	(14.47)
22	Norfolk, VA	0.44		72	Pittsburgh, PA	(14.48)
23	San Francisco, CA	0.36		73	Philadelphia, PA	(15.20)
24	Columbus, GA	0.13		74	Charlotte, NC	(15.41)
25	Wichita, KS	(0.53)		75	Oakland, CA	(15.46)
26	Greensboro, NC	(0.56)		76	Virginia Beach, VA	(16.00)
27	Garland, TX	(1.18)		77	Colorado Springs, CO	(16.52)
28	Aurora, CO	(1.70)		78	New York, NY	(17.46)
29	Chicago, IL	(2.37)		79	Long Beach, CA	(17.61)
30	Shreveport, LA	(3.19)		80	Boston, MA	(17.96)
31	Sacramento, CA	(3.34)		81	Lubbock, TX	(18.32)
32	Tampa, FL	(3.61)		82	Phoenix, AZ	(18.36)
33	Akron, OH	(3.76)		83	Columbus, OH	(18.69)
33	Lincoln, NE	(3.76)		84	Tulsa, OK	(19.18)
33	Oklahoma City, OK	(3.76)		85	Glendale, CA	(19.35)
36	Austin, TX	(4.56)		86	Arlington, TX	(20.44)
37	Louisville, KY	(4.65)		87	Atlanta, GA	(20.47)
38	Lexington, KY	(4.72)		88	Tacoma, WA	(21.90)
39	Detroit, MI	(4.92)		89	San Antonio, TX	(24.13)
40	Kansas City, MO	(4.93)		90	Jersey City, NJ	(24.34)
41	Newark, NJ	(5.13)		91	El Paso, TX	(24.52)
42	Huntington Beach, CA	(5.21)		92	Madison, WI	(24.71)
43	Grand Rapids, MI	(5.79)		93	San Diego, CA	(26.85)
44	Jacksonville, FL	(6.14)		94	St. Petersburg, FL	(29.28)
45	New Orleans, LA	(6.83)		95	Santa Ana, CA	(30.01)
46	Corpus Christi, TX	(7.00)		96	Houston, TX	(30.41)
47	Fort Wayne, IN	(7.05)		97	Fort Worth, TX	(34.59)
48	Los Angeles, CA	(7.51)		98	Dallas, TX	(39.05)
49	Mobile, AL	(7.55)		–	San Bernardino, CA**	NA
50	Fresno, CA	(8.12)		–	Tucson, AZ**	NA

Source: Morgan Quitno Corporation using data from U.S. Department of Justice, Federal Bureau of Investigation "Crime in the United States 1993" (Uniform Crime Reports, December 4, 1994)
*Property crimes are offenses of burglary, larceny-theft and motor vehicle theft. They consist of taking money or property but there is no force or threat of force against victims.
**Not available.

69. Burglaries in 1993

National Total = 2,834,808 Burglaries*

RANK	CITY	BURGLARY	RANK	CITY	BURGLARY
79	Akron, OH	3,367	69	Louisville, KY	4,204
36	Albuquerque, NM	8,199	88	Lubbock, TX	2,541
73	Anaheim, CA	3,942	98	Madison, WI	1,606
96	Anchorage, AK	1,880	10	Memphis, TN	15,314
72	Arlington, TX	3,977	64	Mesa, AZ	4,664
14	Atlanta, GA	13,168	17	Miami, FL	12,277
86	Aurora, CO	2,909	35	Milwaukee, WI	8,250
33	Austin, TX	8,453	26	Minneapolis, MN	9,358
76	Bakersfield, CA	3,650	60	Mobile, AL	4,884
8	Baltimore, MD	17,901	78	Montgomery, AL	3,558
43	Baton Rouge, LA	7,543	29	Nashville, TN	9,149
49	Birmingham, AL	6,628	20	New Orleans, LA	11,184
39	Boston, MA	7,982	1	New York, NY	99,207
42	Buffalo, NY	7,597	47	Newark, NJ	6,879
22	Charlotte, NC	10,691	91	Newport News, VA	2,101
3	Chicago, IL	45,670	75	Norfolk, VA	3,732
51	Cincinnati, OH	6,154	34	Oakland, CA	8,355
38	Cleveland, OH	8,031	24	Oklahoma City, OK	10,000
77	Colorado Springs, CO	3,645	67	Orlando, FL	4,352
90	Columbus, GA	2,309	12	Philadelphia, PA	15,117
15	Columbus, OH	13,055	7	Phoenix, AZ	20,617
66	Corpus Christi, TX	4,600	65	Pittsburgh, PA	4,611
6	Dallas, TX	20,975	40	Portland, OR	7,845
68	Dayton, OH	4,303	85	Raleigh, NC	2,947
30	Denver, CO	9,128	58	Richmond, VA	5,081
93	Des Moines, IA	1,986	59	Riverside, CA	4,975
5	Detroit, MI	23,092	50	Rochester, NY	6,340
55	El Paso, TX	5,643	37	Sacramento, CA	8,080
92	Fort Wayne, IN	2,028	9	San Antonio, TX	17,866
23	Fort Worth, TX	10,505	63	San Bernardino, CA	4,740
100	Fremont, CA	1,584	13	San Diego, CA	14,583
32	Fresno, CA	8,472	21	San Francisco, CA	11,153
89	Garland, TX	2,522	52	San Jose, CA	6,014
99	Glendale, CA	1,596	84	Santa Ana, CA	2,950
83	Grand Rapids, MI	3,161	28	Seattle, WA	9,247
82	Greensboro, NC	3,177	62	Shreveport, LA	4,774
27	Honolulu, HI	9,296	87	Spokane, WA	2,699
4	Houston, TX	27,022	57	Stockton, CA	5,362
94	Huntington Beach, CA	1,984	16	St. Louis, MO	12,400
41	Indianapolis, IN	7,629	71	St. Paul, MN	4,023
46	Jackson, MS	7,071	61	St. Petersburg, FL	4,828
11	Jacksonville, FL	15,127	74	Tacoma, WA	3,915
70	Jersey City, NJ	4,190	31	Tampa, FL	8,987
18	Kansas City, MO	12,106	56	Toledo, OH	5,502
25	Las Vegas, NV	9,783	44	Tucson, AZ	7,363
81	Lexington, KY	3,187	45	Tulsa, OK	7,196
94	Lincoln, NE	1,984	80	Virginia Beach, VA	3,261
54	Little Rock, AR	5,796	19	Washington, DC	11,532
48	Long Beach, CA	6,780	53	Wichita, KS	5,847
2	Los Angeles, CA	50,232	97	Yonkers, NY	1,682

Source: U.S. Department of Justice, Federal Bureau of Investigation
  "Crime in the United States 1993" (Uniform Crime Reports, December 4, 1994)
*Burglary is the unlawful entry of a structure to commit a felony or theft. Attempts are included.

69. Burglaries in 1993 (continued)

National Total = 2,834,808 Burglaries*

RANK	CITY	BURGLARY	RANK	CITY	BURGLARY
1	New York, NY	99,207	51	Cincinnati, OH	6,154
2	Los Angeles, CA	50,232	52	San Jose, CA	6,014
3	Chicago, IL	45,670	53	Wichita, KS	5,847
4	Houston, TX	27,022	54	Little Rock, AR	5,796
5	Detroit, MI	23,092	55	El Paso, TX	5,643
6	Dallas, TX	20,975	56	Toledo, OH	5,502
7	Phoenix, AZ	20,617	57	Stockton, CA	5,362
8	Baltimore, MD	17,901	58	Richmond, VA	5,081
9	San Antonio, TX	17,866	59	Riverside, CA	4,975
10	Memphis, TN	15,314	60	Mobile, AL	4,884
11	Jacksonville, FL	15,127	61	St. Petersburg, FL	4,828
12	Philadelphia, PA	15,117	62	Shreveport, LA	4,774
13	San Diego, CA	14,583	63	San Bernardino, CA	4,740
14	Atlanta, GA	13,168	64	Mesa, AZ	4,664
15	Columbus, OH	13,055	65	Pittsburgh, PA	4,611
16	St. Louis, MO	12,400	66	Corpus Christi, TX	4,600
17	Miami, FL	12,277	67	Orlando, FL	4,352
18	Kansas City, MO	12,106	68	Dayton, OH	4,303
19	Washington, DC	11,532	69	Louisville, KY	4,204
20	New Orleans, LA	11,184	70	Jersey City, NJ	4,190
21	San Francisco, CA	11,153	71	St. Paul, MN	4,023
22	Charlotte, NC	10,691	72	Arlington, TX	3,977
23	Fort Worth, TX	10,505	73	Anaheim, CA	3,942
24	Oklahoma City, OK	10,000	74	Tacoma, WA	3,915
25	Las Vegas, NV	9,783	75	Norfolk, VA	3,732
26	Minneapolis, MN	9,358	76	Bakersfield, CA	3,650
27	Honolulu, HI	9,296	77	Colorado Springs, CO	3,645
28	Seattle, WA	9,247	78	Montgomery, AL	3,558
29	Nashville, TN	9,149	79	Akron, OH	3,367
30	Denver, CO	9,128	80	Virginia Beach, VA	3,261
31	Tampa, FL	8,987	81	Lexington, KY	3,187
32	Fresno, CA	8,472	82	Greensboro, NC	3,177
33	Austin, TX	8,453	83	Grand Rapids, MI	3,161
34	Oakland, CA	8,355	84	Santa Ana, CA	2,950
35	Milwaukee, WI	8,250	85	Raleigh, NC	2,947
36	Albuquerque, NM	8,199	86	Aurora, CO	2,909
37	Sacramento, CA	8,080	87	Spokane, WA	2,699
38	Cleveland, OH	8,031	88	Lubbock, TX	2,541
39	Boston, MA	7,982	89	Garland, TX	2,522
40	Portland, OR	7,845	90	Columbus, GA	2,309
41	Indianapolis, IN	7,629	91	Newport News, VA	2,101
42	Buffalo, NY	7,597	92	Fort Wayne, IN	2,028
43	Baton Rouge, LA	7,543	93	Des Moines, IA	1,986
44	Tucson, AZ	7,363	94	Huntington Beach, CA	1,984
45	Tulsa, OK	7,196	94	Lincoln, NE	1,984
46	Jackson, MS	7,071	96	Anchorage, AK	1,880
47	Newark, NJ	6,879	97	Yonkers, NY	1,682
48	Long Beach, CA	6,780	98	Madison, WI	1,606
49	Birmingham, AL	6,628	99	Glendale, CA	1,596
50	Rochester, NY	6,340	100	Fremont, CA	1,584

Source: U.S. Department of Justice, Federal Bureau of Investigation
"Crime in the United States 1993" (Uniform Crime Reports, December 4, 1994)
*Burglary is the unlawful entry of a structure to commit a felony or theft. Attempts are included.

70. Burglary Rate in 1993

National Rate = 1,099.2 Burglaries per 100,000 Population*

RANK	CITY	RATE	RANK	CITY	RATE
65	Akron, OH	1,496.2	61	Louisville, KY	1,536.8
37	Albuquerque, NM	2,013.1	76	Lubbock, TX	1,325.9
70	Anaheim, CA	1,424.7	97	Madison, WI	815.6
99	Anchorage, AK	749.8	15	Memphis, TN	2,474.1
71	Arlington, TX	1,413.6	62	Mesa, AZ	1,530.7
4	Atlanta, GA	3,268.5	3	Miami, FL	3,295.7
84	Aurora, CO	1,179.6	77	Milwaukee, WI	1,324.0
53	Austin, TX	1,683.8	11	Minneapolis, MN	2,552.4
41	Bakersfield, CA	1,922.0	21	Mobile, AL	2,390.8
18	Baltimore, MD	2,442.3	45	Montgomery, AL	1,830.3
2	Baton Rouge, LA	3,344.4	48	Nashville, TN	1,781.2
16	Birmingham, AL	2,466.1	24	New Orleans, LA	2,274.9
68	Boston, MA	1,441.1	75	New York, NY	1,350.3
22	Buffalo, NY	2,338.6	12	Newark, NJ	2,548.8
13	Charlotte, NC	2,528.2	85	Newport News, VA	1,167.4
58	Chicago, IL	1,637.5	67	Norfolk, VA	1,448.7
54	Cincinnati, OH	1,678.7	29	Oakland, CA	2,216.0
59	Cleveland, OH	1,588.0	30	Oklahoma City, OK	2,186.0
83	Colorado Springs, CO	1,197.3	17	Orlando, FL	2,462.3
82	Columbus, GA	1,213.1	93	Philadelphia, PA	969.3
36	Columbus, OH	2,018.0	40	Phoenix, AZ	1,983.6
52	Corpus Christi, TX	1,693.9	81	Pittsburgh, PA	1,251.4
38	Dallas, TX	2,011.8	51	Portland, OR	1,724.6
23	Dayton, OH	2,334.1	78	Raleigh, NC	1,315.3
44	Denver, CO	1,831.5	14	Richmond, VA	2,474.5
91	Des Moines, IA	1,015.9	33	Riverside, CA	2,064.0
26	Detroit, MI	2,263.8	10	Rochester, NY	2,694.4
89	El Paso, TX	1,017.6	31	Sacramento, CA	2,089.3
86	Fort Wayne, IN	1,156.2	47	San Antonio, TX	1,813.0
25	Fort Worth, TX	2,267.1	9	San Bernardino, CA	2,720.8
96	Fremont, CA	874.5	80	San Diego, CA	1,256.5
28	Fresno, CA	2,229.6	64	San Francisco, CA	1,514.6
79	Garland, TX	1,293.8	100	San Jose, CA	742.9
95	Glendale, CA	889.2	90	Santa Ana, CA	1,017.0
57	Grand Rapids, MI	1,645.3	49	Seattle, WA	1,740.5
56	Greensboro, NC	1,646.5	19	Shreveport, LA	2,418.7
87	Honolulu, HI	1,061.8	72	Spokane, WA	1,409.3
60	Houston, TX	1,567.1	20	Stockton, CA	2,416.8
88	Huntington Beach, CA	1,061.3	6	St. Louis, MO	3,203.7
35	Indianapolis, IN	2,019.7	66	St. Paul, MN	1,483.4
1	Jackson, MS	3,567.1	34	St. Petersburg, FL	2,022.4
27	Jacksonville, FL	2,250.0	32	Tacoma, WA	2,083.6
46	Jersey City, NJ	1,819.4	7	Tampa, FL	3,111.0
8	Kansas City, MO	2,780.3	55	Toledo, OH	1,660.1
73	Las Vegas, NV	1,363.6	50	Tucson, AZ	1,727.0
74	Lexington, KY	1,355.6	42	Tulsa, OK	1,901.9
92	Lincoln, NE	1,000.9	98	Virginia Beach, VA	770.2
5	Little Rock, AR	3,239.4	39	Washington, DC	1,995.2
63	Long Beach, CA	1,529.6	43	Wichita, KS	1,864.5
69	Los Angeles, CA	1,424.9	94	Yonkers, NY	899.6

Source: U.S. Department of Justice, Federal Bureau of Investigation
  "Crime in the United States 1993" (Uniform Crime Reports, December 4, 1994)
*Burglary is the unlawful entry of a structure to commit a felony or theft. Attempts are included.

70. Burglary Rate in 1993 (continued)

National Rate = 1,099.2 Burglaries per 100,000 Population*

RANK	CITY	RATE	RANK	CITY	RATE
1	Jackson, MS	3,567.1	51	Portland, OR	1,724.6
2	Baton Rouge, LA	3,344.4	52	Corpus Christi, TX	1,693.9
3	Miami, FL	3,295.7	53	Austin, TX	1,683.8
4	Atlanta, GA	3,268.5	54	Cincinnati, OH	1,678.7
5	Little Rock, AR	3,239.4	55	Toledo, OH	1,660.1
6	St. Louis, MO	3,203.7	56	Greensboro, NC	1,646.5
7	Tampa, FL	3,111.0	57	Grand Rapids, MI	1,645.3
8	Kansas City, MO	2,780.3	58	Chicago, IL	1,637.5
9	San Bernardino, CA	2,720.8	59	Cleveland, OH	1,588.0
10	Rochester, NY	2,694.4	60	Houston, TX	1,567.1
11	Minneapolis, MN	2,552.4	61	Louisville, KY	1,536.8
12	Newark, NJ	2,548.8	62	Mesa, AZ	1,530.7
13	Charlotte, NC	2,528.2	63	Long Beach, CA	1,529.6
14	Richmond, VA	2,474.5	64	San Francisco, CA	1,514.6
15	Memphis, TN	2,474.1	65	Akron, OH	1,496.2
16	Birmingham, AL	2,466.1	66	St. Paul, MN	1,483.4
17	Orlando, FL	2,462.3	67	Norfolk, VA	1,448.7
18	Baltimore, MD	2,442.3	68	Boston, MA	1,441.1
19	Shreveport, LA	2,418.7	69	Los Angeles, CA	1,424.9
20	Stockton, CA	2,416.8	70	Anaheim, CA	1,424.7
21	Mobile, AL	2,390.8	71	Arlington, TX	1,413.6
22	Buffalo, NY	2,338.6	72	Spokane, WA	1,409.3
23	Dayton, OH	2,334.1	73	Las Vegas, NV	1,363.6
24	New Orleans, LA	2,274.9	74	Lexington, KY	1,355.6
25	Fort Worth, TX	2,267.1	75	New York, NY	1,350.3
26	Detroit, MI	2,263.8	76	Lubbock, TX	1,325.9
27	Jacksonville, FL	2,250.0	77	Milwaukee, WI	1,324.0
28	Fresno, CA	2,229.6	78	Raleigh, NC	1,315.3
29	Oakland, CA	2,216.0	79	Garland, TX	1,293.8
30	Oklahoma City, OK	2,186.0	80	San Diego, CA	1,256.5
31	Sacramento, CA	2,089.3	81	Pittsburgh, PA	1,251.4
32	Tacoma, WA	2,083.6	82	Columbus, GA	1,213.1
33	Riverside, CA	2,064.0	83	Colorado Springs, CO	1,197.3
34	St. Petersburg, FL	2,022.4	84	Aurora, CO	1,179.6
35	Indianapolis, IN	2,019.7	85	Newport News, VA	1,167.4
36	Columbus, OH	2,018.0	86	Fort Wayne, IN	1,156.2
37	Albuquerque, NM	2,013.1	87	Honolulu, HI	1,061.8
38	Dallas, TX	2,011.8	88	Huntington Beach, CA	1,061.3
39	Washington, DC	1,995.2	89	El Paso, TX	1,017.6
40	Phoenix, AZ	1,983.6	90	Santa Ana, CA	1,017.0
41	Bakersfield, CA	1,922.0	91	Des Moines, IA	1,015.9
42	Tulsa, OK	1,901.9	92	Lincoln, NE	1,000.9
43	Wichita, KS	1,864.5	93	Philadelphia, PA	969.3
44	Denver, CO	1,831.5	94	Yonkers, NY	899.6
45	Montgomery, AL	1,830.3	95	Glendale, CA	889.2
46	Jersey City, NJ	1,819.4	96	Fremont, CA	874.5
47	San Antonio, TX	1,813.0	97	Madison, WI	815.6
48	Nashville, TN	1,781.2	98	Virginia Beach, VA	770.2
49	Seattle, WA	1,740.5	99	Anchorage, AK	749.8
50	Tucson, AZ	1,727.0	100	San Jose, CA	742.9

Source: U.S. Department of Justice, Federal Bureau of Investigation
"Crime in the United States 1993" (Uniform Crime Reports, December 4, 1994)
*Burglary is the unlawful entry of a structure to commit a felony or theft. Attempts are included.

71. Percent Change in Burglary Rate: 1992 to 1993

National Percent Change = 5.9% Decrease*

RANK	CITY	% CHANGE	RANK	CITY	% CHANGE
29	Akron, OH	1.07	30	Louisville, KY	0.83
54	Albuquerque, NM	(7.20)	80	Lubbock, TX	(12.09)
32	Anaheim, CA	(0.61)	94	Madison, WI	(18.37)
100	Anchorage, AK	(31.65)	42	Memphis, TN	(4.45)
68	Arlington, TX	(10.36)	20	Mesa, AZ	3.35
23	Atlanta, GA	2.79	27	Miami, FL	1.97
55	Aurora, CO	(7.24)	37	Milwaukee, WI	(2.61)
96	Austin, TX	(20.17)	19	Minneapolis, MN	3.49
31	Bakersfield, CA	(0.40)	44	Mobile, AL	(5.00)
7	Baltimore, MD	13.22	34	Montgomery, AL	(1.26)
2	Baton Rouge, LA	17.03	69	Nashville, TN	(10.44)
64	Birmingham, AL	(9.79)	18	New Orleans, LA	4.76
46	Boston, MA	(5.31)	39	New York, NY	(3.76)
50	Buffalo, NY	(5.87)	3	Newark, NJ	15.57
92	Charlotte, NC	(17.72)	59	Newport News, VA	(8.54)
47	Chicago, IL	(5.42)	22	Norfolk, VA	3.04
81	Cincinnati, OH	(12.29)	38	Oakland, CA	(3.54)
63	Cleveland, OH	(9.40)	77	Oklahoma City, OK	(11.73)
52	Colorado Springs, CO	(6.28)	51	Orlando, FL	(5.99)
86	Columbus, GA	(13.76)	41	Philadelphia, PA	(4.04)
85	Columbus, OH	(13.61)	36	Phoenix, AZ	(2.38)
84	Corpus Christi, TX	(13.59)	67	Pittsburgh, PA	(10.05)
88	Dallas, TX	(15.12)	66	Portland, OR	(9.82)
45	Dayton, OH	(5.20)	97	Raleigh, NC	(25.20)
28	Denver, CO	1.42	8	Richmond, VA	10.73
21	Des Moines, IA	3.20	9	Riverside, CA	10.25
16	Detroit, MI	7.21	61	Rochester, NY	(9.10)
99	El Paso, TX	(28.79)	12	Sacramento, CA	9.57
87	Fort Wayne, IN	(14.56)	95	San Antonio, TX	(19.71)
98	Fort Worth, TX	(26.26)	60	San Bernardino, CA	(8.72)
13	Fremont, CA	8.35	78	San Diego, CA	(11.95)
82	Fresno, CA	(12.98)	40	San Francisco, CA	(3.87)
91	Garland, TX	(16.52)	72	San Jose, CA	(11.05)
48	Glendale, CA	(5.44)	93	Santa Ana, CA	(18.27)
90	Grand Rapids, MI	(16.36)	25	Seattle, WA	2.54
53	Greensboro, NC	(6.66)	5	Shreveport, LA	14.03
26	Honolulu, HI	2.07	49	Spokane, WA	(5.57)
79	Houston, TX	(12.05)	4	Stockton, CA	14.52
24	Huntington Beach, CA	2.78	17	St. Louis, MO	4.83
1	Indianapolis, IN	22.97	73	St. Paul, MN	(11.28)
43	Jackson, MS	(4.79)	83	St. Petersburg, FL	(13.31)
58	Jacksonville, FL	(8.38)	6	Tacoma, WA	13.26
56	Jersey City, NJ	(7.92)	62	Tampa, FL	(9.23)
35	Kansas City, MO	(2.27)	57	Toledo, OH	(8.22)
70	Las Vegas, NV	(10.51)	15	Tucson, AZ	7.41
10	Lexington, KY	9.95	75	Tulsa, OK	(11.40)
76	Lincoln, NE	(11.57)	89	Virginia Beach, VA	(15.87)
14	Little Rock, AR	7.84	11	Washington, DC	9.63
65	Long Beach, CA	(9.81)	73	Wichita, KS	(11.28)
71	Los Angeles, CA	(10.83)	33	Yonkers, NY	(1.10)

Source: Morgan Quitno Corporation using data from U.S. Department of Justice, Federal Bureau of Investigation "Crime in the United States 1993" (Uniform Crime Reports, December 4, 1994)
*Burglary is the unlawful entry of a structure to commit a felony or theft. Attempts are included.

71. Percent Change in Burglary Rate: 1992 to 1993 (continued)

National Percent Change = 5.9% Decrease*

RANK	CITY	% CHANGE		RANK	CITY	% CHANGE
1	Indianapolis,IN	22.97		51	Orlando, FL	(5.99)
2	Baton Rouge, LA	17.03		52	Colorado Springs, CO	(6.28)
3	Newark, NJ	15.57		53	Greensboro, NC	(6.66)
4	Stockton, CA	14.52		54	Albuquerque, NM	(7.20)
5	Shreveport, LA	14.03		55	Aurora, CO	(7.24)
6	Tacoma, WA	13.26		56	Jersey City, NJ	(7.92)
7	Baltimore, MD	13.22		57	Toledo, OH	(8.22)
8	Richmond, VA	10.73		58	Jacksonville, FL	(8.38)
9	Riverside, CA	10.25		59	Newport News, VA	(8.54)
10	Lexington, KY	9.95		60	San Bernardino, CA	(8.72)
11	Washington, DC	9.63		61	Rochester, NY	(9.10)
12	Sacramento, CA	9.57		62	Tampa, FL	(9.23)
13	Fremont, CA	8.35		63	Cleveland, OH	(9.40)
14	Little Rock, AR	7.84		64	Birmingham, AL	(9.79)
15	Tucson, AZ	7.41		65	Long Beach, CA	(9.81)
16	Detroit, MI	7.21		66	Portland, OR	(9.82)
17	St. Louis, MO	4.83		67	Pittsburgh, PA	(10.05)
18	New Orleans, LA	4.76		68	Arlington, TX	(10.36)
19	Minneapolis, MN	3.49		69	Nashville, TN	(10.44)
20	Mesa, AZ	3.35		70	Las Vegas, NV	(10.51)
21	Des Moines, IA	3.20		71	Los Angeles, CA	(10.83)
22	Norfolk, VA	3.04		72	San Jose, CA	(11.05)
23	Atlanta, GA	2.79		73	St. Paul, MN	(11.28)
24	Huntington Beach, CA	2.78		73	Wichita, KS	(11.28)
25	Seattle, WA	2.54		75	Tulsa, OK	(11.40)
26	Honolulu, HI	2.07		76	Lincoln, NE	(11.57)
27	Miami, FL	1.97		77	Oklahoma City, OK	(11.73)
28	Denver, CO	1.42		78	San Diego, CA	(11.95)
29	Akron, OH	1.07		79	Houston, TX	(12.05)
30	Louisville, KY	0.83		80	Lubbock, TX	(12.09)
31	Bakersfield, CA	(0.40)		81	Cincinnati, OH	(12.29)
32	Anaheim, CA	(0.61)		82	Fresno, CA	(12.98)
33	Yonkers, NY	(1.10)		83	St. Petersburg, FL	(13.31)
34	Montgomery, AL	(1.26)		84	Corpus Christi, TX	(13.59)
35	Kansas City, MO	(2.27)		85	Columbus, OH	(13.61)
36	Phoenix, AZ	(2.38)		86	Columbus, GA	(13.76)
37	Milwaukee, WI	(2.61)		87	Fort Wayne, IN	(14.56)
38	Oakland, CA	(3.54)		88	Dallas, TX	(15.12)
39	New York, NY	(3.76)		89	Virginia Beach, VA	(15.87)
40	San Francisco, CA	(3.87)		90	Grand Rapids, MI	(16.36)
41	Philadelphia, PA	(4.04)		91	Garland, TX	(16.52)
42	Memphis, TN	(4.45)		92	Charlotte, NC	(17.72)
43	Jackson, MS	(4.79)		93	Santa Ana, CA	(18.27)
44	Mobile, AL	(5.00)		94	Madison, WI	(18.37)
45	Dayton, OH	(5.20)		95	San Antonio, TX	(19.71)
46	Boston, MA	(5.31)		96	Austin, TX	(20.17)
47	Chicago, IL	(5.42)		97	Raleigh, NC	(25.20)
48	Glendale, CA	(5.44)		98	Fort Worth, TX	(26.26)
49	Spokane, WA	(5.57)		99	El Paso, TX	(28.79)
50	Buffalo, NY	(5.87)		100	Anchorage, AK	(31.65)

Source: Morgan Quitno Corporation using data from U.S. Department of Justice, Federal Bureau of Investigation
"Crime in the United States 1993" (Uniform Crime Reports, December 4, 1994)
*Burglary is the unlawful entry of a structure to commit a felony or theft. Attempts are included.

72. Percent Change in Burglary Rate: 1989 to 1993

National Percent Change = 13.9% Decrease*

RANK	CITY	% CHANGE	RANK	CITY	% CHANGE
60	Akron, OH	11.53	46	Louisville, KY	20.24
30	Albuquerque, NM	42.10	71	Lubbock, TX	4.25
64	Anaheim, CA	9.28	26	Madison, WI	44.99
5	Anchorage, AK	85.96	22	Memphis, TN	49.29
54	Arlington, TX	18.78	6	Mesa, AZ	80.67
84	Atlanta, GA	(5.84)	79	Miami, FL	(0.58)
8	Aurora, CO	74.48	15	Milwaukee, WI	60.61
28	Austin, TX	42.52	48	Minneapolis, MN	19.64
91	Bakersfield, CA	(20.39)	27	Mobile, AL	43.61
14	Baltimore, MD	61.76	4	Montgomery, AL	89.08
1	Baton Rouge, LA	165.08	13	Nashville, TN	64.45
78	Birmingham, AL	(0.08)	75	New Orleans, LA	2.19
95	Boston, MA	(27.14)	85	New York, NY	(7.62)
19	Buffalo, NY	53.28	39	Newark, NJ	29.02
47	Charlotte, NC	20.02	3	Newport News, VA	128.29
51	Chicago, IL	19.35	11	Norfolk, VA	69.46
12	Cincinnati, OH	65.48	31	Oakland, CA	37.39
62	Cleveland, OH	10.05	77	Oklahoma City, OK	0.69
70	Colorado Springs, CO	4.50	89	Orlando, FL	(15.62)
65	Columbus, GA	8.22	49	Philadelphia, PA	19.37
63	Columbus, OH	9.96	52	Phoenix, AZ	19.13
88	Corpus Christi, TX	(13.44)	56	Pittsburgh, PA	15.10
94	Dallas, TX	(24.90)	90	Portland, OR	(19.11)
80	Dayton, OH	(1.91)	7	Raleigh, NC	76.61
24	Denver, CO	45.90	20	Richmond, VA	53.15
93	Des Moines, IA	(24.51)	34	Riverside, CA	35.16
55	Detroit, MI	16.38	32	Rochester, NY	36.79
40	El Paso, TX	27.43	41	Sacramento, CA	25.38
69	Fort Wayne, IN	4.52	67	San Antonio, TX	5.92
76	Fort Worth, TX	1.26	-	San Bernardino, CA**	NA
37	Fremont, CA	30.02	42	San Diego, CA	22.80
16	Fresno, CA	56.61	10	San Francisco, CA	72.26
18	Garland, TX	53.68	59	San Jose, CA	11.58
44	Glendale, CA	20.76	29	Santa Ana, CA	42.12
33	Grand Rapids, MI	36.08	68	Seattle, WA	5.61
49	Greensboro, NC	19.37	61	Shreveport, LA	10.46
38	Honolulu, HI	29.06	87	Spokane, WA	(12.08)
-	Houston, TX**	NA	57	Stockton, CA	14.43
53	Huntington Beach, CA	19.05	17	St. Louis, MO	54.33
25	Indianapolis, IN	45.46	66	St. Paul, MN	7.65
2	Jackson, MS	136.29	96	St. Petersburg, FL	(28.06)
86	Jacksonville, FL	(10.92)	97	Tacoma, WA	(28.11)
74	Jersey City, NJ	2.59	83	Tampa, FL	(5.29)
73	Kansas City, MO	2.93	72	Toledo, OH	4.04
36	Las Vegas, NV	30.48	-	Tucson, AZ**	NA
23	Lexington, KY	47.36	92	Tulsa, OK	(21.86)
43	Lincoln, NE	22.33	9	Virginia Beach, VA	73.46
81	Little Rock, AR	(1.99)	58	Washington, DC	13.55
82	Long Beach, CA	(5.06)	34	Wichita, KS	35.16
45	Los Angeles, CA	20.73	21	Yonkers, NY	50.59

Source: Morgan Quitno Corporation using data from U.S. Department of Justice, Federal Bureau of Investigation
"Crime in the United States 1993" (Uniform Crime Reports, December 4, 1994)
*Burglary is the unlawful entry of a structure to commit a felony or theft. Attempts are included.

72. Percent Change in Burglary Rate: 1989 to 1993 (continued)

National Percent Change = 13.9% Decrease*

RANK	CITY	% CHANGE	RANK	CITY	% CHANGE
1	Baton Rouge, LA	165.08	51	Chicago, IL	19.35
2	Jackson, MS	136.29	52	Phoenix, AZ	19.13
3	Newport News, VA	128.29	53	Huntington Beach, CA	19.05
4	Montgomery, AL	89.08	54	Arlington, TX	18.78
5	Anchorage, AK	85.96	55	Detroit, MI	16.38
6	Mesa, AZ	80.67	56	Pittsburgh, PA	15.10
7	Raleigh, NC	76.61	57	Stockton, CA	14.43
8	Aurora, CO	74.48	58	Washington, DC	13.55
9	Virginia Beach, VA	73.46	59	San Jose, CA	11.58
10	San Francisco, CA	72.26	60	Akron, OH	11.53
11	Norfolk, VA	69.46	61	Shreveport, LA	10.46
12	Cincinnati, OH	65.48	62	Cleveland, OH	10.05
13	Nashville, TN	64.45	63	Columbus, OH	9.96
14	Baltimore, MD	61.76	64	Anaheim, CA	9.28
15	Milwaukee, WI	60.61	65	Columbus, GA	8.22
16	Fresno, CA	56.61	66	St. Paul, MN	7.65
17	St. Louis, MO	54.33	67	San Antonio, TX	5.92
18	Garland, TX	53.68	68	Seattle, WA	5.61
19	Buffalo, NY	53.28	69	Fort Wayne, IN	4.52
20	Richmond, VA	53.15	70	Colorado Springs, CO	4.50
21	Yonkers, NY	50.59	71	Lubbock, TX	4.25
22	Memphis, TN	49.29	72	Toledo, OH	4.04
23	Lexington, KY	47.36	73	Kansas City, MO	2.93
24	Denver, CO	45.90	74	Jersey City, NJ	2.59
25	Indianapolis, IN	45.46	75	New Orleans, LA	2.19
26	Madison, WI	44.99	76	Fort Worth, TX	1.26
27	Mobile, AL	43.61	77	Oklahoma City, OK	0.69
28	Austin, TX	42.52	78	Birmingham, AL	(0.08)
29	Santa Ana, CA	42.12	79	Miami, FL	(0.58)
30	Albuquerque, NM	42.10	80	Dayton, OH	(1.91)
31	Oakland, CA	37.39	81	Little Rock, AR	(1.99)
32	Rochester, NY	36.79	82	Long Beach, CA	(5.06)
33	Grand Rapids, MI	36.08	83	Tampa, FL	(5.29)
34	Riverside, CA	35.16	84	Atlanta, GA	(5.84)
34	Wichita, KS	35.16	85	New York, NY	(7.62)
36	Las Vegas, NV	30.48	86	Jacksonville, FL	(10.92)
37	Fremont, CA	30.02	87	Spokane, WA	(12.08)
38	Honolulu, HI	29.06	88	Corpus Christi, TX	(13.44)
39	Newark, NJ	29.02	89	Orlando, FL	(15.62)
40	El Paso, TX	27.43	90	Portland, OR	(19.11)
41	Sacramento, CA	25.38	91	Bakersfield, CA	(20.39)
42	San Diego, CA	22.80	92	Tulsa, OK	(21.86)
43	Lincoln, NE	22.33	93	Des Moines, IA	(24.51)
44	Glendale, CA	20.76	94	Dallas, TX	(24.90)
45	Los Angeles, CA	20.73	95	Boston, MA	(27.14)
46	Louisville, KY	20.24	96	St. Petersburg, FL	(28.06)
47	Charlotte, NC	20.02	97	Tacoma, WA	(28.11)
48	Minneapolis, MN	19.64	-	Houston, TX**	NA
49	Greensboro, NC	19.37	-	San Bernardino, CA**	NA
49	Philadelphia, PA	19.37	-	Tucson, AZ**	NA

Source: Morgan Quitno Corporation using data from U.S. Department of Justice, Federal Bureau of Investigation "Crime in the United States 1993" (Uniform Crime Reports, December 4, 1994)
*Burglary is the unlawful entry of a structure to commit a felony or theft. Attempts are included.

Alpha Order – City

73. Larceny and Theft in 1993

National Total = 7,820,909 Larcenies and Thefts*

RANK	CITY	THEFTS
86	Akron, OH	8,675
36	Albuquerque, NM	20,552
83	Anaheim, CA	9,145
73	Anchorage, AK	10,660
68	Arlington, TX	11,514
21	Atlanta, GA	31,249
69	Aurora, CO	11,512
14	Austin, TX	35,647
87	Bakersfield, CA	8,498
9	Baltimore, MD	41,451
42	Baton Rouge, LA	18,156
47	Birmingham, AL	14,926
30	Boston, MA	24,798
61	Buffalo, NY	12,714
27	Charlotte, NC	26,370
2	Chicago, IL	121,314
44	Cincinnati, OH	17,085
57	Cleveland, OH	13,494
58	Colorado Springs, CO	13,391
91	Columbus, GA	7,752
24	Columbus, OH	29,051
39	Corpus Christi, TX	18,919
6	Dallas, TX	54,183
81	Dayton, OH	9,473
43	Denver, CO	17,858
63	Des Moines, IA	11,763
8	Detroit, MI	42,818
22	El Paso, TX	29,440
76	Fort Wayne, IN	10,016
28	Fort Worth, TX	26,310
100	Fremont, CA	3,945
49	Fresno, CA	14,518
92	Garland, TX	7,657
99	Glendale, CA	4,501
85	Grand Rapids, MI	8,827
79	Greensboro, NC	9,657
10	Honolulu, HI	40,148
4	Houston, TX	61,569
97	Huntington Beach, CA	5,042
51	Indianapolis, IN	14,383
66	Jackson, MS	11,603
18	Jacksonville, FL	31,936
95	Jersey City, NJ	6,331
32	Kansas City, MO	23,611
31	Las Vegas, NV	23,855
78	Lexington, KY	9,684
75	Lincoln, NE	10,023
52	Little Rock, AR	14,306
53	Long Beach, CA	14,108
3	Los Angeles, CA	119,092
89	Louisville, KY	8,076
90	Lubbock, TX	7,927
93	Madison, WI	7,466
33	Memphis, TN	23,434
50	Mesa, AZ	14,430
19	Miami, FL	31,871
29	Milwaukee, WI	25,553
37	Minneapolis, MN	19,952
77	Mobile, AL	9,926
96	Montgomery, AL	5,843
16	Nashville, TN	32,456
34	New Orleans, LA	22,019
1	New York, NY	235,132
74	Newark, NJ	10,420
94	Newport News, VA	7,267
55	Norfolk, VA	13,535
38	Oakland, CA	18,991
23	Oklahoma City, OK	29,316
65	Orlando, FL	11,655
11	Philadelphia, PA	39,181
7	Phoenix, AZ	48,382
59	Pittsburgh, PA	13,017
25	Portland, OR	27,016
82	Raleigh, NC	9,395
67	Richmond, VA	11,571
80	Riverside, CA	9,635
56	Rochester, NY	13,522
40	Sacramento, CA	18,670
5	San Antonio, TX	61,284
88	San Bernardino, CA	8,410
13	San Diego, CA	37,862
15	San Francisco, CA	34,558
35	San Jose, CA	21,398
84	Santa Ana, CA	8,973
12	Seattle, WA	39,176
54	Shreveport, LA	13,784
72	Spokane, WA	10,965
62	Stockton, CA	12,291
26	St. Louis, MO	26,975
71	St. Paul, MN	11,329
64	St. Petersburg, FL	11,729
70	Tacoma, WA	11,355
41	Tampa, FL	18,534
46	Toledo, OH	15,251
17	Tucson, AZ	32,076
60	Tulsa, OK	12,790
48	Virginia Beach, VA	14,812
20	Washington, DC	31,466
45	Wichita, KS	16,264
98	Yonkers, NY	4,593

Source: U.S. Department of Justice, Federal Bureau of Investigation
"Crime in the United States 1993" (Uniform Crime Reports, December 4, 1994)
*Larceny and theft is the unlawful taking of property without use of force, violence or fraud. Attempts are included. Motor vehicle thefts are excluded.
**Not available.

228

73. Larceny and Theft in 1993 (continued)

National Total = 7,820,909 Larcenies and Thefts*

RANK	CITY	THEFTS	RANK	CITY	THEFTS
1	New York, NY	235,132	51	Indianapolis, IN	14,383
2	Chicago, IL	121,314	52	Little Rock, AR	14,306
3	Los Angeles, CA	119,092	53	Long Beach, CA	14,108
4	Houston, TX	61,569	54	Shreveport, LA	13,784
5	San Antonio, TX	61,284	55	Norfolk, VA	13,535
6	Dallas, TX	54,183	56	Rochester, NY	13,522
7	Phoenix, AZ	48,382	57	Cleveland, OH	13,494
8	Detroit, MI	42,818	58	Colorado Springs, CO	13,391
9	Baltimore, MD	41,451	59	Pittsburgh, PA	13,017
10	Honolulu, HI	40,148	60	Tulsa, OK	12,790
11	Philadelphia, PA	39,181	61	Buffalo, NY	12,714
12	Seattle, WA	39,176	62	Stockton, CA	12,291
13	San Diego, CA	37,862	63	Des Moines, IA	11,763
14	Austin, TX	35,647	64	St. Petersburg, FL	11,729
15	San Francisco, CA	34,558	65	Orlando, FL	11,655
16	Nashville, TN	32,456	66	Jackson, MS	11,603
17	Tucson, AZ	32,076	67	Richmond, VA	11,571
18	Jacksonville, FL	31,936	68	Arlington, TX	11,514
19	Miami, FL	31,871	69	Aurora, CO	11,512
20	Washington, DC	31,466	70	Tacoma, WA	11,355
21	Atlanta, GA	31,249	71	St. Paul, MN	11,329
22	El Paso, TX	29,440	72	Spokane, WA	10,965
23	Oklahoma City, OK	29,316	73	Anchorage, AK	10,660
24	Columbus, OH	29,051	74	Newark, NJ	10,420
25	Portland, OR	27,016	75	Lincoln, NE	10,023
26	St. Louis, MO	26,975	76	Fort Wayne, IN	10,016
27	Charlotte, NC	26,370	77	Mobile, AL	9,926
28	Fort Worth, TX	26,310	78	Lexington, KY	9,684
29	Milwaukee, WI	25,553	79	Greensboro, NC	9,657
30	Boston, MA	24,798	80	Riverside, CA	9,635
31	Las Vegas, NV	23,855	81	Dayton, OH	9,473
32	Kansas City, MO	23,611	82	Raleigh, NC	9,395
33	Memphis, TN	23,434	83	Anaheim, CA	9,145
34	New Orleans, LA	22,019	84	Santa Ana, CA	8,973
35	San Jose, CA	21,398	85	Grand Rapids, MI	8,827
36	Albuquerque, NM	20,552	86	Akron, OH	8,675
37	Minneapolis, MN	19,952	87	Bakersfield, CA	8,498
38	Oakland, CA	18,991	88	San Bernardino, CA	8,410
39	Corpus Christi, TX	18,919	89	Louisville, KY	8,076
40	Sacramento, CA	18,670	90	Lubbock, TX	7,927
41	Tampa, FL	18,534	91	Columbus, GA	7,752
42	Baton Rouge, LA	18,156	92	Garland, TX	7,657
43	Denver, CO	17,858	93	Madison, WI	7,466
44	Cincinnati, OH	17,085	94	Newport News, VA	7,267
45	Wichita, KS	16,264	95	Jersey City, NJ	6,331
46	Toledo, OH	15,251	96	Montgomery, AL	5,843
47	Birmingham, AL	14,926	97	Huntington Beach, CA	5,042
48	Virginia Beach, VA	14,812	98	Yonkers, NY	4,593
49	Fresno, CA	14,518	99	Glendale, CA	4,501
50	Mesa, AZ	14,430	100	Fremont, CA	3,945

Source: U.S. Department of Justice, Federal Bureau of Investigation
   "Crime in the United States 1993" (Uniform Crime Reports, December 4, 1994)
*Larceny and theft is the unlawful taking of property without use of force, violence or fraud. Attempts are included. Motor vehicle thefts are excluded.
**Not available.

74. Larceny and Theft Rate in 1993

National Rate = 3,032.4 Larcenies and Thefts per 100,000 Population*

RANK	CITY	RATE	RANK	CITY	RATE
74	Akron, OH	3,854.9	92	Louisville, KY	2,952.1
38	Albuquerque, NM	5,046.1	64	Lubbock, TX	4,136.4
86	Anaheim, CA	3,305.1	77	Madison, WI	3,791.4
60	Anchorage, AK	4,251.8	78	Memphis, TN	3,785.9
67	Arlington, TX	4,092.6	46	Mesa, AZ	4,735.9
4	Atlanta, GA	7,756.5	1	Miami, FL	8,555.5
48	Aurora, CO	4,668.1	66	Milwaukee, WI	4,100.9
7	Austin, TX	7,100.7	30	Minneapolis, MN	5,441.8
57	Bakersfield, CA	4,474.8	42	Mobile, AL	4,858.9
25	Baltimore, MD	5,655.2	91	Montgomery, AL	3,005.7
2	Baton Rouge, LA	8,049.9	14	Nashville, TN	6,318.7
27	Birmingham, AL	5,553.5	55	New Orleans, LA	4,478.9
56	Boston, MA	4,477.2	88	New York, NY	3,200.3
72	Buffalo, NY	3,913.7	73	Newark, NJ	3,860.8
15	Charlotte, NC	6,236.1	69	Newport News, VA	4,037.8
59	Chicago, IL	4,349.7	33	Norfolk, VA	5,253.9
49	Cincinnati, OH	4,660.5	39	Oakland, CA	5,036.9
95	Cleveland, OH	2,668.2	13	Oklahoma City, OK	6,408.6
58	Colorado Springs, CO	4,398.6	11	Orlando, FL	6,594.1
68	Columbus, GA	4,072.9	97	Philadelphia, PA	2,512.4
54	Columbus, OH	4,490.6	50	Phoenix, AZ	4,654.9
10	Corpus Christi, TX	6,966.7	81	Pittsburgh, PA	3,532.7
34	Dallas, TX	5,196.8	19	Portland, OR	5,939.0
36	Dayton, OH	5,138.5	62	Raleigh, NC	4,193.1
79	Denver, CO	3,583.1	26	Richmond, VA	5,635.3
18	Des Moines, IA	6,017.3	70	Riverside, CA	3,997.2
61	Detroit, MI	4,197.6	21	Rochester, NY	5,746.7
32	El Paso, TX	5,309.1	43	Sacramento, CA	4,827.6
23	Fort Wayne, IN	5,710.2	16	San Antonio, TX	6,218.8
24	Fort Worth, TX	5,677.9	44	San Bernardino, CA	4,827.4
100	Fremont, CA	2,177.9	87	San Diego, CA	3,262.3
75	Fresno, CA	3,820.8	47	San Francisco, CA	4,693.0
71	Garland, TX	3,928.1	96	San Jose, CA	2,643.3
98	Glendale, CA	2,507.7	90	Santa Ana, CA	3,093.4
52	Grand Rapids, MI	4,594.5	6	Seattle, WA	7,374.0
40	Greensboro, NC	5,004.9	8	Shreveport, LA	6,983.5
53	Honolulu, HI	4,586.0	22	Spokane, WA	5,725.5
80	Houston, TX	3,570.6	28	Stockton, CA	5,539.8
94	Huntington Beach, CA	2,697.0	9	St. Louis, MO	6,969.3
76	Indianapolis, IN	3,807.8	63	St. Paul, MN	4,177.2
20	Jackson, MS	5,853.4	41	St. Petersburg, FL	4,913.1
45	Jacksonville, FL	4,750.2	17	Tacoma, WA	6,043.3
93	Jersey City, NJ	2,749.0	12	Tampa, FL	6,415.9
31	Kansas City, MO	5,422.5	51	Toledo, OH	4,601.8
85	Las Vegas, NV	3,325.0	5	Tucson, AZ	7,523.5
65	Lexington, KY	4,119.2	83	Tulsa, OK	3,380.5
37	Lincoln, NE	5,056.3	82	Virginia Beach, VA	3,498.5
3	Little Rock, AR	7,995.6	29	Washington, DC	5,443.9
89	Long Beach, CA	3,182.8	35	Wichita, KS	5,186.3
84	Los Angeles, CA	3,378.2	99	Yonkers, NY	2,456.6

Source: U.S. Department of Justice, Federal Bureau of Investigation
   "Crime in the United States 1993" (Uniform Crime Reports, December 4, 1994)
Larceny and theft is the unlawful taking of property without use of force, violence or fraud. Attempts are included. Motor vehicle thefts are excluded.
**Not available.*

74. Larceny and Theft Rate in 1993 (continued)

National Rate = 3,032.4 Larcenies and Thefts per 100,000 Population*

RANK	CITY	RATE	RANK	CITY	RATE
1	Miami, FL	8,555.5	51	Toledo, OH	4,601.8
2	Baton Rouge, LA	8,049.9	52	Grand Rapids, MI	4,594.5
3	Little Rock, AR	7,995.6	53	Honolulu, HI	4,586.0
4	Atlanta, GA	7,756.5	54	Columbus, OH	4,490.6
5	Tucson, AZ	7,523.5	55	New Orleans, LA	4,478.9
6	Seattle, WA	7,374.0	56	Boston, MA	4,477.2
7	Austin, TX	7,100.7	57	Bakersfield, CA	4,474.8
8	Shreveport, LA	6,983.5	58	Colorado Springs, CO	4,398.6
9	St. Louis, MO	6,969.3	59	Chicago, IL	4,349.7
10	Corpus Christi, TX	6,966.7	60	Anchorage, AK	4,251.8
11	Orlando, FL	6,594.1	61	Detroit, MI	4,197.6
12	Tampa, FL	6,415.9	62	Raleigh, NC	4,193.1
13	Oklahoma City, OK	6,408.6	63	St. Paul, MN	4,177.2
14	Nashville, TN	6,318.7	64	Lubbock, TX	4,136.4
15	Charlotte, NC	6,236.1	65	Lexington, KY	4,119.2
16	San Antonio, TX	6,218.8	66	Milwaukee, WI	4,100.9
17	Tacoma, WA	6,043.3	67	Arlington, TX	4,092.6
18	Des Moines, IA	6,017.3	68	Columbus, GA	4,072.9
19	Portland, OR	5,939.0	69	Newport News, VA	4,037.8
20	Jackson, MS	5,853.4	70	Riverside, CA	3,997.2
21	Rochester, NY	5,746.7	71	Garland, TX	3,928.1
22	Spokane, WA	5,725.5	72	Buffalo, NY	3,913.7
23	Fort Wayne, IN	5,710.2	73	Newark, NJ	3,860.8
24	Fort Worth, TX	5,677.9	74	Akron, OH	3,854.9
25	Baltimore, MD	5,655.2	75	Fresno, CA	3,820.8
26	Richmond, VA	5,635.3	76	Indianapolis, IN	3,807.8
27	Birmingham, AL	5,553.5	77	Madison, WI	3,791.4
28	Stockton, CA	5,539.8	78	Memphis, TN	3,785.9
29	Washington, DC	5,443.9	79	Denver, CO	3,583.1
30	Minneapolis, MN	5,441.8	80	Houston, TX	3,570.6
31	Kansas City, MO	5,422.5	81	Pittsburgh, PA	3,532.7
32	El Paso, TX	5,309.1	82	Virginia Beach, VA	3,498.5
33	Norfolk, VA	5,253.9	83	Tulsa, OK	3,380.5
34	Dallas, TX	5,196.8	84	Los Angeles, CA	3,378.2
35	Wichita, KS	5,186.3	85	Las Vegas, NV	3,325.0
36	Dayton, OH	5,138.5	86	Anaheim, CA	3,305.1
37	Lincoln, NE	5,056.3	87	San Diego, CA	3,262.3
38	Albuquerque, NM	5,046.1	88	New York, NY	3,200.3
39	Oakland, CA	5,036.9	89	Long Beach, CA	3,182.8
40	Greensboro, NC	5,004.9	90	Santa Ana, CA	3,093.4
41	St. Petersburg, FL	4,913.1	91	Montgomery, AL	3,005.7
42	Mobile, AL	4,858.9	92	Louisville, KY	2,952.1
43	Sacramento, CA	4,827.6	93	Jersey City, NJ	2,749.0
44	San Bernardino, CA	4,827.4	94	Huntington Beach, CA	2,697.0
45	Jacksonville, FL	4,750.2	95	Cleveland, OH	2,668.2
46	Mesa, AZ	4,735.9	96	San Jose, CA	2,643.3
47	San Francisco, CA	4,693.0	97	Philadelphia, PA	2,512.4
48	Aurora, CO	4,668.1	98	Glendale, CA	2,507.7
49	Cincinnati, OH	4,660.5	99	Yonkers, NY	2,456.6
50	Phoenix, AZ	4,654.9	100	Fremont, CA	2,177.9

Source: U.S. Department of Justice, Federal Bureau of Investigation
  "Crime in the United States 1993" (Uniform Crime Reports, December 4, 1994)
*Larceny and theft is the unlawful taking of property without use of force, violence or fraud. Attempts are included. Motor vehicle thefts are excluded.
**Not available.

Alpha Order – City

75. Percent Change in Larceny and Theft Rate: 1992 to 1993

National Percent Change = 2.3% Decrease*

RANK	CITY	% CHANGE	RANK	CITY	% CHANGE
67	Akron, OH	(3.73)	87	Louisville, KY	(7.94)
35	Albuquerque, NM	0.06	79	Lubbock, TX	(5.88)
71	Anaheim, CA	(4.33)	91	Madison, WI	(9.58)
75	Anchorage, AK	(5.01)	17	Memphis, TN	5.01
100	Arlington, TX	(19.32)	3	Mesa, AZ	17.51
80	Atlanta, GA	(6.00)	21	Miami, FL	4.40
64	Aurora, CO	(3.36)	39	Milwaukee, WI	(0.26)
59	Austin, TX	(2.75)	63	Minneapolis, MN	(3.24)
34	Bakersfield, CA	0.59	98	Mobile, AL	(16.95)
18	Baltimore, MD	4.93	85	Montgomery, AL	(7.64)
4	Baton Rouge, LA	13.79	1	Nashville, TN	24.59
42	Birmingham, AL	(0.68)	7	New Orleans, LA	11.19
22	Boston, MA	4.26	36	New York, NY	(0.06)
47	Buffalo, NY	(1.16)	44	Newark, NJ	(0.98)
78	Charlotte, NC	(5.60)	76	Newport News, VA	(5.51)
26	Chicago, IL	2.95	32	Norfolk, VA	1.32
58	Cincinnati, OH	(2.63)	89	Oakland, CA	(8.74)
68	Cleveland, OH	(3.79)	12	Oklahoma City, OK	6.97
77	Colorado Springs, CO	(5.55)	20	Orlando, FL	4.67
16	Columbus, GA	5.29	29	Philadelphia, PA	1.54
46	Columbus, OH	(1.14)	33	Phoenix, AZ	1.17
25	Corpus Christi, TX	3.28	27	Pittsburgh, PA	2.58
96	Dallas, TX	(13.78)	28	Portland, OR	2.43
48	Dayton, OH	(1.29)	65	Raleigh, NC	(3.66)
49	Denver, CO	(1.34)	53	Richmond, VA	(2.10)
90	Des Moines, IA	(8.87)	11	Riverside, CA	7.94
14	Detroit, MI	5.85	94	Rochester, NY	(12.31)
66	El Paso, TX	(3.71)	30	Sacramento, CA	1.53
81	Fort Wayne, IN	(6.03)	84	San Antonio, TX	(7.37)
99	Fort Worth, TX	(17.78)	70	San Bernardino, CA	(4.11)
83	Fremont, CA	(6.86)	86	San Diego, CA	(7.89)
97	Fresno, CA	(16.00)	88	San Francisco, CA	(8.17)
53	Garland, TX	(2.10)	92	San Jose, CA	(9.91)
13	Glendale, CA	6.26	72	Santa Ana, CA	(4.36)
61	Grand Rapids, MI	(2.95)	55	Seattle, WA	(2.29)
73	Greensboro, NC	(4.77)	8	Shreveport, LA	9.78
23	Honolulu, HI	4.09	37	Spokane, WA	(0.09)
60	Houston, TX	(2.84)	40	Stockton, CA	(0.41)
5	Huntington Beach, CA	11.47	9	St. Louis, MO	9.60
2	Indianapolis, IN	19.42	43	St. Paul, MN	(0.75)
57	Jackson, MS	(2.62)	51	St. Petersburg, FL	(1.50)
74	Jacksonville, FL	(4.83)	38	Tacoma, WA	(0.21)
69	Jersey City, NJ	(3.84)	45	Tampa, FL	(1.02)
10	Kansas City, MO	9.50	62	Toledo, OH	(3.11)
95	Las Vegas, NV	(13.63)	6	Tucson, AZ	11.38
31	Lexington, KY	1.50	52	Tulsa, OK	(1.99)
93	Lincoln, NE	(10.10)	82	Virginia Beach, VA	(6.19)
24	Little Rock, AR	3.76	19	Washington, DC	4.72
56	Long Beach, CA	(2.50)	41	Wichita, KS	(0.58)
50	Los Angeles, CA	(1.39)	15	Yonkers, NY	5.35

Source: Morgan Quitno Corporation using data from U.S. Department of Justice, Federal Bureau of Investigation "Crime in the United States 1993" (Uniform Crime Reports, December 4, 1994)
*Larceny and theft is the unlawful taking of property without use of force, violence or fraud. Attempts are included. Motor vehicle thefts are excluded.
**Not available.

232

75. Percent Change in Larceny and Theft Rate: 1992 to 1993 (continued)

National Percent Change = 2.3% Decrease*

RANK	CITY	% CHANGE	RANK	CITY	% CHANGE
1	Nashville, TN	24.59	51	St. Petersburg, FL	(1.50)
2	Indianapolis, IN	19.42	52	Tulsa, OK	(1.99)
3	Mesa, AZ	17.51	53	Garland, TX	(2.10)
4	Baton Rouge, LA	13.79	53	Richmond, VA	(2.10)
5	Huntington Beach, CA	11.47	55	Seattle, WA	(2.29)
6	Tucson, AZ	11.38	56	Long Beach, CA	(2.50)
7	New Orleans, LA	11.19	57	Jackson, MS	(2.62)
8	Shreveport, LA	9.78	58	Cincinnati, OH	(2.63)
9	St. Louis, MO	9.60	59	Austin, TX	(2.75)
10	Kansas City, MO	9.50	60	Houston, TX	(2.84)
11	Riverside, CA	7.94	61	Grand Rapids, MI	(2.95)
12	Oklahoma City, OK	6.97	62	Toledo, OH	(3.11)
13	Glendale, CA	6.26	63	Minneapolis, MN	(3.24)
14	Detroit, MI	5.85	64	Aurora, CO	(3.36)
15	Yonkers, NY	5.35	65	Raleigh, NC	(3.66)
16	Columbus, GA	5.29	66	El Paso, TX	(3.71)
17	Memphis, TN	5.01	67	Akron, OH	(3.73)
18	Baltimore, MD	4.93	68	Cleveland, OH	(3.79)
19	Washington, DC	4.72	69	Jersey City, NJ	(3.84)
20	Orlando, FL	4.67	70	San Bernardino, CA	(4.11)
21	Miami, FL	4.40	71	Anaheim, CA	(4.33)
22	Boston, MA	4.26	72	Santa Ana, CA	(4.36)
23	Honolulu, HI	4.09	73	Greensboro, NC	(4.77)
24	Little Rock, AR	3.76	74	Jacksonville, FL	(4.83)
25	Corpus Christi, TX	3.28	75	Anchorage, AK	(5.01)
26	Chicago, IL	2.95	76	Newport News, VA	(5.51)
27	Pittsburgh, PA	2.58	77	Colorado Springs, CO	(5.55)
28	Portland, OR	2.43	78	Charlotte, NC	(5.60)
29	Philadelphia, PA	1.54	79	Lubbock, TX	(5.88)
30	Sacramento, CA	1.53	80	Atlanta, GA	(6.00)
31	Lexington, KY	1.50	81	Fort Wayne, IN	(6.03)
32	Norfolk, VA	1.32	82	Virginia Beach, VA	(6.19)
33	Phoenix, AZ	1.17	83	Fremont, CA	(6.86)
34	Bakersfield, CA	0.59	84	San Antonio, TX	(7.37)
35	Albuquerque, NM	0.06	85	Montgomery, AL	(7.64)
36	New York, NY	(0.06)	86	San Diego, CA	(7.89)
37	Spokane, WA	(0.09)	87	Louisville, KY	(7.94)
38	Tacoma, WA	(0.21)	88	San Francisco, CA	(8.17)
39	Milwaukee, WI	(0.26)	89	Oakland, CA	(8.74)
40	Stockton, CA	(0.41)	90	Des Moines, IA	(8.87)
41	Wichita, KS	(0.58)	91	Madison, WI	(9.58)
42	Birmingham, AL	(0.68)	92	San Jose, CA	(9.91)
43	St. Paul, MN	(0.75)	93	Lincoln, NE	(10.10)
44	Newark, NJ	(0.98)	94	Rochester, NY	(12.31)
45	Tampa, FL	(1.02)	95	Las Vegas, NV	(13.63)
46	Columbus, OH	(1.14)	96	Dallas, TX	(13.78)
47	Buffalo, NY	(1.16)	97	Fresno, CA	(16.00)
48	Dayton, OH	(1.29)	98	Mobile, AL	(16.95)
49	Denver, CO	(1.34)	99	Fort Worth, TX	(17.78)
50	Los Angeles, CA	(1.39)	100	Arlington, TX	(19.32)

Source: Morgan Quitno Corporation using data from U.S. Department of Justice, Federal Bureau of Investigation
"Crime in the United States 1993" (Uniform Crime Reports, December 4, 1994)
*Larceny and theft is the unlawful taking of property without use of force, violence or fraud. Attempts are included. Motor vehicle thefts are excluded.
**Not available.

76. Percent Change in Larceny and Theft Rate: 1989 to 1993

National Percent Change = 4.4% Decrease*

RANK	CITY	% CHANGE	RANK	CITY	% CHANGE
56	Akron, OH	(9.47)	41	Louisville, KY	(3.24)
60	Albuquerque, NM	(10.40)	69	Lubbock, TX	(14.87)
55	Anaheim, CA	(9.06)	88	Madison, WI	(23.05)
8	Anchorage, AK	15.55	12	Memphis, TN	11.15
80	Arlington, TX	(18.33)	10	Mesa, AZ	12.83
86	Atlanta, GA	(22.46)	22	Miami, FL	4.30
29	Aurora, CO	0.22	77	Milwaukee, WI	(18.03)
33	Austin, TX	(0.78)	62	Minneapolis, MN	(11.61)
67	Bakersfield, CA	(13.74)	43	Mobile, AL	(4.08)
3	Baltimore, MD	29.73	92	Montgomery, AL	(26.12)
6	Baton Rouge, LA	21.35	1	Nashville, TN	66.84
4	Birmingham, AL	27.60	44	New Orleans, LA	(5.05)
72	Boston, MA	(15.66)	78	New York, NY	(18.04)
23	Buffalo, NY	4.27	36	Newark, NJ	(1.63)
61	Charlotte, NC	(11.41)	11	Newport News, VA	11.74
32	Chicago, IL	(0.13)	34	Norfolk, VA	(1.53)
18	Cincinnati, OH	5.76	87	Oakland, CA	(22.93)
59	Cleveland, OH	(10.31)	7	Oklahoma City, OK	16.63
63	Colorado Springs, CO	(12.48)	25	Orlando, FL	3.36
19	Columbus, GA	5.39	76	Philadelphia, PA	(17.98)
81	Columbus, OH	(18.51)	89	Phoenix, AZ	(24.61)
28	Corpus Christi, TX	1.19	21	Pittsburgh, PA	4.96
96	Dallas, TX	(34.68)	47	Portland, OR	(6.00)
73	Dayton, OH	(17.27)	63	Raleigh, NC	(12.48)
39	Denver, CO	(2.48)	24	Richmond, VA	3.59
58	Des Moines, IA	(9.57)	16	Riverside, CA	6.43
30	Detroit, MI	0.14	83	Rochester, NY	(19.05)
74	El Paso, TX	(17.65)	50	Sacramento, CA	(6.64)
49	Fort Wayne, IN	(6.54)	75	San Antonio, TX	(17.73)
95	Fort Worth, TX	(29.46)	-	San Bernardino, CA**	NA
27	Fremont, CA	1.61	94	San Diego, CA	(28.01)
98	Fresno, CA	(35.44)	46	San Francisco, CA	(5.56)
13	Garland, TX	8.32	71	San Jose, CA	(15.31)
79	Glendale, CA	(18.23)	97	Santa Ana, CA	(35.33)
20	Grand Rapids, MI	5.19	42	Seattle, WA	(4.07)
31	Greensboro, NC	0.09	37	Shreveport, LA	(2.08)
15	Honolulu, HI	7.18	26	Spokane, WA	1.82
90	Houston, TX	(25.17)	68	Stockton, CA	(14.42)
51	Huntington Beach, CA	(6.98)	17	St. Louis, MO	5.85
2	Indianapolis, IN	40.47	45	St. Paul, MN	(5.10)
5	Jackson, MS	22.68	93	St. Petersburg, FL	(26.32)
48	Jacksonville, FL	(6.51)	84	Tacoma, WA	(21.87)
91	Jersey City, NJ	(25.71)	56	Tampa, FL	(9.47)
52	Kansas City, MO	(7.62)	53	Toledo, OH	(7.98)
82	Las Vegas, NV	(18.71)	-	Tucson, AZ**	NA
35	Lexington, KY	(1.61)	66	Tulsa, OK	(13.63)
38	Lincoln, NE	(2.43)	70	Virginia Beach, VA	(15.11)
14	Little Rock, AR	7.72	9	Washington, DC	12.94
85	Long Beach, CA	(22.22)	40	Wichita, KS	(2.85)
54	Los Angeles, CA	(8.17)	65	Yonkers, NY	(12.88)

Source: Morgan Quitno Corporation using data from U.S. Department of Justice, Federal Bureau of Investigation "Crime in the United States 1993" (Uniform Crime Reports, December 4, 1994)
*Larceny and theft is the unlawful taking of property without use of force, violence or fraud. Attempts are included. Motor vehicle thefts are excluded.
**Not available.

76. Percent Change in Larceny and Theft Rate: 1989 to 1993 (continued)

National Percent Change = 4.4% Decrease*

RANK	CITY	% CHANGE	RANK	CITY	% CHANGE
1	Nashville, TN	66.84	51	Huntington Beach, CA	(6.98)
2	Indianapolis, IN	40.47	52	Kansas City, MO	(7.62)
3	Baltimore, MD	29.73	53	Toledo, OH	(7.98)
4	Birmingham, AL	27.60	54	Los Angeles, CA	(8.17)
5	Jackson, MS	22.68	55	Anaheim, CA	(9.06)
6	Baton Rouge, LA	21.35	56	Akron, OH	(9.47)
7	Oklahoma City, OK	16.63	56	Tampa, FL	(9.47)
8	Anchorage, AK	15.55	58	Des Moines, IA	(9.57)
9	Washington, DC	12.94	59	Cleveland, OH	(10.31)
10	Mesa, AZ	12.83	60	Albuquerque, NM	(10.40)
11	Newport News, VA	11.74	61	Charlotte, NC	(11.41)
12	Memphis, TN	11.15	62	Minneapolis, MN	(11.61)
13	Garland, TX	8.32	63	Colorado Springs, CO	(12.48)
14	Little Rock, AR	7.72	63	Raleigh, NC	(12.48)
15	Honolulu, HI	7.18	65	Yonkers, NY	(12.88)
16	Riverside, CA	6.43	66	Tulsa, OK	(13.63)
17	St. Louis, MO	5.85	67	Bakersfield, CA	(13.74)
18	Cincinnati, OH	5.76	68	Stockton, CA	(14.42)
19	Columbus, GA	5.39	69	Lubbock, TX	(14.87)
20	Grand Rapids, MI	5.19	70	Virginia Beach, VA	(15.11)
21	Pittsburgh, PA	4.96	71	San Jose, CA	(15.31)
22	Miami, FL	4.30	72	Boston, MA	(15.66)
23	Buffalo, NY	4.27	73	Dayton, OH	(17.27)
24	Richmond, VA	3.59	74	El Paso, TX	(17.65)
25	Orlando, FL	3.36	75	San Antonio, TX	(17.73)
26	Spokane, WA	1.82	76	Philadelphia, PA	(17.98)
27	Fremont, CA	1.61	77	Milwaukee, WI	(18.03)
28	Corpus Christi, TX	1.19	78	New York, NY	(18.04)
29	Aurora, CO	0.22	79	Glendale, CA	(18.23)
30	Detroit, MI	0.14	80	Arlington, TX	(18.33)
31	Greensboro, NC	0.09	81	Columbus, OH	(18.51)
32	Chicago, IL	(0.13)	82	Las Vegas, NV	(18.71)
33	Austin, TX	(0.78)	83	Rochester, NY	(19.05)
34	Norfolk, VA	(1.53)	84	Tacoma, WA	(21.87)
35	Lexington, KY	(1.61)	85	Long Beach, CA	(22.22)
36	Newark, NJ	(1.63)	86	Atlanta, GA	(22.46)
37	Shreveport, LA	(2.08)	87	Oakland, CA	(22.93)
38	Lincoln, NE	(2.43)	88	Madison, WI	(23.05)
39	Denver, CO	(2.48)	89	Phoenix, AZ	(24.61)
40	Wichita, KS	(2.85)	90	Houston, TX	(25.17)
41	Louisville, KY	(3.24)	91	Jersey City, NJ	(25.71)
42	Seattle, WA	(4.07)	92	Montgomery, AL	(26.12)
43	Mobile, AL	(4.08)	93	St. Petersburg, FL	(26.32)
44	New Orleans, LA	(5.05)	94	San Diego, CA	(28.01)
45	St. Paul, MN	(5.10)	95	Fort Worth, TX	(29.46)
46	San Francisco, CA	(5.56)	96	Dallas, TX	(34.68)
47	Portland, OR	(6.00)	97	Santa Ana, CA	(35.33)
48	Jacksonville, FL	(6.51)	98	Fresno, CA	(35.44)
49	Fort Wayne, IN	(6.54)	–	San Bernardino, CA**	NA
50	Sacramento, CA	(6.64)	–	Tucson, AZ**	NA

Source: Morgan Quitno Corporation using data from U.S. Department of Justice, Federal Bureau of Investigation "Crime in the United States 1993" (Uniform Crime Reports, December 4, 1994)
Larceny and theft is the unlawful taking of property without use of force, violence or fraud. Attempts are included. Motor vehicle thefts are excluded.
**Not available.*

235

77. Motor Vehicle Thefts in 1993

National Total = 1,561,047 Motor Vehicle Thefts*

RANK	CITY	THEFTS	RANK	CITY	THEFTS
72	Akron, OH	2,043	67	Louisville, KY	2,325
56	Albuquerque, NM	3,578	98	Lubbock, TX	610
54	Anaheim, CA	3,607	91	Madison, WI	913
82	Anchorage, AK	1,387	10	Memphis, TN	13,289
64	Arlington, TX	2,452	63	Mesa, AZ	2,717
22	Atlanta, GA	9,216	14	Miami, FL	11,178
80	Aurora, CO	1,489	18	Milwaukee, WI	10,615
47	Austin, TX	4,357	43	Minneapolis, MN	4,672
77	Bakersfield, CA	1,595	78	Mobile, AL	1,537
17	Baltimore, MD	10,623	85	Montgomery, AL	1,214
50	Baton Rouge, LA	4,006	42	Nashville, TN	4,731
58	Birmingham, AL	3,544	21	New Orleans, LA	9,546
12	Boston, MA	11,932	1	New York, NY	112,464
39	Buffalo, NY	5,519	16	Newark, NJ	10,993
59	Charlotte, NC	2,972	97	Newport News, VA	684
3	Chicago, IL	40,438	69	Norfolk, VA	2,173
71	Cincinnati, OH	2,063	29	Oakland, CA	7,772
19	Cleveland, OH	10,170	38	Oklahoma City, OK	5,539
90	Colorado Springs, CO	1,017	74	Orlando, FL	1,806
88	Columbus, GA	1,042	6	Philadelphia, PA	23,785
33	Columbus, OH	7,070	9	Phoenix, AZ	15,566
76	Corpus Christi, TX	1,672	35	Pittsburgh, PA	6,506
8	Dallas, TX	17,465	26	Portland, OR	8,459
61	Dayton, OH	2,939	92	Raleigh, NC	883
31	Denver, CO	7,558	68	Richmond, VA	2,215
93	Des Moines, IA	854	57	Riverside, CA	3,562
4	Detroit, MI	28,061	60	Rochester, NY	2,954
37	El Paso, TX	5,546	28	Sacramento, CA	7,885
75	Fort Wayne, IN	1,786	13	San Antonio, TX	11,796
36	Fort Worth, TX	6,007	55	San Bernardino, CA	3,596
94	Fremont, CA	824	7	San Diego, CA	19,319
11	Fresno, CA	13,083	15	San Francisco, CA	11,056
89	Garland, TX	1,033	49	San Jose, CA	4,014
81	Glendale, CA	1,447	51	Santa Ana, CA	3,958
87	Grand Rapids, MI	1,075	34	Seattle, WA	6,819
95	Greensboro, NC	749	79	Shreveport, LA	1,503
45	Honolulu, HI	4,460	96	Spokane, WA	730
5	Houston, TX	27,519	52	Stockton, CA	3,696
84	Huntington Beach, CA	1,219	20	St. Louis, MO	10,065
40	Indianapolis, IN	5,226	66	St. Paul, MN	2,326
48	Jackson, MS	4,054	83	St. Petersburg, FL	1,292
23	Jacksonville, FL	9,033	65	Tacoma, WA	2,335
53	Jersey City, NJ	3,655	25	Tampa, FL	8,473
24	Kansas City, MO	8,487	44	Toledo, OH	4,517
32	Las Vegas, NV	7,446	41	Tucson, AZ	5,143
98	Lexington, KY	610	46	Tulsa, OK	4,447
100	Lincoln, NE	429	86	Virginia Beach, VA	1,195
70	Little Rock, AR	2,081	27	Washington, DC	8,060
30	Long Beach, CA	7,626	62	Wichita, KS	2,883
2	Los Angeles, CA	59,764	73	Yonkers, NY	1,868

Source: U.S. Department of Justice, Federal Bureau of Investigation
 "Crime in the United States 1993" (Uniform Crime Reports, December 4, 1994)
*Includes the theft or attempted theft of a self-propelled vehicle. Excludes motorboats, construction equipment, airplanes and farming equipment.

77. Motor Vehicle Thefts in 1993 (continued)

National Total = 1,561,047 Motor Vehicle Thefts*

RANK	CITY	THEFTS	RANK	CITY	THEFTS
1	New York, NY	112,464	51	Santa Ana, CA	3,958
2	Los Angeles, CA	59,764	52	Stockton, CA	3,696
3	Chicago, IL	40,438	53	Jersey City, NJ	3,655
4	Detroit, MI	28,061	54	Anaheim, CA	3,607
5	Houston, TX	27,519	55	San Bernardino, CA	3,596
6	Philadelphia, PA	23,785	56	Albuquerque, NM	3,578
7	San Diego, CA	19,319	57	Riverside, CA	3,562
8	Dallas, TX	17,465	58	Birmingham, AL	3,544
9	Phoenix, AZ	15,566	59	Charlotte, NC	2,972
10	Memphis, TN	13,289	60	Rochester, NY	2,954
11	Fresno, CA	13,083	61	Dayton, OH	2,939
12	Boston, MA	11,932	62	Wichita, KS	2,883
13	San Antonio, TX	11,796	63	Mesa, AZ	2,717
14	Miami, FL	11,178	64	Arlington, TX	2,452
15	San Francisco, CA	11,056	65	Tacoma, WA	2,335
16	Newark, NJ	10,993	66	St. Paul, MN	2,326
17	Baltimore, MD	10,623	67	Louisville, KY	2,325
18	Milwaukee, WI	10,615	68	Richmond, VA	2,215
19	Cleveland, OH	10,170	69	Norfolk, VA	2,173
20	St. Louis, MO	10,065	70	Little Rock, AR	2,081
21	New Orleans, LA	9,546	71	Cincinnati, OH	2,063
22	Atlanta, GA	9,216	72	Akron, OH	2,043
23	Jacksonville, FL	9,033	73	Yonkers, NY	1,868
24	Kansas City, MO	8,487	74	Orlando, FL	1,806
25	Tampa, FL	8,473	75	Fort Wayne, IN	1,786
26	Portland, OR	8,459	76	Corpus Christi, TX	1,672
27	Washington, DC	8,060	77	Bakersfield, CA	1,595
28	Sacramento, CA	7,885	78	Mobile, AL	1,537
29	Oakland, CA	7,772	79	Shreveport, LA	1,503
30	Long Beach, CA	7,626	80	Aurora, CO	1,489
31	Denver, CO	7,558	81	Glendale, CA	1,447
32	Las Vegas, NV	7,446	82	Anchorage, AK	1,387
33	Columbus, OH	7,070	83	St. Petersburg, FL	1,292
34	Seattle, WA	6,819	84	Huntington Beach, CA	1,219
35	Pittsburgh, PA	6,506	85	Montgomery, AL	1,214
36	Fort Worth, TX	6,007	86	Virginia Beach, VA	1,195
37	El Paso, TX	5,546	87	Grand Rapids, MI	1,075
38	Oklahoma City, OK	5,539	88	Columbus, GA	1,042
39	Buffalo, NY	5,519	89	Garland, TX	1,033
40	Indianapolis,IN	5,226	90	Colorado Springs, CO	1,017
41	Tucson, AZ	5,143	91	Madison, WI	913
42	Nashville, TN	4,731	92	Raleigh, NC	883
43	Minneapolis, MN	4,672	93	Des Moines, IA	854
44	Toledo, OH	4,517	94	Fremont, CA	824
45	Honolulu, HI	4,460	95	Greensboro, NC	749
46	Tulsa, OK	4,447	96	Spokane, WA	730
47	Austin, TX	4,357	97	Newport News, VA	684
48	Jackson, MS	4,054	98	Lexington, KY	610
49	San Jose, CA	4,014	98	Lubbock, TX	610
50	Baton Rouge, LA	4,006	100	Lincoln, NE	429

Source: U.S. Department of Justice, Federal Bureau of Investigation
   "Crime in the United States 1993" (Uniform Crime Reports, December 4, 1994)
*Includes the theft or attempted theft of a self-propelled vehicle. Excludes motorboats, construction equipment, airplanes and farming equipment.

78. Motor Vehicle Theft Rate in 1993

National Rate = 605.3 Motor Vehicle Thefts per 100,000 Population*

RANK	CITY	RATE	RANK	CITY	RATE
64	Akron, OH	907.8	70	Louisville, KY	849.9
66	Albuquerque, NM	878.5	97	Lubbock, TX	318.3
44	Anaheim, CA	1,303.6	89	Madison, WI	463.6
83	Anchorage, AK	553.2	9	Memphis, TN	2,146.9
67	Arlington, TX	871.6	65	Mesa, AZ	891.7
7	Atlanta, GA	2,287.5	3	Miami, FL	3,000.7
80	Aurora, CO	603.8	21	Milwaukee, WI	1,703.5
68	Austin, TX	867.9	47	Minneapolis, MN	1,274.3
72	Bakersfield, CA	839.9	75	Mobile, AL	752.4
37	Baltimore, MD	1,449.3	78	Montgomery, AL	624.5
18	Baton Rouge, LA	1,776.2	62	Nashville, TN	921.1
43	Birmingham, AL	1,318.6	16	New Orleans, LA	1,941.7
8	Boston, MA	2,154.3	30	New York, NY	1,530.7
22	Buffalo, NY	1,698.9	1	Newark, NJ	4,073.1
76	Charlotte, NC	702.8	95	Newport News, VA	380.1
36	Chicago, IL	1,449.9	71	Norfolk, VA	843.5
81	Cincinnati, OH	562.8	11	Oakland, CA	2,061.3
14	Cleveland, OH	2,011.0	50	Oklahoma City, OK	1,210.8
96	Colorado Springs, CO	334.1	58	Orlando, FL	1,021.8
84	Columbus, GA	547.5	31	Philadelphia, PA	1,525.1
55	Columbus, OH	1,092.8	34	Phoenix, AZ	1,497.6
79	Corpus Christi, TX	615.7	19	Pittsburgh, PA	1,765.7
24	Dallas, TX	1,675.1	17	Portland, OR	1,859.6
28	Dayton, OH	1,594.2	92	Raleigh, NC	394.1
32	Denver, CO	1,516.4	56	Richmond, VA	1,078.7
91	Des Moines, IA	436.9	35	Riverside, CA	1,477.8
5	Detroit, MI	2,750.9	48	Rochester, NY	1,255.4
60	El Paso, TX	1,000.2	13	Sacramento, CA	2,038.9
59	Fort Wayne, IN	1,018.2	52	San Antonio, TX	1,197.0
45	Fort Worth, TX	1,296.4	10	San Bernardino, CA	2,064.1
90	Fremont, CA	454.9	26	San Diego, CA	1,664.6
2	Fresno, CA	3,443.1	33	San Francisco, CA	1,501.4
86	Garland, TX	529.9	88	San Jose, CA	495.8
73	Glendale, CA	806.2	40	Santa Ana, CA	1,364.5
82	Grand Rapids, MI	559.5	46	Seattle, WA	1,283.5
93	Greensboro, NC	388.2	74	Shreveport, LA	761.5
87	Honolulu, HI	509.4	94	Spokane, WA	381.2
27	Houston, TX	1,595.9	25	Stockton, CA	1,665.9
77	Huntington Beach, CA	652.1	6	St. Louis, MO	2,600.4
39	Indianapolis,IN	1,383.6	69	St. Paul, MN	857.6
12	Jackson, MS	2,045.1	85	St. Petersburg, FL	541.2
42	Jacksonville, FL	1,343.6	49	Tacoma, WA	1,242.7
29	Jersey City, NJ	1,587.1	4	Tampa, FL	2,933.1
15	Kansas City, MO	1,949.1	41	Toledo, OH	1,362.9
57	Las Vegas, NV	1,037.9	51	Tucson, AZ	1,206.3
99	Lexington, KY	259.5	53	Tulsa, OK	1,175.4
100	Lincoln, NE	216.4	98	Virginia Beach, VA	282.2
54	Little Rock, AR	1,163.1	38	Washington, DC	1,394.5
20	Long Beach, CA	1,720.4	63	Wichita, KS	919.3
23	Los Angeles, CA	1,695.3	61	Yonkers, NY	999.1

Source: U.S. Department of Justice, Federal Bureau of Investigation
"Crime in the United States 1993" (Uniform Crime Reports, December 4, 1994)
*Includes the theft or attempted theft of a self-propelled vehicle. Excludes motorboats, construction equipment, airplanes and farming equipment.

78. Motor Vehicle Theft Rate in 1993 (continued)

National Rate = 605.3 Motor Vehicle Thefts per 100,000 Population*

RANK	CITY	RATE	RANK	CITY	RATE
1	Newark, NJ	4,073.1	51	Tucson, AZ	1,206.3
2	Fresno, CA	3,443.1	52	San Antonio, TX	1,197.0
3	Miami, FL	3,000.7	53	Tulsa, OK	1,175.4
4	Tampa, FL	2,933.1	54	Little Rock, AR	1,163.1
5	Detroit, MI	2,750.9	55	Columbus, OH	1,092.8
6	St. Louis, MO	2,600.4	56	Richmond, VA	1,078.7
7	Atlanta, GA	2,287.5	57	Las Vegas, NV	1,037.9
8	Boston, MA	2,154.3	58	Orlando, FL	1,021.8
9	Memphis, TN	2,146.9	59	Fort Wayne, IN	1,018.2
10	San Bernardino, CA	2,064.1	60	El Paso, TX	1,000.2
11	Oakland, CA	2,061.3	61	Yonkers, NY	999.1
12	Jackson, MS	2,045.1	62	Nashville, TN	921.1
13	Sacramento, CA	2,038.9	63	Wichita, KS	919.3
14	Cleveland, OH	2,011.0	64	Akron, OH	907.8
15	Kansas City, MO	1,949.1	65	Mesa, AZ	891.7
16	New Orleans, LA	1,941.7	66	Albuquerque, NM	878.5
17	Portland, OR	1,859.6	67	Arlington, TX	871.6
18	Baton Rouge, LA	1,776.2	68	Austin, TX	867.9
19	Pittsburgh, PA	1,765.7	69	St. Paul, MN	857.6
20	Long Beach, CA	1,720.4	70	Louisville, KY	849.9
21	Milwaukee, WI	1,703.5	71	Norfolk, VA	843.5
22	Buffalo, NY	1,698.9	72	Bakersfield, CA	839.9
23	Los Angeles, CA	1,695.3	73	Glendale, CA	806.2
24	Dallas, TX	1,675.1	74	Shreveport, LA	761.5
25	Stockton, CA	1,665.9	75	Mobile, AL	752.4
26	San Diego, CA	1,664.6	76	Charlotte, NC	702.8
27	Houston, TX	1,595.9	77	Huntington Beach, CA	652.1
28	Dayton, OH	1,594.2	78	Montgomery, AL	624.5
29	Jersey City, NJ	1,587.1	79	Corpus Christi, TX	615.7
30	New York, NY	1,530.7	80	Aurora, CO	603.8
31	Philadelphia, PA	1,525.1	81	Cincinnati, OH	562.8
32	Denver, CO	1,516.4	82	Grand Rapids, MI	559.5
33	San Francisco, CA	1,501.4	83	Anchorage, AK	553.2
34	Phoenix, AZ	1,497.6	84	Columbus, GA	547.5
35	Riverside, CA	1,477.8	85	St. Petersburg, FL	541.2
36	Chicago, IL	1,449.9	86	Garland, TX	529.9
37	Baltimore, MD	1,449.3	87	Honolulu, HI	509.4
38	Washington, DC	1,394.5	88	San Jose, CA	495.8
39	Indianapolis,IN	1,383.6	89	Madison, WI	463.6
40	Santa Ana, CA	1,364.5	90	Fremont, CA	454.9
41	Toledo, OH	1,362.9	91	Des Moines, IA	436.9
42	Jacksonville, FL	1,343.6	92	Raleigh, NC	394.1
43	Birmingham, AL	1,318.6	93	Greensboro, NC	388.2
44	Anaheim, CA	1,303.6	94	Spokane, WA	381.2
45	Fort Worth, TX	1,296.4	95	Newport News, VA	380.1
46	Seattle, WA	1,283.5	96	Colorado Springs, CO	334.1
47	Minneapolis, MN	1,274.3	97	Lubbock, TX	318.3
48	Rochester, NY	1,255.4	98	Virginia Beach, VA	282.2
49	Tacoma, WA	1,242.7	99	Lexington, KY	259.5
50	Oklahoma City, OK	1,210.8	100	Lincoln, NE	216.4

Source: U.S. Department of Justice, Federal Bureau of Investigation
"Crime in the United States 1993" (Uniform Crime Reports, December 4, 1994)
*Includes the theft or attempted theft of a self-propelled vehicle. Excludes motorboats, construction equipment, airplanes and farming equipment.

79. Percent Change in Motor Vehicle Theft Rate: 1992 to 1993

National Percent Change = 4.1% Decrease*

RANK	CITY	% CHANGE	RANK	CITY	% CHANGE
63	Akron, OH	(5.25)	84	Louisville, KY	(13.59)
10	Albuquerque, NM	21.34	85	Lubbock, TX	(14.20)
36	Anaheim, CA	3.62	2	Madison, WI	44.06
88	Anchorage, AK	(17.05)	40	Memphis, TN	2.17
92	Arlington, TX	(19.54)	25	Mesa, AZ	7.05
17	Atlanta, GA	11.22	5	Miami, FL	28.77
87	Aurora, CO	(15.78)	96	Milwaukee, WI	(23.08)
72	Austin, TX	(8.09)	66	Minneapolis, MN	(6.97)
12	Bakersfield, CA	20.48	99	Mobile, AL	(33.81)
57	Baltimore, MD	(3.10)	42	Montgomery, AL	1.10
37	Baton Rouge, LA	2.62	70	Nashville, TN	(7.71)
58	Birmingham, AL	(3.72)	23	New Orleans, LA	7.47
21	Boston, MA	8.14	82	New York, NY	(11.08)
39	Buffalo, NY	2.36	91	Newark, NJ	(18.85)
14	Charlotte, NC	17.11	95	Newport News, VA	(21.35)
74	Chicago, IL	(8.70)	33	Norfolk, VA	4.12
54	Cincinnati, OH	(1.76)	38	Oakland, CA	2.48
59	Cleveland, OH	(4.07)	68	Oklahoma City, OK	(7.58)
73	Colorado Springs, CO	(8.21)	67	Orlando, FL	(7.08)
1	Columbus, GA	50.66	19	Philadelphia, PA	9.11
43	Columbus, OH	0.93	48	Phoenix, AZ	(0.05)
64	Corpus Christi, TX	(5.86)	90	Pittsburgh, PA	(18.75)
86	Dallas, TX	(14.54)	22	Portland, OR	7.83
49	Dayton, OH	(0.73)	80	Raleigh, NC	(10.76)
68	Denver, CO	(7.58)	65	Richmond, VA	(6.44)
7	Des Moines, IA	26.90	50	Riverside, CA	(0.89)
32	Detroit, MI	5.04	28	Rochester, NY	6.08
52	El Paso, TX	(1.35)	60	Sacramento, CA	(4.50)
35	Fort Wayne, IN	3.91	94	San Antonio, TX	(20.90)
100	Fort Worth, TX	(39.32)	31	San Bernardino, CA	5.23
3	Fremont, CA	38.60	62	San Diego, CA	(5.23)
55	Fresno, CA	(2.78)	81	San Francisco, CA	(11.01)
89	Garland, TX	(17.50)	29	San Jose, CA	6.05
24	Glendale, CA	7.31	51	Santa Ana, CA	(1.04)
56	Grand Rapids, MI	(3.05)	76	Seattle, WA	(9.14)
18	Greensboro, NC	10.10	77	Shreveport, LA	(9.82)
6	Honolulu, HI	27.13	34	Spokane, WA	4.07
83	Houston, TX	(12.55)	45	Stockton, CA	0.57
30	Huntington Beach, CA	6.02	9	St. Louis, MO	24.20
4	Indianapolis, IN	30.95	47	St. Paul, MN	0.20
44	Jackson, MS	0.70	98	St. Petersburg, FL	(25.50)
41	Jacksonville, FL	1.52	8	Tacoma, WA	25.58
97	Jersey City, NJ	(23.94)	15	Tampa, FL	16.67
26	Kansas City, MO	6.92	16	Toledo, OH	11.61
61	Las Vegas, NV	(4.85)	13	Tucson, AZ	17.21
75	Lexington, KY	(9.01)	71	Tulsa, OK	(7.93)
20	Lincoln, NE	8.96	53	Virginia Beach, VA	(1.43)
93	Little Rock, AR	(20.23)	79	Washington, DC	(9.91)
11	Long Beach, CA	21.28	46	Wichita, KS	0.33
78	Los Angeles, CA	(9.84)	27	Yonkers, NY	6.56

Source: Morgan Quitno Corporation using data from U.S. Department of Justice, Federal Bureau of Investigation "Crime in the United States 1993" (Uniform Crime Reports, December 4, 1994)
Includes the theft or attempted theft of a self-propelled vehicle. Excludes motorboats, construction equipment, airplanes and farming equipment.

79. Percent Change in Motor Vehicle Theft Rate: 1992 to 1993 (continued)

National Percent Change = 4.1% Decrease*

RANK	CITY	% CHANGE	RANK	CITY	% CHANGE
1	Columbus, GA	50.66	51	Santa Ana, CA	(1.04)
2	Madison, WI	44.06	52	El Paso, TX	(1.35)
3	Fremont, CA	38.60	53	Virginia Beach, VA	(1.43)
4	Indianapolis, IN	30.95	54	Cincinnati, OH	(1.76)
5	Miami, FL	28.77	55	Fresno, CA	(2.78)
6	Honolulu, HI	27.13	56	Grand Rapids, MI	(3.05)
7	Des Moines, IA	26.90	57	Baltimore, MD	(3.10)
8	Tacoma, WA	25.58	58	Birmingham, AL	(3.72)
9	St. Louis, MO	24.20	59	Cleveland, OH	(4.07)
10	Albuquerque, NM	21.34	60	Sacramento, CA	(4.50)
11	Long Beach, CA	21.28	61	Las Vegas, NV	(4.85)
12	Bakersfield, CA	20.48	62	San Diego, CA	(5.23)
13	Tucson, AZ	17.21	63	Akron, OH	(5.25)
14	Charlotte, NC	17.11	64	Corpus Christi, TX	(5.86)
15	Tampa, FL	16.67	65	Richmond, VA	(6.44)
16	Toledo, OH	11.61	66	Minneapolis, MN	(6.97)
17	Atlanta, GA	11.22	67	Orlando, FL	(7.08)
18	Greensboro, NC	10.10	68	Denver, CO	(7.58)
19	Philadelphia, PA	9.11	68	Oklahoma City, OK	(7.58)
20	Lincoln, NE	8.96	70	Nashville, TN	(7.71)
21	Boston, MA	8.14	71	Tulsa, OK	(7.93)
22	Portland, OR	7.83	72	Austin, TX	(8.09)
23	New Orleans, LA	7.47	73	Colorado Springs, CO	(8.21)
24	Glendale, CA	7.31	74	Chicago, IL	(8.70)
25	Mesa, AZ	7.05	75	Lexington, KY	(9.01)
26	Kansas City, MO	6.92	76	Seattle, WA	(9.14)
27	Yonkers, NY	6.56	77	Shreveport, LA	(9.82)
28	Rochester, NY	6.08	78	Los Angeles, CA	(9.84)
29	San Jose, CA	6.05	79	Washington, DC	(9.91)
30	Huntington Beach, CA	6.02	80	Raleigh, NC	(10.76)
31	San Bernardino, CA	5.23	81	San Francisco, CA	(11.01)
32	Detroit, MI	5.04	82	New York, NY	(11.08)
33	Norfolk, VA	4.12	83	Houston, TX	(12.55)
34	Spokane, WA	4.07	84	Louisville, KY	(13.59)
35	Fort Wayne, IN	3.91	85	Lubbock, TX	(14.20)
36	Anaheim, CA	3.62	86	Dallas, TX	(14.54)
37	Baton Rouge, LA	2.62	87	Aurora, CO	(15.78)
38	Oakland, CA	2.48	88	Anchorage, AK	(17.05)
39	Buffalo, NY	2.36	89	Garland, TX	(17.50)
40	Memphis, TN	2.17	90	Pittsburgh, PA	(18.75)
41	Jacksonville, FL	1.52	91	Newark, NJ	(18.85)
42	Montgomery, AL	1.10	92	Arlington, TX	(19.54)
43	Columbus, OH	0.93	93	Little Rock, AR	(20.23)
44	Jackson, MS	0.70	94	San Antonio, TX	(20.90)
45	Stockton, CA	0.57	95	Newport News, VA	(21.35)
46	Wichita, KS	0.33	96	Milwaukee, WI	(23.08)
47	St. Paul, MN	0.20	97	Jersey City, NJ	(23.94)
48	Phoenix, AZ	(0.05)	98	St. Petersburg, FL	(25.50)
49	Dayton, OH	(0.73)	99	Mobile, AL	(33.81)
50	Riverside, CA	(0.89)	100	Fort Worth, TX	(39.32)

Source: Morgan Quitno Corporation using data from U.S. Department of Justice, Federal Bureau of Investigation "Crime in the United States 1993" (Uniform Crime Reports, December 4, 1994)
*Includes the theft or attempted theft of a self-propelled vehicle. Excludes motorboats, construction equipment, airplanes and farming equipment.

80. Percent Change in Motor Vehicle Theft Rate: 1989 to 1993

National Percent Change = 4.0% Decrease*

RANK	CITY	% CHANGE	RANK	CITY	% CHANGE
24	Akron, OH	23.21	30	Louisville, KY	19.30
16	Albuquerque, NM	46.59	74	Lubbock, TX	(12.58)
47	Anaheim, CA	8.52	35	Madison, WI	16.19
48	Anchorage, AK	6.71	43	Memphis, TN	11.38
75	Arlington, TX	(13.93)	18	Mesa, AZ	38.92
77	Atlanta, GA	(15.37)	25	Miami, FL	22.45
46	Aurora, CO	8.77	42	Milwaukee, WI	12.03
14	Austin, TX	50.34	84	Minneapolis, MN	(19.11)
49	Bakersfield, CA	6.44	17	Mobile, AL	44.50
21	Baltimore, MD	35.32	10	Montgomery, AL	62.59
2	Baton Rouge, LA	98.10	5	Nashville, TN	73.04
60	Birmingham, AL	(0.89)	72	New Orleans, LA	(10.52)
87	Boston, MA	(23.84)	78	New York, NY	(15.73)
8	Buffalo, NY	66.54	83	Newark, NJ	(18.45)
61	Charlotte, NC	(3.05)	31	Newport News, VA	19.08
66	Chicago, IL	(5.60)	59	Norfolk, VA	0.07
19	Cincinnati, OH	38.86	37	Oakland, CA	15.38
45	Cleveland, OH	9.63	86	Oklahoma City, OK	(20.77)
97	Colorado Springs, CO	(40.96)	68	Orlando, FL	(8.19)
11	Columbus, GA	57.46	56	Philadelphia, PA	0.62
71	Columbus, OH	(10.42)	44	Phoenix, AZ	11.03
20	Corpus Christi, TX	36.46	81	Pittsburgh, PA	(17.44)
96	Dallas, TX	(38.86)	39	Portland, OR	13.67
32	Dayton, OH	18.81	80	Raleigh, NC	(16.91)
22	Denver, CO	33.31	36	Richmond, VA	15.47
38	Des Moines, IA	14.13	63	Riverside, CA	(3.68)
53	Detroit, MI	1.69	15	Rochester, NY	48.34
64	El Paso, TX	(4.36)	50	Sacramento, CA	5.11
12	Fort Wayne, IN	55.12	89	San Antonio, TX	(25.52)
95	Fort Worth, TX	(37.76)	-	San Bernardino, CA**	NA
23	Fremont, CA	29.86	92	San Diego, CA	(28.51)
3	Fresno, CA	86.45	34	San Francisco, CA	16.52
67	Garland, TX	(6.87)	76	San Jose, CA	(15.09)
85	Glendale, CA	(20.21)	73	Santa Ana, CA	(12.28)
94	Grand Rapids, MI	(35.11)	40	Seattle, WA	13.52
55	Greensboro, NC	1.36	4	Shreveport, LA	85.23
28	Honolulu, HI	20.06	79	Spokane, WA	(15.96)
90	Houston, TX	(26.10)	29	Stockton, CA	19.35
41	Huntington Beach, CA	12.08	33	St. Louis, MO	17.93
7	Indianapolis, IN	67.57	82	St. Paul, MN	(18.03)
1	Jackson, MS	281.26	98	St. Petersburg, FL	(46.88)
6	Jacksonville, FL	68.31	57	Tacoma, WA	0.53
93	Jersey City, NJ	(34.54)	9	Tampa, FL	62.96
65	Kansas City, MO	(5.41)	62	Toledo, OH	(3.50)
27	Las Vegas, NV	21.48	-	Tucson, AZ**	NA
88	Lexington, KY	(25.32)	91	Tulsa, OK	(27.85)
52	Lincoln, NE	2.46	58	Virginia Beach, VA	0.28
26	Little Rock, AR	22.21	54	Washington, DC	1.59
51	Long Beach, CA	4.49	13	Wichita, KS	51.72
69	Los Angeles, CA	(8.83)	70	Yonkers, NY	(10.26)

Source: Morgan Quitno Corporation using data from U.S. Department of Justice, Federal Bureau of Investigation
"Crime in the United States 1993" (Uniform Crime Reports, December 4, 1994)
*Includes the theft or attempted theft of a self-propelled vehicle. Excludes motorboats, construction equipment, airplanes and farming equipment.
**Not available.

80. Percent Change in Motor Vehicle Theft Rate: 1989 to 1993 (continued)

National Percent Change = 4.0% Decrease*

RANK	CITY	% CHANGE	RANK	CITY	% CHANGE
1	Jackson, MS	281.26	51	Long Beach, CA	4.49
2	Baton Rouge, LA	98.10	52	Lincoln, NE	2.46
3	Fresno, CA	86.45	53	Detroit, MI	1.69
4	Shreveport, LA	85.23	54	Washington, DC	1.59
5	Nashville, TN	73.04	55	Greensboro, NC	1.36
6	Jacksonville, FL	68.31	56	Philadelphia, PA	0.62
7	Indianapolis,IN	67.57	57	Tacoma, WA	0.53
8	Buffalo, NY	66.54	58	Virginia Beach, VA	0.28
9	Tampa, FL	62.96	59	Norfolk, VA	0.07
10	Montgomery, AL	62.59	60	Birmingham, AL	(0.89)
11	Columbus, GA	57.46	61	Charlotte, NC	(3.05)
12	Fort Wayne, IN	55.12	62	Toledo, OH	(3.50)
13	Wichita, KS	51.72	63	Riverside, CA	(3.68)
14	Austin, TX	50.34	64	El Paso, TX	(4.36)
15	Rochester, NY	48.34	65	Kansas City, MO	(5.41)
16	Albuquerque, NM	46.59	66	Chicago, IL	(5.60)
17	Mobile, AL	44.50	67	Garland, TX	(6.87)
18	Mesa, AZ	38.92	68	Orlando, FL	(8.19)
19	Cincinnati, OH	38.86	69	Los Angeles, CA	(8.83)
20	Corpus Christi, TX	36.46	70	Yonkers, NY	(10.26)
21	Baltimore, MD	35.32	71	Columbus, OH	(10.42)
22	Denver, CO	33.31	72	New Orleans, LA	(10.52)
23	Fremont, CA	29.86	73	Santa Ana, CA	(12.28)
24	Akron, OH	23.21	74	Lubbock, TX	(12.58)
25	Miami, FL	22.45	75	Arlington, TX	(13.93)
26	Little Rock, AR	22.21	76	San Jose, CA	(15.09)
27	Las Vegas, NV	21.48	77	Atlanta, GA	(15.37)
28	Honolulu, HI	20.06	78	New York, NY	(15.73)
29	Stockton, CA	19.35	79	Spokane, WA	(15.96)
30	Louisville, KY	19.30	80	Raleigh, NC	(16.91)
31	Newport News, VA	19.08	81	Pittsburgh, PA	(17.44)
32	Dayton, OH	18.81	82	St. Paul, MN	(18.03)
33	St. Louis, MO	17.93	83	Newark, NJ	(18.45)
34	San Francisco, CA	16.52	84	Minneapolis, MN	(19.11)
35	Madison, WI	16.19	85	Glendale, CA	(20.21)
36	Richmond, VA	15.47	86	Oklahoma City, OK	(20.77)
37	Oakland, CA	15.38	87	Boston, MA	(23.84)
38	Des Moines, IA	14.13	88	Lexington, KY	(25.32)
39	Portland, OR	13.67	89	San Antonio, TX	(25.52)
40	Seattle, WA	13.52	90	Houston, TX	(26.10)
41	Huntington Beach, CA	12.08	91	Tulsa, OK	(27.85)
42	Milwaukee, WI	12.03	92	San Diego, CA	(28.51)
43	Memphis, TN	11.38	93	Jersey City, NJ	(34.54)
44	Phoenix, AZ	11.03	94	Grand Rapids, MI	(35.11)
45	Cleveland, OH	9.63	95	Fort Worth, TX	(37.76)
46	Aurora, CO	8.77	96	Dallas, TX	(38.86)
47	Anaheim, CA	8.52	97	Colorado Springs, CO	(40.96)
48	Anchorage, AK	6.71	98	St. Petersburg, FL	(46.88)
49	Bakersfield, CA	6.44	–	San Bernardino, CA**	NA
50	Sacramento, CA	5.11	–	Tucson, AZ**	NA

Source: Morgan Quitno Corporation using data from U.S. Department of Justice, Federal Bureau of Investigation "Crime in the United States 1993" (Uniform Crime Reports, December 4, 1994)
Includes the theft or attempted theft of a self-propelled vehicle. Excludes motorboats, construction equipment, airplanes and farming equipment.
**Not available.*

81. Police Officers in 1993

National Total = 553,773 Officers*

RANK	CITY	OFFICERS	RANK	CITY	OFFICERS
68	Akron, OH	455	56	Louisville, KY	627
48	Albuquerque, NM	751	88	Lubbock, TX	312
84	Anaheim, CA	347	89	Madison, WI	302
92	Anchorage, AK	267	23	Memphis, TN	1,437
80	Arlington, TX	381	66	Mesa, AZ	467
18	Atlanta, GA	1,626	33	Miami, FL	1,062
76	Aurora, CO	391	10	Milwaukee, WI	2,079
39	Austin, TX	881	41	Minneapolis, MN	876
97	Bakersfield, CA	234	71	Mobile, AL	425
8	Baltimore, MD	2,947	74	Montgomery, AL	412
55	Baton Rouge, LA	649	30	Nashville, TN	1,099
46	Birmingham, AL	770	20	New Orleans, LA	1,513
12	Boston, MA	1,944	1	New York, NY	29,327
38	Buffalo, NY	931	29	Newark, NJ	1,151
36	Charlotte, NC	940	87	Newport News, VA	318
2	Chicago, IL	12,093	52	Norfolk, VA	664
37	Cincinnati, OH	933	50	Oakland, CA	719
16	Cleveland, OH	1,699	34	Oklahoma City, OK	988
65	Colorado Springs, CO	468	59	Orlando, FL	552
81	Columbus, GA	369	4	Philadelphia, PA	6,225
19	Columbus, OH	1,543	11	Phoenix, AZ	1,978
79	Corpus Christi, TX	385	31	Pittsburgh, PA	1,095
9	Dallas, TX	2,807	39	Portland, OR	881
64	Dayton, OH	486	67	Raleigh, NC	461
24	Denver, CO	1,394	53	Richmond, VA	659
82	Des Moines, IA	353	89	Riverside, CA	302
7	Detroit, MI	3,860	51	Rochester, NY	670
42	El Paso, TX	850	58	Sacramento, CA	578
86	Fort Wayne, IN	322	17	San Antonio, TX	1,662
32	Fort Worth, TX	1,074	95	San Bernardino, CA	251
100	Fremont, CA	180	14	San Diego, CA	1,861
70	Fresno, CA	432	15	San Francisco, CA	1,804
96	Garland, TX	240	27	San Jose, CA	1,203
99	Glendale, CA	216	77	Santa Ana, CA	387
91	Grand Rapids, MI	275	26	Seattle, WA	1,245
72	Greensboro, NC	422	69	Shreveport, LA	452
13	Honolulu, HI	1,921	93	Spokane, WA	261
5	Houston, TX	4,734	85	Stockton, CA	324
98	Huntington Beach, CA	231	21	St. Louis, MO	1,448
35	Indianapolis, IN	967	60	St. Paul, MN	521
73	Jackson, MS	413	61	St. Petersburg, FL	508
25	Jacksonville, FL	1,253	83	Tacoma, WA	350
43	Jersey City, NJ	821	45	Tampa, FL	771
28	Kansas City, MO	1,191	54	Toledo, OH	654
22	Las Vegas, NV	1,445	47	Tucson, AZ	759
77	Lexington, KY	387	49	Tulsa, OK	738
94	Lincoln, NE	256	57	Virginia Beach, VA	614
75	Little Rock, AR	395	6	Washington, DC	4,372
44	Long Beach, CA	791	63	Wichita, KS	496
3	Los Angeles, CA	7,637	62	Yonkers, NY	506

Source: U.S. Department of Justice, Federal Bureau of Investigation
  "Crime in the United States 1993" (Uniform Crime Reports, December 4, 1994)
*Does not include civilian employees.

81. Police Officers in 1993 (continued)

National Total = 553,773 Officers*

RANK	CITY	OFFICERS	RANK	CITY	OFFICERS
1	New York, NY	29,327	51	Rochester, NY	670
2	Chicago, IL	12,093	52	Norfolk, VA	664
3	Los Angeles, CA	7,637	53	Richmond, VA	659
4	Philadelphia, PA	6,225	54	Toledo, OH	654
5	Houston, TX	4,734	55	Baton Rouge, LA	649
6	Washington, DC	4,372	56	Louisville, KY	627
7	Detroit, MI	3,860	57	Virginia Beach, VA	614
8	Baltimore, MD	2,947	58	Sacramento, CA	578
9	Dallas, TX	2,807	59	Orlando, FL	552
10	Milwaukee, WI	2,079	60	St. Paul, MN	521
11	Phoenix, AZ	1,978	61	St. Petersburg, FL	508
12	Boston, MA	1,944	62	Yonkers, NY	506
13	Honolulu, HI	1,921	63	Wichita, KS	496
14	San Diego, CA	1,861	64	Dayton, OH	486
15	San Francisco, CA	1,804	65	Colorado Springs, CO	468
16	Cleveland, OH	1,699	66	Mesa, AZ	467
17	San Antonio, TX	1,662	67	Raleigh, NC	461
18	Atlanta, GA	1,626	68	Akron, OH	455
19	Columbus, OH	1,543	69	Shreveport, LA	452
20	New Orleans, LA	1,513	70	Fresno, CA	432
21	St. Louis, MO	1,448	71	Mobile, AL	425
22	Las Vegas, NV	1,445	72	Greensboro, NC	422
23	Memphis, TN	1,437	73	Jackson, MS	413
24	Denver, CO	1,394	74	Montgomery, AL	412
25	Jacksonville, FL	1,253	75	Little Rock, AR	395
26	Seattle, WA	1,245	76	Aurora, CO	391
27	San Jose, CA	1,203	77	Lexington, KY	387
28	Kansas City, MO	1,191	77	Santa Ana, CA	387
29	Newark, NJ	1,151	79	Corpus Christi, TX	385
30	Nashville, TN	1,099	80	Arlington, TX	381
31	Pittsburgh, PA	1,095	81	Columbus, GA	369
32	Fort Worth, TX	1,074	82	Des Moines, IA	353
33	Miami, FL	1,062	83	Tacoma, WA	350
34	Oklahoma City, OK	988	84	Anaheim, CA	347
35	Indianapolis, IN	967	85	Stockton, CA	324
36	Charlotte, NC	940	86	Fort Wayne, IN	322
37	Cincinnati, OH	933	87	Newport News, VA	318
38	Buffalo, NY	931	88	Lubbock, TX	312
39	Austin, TX	881	89	Madison, WI	302
39	Portland, OR	881	89	Riverside, CA	302
41	Minneapolis, MN	876	91	Grand Rapids, MI	275
42	El Paso, TX	850	92	Anchorage, AK	267
43	Jersey City, NJ	821	93	Spokane, WA	261
44	Long Beach, CA	791	94	Lincoln, NE	256
45	Tampa, FL	771	95	San Bernardino, CA	251
46	Birmingham, AL	770	96	Garland, TX	240
47	Tucson, AZ	759	97	Bakersfield, CA	234
48	Albuquerque, NM	751	98	Huntington Beach, CA	231
49	Tulsa, OK	738	99	Glendale, CA	216
50	Oakland, CA	719	100	Fremont, CA	180

Source: U.S. Department of Justice, Federal Bureau of Investigation
   "Crime in the United States 1993" (Uniform Crime Reports, December 4, 1994)
*Does not include civilian employees.

82. Rate of Police Officers in 1993

National Rate = 227 Officers per 100,000 Population*

RANK	CITY	RATE	RANK	CITY	RATE
53	Akron, OH	202	39	Louisville, KY	229
64	Albuquerque, NM	184	73	Lubbock, TX	163
92	Anaheim, CA	125	78	Madison, WI	153
99	Anchorage, AK	106	37	Memphis, TN	232
89	Arlington, TX	135	78	Mesa, AZ	153
4	Atlanta, GA	404	21	Miami, FL	285
75	Aurora, CO	159	13	Milwaukee, WI	334
70	Austin, TX	175	34	Minneapolis, MN	239
95	Bakersfield, CA	123	50	Mobile, AL	208
5	Baltimore, MD	402	49	Montgomery, AL	212
18	Baton Rouge, LA	288	47	Nashville, TN	214
20	Birmingham, AL	286	16	New Orleans, LA	308
11	Boston, MA	351	6	New York, NY	399
19	Buffalo, NY	287	3	Newark, NJ	426
41	Charlotte, NC	222	69	Newport News, VA	177
2	Chicago, IL	434	30	Norfolk, VA	258
32	Cincinnati, OH	255	60	Oakland, CA	191
12	Cleveland, OH	336	46	Oklahoma City, OK	216
77	Colorado Springs, CO	154	15	Orlando, FL	312
57	Columbus, GA	194	6	Philadelphia, PA	399
34	Columbus, OH	239	61	Phoenix, AZ	190
87	Corpus Christi, TX	142	17	Pittsburgh, PA	297
27	Dallas, TX	269	57	Portland, OR	194
29	Dayton, OH	264	52	Raleigh, NC	206
23	Denver, CO	280	14	Richmond, VA	321
66	Des Moines, IA	181	92	Riverside, CA	125
8	Detroit, MI	378	21	Rochester, NY	285
78	El Paso, TX	153	81	Sacramento, CA	149
64	Fort Wayne, IN	184	71	San Antonio, TX	169
37	Fort Worth, TX	232	85	San Bernardino, CA	144
100	Fremont, CA	99	74	San Diego, CA	160
98	Fresno, CA	114	33	San Francisco, CA	245
95	Garland, TX	123	81	San Jose, CA	149
97	Glendale, CA	120	90	Santa Ana, CA	133
86	Grand Rapids, MI	143	36	Seattle, WA	234
43	Greensboro, NC	219	39	Shreveport, LA	229
43	Honolulu, HI	219	88	Spokane, WA	136
24	Houston, TX	275	83	Stockton, CA	146
94	Huntington Beach, CA	124	9	St. Louis, MO	374
31	Indianapolis,IN	256	59	St. Paul, MN	192
50	Jackson, MS	208	48	St. Petersburg, FL	213
62	Jacksonville, FL	186	62	Tacoma, WA	186
10	Jersey City, NJ	356	28	Tampa, FL	267
25	Kansas City, MO	274	55	Toledo, OH	197
54	Las Vegas, NV	201	67	Tucson, AZ	178
72	Lexington, KY	165	56	Tulsa, OK	195
91	Lincoln, NE	129	84	Virginia Beach, VA	145
42	Little Rock, AR	221	1	Washington, DC	756
67	Long Beach, CA	178	76	Wichita, KS	158
45	Los Angeles, CA	217	26	Yonkers, NY	271

Source: Morgan Quitno Corporation using data from U.S. Department of Justice, Federal Bureau of Investigation
"Crime in the United States 1993" (Uniform Crime Reports, December 4, 1994)
*Based on sworn officers only. Does not include civilian employees.

82. Rate of Police Officers in 1993 (continued)

National Rate = 227 Officers per 100,000 Population*

RANK	CITY	RATE	RANK	CITY	RATE
1	Washington, DC	756	50	Mobile, AL	208
2	Chicago, IL	434	52	Raleigh, NC	206
3	Newark, NJ	426	53	Akron, OH	202
4	Atlanta, GA	404	54	Las Vegas, NV	201
5	Baltimore, MD	402	55	Toledo, OH	197
6	New York, NY	399	56	Tulsa, OK	195
6	Philadelphia, PA	399	57	Columbus, GA	194
8	Detroit, MI	378	57	Portland, OR	194
9	St. Louis, MO	374	59	St. Paul, MN	192
10	Jersey City, NJ	356	60	Oakland, CA	191
11	Boston, MA	351	61	Phoenix, AZ	190
12	Cleveland, OH	336	62	Jacksonville, FL	186
13	Milwaukee, WI	334	62	Tacoma, WA	186
14	Richmond, VA	321	64	Albuquerque, NM	184
15	Orlando, FL	312	64	Fort Wayne, IN	184
16	New Orleans, LA	308	66	Des Moines, IA	181
17	Pittsburgh, PA	297	67	Long Beach, CA	178
18	Baton Rouge, LA	288	67	Tucson, AZ	178
19	Buffalo, NY	287	69	Newport News, VA	177
20	Birmingham, AL	286	70	Austin, TX	175
21	Miami, FL	285	71	San Antonio, TX	169
21	Rochester, NY	285	72	Lexington, KY	165
23	Denver, CO	280	73	Lubbock, TX	163
24	Houston, TX	275	74	San Diego, CA	160
25	Kansas City, MO	274	75	Aurora, CO	159
26	Yonkers, NY	271	76	Wichita, KS	158
27	Dallas, TX	269	77	Colorado Springs, CO	154
28	Tampa, FL	267	78	El Paso, TX	153
29	Dayton, OH	264	78	Madison, WI	153
30	Norfolk, VA	258	78	Mesa, AZ	153
31	Indianapolis, IN	256	81	Sacramento, CA	149
32	Cincinnati, OH	255	81	San Jose, CA	149
33	San Francisco, CA	245	83	Stockton, CA	146
34	Columbus, OH	239	84	Virginia Beach, VA	145
34	Minneapolis, MN	239	85	San Bernardino, CA	144
36	Seattle, WA	234	86	Grand Rapids, MI	143
37	Fort Worth, TX	232	87	Corpus Christi, TX	142
37	Memphis, TN	232	88	Spokane, WA	136
39	Louisville, KY	229	89	Arlington, TX	135
39	Shreveport, LA	229	90	Santa Ana, CA	133
41	Charlotte, NC	222	91	Lincoln, NE	129
42	Little Rock, AR	221	92	Anaheim, CA	125
43	Greensboro, NC	219	92	Riverside, CA	125
43	Honolulu, HI	219	94	Huntington Beach, CA	124
45	Los Angeles, CA	217	95	Bakersfield, CA	123
46	Oklahoma City, OK	216	95	Garland, TX	123
47	Nashville, TN	214	97	Glendale, CA	120
48	St. Petersburg, FL	213	98	Fresno, CA	114
49	Montgomery, AL	212	99	Anchorage, AK	106
50	Jackson, MS	208	100	Fremont, CA	99

Source: Morgan Quitno Corporation using data from U.S. Department of Justice, Federal Bureau of Investigation "Crime in the United States 1993" (Uniform Crime Reports, December 4, 1994)
Based on sworn officers only. Does not include civilian employees.

83. Percent Change in Rate of Police Officers: 1992 to 1993

National Percent Change = 0.89% Increase*

RANK	CITY	% CHANGE	RANK	CITY	% CHANGE
26	Akron, OH	5.21	52	Louisville, KY	0.88
95	Albuquerque, NM	(6.12)	38	Lubbock, TX	3.16
72	Anaheim, CA	(1.57)	94	Madison, WI	(5.56)
58	Anchorage, AK	0.00	20	Memphis, TN	6.42
64	Arlington, TX	(0.74)	8	Mesa, AZ	10.07
9	Atlanta, GA	8.89	29	Miami, FL	4.40
96	Aurora, CO	(8.62)	15	Milwaukee, WI	7.40
39	Austin, TX	2.94	10	Minneapolis, MN	8.64
97	Bakersfield, CA	(8.89)	92	Mobile, AL	(5.02)
18	Baltimore, MD	6.91	61	Montgomery, AL	(0.47)
-	Baton Rouge, LA**	NA	25	Nashville, TN	5.42
44	Birmingham, AL	2.14	-	New Orleans, LA**	NA
36	Boston, MA	3.54	32	New York, NY	4.18
14	Buffalo, NY	7.49	7	Newark, NJ	10.36
31	Charlotte, NC	4.23	19	Newport News, VA	6.63
56	Chicago, IL	0.46	35	Norfolk, VA	3.61
71	Cincinnati, OH	(1.54)	41	Oakland, CA	2.69
28	Cleveland, OH	4.67	46	Oklahoma City, OK	1.89
42	Colorado Springs, CO	2.67	80	Orlando, FL	(2.19)
70	Columbus, GA	(1.52)	43	Philadelphia, PA	2.57
16	Columbus, OH	7.17	77	Phoenix, AZ	(2.06)
49	Corpus Christi, TX	1.43	50	Pittsburgh, PA	1.37
79	Dallas, TX	(2.18)	45	Portland, OR	2.11
53	Dayton, OH	0.76	75	Raleigh, NC	(1.90)
37	Denver, CO	3.32	17	Richmond, VA	7.00
62	Des Moines, IA	(0.55)	85	Riverside, CA	(3.85)
40	Detroit, MI	2.72	58	Rochester, NY	0.00
68	El Paso, TX	(1.29)	88	Sacramento, CA	(4.49)
74	Fort Wayne, IN	(1.60)	21	San Antonio, TX	6.29
27	Fort Worth, TX	4.98	84	San Bernardino, CA	(3.36)
76	Fremont, CA	(1.98)	98	San Diego, CA	(18.37)
47	Fresno, CA	1.79	2	San Francisco, CA	53.13
93	Garland, TX	(5.38)	88	San Jose, CA	(4.49)
12	Glendale, CA	8.11	34	Santa Ana, CA	3.91
86	Grand Rapids, MI	(4.03)	1	Seattle, WA	53.95
87	Greensboro, NC	(4.37)	11	Shreveport, LA	8.53
66	Honolulu, HI	(0.90)	63	Spokane, WA	(0.73)
6	Houston, TX	10.89	30	Stockton, CA	4.29
48	Huntington Beach, CA	1.64	3	St. Louis, MO	34.05
4	Indianapolis, IN	29.29	23	St. Paul, MN	5.49
5	Jackson, MS	20.23	24	St. Petersburg, FL	5.45
67	Jacksonville, FL	(1.06)	73	Tacoma, WA	(1.59)
69	Jersey City, NJ	(1.39)	82	Tampa, FL	(2.91)
32	Kansas City, MO	4.18	22	Toledo, OH	5.91
91	Las Vegas, NV	(4.74)	58	Tucson, AZ	0.00
81	Lexington, KY	(2.37)	83	Tulsa, OK	(2.99)
65	Lincoln, NE	(0.77)	90	Virginia Beach, VA	(4.61)
51	Little Rock, AR	0.91	54	Washington, DC	0.67
13	Long Beach, CA	7.88	55	Wichita, KS	0.64
56	Los Angeles, CA	0.46	78	Yonkers, NY	(2.17)

Source: Morgan Quitno Corporation using data from U.S. Department of Justice, Federal Bureau of Investigation "Crime in the United States 1993" (Uniform Crime Reports, December 4, 1994)
*Based on sworn officers only. Does not include civilian employees.

83. Percent Change in Rate of Police Officers: 1992 to 1993 (continued)

National Percent Change = 0.89% Increase*

RANK	CITY	% CHANGE		RANK	CITY	% CHANGE
1	Seattle, WA	53.95		51	Little Rock, AR	0.91
2	San Francisco, CA	53.13		52	Louisville, KY	0.88
3	St. Louis, MO	34.05		53	Dayton, OH	0.76
4	Indianapolis, IN	29.29		54	Washington, DC	0.67
5	Jackson, MS	20.23		55	Wichita, KS	0.64
6	Houston, TX	10.89		56	Chicago, IL	0.46
7	Newark, NJ	10.36		56	Los Angeles, CA	0.46
8	Mesa, AZ	10.07		58	Anchorage, AK	0.00
9	Atlanta, GA	8.89		58	Rochester, NY	0.00
10	Minneapolis, MN	8.64		58	Tucson, AZ	0.00
11	Shreveport, LA	8.53		61	Montgomery, AL	(0.47)
12	Glendale, CA	8.11		62	Des Moines, IA	(0.55)
13	Long Beach, CA	7.88		63	Spokane, WA	(0.73)
14	Buffalo, NY	7.49		64	Arlington, TX	(0.74)
15	Milwaukee, WI	7.40		65	Lincoln, NE	(0.77)
16	Columbus, OH	7.17		66	Honolulu, HI	(0.90)
17	Richmond, VA	7.00		67	Jacksonville, FL	(1.06)
18	Baltimore, MD	6.91		68	El Paso, TX	(1.29)
19	Newport News, VA	6.63		69	Jersey City, NJ	(1.39)
20	Memphis, TN	6.42		70	Columbus, GA	(1.52)
21	San Antonio, TX	6.29		71	Cincinnati, OH	(1.54)
22	Toledo, OH	5.91		72	Anaheim, CA	(1.57)
23	St. Paul, MN	5.49		73	Tacoma, WA	(1.59)
24	St. Petersburg, FL	5.45		74	Fort Wayne, IN	(1.60)
25	Nashville, TN	5.42		75	Raleigh, NC	(1.90)
26	Akron, OH	5.21		76	Fremont, CA	(1.98)
27	Fort Worth, TX	4.98		77	Phoenix, AZ	(2.06)
28	Cleveland, OH	4.67		78	Yonkers, NY	(2.17)
29	Miami, FL	4.40		79	Dallas, TX	(2.18)
30	Stockton, CA	4.29		80	Orlando, FL	(2.19)
31	Charlotte, NC	4.23		81	Lexington, KY	(2.37)
32	Kansas City, MO	4.18		82	Tampa, FL	(2.91)
32	New York, NY	4.18		83	Tulsa, OK	(2.99)
34	Santa Ana, CA	3.91		84	San Bernardino, CA	(3.36)
35	Norfolk, VA	3.61		85	Riverside, CA	(3.85)
36	Boston, MA	3.54		86	Grand Rapids, MI	(4.03)
37	Denver, CO	3.32		87	Greensboro, NC	(4.37)
38	Lubbock, TX	3.16		88	Sacramento, CA	(4.49)
39	Austin, TX	2.94		88	San Jose, CA	(4.49)
40	Detroit, MI	2.72		90	Virginia Beach, VA	(4.61)
41	Oakland, CA	2.69		91	Las Vegas, NV	(4.74)
42	Colorado Springs, CO	2.67		92	Mobile, AL	(5.02)
43	Philadelphia, PA	2.57		93	Garland, TX	(5.38)
44	Birmingham, AL	2.14		94	Madison, WI	(5.56)
45	Portland, OR	2.11		95	Albuquerque, NM	(6.12)
46	Oklahoma City, OK	1.89		96	Aurora, CO	(8.62)
47	Fresno, CA	1.79		97	Bakersfield, CA	(8.89)
48	Huntington Beach, CA	1.64		98	San Diego, CA	(18.37)
49	Corpus Christi, TX	1.43		-	Baton Rouge, LA**	NA
50	Pittsburgh, PA	1.37		-	New Orleans, LA**	NA

Source: Morgan Quitno Corporation using data from U.S. Department of Justice, Federal Bureau of Investigation
"Crime in the United States 1993" (Uniform Crime Reports, December 4, 1994)
*Based on sworn officers only. Does not include civilian employees.

84. Percent Change in Rate of Police Officers: 1989 to 1993

National Percent Change = 5.09% Increase*

RANK	CITY	% CHANGE	RANK	CITY	% CHANGE
61	Akron, OH	0.50	72	Louisville, KY	(2.55)
81	Albuquerque, NM	(7.07)	67	Lubbock, TX	(1.21)
70	Anaheim, CA	(2.34)	85	Madison, WI	(8.38)
65	Anchorage, AK	(0.93)	22	Memphis, TN	11.54
62	Arlington, TX	0.00	7	Mesa, AZ	17.69
19	Atlanta, GA	13.48	71	Miami, FL	(2.40)
87	Aurora, CO	(9.14)	53	Milwaukee, WI	2.77
27	Austin, TX	8.70	21	Minneapolis, MN	12.74
94	Bakersfield, CA	(16.89)	5	Mobile, AL	21.64
42	Baltimore, MD	5.24	68	Montgomery, AL	(1.85)
31	Baton Rouge, LA	8.27	44	Nashville, TN	4.90
18	Birmingham, AL	13.49	–	New Orleans, LA**	NA
–	Boston, MA**	NA	17	New York, NY	13.68
93	Buffalo, NY	(13.29)	2	Newark, NJ	25.66
16	Charlotte, NC	13.85	33	Newport News, VA	7.27
25	Chicago, IL	9.60	8	Norfolk, VA	17.27
59	Cincinnati, OH	1.59	15	Oakland, CA	14.37
60	Cleveland, OH	0.90	13	Oklahoma City, OK	14.89
29	Colorado Springs, CO	8.45	66	Orlando, FL	(0.95)
75	Columbus, GA	(4.90)	41	Philadelphia, PA	5.28
54	Columbus, OH	2.58	80	Phoenix, AZ	(6.86)
43	Corpus Christi, TX	5.19	48	Pittsburgh, PA	3.85
28	Dallas, TX	8.47	23	Portland, OR	10.86
78	Dayton, OH	(5.71)	86	Raleigh, NC	(8.44)
50	Denver, CO	3.70	20	Richmond, VA	13.03
52	Des Moines, IA	2.84	84	Riverside, CA	(8.09)
96	Detroit, MI	(17.29)	55	Rochester, NY	2.52
45	El Paso, TX	4.08	92	Sacramento, CA	(12.87)
32	Fort Wayne, IN	7.60	30	San Antonio, TX	8.33
57	Fort Worth, TX	1.75	–	San Bernardino, CA**	NA
90	Fremont, CA	(11.61)	77	San Diego, CA	(5.33)
91	Fresno, CA	(11.63)	49	San Francisco, CA	3.81
39	Garland, TX	6.03	38	San Jose, CA	6.43
34	Glendale, CA	7.14	89	Santa Ana, CA	(10.14)
51	Grand Rapids, MI	2.88	58	Seattle, WA	1.74
64	Greensboro, NC	(0.90)	1	Shreveport, LA	38.79
40	Honolulu, HI	5.80	63	Spokane, WA	(0.73)
12	Houston, TX	15.06	6	Stockton, CA	17.74
24	Huntington Beach, CA	10.71	73	St. Louis, MO	(2.86)
3	Indianapolis, IN	24.27	79	St. Paul, MN	(6.34)
11	Jackson, MS	15.56	9	St. Petersburg, FL	15.76
46	Jacksonville, FL	3.91	56	Tacoma, WA	2.20
95	Jersey City, NJ	(17.21)	47	Tampa, FL	3.89
37	Kansas City, MO	6.61	74	Toledo, OH	(4.37)
88	Las Vegas, NV	(9.87)	–	Tucson, AZ**	NA
34	Lexington, KY	7.14	34	Tulsa, OK	7.14
69	Lincoln, NE	(2.27)	83	Virginia Beach, VA	(7.64)
4	Little Rock, AR	22.10	13	Washington, DC	14.89
10	Long Beach, CA	15.58	26	Wichita, KS	8.97
76	Los Angeles, CA	(5.24)	82	Yonkers, NY	(7.19)

Source: Morgan Quitno Corporation using data from U.S. Department of Justice, Federal Bureau of Investigation
"Crime in the United States 1993" (Uniform Crime Reports, December 4, 1994)
*Based on sworn officers only. Does not include civilian employees.

84. Percent Change in Rate of Police Officers: 1989 to 1993 (continued)

National Percent Change = 5.09% Increase*

RANK	CITY	% CHANGE	RANK	CITY	% CHANGE
1	Shreveport, LA	38.79	51	Grand Rapids, MI	2.88
2	Newark, NJ	25.66	52	Des Moines, IA	2.84
3	Indianapolis, IN	24.27	53	Milwaukee, WI	2.77
4	Little Rock, AR	22.10	54	Columbus, OH	2.58
5	Mobile, AL	21.64	55	Rochester, NY	2.52
6	Stockton, CA	17.74	56	Tacoma, WA	2.20
7	Mesa, AZ	17.69	57	Fort Worth, TX	1.75
8	Norfolk, VA	17.27	58	Seattle, WA	1.74
9	St. Petersburg, FL	15.76	59	Cincinnati, OH	1.59
10	Long Beach, CA	15.58	60	Cleveland, OH	0.90
11	Jackson, MS	15.56	61	Akron, OH	0.50
12	Houston, TX	15.06	62	Arlington, TX	0.00
13	Oklahoma City, OK	14.89	63	Spokane, WA	(0.73)
13	Washington, DC	14.89	64	Greensboro, NC	(0.90)
15	Oakland, CA	14.37	65	Anchorage, AK	(0.93)
16	Charlotte, NC	13.85	66	Orlando, FL	(0.95)
17	New York, NY	13.68	67	Lubbock, TX	(1.21)
18	Birmingham, AL	13.49	68	Montgomery, AL	(1.85)
19	Atlanta, GA	13.48	69	Lincoln, NE	(2.27)
20	Richmond, VA	13.03	70	Anaheim, CA	(2.34)
21	Minneapolis, MN	12.74	71	Miami, FL	(2.40)
22	Memphis, TN	11.54	72	Louisville, KY	(2.55)
23	Portland, OR	10.86	73	St. Louis, MO	(2.86)
24	Huntington Beach, CA	10.71	74	Toledo, OH	(4.37)
25	Chicago, IL	9.60	75	Columbus, GA	(4.90)
26	Wichita, KS	8.97	76	Los Angeles, CA	(5.24)
27	Austin, TX	8.70	77	San Diego, CA	(5.33)
28	Dallas, TX	8.47	78	Dayton, OH	(5.71)
29	Colorado Springs, CO	8.45	79	St. Paul, MN	(6.34)
30	San Antonio, TX	8.33	80	Phoenix, AZ	(6.86)
31	Baton Rouge, LA	8.27	81	Albuquerque, NM	(7.07)
32	Fort Wayne, IN	7.60	82	Yonkers, NY	(7.19)
33	Newport News, VA	7.27	83	Virginia Beach, VA	(7.64)
34	Glendale, CA	7.14	84	Riverside, CA	(8.09)
34	Lexington, KY	7.14	85	Madison, WI	(8.38)
34	Tulsa, OK	7.14	86	Raleigh, NC	(8.44)
37	Kansas City, MO	6.61	87	Aurora, CO	(9.14)
38	San Jose, CA	6.43	88	Las Vegas, NV	(9.87)
39	Garland, TX	6.03	89	Santa Ana, CA	(10.14)
40	Honolulu, HI	5.80	90	Fremont, CA	(11.61)
41	Philadelphia, PA	5.28	91	Fresno, CA	(11.63)
42	Baltimore, MD	5.24	92	Sacramento, CA	(12.87)
43	Corpus Christi, TX	5.19	93	Buffalo, NY	(13.29)
44	Nashville, TN	4.90	94	Bakersfield, CA	(16.89)
45	El Paso, TX	4.08	95	Jersey City, NJ	(17.21)
46	Jacksonville, FL	3.91	96	Detroit, MI	(17.29)
47	Tampa, FL	3.89	–	Boston, MA**	NA
48	Pittsburgh, PA	3.85	–	New Orleans, LA**	NA
49	San Francisco, CA	3.81	–	San Bernardino, CA**	NA
50	Denver, CO	3.70	–	Tucson, AZ**	NA

Source: Morgan Quitno Corporation using data from U.S. Department of Justice, Federal Bureau of Investigation "Crime in the United States 1993" (Uniform Crime Reports, December 4, 1994)
Based on sworn officers only. Does not include civilian employees.

251

III. APPENDICES

85. Metropolitan Population in 1993

National Total = 257,908,000 Population*

RANK	METRO AREA	POP	RANK	METRO AREA	POP	RANK	METRO AREA	POP
238	Abilene, TX	122,927	272	Cheyenne, WY	76,880	28	Fort Worth–Arlington, TX	1,538,831
66	Akron, OH	667,989	–	Chicago, IL**	NA	61	Fresno, CA	812,859
247	Albany, GA	117,680	178	Chico–Paradise, CA	190,302	260	Gadsden, AL	100,556
–	Albany, NY**	NA	26	Cincinnati, OH–KY–IN	1,571,218	176	Gainesville, FL	192,158
70	Albuquerque, NM	629,814	185	Clarksville–Hopkinsville, TN–KY	180,407	159	Galveston–Texas City, TX	232,567
231	Alexandria, LA	131,041	–	Cleveland, OH**	NA	71	Gary–Hammond, IN	622,774
229	Altoona, PA	131,894	97	Colorado Springs, CO	433,461	239	Glens Falls, NY	121,523
174	Amarillo, TX	195,405	245	Columbia, MO	117,862	253	Goldsboro, NC	109,427
150	Anchorage, AK	250,720	86	Columbia, SC	477,627	257	Grand Forks, ND–MN	103,652
83	Ann Arbor, MI	503,897	141	Columbus, GA–AL	278,325	51	Grand Rapids–Muskegon–Holland, MI	968,826
246	Anniston, AL	117,781	33	Columbus, OH	1,401,383	216	Greeley, CO	139,826
121	Appleton–Oshkosh–Neenah, WI	329,973	113	Corpus Christi, TX	369,485	170	Green Bay, WI	203,170
173	Asheville, NC	200,605	258	Cumberland, MD–WV	102,409	41	Greensboro–Winston Salem–High Point, NC	1,096,140
203	Athens, GA	154,465	10	Dallas, TX	2,751,065	250	Greenville, NC	112,149
8	Atlanta, GA	3,225,549	193	Danbury, CT	162,590	60	Greenville–Spartanburg–Anderson, SC	863,667
124	Atlantic City, NJ	328,721	252	Danville, VA	110,979	235	Hagerstown, MD	126,701
90	Augusta–Aiken, GA–SC	451,500	99	Daytona Beach, FL	427,877	73	Harrisburg–Lebanon–Carlisle, PA	604,920
56	Austin–San Marcos, TX	918,765	52	Dayton–Springfield, OH	968,224	44	Hartford, CT	1,053,803
74	Bakersfield, CA	593,687	223	Decatur, AL	136,793	130	Hickory–Morganton, NC	303,975
15	Baltimore, MD	2,457,276	23	Denver, CO	1,757,721	58	Honolulu, HI	875,455
273	Bangor, ME	67,623	102	Des Moines, IA	408,171	179	Houma, LA	187,213
221	Barnstable–Yarmouth, MA	137,118	5	Detroit, MI	4,330,568	6	Houston, TX	3,600,764
77	Baton Rouge, LA	548,361	228	Dothan, AL	134,860	126	Huntington–Ashland, WV–KY–OH	317,163
109	Beaumont–Port Arthur, TX	377,093	266	Dubuque, IA	87,612	127	Huntsville, AL	311,694
215	Bellingham, WA	140,914	154	Duluth–Superior, MN–WI	243,527	–	Indianapolis, IN**	NA
194	Benton Harbor, MI	162,208	146	Dutchess County, NY	264,128	206	Jackson, MI	152,438
36	Bergen–Passaic, NJ	1,300,853	214	Eau Claire, WI	141,145	101	Jackson, MS	409,223
145	Binghamton, NY	267,981	68	El Paso, TX	640,839	270	Jackson, TN	81,410
59	Birmingham, AL	869,321	195	Elkhart–Goshen, IN	160,863	53	Jacksonville, FL	966,411
268	Bismarck, ND	86,183	274	Enid, OK	56,818	209	Jacksonville, NC	146,832
249	Bloomington, IN	112,184	139	Erie, PA	280,843	212	Janesville–Beloit, WI	144,047
122	Boise, ID	329,652	133	Eugene–Springfield, OR	296,820	76	Jersey City, NJ	559,129
7	Boston, MA–NH	3,393,227	135	Evansville–Henderson, IN–KY	285,569	91	Johnson City–Kingsport–Bristol, TN–VA	450,919
153	Boulder–Longmont, CO	245,117	198	Fargo–Moorhead, ND–MN	158,369	155	Johnstown, PA	241,842
167	Brazoria, TX	207,861	138	Fayetteville, NC	281,740	219	Joplin, MO	138,638
165	Bremerton, WA	215,355	161	Fayetteville–Springdale–Rogers, AR	228,557	93	Kalamazoo–Battle Creek, MI	438,379
89	Bridgeport, CT	452,865	222	Fitchburg–Leominster, MA	136,990	–	Kansas City, MO–KS**	NA
152	Brockton, MA	246,237	96	Flint, MI	435,436	227	Kenosha, WI	135,181
136	Brownsville–Harlingen–San Benito, TX	284,168	226	Florence, AL	135,811	147	Killeen–Temple, TX	259,871
233	Bryan–College Station, TX	127,620	243	Florence, SC	119,908	261	Kokomo, IN	99,536
39	Buffalo–Niagara Falls, NY	1,201,686	168	Fort Collins–Loveland, CO	203,897	244	La Crosse, WI–MN	119,099
105	Canton–Massillon, OH	401,855	35	Fort Lauderdale, FL	1,320,180	191	Lafayette, IN	166,449
148	Charleston, WV	254,300	115	Fort Myers–Cape Coral, FL	357,168	116	Lafayette, LA	354,604
79	Charleston–North Charleston, SC	534,445	144	Fort Pierce–Port St. Lucie, FL	269,255	188	Lake Charles, LA	172,146
224	Charlottesville, VA	136,484	182	Fort Smith, AR–OK	182,651	100	Lakeland–Winter Haven, FL	425,061
38	Charlotte–Gastonia–Rock Hill, NC–SC	1,230,964	201	Fort Walton Beach, FL	155,654	95	Lancaster, PA	436,325
94	Chattanooga, TN–GA	438,176	88	Fort Wayne, IN	467,750	92	Lansing–East Lansing, MI	438,470

Source: U.S. Bureau of the Census as reported by U.S. Department of Justice, Federal Bureau of Investigation
"Crime in the United States 1993" (Uniform Crime Reports, December 4, 1994)
Estimates as of July 1, 1993.
**Not available.

85. Metropolitan Population in 1993 (continued)

National Total = 257,908,000 Population*

RANK	METRO AREA	POP	RANK	METRO AREA	POP	RANK	METRO AREA	POP
207	Laredo, TX	151,386	184	Olympia, WA	180,410	20	Seattle-Bellevue-Everett, WA	2,075,927
48	Las Vegas, NV-AZ	1,007,944	–	Omaha, NE**	NA	255	Sheboygan, WI	105,984
134	Lawrence, MA-NH	295,930	14	Orange County, CA	2,510,193	264	Sherman-Denison, TX	96,941
240	Lawton, OK	121,443	34	Orlando, FL	1,323,652	111	Shreveport-Bossier City, LA	375,630
256	Lewiston-Auburn, ME	104,092	265	Owensboro, KY	89,640	248	Sioux City, IA-NE	117,570
114	Lexington, KY	364,218	225	Panama City, FL	135,954	208	Sioux Falls, SD	148,358
164	Lincoln, NE	220,404	3	Philadelphia, PA-NJ	4,969,334	149	South Bend, IN	252,959
80	Little Rock-North Little Rock, AR	532,157	17	Phoenix-Mesa, AZ	2,393,251	107	Spokane, WA	389,486
169	Longview-Marshall, TX	203,855	267	Pine Bluff, AR	86,325	78	Springfield, MA	539,699
1	Los Angeles-Long Beach, CA	9,146,057	16	Pittsburgh, PA	2,423,968	142	Springfield, MO	277,899
50	Louisville, KY-IN	976,668	263	Pittsfield, MA	98,519	123	Stamford-Norwalk, CT	329,636
162	Lubbock, TX	228,251	157	Portland, ME	233,775	213	Steubenville-Weirton, OH-WV	142,406
172	Lynchburg, VA	201,399	25	Portland-Vancouver, OR-WA	1,640,863	81	Stockton-Lodi, CA	509,244
129	Macon, GA	304,968	54	Providence-Fall River-Warwick, RI-MA	956,796	204	St. Cloud, MN	154,366
110	Madison, WI	376,681	137	Provo-Orem, UT	282,500	262	St. Joseph, MO	98,796
190	Manchester, NH	166,876	234	Pueblo, CO	127,363	–	St. Louis, MO-IL**	NA
186	Mansfield, OH	176,573	242	Punta Gorda, FL	120,986	254	Sumter, SC	106,524
98	McAllen-Edinburg-Mission, TX	429,233	183	Racine, WI	181,121	62	Syracuse, NY	756,865
200	Medford-Ashland, OR	157,196	55	Raleigh-Durham-Chapel Hill, NC	923,111	69	Tacoma, WA	633,847
45	Memphis, TN-AR-MS	1,048,342	269	Rapid City, SD	85,853	151	Tallahassee, FL	248,840
177	Merced, CA	191,038	118	Reading, PA	344,635	19	Tampa-St. Petersburg-Clearwater, FL	2,137,896
21	Miami, FL	2,037,568	197	Redding, CA	159,209	237	Texarkana, TX-AR	123,027
43	Middlesex-Sommerset-Hunterdon, NJ	1,054,645	140	Reno, NV	279,191	72	Toledo, OH	619,203
30	Milwaukee-Waukesha, WI	1,453,647	192	Richland-Kennewick-Pasco, WA	164,404	120	Trenton, NJ	330,159
11	Minneapolis-St. Paul, MN-WI	2,648,322	57	Richmond-Petersburg, VA	909,654	64	Tucson, AZ	708,931
84	Mobile, AL	501,440	9	Riverside-San Bernardino, CA	2,837,569	63	Tulsa, OK	737,648
106	Modesto, CA	399,253	160	Roanoke, VA	229,712	202	Tuscaloosa, AL	155,452
47	Monmouth-Ocean, NJ	1,010,250	251	Rochester, MN	111,693	199	Tyler, TX	157,425
211	Monroe, LA	145,451	42	Rochester, NY	1,086,478	125	Utica-Rome, NY	317,581
128	Montgomery, AL	309,452	218	Rocky Mount, NC	139,396	85	Vallejo-Fairfield-Napa, CA	479,963
205	Myrtle Beach, SC	154,007	31	Sacramento, CA	1,433,067	65	Ventura, CA	693,577
189	Naples, FL	167,124	104	Saginaw-Bay City-Midland, MI	404,419	271	Victoria, TX	78,557
196	Nashua, NH	160,383	132	Salem, OR	297,177	217	Vineland-Millville-Bridgeton, NJ	139,537
46	Nashville, TN	1,038,512	112	Salinas, CA	372,077	119	Visalia-Tulare-Porterville, CA	334,462
12	Nassau-Suffolk, NY	2,628,063	40	Salt Lake City-Ogden, UT	1,158,462	175	Waco, TX	195,325
187	New Bedford, MA	174,609	259	San Angelo, TX	101,060	4	Washington, DC-MD-VA-WV	4,399,049
75	New Haven-Meriden, CT	562,831	32	San Antonio, TX	1,405,738	180	Waterbury, CT	185,361
131	New London-Norwich, CT-RI	301,303	13	San Diego, CA	2,627,659	236	Waterloo-Cedar Falls, IA	125,885
37	New Orleans, LA	1,260,951	24	San Francisco, CA	1,642,731	220	Wausau, WI	138,369
2	New York, NY	8,619,661	27	San Jose, CA	1,544,156	–	West Palm Beach-Boca Raton, FL**	NA
22	Newark, NJ	1,937,773	163	San Luis Obispo-Atascadero, CA	222,812	232	Wichita Falls, TX	130,603
117	Newburgh, NY-PA	349,972	108	Santa Barbara-Santa Maria-Lompoc, CA	379,359	241	Williamsport, PA	120,995
29	Norfolk-Va Beach-Newport News, VA-NC	1,519,381	158	Santa Cruz-Watsonville, CA	233,352	181	Wilmington, NC	185,143
18	Oakland, CA	2,170,116	103	Santa Rosa, CA	405,090	87	Worcester, MA-CT	470,774
166	Ocala, FL	211,008	82	Sarasota-Bradenton, FL	506,026	171	Yakima, WA	202,331
156	Odessa-Midland, TX	238,376	143	Savannah, GA	273,038	210	Yolo, CA	146,290
49	Oklahoma City, OK	991,503	67	Scranton-Wilkes-Barre-Hazleton, PA	641,457	230	Yuba City, CA	131,663

Source: U.S. Bureau of the Census as reported by U.S. Department of Justice, Federal Bureau of Investigation
"Crime in the United States 1993" (Uniform Crime Reports, December 4, 1994)

*Estimates as of July 1, 1993.

**Not available.

85. Metropolitan Population in 1993 (continued)

National Total = 257,908,000 Population*

RANK	METRO AREA	POP	RANK	METRO AREA	POP	RANK	METRO AREA	POP
1	Los Angeles–Long Beach, CA	9,146,057	48	Las Vegas, NV–AZ	1,007,944	95	Lancaster, PA	436,325
2	New York, NY	8,619,661	49	Oklahoma City, OK	991,503	96	Flint, MI	435,436
3	Philadelphia, PA–NJ	4,969,334	50	Louisville, KY–IN	976,668	97	Colorado Springs, CO	433,461
4	Washington, DC–MD–VA–WV	4,399,049	51	Grand Rapids–Muskegon–Holland, MI	968,826	98	McAllen–Edinburg–Mission, TX	429,233
5	Detroit, MI	4,330,568	52	Dayton–Springfield, OH	968,224	99	Daytona Beach, FL	427,877
6	Houston, TX	3,600,764	53	Jacksonville, FL	966,411	100	Lakeland–Winter Haven, FL	425,061
7	Boston, MA–NH	3,393,227	54	Providence–Fall River–Warwick, RI–MA	956,796	101	Jackson, MS	409,223
8	Atlanta, GA	3,225,549	55	Raleigh–Durham–Chapel Hill, NC	923,111	102	Des Moines, IA	408,171
9	Riverside–San Bernardino, CA	2,837,569	56	Austin–San Marcos, TX	918,765	103	Santa Rosa, CA	405,090
10	Dallas, TX	2,751,065	57	Richmond–Petersburg, VA	909,654	104	Saginaw–Bay City–Midland, MI	404,419
11	Minneapolis–St. Paul, MN–WI	2,648,322	58	Honolulu, HI	875,455	105	Canton–Massillon, OH	401,855
12	Nassau–Suffolk, NY	2,628,063	59	Birmingham, AL	869,321	106	Modesto, CA	399,253
13	San Diego, CA	2,627,659	60	Greenville–Spartanburg–Anderson, SC	863,667	107	Spokane, WA	389,486
14	Orange County, CA	2,510,193	61	Fresno, CA	812,859	108	Santa Barbara–Santa Maria–Lompoc, CA	379,359
15	Baltimore, MD	2,457,276	62	Syracuse, NY	756,865	109	Beaumont–Port Arthur, TX	377,093
16	Pittsburgh, PA	2,423,968	63	Tulsa, OK	737,648	110	Madison, WI	376,681
17	Phoenix–Mesa, AZ	2,393,251	64	Tucson, AZ	708,931	111	Shreveport–Bossier City, LA	375,630
18	Oakland, CA	2,170,116	65	Ventura, CA	693,577	112	Salinas, CA	372,077
19	Tampa–St. Petersburg–Clearwater, FL	2,137,896	66	Akron, OH	667,989	113	Corpus Christi, TX	369,485
20	Seattle–Bellevue–Everett, WA	2,075,927	67	Scranton–Wilkes-Barre–Hazleton, PA	641,457	114	Lexington, KY	364,218
21	Miami, FL	2,037,568	68	El Paso, TX	640,839	115	Fort Myers–Cape Coral, FL	357,168
22	Newark, NJ	1,937,773	69	Tacoma, WA	633,847	116	Lafayette, LA	354,604
23	Denver, CO	1,757,721	70	Albuquerque, NM	629,814	117	Newburgh, NY–PA	349,972
24	San Francisco, CA	1,642,731	71	Gary–Hammond, IN	622,774	118	Reading, PA	344,635
25	Portland–Vancouver, OR–WA	1,640,863	72	Toledo, OH	619,203	119	Visalia–Tulare–Porterville, CA	334,462
26	Cincinnati, OH–KY–IN	1,571,218	73	Harrisburg–Lebanon–Carlisle, PA	604,920	120	Trenton, NJ	330,159
27	San Jose, CA	1,544,156	74	Bakersfield, CA	593,687	121	Appleton–Oshkosh–Neenah, WI	329,973
28	Fort Worth–Arlington, TX	1,538,831	75	New Haven–Meriden, CT	562,831	122	Boise, ID	329,652
29	Norfolk–Va Beach–Newport News, VA–NC	1,519,381	76	Jersey City, NJ	559,129	123	Stamford–Norwalk, CT	329,636
30	Milwaukee–Waukesha, WI	1,453,647	77	Baton Rouge, LA	548,361	124	Atlantic City, NJ	328,721
31	Sacramento, CA	1,433,067	78	Springfield, MA	539,699	125	Utica–Rome, NY	317,581
32	San Antonio, TX	1,405,738	79	Charleston–North Charleston, SC	534,445	126	Huntington–Ashland, WV–KY–OH	317,163
33	Columbus, OH	1,401,383	80	Little Rock–North Little Rock, AR	532,157	127	Huntsville, AL	311,694
34	Orlando, FL	1,323,652	81	Stockton–Lodi, CA	509,244	128	Montgomery, AL	309,452
35	Fort Lauderdale, FL	1,320,180	82	Sarasota–Bradenton, FL	506,026	129	Macon, GA	304,968
36	Bergen–Passaic, NJ	1,300,853	83	Ann Arbor, MI	503,897	130	Hickory–Morganton, NC	303,975
37	New Orleans, LA	1,260,951	84	Mobile, AL	501,440	131	New London–Norwich, CT–RI	301,303
38	Charlotte–Gastonia–Rock Hill, NC–SC	1,230,964	85	Vallejo–Fairfield–Napa, CA	479,963	132	Salem, OR	297,177
39	Buffalo–Niagara Falls, NY	1,201,686	86	Columbia, SC	477,627	133	Eugene–Springfield, OR	296,820
40	Salt Lake City–Ogden, UT	1,158,462	87	Worcester, MA–CT	470,774	134	Lawrence, MA–NH	295,930
41	Greensboro–Winston Salem–High Point, NC	1,096,140	88	Fort Wayne, IN	467,750	135	Evansville–Henderson, IN–KY	285,569
42	Rochester, NY	1,086,478	89	Bridgeport, CT	452,865	136	Brownsville–Harlingen–San Benito, TX	284,168
43	Middlesex–Sommerset–Hunterdon, NJ	1,054,645	90	Augusta–Aiken, GA–SC	451,500	137	Provo–Orem, UT	282,500
44	Hartford, CT	1,053,803	91	Johnson City–Kingsport–Bristol, TN–VA	450,919	138	Fayetteville, NC	281,740
45	Memphis, TN–AR–MS	1,048,342	92	Lansing–East Lansing, MI	438,470	139	Erie, PA	280,843
46	Nashville, TN	1,038,512	93	Kalamazoo–Battle Creek, MI	438,379	140	Reno, NV	279,191
47	Monmouth–Ocean, NJ	1,010,250	94	Chattanooga, TN–GA	438,176	141	Columbus, GA–AL	278,325

Source: U.S. Bureau of the Census as reported by U.S. Department of Justice, Federal Bureau of Investigation
    "Crime in the United States 1993" (Uniform Crime Reports, December 4, 1994)
*Estimates as of July 1, 1993.
**Not available.

85. Metropolitan Population in 1993 (continued)

National Total = 257,908,000 Population*

RANK	METRO AREA	POP	RANK	METRO AREA	POP	RANK	METRO AREA	POP
142	Springfield, MO	277,899	189	Naples, FL	167,124	236	Waterloo-Cedar Falls, IA	125,885
143	Savannah, GA	273,038	190	Manchester, NH	166,876	237	Texarkana, TX-AR	123,027
144	Fort Pierce-Port St. Lucie, FL	269,255	191	Lafayette, IN	166,449	238	Abilene, TX	122,927
145	Binghamton, NY	267,981	192	Richland-Kennewick-Pasco, WA	164,404	239	Glens Falls, NY	121,523
146	Dutchess County, NY	264,128	193	Danbury, CT	162,590	240	Lawton, OK	121,443
147	Killeen-Temple, TX	259,871	194	Benton Harbor, MI	162,208	241	Williamsport, PA	120,995
148	Charleston, WV	254,300	195	Elkhart-Goshen, IN	160,863	242	Punta Gorda, FL	120,986
149	South Bend, IN	252,959	196	Nashua, NH	160,383	243	Florence, SC	119,908
150	Anchorage, AK	250,720	197	Redding, CA	159,209	244	La Crosse, WI-MN	119,099
151	Tallahassee, FL	248,840	198	Fargo-Moorhead, ND-MN	158,369	245	Columbia, MO	117,862
152	Brockton, MA	246,237	199	Tyler, TX	157,425	246	Anniston, AL	117,781
153	Boulder-Longmont, CO	245,117	200	Medford-Ashland, OR	157,196	247	Albany, GA	117,680
154	Duluth-Superior, MN-WI	243,527	201	Fort Walton Beach, FL	155,654	248	Sioux City, IA-NE	117,570
155	Johnstown, PA	241,842	202	Tuscaloosa, AL	155,452	249	Bloomington, IN	112,184
156	Odessa-Midland, TX	238,376	203	Athens, GA	154,465	250	Greenville, NC	112,149
157	Portland, ME	233,775	204	St. Cloud, MN	154,366	251	Rochester, MN	111,693
158	Santa Cruz-Watsonville, CA	233,352	205	Myrtle Beach, SC	154,007	252	Danville, VA	110,979
159	Galveston-Texas City, TX	232,567	206	Jackson, MI	152,438	253	Goldsboro, NC	109,427
160	Roanoke, VA	229,712	207	Laredo, TX	151,386	254	Sumter, SC	106,524
161	Fayetteville-Springdale-Rogers, AR	228,557	208	Sioux Falls, SD	148,358	255	Sheboygan, WI	105,984
162	Lubbock, TX	228,251	209	Jacksonville, NC	146,832	256	Lewiston-Auburn, ME	104,092
163	San Luis Obispo-Atascadero, CA	222,812	210	Yolo, CA	146,290	257	Grand Forks, ND-MN	103,652
164	Lincoln, NE	220,404	211	Monroe, LA	145,451	258	Cumberland, MD-WV	102,409
165	Bremerton, WA	215,355	212	Janesville-Beloit, WI	144,047	259	San Angelo, TX	101,060
166	Ocala, FL	211,008	213	Steubenville-Weirton, OH-WV	142,406	260	Gadsden, AL	100,556
167	Brazoria, TX	207,861	214	Eau Claire, WI	141,145	261	Kokomo, IN	99,536
168	Fort Collins-Loveland, CO	203,897	215	Bellingham, WA	140,914	262	St. Joseph, MO	98,796
169	Longview-Marshall, TX	203,855	216	Greeley, CO	139,826	263	Pittsfield, MA	98,519
170	Green Bay, WI	203,170	217	Vineland-Millville-Bridgeton, NJ	139,537	264	Sherman-Denison, TX	96,941
171	Yakima, WA	202,331	218	Rocky Mount, NC	139,396	265	Owensboro, KY	89,640
172	Lynchburg, VA	201,399	219	Joplin, MO	138,638	266	Dubuque, IA	87,612
173	Asheville, NC	200,605	220	Wausau, WI	138,369	267	Pine Bluff, AR	86,325
174	Amarillo, TX	195,405	221	Barnstable-Yarmouth, MA	137,118	268	Bismarck, ND	86,183
175	Waco, TX	195,325	222	Fitchburg-Leominster, MA	136,990	269	Rapid City, SD	85,853
176	Gainesville, FL	192,158	223	Decatur, AL	136,793	270	Jackson, TN	81,410
177	Merced, CA	191,038	224	Charlottesville, VA	136,484	271	Victoria, TX	78,557
178	Chico-Paradise, CA	190,302	225	Panama City, FL	135,954	272	Cheyenne, WY	76,880
179	Houma, LA	187,213	226	Florence, AL	135,811	273	Bangor, ME	67,623
180	Waterbury, CT	185,361	227	Kenosha, WI	135,181	274	Enid, OK	56,818
181	Wilmington, NC	185,143	228	Dothan, AL	134,860	–	Albany, NY**	NA
182	Fort Smith, AR-OK	182,651	229	Altoona, PA	131,894	–	Chicago, IL**	NA
183	Racine, WI	181,121	230	Yuba City, CA	131,663	–	Cleveland, OH**	NA
184	Olympia, WA	180,410	231	Alexandria, LA	131,041	–	Indianapolis, IN**	NA
185	Clarksville-Hopkinsville, TN-KY	180,407	232	Wichita Falls, TX	130,603	–	Kansas City, MO-KS**	NA
186	Mansfield, OH	176,573	233	Bryan-College Station, TX	127,620	–	Omaha, NE**	NA
187	New Bedford, MA	174,609	234	Pueblo, CO	127,363	–	St. Louis, MO-IL**	NA
188	Lake Charles, LA	172,146	235	Hagerstown, MD	126,701	–	West Palm Beach-Boca Raton, FL**	NA

Source: U.S. Bureau of the Census as reported by U.S. Department of Justice, Federal Bureau of Investigation
  "Crime in the United States 1993" (Uniform Crime Reports, December 4, 1994)
*Estimates as of July 1, 1993.
**Not available.

86. Metropolitan Population in 1992

National Total = 255,078,000 Population*

RANK	METRO AREA	POP	RANK	METRO AREA	POP	RANK	METRO AREA	POP
220	Abilene, TX	124,367	254	Cheyenne, WY	75,173	28	Fort Worth-Arlington, TX	1,503,718
64	Akron, OH	662,347	2	Chicago, IL	7,541,468	59	Fresno, CA	783,669
228	Albany, GA	117,295	167	Chico-Paradise, CA	188,887	242	Gadsden, AL	101,739
–	Albany, NY**	NA	27	Cincinnati, OH-KY-IN	1,551,617	166	Gainesville, FL	189,308
70	Albuquerque, NM	614,855	174	Clarksville-Hopkinsville, TN-KY	173,761	153	Galveston-Texas City, TX	225,957
212	Alexandria, LA	133,640	17	Cleveland, OH	2,241,943	68	Gary-Hammond, IN	617,359
214	Altoona, PA	131,927	91	Colorado Springs, CO	418,167	224	Glens Falls, NY	119,373
165	Amarillo, TX	194,935	229	Columbia, MO	114,043	235	Goldsboro, NC	108,045
146	Anchorage, AK	241,565	81	Columbia, SC	468,978	240	Grand Forks, ND-MN	103,641
79	Ann Arbor, MI	494,333	133	Columbus, GA-AL	273,715	49	Grand Rapids-Muskegon-Holland, MI	952,154
226	Anniston, AL	118,767	34	Columbus, OH	1,365,279	201	Greeley, CO	138,846
117	Appleton-Oshkosh-Neenah, WI	320,573	108	Corpus Christi, TX	364,607	162	Green Bay, WI	199,174
163	Asheville, NC	198,220	239	Cumberland, MD-WV	103,894	40	Greensboro-Winston Salem-High Point, NC	1,084,803
187	Athens, GA	153,543	8	Dallas, TX	2,685,255	233	Greenville, NC	109,407
7	Atlanta, GA	3,101,010	178	Danbury, CT	162,257	58	Greenville-Spartanburg-Anderson, SC	859,369
116	Atlantic City, NJ	321,815	231	Danville, VA	112,038	219	Hagerstown, MD	124,602
94	Augusta-Aiken, GA-SC	410,465	92	Daytona Beach, FL	416,379	71	Harrisburg-Lebanon-Carlisle, PA	595,094
55	Austin-San Marcos, TX	879,556	47	Dayton-Springfield, OH	966,619	42	Hartford, CT	1,055,773
72	Bakersfield, CA	563,678	211	Decatur, AL	133,829	122	Hickory-Morganton, NC	301,844
14	Baltimore, MD	2,445,286	22	Denver, CO	1,701,831	56	Honolulu, HI	875,297
255	Bangor, ME	66,952	100	Des Moines, IA	398,124	169	Houma, LA	185,738
208	Barnstable-Yarmouth, MA	134,532	4	Detroit, MI	4,334,397	6	Houston, TX	3,453,675
80	Baton Rouge, LA	477,506	210	Dothan, AL	134,044	126	Huntington-Ashland, WV-KY-OH	292,220
105	Beaumont-Port Arthur, TX	375,447	248	Dubuque, IA	87,553	124	Huntsville, AL	299,958
207	Bellingham, WA	134,845	142	Duluth-Superior, MN-WI	245,840	31	Indianapolis, IN	1,410,497
177	Benton Harbor, MI	163,823	–	Dutchess County, NY**	NA	191	Jackson, MI	152,027
–	Bergen-Passaic, NJ**	NA	199	Eau Claire, WI	140,774	97	Jackson, MS	401,856
137	Binghamton, NY	267,248	69	El Paso, TX	614,927	252	Jackson, TN	80,327
57	Birmingham, AL	860,254	179	Elkhart-Goshen, IN	159,516	50	Jacksonville, FL	945,413
250	Bismarck, ND	83,458	256	Enid, OK	57,929	184	Jacksonville, NC	154,676
232	Bloomington, IN	111,293	131	Erie, PA	278,512	198	Janesville-Beloit, WI	142,786
119	Boise, ID	313,650	125	Eugene-Springfield, OR	296,305	–	Jersey City, NJ**	NA
–	Boston, MA-NH**	NA	128	Evansville-Henderson, IN-KY	284,809	85	Johnson City-Kingsport-Bristol, TN-VA	448,917
148	Boulder-Longmont, CO	237,321	185	Fargo-Moorhead, ND-MN	154,146	144	Johnstown, PA	243,777
161	Brazoria, TX	199,250	129	Fayetteville, NC	283,441	–	Joplin, MO**	NA
158	Bremerton, WA	200,225	155	Fayetteville-Springdale-Rogers, AR	215,225	88	Kalamazoo-Battle Creek, MI	435,967
84	Bridgeport, CT	452,801	–	Fitchburg-Leominster, MA**	NA	24	Kansas City, MO-KS	1,608,411
143	Brockton, MA	244,950	87	Flint, MI	436,895	215	Kenosha, WI	131,196
134	Brownsville-Harlingen-San Benito, TX	270,362	209	Florence, AL	134,416	138	Killeen-Temple, TX	265,354
218	Bryan-College Station, TX	126,663	227	Florence, SC	118,150	245	Kokomo, IN	99,004
–	Buffalo-Niagara Falls, NY**	NA	–	Fort Collins-Loveland, CO**	NA	225	La Crosse, WI-MN	119,143
98	Canton-Massillon, OH	400,223	35	Fort Lauderdale, FL	1,308,841	176	Lafayette, IN	165,002
140	Charleston, WV	252,438	111	Fort Myers-Cape Coral, FL	349,357	110	Lafayette, LA	350,419
76	Charleston-North Charleston, SC	523,763	139	Fort Pierce-Port St. Lucie, FL	261,737	–	Lake Charles, LA**	NA
206	Charlottesville, VA	135,122	171	Fort Smith, AR-OK	179,528	90	Lakeland-Winter Haven, FL	422,603
38	Charlotte-Gastonia-Rock Hill, NC-SC	1,199,979	192	Fort Walton Beach, FL	149,885	89	Lancaster, PA	427,316
93	Chattanooga, TN-GA	412,862	83	Fort Wayne, IN	465,968	86	Lansing-East Lansing, MI	439,243

Source: U.S. Bureau of the Census as reported by U.S. Department of Justice, Federal Bureau of Investigation
   "Crime in the United States 1992" (Uniform Crime Reports, October 3, 1993)
*Estimates as of July 1, 1992.
**Not available. Data for the metro areas of Boston and New York were reported for areas reported as separate metro areas in 1989 and 1993. Accordingly, 1992 data are not comparable.

86. Metropolitan Population in 1992 (continued)

National Total = 255,078,000 Population*

RANK	METRO AREA	POP	RANK	METRO AREA	POP	RANK	METRO AREA	POP
202	Laredo, TX	138,488	175	Olympia, WA	170,155	20	Seattle-Bellevue-Everett, WA	2,052,699
51	Las Vegas, NV–AZ	936,084	–	Omaha, NE**	NA	236	Sheboygan, WI	106,320
–	Lawrence, MA–NH**	NA	13	Orange County, CA	2,500,181	246	Sherman-Denison, TX	98,762
230	Lawton, OK	113,838	36	Orlando, FL	1,276,893	103	Shreveport-Bossier City, LA	382,299
238	Lewiston-Auburn, ME	105,861	247	Owensboro, KY	88,836	–	Sioux City, IA–NE**	NA
109	Lexington, KY	355,006	213	Panama City, FL	132,386	197	Sioux Falls, SD	143,795
154	Lincoln, NE	217,458	3	Philadelphia, PA–NJ	4,972,026	141	South Bend, IN	252,302
75	Little Rock-North Little Rock, AR	523,823	16	Phoenix-Mesa, AZ	2,340,390	104	Spokane, WA	381,358
156	Longview-Marshall, TX	203,936	249	Pine Bluff, AR	87,241	74	Springfield, MA	540,224
1	Los Angeles-Long Beach, CA	9,193,319	15	Pittsburgh, PA	2,427,233	136	Springfield, MO	268,266
46	Louisville, KY–IN	967,561	243	Pittsfield, MA	99,614	113	Stamford-Norwalk, CT	329,312
152	Lubbock, TX	230,588	150	Portland, ME	233,596	196	Steubenville-Weirton, OH–WV	144,400
159	Lynchburg, VA	200,006	25	Portland-Vancouver, OR–WA	1,591,835	78	Stockton-Lodi, CA	498,497
121	Macon, GA	303,144	48	Providence-Fall River-Warwick, RI–MA	960,912	189	St. Cloud, MN	152,536
106	Madison, WI	368,920	132	Provo-Orem, UT	277,368	244	St. Joseph, MO	99,160
–	Manchester, NH**	NA	216	Pueblo, CO	129,722	12	St. Louis, MO–IL	2,542,160
173	Mansfield, OH	176,706	–	Punta Gorda, FL**	NA	237	Sumter, SC	106,058
99	McAllen-Edinburg-Mission, TX	398,648	172	Racine, WI	179,150	60	Syracuse, NY	747,819
188	Medford-Ashland, OR	153,315	54	Raleigh-Durham-Chapel Hill, NC	882,596	67	Tacoma, WA	619,402
43	Memphis, TN–AR–MS	1,036,313	251	Rapid City, SD	83,145	145	Tallahassee, FL	243,524
170	Merced, CA	185,030	112	Reading, PA	340,092	19	Tampa-St. Petersburg-Clearwater, FL	2,156,055
21	Miami, FL	2,019,426	190	Redding, CA	152,501	222	Texarkana, TX–AR	124,132
–	Middlesex-Somerset-Hunterdon, NJ**	NA	130	Reno, NV	281,188	66	Toledo, OH	623,669
30	Milwaukee-Waukesha, WI	1,456,232	182	Richland-Kennewick-Pasco, WA	158,329	114	Trenton, NJ	328,290
10	Minneapolis-St. Paul, MN–WI	2,600,929	53	Richmond-Petersburg, VA	892,158	62	Tucson, AZ	697,220
–	Mobile, AL**	NA	9	Riverside-San Bernardino, CA	2,671,120	61	Tulsa, OK	724,036
101	Modesto, CA	384,293	151	Roanoke, VA	231,351	186	Tuscaloosa, AL	154,032
–	Monmouth-Ocean, NJ**	NA	234	Rochester, MN	109,020	183	Tyler, TX	157,197
195	Monroe, LA	144,445	41	Rochester, NY	1,070,013	118	Utica-Rome, NY	316,531
123	Montgomery, AL	301,633	203	Rocky Mount, NC	138,023	82	Vallejo-Fairfield-Napa, CA	467,955
193	Myrtle Beach, SC	148,849	32	Sacramento, CA	1,389,836	63	Ventura, CA	693,890
181	Naples, FL	158,565	95	Saginaw-Bay City-Midland, MI	405,376	253	Victoria, TX	77,290
180	Nashua, NH	159,026	127	Salem, OR	290,605	200	Vineland-Millville-Bridgeton, NJ	139,100
44	Nashville, TN	1,014,815	107	Salinas, CA	368,875	115	Visalia-Tulare-Porterville, CA	323,513
–	Nassau-Suffolk, NY**	NA	39	Salt Lake City-Ogden, UT	1,128,406	164	Waco, TX	196,563
–	New Bedford, MA**	NA	241	San Angelo, TX	102,337	5	Washington, DC–MD–VA–WV	4,306,943
73	New Haven-Meriden, CT	561,661	33	San Antonio, TX	1,376,937	168	Waterbury, CT	186,481
120	New London-Norwich, CT–RI	306,916	11	San Diego, CA	2,590,916	–	Waterloo-Cedar Falls, IA**	NA
37	New Orleans, LA	1,258,657	23	San Francisco, CA	1,663,297	204	Wausau, WI	137,540
–	New York, NY**	NA	26	San Jose, CA	1,553,258	52	West Palm Beach-Boca Raton, FL	900,197
–	Newark, NJ**	NA	–	San Luis Obispo-Atascadero, CA**	NA	205	Wichita Falls, TX	135,484
–	Newburgh, NY–PA**	NA	102	Santa Barbara-Santa Maria-Lompoc, CA	383,348	223	Williamsport, PA	119,972
29	Norfolk-Va Beach-Newport News, VA–NC	1,487,600	147	Santa Cruz-Watsonville, CA	238,272	221	Wilmington, NC	124,169
18	Oakland, CA	2,160,350	96	Santa Rosa, CA	402,652	–	Worcester, MA–CT**	NA
157	Ocala, FL	203,112	77	Sarasota-Bradenton, FL	510,282	160	Yakima, WA	199,259
149	Odessa-Midland, TX	234,431	135	Savannah, GA	268,912	194	Yolo, CA	146,334
45	Oklahoma City, OK	979,343	65	Scranton-Wilkes-Barre-Hazleton, PA	645,218	217	Yuba City, CA	127,199

Source: U.S. Bureau of the Census as reported by U.S. Department of Justice, Federal Bureau of Investigation
"Crime in the United States 1992" (Uniform Crime Reports, October 3, 1993)
*Estimates as of July 1, 1992.
**Not available. Data for the metro areas of Boston and New York were reported for areas reported as separate metro areas in 1989 and 1993. Accordingly, 1992 data are not comparable.

86. Metropolitan Population in 1992 (continued)

National Total = 255,078,000 Population*

RANK	METRO AREA	POP	RANK	METRO AREA	POP	RANK	METRO AREA	POP
1	Los Angeles–Long Beach, CA	9,193,319	48	Providence–Fall River–Warwick, RI–MA	960,912	95	Saginaw–Bay City–Midland, MI	405,376
2	Chicago, IL	7,541,468	49	Grand Rapids–Muskegon–Holland, MI	952,154	96	Santa Rosa, CA	402,652
3	Philadelphia, PA–NJ	4,972,026	50	Jacksonville, FL	945,413	97	Jackson, MS	401,856
4	Detroit, MI	4,334,397	51	Las Vegas, NV–AZ	936,084	98	Canton–Massillon, OH	400,223
5	Washington, DC–MD–VA–WV	4,306,943	52	West Palm Beach–Boca Raton, FL	900,197	99	McAllen–Edinburg–Mission, TX	398,648
6	Houston, TX	3,453,675	53	Richmond–Petersburg, VA	892,158	100	Des Moines, IA	398,124
7	Atlanta, GA	3,101,010	54	Raleigh–Durham–Chapel Hill, NC	882,596	101	Modesto, CA	384,293
8	Dallas, TX	2,685,255	55	Austin–San Marcos, TX	879,556	102	Santa Barbara–Santa Maria–Lompoc, CA	383,348
9	Riverside–San Bernardino, CA	2,671,120	56	Honolulu, HI	875,297	103	Shreveport–Bossier City, LA	382,299
10	Minneapolis–St. Paul, MN–WI	2,600,929	57	Birmingham, AL	860,254	104	Spokane, WA	381,358
11	San Diego, CA	2,590,916	58	Greenville–Spartanburg–Anderson, SC	859,369	105	Beaumont–Port Arthur, TX	375,447
12	St. Louis, MO–IL	2,542,160	59	Fresno, CA	783,669	106	Madison, WI	368,920
13	Orange County, CA	2,500,181	60	Syracuse, NY	747,819	107	Salinas, CA	368,875
14	Baltimore, MD	2,445,286	61	Tulsa, OK	724,036	108	Corpus Christi, TX	364,607
15	Pittsburgh, PA	2,427,233	62	Tucson, AZ	697,220	109	Lexington, KY	355,006
16	Phoenix–Mesa, AZ	2,340,390	63	Ventura, CA	693,890	110	Lafayette, LA	350,419
17	Cleveland, OH	2,241,943	64	Akron, OH	662,347	111	Fort Myers–Cape Coral, FL	349,357
18	Oakland, CA	2,160,350	65	Scranton–Wilkes-Barre–Hazleton, PA	645,218	112	Reading, PA	340,092
19	Tampa–St. Petersburg–Clearwater, FL	2,156,055	66	Toledo, OH	623,669	113	Stamford–Norwalk, CT	329,312
20	Seattle–Bellevue–Everett, WA	2,052,699	67	Tacoma, WA	619,402	114	Trenton, NJ	328,290
21	Miami, FL	2,019,426	68	Gary–Hammond, IN	617,359	115	Visalia–Tulare–Porterville, CA	323,513
22	Denver, CO	1,701,831	69	El Paso, TX	614,927	116	Atlantic City, NJ	321,815
23	San Francisco, CA	1,663,297	70	Albuquerque, NM	614,855	117	Appleton–Oshkosh–Neenah, WI	320,573
24	Kansas City, MO–KS	1,608,411	71	Harrisburg–Lebanon–Carlisle, PA	595,094	118	Utica–Rome, NY	316,531
25	Portland–Vancouver, OR–WA	1,591,835	72	Bakersfield, CA	563,678	119	Boise, ID	313,650
26	San Jose, CA	1,553,258	73	New Haven–Meriden, CT	561,661	120	New London–Norwich, CT–RI	306,916
27	Cincinnati, OH–KY–IN	1,551,617	74	Springfield, MA	540,224	121	Macon, GA	303,144
28	Fort Worth–Arlington, TX	1,503,718	75	Little Rock–North Little Rock, AR	523,823	122	Hickory–Morganton, NC	301,844
29	Norfolk–Va Beach–Newport News, VA–NC	1,487,600	76	Charleston–North Charleston, SC	523,763	123	Montgomery, AL	301,633
30	Milwaukee–Waukesha, WI	1,456,232	77	Sarasota–Bradenton, FL	510,282	124	Huntsville, AL	299,958
31	Indianapolis, IN	1,410,497	78	Stockton–Lodi, CA	498,497	125	Eugene–Springfield, OR	296,305
32	Sacramento, CA	1,389,836	79	Ann Arbor, MI	494,333	126	Huntington–Ashland, WV–KY–OH	292,220
33	San Antonio, TX	1,376,937	80	Baton Rouge, LA	477,506	127	Salem, OR	290,605
34	Columbus, OH	1,365,279	81	Columbia, SC	468,978	128	Evansville–Henderson, IN–KY	284,809
35	Fort Lauderdale, FL	1,308,841	82	Vallejo–Fairfield–Napa, CA	467,955	129	Fayetteville, NC	283,441
36	Orlando, FL	1,276,893	83	Fort Wayne, IN	465,968	130	Reno, NV	281,188
37	New Orleans, LA	1,258,657	84	Bridgeport, CT	452,801	131	Erie, PA	278,512
38	Charlotte–Gastonia–Rock Hill, NC–SC	1,199,979	85	Johnson City–Kingsport–Bristol, TN–VA	448,917	132	Provo–Orem, UT	277,368
39	Salt Lake City–Ogden, UT	1,128,406	86	Lansing–East Lansing, MI	439,243	133	Columbus, GA–AL	273,715
40	Greensboro–Winston Salem–High Point, NC	1,084,803	87	Flint, MI	436,895	134	Brownsville–Harlingen–San Benito, TX	270,362
41	Rochester, NY	1,070,013	88	Kalamazoo–Battle Creek, MI	435,967	135	Savannah, GA	268,912
42	Hartford, CT	1,055,773	89	Lancaster, PA	427,316	136	Springfield, MO	268,266
43	Memphis, TN–AR–MS	1,036,313	90	Lakeland–Winter Haven, FL	422,603	137	Binghamton, NY	267,248
44	Nashville, TN	1,014,815	91	Colorado Springs, CO	418,167	138	Killeen–Temple, TX	265,354
45	Oklahoma City, OK	979,343	92	Daytona Beach, FL	416,379	139	Fort Pierce–Port St. Lucie, FL	261,737
46	Louisville, KY–IN	967,561	93	Chattanooga, TN–GA	412,862	140	Charleston, WV	252,438
47	Dayton–Springfield, OH	966,619	94	Augusta–Aiken, GA–SC	410,465	141	South Bend, IN	252,302

Source: U.S. Bureau of the Census as reported by U.S. Department of Justice, Federal Bureau of Investigation
   "Crime in the United States 1992" (Uniform Crime Reports, October 3, 1993)
Estimates as of July 1, 1992.
**Not available. Data for the metro areas of Boston and New York were reported for areas reported as separate metro areas in 1989 and 1993. Accordingly, 1992 data are not comparable.*

86. Metropolitan Population in 1992 (continued)

National Total = 255,078,000 Population*

RANK	METRO AREA	POP	RANK	METRO AREA	POP	RANK	METRO AREA	POP
142	Duluth–Superior, MN–WI	245,840	189	St. Cloud, MN	152,536	236	Sheboygan, WI	106,320
143	Brockton, MA	244,950	190	Redding, CA	152,501	237	Sumter, SC	106,058
144	Johnstown, PA	243,777	191	Jackson, MI	152,027	238	Lewiston–Auburn, ME	105,861
145	Tallahassee, FL	243,524	192	Fort Walton Beach, FL	149,885	239	Cumberland, MD–WV	103,894
146	Anchorage, AK	241,565	193	Myrtle Beach, SC	148,849	240	Grand Forks, ND–MN	103,641
147	Santa Cruz–Watsonville, CA	238,272	194	Yolo, CA	146,334	241	San Angelo, TX	102,337
148	Boulder–Longmont, CO	237,321	195	Monroe, LA	144,445	242	Gadsden, AL	101,739
149	Odessa–Midland, TX	234,431	196	Steubenville–Weirton, OH–WV	144,400	243	Pittsfield, MA	99,614
150	Portland, ME	233,596	197	Sioux Falls, SD	143,795	244	St. Joseph, MO	99,160
151	Roanoke, VA	231,351	198	Janesville–Beloit, WI	142,786	245	Kokomo, IN	99,004
152	Lubbock, TX	230,588	199	Eau Claire, WI	140,774	246	Sherman–Denison, TX	98,762
153	Galveston–Texas City, TX	225,957	200	Vineland–Millville–Bridgeton, NJ	139,100	247	Owensboro, KY	88,836
154	Lincoln, NE	217,458	201	Greeley, CO	138,846	248	Dubuque, IA	87,553
155	Fayetteville–Springdale–Rogers, AR	215,225	202	Laredo, TX	138,488	249	Pine Bluff, AR	87,241
156	Longview–Marshall, TX	203,936	203	Rocky Mount, NC	138,023	250	Bismarck, ND	83,458
157	Ocala, FL	203,112	204	Wausau, WI	137,540	251	Rapid City, SD	83,145
158	Bremerton, WA	200,225	205	Wichita Falls, TX	135,484	252	Jackson, TN	80,327
159	Lynchburg, VA	200,006	206	Charlottesville, VA	135,122	253	Victoria, TX	77,290
160	Yakima, WA	199,259	207	Bellingham, WA	134,845	254	Cheyenne, WY	75,173
161	Brazoria, TX	199,250	208	Barnstable–Yarmouth, MA	134,532	255	Bangor, ME	66,952
162	Green Bay, WI	199,174	209	Florence, AL	134,416	256	Enid, OK	57,929
163	Asheville, NC	198,220	210	Dothan, AL	134,044	–	Albany, NY**	NA
164	Waco, TX	196,563	211	Decatur, AL	133,829	–	Bergen–Passaic, NJ**	NA
165	Amarillo, TX	194,935	212	Alexandria, LA	133,640	–	Boston, MA–NH**	NA
166	Gainesville, FL	189,308	213	Panama City, FL	132,386	–	Buffalo–Niagara Falls, NY**	NA
167	Chico–Paradise, CA	188,887	214	Altoona, PA	131,927	–	Dutchess County, NY**	NA
168	Waterbury, CT	186,481	215	Kenosha, WI	131,196	–	Fitchburg–Leominster, MA**	NA
169	Houma, LA	185,738	216	Pueblo, CO	129,722	–	Fort Collins–Loveland, CO**	NA
170	Merced, CA	185,030	217	Yuba City, CA	127,199	–	Jersey City, NJ**	NA
171	Fort Smith, AR–OK	179,528	218	Bryan–College Station, TX	126,663	–	Joplin, MO**	NA
172	Racine, WI	179,150	219	Hagerstown, MD	124,602	–	Lake Charles, LA**	NA
173	Mansfield, OH	176,706	220	Abilene, TX	124,367	–	Lawrence, MA–NH**	NA
174	Clarksville–Hopkinsville, TN–KY	173,761	221	Wilmington, NC	124,169	–	Manchester, NH**	NA
175	Olympia, WA	170,155	222	Texarkana, TX–AR	124,132	–	Middlesex–Somerset–Hunterdon, NJ**	NA
176	Lafayette, IN	165,002	223	Williamsport, PA	119,972	–	Mobile, AL**	NA
177	Benton Harbor, MI	163,823	224	Glens Falls, NY	119,373	–	Monmouth–Ocean, NJ**	NA
178	Danbury, CT	162,257	225	La Crosse, WI–MN	119,143	–	Nassau–Suffolk, NY**	NA
179	Elkhart–Goshen, IN	159,516	226	Anniston, AL	118,767	–	New Bedford, MA**	NA
180	Nashua, NH	159,026	227	Florence, SC	118,150	–	New York, NY**	NA
181	Naples, FL	158,565	228	Albany, GA	117,295	–	Newark, NJ**	NA
182	Richland–Kennewick–Pasco, WA	158,329	229	Columbia, MO	114,043	–	Newburgh, NY–PA**	NA
183	Tyler, TX	157,197	230	Lawton, OK	113,838	–	Omaha, NE**	NA
184	Jacksonville, NC	154,676	231	Danville, VA	112,038	–	Punta Gorda, FL**	NA
185	Fargo–Moorhead, ND–MN	154,146	232	Bloomington, IN	111,293	–	San Luis Obispo–Atascadero, CA**	NA
186	Tuscaloosa, AL	154,032	233	Greenville, NC	109,407	–	Sioux City, IA–NE**	NA
187	Athens, GA	153,543	234	Rochester, MN	109,020	–	Waterloo–Cedar Falls, IA**	NA
188	Medford–Ashland, OR	153,315	235	Goldsboro, NC	108,045	–	Worcester, MA–CT**	NA

Source: U.S. Bureau of the Census as reported by U.S. Department of Justice, Federal Bureau of Investigation
"Crime in the United States 1992" (Uniform Crime Reports, October 3, 1993)
*Estimates as of July 1, 1992.
**Not available. Data for the metro areas of Boston and New York were reported for areas reported as separate metro areas in 1989 and 1993. Accordingly, 1992 data are not comparable.

87. Metropolitan Population in 1989

National Total = 248,239,000 Population*

RANK	METRO AREA	POP	RANK	METRO AREA	POP	RANK	METRO AREA	POP
217	Abilene, TX	122,905	251	Cheyenne, WY	74,523	33	Fort Worth–Arlington, TX	1,388,527
–	Akron, OH**	NA	3	Chicago, IL	6,196,105	69	Fresno, CA	631,072
225	Albany, GA	118,033	168	Chico–Paradise, CA	179,119	236	Gadsden, AL	102,776
57	Albany, NY	852,838	29	Cincinnati, OH–KY–IN	1,455,227	153	Gainesville, FL	213,254
83	Albuquerque, NM	501,336	179	Clarksville–Hopkinsville, TN–KY	159,846	155	Galveston–Texas City, TX	211,906
197	Alexandria, LA	136,993	24	Cleveland, OH	1,853,974	73	Gary–Hammond, IN	616,166
204	Altoona, PA	132,917	100	Colorado Springs, CO	395,809	227	Glens Falls, NY	116,465
158	Amarillo, TX	198,182	231	Columbia, MO	106,158	–	Goldsboro, NC**	NA
151	Anchorage, AK	223,363	86	Columbia, SC	462,561	252	Grand Forks, ND–MN	69,677
133	Ann Arbor, MI	265,500	138	Columbus, GA–AL	249,895	60	Grand Rapids–Muskegon–Holland, MI	834,669
215	Anniston, AL	123,706	34	Columbus, OH	1,350,738	198	Greeley, CO	136,880
121	Appleton–Oshkosh–Neenah, WI	311,726	108	Corpus Christi, TX	362,247	160	Green Bay, WI	191,696
170	Asheville, NC	175,336	234	Cumberland, MD–WV	103,289	53	Greensboro–Winston Salem–High Point, NC	938,114
190	Athens, GA	146,749	14	Dallas, TX	2,404,726	–	Greenville, NC**	NA
9	Atlanta, GA	2,777,665	177	Danbury, CT	163,093	70	Greenville–Spartanburg–Anderson, SC	630,206
123	Atlantic City, NJ	309,796	230	Danville, VA	109,584	221	Hagerstown, MD	119,640
98	Augusta–Aiken, GA–SC	401,895	111	Daytona Beach, FL	357,887	–	Harrisburg–Lebanon–Carlisle, PA**	NA
62	Austin–San Marcos, TX	755,191	52	Dayton–Springfield, OH	953,334	61	Hartford, CT	762,461
78	Bakersfield, CA	533,763	203	Decatur, AL	133,649	–	Hickory–Morganton, NC**	NA
15	Baltimore, MD	2,378,992	25	Denver, CO	1,640,296	58	Honolulu, HI	848,959
253	Bangor, ME	65,854	101	Des Moines, IA	392,600	–	Houma, LA**	NA
–	Barnstable–Yarmouth, MA**	NA	5	Detroit, MI	4,370,346	7	Houston, TX	3,276,259
80	Baton Rouge, LA	533,360	205	Dothan, AL	131,531	118	Huntington–Ashland, WV–KY–OH	321,199
106	Beaumont–Port Arthur, TX	367,202	244	Dubuque, IA	91,146	143	Huntsville, AL	237,479
219	Bellingham, WA	121,583	140	Duluth–Superior, MN–WI	243,657	38	Indianapolis, IN	1,245,515
176	Benton Harbor, MI	167,199	–	Dutchess County, NY**	NA	183	Jackson, MI	150,037
37	Bergen–Passaic, NJ	1,294,794	195	Eau Claire, WI	138,759	99	Jackson, MS	396,399
134	Binghamton, NY	261,615	74	El Paso, TX	591,217	249	Jackson, TN	78,914
54	Birmingham, AL	929,861	182	Elkhart–Goshen, IN	152,079	55	Jacksonville, FL	922,557
247	Bismarck, ND	84,798	254	Enid, OK	57,978	210	Jacksonville, NC	128,134
233	Bloomington, IN	103,768	128	Erie, PA	277,872	199	Janesville–Beloit, WI	136,654
157	Boise, ID	202,940	129	Eugene–Springfield, OR	275,323	77	Jersey City, NJ	543,246
8	Boston, MA–NH	2,868,381	127	Evansville–Henderson, IN–KY	282,890	89	Johnson City–Kingsport–Bristol, TN–VA	446,376
152	Boulder–Longmont, CO	218,936	187	Fargo–Moorhead, ND–MN	147,747	–	Johnstown, PA**	NA
163	Brazoria, TX	186,275	135	Fayetteville, NC	259,003	200	Joplin, MO	136,360
–	Bremerton, WA**	NA	229	Fayetteville–Springdale–Rogers, AR	111,117	109	Kalamazoo–Battle Creek, MI	358,383
88	Bridgeport, CT	454,602	240	Fitchburg–Leominster, MA	98,942	27	Kansas City, MO–KS	1,583,141
–	Brockton, MA**	NA	91	Flint, MI	432,148	216	Kenosha, WI	122,918
132	Brownsville–Harlingen–San Benito, TX	266,396	201	Florence, AL	135,946	141	Killeen–Temple, TX	241,774
226	Bryan–College Station, TX	117,658	222	Florence, SC	119,459	239	Kokomo, IN	99,541
41	Buffalo–Niagara Falls, NY	1,179,892	165	Fort Collins–Loveland, CO	182,882	242	La Crosse, WI–MN	95,748
97	Canton–Massillon, OH	403,252	39	Fort Lauderdale, FL	1,219,323	156	Lafayette, IN	208,473
81	Charleston, WV	517,117	120	Fort Myers–Cape Coral, FL	317,517	211	Lafayette, LA	126,212
136	Charleston–North Charleston, SC	257,418	142	Fort Pierce–Port St. Lucie, FL	238,112	175	Lake Charles, LA	171,391
214	Charlottesville, VA	125,500	167	Fort Smith, AR–OK	181,179	96	Lakeland–Winter Haven, FL	406,578
42	Charlotte–Gastonia–Rock Hill, NC–SC	1,126,294	180	Fort Walton Beach, FL	154,701	94	Lancaster, PA	415,404
90	Chattanooga, TN–GA	442,433	105	Fort Wayne, IN	369,680	93	Lansing–East Lansing, MI	429,839

*Source: U.S. Bureau of the Census as reported by U.S. Department of Justice, Federal Bureau of Investigation
"Crime in the United States 1989" (Uniform Crime Reports, August 5, 1990)*
Estimates as of July 1, 1989.
**Not available.*

87. Metropolitan Population in 1989 (continued)

National Total = 248,239,000 Population*

RANK	METRO AREA	POP	RANK	METRO AREA	POP	RANK	METRO AREA	POP
206	Laredo, TX	130,070	178	Olympia, WA	160,404	21	Seattle-Bellevue-Everett, WA	1,906,244
65	Las Vegas, NV-AZ	665,377	71	Omaha, NE	624,713	235	Sheboygan, WI	103,267
104	Lawrence, MA-NH	372,299	16	Orange County, CA	2,316,738	241	Sherman-Denison, TX	98,788
224	Lawton, OK	118,641	44	Orlando, FL	997,545	112	Shreveport-Bossier City, LA	356,998
232	Lewiston-Auburn, ME	104,688	245	Owensboro, KY	87,885	228	Sioux City, IA-NE	115,996
115	Lexington, KY	348,337	208	Panama City, FL	128,918	212	Sioux Falls, SD	125,835
154	Lincoln, NE	212,762	4	Philadelphia, PA-NJ	4,934,532	–	South Bend, IN**	NA
82	Little Rock-North Little Rock, AR	515,504	18	Phoenix-Mesa, AZ	2,069,480	107	Spokane, WA	365,057
173	Longview-Marshall, TX	173,571	243	Pine Bluff, AR	91,225	79	Springfield, MA	533,762
1	Los Angeles-Long Beach, CA	8,815,101	17	Pittsburgh, PA	2,289,148	144	Springfield, MO	235,093
50	Louisville, KY-IN	968,846	–	Pittsfield, MA**	NA	119	Stamford-Norwalk, CT	318,560
149	Lubbock, TX	228,091	148	Portland, ME	230,768	–	Steubenville-Weirton, OH-WV**	NA
188	Lynchburg, VA	147,498	40	Portland-Vancouver, OR-WA	1,210,973	85	Stockton-Lodi, CA	467,761
126	Macon, GA	290,972	67	Providence-Fall River-Warwick, RI-MA	660,775	164	St. Cloud, MN	183,152
116	Madison, WI	346,898	–	Provo-Orem, UT**	NA	246	St. Joseph, MO	85,689
189	Manchester, NH	146,841	209	Pueblo, CO	128,218	11	St. Louis, MO-IL	2,486,269
207	Mansfield, OH	129,628	–	Punta Gorda, FL**	NA	–	Sumter, SC**	NA
102	McAllen-Edinburg-Mission, TX	391,420	172	Racine, WI	174,251	68	Syracuse, NY	652,212
185	Medford-Ashland, OR	148,721	64	Raleigh-Durham-Chapel Hill, NC	691,710	75	Tacoma, WA	573,254
45	Memphis, TN-AR-MS	987,409	248	Rapid City, SD	82,218	145	Tallahassee, FL	234,825
171	Merced, CA	174,500	–	Reading, PA**	NA	20	Tampa-St. Petersburg-Clearwater, FL	2,049,429
23	Miami, FL	1,862,881	192	Redding, CA	143,398	220	Texarkana, TX-AR	120,411
48	Middlesex-Sommerset-Hunterdon, NJ	980,189	137	Reno, NV	252,639	72	Toledo, OH	619,498
31	Milwaukee-Waukesha, WI	1,401,428	184	Richland-Kennewick-Pasco, WA	149,956	117	Trenton, NJ	331,639
13	Minneapolis-St. Paul, MN-WI	2,412,207	56	Richmond-Petersburg, VA	855,894	–	Tucson, AZ**	NA
84	Mobile, AL	487,191	–	Riverside-San Bernardino, CA**	NA	63	Tulsa, OK	723,583
114	Modesto, CA	350,026	150	Roanoke, VA	224,643	191	Tuscaloosa, AL	145,838
49	Monmouth-Ocean, NJ	971,371	237	Rochester, MN	102,088	181	Tyler, TX	153,925
193	Monroe, LA	143,157	46	Rochester, NY	982,433	122	Utica-Rome, NY	310,797
125	Montgomery, AL	304,607	–	Rocky Mount, NC**	NA	92	Vallejo-Fairfield-Napa, CA	431,835
–	Myrtle Beach, SC**	NA	30	Sacramento, CA	1,421,863	66	Ventura, CA	664,433
194	Naples, FL	142,272	95	Saginaw-Bay City-Midland, MI	407,659	250	Victoria, TX	74,974
169	Nashua, NH	177,851	131	Salem, OR	274,376	196	Vineland-Millville-Bridgeton, NJ	138,667
47	Nashville, TN	980,876	110	Salinas, CA	358,032	124	Visalia-Tulare-Porterville, CA	305,785
10	Nassau-Suffolk, NY	2,644,912	43	Salt Lake City-Ogden, UT	1,075,905	162	Waco, TX	189,706
174	New Bedford, MA	171,764	238	San Angelo, TX	100,201	6	Washington, DC-MD-VA-WV	3,767,093
76	New Haven-Meriden, CT	558,293	35	San Antonio, TX	1,335,208	166	Waterbury, CT	182,539
130	New London-Norwich, CT-RI	274,896	12	San Diego, CA	2,433,139	186	Waterloo-Cedar Falls, IA	148,103
36	New Orleans, LA	1,299,252	26	San Francisco, CA	1,632,084	202	Wausau, WI	133,846
2	New York, NY	8,586,420	28	San Jose, CA	1,469,902	59	West Palm Beach-Boca Raton, FL	840,789
22	Newark, NJ	1,889,840	–	San Luis Obispo-Atascadero, CA**	NA	213	Wichita Falls, TX	125,731
–	Newburgh, NY-PA**	NA	113	Santa Barbara-Santa Maria-Lompoc, CA	352,181	–	Williamsport, PA**	NA
32	Norfolk-Va Beach-Newport News, VA-NC	1,399,252	147	Santa Cruz-Watsonville, CA	232,700	223	Wilmington, NC	118,815
19	Oakland, CA	2,059,402	103	Santa Rosa, CA	375,687	–	Worcester, MA-CT**	NA
159	Ocala, FL	194,968	87	Sarasota-Bradenton, FL	455,865	161	Yakima, WA	190,006
146	Odessa-Midland, TX	234,106	139	Savannah, GA	248,042	–	Yolo, CA**	NA
51	Oklahoma City, OK	958,530	–	Scranton-Wilkes-Barre-Hazleton, PA**	NA	218	Yuba City, CA	121,636

Source: U.S. Bureau of the Census as reported by U.S. Department of Justice, Federal Bureau of Investigation
  "Crime in the United States 1989" (Uniform Crime Reports, August 5, 1990)
*Estimates as of July 1, 1989.
**Not available.

87. Metropolitan Population in 1989 (continued)

National Total = 248,239,000 Population*

RANK	METRO AREA	POP	RANK	METRO AREA	POP	RANK	METRO AREA	POP
1	Los Angeles–Long Beach, CA	8,815,101	48	Middlesex–Sommerset–Hunterdon, NJ	980,189	95	Saginaw–Bay City–Midland, MI	407,659
2	New York, NY	8,586,420	49	Monmouth–Ocean, NJ	971,371	96	Lakeland–Winter Haven, FL	406,578
3	Chicago, IL	6,196,105	50	Louisville, KY–IN	968,846	97	Canton–Massillon, OH	403,252
4	Philadelphia, PA–NJ	4,934,532	51	Oklahoma City, OK	958,530	98	Augusta–Aiken, GA–SC	401,895
5	Detroit, MI	4,370,346	52	Dayton–Springfield, OH	953,334	99	Jackson, MS	396,399
6	Washington, DC–MD–VA–WV	3,767,093	53	Greensboro–Winston Salem–High Point, NC	938,114	100	Colorado Springs, CO	395,809
7	Houston, TX	3,276,259	54	Birmingham, AL	929,861	101	Des Moines, IA	392,600
8	Boston, MA–NH	2,868,381	55	Jacksonville, FL	922,557	102	McAllen–Edinburg–Mission, TX	391,420
9	Atlanta, GA	2,777,665	56	Richmond–Petersburg, VA	855,894	103	Santa Rosa, CA	375,687
10	Nassau–Suffolk, NY	2,644,912	57	Albany, NY	852,838	104	Lawrence, MA–NH	372,299
11	St. Louis, MO–IL	2,486,269	58	Honolulu, HI	848,959	105	Fort Wayne, IN	369,680
12	San Diego, CA	2,433,139	59	West Palm Beach–Boca Raton, FL	840,789	106	Beaumont–Port Arthur, TX	367,202
13	Minneapolis–St. Paul, MN–WI	2,412,207	60	Grand Rapids–Muskegon–Holland, MI	834,669	107	Spokane, WA	365,057
14	Dallas, TX	2,404,726	61	Hartford, CT	762,461	108	Corpus Christi, TX	362,247
15	Baltimore, MD	2,378,992	62	Austin–San Marcos, TX	755,191	109	Kalamazoo–Battle Creek, MI	358,383
16	Orange County, CA	2,316,738	63	Tulsa, OK	723,583	110	Salinas, CA	358,032
17	Pittsburgh, PA	2,289,148	64	Raleigh–Durham–Chapel Hill, NC	691,710	111	Daytona Beach, FL	357,887
18	Phoenix–Mesa, AZ	2,069,480	65	Las Vegas, NV–AZ	665,377	112	Shreveport–Bossier City, LA	356,998
19	Oakland, CA	2,059,402	66	Ventura, CA	664,433	113	Santa Barbara–Santa Maria–Lompoc, CA	352,181
20	Tampa–St. Petersburg–Clearwater, FL	2,049,429	67	Providence–Fall River–Warwick, RI–MA	660,775	114	Modesto, CA	350,026
21	Seattle–Bellevue–Everett, WA	1,906,244	68	Syracuse, NY	652,212	115	Lexington, KY	348,337
22	Newark, NJ	1,889,840	69	Fresno, CA	631,072	116	Madison, WI	346,898
23	Miami, FL	1,862,881	70	Greenville–Spartanburg–Anderson, SC	630,206	117	Trenton, NJ	331,639
24	Cleveland, OH	1,853,974	71	Omaha, NE	624,713	118	Huntington–Ashland, WV–KY–OH	321,199
25	Denver, CO	1,640,296	72	Toledo, OH	619,498	119	Stamford–Norwalk, CT	318,560
26	San Francisco, CA	1,632,084	73	Gary–Hammond, IN	616,166	120	Fort Myers–Cape Coral, FL	317,517
27	Kansas City, MO–KS	1,583,141	74	El Paso, TX	591,217	121	Appleton–Oshkosh–Neenah, WI	311,726
28	San Jose, CA	1,469,902	75	Tacoma, WA	573,254	122	Utica–Rome, NY	310,797
29	Cincinnati, OH–KY–IN	1,455,227	76	New Haven–Meriden, CT	558,293	123	Atlantic City, NJ	309,796
30	Sacramento, CA	1,421,863	77	Jersey City, NJ	543,246	124	Visalia–Tulare–Porterville, CA	305,785
31	Milwaukee–Waukesha, WI	1,401,428	78	Bakersfield, CA	533,763	125	Montgomery, AL	304,607
32	Norfolk–Va Beach–Newport News, VA–NC	1,399,252	79	Springfield, MA	533,762	126	Macon, GA	290,972
33	Fort Worth–Arlington, TX	1,388,527	80	Baton Rouge, LA	533,360	127	Evansville–Henderson, IN–KY	282,890
34	Columbus, OH	1,350,738	81	Charleston, WV	517,117	128	Erie, PA	277,872
35	San Antonio, TX	1,335,208	82	Little Rock–North Little Rock, AR	515,504	129	Eugene–Springfield, OR	275,323
36	New Orleans, LA	1,299,252	83	Albuquerque, NM	501,336	130	New London–Norwich, CT–RI	274,896
37	Bergen–Passaic, NJ	1,294,794	84	Mobile, AL	487,191	131	Salem, OR	274,376
38	Indianapolis, IN	1,245,515	85	Stockton–Lodi, CA	467,761	132	Brownsville–Harlingen–San Benito, TX	266,396
39	Fort Lauderdale, FL	1,219,323	86	Columbia, SC	462,561	133	Ann Arbor, MI	265,500
40	Portland–Vancouver, OR–WA	1,210,973	87	Sarasota–Bradenton, FL	455,865	134	Binghamton, NY	261,615
41	Buffalo–Niagara Falls, NY	1,179,892	88	Bridgeport, CT	454,602	135	Fayetteville, NC	259,003
42	Charlotte–Gastonia–Rock Hill, NC–SC	1,126,294	89	Johnson City–Kingsport–Bristol, TN–VA	446,376	136	Charleston–North Charleston, SC	257,418
43	Salt Lake City–Ogden, UT	1,075,905	90	Chattanooga, TN–GA	442,433	137	Reno, NV	252,639
44	Orlando, FL	997,545	91	Flint, MI	432,148	138	Columbus, GA–AL	249,895
45	Memphis, TN–AR–MS	987,409	92	Vallejo–Fairfield–Napa, CA	431,835	139	Savannah, GA	248,042
46	Rochester, NY	982,433	93	Lansing–East Lansing, MI	429,839	140	Duluth–Superior, MN–WI	243,657
47	Nashville, TN	980,876	94	Lancaster, PA	415,404	141	Killeen–Temple, TX	241,774

Source: U.S. Bureau of the Census as reported by U.S. Department of Justice, Federal Bureau of Investigation
   "Crime in the United States 1989" (Uniform Crime Reports, August 5, 1990)
*Estimates as of July 1, 1989.
**Not available.

87. Metropolitan Population in 1989 (continued)

National Total = 248,239,000 Population*

RANK	METRO AREA	POP	RANK	METRO AREA	POP	RANK	METRO AREA	POP
142	Fort Pierce–Port St. Lucie, FL	238,112	189	Manchester, NH	146,841	236	Gadsden, AL	102,776
143	Huntsville, AL	237,479	190	Athens, GA	146,749	237	Rochester, MN	102,088
144	Springfield, MO	235,093	191	Tuscaloosa, AL	145,838	238	San Angelo, TX	100,201
145	Tallahassee, FL	234,825	192	Redding, CA	143,398	239	Kokomo, IN	99,541
146	Odessa–Midland, TX	234,106	193	Monroe, LA	143,157	240	Fitchburg–Leominster, MA	98,942
147	Santa Cruz–Watsonville, CA	232,700	194	Naples, FL	142,272	241	Sherman–Denison, TX	98,788
148	Portland, ME	230,768	195	Eau Claire, WI	138,759	242	La Crosse, WI–MN	95,748
149	Lubbock, TX	228,091	196	Vineland–Millville–Bridgeton, NJ	138,667	243	Pine Bluff, AR	91,225
150	Roanoke, VA	224,643	197	Alexandria, LA	136,993	244	Dubuque, IA	91,146
151	Anchorage, AK	223,363	198	Greeley, CO	136,880	245	Owensboro, KY	87,885
152	Boulder–Longmont, CO	218,936	199	Janesville–Beloit, WI	136,654	246	St. Joseph, MO	85,689
153	Gainesville, FL	213,254	200	Joplin, MO	136,360	247	Bismarck, ND	84,798
154	Lincoln, NE	212,762	201	Florence, AL	135,946	248	Rapid City, SD	82,218
155	Galveston–Texas City, TX	211,906	202	Wausau, WI	133,846	249	Jackson, TN	78,914
156	Lafayette, IN	208,473	203	Decatur, AL	133,649	250	Victoria, TX	74,974
157	Boise, ID	202,940	204	Altoona, PA	132,917	251	Cheyenne, WY	74,523
158	Amarillo, TX	198,182	205	Dothan, AL	131,531	252	Grand Forks, ND–MN	69,677
159	Ocala, FL	194,968	206	Laredo, TX	130,070	253	Bangor, ME	65,854
160	Green Bay, WI	191,696	207	Mansfield, OH	129,628	254	Enid, OK	57,978
161	Yakima, WA	190,006	208	Panama City, FL	128,918	–	Akron, OH**	NA
162	Waco, TX	189,706	209	Pueblo, CO	128,218	–	Barnstable–Yarmouth, MA**	NA
163	Brazoria, TX	186,275	210	Jacksonville, NC	128,134	–	Bremerton, WA**	NA
164	St. Cloud, MN	183,152	211	Lafayette, LA	126,212	–	Brockton, MA**	NA
165	Fort Collins–Loveland, CO	182,882	212	Sioux Falls, SD	125,835	–	Dutchess County, NY**	NA
166	Waterbury, CT	182,539	213	Wichita Falls, TX	125,731	–	Goldsboro, NC**	NA
167	Fort Smith, AR–OK	181,179	214	Charlottesville, VA	125,500	–	Greenville, NC**	NA
168	Chico–Paradise, CA	179,119	215	Anniston, AL	123,706	–	Harrisburg–Lebanon–Carlisle, PA**	NA
169	Nashua, NH	177,851	216	Kenosha, WI	122,918	–	Hickory–Morganton, NC**	NA
170	Asheville, NC	175,336	217	Abilene, TX	122,905	–	Houma, LA**	NA
171	Merced, CA	174,500	218	Yuba City, CA	121,636	–	Johnstown, PA**	NA
172	Racine, WI	174,251	219	Bellingham, WA	121,583	–	Myrtle Beach, SC**	NA
173	Longview–Marshall, TX	173,571	220	Texarkana, TX–AR	120,411	–	Newburgh, NY–PA**	NA
174	New Bedford, MA	171,764	221	Hagerstown, MD	119,640	–	Pittsfield, MA**	NA
175	Lake Charles, LA	171,391	222	Florence, SC	119,459	–	Provo–Orem, UT**	NA
176	Benton Harbor, MI	167,199	223	Wilmington, NC	118,815	–	Punta Gorda, FL**	NA
177	Danbury, CT	163,093	224	Lawton, OK	118,641	–	Reading, PA**	NA
178	Olympia, WA	160,404	225	Albany, GA	118,033	–	Riverside–San Bernardino, CA**	NA
179	Clarksville–Hopkinsville, TN–KY	159,846	226	Bryan–College Station, TX	117,658	–	Rocky Mount, NC**	NA
180	Fort Walton Beach, FL	154,701	227	Glens Falls, NY	116,465	–	San Luis Obispo–Atascadero, CA**	NA
181	Tyler, TX	153,925	228	Sioux City, IA–NE	115,996	–	Scranton–Wilkes-Barre–Hazleton, PA**	NA
182	Elkhart–Goshen, IN	152,079	229	Fayetteville–Springdale–Rogers, AR	111,117	–	South Bend, IN**	NA
183	Jackson, MI	150,037	230	Danville, VA	109,584	–	Steubenville–Weirton, OH–WV**	NA
184	Richland–Kennewick–Pasco, WA	149,956	231	Columbia, MO	106,158	–	Sumter, SC**	NA
185	Medford–Ashland, OR	148,721	232	Lewiston–Auburn, ME	104,688	–	Tucson, AZ**	NA
186	Waterloo–Cedar Falls, IA	148,103	233	Bloomington, IN	103,768	–	Williamsport, PA**	NA
187	Fargo–Moorhead, ND–MN	147,747	234	Cumberland, MD–WV	103,289	–	Worcester, MA–CT**	NA
188	Lynchburg, VA	147,498	235	Sheboygan, WI	103,267	–	Yolo, CA**	NA

Source: U.S. Bureau of the Census as reported by U.S. Department of Justice, Federal Bureau of Investigation
"Crime in the United States 1989" (Uniform Crime Reports, August 5, 1990)
*Estimates as of July 1, 1989.
**Not available.

88. City Population in 1993

National Total = 257,908,000*

RANK	CITY	POP	RANK	CITY	POP
72	Akron, OH	225,040	58	Louisville, KY	273,564
37	Albuquerque, NM	407,286	86	Lubbock, TX	191,639
57	Anaheim, CA	276,696	80	Madison, WI	196,919
64	Anchorage, AK	250,720	19	Memphis, TN	618,981
56	Arlington, TX	281,336	52	Mesa, AZ	304,695
38	Atlanta, GA	402,877	45	Miami, FL	372,519
65	Aurora, CO	246,610	18	Milwaukee, WI	623,114
26	Austin, TX	502,018	47	Minneapolis, MN	366,642
89	Bakersfield, CA	189,908	76	Mobile, AL	204,286
14	Baltimore, MD	732,968	83	Montgomery, AL	194,399
71	Baton Rouge, LA	225,544	24	Nashville, TN	513,648
62	Birmingham, AL	268,768	28	New Orleans, LA	491,619
22	Boston, MA	553,870	1	New York, NY	7,347,257
50	Buffalo, NY	324,855	61	Newark, NJ	269,892
36	Charlotte, NC	422,862	95	Newport News, VA	179,975
3	Chicago, IL	2,788,996	63	Norfolk, VA	257,617
48	Cincinnati, OH	366,591	44	Oakland, CA	377,037
25	Cleveland, OH	505,730	30	Oklahoma City, OK	457,448
53	Colorado Springs, CO	304,438	98	Orlando, FL	176,748
88	Columbus, GA	190,331	5	Philadelphia, PA	1,559,534
17	Columbus, OH	646,933	8	Phoenix, AZ	1,039,369
59	Corpus Christi, TX	271,564	46	Pittsburgh, PA	368,473
7	Dallas, TX	1,042,619	31	Portland, OR	454,889
93	Dayton, OH	184,352	73	Raleigh, NC	224,057
27	Denver, CO	498,402	75	Richmond, VA	205,331
81	Des Moines, IA	195,485	66	Riverside, CA	241,041
9	Detroit, MI	1,020,062	68	Rochester, NY	235,301
21	El Paso, TX	554,515	40	Sacramento, CA	386,732
99	Fort Wayne, IN	175,405	10	San Antonio, TX	985,456
29	Fort Worth, TX	463,373	100	San Bernardino, CA	174,215
94	Fremont, CA	181,134	6	San Diego, CA	1,160,603
41	Fresno, CA	379,977	13	San Francisco, CA	736,377
82	Garland, TX	194,930	12	San Jose, CA	809,528
96	Glendale, CA	179,488	54	Santa Ana, CA	290,070
85	Grand Rapids, MI	192,121	23	Seattle, WA	531,274
84	Greensboro, NC	192,951	79	Shreveport, LA	197,379
11	Honolulu, HI	875,455	87	Spokane, WA	191,511
4	Houston, TX	1,724,327	74	Stockton, CA	221,867
92	Huntington Beach, CA	186,948	39	St. Louis, MO	387,053
43	Indianapolis,IN	377,723	60	St. Paul, MN	271,208
78	Jackson, MS	198,227	67	St. Petersburg, FL	238,727
16	Jacksonville, FL	672,310	90	Tacoma, WA	187,895
70	Jersey City, NJ	230,298	55	Tampa, FL	288,877
33	Kansas City, MO	435,428	49	Toledo, OH	331,416
15	Las Vegas, NV	717,441	34	Tucson, AZ	426,344
69	Lexington, KY	235,094	42	Tulsa, OK	378,350
77	Lincoln, NE	198,228	35	Virginia Beach, VA	423,387
97	Little Rock, AR	178,924	20	Washington, DC	578,000
32	Long Beach, CA	443,259	51	Wichita, KS	313,597
2	Los Angeles, CA	3,525,317	91	Yonkers, NY	186,967

Source: U.S. Bureau of the Census as reported by U.S. Department of Justice, Federal Bureau of Investigation "Crime in the United States 1993" (Uniform Crime Reports, December 4, 1994)
Estimates as of July 1, 1993. Omaha, NE ranks 48th with a population of 304,000 and Hialeah, FL ranks 84th with a population of 192,000. However, crime statistics were not available through the FBI and the cities are not shown. Las Vegas, NV has a population of 296,000 but is shown with the population the FBI reports for the jurisdiction of the Las Vegas Metro Police.

266

88. City Population in 1993 (continued)

National Total = 257,908,000*

RANK	CITY	POP		RANK	CITY	POP
1	New York, NY	7,347,257		51	Wichita, KS	313,597
2	Los Angeles, CA	3,525,317		52	Mesa, AZ	304,695
3	Chicago, IL	2,788,996		53	Colorado Springs, CO	304,438
4	Houston, TX	1,724,327		54	Santa Ana, CA	290,070
5	Philadelphia, PA	1,559,534		55	Tampa, FL	288,877
6	San Diego, CA	1,160,603		56	Arlington, TX	281,336
7	Dallas, TX	1,042,619		57	Anaheim, CA	276,696
8	Phoenix, AZ	1,039,369		58	Louisville, KY	273,564
9	Detroit, MI	1,020,062		59	Corpus Christi, TX	271,564
10	San Antonio, TX	985,456		60	St. Paul, MN	271,208
11	Honolulu, HI	875,455		61	Newark, NJ	269,892
12	San Jose, CA	809,528		62	Birmingham, AL	268,768
13	San Francisco, CA	736,377		63	Norfolk, VA	257,617
14	Baltimore, MD	732,968		64	Anchorage, AK	250,720
15	Las Vegas, NV	717,441		65	Aurora, CO	246,610
16	Jacksonville, FL	672,310		66	Riverside, CA	241,041
17	Columbus, OH	646,933		67	St. Petersburg, FL	238,727
18	Milwaukee, WI	623,114		68	Rochester, NY	235,301
19	Memphis, TN	618,981		69	Lexington, KY	235,094
20	Washington, DC	578,000		70	Jersey City, NJ	230,298
21	El Paso, TX	554,515		71	Baton Rouge, LA	225,544
22	Boston, MA	553,870		72	Akron, OH	225,040
23	Seattle, WA	531,274		73	Raleigh, NC	224,057
24	Nashville, TN	513,648		74	Stockton, CA	221,867
25	Cleveland, OH	505,730		75	Richmond, VA	205,331
26	Austin, TX	502,018		76	Mobile, AL	204,286
27	Denver, CO	498,402		77	Lincoln, NE	198,228
28	New Orleans, LA	491,619		78	Jackson, MS	198,227
29	Fort Worth, TX	463,373		79	Shreveport, LA	197,379
30	Oklahoma City, OK	457,448		80	Madison, WI	196,919
31	Portland, OR	454,889		81	Des Moines, IA	195,485
32	Long Beach, CA	443,259		82	Garland, TX	194,930
33	Kansas City, MO	435,428		83	Montgomery, AL	194,399
34	Tucson, AZ	426,344		84	Greensboro, NC	192,951
35	Virginia Beach, VA	423,387		85	Grand Rapids, MI	192,121
36	Charlotte, NC	422,862		86	Lubbock, TX	191,639
37	Albuquerque, NM	407,286		87	Spokane, WA	191,511
38	Atlanta, GA	402,877		88	Columbus, GA	190,331
39	St. Louis, MO	387,053		89	Bakersfield, CA	189,908
40	Sacramento, CA	386,732		90	Tacoma, WA	187,895
41	Fresno, CA	379,977		91	Yonkers, NY	186,967
42	Tulsa, OK	378,350		92	Huntington Beach, CA	186,948
43	Indianapolis, IN	377,723		93	Dayton, OH	184,352
44	Oakland, CA	377,037		94	Fremont, CA	181,134
45	Miami, FL	372,519		95	Newport News, VA	179,975
46	Pittsburgh, PA	368,473		96	Glendale, CA	179,488
47	Minneapolis, MN	366,642		97	Little Rock, AR	178,924
48	Cincinnati, OH	366,591		98	Orlando, FL	176,748
49	Toledo, OH	331,416		99	Fort Wayne, IN	175,405
50	Buffalo, NY	324,855		100	San Bernardino, CA	174,215

Source: U.S. Bureau of the Census as reported by U.S. Department of Justice, Federal Bureau of Investigation
   "Crime in the United States 1993" (Uniform Crime Reports, December 4, 1994)
*Estimates as of July 1, 1993. Omaha, NE ranks 48th with a population of 304,000 and Hialeah, FL ranks 84th
with a population of 192,000. However, crime statistics were not available through the FBI and the cities are not
shown. Las Vegas, NV has a population of 296,000 but is shown with the population the FBI reports for the
jurisdiction of the Las Vegas Metro Police.   267

89. City Population in 1992

National Total = 255,078,000*

RANK	CITY	POP	RANK	CITY	POP
72	Akron, OH	226,490	59	Louisville, KY	274,312
40	Albuquerque, NM	401,259	82	Lubbock, TX	193,545
58	Anaheim, CA	276,314	79	Madison, WI	195,767
65	Anchorage, AK	241,565	19	Memphis, TN	628,865
61	Arlington, TX	272,037	53	Mesa, AZ	301,200
36	Atlanta, GA	410,876	46	Miami, FL	373,791
68	Aurora, CO	233,939	18	Milwaukee, WI	643,017
29	Austin, TX	483,975	43	Minneapolis, MN	377,345
94	Bakersfield, CA	181,321	77	Mobile, AL	200,911
13	Baltimore, MD	755,517	84	Montgomery, AL	191,522
66	Baton Rouge, LA	237,390	24	Nashville, TN	514,771
60	Birmingham, AL	272,407	26	New Orleans, LA	505,008
21	Boston, MA	572,822	1	New York, NY	7,375,097
50	Buffalo, NY	330,466	57	Newark, NJ	277,544
37	Charlotte, NC	408,951	98	Newport News, VA	175,256
3	Chicago, IL	2,832,901	62	Norfolk, VA	269,347
47	Cincinnati, OH	369,707	41	Oakland, CA	386,086
25	Cleveland, OH	513,487	32	Oklahoma City, OK	454,255
54	Colorado Springs, CO	296,124	99	Orlando, FL	171,694
90	Columbus, GA	186,826	5	Philadelphia, PA	1,603,638
17	Columbus, OH	643,028	9	Phoenix, AZ	999,900
63	Corpus Christi, TX	267,601	45	Pittsburgh, PA	373,842
7	Dallas, TX	1,046,562	31	Portland, OR	458,132
93	Dayton, OH	184,877	74	Raleigh, NC	214,674
28	Denver, CO	492,672	75	Richmond, VA	209,279
80	Des Moines, IA	195,752	67	Riverside, CA	234,929
8	Detroit, MI	1,044,128	69	Rochester, NY	233,289
23	El Paso, TX	535,655	42	Sacramento, CA	383,102
97	Fort Wayne, IN	176,751	39	San Antonio, TX	402,573
30	Fort Worth, TX	465,262	100	San Bernardino, CA	170,269
95	Fremont, CA	179,785	10	San Diego, CA	972,824
48	Fresno, CA	367,376	6	San Francisco, CA	1,151,853
88	Garland, TX	187,770	14	San Jose, CA	750,885
91	Glendale, CA	186,734	52	Santa Ana, CA	304,666
83	Grand Rapids, MI	192,008	12	Seattle, WA	811,342
85	Greensboro, NC	189,454	76	Shreveport, LA	201,676
11	Honolulu, HI	875,297	89	Spokane, WA	187,002
4	Houston, TX	1,695,239	73	Stockton, CA	218,787
87	Huntington Beach, CA	188,270	22	St. Louis, MO	544,940
27	Indianapolis, IN	493,298	56	St. Paul, MN	278,762
78	Jackson, MS	199,964	64	St. Petersburg, FL	248,774
16	Jacksonville, FL	663,899	92	Tacoma, WA	186,440
70	Jersey City, NJ	230,277	55	Tampa, FL	291,920
34	Kansas City, MO	441,162	49	Toledo, OH	338,126
15	Las Vegas, NV	678,385	35	Tucson, AZ	423,836
71	Lexington, KY	229,628	44	Tulsa, OK	375,053
81	Lincoln, NE	195,329	38	Virginia Beach, VA	405,116
96	Little Rock, AR	179,498	20	Washington, DC	589,000
33	Long Beach, CA	445,405	51	Wichita, KS	309,955
2	Los Angeles, CA	3,615,355	86	Yonkers, NY	189,425

Source: U.S. Bureau of the Census as reported by U.S. Department of Justice, Federal Bureau of Investigation "Crime in the United States 1993" (Uniform Crime Reports, December 4, 1994)
*Estimates as of July 1, 1992. Cities shown are 100 largest based on 1993 population (see footnote for table 88 regarding Omaha, NE, Hialeah, FL). Las Vegas, NV is shown with the population the FBI reports for the jurisdiction of the Las Vegas Metro Police.

89. City Population in 1992 (continued)

National Total = 255,078,000*

RANK	CITY	POP	RANK	CITY	POP
1	New York, NY	7,375,097	51	Wichita, KS	309,955
2	Los Angeles, CA	3,615,355	52	Santa Ana, CA	304,666
3	Chicago, IL	2,832,901	53	Mesa, AZ	301,200
4	Houston, TX	1,695,239	54	Colorado Springs, CO	296,124
5	Philadelphia, PA	1,603,638	55	Tampa, FL	291,920
6	San Francisco, CA	1,151,853	56	St. Paul, MN	278,762
7	Dallas, TX	1,046,562	57	Newark, NJ	277,544
8	Detroit, MI	1,044,128	58	Anaheim, CA	276,314
9	Phoenix, AZ	999,900	59	Louisville, KY	274,312
10	San Diego, CA	972,824	60	Birmingham, AL	272,407
11	Honolulu, HI	875,297	61	Arlington, TX	272,037
12	Seattle, WA	811,342	62	Norfolk, VA	269,347
13	Baltimore, MD	755,517	63	Corpus Christi, TX	267,601
14	San Jose, CA	750,885	64	St. Petersburg, FL	248,774
15	Las Vegas, NV	678,385	65	Anchorage, AK	241,565
16	Jacksonville, FL	663,899	66	Baton Rouge, LA	237,390
17	Columbus, OH	643,028	67	Riverside, CA	234,929
18	Milwaukee, WI	643,017	68	Aurora, CO	233,939
19	Memphis, TN	628,865	69	Rochester, NY	233,289
20	Washington, DC	589,000	70	Jersey City, NJ	230,277
21	Boston, MA	572,822	71	Lexington, KY	229,628
22	St. Louis, MO	544,940	72	Akron, OH	226,490
23	El Paso, TX	535,655	73	Stockton, CA	218,787
24	Nashville, TN	514,771	74	Raleigh, NC	214,674
25	Cleveland, OH	513,487	75	Richmond, VA	209,279
26	New Orleans, LA	505,008	76	Shreveport, LA	201,676
27	Indianapolis, IN	493,298	77	Mobile, AL	200,911
28	Denver, CO	492,672	78	Jackson, MS	199,964
29	Austin, TX	483,975	79	Madison, WI	195,767
30	Fort Worth, TX	465,262	80	Des Moines, IA	195,752
31	Portland, OR	458,132	81	Lincoln, NE	195,329
32	Oklahoma City, OK	454,255	82	Lubbock, TX	193,545
33	Long Beach, CA	445,405	83	Grand Rapids, MI	192,008
34	Kansas City, MO	441,162	84	Montgomery, AL	191,522
35	Tucson, AZ	423,836	85	Greensboro, NC	189,454
36	Atlanta, GA	410,876	86	Yonkers, NY	189,425
37	Charlotte, NC	408,951	87	Huntington Beach, CA	188,270
38	Virginia Beach, VA	405,116	88	Garland, TX	187,770
39	San Antonio, TX	402,573	89	Spokane, WA	187,002
40	Albuquerque, NM	401,259	90	Columbus, GA	186,826
41	Oakland, CA	386,086	91	Glendale, CA	186,734
42	Sacramento, CA	383,102	92	Tacoma, WA	186,440
43	Minneapolis, MN	377,345	93	Dayton, OH	184,877
44	Tulsa, OK	375,053	94	Bakersfield, CA	181,321
45	Pittsburgh, PA	373,842	95	Fremont, CA	179,785
46	Miami, FL	373,791	96	Little Rock, AR	179,498
47	Cincinnati, OH	369,707	97	Fort Wayne, IN	176,751
48	Fresno, CA	367,376	98	Newport News, VA	175,256
49	Toledo, OH	338,126	99	Orlando, FL	171,694
50	Buffalo, NY	330,466	100	San Bernardino, CA	170,269

Source: U.S. Bureau of the Census as reported by U.S. Department of Justice, Federal Bureau of Investigation "Crime in the United States 1993" (Uniform Crime Reports, December 4, 1994)
*Estimates as of July 1, 1992. Cities shown are 100 largest based on 1993 population (see footnote for table 88 regarding Omaha, NE, Hialeah, FL). Las Vegas, NV is shown with the population the FBI reports for the jurisdiction of the Las Vegas Metro Police.

90. City Population in 1989

National Total = 248,239,000*

RANK	CITY	POP	RANK	CITY	POP
68	Akron, OH	222,588	56	Louisville, KY	282,153
37	Albuquerque, NM	384,801	80	Lubbock, TX	189,797
61	Anaheim, CA	251,146	90	Madison, WI	178,942
67	Anchorage, AK	223,363	16	Memphis, TN	651,081
60	Arlington, TX	259,796	54	Mesa, AZ	285,883
33	Atlanta, GA	426,482	38	Miami, FL	381,206
69	Aurora, CO	219,780	18	Milwaukee, WI	600,898
29	Austin, TX	468,907	45	Minneapolis, MN	348,384
97	Bakersfield, CA	161,823	74	Mobile, AL	209,507
12	Baltimore, MD	763,138	77	Montgomery, AL	194,196
64	Baton Rouge, LA	233,893	26	Nashville, TN	501,398
57	Birmingham, AL	278,011	22	New Orleans, LA	528,589
19	Boston, MA	580,095	1	New York, NY	7,369,454
49	Buffalo, NY	314,284	50	Newark, NJ	313,839
40	Charlotte, NC	372,612	96	Newport News, VA	162,298
3	Chicago, IL	2,988,260	52	Norfolk, VA	290,434
41	Cincinnati, OH	372,282	43	Oakland, CA	366,305
23	Cleveland, OH	523,906	31	Oklahoma City, OK	431,982
55	Colorado Springs, CO	284,482	98	Orlando, FL	160,197
89	Columbus, GA	180,328	5	Philadelphia, PA	1,652,188
20	Columbus, OH	572,341	10	Phoenix, AZ	941,948
58	Corpus Christi, TX	263,298	39	Pittsburgh, PA	376,412
8	Dallas, TX	996,320	35	Portland, OR	425,788
91	Dayton, OH	178,866	81	Raleigh, NC	189,132
27	Denver, CO	494,589	72	Richmond, VA	216,229
78	Des Moines, IA	193,305	73	Riverside, CA	216,205
7	Detroit, MI	1,039,599	65	Rochester, NY	230,303
24	El Paso, TX	515,607	46	Sacramento, CA	347,172
87	Fort Wayne, IN	180,975	9	San Antonio, TX	949,691
32	Fort Worth, TX	430,831	-	San Bernardino, CA**	NA
93	Fremont, CA	170,999	6	San Diego, CA	1,098,639
48	Fresno, CA	315,218	14	San Francisco, CA	750,964
86	Garland, TX	182,088	13	San Jose, CA	757,964
95	Glendale, CA	165,477	62	Santa Ana, CA	245,880
83	Grand Rapids, MI	186,036	25	Seattle, WA	514,398
84	Greensboro, NC	184,321	71	Shreveport, LA	216,734
11	Honolulu, HI	848,959	92	Spokane, WA	175,051
4	Houston, TX	1,713,499	76	Stockton, CA	195,727
79	Huntington Beach, CA	191,826	36	St. Louis, MO	405,066
28	Indianapolis, IN	484,056	59	St. Paul, MN	261,902
75	Jackson, MS	201,350	63	St. Petersburg, FL	241,862
15	Jacksonville, FL	654,737	94	Tacoma, WA	167,943
70	Jersey City, NJ	218,020	53	Tampa, FL	289,463
30	Kansas City, MO	440,435	47	Toledo, OH	342,418
21	Las Vegas, NV	536,148	-	Tucson, AZ**	NA
66	Lexington, KY	225,918	44	Tulsa, OK	366,297
82	Lincoln, NE	188,922	42	Virginia Beach, VA	370,316
88	Little Rock, AR	180,932	17	Washington, DC	604,000
34	Long Beach, CA	426,025	51	Wichita, KS	297,391
2	Los Angeles, CA	3,441,449	85	Yonkers, NY	183,417

Source: U.S. Department of Justice, Federal Bureau of Investigation
"Crime in the United States 1989" (Uniform Crime Reports, August 5, 1990)
Estimates as of July 1, 1989. Cities shown are 100 largest based on 1993 population (see footnote for table 88 regarding Omaha, NE, Hialeah, FL). Las Vegas, NV is shown with the population the FBI reports for the jurisdiction of the Las Vegas Metro Police.

90. City Population in 1989 (continued)

National Total = 248,239,000*

RANK	CITY	POP	RANK	CITY	POP
1	New York, NY	7,369,454	51	Wichita, KS	297,391
2	Los Angeles, CA	3,441,449	52	Norfolk, VA	290,434
3	Chicago, IL	2,988,260	53	Tampa, FL	289,463
4	Houston, TX	1,713,499	54	Mesa, AZ	285,883
5	Philadelphia, PA	1,652,188	55	Colorado Springs, CO	284,482
6	San Diego, CA	1,098,639	56	Louisville, KY	282,153
7	Detroit, MI	1,039,599	57	Birmingham, AL	278,011
8	Dallas, TX	996,320	58	Corpus Christi, TX	263,298
9	San Antonio, TX	949,691	59	St. Paul, MN	261,902
10	Phoenix, AZ	941,948	60	Arlington, TX	259,796
11	Honolulu, HI	848,959	61	Anaheim, CA	251,146
12	Baltimore, MD	763,138	62	Santa Ana, CA	245,880
13	San Jose, CA	757,964	63	St. Petersburg, FL	241,862
14	San Francisco, CA	750,964	64	Baton Rouge, LA	233,893
15	Jacksonville, FL	654,737	65	Rochester, NY	230,303
16	Memphis, TN	651,081	66	Lexington, KY	225,918
17	Washington, DC	604,000	67	Anchorage, AK	223,363
18	Milwaukee, WI	600,898	68	Akron, OH	222,588
19	Boston, MA	580,095	69	Aurora, CO	219,780
20	Columbus, OH	572,341	70	Jersey City, NJ	218,020
21	Las Vegas, NV	536,148	71	Shreveport, LA	216,734
22	New Orleans, LA	528,589	72	Richmond, VA	216,229
23	Cleveland, OH	523,906	73	Riverside, CA	216,205
24	El Paso, TX	515,607	74	Mobile, AL	209,507
25	Seattle, WA	514,398	75	Jackson, MS	201,350
26	Nashville, TN	501,398	76	Stockton, CA	195,727
27	Denver, CO	494,589	77	Montgomery, AL	194,196
28	Indianapolis,IN	484,056	78	Des Moines, IA	193,305
29	Austin, TX	468,907	79	Huntington Beach, CA	191,826
30	Kansas City, MO	440,435	80	Lubbock, TX	189,797
31	Oklahoma City, OK	431,982	81	Raleigh, NC	189,132
32	Fort Worth, TX	430,831	82	Lincoln, NE	188,922
33	Atlanta, GA	426,482	83	Grand Rapids, MI	186,036
34	Long Beach, CA	426,025	84	Greensboro, NC	184,321
35	Portland, OR	425,788	85	Yonkers, NY	183,417
36	St. Louis, MO	405,066	86	Garland, TX	182,088
37	Albuquerque, NM	384,801	87	Fort Wayne, IN	180,975
38	Miami, FL	381,206	88	Little Rock, AR	180,932
39	Pittsburgh, PA	376,412	89	Columbus, GA	180,328
40	Charlotte, NC	372,612	90	Madison, WI	178,942
41	Cincinnati, OH	372,282	91	Dayton, OH	178,866
42	Virginia Beach, VA	370,316	92	Spokane, WA	175,051
43	Oakland, CA	366,305	93	Fremont, CA	170,999
44	Tulsa, OK	366,297	94	Tacoma, WA	167,943
45	Minneapolis, MN	348,384	95	Glendale, CA	165,477
46	Sacramento, CA	347,172	96	Newport News, VA	162,298
47	Toledo, OH	342,418	97	Bakersfield, CA	161,823
48	Fresno, CA	315,218	98	Orlando, FL	160,197
49	Buffalo, NY	314,284	-	San Bernardino, CA**	NA
50	Newark, NJ	313,839	-	Tucson, AZ**	NA

Source: U.S. Department of Justice, Federal Bureau of Investigation
"Crime in the United States 1989" (Uniform Crime Reports, August 5, 1990)
Estimates as of July 1, 1989. Cities shown are 100 largest based on 1993 population (see footnote for table 88 regarding Omaha, NE, Hialeah, FL). Las Vegas, NV is shown with the population the FBI reports for the jurisdiction of the Las Vegas Metro Police.

DESCRIPTIONS OF METROPOLITAN AREAS IN 1993

Abilene, TX includes Taylor County

Akron, OH includes Portage and Summit Counties

Albany, GA includes Dougherty and Lee Counties

Albuquerque, NM includes Bernailillo, Sandoval and Valencia Counties

Alexandria, LA includes Rapides County

Altoona, PA includes Blair County

Amarillo, TX includes Potter and Randall Counties

Anchorage, AK includes Anchorage Bourough

Ann Arbor, MI includes Lenawee, Livingston and Washtenaw Counties

Anniston, AL includes Calhoun County

Appleton-Oshkosh-Neenah, WI includes Calumet, Outagamie and Winnebago Counties

Asheville, NC includes Buncombe County

Athens, GA includes Clark, Madison and Oconee Counties

Atlanta, GA includes Barrow, Bartow, Carroll, Cherokee, Clayton, Cobb, Coweta, DeKalb, Douglas, Fayette, Forsythe, Fulton, Gwinnett, Henry, Newton, Paulding, Pickens, Rockdale, Spalding and Walton Counties

Atlantic City, NJ includes Atlantic and Cape May Counties

Augusta-Aiken, GA-SC includes Columbia, GA, McDuffie, GA, Richmond, GA, Aiken, SC and Edgefield, SC Counties

Austin-San Marcos, TX includes Bastrop, Caldwell, Hays, Travis and Williamson Counties

Bakersfield, CA includes Kern County

Baltimore, MD includes Baltimore City and Anne Arundel, Baltimore, Carroll, Hartford, Howard and Queen Anne's Counties

Bangor, ME includes part of Penobscot and Waldo Counties

Barnstable-Yarmouth, MA includes part of Barnstable County

Baton Rouge, LA includes Ascension, East Baton Rouge, Livingston and West Baton Rouge Parishes

Beaumont-Port Arthur, TX includes Hardin, Jefferson and Orange Counties

Bellingham, WA includes Whatcom County

Benton Harbor, MI includes Berrien County

Bergen-Passaic, NJ includes Bergen and Passaic Counties

Binghamton, NY includes Broome and Tioga Counties

Birmingham, AL includes Blount, Jefferson, St. Clair and Shelby Counties

Bismarck, ND includes Burleigh and Morton Counties

Bloomington, IN includes Monroe County

Boise, ID includes Ada and Canyon Counties

Boston, MA-NH includes part of Bristol, MA, Essex, MA, Middlesex, MA, Plymouth, MA, Suffolk, MA, Worcester, MA and Rockingham, NH Counties

Boulder-Longmont, CO includes Boulder County

Brazoria, TX includes Brazoria County

Bremerton, WA includes Kitsap County

Bridgeport, CT includes part of Fairfield and New Haven Counties

Brockton, MA includes part of Bristol, Norfolk and Plymouth Counties

Brownsville-Harlingen-San Benito, TX includes Cameron County

Bryan-College Station, TX includes Brazos County

Buffalo-Niagara Falls, NY includes Erie and Niagara Counties

Canton-Massillon, OH includes Carroll and Stark Counties

Charleston, WV includes Kanawha and Putnam Counties

Charleston-North Charleston, SC includes Berkeley, Charleston and Dorchester Counties

Charlottesville, VA includes Albemarle, Fluvanna and Greene Counties and City of Charlottesville

Charlotte-Gastonia-Rock Hill, NC-SC includes Cabarrus, NC, Gaston, NC, Lincoln, NC, Mecklenburg, NC, Rowan, NC, Union, NC and York, SC Counties

Chattanooga, TN-GA includes Hamilton, TN, Marion, TN, Catoosa, GA, Dade, GA and Walker, GA Counties

Cheyenne, WY includes Laramie County

Chicago, IL includes Cook, Dekalb, DuPage, Grundy, Kane, Kendall, Lake, McHenry and Will Counties (1993 metro data not available)

Chico-Paradise, CA includes Butte County

Cincinnati, OH-KY-IN includes Brown, OH, Clermont, OH, Hamilton, OH, Warren, OH, Boone, KY, Campbell, KY, Gallatin, KY, Grant, KY, Kenton, KY, Pendleton, KY, Dearborn, IN and Ohio, IN Counties

DESCRIPTIONS OF METROPOLITAN AREAS IN 1993 (continued)

Clarksville-Hopkinsville, TN-KY includes Christian, KY and Montgomery, TN Counties

Cleveland, OH includes Ashtabula, Cuyahoga, Geauga, Lake, Lorain and Medina Counties (1993 data not available)

Colorado Springs, CO includes El Paso County

Columbia, MO includes Boone County

Columbia, SC includes Lexington and Richland Counties

Columbus, GA-AL includes Chattahoochee, GA, Harris, GA, Muscogee, GA and Russell, AL Counties

Columbus, OH includes Delaware, Fairfield, Franklin, Licking, Madison and Pickaway Counties

Corpus Christi, TX includes Nueces and San Patricio Counties

Cumberland, MD-WV includes Allegany, MD and Mineral, WV Counties

Dallas, TX includes Collin, Dallas, Denton, Ellis, Henderson, Kaufman and Rockwall Counties

Danbury, CT includes part of Fairfield, Litchfield and New Haven Counties

Danville, VA includes Pittsylvania County and City of Danville

Daytona Beach, FL includes Flagler and Volusia Counties

Dayton-Springfield, OH includes Clark, Greene, Miami and Montgomery Counties

Decatur, AL includes Lawrence and Morgan Counties

Denver, CO includes Adams, Arapahoe, Denver, Douglas and Jefferson Counties

Des Moines, IA includes Dallas, Polk and Warren Counties

Detroit, MI includes Lapeer, Macomb, Monroe, Oakland, St. Clair and Wayne Counties

Dothan, AL includes Dale and Houston Counties

Dubuque, IA includes Dubuque County

Duluth-Superior, MN-WI includes St. Louis, MN and Douglas, WI Counties

Dutchess County, NY includes Dutchess County

Eau Claire, WI includes Chippewa and Eau Claire Counties

El Paso, TX includes El Paso County

Elkhart-Goshen, IN includes Elkhart County

Enid, OK includes Garfield County

Erie, PA includes Erie County

Eugene-Springfield, OR includes Lane County

Evansville-Henderson, IN-KY includes Posey, IN, Vanderburgh, IN, Warrick, IN and Henderson, KY Counties

Fargo-Moorhead, ND-MN includes Cass, ND and Clay, MN Counties

Fayetteville, NC includes Cumberland County

Fayetteville-Springdale-Rogers, AR includes Benton and Washington Counties

Fitchburg-Leominster, MA includes part of Middlesex and Worcester Counties

Flint, MI includes Genesee County

Florence, AL includes Colbert and Lauderdale Counties

Florence, SC includes Florence County

Fort Collins-Loveland, CO includes Larimar County

Fort Lauderdale, FL includes Broward County

Fort Myers-Cape Coral, FL includes Lee County

Fort Pierce-Port St. Lucie, FL includes Martin and St. Lucie Counties

Fort Smith, AR-OK includes Crawford, AR, Sebastian, AR and Sequoyah, OK Counties

Fort Walton Beach, FL includes Okaloosa County

Fort Wayne, IN includes Adams, Allen, De Kalb, Huntington and Whitley Counties

Fort Worth-Arlington, TX includes Johnson, Parker and Tarrant Counties

Fresno, CA includes Fresno and Madera Counties

Gadsden, AL includes Etowah County

Gainesville, FL includes Alachua County

Galveston-Texas City, TX includes Galveston County

Gary-Hammond, IN includes Lake and Porter Counties

Glens Falls, NY includes Warren and Washington Counties

Goldsboro, NC includes Wayne County

Grand Forks, ND-MN includes Grand Forks, ND and Polk, MN Counties

Grand Rapids-Muskegon-Holland, MI includes Allegan, Kent, Muskegon and Ottawa Counties

Greeley, CO includes Weld County

Green Bay, WI includes Brown County

Greensboro-Winston Salem-High Point, NC includes Alamance, Davidson, Davie, Forsythe, Guilford, Randolph, Stokes and Yadkin Counties

Greenville, NC includes Pitt County

Greenville-Spartanburg-Anderson, SC includes Anderson, Cherokee, Greenville, Pickens and Spartanburg Counties

Hagerstown, MD includes Washington County

Harrisburg-Lebanon-Carlisle, PA includes Cumberland, Dauphin, Lebanon and Perry Counties

Hartford, CT includes all of Hartford County and part of Litchfield, Middlesex, New London, Tolland and Windham Counties

Hickory-Morganton, NC includes Alexander, Burke, Caldwell and Catawba Counties

Honolulu, HI includes Honolulu County

Houma, LA includes Lafourche and Terrebonne Parishes

Houston, TX includes Chambers, Fort Bend, Harris, Liberty, Montgomery and Waller Counties

Huntington-Ashland, WV-KY-OK includes Cabell, WV, Wayne, WV, Boyd, KY, Carter, KY, Greenup, KY and Lawrence, OH Counties

Huntsville, AL includes Limestone and Madison Counties

Indianapolis, IN includes Boone, Hamilton, Hancock, Hendricks, Johnson, Madison, Marion, Morgan and Shelby Counties (1993 data not available)

Jackson, MI includes Jackson County

Jackson, MS includes Hinds, Madison and Rankin Counties

Jackson, TN includes Madison County

Jacksonville, FL includes Clay, Duval, Nassau and St. Johns Counties

Jacksonville, NC includes Onslow County

Janesville-Beloit, WI includes Rock County

Jersey City, NJ includes Hudson County

Johnson City-Kingsport-Bristol, TN-VA includes Carter, TN, Hawkins, TN, Sullivan, TN, Unicoi, TN, Washington, TN, Bristol, VA, Scott, VA and Washington, VA Counties and City of Bristol, VA

Johnstown, PA includes Cambria and Somerset Counties

Joplin, MO includes Jasper and Newton Counties

Kalamazoo-Battle Creek, MI includes Calhoun, Kalamazoo and Van Buren Counties

Kansas City, MO-KS includes Cass, MO, Clay, MO, Clinton, MO, Jackson, MO, Lafayette, MO, Platte, MO, Ray, MO, Johnson, KS, Leavenworth, KS, Miami, KS and Wyandotte, KS Counties (1993 data not available)

Kenosha, WI includes Kenosha County

Killeen-Temple, TX includes Bell and Coryell Counties

Kokomo, IN includes Howard and Tipton Counties

La Crosse, WI-MN includes La Crosse, WI and Houston, MN Counties

Lafayette, IN includes Clinton and Tippecanoe Counties

Lafayette, LA includes Acadia, Lafayette, St. Landry and St. Martin Parishes

Lake Charles, LA includes Calcasieu Parish

Lakeland-Winter Haven, FL includes Polk County

Lancaster, PA includes Lancaster County

Lansing-East Lansing, MI includes Clinton, Eaton and Ingham Counties

Laredo, TX includes Webb County

Las Vegas, NV-AZ includes Clark, NV, Nye, NV and Mohave, AZ Counties

Lawrence, MA-NH includes part of Essex, MA and Rockingham, NH

Lawton, OK includes Comanche County

Lewiston-Auburn, ME includes part of Androscoggin County

Lexington, KY includes Bourbon, Clark, Fayette, Jessamine, Scott and Woodford Counties

Lincoln, NE includes Lancaster County

Little Rock-North Little Rock, AR includes Faulkner, Lonoke, Pulaski and Saline Counties

Longview-Marshall, TX includes Gregg, Harrison and Upshur Counties

Los Angeles-Long Beach, CA includes Los Angeles County

Louisville, KY-IN includes Bullitt, KY, Jefferson, KY, Oldham, KY, Clark, IN, Floyd, IN, Harrison, IN and Scott, IN Counties

Lubbock, TX includes Lubbock County

Lynchburg, VA includes Amherst, Bedford and Campbell Counties and Cities of Lynchburg and Beford

Macon, GA includes Bibb, Houston, Jones, Peach and Twiggs Counties

Madison, WI includes Dane County

Manchester, NH includes part of Hillsborough, Merrimack and Rockingham Counties

DESCRIPTIONS OF METROPOLITAN AREAS IN 1993 (continued)

Mansfield, OH includes Crawford and Richland Counties

McAllen-Edinburg-Mission, TX includes Hidalgo County

Medford-Ashland, OR includes Jackson County

Memphis, TN-AR-MS includes Fayette, TN, Shelby, TN, Tipton, TN, Crittenden, AR and De Soto, MS Counties

Merced, CA includes Merced County

Miami, FL includes Dade County

Middlesex-Somerset-Hunterdon, NJ includes Hunterdon, Middlesex and Somerset Counties

Milwaukee-Waukesha, WI includes Milwaukee, Ozaukee, Washington and Waukesha Counties

Minneapolis-St. Paul, MN-WI includes Anoka, MN, Carver, MN, Chisago, MN, Dakota, MN, Hennepin, MN, Isanti, MN, Ramsey, MN, Scott, MN, Sherburne, MN, Wright, MN, Pierce, WI and St. Croix, WI Counties

Mobile, AL includes Baldwin and Mobile Counties

Modesto, CA includes Stanislaus County

Monmouth-Ocean, NJ includes Monmouth and Ocean Counties

Monroe, LA includes Ouachita Parish

Montgomery, AL includes Autauga, Elmore and Montgomery Counties

Myrtle Beach, SC includes Horry County

Naples, FL includes Collier County

Nashua, NH includes part of Hillsborough County

Nashville, TN includes Cheatham, Davidson, Dickson, Robertson, Rutherford, Williamson and Wilson Counties

Nassau-Suffolk, NY includes Nassau and Suffolk Counties

Newark, NJ includes Essex, Morris, Sussex, Union and Warren Counties

New Bedford, MA includes part of Bristol and Plymouth Counties

Newburgh, NY-PA includes Orange, NY and Pike, PA Counties

New Haven-Meriden, CT includes part of Middlesex and New Haven Counties

New London-Norwich, CT-RI includes part of Middlesex, CT, New London, CT and Washington, RI Counties

New Orleans, LA includes Jefferson, Orleans, Plaquemines, St. Bernard, St. Charles, St. James, St. John the Baptist, and St. Tammany Parishes

New York, NY includes Bronx, Kings, New York, Putnam, Queens, Richmond, Rockland and Westchester Counties

Norfolk-Virginia Beach-Newport News, VA-NC includes Gloucester, VA, Isle of Wright, VA, James City, VA, Mathews, VA, York, VA and Currituck, NC Counties and Cities of Chesapeake, VA, Hampton, VA, Newport News, VA, Portsmouth, VA, Poquoson, VA, Suffolk, VA, Virginia Beach, VA and Williamsburg, VA

Oakland, CA includes Alameda and Contra Cost Counties

Ocala, FL includes Marion County

Odessa-Midland, TX includes Ector and Midland Counties

Oklahoma City, OK includes Canadian, Cleveland, Logan, McClain, Oklahoma and Pottawatomie Counties

Olympia, WA includes Thurston County

Orange County, CA includes Orange County

Orlando, FL includes Lake, Orange, Osceola and Seminole Counties

Owensboro, KY includes Daviess County

Panama City, FL includes Bay County

Philadelphia, PA-NJ includes Bucks, PA, Chester, PA, Delaware, PA, Montgomery, PA, Philadelphia, PA, Burlington, NJ, Camden, NJ, Gloucester, NJ and Salem, NJ Counties

Phoenix-Mesa, AZ includes Maricopa and Pinal Counties

Pine Bluff, AR includes Jefferson County

Pittsburgh, PA includes Allegheny, Beaver, Butler, Fayette and Westmoreland Counties

Pittsfield, MA includes part of Berkshire County

Portland, ME includes part of Cumberland and York Counties

Portland-Vancouver, OR-WA includes Clackamas, OR, Columbia, OR, Multnomah, OR, Washington, OR, Yamhill, OR and Clark, WA Counties

Providence-Fall River-Warwick, RI-MA includes part of Bristol, RI, Kent, RI, Newport, RI, Providence, RI, Washington, RI and Bristol, MA Counties

Provo-Orem, UT includes Utah County

Pueblo, CO includes Pueblo County

Punta Gorda, FL includes Charlotte County

Racine, WI includes Racine County

Raleigh-Durham-Chapel Hill, NC includes Chatham, Durham, Franklin, Johnston, Orange and Wake Counties

DESCRIPTIONS OF METROPOLITAN AREAS IN 1993 (continued)

Rapid City, SD includes Pennington County

Reading, PA includes Berks County

Redding, CA includes Shasta County

Reno, NV includes Washoe County

Richland-Kennewick-Pasco, WA includes Benton and Franklin Counties

Richmond-Petersburg, VA includes Charles City, Chesterfield, Dinwiddie, Goochland, Hanover, Henrico, New Kent, Powhatan and Prince George Counties and Cities of Colonial Heights, Hopewell, Petersburg and Richmond

Riverside-San Bernardino, CA includes Riverside and San Bernardino Counties

Roanoke, VA includes Botetourt and Roanoke Counties and Cities of Roanoke and Salem

Rochester, MN includes Olmsted County

Rochester, NY includes Genesee, Livingston, Monroe, Ontario, Orleans and Wayne Counties

Rocky Mount, NC includes Edgecombe and Nash Counties

Sacramento, CA includes El Dorado, Placer and Sacramento Counties

Saginaw-Bay City-Midland, MI includes Bay, Midland and Saginaw Counties

Salem, OR includes Marion and Polk Counties

Salinas, CA includes Monterey County

Salt Lake City-Ogden, UT includes Davis, Salt Lake and Weber Counties

San Angelo, TX includes Tom Green County

San Antonio, TX includes Bexar, Comal, Guadalupe and Wilson Counties

San Diego, CA includes San Diego County

San Francisco, CA includes Marin, San Francisco and San Mateo Counties

San Jose, CA includes Santa Clara County

San Luis Obispo-Atascadero, CA includes San Luis Obispo County

Santa Barbara-Santa Maria-Lompoc, CA includes Santa Barbara County

Santa Cruz-Watsonville, CA includes Santa Cruz County

Santa Rosa, CA includes Sonoma County

Sarasota-Bradenton, FL includes Manatee and Sarasota Counties

Savannah, GA includes Bryan, Chatham and Effingham Counties

Scranton-Wilkes-Barre-Hazleton, PA includes Columbia, Lackawanna, Luzerne and Wyoming Counties

Seattle-Bellevue-Everett, WA includes Island, King and Snohomish Counties

Sheboygan, WI includes Sheboygan County

Sherman-Denison, TX includes Grayson County

Shreveport-Bossier City, LA includes Bossier, Caddo and Webster Parishes

Sioux City, IA-NE includes Woodbury, IA and Dakota, NE Counties

Sioux Falls, SD includes Lincoln and Minnehaha Counties

South Bend, IN includes St. Joseph County

Spokane, WA includes Spokane County

Springfield, MA includes part of Franklin, Hampden and Hampshire Counties

Springfield, MO includes Christian, Greene and Webster Counties

Stamford-Norwalk, CT includes part of Fairfield County

Steubenville-Weirton, OH-WV includes Jefferson, OH, Brooke, WV and Hancock, WV Counties

Stockton-Lodi, CA includes San Joaquin County

St. Cloud, MN includes Benton and Stearns Counties

St. Joseph, MO includes Andrew and Buchanan Counties

St. Louis, MO-IL includes Franklin, MO, Jefferson, MO, Lincoln, MO, St. Charles, MO, St, Louis, MO, Warren, MO, Jersey, IL, Madison, IL, Monroe, IL and St, Clair, IL Counties (1993 data not available)

Sumter, SC includes Sumter County

Syracuse, NY includes Cayuga, Madison, Onondaga and Oswego Counties

Tacoma, WA includes Pierce County

Tallahassee, FL includes Gadsden and Leon Counties

Tampa-St. Petersburg-Clearwater, FL includes Hernando, Hillsborough, Pasco and Pinellas Counties

Texarkana, TX-AR includes Bowie, TX and Miller, AR Counties

Toledo, OH includes Fulton, Lucas and Wood Counties

Trenton, NJ includes Mercer County

Tucson, AZ includes Pima County

Tulsa, OK includes Creek, Osage, Rogers, Tulsa and Wagoner Counties

Tuscaloosa, AL includes Tuscaloosa County	Williamsport, PA includes Lycoming County	
Tyler, TX includes Smith County	Wilmington, NC includes New Hanover County	
Utica-Rome, NY includes Herkimer and Oneida Counties	Worcester, MA-CT includes part of Hampden, MA, Worcester, MA and Windham, CT Counties	
Vallejo-Fairfield-Napa, CA includes Napa and Solano Counties	Yakima, WA includes Yakima County	
Ventura, CA includes Ventura County	Yolo, CA includes Yolo County	
Victoria, TX includes Victoria County	Yuba City, CA includes Sutter and Yuba Counties	
Vineland-Millville-Bridgeton, NJ includes Cumberland County		
Visalia-Tulare-Poterville, CA includes Tulare County		
Waco, TX includes McLennan County		
Washington, DC-MD-VA-WV includes Calvert, MD, Charles, MD, Frederick, MD, Montgmery, MD, Prince Georges, MD, Arlington, VA, Clarke, VA, Culpeper, VA, Fairfax, VA, Fauquier, VA, King George, VA, Loudoun, VA, Prince William, VA, Spotsylvania, VA, Stafford, VA, Warren, VA, Berkeley, WV and Jefferson, WV Counties and Cities of Alexandria, VA, Fairfax, VA, Falls Church, VA, Fredericksburg, VA, Manassas, VA and Manassas Park, VA		
Waterbury, CT includes part of Litchfield and New Haven Counties		
Waterloo-Cedar Falls, IA includes Black Hawk County		
Wausau, WI includes Marathon County		
West Palm Beach-Boca Raton, FL includes Palm Beach County (1993 data not available)		
Wichita, KS includes Butler, Harvey and Sedgwick Counties (1993 data not available)		
Wichita Falls, TX includes Archer and Wichita Counties		

GAVILAN COLLEGE LIBRARY

COUNTY INDEX: 1993

COUNTY:	IS IN METROPOLITAN:	COUNTY:	IS IN METROPOLITAN:
Acadia, LA	Lafayette, LA	Bristol, MA (part)	New Bedford, MA
Ada, ID	Boise, ID	Bristol, MA (part)	Providence-Fall River-Warwick, RI-MA
Adams, CO	Denver, CO	Bristol, RI (part)	Providence-Fall River-Warwick, RI-MA
Adams, IN	Fort Wayne, IN	Bristol, VA-City of	Johnson City-Kingsport-Bristol, TN-VA
Aiken, SC	Augusta-Aiken, GA-SC	Bronx, NY	New York, NY
Alachua, FL	Gainesville, FL	Brooke, WV	Steubenville-Weirton, OH-WV
Alamance, NC	Greensboro-Winston Salem-High Point, NC	Broome, NY	Binghamton, NY
Alameda, CA	Oakland, CA	Broward, FL	Fort Lauderdale, FL
Albemarle, VA	Charlottesville, VA	Brown, OH	Cincinnati, OH-KY-IN
Alexander, NC	Hickory-Morganton, NC	Brown, WI	Green Bay, WI
Alexandria, VA-City of	Washington, DC-MD-VA-WV	Brunswick, NC	Wilmington, NC
Allegan, MI	Grand Rapids-Muskegon-Holland, MI	Bryan, GA	Savannah, GA
Allegany, MD	Cumberland, MD-WV	Buchanan, MO	St. Joseph, MO
Allegheny, PA	Pittsburgh, PA	Bucks, PA	Philadelphia, PA-NJ
Allen, IN	Fort Wayne, IN	Bullitt, KY	Louisville, KY-IN
Amherst, VA	Lynchburg, VA	Buncombe, NC	Asheville, NC
Anchorage, AK	Anchorage, AK	Burke, NC	Hickory-Morganton, NC
Anderson, SC	Greenville-Spartanburg-Anderson, SC	Burleigh, ND	Bismarck, ND
Andrew, MO	St. Joseph, MO	Burlington, NJ	Philadelphia, PA-NJ
Androscoggin, ME (part)	Lewiston-Auburn, ME	Butler, KS	Wichita, KS
Anne Arundel, MD	Baltimore, MD	Butler, PA	Pittsburgh, PA
Anoka, MN	Minneapolis-St. Paul, MN-WI	Butte, CA	Chico-Paradise, CA
Arapahoe, CO	Denver, CO	Cabarrus, NC	Charlotte-Gastonia-Rock Hill, NC-SC
Archer, TX	Wichita Falls, TX	Cabell, WV	Huntington-Ashland, WV-KY-OK
Arlington, VA	Washington, DC-MD-VA-WV	Caddo, LA	Shreveport-Bossier City, LA
Ascension, LA	Baton Rouge, LA	Calcasieu, LA	Lake Charles, LA
Ashtabula, OH	Cleveland, OH	Caldwell, NC	Hickory-Morganton, NC
Atlantic, NJ	Atlantic City, NJ	Caldwell, TX	Austin-San Marcos, TX
Autauga, AL	Montgomery, AL	Calhoun, AL	Anniston, AL
Baldwin, AL	Mobile, AL	Calhoun, MI	Kalamazoo-Battle Creek, MI
Baltimore, MD	Baltimore, MD	Calumet, WI	Appleton-Oshkosh-Neenah, WI
Baltimore, MD-City of	Baltimore, MD	Calvert, MD	Washington, DC-MD-VA-WV
Barnstable, MA (part)	Barnstable-Yarmouth, MA	Cambria, PA	Johnstown, PA
Barrow, GA	Atlanta, GA	Camden, NJ	Philadelphia, PA-NJ
Bartow, GA	Atlanta, GA	Cameron, TX	Brownsville-Harlingen-San Benito, TX
Bastrop, TX	Austin-San Marcos, TX	Campbell, KY	Cincinnati, OH-KY-IN
Bay, FL	Panama City, FL	Campbell, VA	Lynchburg, VA
Bay, MI	Saginaw-Bay City-Midland, MI	Canadian, OK	Oklahoma City, OK
Beaver, PA	Pittsburgh, PA	Canyon, ID	Boise, ID
Bedford, VA	Lynchburg, VA	Cape May, NJ	Atlantic City, NJ
Bedford, VA-City of	Lynchburg, VA	Carroll, GA	Atlanta, GA
Bell, TX	Killeen-Temple, TX	Carroll, MD	Baltimore, MD
Benton, AR	Fayetteville-Springdale-Rogers, AR	Carroll, OH	Canton-Massillon, OH
Benton, MN	St. Cloud, MN	Carter, TN	Johnson City-Kingsport-Bristol, TN-VA
Benton, WA	Richland-Kennewick-Pasco, WA	Carver, MN	Minneapolis-St. Paul, MN-WI
Bergen, NJ	Bergen-Passaic, NJ	Cass, MO	Kansas City, MO-KS
Berkeley, SC	Charleston-North Charleston, SC	Cass, ND	Fargo-Moorhead, ND-MN
Berkeley, WV	Washington, DC-MD-VA-WV	Catawba, NC	Hickory-Morganton, NC
Berks, PA	Reading, PA	Catoosa, GA	Chattanooga, TN-GA
Berkshire, MA (part)	Pittsfield, MA	Cayuga, NY	Syracuse, NY
Bernalillo, NM	Albuquerque, NM	Chambers, TX	Houston, TX
Berrien, MI	Benton Harbor, MI	Charles, MD	Washington, DC-MD-VA-WV
Bexar, TX	San Antonio, TX	Charles City, VA	Richmond-Petersburg, VA
Bibb, GA	Macon, GA	Charleston, SC	Charleston-North Charleston, SC
Black Hawk, IA	Waterloo-Cedar Falls, IA	Charlottesville, VA-City of	Charlottesville, VA
Blair, PA	Altoona, PA	Charolette, FL	Punta Gorda, FL
Blount, AL	Birmingham, AL	Chatham, GA	Savannah, GA
Boone, IN	Indianapolis, IN	Chatham, NC	Raleigh-Durham-Chapel Hill, NC
Boone, KY	Cincinnati, OH-KY-IN	Chattahoochee, GA	Columbus, GA-AL
Boone, MO	Columbia, MO	Cheatham, TN	Nashville, TN
Bossier, LA	Shreveport-Bossier City, LA	Cherokee, GA	Atlanta, GA
Botetourt, VA	Roanoke, VA	Cherokee, SC	Greenville-Spartanburg-Anderson, SC
Boulder, CO	Boulder-Longmont, CO	Chesapeake, VA-City of	Norfolk-Va Beach-Newport News, VA-NC
Bourbon, KY	Lexington, KY	Chester, PA	Philadelphia, PA-NJ
Bowie, TX	Texarkana, TX-AR	Chesterfield, VA	Richmond-Petersburg, VA
Boyd, KY	Huntington-Ashland, WV-KY-OK	Chippewa, WI	Eau Claire, WI
Brazoria, TX	Brazoria, TX	Chisago, MN	Minneapolis-St. Paul, MN-WI
Brazos, TX	Bryan-College Station, TX	Christian, KY	Clarksville-Hopkinsville, TN-KY
Bristol, MA (part)	Boston, MA-NH	Christian, MO	Springfield, MO
Bristol, MA (part)	Brockton, MA	Clackamas, OR	Portland-Vancouver, OR-WA

COUNTY INDEX: 1993 (continued)

COUNTY:	IS IN METROPOLITAN:	COUNTY:	IS IN METROPOLITAN:
Clark, IN	Louisville, KY-IN	Douglas, WI	Duluth-Superior, MN-WI
Clark, KY	Lexington, KY	Dubuque, IA	Dubuque, IA
Clark, NV	Las Vegas, NV-AZ	DuPage, IL	Chicago, IL
Clark, OH	Dayton-Springfield, OH	Durham, NC	Raleigh-Durham-Chapel Hill, NC
Clark, WA	Portland-Vancouver, OR-WA	Dutchess, NY	Dutchess County, NY
Clarke, GA	Athens, GA	Duval, FL	Jacksonville, FL
Clarke, VA	Washington, DC-MD-VA-WV	East Baton Rouge, LA	Baton Rouge, LA
Clay, FL	Jacksonville, FL	Eaton, MI	Lansing-East Lansing, MI
Clay, MN	Fargo-Moorhead, ND-MN	Eau Claire, WI	Eau Claire, WI
Clay, MO	Kansas City, MO-KS	Ector, TX	Odessa-Midland, TX
Clermont, OH	Cincinnati, OH-KY-IN	Edgecombe, NC	Rocky Mount, NC
Cleveland, OK	Oklahoma City, OK	Edgefield, SC	Augusta-Aiken, GA-SC
Clinton, IN	Lafayette, IN	Effingham, GA	Savannah, GA
Clinton, MI	Lansing-East Lansing, MI	El Dorado, CA	Sacramento, CA
Clinton, MO	Kansas City, MO-KS	El Paso, CO	Colorado Springs, CO
Cobb, GA	Atlanta, GA	El Paso, TX	El Paso, TX
Colbert, AL	Florence, AL	Elkhart, IN	Elkhart-Goshen, IN
Collier, FL	Naples, FL	Ellis, TX	Dallas, TX
Collin, TX	Dallas, TX	Elmore, AL	Montgomery, AL
Colonial Heights, VA-City	Richmond-Petersburg, VA	Erie, NY	Buffalo-Niagara Falls, NY
Columbia, GA	Augusta-Aiken, GA-SC	Erie, PA	Erie, PA
Columbia, OR	Portland-Vancouver, OR-WA	Essex, MA (part)	Boston, MA-NH
Columbia, PA	Scranton-Wilkes-Barre-Hazleton, PA	Essex, MA (part)	Lawrence, MA-NH
Comal, TX	San Antonio, TX	Essex, NJ	Newark, NJ
Comanche, OK	Lawton, OK	Etowah, AL	Gadsden, AL
Contra Costa, CA	Oakland, CA	Fairfax, VA	Washington, DC-MD-VA-WV
Cook, IL	Chicago, IL	Fairfax, VA-City of	Washington, DC-MD-VA-WV
Coryell, TX	Killeen-Temple, TX	Fairfield, CT (part)	Bridgeport, CT
Coweta, GA	Atlanta, GA	Fairfield, CT (part)	Danbury, CT
Crawford, AR	Fort Smith, AR-OK	Fairfield, CT (part)	Stamford-Norwalk, CT
Crawford, OH	Mansfield, OH	Fairfield, OH	Columbus, OH
Creek, OK	Tulsa, OK	Falls Church, VA-City of	Washington, DC-MD-VA-WV
Crittenden, AR	Memphis, TN-AR-MS	Faulkner, AR	Little Rock-North Little Rock, AR
Culpeper, VA	Washington, DC-MD-VA-WV	Fauquier, VA	Washington, DC-MD-VA-WV
Cumberland, ME (part)	Portland, ME	Fayette, GA	Atlanta, GA
Cumberland, NC	Fayetteville, NC	Fayette, KY	Lexington, KY
Cumberland, NJ	Vineland-Millville-Bridgeton, NJ	Fayette, PA	Pittsburgh, PA
Cumberland, PA	Harrisburg-Lebanon-Carlisle, PA	Fayette, TN	Memphis, TN-AR-MS
Currituck, NC	Norfolk-Va Beach-Newport News, VA-NC	Flagler, FL	Daytona Beach, FL
Cuyahoga, OH	Cleveland, OH	Florence, SC	Florence, SC
Dade, FL	Miami, FL	Floyd, IN	Louisville, KY-IN
Dade, GA	Chattanooga, TN-GA	Fluvanna, VA	Charlottesville, VA
Dakota, MN	Minneapolis-St. Paul, MN-WI	Forsyth, GA	Atlanta, GA
Dakota, NE	Sioux City, IA-NE	Forsythe, NC	Greensboro-Winston Salem-High Point, NC
Dale, AL	Dothan, AL	Fort Bend, TX	Houston, TX
Dallas, IA	Des Moines, IA	Franklin, MA (part)	Springfield, MA
Dallas, TX	Dallas, TX	Franklin, MO	St. Louis, MO-IL
Dane, WI	Madison, WI	Franklin, NC	Raleigh-Durham-Chapel Hill, NC
Danville, VA-City of	Danville, VA	Franklin, OH	Columbus, OH
Dauphin, PA	Harrisburg-Lebanon-Carlisle, PA	Franklin, WA	Richland-Kennewick-Pasco, WA
Davidson, NC	Greensboro-Winston Salem-High Point, NC	Frederick, MD	Washington, DC-MD-VA-WV
Davidson, TN	Nashville, TN	Fredericksburg, VA-City of	Washington, DC-MD-VA-WV
Davie, NC	Greensboro-Winston Salem-High Point, NC	Fresno, CA	Fresno, CA
Daviess, KY	Owensboro, KY	Fulton, GA	Atlanta, GA
Davis, UT	Salt Lake City-Ogden, UT	Fulton, OH	Toledo, OH
De Kalb, IN	Fort Wayne, IN	Gadsden, FL	Tallahassee, FL
De Soto, MS	Memphis, TN-AR-MS	Gallatin, KY	Cincinnati, OH-KY-IN
Dearborn, IN	Cincinnati, OH-KY-IN	Galveston, TX	Galveston-Texas City, TX
DeKalb, GA	Atlanta, GA	Garfield, OK	Enid, OK
Dekalb, IL	Chicago, IL	Gaston, NC	Charlotte-Gastonia-Rock Hill, NC-SC
Delaware, OH	Columbus, OH	Geauga, OH	Cleveland, OH
Delaware, PA	Philadelphia, PA-NJ	Genesee, MI	Flint, MI
Denton, TX	Dallas, TX	Genesee, NY	Rochester, NY
Denver, CO	Denver, CO	Gloucester, NJ	Philadelphia, PA-NJ
Dickson, TN	Nashville, TN	Gloucester, VA	Norfolk-Va Beach-Newport News, VA-NC
Dinwiddie, VA	Richmond-Petersburg, VA	Goochland, VA	Richmond-Petersburg, VA
Dorchester, SC	Charleston-North Charleston, SC	Grand Forks, ND	Grand Forks, ND-MN
Dougherty, GA	Albany, GA	Grant, KY	Cincinnati, OH-KY-IN
Douglas, CO	Denver, CO	Grayson, TX	Sherman-Denison, TX
Douglas, GA	Atlanta, GA	Greene, MO	Springfield, MO

COUNTY INDEX: 1993 (continued)

COUNTY:	IS IN METROPOLITAN:	COUNTY:	IS IN METROPOLITAN:
Greene, OH	Dayton-Springfield, OH	Jefferson, WV	Washington, DC-MD-VA-WV
Greene, VA	Charlottesville, VA	Jersey, IL	St. Louis, MO-IL
Greenup, KY	Huntington-Ashland, WV-KY-OK	Jessamine, KY	Lexington, KY
Greenville, SC	Greenville-Spartanburg-Anderson, SC	Johnson, IN	Indianapolis, IN
Gregg, TX	Longview-Marshall, TX	Johnson, KS	Kansas City, MO-KS
Grundy, IL	Chicago, IL	Johnson, TX	Fort Worth-Arlington, TX
Guadalupe, TX	San Antonio, TX	Johnston, NC	Raleigh-Durham-Chapel Hill, NC
Guilford, NC	Greensboro-Winston Salem-High Point, NC	Jones, GA	Macon, GA
Gwinnett, GA	Atlanta, GA	Kalamazoo, MI	Kalamazoo-Battle Creek, MI
Hamilton, IN	Indianapolis, IN	Kanawha, WV	Charleston, WV
Hamilton, OH	Cincinnati, OH-KY-IN	Kane, IL	Chicago, IL
Hamilton, TN	Chattanooga, TN-GA	Kaufman, TX	Dallas, TX
Hampden, MA (part)	Springfield, MA	Kendall, IL	Chicago, IL
Hampden, MA (part)	Worcester, MA-CT	Kenosha, WI	Kenosha, WI
Hampshire, MA (part)	Springfield, MA	Kent, MI	Grand Rapids-Muskegon-Holland, MI
Hampton, VA-City of	Norfolk-Va Beach-Newport News, VA-NC	Kent, RI (part)	Providence-Fall River-Warwick, RI-MA
Hancock, IN	Indianapolis, IN	Kenton, KY	Cincinnati, OH-KY-IN
Hancock, WV	Steubenville-Weirton, OH-WV	Kern, CA	Bakersfield, CA
Hanover, VA	Richmond-Petersburg, VA	King, WA	Seattle-Bellevue-Everett, WA
Hardin, TX	Beaumont-Port Arthur, TX	King George, VA	Washington, DC-MD-VA-WV
Harford, MD	Baltimore, MD	Kings, NY	New York, NY
Harris, GA	Columbus, GA-AL	Kitsap, Wa	Bremerton, WA
Harris, TX	Houston, TX	La Crosse, WI	La Crosse, WI-MN
Harrison, IN	Louisville, KY-IN	Lackawanna, PA	Scranton-Wilkes-Barre-Hazleton, PA
Harrison, TX	Longview-Marshall, TX	Lafayette, LA	Lafayette, LA
Hartford, CT	Hartford, CT	Lafayette, MO	Kansas City, MO-KS
Harvey, KS	Wichita, KS	Lafourche, LA	Houma, LA
Hawkins, TN	Johnson City-Kingsport-Bristol, TN-VA	Lake, FL	Orlando, FL
Hays, TX	Austin-San Marcos, TX	Lake, IL	Chicago, IL
Henderson, KY	Evansville-Henderson, IN-KY	Lake, IN	Gary-Hammond, IN
Henderson, TX	Dallas, TX	Lake, OH	Cleveland, OH
Hendricks, IN	Indianapolis, IN	Lancaster, NE	Lincoln, NE
Hennepin, MN	Minneapolis-St. Paul, MN-WI	Lancaster, PA	Lancaster, PA
Henrico, VA	Richmond-Petersburg, VA	Lane, OR	Eugene-Springfield, OR
Henry, GA	Atlanta, GA	Lapeer, MI	Detroit, MI
Herkimer, NY	Utica-Rome, NY	Laramie, WY	Cheyenne, WY
Hernando, FL	Tampa-St. Petersburg-Clearwater, FL	Larimer, CO	Fort Collins-Loveland, CO
Hidalgo, TX	McAllen-Edinburg-Mission, TX	Lauderdale, AL	Florence, AL
Hillsborough, FL	Tampa-St. Petersburg-Clearwater, FL	Lawrence, AL	Decatur, AL
Hillsborough, NH (part)	Manchester, NH	Lawrence, OH	Huntington-Ashland, WV-KY-OK
Hillsborough, NH (part)	Nashua, NH	Leavenworth, KS	Kansas City, MO-KS
Hinds, MS	Jackson, MS	Lebanon, PA	Harrisburg-Lebanon-Carlisle, PA
Honolulu, HI	Honolulu, HI	Lee, FL	Fort Myers-Cape Coral, FL
Hopewell, VA-City of	Richmond-Petersburg, VA	Lee, GA	Albany, GA
Horry, SC	Myrtle Beach, SC	Lenawee, MI	Ann Arbor, MI
Houston, AL	Dothan, AL	Leon, FL	Tallahassee, FL
Houston, GA	Macon, GA	Lexington, SC	Columbia, SC
Houston, MN	La Crosse, WI-MN	Liberty, TX	Houston, TX
Howard, IN	Kokomo, IN	Licking, OH	Columbus, OH
Howard, MD	Baltimore, MD	Limestone, AL	Huntsville, AL
Hudson, NJ	Jersey City, NJ	Lincoln, MO	St. Louis, MO-IL
Hunterdon, NJ	Middlesex-Somerset-Hunterdon, NJ	Lincoln, NC	Charlotte-Gastonia-Rock Hill, NC-SC
Huntington, IN	Fort Wayne, IN	Lincoln, SD	Sioux Falls, SD
Ingham, MI	Lansing-East Lansing, MI	Litchfield, CT (part)	Danbury, CT
Isanti, MN	Minneapolis-St. Paul, MN-WI	Litchfield, CT (part)	Hartford, CT
Island, WA	Seattle-Bellevue-Everett, WA	Litchfield, CT (part)	Waterbury, CT
Isle of Wright, VA	Norfolk-Va Beach-Newport News, VA-NC	Livingston, LA	Baton Rouge, LA
Jackson, MI	Jackson, MI	Livingston, MI	Ann Arbor, MI
Jackson, MO	Kansas City, MO-KS	Livingston, NY	Rochester, NY
Jackson, OR	Medford-Ashland, OR	Logan, OK	Oklahoma City, OK
James City, VA	Norfolk-Va Beach-Newport News, VA-NC	Lonoke, AR	Little Rock-North Little Rock, AR
Jasper, MO	Joplin, MO	Lorain, OH	Cleveland, OH
Jefferson, AL	Birmingham, AL	Los Angeles, CA	Los Angeles-Long Beach, CA
Jefferson, AR	Pine Bluff, AR	Loudoun, VA	Washington, DC-MD-VA-WV
Jefferson, CO	Denver, CO	Lubbock, TX	Lubbock, TX
Jefferson, KY	Louisville, KY-IN	Lucas, OH	Toledo, OH
Jefferson, LA	New Orleans, LA	Luzerne, PA	Scranton-Wilkes-Barre-Hazleton, PA
Jefferson, MO	St. Louis, MO-IL	Lycoming, PA	Williamsport, PA
Jefferson, OH	Steubenville-Weirton, OH-WV	Lynchburg, VA-City of	Lynchburg, VA
Jefferson, TX	Beaumont-Port Arthur, TX	Macomb, MI	Detroit, MI

COUNTY:	IS IN METROPOLITAN:	COUNTY:	IS IN METROPOLITAN:
Madera, CA	Fresno, CA	New Haven, CT (part)	New Haven-Meriden, CT
Madison, AL	Huntsville, AL	New Haven, CT (part)	Waterbury, CT
Madison, GA	Athens, GA	New Kent, VA	Richmond-Petersburg, VA
Madison, IL	St. Louis, MO-IL	New London, CT (part)	Hartford, CT
Madison, IN	Indianapolis, IN	New London, CT (part)	New London-Norwich, CT-RI
Madison, MS	Jackson, MS	New York, NY	New York, NY
Madison, NY	Syracuse, NY	Newport, RI (part)	Providence-Fall River-Warwick, RI-MA
Madison, OH	Columbus, OH	Newport News, VA-City of	Norfolk-Va Beach-Newport News, VA-NC
Madison, TN	Jackson, TN	Newton, GA	Atlanta, GA
Manassas, VA-City of	Washington, DC-MD-VA-WV	Newton, MO	Joplin, MO
Manassas Park, VA-City of	Washington, DC-MD-VA-WV	Niagara, NY	Buffalo-Niagara Falls, NY
Manatee, FL	Sarasota-Bradenton, FL	Norfolk, MA (part)	Brockton, MA
Marathon, WI	Wausau, WI	Nueces, TX	Corpus Christi, TX
Maricopa, AZ	Phoenix-Mesa, AZ	Nye, NV	Las Vegas, NV-AZ
Marin, CA	San Francisco, CA	Oakland, MI	Detroit, MI
Marion, Fl	Ocala, FL	Ocean, NJ	Monmouth-Ocean, NJ
Marion, IN	Indianapolis, IN	Oconee, GA	Athens, GA
Marion, OR	Salem, OR	Ohio, IN	Cincinnati, OH-KY-IN
Marion, TN	Chattanooga, TN-GA	Okaloosa, FL	Fort Walton Beach, FL
Martin, FL	Fort Pierce-Port St. Lucie, FL	Oklahoma, OK	Oklahoma City, OK
Mathews, VA	Norfolk-Va Beach-Newport News, VA-NC	Oldham, KY	Louisville, KY-IN
McClain, OK	Oklahoma City, OK	Olmsted, MN	Rochester, MN
McHenry, IL	Chicago, IL	Oneida, NY	Utica-Rome, NY
McLennan, TX	Waco, TX	Onondaga, NY	Syracuse, NY
Mecklenburg, NC	Charlotte-Gastonia-Rock Hill, NC-SC	Onslow, NC	Jacksonville, NC
Medina, OH	Cleveland, OH	Ontario, NY	Rochester, NY
Merced, CA	Merced, CA	Orange, CA	Orange County, CA
Mercer, NJ	Trenton, NJ	Orange, FL	Orlando, FL
Merrimack, NH (part)	Manchester, NH	Orange, NC	Raleigh-Durham-Chapel Hill, NC
Miami, KS	Kansas City, MO-KS	Orange, NY	Newburgh, NY-PA
Miami, OH	Dayton-Springfield, OH	Orange, TX	Beaumont-Port Arthur, TX
Middlesex, CT (part)	Hartford, CT	Orleans, LA	New Orleans, LA
Middlesex, CT (part)	New Haven-Meriden, CT	Orleans, NY	Rochester, NY
Middlesex, CT (part)	New London-Norwich, CT-RI	Osage, OK	Tulsa, OK
Middlesex, MA (part)	Boston, MA-NH	Osceola, FL	Orlando, FL
Middlesex, MA (part)	Fitchburg-Leominster, MA	Oswego, NY	Syracuse, NY
Middlesex, NJ	Middlesex-Somerset-Hunterdon, NJ	Ottawa, MI	Grand Rapids-Muskegon-Holland, MI
Midland, MI	Saginaw-Bay City-Midland, MI	Ouachita, LA	Monroe, LA
Midland, TX	Odessa-Midland, TX	Outagamie, WI	Appleton-Oshkosh-Neenah, WI
Miller, AR	Texarkana, TX-AR	Ozaukee, WI	Milwaukee-Waukesha, WI
Milwaukee, WI	Milwaukee-Waukesha, WI	Palm Beach, FL	West Palm Beach-Boca Raton, FL
Mineral, WV	Cumberland, MD-WV	Parker, TX	Fort Worth-Arlington, TX
Minnehaha, SD	Sioux Falls, SD	Pasco, FL	Tampa-St. Petersburg-Clearwater, FL
Mobile, AL	Mobile, AL	Passaic, NJ	Bergen-Passaic, NJ
Mohave, AZ	Las Vegas, NV-AZ	Paulding, GA	Atlanta, GA
Monmouth, NJ	Monmouth-Ocean, NJ	Peach, GA	Macon, GA
Monroe, IL	St. Louis, MO-IL	Pendleton, KY	Cincinnati, OH-KY-IN
Monroe, IN	Bloomington, IN	Pennington, SD	Rapid City, SD
Monroe, MI	Detroit, MI	Penobscot, ME (part)	Bangor, ME
Monroe, NY	Rochester, NY	Perry, PA	Harrisburg-Lebanon-Carlisle, PA
Monterey, CA	Salinas, CA	Petersburg, VA-City of	Richmond-Petersburg, VA
Montgomery, AL	Montgomery, AL	Philadelphia, PA	Philadelphia, PA-NJ
Montgomery, MD	Washington, DC-MD-VA-WV	Pickaway, OH	Columbus, OH
Montgomery, OH	Dayton-Springfield, OH	Pickens, GA	Atlanta, GA
Montgomery, PA	Philadelphia, PA-NJ	Pickens, SC	Greenville-Spartanburg-Anderson, SC
Montgomery, TN	Clarksville-Hopkinsville, TN-KY	Pierce, WA	Tacoma, WA
Montgomery, TX	Houston, TX	Pierce, WI	Minneapolis-St. Paul, MN-WI
Morgan, AL	Decatur, AL	Pike, PA	Newburgh, NY-PA
Morgan, IN	Indianapolis, IN	Pima, AZ	Tucson, AZ
Morris, NJ	Newark, NJ	Pinal, AZ	Phoenix-Mesa, AZ
Morton, ND	Bismarck, ND	Pinellas, FL	Tampa-St. Petersburg-Clearwater, FL
Multnomah, OR	Portland-Vancouver, OR-WA	Pitt, NC	Greenville, NC
Muscogee, GA	Columbus, GA-AL	Pittsylvania, VA	Danville, VA
Muskegon, MI	Grand Rapids-Muskegon-Holland, MI	Placer, CA	Sacramento, CA
Napa, CA	Vallejo-Fairfield-Napa, CA	Plaquemines, LA	New Orleans, LA
Nash, NC	Rocky Mount, NC	Platte, MO	Kansas City, MO-KS
Nassau, FL	Jacksonville, FL	Plymouth, MA (part)	Boston, MA-NH
Nassau, NY	Nassau-Suffolk, NY	Plymouth, MA (part)	Brockton, MA
New Hanover, NC	Wilmington, NC	Plymouth, MA (part)	New Bedford, MA
New Haven, CT (part)	Bridgeport, CT	Polk, FL	Lakeland-Winter Haven, FL

COUNTY INDEX: 1993 (continued)

COUNTY:	IS IN METROPOLITAN:	COUNTY:	IS IN METROPOLITAN:
Polk, IA	Des Moines, IA	Sebastian, AR	Fort Smith, AR-OK
Polk, MN	Grand Forks, ND-MN	Sedgwick, KS	Wichita, KS
Polk, OR	Salem, OR	Seminole, FL	Orlando, FL
Poquoson, VA-City of	Norfolk-Va Beach-Newport News, VA-NC	Sequoyah, OK	Fort Smith, AR-OK
Portage, OH	Akron, OH	Shasta, CA	Redding, CA
Porter, IN	Gary-Hammond, IN	Sheboygan, WI	Sheboygan, WI
Portsmouth, VA-City of	Norfolk-Va Beach-Newport News, VA-NC	Shelby, AL	Birmingham, AL
Posey, IN	Evansville-Henderson, IN-KY	Shelby, IN	Indianapolis, IN
Pottawatomie, OK	Oklahoma City, OK	Shelby, TN	Memphis, TN-AR-MS
Potter, TX	Amarillo, TX	Sherburne, MN	Minneapolis-St. Paul, MN-WI
Powhatan, VA	Richmond-Petersburg, VA	Smith, TX	Tyler, TX
Prince George, VA	Richmond-Petersburg, VA	Snohomish, WA	Seattle-Bellevue-Everett, WA
Prince Georges, MD	Washington, DC-MD-VA-WV	Solano, CA	Vallejo-Fairfield-Napa, CA
Prince William, VA	Washington, DC-MD-VA-WV	Somerset, NJ	Middlesex-Somerset-Hunterdon, NJ
Providence, RI (part)	Providence-Fall River-Warwick, RI-MA	Somerset, PA	Johnstown, PA
Pueblo, CO	Pueblo, CO	Sonoma, CA	Santa Rosa, CA
Pulaski, AR	Little Rock-North Little Rock, AR	Spalding, GA	Atlanta, GA
Putnam, NY	New York, NY	Spartanburg, SC	Greenville-Spartanburg-Anderson, SC
Putnam, WV	Charleston, WV	Spokane, WA	Spokane, WA
Queen Anne's, MD	Baltimore, MD	Spotsylvania, VA	Washington, DC-MD-VA-WV
Queens, NY	New York, NY	Stafford, VA	Washington, DC-MD-VA-WV
Racine, WI	Racine, WI	Stanislaus, CA	Modesto, CA
Ramsey, MN	Minneapolis-St. Paul, MN-WI	Stark, OH	Canton-Massillon, OH
Randall, TX	Amarillo, TX	Stearns, MN	St. Cloud, MN
Randolph, NC	Greensboro-Winston Salem-High Point, NC	Stokes, NC	Greensboro-Winston Salem-High Point, NC
Rankin, MS	Jackson, MS	St. Bernard, LA	New Orleans, LA
Rapides, LA	Alexandria, LA	St. Charles, LA	New Orleans, LA
Ray, MO	Kansas City, MO-KS	St. Charles, MO	St. Louis, MO-IL
Richland, OH	Mansfield, OH	St. Clair, AL	Birmingham, AL
Richland, SC	Columbia, SC	St. Clair, IL	St. Louis, MO-IL
Richmond, GA	Augusta-Aiken, GA-SC	St. Clair, MI	Detroit, MI
Richmond, NY	New York, NY	St. Croix, WI	Minneapolis-St. Paul, MN-WI
Richmond, VA-City of	Richmond-Petersburg, VA	St. James, LA	New Orleans, LA
Riverside, CA	Riverside-San Bernardino, CA	St. John the Baptist, LA	New Orleans, LA
Roanoke, VA	Roanoke, VA	St. Johns, FL	Jacksonville, FL
Roanoke, VA-City of	Roanoke, VA	St. Joseph, IN	South Bend, IN
Robertson, TN	Nashville, TN	St. Landry, LA	Lafayette, LA
Rock, WI	Janesville-Beloit, WI	St. Louis, MN	Duluth-Superior, MN-WI
Rockdale, GA	Atlanta, GA	St. Louis, MO	St. Louis, MO-IL
Rockingham, NH (part)	Boston, MA-NH	St. Lucie, FL	Fort Pierce-Port St. Lucie, FL
Rockingham, NH (part)	Lawrence, MA-NH	St. Martin, LA	Lafayette, LA
Rockingham, NH (part)	Manchester, NH	St. Tammany, LA	New Orleans, LA
Rockland, NY	New York, NY	Suffolk, MA (part)	Boston, MA-NH
Rockwall, TX	Dallas, TX	Suffolk, NY	Nassau-Suffolk, NY
Rogers, OK	Tulsa, OK	Sullivan, TN	Johnson City-Kingsport-Bristol, TN-VA
Rowan, NC	Charlotte-Gastonia-Rock Hill, NC-SC	Summit, OH	Akron, OH
Russell, AL	Columbus, GA-AL	Sumner, TN	Nashville, TN
Rutherford, TN	Nashville, TN	Sumter, SC	Sumter, SC
Sacramento, CA	Sacramento, CA	Sussex, NJ	Newark, NJ
Saginaw, MI	Saginaw-Bay City-Midland, MI	Sutter, CA	Yuba City, CA
Salem, NJ	Philadelphia, PA-NJ	Tarrant, TX	Fort Worth-Arlington, TX
Salem, VA-City of	Roanoke, VA	Taylor, TX	Abilene, TX
Saline, AR	Little Rock-North Little Rock, AR	Terrebonne, LA	Houma, LA
Salt Lake, UT	Salt Lake City-Ogden, UT	Thurston, WA	Olympia, WA
San Bernardino, CA	Riverside-San Bernardino, CA	Tioga, NY	Binghamton, NY
San Diego, CA	San Diego, CA	Tippecanoe, IN	Lafayette, IN
San Francisco, CA	San Francisco, CA	Tipton, IN	Kokomo, IN
San Joaquin, CA	Stockton-Lodi, CA	Tipton, TN	Memphis, TN-AR-MS
San Luis Obispo, CA	San Luis Obispo-Atascadero, CA	Tolland, CT (part)	Hartford, CT
San Mateo, CA	San Francisco, CA	Tom Green, TX	San Angelo, TX
San Patricio, TX	Corpus Christi, TX	Travis, TX	Austin-San Marcos, TX
Sandoval, NM	Albuquerque, NM	Tulare, CA	Visalia-Tulare-Poterville, CA
Santa Barbara, CA	Santa Barbara-Santa Maria-Lompoc, CA	Tulsa, OK	Tulsa, OK
Santa Clara, CA	San Jose, CA	Tuscaloosa, AL	Tuscaloosa, AL
Santa Cruz, CA	Santa Cruz-Watsonville, CA	Twiggs, GA	Macon, GA
Sarasota, FL	Sarasota-Bradenton, FL	Unicoi, TN	Johnson City-Kingsport-Bristol, TN-VA
Scott, IN	Louisville, KY-IN	Union, NC	Charlotte-Gastonia-Rock Hill, NC-SC
Scott, KY	Lexington, KY	Union, NJ	Newark, NJ
Scott, MN	Minneapolis-St. Paul, MN-WI	Upshur, TX	Longview-Marshall, TX
Scott, VA	Johnson City-Kingsport-Bristol, TN-VA	Utah, UT	Provo-Orem, UT

COUNTY INDEX: 1993 (continued)

COUNTY:	IS IN METROPOLITAN:	COUNTY:	IS IN METROPOLITAN:
Valencia, NM	Albuquerque, NM	Weber, UT	Salt Lake City-Ogden, UT
Van Buren, MI	Kalamazoo-Battle Creek, MI	Webster, LA	Shreveport-Bossier City, LA
Vanderburgh, IN	Evansville-Henderson, IN-KY	Webster, MO	Springfield, MO
Ventura, CA	Ventura, CA	Weld, CO	Greeley, CO
Victoria, TX	Victoria, TX	West Baton Rouge, LA	Baton Rouge, LA
Virginia Beach, VA-City of	Norfolk-Va Beach-Newport News, VA-NC	Westchester, NY	New York, NY
Volusia, FL	Daytona Beach, FL	Westmoreland, PA	Pittsburgh, PA
Wagoner, OK	Tulsa, OK	Whatcom, WA	Bellingham, WA
Wake, NC	Raleigh-Durham-Chapel Hill, NC	Whitley, IN	Fort Wayne, IN
Waldo, ME (part)	Bangor, ME	Wichita, TX	Wichita Falls, TX
Walker, GA	Chattanooga, TN-GA	Will, IL	Chicago, IL
Waller, TX	Houston, TX	Williamsburg, VA-City of	Norfolk-Va Beach-Newport News, VA-NC
Walton, GA	Atlanta, GA	Williamson, TN	Nashville, TN
Warren, IA	Des Moines, IA	Williamson, TX	Austin-San Marcos, TX
Warren, MO	St. Louis, MO-IL	Wilson, TN	Nashville, TN
Warren, NJ	Newark, NJ	Wilson, TX	San Antonio, TX
Warren, NY	Glens Falls, NY	Windham, CT (part)	Hartford, CT
Warren, OH	Cincinnati, OH-KY-IN	Windham, CT (part)	Worcester, MA-CT
Warren, VA	Washington, DC-MD-VA-WV	Winnebago, WI	Appleton-Oshkosh-Neenah, WI
Warrick, IN	Evansville-Henderson, IN-KY	Wood, OH	Toledo, OH
Washington, AR	Fayetteville-Springdale-Rogers, AR	Woodbury, IA	Sioux City, IA-NE
Washington, MD	Hagerstown, MD	Woodford, KY	Lexington, KY
Washington, NY	Glens Falls, NY	Worcester, MA (part)	Boston, MA-NH
Washington, OR	Portland-Vancouver, OR-WA	Worcester, MA (part)	Fitchburg-Leominster, MA
Washington, RI (part)	New London-Norwich, CT-RI	Worcester, MA (part)	Worcester, MA-CT
Washington, RI (part)	Providence-Fall River-Warwick, RI-MA	Wright, MN	Minneapolis-St. Paul, MN-WI
Washington, TN	Johnson City-Kingsport-Bristol, TN-VA	Wyandotte, KS	Kansas City, MO-KS
Washington, VA	Johnson City-Kingsport-Bristol, TN-VA	Wyoming, PA	Scranton-Wilkes-Barre-Hazleton, PA
Washington, WI	Milwaukee-Waukesha, WI	Yadkin, NC	Greensboro-Winston Salem-High Point, NC
Washoe, NV	Reno, NV	Yakima, Wa	Yakima, WA
Washtenaw, MI	Ann Arbor, MI	Yamhill, OR	Portland-Vancouver, OR-WA
Waukesha, WI	Milwaukee-Waukesha, WI	Yolo, CA	Yolo, CA
Wayne, MI	Detroit, MI	York, ME (part)	Portland, ME
Wayne, NC	Goldsboro, NC	York, SC	Charlotte-Gastonia-Rock Hill, NC-SC
Wayne, NY	Rochester, NY	York, VA	Norfolk-Va Beach-Newport News, VA-NC
Wayne, WV	Huntington-Ashland, WV-KY-OK	Yuba, CA	Yuba City, CA
Webb, TX	Laredo, TX		

GAVILAN COLLEGE LIBRARY

NATIONAL, METROPOLITAN AND CITY CRIME STATISTICS SUMMARY: 1993

	NATIONAL	METRO	100 CITIES
Population	257,908,000	204,951,864	53,282,561
Crimes in 1993	14,140,952	12,389,557	4,287,240
Crime Rate in 1993 (per 100,000 Population)	5,482.1	6,045.1	9,149.0
Percent Change in Crime Rate: 1992 to 1993	(3.1)	(3.6)	(2.4)
Percent Change in Crime Rate: 1989 to 1993	(4.5)	(6.9)	(1.9)
Violent Crimes in 1993	1,924,188	1,746,540	772,360
Violent Crime Rate in 1993 (per 100,000 Population)	746.1	852.2	1,648.2
Percent Change in Violent Crime Rate: 1992 to 1993	(1.5)	(2.2)	(1.2)
Percent Change in Violent Crime Rate: 1989 to 1993	12.5	9.3	16.2
Murders in 1993	24,526	21,712	12,761
Murder Rate in 1993 (per 100,000 Population)	9.5	10.6	23.9
Percent Change in Murder Rate: 1992 to 1993	2.2	1.9	2.6
Percent Change in Murder Rate: 1989 to 1993	9.2	9.3	12.7
Rapes in 1993	104,806	88,611	32,206
Rape Rate in 1993 (per 100,000 Population)	40.6	43.2	65.4
Percent Change in Rape Rate: 1992 to 1993	(5.1)	(6.3)	(7.4)
Percent Change in Rape Rate: 1989 to 1993	6.6	1.6	1.9
Robberies in 1993	659,757	639,413	396,999
Robbery Rate in 1993 (per 100,000 Population)	255.8	312.0	770.0
Percent Change in Robbery Rate: 1992 to 1993	(3.0)	(3.5)	(1.7)
Percent Change in Robbery Rate: 1989 to 1993	9.8	6.7	9.5
Aggravated Assaults in 1993	1,135,099	996,804	440,054
Aggravated Assault Rate in 1993 (per 100,000 Population)	440.1	486.4	865.2
Percent Change in Aggravated Assault Rate: 1992 to 1993	(0.4)	(1.0)	0.9
Percent Change in Aggravated Assault Rate: 1989 to 1993	14.8	11.8	13.1
Property Crimes in 1993	12,216,764	10,643,017	3,987,437
Property Crime Rate in 1993 (per 100,000 Population)	4,736.9	5,192.9	7,483.6
Percent Change in Property Crime Rate: 1992 to 1993	(3.4)	(3.9)	(2.8)
Percent Change in Property Crime Rate: 1989 to 1993	(6.7)	(9.2)	(10.4)
Burglaries in 1993	2,834,808	2,423,097	904,862
Burglary Rate in 1993 (per 100,000 Population)	1,099.2	1,182.3	1,698.2
Percent Change in Burglary Rate: 1992 to 1993	(5.9)	(6.5)	(5.7)
Percent Change in Burglary Rate: 1989 to 1993	(13.9)	(16.3)	(17.9)
Larceny and Theft in 1993	7,820,909	6,741,385	2,325,063
Larceny and Theft Rate in 1993 (per 100,000 Population)	3,032.4	3,289.3	4,363.6
Percent Change in Larceny and Theft Rate: 1992 to 1993	(2.3)	(2.6)	(0.9)
Percent Change in Larceny and Theft Rate: 1989 to 1993	(4.4)	(6.9)	(8.9)
Motor Vehicle Thefts in 1993	1,561,047	1,478,535	757,512
Motor Vehicle Theft Rate in 1993 (per 100,000 Population)	605.3	721.4	1,421.7
Percent Change in Motor Vehicle Theft Rate: 1992 to 1993	(4.1)	(4.8)	(5.0)
Percent Change in Motor Vehicle Theft Rate: 1989 to 1993	(4.0)	(6.4)	(4.9)

Source: U.S. Bureau of the Census as reported by U.S. Department of Justice, Federal Bureau of Investigation "Crime in the United States 1993" (Uniform Crime Reports, December 4, 1994) All city crime data shown on this chart calculated by the editors.